BASKETBALL CARD

PRICE GUIDE
1995

Other **CONFIDENT COLLECTOR** *Titles*
by Allan Kaye and Michael McKeever
from Avon Books

BASEBALL CARD PRICE GUIDE 1995
FOOTBALL CARD PRICE GUIDE 1995
HOCKEY CARD PRICE GUIDE 1995

Coming Soon

BASEBALL PRICE GUIDE 1996

Avon Books are available at special quantity discounts for bulk purchases for sales promotions, premiums, fund raising or educational use. Special books, or book excerpts, can also be created to fit specific needs.

For details write or telephone the office of the Director of Special Markets, Avon Books, Dept. FP, 1350 Avenue of the Americas, New York, New York 10019, 1-800-238-0658.

BASKETBALL CARD

PRICE GUIDE 1995

ALLAN KAYE
AND
MICHAEL McKEEVER

The CONFIDENT COLLECTOR™

AVON BOOKS NEW YORK

If you purchased this book without a cover, you should be aware that this book is stolen property. It was reported as "unsold and destroyed" to the publisher, and neither the author nor the publisher has received any payment for this "stripped book."

THE CONFIDENT COLLECTOR: BASKETBALL CARD PRICE GUIDE (1995) is an original publication of Avon Books. This edition has never before appeared in book form.

AVON BOOKS
A division of
The Hearst Corporation
1350 Avenue of the Americas
New York, New York 10019

Copyright © 1993, 1994 by Michael McKeever
Cover art: Robert Tanenbaum
The Confident Collector and its logo are trademarked properties of Avon Books.
Published by arrangement with the author
Library of Congress Catalog Card Number: 94-94468
ISBN: 0-380-77242-6

All rights reserved, which includes the right to reproduce this book or portions thereof in any form whatsoever except as provided by the U.S. Copyright Law. For more information address Avon Books.

First Avon Books Printing: December 1994

AVON TRADEMARK REG. U.S. PAT. OFF. AND IN OTHER COUNTRIES, MARCA REGISTRADA, HECHO EN U.S.A.

Printed in U.S.A.

OPM 10 9 8 7 6 5 4 3 2 1

Important Notice: All of the information, including valuations, in this book has been compiled from the most reliable sources, and every effort has been made to eliminate errors and questionable data. Nevertheless, the possibility of error always exists in a work of such immense scope. The publisher and the author will not be held responsible for losses which may occur in the purchase, sale, or other transaction of property because of information contained herein. Readers who feel they have discovered errors are invited to *write* the authors in care of Avon Books, so that the errors may be corrected in subsequent editions.

TABLE OF CONTENTS

Acknowledgements 5
Introduction 6
Glossary Of Terms 7
Grading Guide 9
David Robinson Interview 10

Bowman

1948 Bowman 12

Classic

1991 Classic Draft Picks 13
1992 Classic Draft Picks 14
1993 Classic Draft Picks 15
1993 Classic Futures 17

Courtside

1991 Courtside Draft Pix 18

Fleer

1961-62 Fleer 19
1986-87 Fleer 20
1987-88 Fleer 22
1988-89 Fleer 23
1989-90 Fleer 25
1990-91 Fleer 27
1990-91 Fleer Update 30
1991-92 Fleer 31
1992-93 Fleer 37
1992-93 Fleer Ultra 44
1993-94 Fleer 51
1993-94 Fleer All-Stars 55
1993-94 Fleer Internationals 55
1993-94 Fleer First Year
   Phenoms 56
1993-94 Fleer Living Legends 56
1993-94 Fleer NBA Superstars 57
1993-94 Fleer Rookie
   Sensations 57
1993-94 Fleer Sharpshooters 58
1993-94 Fleer Tower Of Power 58
1993-94 Fleer Jam Session 59
1993-94 Fleer Jam Session
   2nd Year Stars 62
1993-94 Fleer Jam Session
   Slam Dunk Heroes 62
1993-94 Fleer Jam Session
   Rookie Standouts 63
1993-94 Fleer Jam Session
   Gamebreakers 63

1993-94 Fleer Ultra 64
1993-94 Fleer Ultra All-NBA 68
1993-94 Fleer Ultra All-Rookie
   Team 68
1993-94 Fleer Ultra
   All-Defensive Team 69
1993-94 Fleer Ultra Award
   Winners 69
1993-94 Fleer Ultra
   Scoring Kings 70
1993-94 Fleer Ultra All-Rookie
   Series 70
1993-94 Fleer Ultra Famous
   Nicknames 71
1993-94 Fleer Ultra
   Inside/Outside 71
1993-94 Fleer Ultra Jam City 72
1993-94 Fleer Ultra Rebound
   Kings 72
1993-94 Fleer Ultra Power
   In The Key 73

Front Row

1991-92 Front Row 73
1991-92 Front Row Update 74
1991-92 Front Row Premier 75
1992-93 Front Row Draft Picks ... 77

Hoops

1989-90 Hoops 78
1990-91 Hoops 82
1991-92 Hoops 86
1992-93 Hoops 93
1993-94 Hoops 99
1993-94 Hoops Admiral's Choice 104
1993-94 Hoops Face-To-Face ... 104
1993-94 Hoops Magic's
   All-Rookies 105
1993-94 Hoops Supreme Court ... 105
1993-94 Hoops Hoops Scoops ... 106

SkyBox

1990-91 SkyBox 106
1991-92 SkyBox 111
1992-93 SkyBox Team USA 117
1992-93 SkyBox 120
1993-94 SkyBox 126
1993-94 SkyBox All-Rookies 130
1993-94 SkyBox Center Stage ... 130
1993-94 SkyBox NBA
   Draft Picks 131

4 - TABLE OF CONTENTS

1993-94 SkyBox Dynamic Dunks 131
1993-94 SkyBox Shaq Talk 132
1993-94 SkyBox Showdown Series 132
1993-94 SkyBox Thunder & Lightning 133

Star Company

1983-84 Star Company 133
1984-85 Star Company 136
1985-86 Star Company 139

Star Pics

1990-91 Star Pics 141
1991-92 Star Pics 142
1992-93 Star Pics 143

Topps

1957-58 Topps 145
1969-70 Topps 146
1970-71 Topps 148
1971-72 Topps 150
1972-73 Topps 153
1973-74 Topps 156
1974-75 Topps 159
1975-76 Topps 163
1976-77 Topps 167
1977-78 Topps 169
1978-79 Topps 171
1979-80 Topps 172
1980-81 Topps 174
1981-82 Topps 179
1992-93 Topps 182
1992-93 Topps Stadium Club ... 186
1993-94 Topps 191
1993-94 Topps Finest 195
1993-94 Topps Stadium Club ... 198

Upper Deck

1991-92 Upper Deck 203
1992-93 Upper Deck 210
1993-94 Upper Deck 220
1993-94 Upper Deck All-NBA Team 225
1993-94 Upper Deck All-Rookie Team 226
1993-94 Upper Deck Jordan's Flight Team 227
1993-94 Upper Deck Future Heroes 227
1993-94 Upper Deck Triple Double 228
1993-94 Upper Deck Locker Talk 228
1993-94 Upper Deck Mr. June 229
1993-94 Upper Deck Rookie Standouts 229
1993-94 Upper Deck Team MVP's 230
1993-94 Upper Deck SE 231

Wild Card

1991-92 Wild Card College 235
1991-92 Wild Card Red Hot Rookies 236

Hot Off The Presses

1994 Classic Draft Picks 239
1994 Classic Dicky V's PTP 240
1994 Classic Picks 241
1994-95 Fleer 241
1994-95 Fleer All-Stars 244
1994-95 Fleer Award Winners ... 244
1994-95 Fleer All-Defensive Team 245
1994-95 Fleer Career Achievements 245
1994-95 Fleer League Leaders ... 246
1994-95 Fleer Pro Visions 246
1994-95 Fleer Rookie Sensations 247
1994-95 Fleer Triple Threats 247
1994-95 Fleer Flair USA Basketball 248
1994-95 Hoops 249
1994-95 Hoops Big Numbers 252
1994-95 Hoops Supreme Court ... 253
1994-95 SkyBox USA Basketball 254
1994-95 SkyBox USA Dream Play 255
1994-95 SkyBox USA Portraits ... 256
1994-95 SkyBox Premium 256
1994-95 Upper Deck USA Basketball 258
1994-95 Upper Deck USA Chalk Talk 260
1994-95 Upper Deck USA Jordan (HL) 260
1994-95 Upper Deck Collectors Choice 261

Acknowledgements

This book would not have been possible without the contributions of dozens of people whose imput and expertise in the areas of card evaluations, research and technical support have significantly enhanced this edition. We sincerely appreciate their efforts and want to thank each of them for their time, dedication and hard work.

Betty and Jonathan Abraham, Cape Coral Cards; Darren Adams, West Coast SportsCards; Michael Balser, Classic Games; Bill Boake, Hall Of Fame Cards; Tim Boyle, Lesnik Public Relations; Rich Bradley, The Upper Deck Company; Scott Bradshaw, Centerfield; John Brenner, Joie Casey, Field Of Dreams; Ken Cicalo, Vivid Graphics; Lou Costanza, Champion Sports; Sylvie Cote; Mike Cramer; Pacific Trading Cards; Dick DeCourcy; Georgia Music & Sports; Larry Dluhy, Sports Collectibles of Houston; Doug Drotman, National Media Group; Chris Eberheart; Dick Engleberg; Joe Esposito, B & E Collectibles; Eddie Fisher, Batter's Box; Larry Fritsch, Larry Fritsch Cards; Richard Galasso, Home Plate Collectibles; Steve Galletta, Touchdown Cards; Tony Galovich, American Card Exchange; Richard Gelman, Card Collector's Company; Dawn Marie Giargiari, Graphic Designer; Dick Gilkeson; Bill Goepner, San Diego Sports Collectibles; David Greenhill, New York Card Company; Wayne Grove, First Base Sports Nostalgia; Bill Goodwin, St. Louis Baseball Cards; Walter Hall, Hall's Nostalgia; Eric Handler, Lapin Public Relations; Don Harrison, The Tenth Inning; Bill Henderson (King Of The Commons); Neil Hoppenworth; Bob Ibach, Lesnik Public Relations; Toby Johnson; Donn Jennings, Donn Jennings Cards; Bill Karaman; Bill Kennedy, No Gum Just Cards; Tim Kilbane, Ron Klasnick, JW International; Rick Kohl, The Strike Zone; David Kohler, SportsCards Plus; Chuck LaPaglia, The SportsCard Report Radio Show; Don Lepore; Lew Lipset; Greg Manning; Jane McKeever; Jim Mayfield; Blake Meyer, Lone Star SportsCards; Chuck Miller; The SportsCard Report Radio Show; Mike Miller; Dick Millerd; Richard Morris; Steve Myland; Donovan Niemi; Joe Pasternack, Card Collectors Company; Frank and Steve Pemper, Ball Four Cards; Jack and Patti Petruzzelli, 59 Innings; Warren Power; Andy Rapoza; Peter Reeves (Our computer guru); Gavin Riley; Alan "Mr. Mint" Rosen; Steve Rotman, Rotman Productions; Murray Rubenfeld, The SportsCard Report Radio Show; Robert Rusnak; Ben Runyan; Kevin Savage, The Sports Gallery; Duke and Smokey Scheinman, Smokey's Baseball Cards; Michelle Serrio; Ira H. Silverman, Silverman, Warren/Kremer, Inc. Eric Slutsky, Edelman Public Relations Worldwide; Nigel Spill, Oldies And Goodies; Jim Stevens; Ted Taylor, Fleer Corp.; Bud Tompkins, Minnesota Connection; Joe Valle, Cardboard Dreams; Eddie Vidal; Tom Wall; Virginia Webster; Bill Wesslund, Portland SportsCards; Chris Widmaier, Silverman, Warren/Kremer, Inc.; Dean Winskill, Argyle SportsCards; Matt Wozniak, Julie Yolles, Star Pics; and Kit Young. We especially want to thank all of the staff at Avon Books.

Introduction

Over the past several years basketball card collecting has become the fastest growing segment in the hobby and basketball card prices have soared in value. When we first started collecting cards there was only one company, Topps. When we published our first hobby magazine there were only three card companies, Donruss, Fleer and Topps. Today more than a dozen companies manufacture cards on a annual basis and collecting has grown from a passive, fun-filled hobby to a huge industry with investment grade cards selling for hundreds, even thousands of dollars.

The purpose of this edition is to provide you with an accurate, up-to-date listing of basketball card values. These prices don't reflect our opinions but are the result of extensive research throughout the marketplace. The prices listed in this volume are actual retail prices obtained by monitoring retail sports card shops, card shows, memorabilia conventions and auctions, hobby publications and mail order catalogues. The card values were then entered in the book just prior to the press run.

We have also tried to make this edition as easy to use as possible. Since rookie cards are among the most popular in the hobby, and are usually a player's most valuable card, we've provided rookie card designations for thousands of players. Look for the (R) symbol next to the player's name.

Since bonus cards and limited edition inserts are among the hottest cards in the hobby we have provided a checklist and values for these special cards following the regular checklist for the set in which they were issued.

Finally, we have provided a complete card grading and conditioning guide to help you analyze the condition of your collection and a glossary with definitions to help you better understand the terminology of the hobby.

Over the past decade card collecting and sports memorabilia has grown from a cottage industry to a $5 billion a year business. It is estimated that 20 million people actively participate in what has become the most popular hobby in America. We sincerely hope this edition will enhance your enjoyment of the hobby and will serve as your official reference guide to the exciting world of basketball cards.

Glossary Of Terms

ABA-American Basketball Association.

AS-All-Star. Players in a subset who made their league's All-Star team the previous season.

AW-Award Winners. Cards that are usually part of a subset that honors a player's achievements from the previous season.

BC-Bonus card. Cards that are not part of a regular set but are often issued in conjunction with the set. Bonus cards are often issued in limited quantities and randomly inserted into selected wax or foil packs.

C-A card depicting a coach.

CL-Checklist. Cards that contain a numerical list of all the cards in a set.

Commons-Applies to the typical card in a set. A card that is not in demand. Most cards in any particular set are commons and have no significant value above the listing for all the common cards in a set.

COR-A card that's been reissued with corrections after an error was discovered on the original.

DP-Draft Pick

ER-Error Card. Signifies that an error exists on a card. Covers such mistakes as misspelling, erroneous statistics or biographical information, wrong photograph or other graphics. The card has no significant value unless a corrected card is issued creating a variation. (See Variation)

HL-Highlight Cards. These cards appear in various sets, primarily Topps, as part of subsets that depict selected players who are honored for special achievements.

HOF-Hall of Famer.

IA-In-Action Cards. Usually appears as part of a subset and features an action photo of a player that differs from the player's regular card in the set.

INSERT-A card that's not part of a regular edition but usually produced in conjunction with that issue. Some insert cards are produced in limited quantities and packed randomly in wax or foil backs.

3 - GLOSSARY

LL-League Leaders. A card in a subset that depicts leaders in various categories such as points, field goal percentage, assists, rebounds and steals that differs from that player's regular card in the set.

MVP-Most Valuable Player.

NBA-National Basketball Association.

OLY-Olympic cards. Usually part of a subset honoring those who played on the US Olympic basketball team.

R-Rookie Card. Indicates the player's first appearance on a card in a regular annual baseball card set, including update, traded and rookie sets. Rookie cards are usually a player's most valuable card.

RB-Record Breaker. A card that's usually part of a subset that honors a player for a particular milestone or record set the previous season.

ROY-Rookie Of The Year.

SP- Short Print. These cards were under-produced and available in lesser quantities than other cards in the same set.

SR-Star Rookies. A popular subset produced by Upper Deck.

TC-Team checklist cards that contain a list of all the player's from a certain team included in a particular card set. Usually found in Upper Deck issues, but have also appeared in other sets.

TL-Team Leaders. The name of a popular subset or insert set.

VAR-Variations. This symbol means that at least two versions of the same card exist. This usually happens when an error card is corrected in future print runs and then put in circulation by the card company.

Grading And Conditioning Guide

All prices quoted in this edition are retail prices, the price the card would sell for in established sports card stores. Buy prices, the price the dealer would pay for a card, range from about one-third of the price listed for common cards to one-half or more for higher valued cards. Regional interest and other factors may cause the value of a card to vary from one part of the country to another.

The values appearing in this edition are intended only to serve as an aid in evaluating your cards. They are not a solicitation to buy or sell on the part of the publisher or any other party.

Mint (MT): A perfect card. Well-centered, with equal borders. Four sharp, square corners. No nicks, creases, scratches, yellowing or fading. The printing must be flawless. No miscut cards or out of register photo's. Cards with gum or wax stains cannot be considered truly mint, even when removed from brand new packs.

Near Mint (NR MT): A nearly perfect card that contains a minor flaw upon close inspection. Must be well-centered and three of the four corners must be perfectly sharp. A slightly off-centered card with four perfect corners would fit this grade. No creases, scratches, yellowing or fading. Card is valued at 50% to 60% of a mint card depending on the scarcity of the card and the demand for the player.

Excellent (EX): Moderate wear, corners still fairly sharp. Card borders might be off-center. No creases, scratches, gum or wax stains on front or back. Surface may show some lack of luster. Card is valued at 40% of mint.

Very Good (VG): Corners rounded or showing minor wear or light creases. Loss of surface luster. All printing must be perfect. No gum or wax stains, no major creases, no writing or markings on the card. Card is valued at 30% to 40% of mint.

Good (G): A well-worn card with rounded corners and a major crease. Could have a small tear, pencil, tape or glue marks on the back. Printing must be intact, but overall, the card shows excessive wear. Card is valued at 20% to 30% of mint.

Fair (F): Card shows major damage such as creases that break the cardboard or pin holes along the border. Shows tape and glue marks. May have a tear or missing a bit of paper. Could have writing or other markings on the back. Card has very little value, less than 10% of mint.

Poor (P): Card fronts have been defaced with pen and ink marks. Corners may be torn off or paper may be missing or ripped-off. Card may have pin holes, glue and tape marks and major cracks through the cardboard. Cards have little or no value, less than 10% of the good (G) value.

Conversation With David Robinson

Since he entered the NBA with the San Antonio Spurs in 1989 David Robinson has established himself as one of the top centers in the game. A perennial All-Star, Robinson won a gold medal as a member of Dream Team I at the 1992 Olympic Games in Barcelona. He led the NBA in scoring in 1993-94 becoming the first center to accomplish the feat in 18 years. In this exclusive interview Robinson talks about his cards and career.

Q. David, you averaged nearly 30 points a game during the '93-'94 season and won the NBA scoring title. Has your role with the Spurs changed?

A. My role changes every year depending upon who's on the team. Two years ago I didn't need to score as much because we had some great shooters on the team. I concentrated on rebounding, dishing off, working the defensive end, and blocking shots. Last year we brought in Dennis (Rodman), one of the best rebounders in the game, and my role switched around a bit. I could score more because he could patrol the boards. In order for us to win I have to do a lot of different things. I can pretty much do whatever the team asks of me. I know what my strengths are. Something I'll never turn away from is my defense, my rebounding, blocking shots. Those are the basics of my game.

Q. You scored a career high 71 points on the final night of the regular season to clinch the scoring title. Did you and your teammates concentrate on getting you the title that night?

A. No not really. Going into that game, it was against the Clippers, we didn't know how many points it would take to win the scoring title. Early in the second half we had the game pretty well in hand and I started getting the ball and the shots were just dropping.
At that point I thought I might have a chance and as it turned out I needed everyone of those 71 points to win it.

Q. In a career filled with highlights is there one or two that stand out?

A. Well, there's been a lot of great things that have happened to me along the way but I would say the Dream Team would have to rank at the top of the list. Being around all of those amazing players, together at one event, I don't think anything even approaches that level of excitement. Winning the gold medal was great, but getting to know these guys on a different level was probably the best thing about it. You see these guys all year, you play against them and beat each other up for 48 minutes and then go our separate ways. But at the Olympics we got to know each other on a more personal level, we saw each other in a different light. I wouldn't trade that experience for anything. Winning an NBA championship would be great but I haven't experienced that one yet.

DAVID ROBINSON - 11

Q. Every night you go head-to-head against the best centers in the NBA. Who's your toughest opponent?

A. There are so many great centers in the game today and it seems like they all had career years last season. But for my style of play I think Hakeem (Olajuwon) is the most difficult for me. He does a lot of the same things I do only he's bigger and stronger than I am. He's a quick leaper. You always have to know where he's at on the court. And he never lets up. You know he's going to get the ball 40 times a game and he's going to shoot it 30 times. Handling his quickness and his strength is a tough assignment and, of course, he's in our division so we see him more often than the other centers.

Q. Turning to the hobby, your 1989 Hoops rookie card is valued in the $25-$30 range. Some of your limited insert cards command up to $50. Are you surprised at the value of those cards?

A. I really don't know what drives the value of those cards. I hear it's supply and demand and the rarer the card the more it's worth. Whatever it is I'm flattered that my cards are popular. There are so many different cards out there it's hard to keep up with them all. As you know I'm a spokesman for SkyBox and I think the cards can play a positive role for kids. They go right into the home and if they can carry the right message I believe they can become an important resource in reaching some of these kids.

Q. Did you collect cards as a kid and, if so, who were some of your heroes?

A. I collected a lot of cards when I was young, mostly baseball cards. Unfortunately they got thrown out along the way. I wish I had them now. Reggie Jackson was a hero. I liked watching him when I was growing up. As far as basketball goes, I'd have to say Dr. J., Julius Erving, was my favorite. I wasn't really into sports all that much as a kid. I had a lot of different interests, school, music and church among other things.

Q. The NBA has never been more popular. How do you feel about the future of the league?

A. The way the NBA has grown, the way the popularity has really picked up, anything is possible. We're expanding into Canada, Toronto and Vancouver. That's a big step. Who knows, maybe one of these days we might be flying to Europe to play. The game has gotten extremely popular around the world and I think that's good for the sport.

12 • 1948 BOWMAN

BOWMAN

1948 Bowman

This 72-card set is considered the first modern basketball card set and was Bowman's only basketball set. The set consists of the top players of the day along with cards that diagram basketball plays. The fronts feature posed pictures on gray backgrounds with red and blue print. Some cards in Series II (37-72) were made without the red and blue print and are considered scarce. Card backs contain player highlights. All cards measure 2-1/16" by 2-1/2".

	NR/MT	EX
Complete Set (72)	8,250.00	4,000.00
Commons (1-36)	48.00	22.00
Commons (37-72)	90.00	42.00
Basketball Plays	30.00	12.00

#	Player	NR/MT	EX
1	Ernie Calverley (R)	150.00	70.00
2	Ralph Hamilton (R)	48.00	22.00
3	Gale Bishop (R)	48.00	22.00
4	Fred Lewis (R)	60.00	28.00
5	Basketball Play	30.00	12.00
6	Bob Ferrick (R)	60.00	28.00
7	John Logan (R)	48.00	22.00
8	Mel Riebe (R)	48.00	22.00
9	Andy Phillip (R)	110.00	50.00
10	Bob Davies (R)	125.00	60.00
11	Basketball Play	30.00	12.00
12	Kenny Sailors (R)	55.00	25.00
13	Paul Armstrong (R)	48.00	22.00
14	Howard Dallmar (R)	55.00	25.00
15	Bruce Hale (R)	60.00	28.00
16	Sid Hertzberg (R)	48.00	22.00
17	Basketball Play	30.00	12.00
18	Red Rocha (R)	48.00	22.00
19	Eddie Ehlers (R)	48.00	22.00
20	Gene Vance (R)	48.00	22.00
21	Fuzzy Levane (R)	55.00	25.00
22	Earl Shannon (R)	48.00	22.00
23	Basketball Play	30.00	12.00
24	Leo Klier (R)	48.00	22.00
25	George Senesky (R)	48.00	22.00
26	Price Brookfield (R)	48.00	22.00
27	John Norlander (R)	48.00	22.00
28	Don Putman (R)	48.00	22.00
29	Basketball Play	30.00	12.00
30	Jack Garfinkel (R)	48.00	22.00
31	Chuck Gilmur (R)	48.00	22.00
32	Red Holzman (R)	450.00	210.00
33	Jack Smiley (R)	48.00	22.00
34	Joe Fulks (R)	400.00	185.00
35	Basketball Play	30.00	12.00
36	Hal Tidrick (R)	48.00	22.00
37	Don Carlson (R)	90.00	42.00
38	Buddy Jeanette (R)	110.00	50.00
39	Ray Kuka (R)	90.00	42.00
40	Stan Miasek (R)	90.00	42.00
41	Basketball Play	35.00	15.00
42	George Nostrand (R)	90.00	42.00
43	Chuck Halbert (R)	100.00	48.00
44	Arnie Johnson (R)	90.00	42.00
45	Bob Doll (R)	90.00	42.00
46	Horace McKinney (R)	125.00	55.00
47	Basketball Play	35.00	15.00
48	Ed Sadowski (R)	90.00	42.00
49	Bob Kinney (R)	90.00	42.00
50	Charles Black	90.00	42.00
51	Jack Dwan (R)	90.00	42.00
52	Cornelius Simmons (R)	95.00	45.00
53	Basketball Play	35.00	15.00
54	Bud Palmer (R)	110.00	50.00
55	Max Zaslofsky (R)	260.00	125.00
56	Lee Roy Robbins (R)	90.00	42.00
57	Arthur Spector (R)	90.00	42.00
58	Arnie Risen (R)	110.00	50.00
59	Basketball Play	35.00	15.00
60	Ariel Maughan (R)	90.00	42.00
61	Dick O'Keefe (R)	90.00	42.00
62	Herman Schaefer (R)	90.00	42.00
63	John Manhken (R)	90.00	42.00
64	Tommy Byrnes (R)	90.00	42.00
65	Basketball Play	35.00	15.00
66	Jim Pollard (R)	375.00	180.00
67	Lee Mogus (R)	90.00	42.00
68	Lee Knorek (R)	90.00	42.00

1991 CLASSIC DRAFT PICKS • 13

		MINT	NR/MT
69	George Mikan (R)	4,850.00	2200.00
70	Walter Budko (R)	90.00	42.00
71	Basketball Play	35.00	15.00
72	Carl Braun (R)	200.00	90.00

CLASSIC

1991 Classic Draft Picks

This set marks Classic's first basketball draft picks set. The cards feature full color photos of players wearing their college uniforms. The photos are framed by light green borders. The backs contain personal data, college stats and profiles of each player's strengths and weaknesses. 10-Limited Print insert cards (LP) were randomly distributed in Classic's foil packs. Those cards are listed at the end of this checklist. All cards measure 2-1/2" by 3-1/2".

		MINT	NR/MT
	Complete Set (50)	7.50	4.50
	Commons	.05	.02
1	Larry Johnson	2.00	1.25
2	Billy Owens	.50	.30
3	Dikembe Mutombo	1.00	.70
4	Mark Macon	.12	.07
5	Brian Williams	.20	.12
6	Terrell Brandon	.20	.12
7	Greg Anthony	.25	.15
8	Dale Davis	.35	.20
9	Anthony Avent	.12	.07
10	Chris Gatling	.15	.10
11	Victor Alexander	.12	.07
12	Kevin Brooks	.10	.06
13	Eric Murdock	.40	.25
14	LeRon Ellis	.20	.12
15	Stanley Roberts	.12	.07
16	Rick Fox	.30	.18
17	Pete Chilcutt	.15	.10
18	Kevin Lynch	.05	.02
19	George Ackles	.07	.04
20	Rodney Monroe	.05	.02
21	Randy Brown	.15	.10
22	Chad Gallagher	.05	.02
23	Donald Hodge	.10	.06
24	Myron Brown	.05	.02
25	Mike Luzzolino	.07	.04
26	Chris Corchiani	.10	.06
27	Elliott Perry	.05	.02
28	Joe Wylie	.07	.04
29	Jimmy Oliver	.08	.05
30	Doug Overton	.12	.07
31	Sean Green	.05	.02
32	Steve Hood	.05	.02
33	Lamont Strothers	.05	.02
34	Alvaro Teheran	.05	.02
35	Bobby Phills	.12	.07
36	Richard Dumas	.25	.15
37	Keith Hughes	.05	.02
38	Isaac Austin	.05	.02
39	Greg Sutton	.05	.02
40	Joey Wright	.05	.02
41	Anthony Jones	.07	.04
42	Von McDade	.05	.02
43	Marcus Kennedy	.05	.02
44	Larry Johnson	.75	.45
45	Larry Johnson/ Billy Owens	.75	.45
46	Anderson Hunt	.07	.04
47	Darrin Chancellor	.05	.02
48	Damon Lopez	.05	.02
49	Thomas Jordan	.05	.02
50	Tony Farmer	.05	.02
LP1	Rocket Ismail	.75	.45
LP2	Rocket Ismail	.75	.45
LP3	Rocket Ismail	.75	.45
LP4	Rocket Ismail	.75	.45
LP5	Rocket Ismail	.75	.45
LP6	Larry Johnson	3.00	1.75

14 • 1991 CLASSIC DRAFT PICKS

LP7	Brien Taylor	.30	.18
LP8	Classic Gold	7.00	4.00
LP9	Larry Johnson/ Billy Owens	3.00	1.75
LP10	Russell Maryland	.35	.20

1992 Classic Draft Picks

Classic increased the size of their set to 100-cards and featured the only 1992 card of Shaquille O'Neal. The card fronts consist of full color glossy action photos wrapped by a white border. The player's name appears in a silver bar under the photo. The backs contain another photograph, personal data, college stats and a scouting report. A 4-card subset called Flashbacks (FB) is included in the set. A Christian Laettner Bonus Card (BC) was inserted in Blister packs and is listed at the end of this checklist along with Classic's Limited Print inserts (LP) and Classic's Basketball Draft Preview Cards (PC) which were randomly inserted into their football foil packs. All cards measure 2-1/2" by 3-1/2".

	MINT	NR/MT
Complete Set (100)	16.00	10.00
Commons	.05	.02

1	Shaquille O'Neal	7.00	4.00
2	Walt Williams	.40	.25
3	Lee Mayberry	.15	.10
4	Tony Bennett	.10	.06
5	Litterial Green	.12	.07
6	Chris Smith	.15	.10
7	Henry Williams	.05	.02
8	Terrell Lowery	.20	.12
9	Radenko Dobras	.08	.05
10	Curtis Blair	.05	.02
11	Randy Woods	.10	.06
12	Todd Day	.40	.25
13	Anthony Peeler	.50	.28
14	Darin Archbold	.05	.02
15	Benford Williams	.05	.02
16	Terrence Lewis	.05	.02
17	James McCoy	.05	.02
18	Damon Patterson	.05	.02
19	Bryant Stith	.40	.25
20	Doug Christie	.50	.30
21	Latrell Sprewell	2.00	1.25
22	Hubert Davis	.40	.25
23	David Booth	.05	.02
24	David Johnson	.07	.04
25	Jon Barry	.15	.10
26	Everick Sullivan	.05	.02
27	Brian Davis	.08	.05
28	Clarence Weatherspoon	.80	.50
29	Malik Sealy	.15	.10
30	Matt Geiger	.20	.12
31	Jimmy Jackson	1.50	.90
32	Matt Steigenga	.05	.02
33	Robert Horry	1.00	.70
34	Marlon Maxey	.12	.07
35	Reggie Slater	.05	.02
36	Lucius Davis	.05	.02
37	Chris King	.05	.02
38	Dexter Cambridge	.08	.05
39	Alonzo Jamison	.05	.02
40	Anthony Tucker	.05	.02
41	Tracy Murray	.20	.12
42	Vernel Singleton	.07	.04
43	Christian Laettner	.80	.50
44	Don MacLean	.60	.35
45	Adam Keefe	.15	.10
46	Tom Gugliotta	.90	.55
47	LaPhonso Ellis	1.00	.70
48	Byron Houston	.20	.12
49	Oliver Miller	.75	.45
50	Popeye Jones	.08	.05
51	P.J. Brown	.05	.02
52	Eric Anderson	.08	.05
53	Darren Morningstar	.05	.02
54	Isaiah Morris	.05	.02
55	Stephen Howard	.05	.02
56	Reggie Smith	.08	.05
57	Elmore Spencer	.25	.15

1993 CLASSIC DRAFT PICKS • 15

58	Sean Rooks	.20	.12
59	Robert Werdann	.08	.05
60	Alonzo Mourning	3.00	1.75
61	Steve Rogers	.05	.02
62	Tim Burroughs	.05	.02
63	Ed Book	.05	.02
64	Herb Jones	.05	.02
65	Mik Kilgore	.05	.02
66	Ken Leeks	.05	.02
67	Sam Mack	.05	.02
68	Sean Miller	.05	.02
69	Craig Upchurch	.05	.02
70	Van Usher	.05	.02
71	Corey Williams	.07	.04
72	Duane Cooper	.07	.04
73	Brett Roberts	.08	.05
74	Elmer Bennett	.05	.02
75	Brent Price	.12	.07
76	Daimon Sweet	.05	.02
77	Darrick Martin	.05	.02
78	Gerald Madkins	.08	.05
79	Jo Jo English	.12	.07
80	Alex Blackwell	.05	.02
81	Anthony Dade	.05	.02
82	Matt Fish	.05	.02
83	Byron Tucker	.05	.02
84	Harold Miner	.60	.35
85	Greg Dennis	.05	.02
86	Jeff Roulston	.05	.02
87	Keir Rogers	.05	.02
88	Billy Law	.05	.02
89	Geoff Lear	.05	.02
90	Lambert Shell	.05	.02
91	Elbert Rogers	.05	.02
92	Ron Ellis	.05	.02
93	Predrag Danilovic	.05	.02
94	Calvin Talford	.05	.02
95	Stacey Augmon (FB)	.10	.06
96	Steve Smith (FB)	.15	.10
97	Billy Owens (FB)	.15	.10
98	Dikembe Mutombo (FB)	.20	.12
99	Checklist (1-50)	.05	.02
100	Checklist (51-100)	.05	.02
BC1	Christian Laettner	1.50	.90
LP1	Shaquille O'Neal	70.00	40.00
LP2	Alonzo Mourning	35.00	20.00
LP3	Christian Laettner	8.00	5.00
LP4	Jimmy Jackson	14.00	9.00
LP5	LaPhonso Ellis	8.00	5.00
LP6	Tom Gugliota	10.00	6.50
LP7	Walt Williams	5.00	3.00
LP8	Todd Day	4.00	2.50
LP9	Clarence Weatherspoon	8.00	5.00
LP10	Adam Keefe	1.00	.70
PC1	Shaquille O'Neal	125.00	80.00
PC2	Alonzo Mourning	50.00	32.00
PC3	Don MacLean	12.00	7.00
PC4	Walt Williams	10.00	6.50
PC5	Christian Laettner	15.00	10.00

1993 Classic Draft Picks

The cards in this set depict the top NBA draft picks pictured in their college uniforms. The card fronts feature full-color game action photos framed by a brown pinstriped border. The player's name and position appear in a white bar centered under his photograph. A gold Classic logo also appears along the bar. The card backs consist of another full-color action photo along with personal data, stats and a brief biography. A gold version of each card was also produced and originally packaged as a factory set. Those cards are valued at 3X to 6 X the values listed below. Autographed inserts of Chris Webber and Jamal Mashburn were distributed in the Classic gold set and 10 Limited Print inserts (LP) were randomly distributed in Classic foil packs. 5 additional insert cards, unnumbered and produced on clear Acetate (ACE), were also distributed randomly in Classic foil packs. All of those values are listed at the end of this checklist. All cards measure 2-1/2" by 3-1/2".

16 • 1993 CLASSIC DRAFT PICKS

	MINT	NR/MT
Complete Set (110)	12.00	7.50
Commons	.05	.02
Complete Set (Gold)	200.00	125.00
Commons (Gold)	.15	.10

#	Player	MINT	NR/MT
1	Chris Webber	3.50	2.00
2	Anfernee Hardaway	3.00	1.75
3	Jamal Mashburn	1.50	.90
4	Isaiah Rider	1.50	.90
5	Vin Baker	.80	.50
6	Rodney Rogers	.50	.30
7	Lindsey Hunter	.35	.20
8	Allan Houston	.25	.15
9	George Lynch	.40	.25
10	Toni Kukoc	.75	.45
11	Ashraf Amaya	.05	.02
12	Mark Bell	.05	.02
13	John Best	.05	.02
14	Corie Blount	.10	.06
15	Dexter Boney	.05	.02
16	Tim Brooks	.07	.04
17	James Bryson	.05	.02
18	Evers Burns	.08	.04
19	Scott Burrell	.15	.10
20	Sam Cassell	.50	.30
21	Derrick Chandler	.05	.02
22	Sam Crawford	.07	.04
23	Ron Curry	.05	.02
24	William Davis	.05	.02
25	Rodney Dobard	.05	.02
26	Tony Dunkin	.08	.05
27	Spencer Dunkley	.05	.02
28	Bill Edwards	.05	.02
29	Bryan Edwards	.05	.02
30	Doug Edwards	.12	.07
31	Chuck Evans	.05	.02
32	Terry Evans	.05	.02
33	Will Flemons	.05	.02
34	Alphonso Ford	.05	.02
35	Brian Gilgeous	.05	.02
36	Josh Grant	.12	.07
37	Evric Gray	.10	.06
38	Geert Hammink	.08	.05
39	Lucious Harris	.12	.07
40	Joe Harvell	.05	.02
41	Antonio Harvey	.10	.06
42	Scott Haskin	.10	.06
43	Brian Hendrick	.05	.02
44	Sascha Hupmann	.05	.02
45	Stanley Jackson	.08	.05
46	Ervin Johnson	.12	.07
47	Adonis Jordan	.08	.05
48	Warren Kidd	.08	.05
49	Malcolm Mackey	.15	.10
50	Rich Manning	.05	.02
51	Chris McNeal	.05	.02
52	Conrad McRae	.10	.06
53	Lance Miller	.05	.02
54	Chris Mills	.40	.25
55	Matt Nover	.08	.05
56	Charles Outlaw	.08	.05
57	Eric Pauley	.08	.05
58	Mike Peplowski	.10	.06
59	Stacey Poole	.07	.04
60	Anthony Reed	.07	.04
61	Eric Riley	.10	.06
62	Darrin Robinson	.05	.02
63	Jackie Robinson	.05	.02
64	James Robinson	.12	.07
65	Byron Russell	.12	.07
66	Brent Scott	.05	.02
67	Bennie Seltzer	.05	.02
68	Ed Stokes	.08	.05
69	Antoine Stoudamire	.07	.04
70	Dirkk Surles	.05	.02
71	Justus Thigpen	.05	.02
72	Kevin Thompson	.08	.05
73	Ray Thompson	.05	.02
74	Gary Trost	.05	.02
75	Nick Van Exel	.75	.45
76	Jerry Walker	.05	.02
77	Rex Walters	.12	.07
78	Leonard White	.05	.02
79	Chris Whitney	.08	.05
80	Steve Worthy	.05	.02
81	Alex Wright	.05	.02
82	Luther Wright	.15	.10
83	Mark Buford	.05	.02
84	Keith Bullock	.05	.02
85	Mitchell Butler	.15	.10
86	Brian Clifford	.05	.02
87	Terry Dehere	.15	.10
88	Acie Earl	.15	.10
89	Greg Graham	.10	.06
90	Angelo Hamilton	.05	.02
91	Thomas Hill	.05	.02
92	Alex Holcombe	.05	.02
93	Khari Jaxon	.05	.02
94	Darnell Mee	.12	.07
95	Sherron Mills	.05	.02
96	Gheorge Muresan	.25	.15
97	Eddie Rivera	.05	.02
98	Julius Nwosu	.05	.02
99	Richard Petruska	.12	.07
100	Bryan Sallier	.05	.02
101	Harper Williams	.05	.02
102	Ike Williams	.05	.02
103	Byron Wilson	.05	.02
104	Shaquille O'Neal (FB)	1.00	.70
105	Alonzo Mourning (FB)	.60	.35
106	Christian Laettner (FB)	.12	.07
107	Jimmy Jackson (FB)	.25	.15

1993 CLASSIC FUTURES • 17

108	Harold Miner (FB)	.10	.06
109	Checklist	.05	.02
110	Checklist	.05	.02
LP1	Chris Webber	10.00	6.50
LP2	Anfernee Hardaway	8.00	5.00
LP3	Jamal Mashburn	5.00	3.00
LP4	Isaiah Rider	5.00	3.00
LP5	Vin Baker	2.50	1.50
LP6	Rodney Rogers	1.75	1.00
LP7	Lindsey Hunter	1.00	.70
LP8	Toni Kukoc	3.50	2.00
LP9	Shaquille O'Neal	7.50	4.50
LP10	Alonzo Mourning	3.50	2.00
___	Chris Webber (Auto)	100.00	65.00
___	Jamal Mashburn (Auto)	50.00	28.00
ACE1	Anfernee Hardaway	12.00	7.50
ACE2	Jamal Mashburn	7.00	4.00
ACE3	Isaiah Rider	7.00	4.00
ACE4	Rodney Rogers	3.00	1.75
ACE5	Chris Webber	14.00	9.00

1993 Classic Futures

The cards in this set measure 2-1/2" by 4-11/16" and feature full-color action photos on the front depicting players in their college uniforms. The photos are framed at the top and bottom by a white border. The player's name and position are printed in gold across the lower border under a small gold Classic log. The words "Classic Futures" are printed in gold across the top. Card backs contain another small photo, personal data and stats. 5 Limited Prints (LP) were issued randomly in packs and also sold as sets on cable television shopping channels. 5 additional inserts called Classic Futures Team (FT) were also randomly inserted into packs. Those inserts are listed at the end of this checklist but not included in the complete set price below.

		MINT	NR/MT
	Complete Set (100)	14.00	9.00
	Commons	.08	.05
1	Chris Webber	4.00	2.50
2	Bill Edwards	.08	.05
3	Anfernee Hardaway	3.00	1.75
4	Bryan Edwards	.08	.05
5	Jamal Mashburn	2.50	1.50
6	Doug Edwards	.12	.07
7	Isaiah Rider	2.00	1.25
8	Chuck Evans	.08	.05
9	Vin Baker	1.00	.70
10	Terry Evans	.08	.05
11	Rodney Rogers	.75	.45
12	Will Flemons	.08	.05
13	Lindsey Hunter	.35	.20
14	Alphonso Ford	.08	.05
15	Allan Houston	.30	.18
16	Josh Grant	.12	.07
17	George Lynch	.60	.35
18	Evric Gray	.12	.07
19	Toni Kukoc	.80	.50
20	Geert Hammink	.10	.06
21	Ashraf Amaya	.08	.05
22	Lucious Harris	.15	.10
23	Mark Bell	.08	.05
24	Joe Harvell	.08	.05
25	Corie Blount	.12	.07
26	Antonio Harvey	.12	.07
27	Dexter Boney	.08	.05
28	Scott Haskin	.12	.07
29	Tim Brooks	.10	.06
30	Brian Hendrick	.08	.05
31	James Bryson	.08	.05
32	Sascha Hupmann	.08	.05
33	Evers Burns	.12	.07
34	Stanley Jackson	.12	.07

18 • 1993 CLASSIC FUTURES

#	Player		
35	Scott Burrell	.20	.12
36	Ervin Johnson	.15	.10
37	Sam Cassell	.60	.35
38	Adonis Jordan	.10	.06
39	Sam Crawford	.10	.06
40	Warren Kidd	.12	.07
41	Ron Curry	.08	.05
42	Malcolm Mackey	.15	.10
43	William Davis	.08	.05
44	Rich Manning	.08	.05
45	Rodney Dobard	.08	.05
46	Chris McNeal	.08	.05
47	Tony Dunkin	.10	.06
48	Conrad McRae	.10	.06
49	Spencer Dunkley	.08	.05
50	Lance Miller	.08	.05
51	Chris Mills	.60	.35
52	Chris Whitney	.12	.07
53	Matt Nover	.10	.06
54	Steve Worthy	.08	.05
55	Charles Outlaw	.12	.07
56	Luther Wright	.20	.12
57	Eric Pauley	.12	.07
58	Mark Buford	.08	.05
59	Mike Peplowski	.12	.07
60	Mitchell Butler	.20	.12
61	Stacey Poole	.08	.05
62	Brian Clifford	.08	.05
63	Anthony Reed	.08	.05
64	Terry Dehere	.20	.12
65	Eric Riley	.12	.07
66	Acie Earl	.20	.12
67	Darrin Robinson	.08	.05
68	Greg Graham	.12	.07
69	James Robinson	.20	.12
70	Angelo Hamilton	.08	.05
71	Bryon Russell	.15	.10
72	Thomas Hill	.10	.06
73	Brent Scott	.08	.05
74	Khari Jaxon	.08	.05
75	Bennie Seltzer	.08	.05
76	Darnell Mee	.20	.12
77	Ed Stokes	.08	.05
78	Sherron Mills	.08	.05
79	Antoine Stoudamire	.08	.05
80	Gheorghe Muresan	.25	.15
81	Dirkk Surles	.08	.05
82	Eddie Rivera	.08	.05
83	Justus Thigpen	.08	.05
84	Julius Nwosu	.08	.05
85	Kevin Thompson	.12	.07
86	Richard Petruska	.12	.07
87	Ray Thompson	.08	.05
88	Bryan Sallier	.08	.05
89	Gary Trost	.08	.05
90	Harper Williams	.08	.05
91	Nick Van Exel	.75	.45
92	Ike Williams	.08	.05
93	Jerry Walker	.08	.05
94	Byron Wilson	.08	.05
95	Rex Walters	.15	.10
96	Alex Holcombe	.08	.05
97	Leonard White	.08	.05
98	Alex Wright	.08	.05
99	Checklist	.08	.05
100	Checklist	.08	.05
LP	Chris Webber	15.00	10.00
LP	Anfernee Hardaway	12.00	7.50
LP	Jamal Mashburn	8.00	5.00
LP	Isaiah Rider	7.50	4.50
LP	Toni Kukoc	5.00	3.00
FT	Chris Webber	10.00	6.50
FT	Anfernee Hardaway	8.00	5.00
FT	Jamal Mashburn	5.00	3.00
FT	Isaiah Rider	5.00	3.00
FT	Toni Kukoc	3.00	1.75

1991 Courtside Draft Pix

This 45-card set features some of the top NBA draft picks from the 1991 draft. The card fronts feature full color photos superimposed over a color rectangle. Color bars appear along the top and right border of the front while the player's name is printed in the upper right corner. The backs include a small head shot, college stats and highlights. All cards measure 2-1/2" by 3-1/2".

		MINT	NR/MT
Complete Set (45)		7.00	4.00
Commons		.05	.02
1	Larry Johnson	.60	.35
2	George Ackles	.05	.02
3	Kenny Anderson	.60	.35
4	Greg Anthony	.20	.12
5	Anthony Avent	.12	.07
6	Terrell Brandon	.15	.10
7	Kevin Brooks	.10	.06
8	Marc Brown	.05	.02
9	Myron Brown	.05	.02
10	Randy Brown	.12	.07
11	Darrin Chancellor	.05	.02
12	Pete Chilcutt	.12	.07
13	Chris Corchiani	.08	.05
14	John Crotty	.08	.05
15	Dale Davis	.50	.30
16	Marty Dow	.05	.02
17	Richard Dumas	.15	.10
18	LeRon Ellis	.25	.15
19	Tony Farmer	.05	.02
20	Roy Fisher	.05	.02
21	Rick Fox	.25	.15
22	Chad Gallagher	.05	.02
23	Chris Gatling	.15	.10
24	Sean Green	.07	.04
25	Reggie Hanson	.05	.02
26	Donald Hodge	.12	.07
27	Steve Hood	.05	.02
28	Keith Hughes	.05	.02
29	Mike Iuzzolino	.07	.04
30	Keith Jennings	.12	.07
31	Larry Johnson	2.00	1.25
32	Treg Lee	.05	.02
33	Cedric Lewis	.05	.02
34	Kevin Lynch	.08	.05
35	Mark Macon	.12	.07
36	Jason Matthews	.05	.02
37	Eric Murdock	.25	.15
38	Jimmy Oliver	.10	.06
39	Doug Overton	.10	.06
40	Elliot Perry	.05	.02
41	Brian Shorter	.05	.02
42	Alvaro Tejeram	.05	.02
43	Joey Wright	.05	.02
44	Joe Wylie	.05	.02
45	Larry Johnson	.60	.35
SP1	Larry Johnson (Mail-In Offer)	4.50	2.75

1961-62 Fleer

This set marks Fleer's first basketball edition. The card fronts feature both action shots and posed photos on the lower two-thirds of the front with the player's team name and team logo in a color box at the top of the card and his name directly above his picture.

The backs contain personal data, highlights and statistics from the previous year and career statistics. The only subset is Action Cards (IA)(45-66). This is a tough set to find in mint condition due to off-centering problems. All cards measure 2-1/2" by 3-1/2".

		NR/MT	EX
Complete Set (66)		4,700.00	2,250.00
Commons		18.00	8.00
1	Al Attles (R)	85.00	40.00
2	Paul Arizin	35.00	15.00
3	Elgin Baylor (R)	400.00	180.00
4	Walt Bellamy (R)	48.00	22.00
5	Arlen Bockhorn	18.00	8.00
6	Bob Boozer (R)	20.00	9.00
7	Carl Bran	18.00	8.00
8	Wilt Chamberlain (R)	1,600.00	750.00
9	Larry Costello	20.00	8.75
10	Bob Cousy	240.00	110.00
11	Walter Dukes	18.00	8.00
12	Wayne Embry (R)	35.00	16.00
13	Dave Gambee	18.00	8.00

20 • 1961-62 FLEER

14	Tom Gola	40.00	18.00
15	Sihugo Green (R)	18.00	8.00
16	Hal Greer (R)	80.00	35.00
17	Richie Guerin (R)	40.00	18.00
18	Cliff Hagan	40.00	18.00
19	Tom Heinsohn	80.00	35.00
20	Bailey Howell (R)	35.00	16.00
21	Rod Hundley	40.00	18.00
22	K.C. Jones (R)	80.00	35.00
23	Sam Jones (R)	70.00	30.00
24	Phil Jordan	18.00	8.00
25	John Kerr	32.00	15.00
26	Rudy LaRusso (R)	32.00	15.00
27	George Lee	18.00	8.00
28	Bob Leonard	20.00	8.75
29	Clyde Lovellette	28.00	13.00
30	John McCarthy	18.00	8.00
31	Tom Meschery (R)	22.00	10.00
32	Willie Naulls	20.00	8.75
33	Don Ohl	18.00	8.00
34	Bob Pettit	80.00	35.00
35	Frank Ramsey	30.00	14.00
36	Oscar Robertson (R)	600.00	280.00
37	Guy Rodgers (R)	22.00	9.50
38	Bill Russell	525.00	245.00
39	Dolph Schayes	35.00	16.00
40	Frank Selvy	22.00	9.50
41	Gene Shue	22.00	9.50
42	Jack Twyman	30.00	14.00
43	Jerry West (R)	750.00	360.00
44	Len Wilkens (R)	150.00	70.00
45	Paul Arizin (IA)	20.00	8.75
46	Elgin Baylor (IA)	110.00	50.00
47	Wilt Chamberlain IA	400.00	180.00
48	Larry Costello (IA)	20.00	8.75
49	Bob Cousy (IA)	80.00	35.00
50	Walter Dukes (IA)	18.00	8.00
51	Tom Gola (IA)	18.00	8.00
52	Richie Guerin (IA)	18.00	8.00
53	Cliff Hagan (IA)	20.00	8.75
54	Tom Heinsohn (IA)	35.00	16.00
55	Bailey Howell (IA)	20.00	8.75
56	John Kerr (IA)	2.00	9.00
57	Rudy LaRusso (IA)	20.00	8.75
58	Clyde Lovellette (IA)	20.00	8.75
59	Bob Pettit (IA)	40.00	18.00
60	Frank Ramsey (IA)	20.00	8.75
61	Oscar Robertson(IA)	175.00	80.00
62	Bill Russell (IA)	240.00	110.00
63	Dolph Schayes (IA)	20.00	8.75
64	Gene Shue (IA)	18.00	8.00
65	Jack Twyman (IA)	18.00	8.00
66	Jerry West (IA)	280.00	130.00

1986-87 Fleer

This 132-card set is Fleer's first regular issue basketball set since the 1961-62 season. The card fronts contain full color action pictures framed by a red, white and blue border. The word "premier" is printed under the Fleer logo. The flip side includes personal data and year-by-year statistics. All cards measure 2-1/2" by 3-1/2".

		MINT	NR/MT
Complete Set (132)		1,650.00	1,000.00
Commons		2.00	1.25

1	Kareem Abdul-Jabbar	14.00	9.00
2	Alvan Adams	2.00	1.25
3	Mark Aguirre (R)	4.00	2.50
4	Danny Ainge (R)	18.00	10.00
5	John Bagley (R)	2.50	1.50
6	Thurl Bailey (R)	2.75	1.60
7	Charles Barkley (R)	240.00	140.00
8	Benoit Benjamin (R)	2.50	1.50
9	Larry Bird	50.00	30.00
10	Otis Birdsong	2.00	1.25
11	Rolando Blackman (R)	7.00	4.00
12	Manute Bol	2.75	1.60
13	Sam Bowie (R)	3.50	2.00
14	Joe Barry Carroll (R)	2.50	1.50
15	Tom Chambers (R)	12.00	7.00
16	Maurice Cheeks	3.50	2.00
17	Michael Cooper	3.00	1.75
18	Wayne Cooper	2.00	1.25
19	Pat Cummings	2.00	1.25

1986-87 FLEER • 21

#	Player		
20	Terry Cummings (R)	5.00	3.00
21	Adrian Dantley	3.00	1.75
22	Brad Davis (R)	2.50	1.50
23	Walter Davis	3.00	1.75
24	Darryl Dawkins	3.00	1.75
25	Larry Drew	2.00	1.25
26	Clyde Drexler (R)	50.00	30.00
27	Joe Dumars (R)	30.00	18.00
28	Mark Eaton (R)	3.00	1.75
29	James Edwards	2.75	1.60
30	Alex English	3.50	2.00
31	Julius Erving	20.00	12.50
32	Patrick Ewing (R)	95.00	55.00
33	Vern Fleming (R)	3.50	2.00
34	Sleepy Floyd (R)	3.00	1.75
35	World B. Free	2.00	1.25
36	George Gervin	5.00	3.00
37	Artis Gilmore	3.50	2.00
38	Mike Gminski	2.00	1.25
39	Rickey Green	2.00	1.25
40	Sidney Green	2.00	1.25
41	David Greenwood	2.00	1.25
42	Darrell Griffith	2.75	1.60
43	Bill Hanzlik	2.00	1.25
44	Derek Harper (R)	7.50	4.50
45	Gerald Henderson	2.00	1.25
46	Roy Hinson	2.00	1.25
47	Craig Hodges (R)	2.75	1.75
48	Phil Hubbard	2.00	1.25
49	Jay Humphries (R)	3.00	1.75
50	Dennis Johnson	3.50	2.00
51	Eddie Johnson (R)	5.00	3.00
52	Frank Johnson (R)	2.50	1.50
53	Magic Johnson	50.00	32.00
54	Marques Johnson	2.75	1.60
55	Steve Johnson (R)	2.00	1.25
56	Vinnie Johnson	2.00	1.25
57	Michael Jordan (R)	900.00	550.00
58	Clark Kellogg (R)	2.75	1.60
59	Albert King	2.00	1.25
60	Bernard King	3.00	1.75
61	Bill Laimbeer	2.75	1.60
62	Allen Leavell (R)	2.00	1.25
63	Lafayette Lever (R)	2.00	1.25
64	Alton Lister (R)	2.00	1.25
65	Lewis Lloyd (R)	2.00	1.25
66	Maurice Lucas	2.00	1.25
67	Jeff Malone (R)	7.00	4.00
68	Karl Malone (R)	75.00	45.00
69	Moses Malone	5.00	3.00
70	Cedric Maxwell	2.00	1.25
71	Rodney McCray (R)	2.75	1.60
72	Xavier McDaniel (R)	7.50	4.50
73	Kevin McHale	6.50	3.75
74	Mike Mitchell	2.00	1.25
75	Sidney Moncrief	3.00	1.75
76	Johnny Moore	2.00	1.25
77	Chris Mullin (R)	40.00	28.00
78	Larry Nance (R)	14.00	9.00
79	Calvin Natt	2.00	1.25
80	Norm Nixon	2.00	1.25
81	Charles Oakley (R)	10.00	6.50
82	Hakeem Olajuwon(R)	175.00	100.00
83	Louis Orr	2.00	1.25
84	Robert Parish	6.00	3.50
85	Jim Paxson	2.75	1.60
86	Sam Perkins (R)	10.00	6.50
87	Ricky Pierce (R)	8.00	5.00
88	Paul Pressey (R)	2.50	1.50
89	Kurt Rambis (R)	2.75	1.60
90	Robert Reid	2.00	1.25
91	Doc Rivers (R)	5.00	3.00
92	Alvin Robertson (R)	4.00	2.50
93	Cliff Robinson	2.00	1.25
94	Tree Rollins	2.00	1.25
95	Dan Roundfield	2.00	1.25
96	Jeff Ruland	2.00	1.25
97	Ralph Sampson (R)	3.00	1.75
98	Danny Schayes (R)	2.50	1.50
99	Byron Scott (R)	5.00	3.00
100	Purvis Short	2.00	1.25
101	Jerry Sichting	2.00	1.25
102	Jack Sikma	2.75	1.60
103	Derek Smith (R)	2.00	1.25
104	Larry Smith	2.00	1.25
105	Rory Sparrow (R)	2.00	1.25
106	Steve Stipanovich (R)	2.00	1.25
107	Terry Teagle (R)	2.00	1.25
108	Reggie Theus	2.75	1.60
109	Isiah Thomas (R)	35.00	20.00
110	LaSalle Thompson (R)	2.75	1.60
111	Mychal Thompson (R)	2.50	1.50
112	Sedale Threatt (R)	5.00	3.00
113	Wayman Tisdale (R)	6.00	3.50
114	Andrew Toney	2.00	1.25
115	Kelly Tripucka	2.00	1.25
116	Mel Turpin (R)	2.00	1.25
117	Kiki Vandeweghe (R)	3.50	2.00
118	Jay Vincent	2.00	1.25
119	Bill Walton	7.50	4.50
120	Spud Webb (R)	8.00	5.00
121	Dominique Wilkins(R)	80.00	48.00
122	Gerald Wilkins (R)	6.00	3.75
123	Buck Williams (R)	10.00	6.50
124	Gus Williams	2.50	1.50
125	Herb Williams (R)	2.50	1.50
126	Kevin Willis (R)	12.50	7.50
127	Randy Wittman	2.00	1.25
128	Al Wood	2.00	1.25
129	Mike Woodson	2.00	1.25
130	Orlando Woolridge (R)	4.00	2.50
131	James Worthy (R)	24.00	14.00
132	Checklist (1-132)	8.00	3.00

/ 1987-88 FLEER

1987-88 Fleer

The cards in this set feature full color action photos on the card front framed by a white border on the sides with gray horizontal stripes at the top and bottom. The player's name and position appear under the picture while his team name is printed across the top. The flip side, in red, white and blue, includes personal data and statistics. All cards measure 2-1/2" by 3-1/2".

		MINT	NR/MT
Complete Set (132)		335.00	190.00
Commons		.90	.55
1	Kareem Abdul-Jabbar	10.00	6.50
2	Alvan Adams	.90	.55
3	Mark Aguirre	1.50	.90
4	Danny Ainge	5.00	3.00
5	John Bagley	.90	.55
6	Thurl Bailey	.90	.55
7	Greg Ballard	.90	.55
8	Gene Banks	.90	.55
9	Charles Barkley	50.00	30.00
10	Benoit Benjamin	1.00	.60
11	Larry Bird	30.00	18.00
12	Rolando Blackman	1.75	1.00
13	Manute Bol	.90	.55
14	Tony Brown	.90	.55
15	Michael Cage (R)	1.50	.90
16	Joe Barry Carroll	.90	.55
17	Bill Cartwright	1.50	.90
18	Terry Catledge (R)	1.25	.70
19	Tom Chambers	3.00	1.75
20	Maurice Cheeks	1.50	.90
21	Michael Cooper	1.25	.70
22	Dave Corzine	.90	.55
23	Terry Cummings	1.50	.90
24	Adrian Dantley	1.50	.90
25	Brad Daugherty (R)	20.00	12.50
26	Walter Davis	1.50	.90
27	Johnny Dawkins (R)	2.25	1.40
28	James Donaldson	.90	.55
29	Larry Drew	.90	.55
30	Clyde Drexler	16.00	9.50
31	Joe Dumars	9.00	5.50
32	Mark Eaton	.90	.55
33	Dale Ellis (R)	4.50	2.75
34	Alex English	1.50	.90
35	Julius Erving	12.00	7.50
36	Mike Evans	.90	.55
37	Patrick Ewing	24.00	14.00
38	Vern Fleming	.90	.55
39	Sleepy Floyd	.90	.55
40	Artis Gilmore	1.50	.90
41	Mike Gminski	.90	.55
42	A.C. Green (R)	10.00	6.50
43	Rickey Green	.90	.55
44	Sidney Green	.90	.55
45	David Greenwood	.90	.55
46	Darrell Griffith	.90	.55
47	Bill Hanzlik	.90	.55
48	Derek Harper	1.50	.90
49	Ron Harper (R)	8.00	5.00
50	Gerald Henderson	.90	.55
51	Roy Hinson	.90	.55
52	Craig Hodges	.90	.55
53	Phil Hubbard	.90	.55
54	Dennis Johnson	1.50	.90
55	Eddie Johnson	1.25	.70
56	Magic Johnson	32.00	19.00
57	Steve Johnson	.90	.55
58	Vinnie Johnson	.90	.55
59	Michael Jordan	200.00	125.00
60	Jerome Kersey (R)	3.50	2.00
61	Bill Laimbeer	1.75	1.00
62	Lafayette Lever	.90	.55
63	Cliff Levingston	.90	.55
64	Alton Lister	.90	.55
65	John Long	.90	.55
66	John Lucas	1.50	.90
67	Jeff Malone	2.00	1.25
68	Karl Malone	18.00	11.00
69	Moses Malone	3.00	1.75
70	Cedric Maxwell	.90	.55
71	Tim McCormick	.90	.55
72	Rodney McCray	1.00	.60
73	Xavier McDaniel	2.50	1.50
74	Kevin McHale	3.50	2.00
75	Nate McMillan (R)	4.50	2.75
76	Sidney Moncrief	1.50	.90

#	Name	MINT	NR/MT
77	Chris Mullin	10.00	6.50
78	Larry Nance	3.00	1.75
79	Charles Oakley	2.50	1.50
80	Hakeem Olajuwon	48.00	28.00
81	Robert Parish	3.50	2.00
82	Jim Paxson	.90	.55
83	John Paxson (R)	6.00	3.50
84	Sam Perkins	2.50	1.50
85	Chuck Person (R)	5.00	3.00
86	Jim Peterson (R)	.90	.55
87	Ricky Pierce	1.50	.90
88	Ed Pinckney (R)	1.25	.70
89	Terry Porter (R)	10.00	6.50
90	Paul Pressey	.90	.55
91	Robert Reid	.90	.55
92	Doc Rivers	1.25	.70
93	Alvin Robertson	1.00	.60
94	Tree Rollins	.90	.55
95	Ralph Sampson	1.00	.60
96	Mike Sanders	.90	.55
97	Detlef Schrempf (R)	20.00	12.50
98	Byron Scott	1.50	.90
99	Jerry Sichting	.90	.55
100	Jack Sikma	1.25	.70
101	Larry Smith	.90	.55
102	Rory Sparrow	.90	.55
103	Steve Sipanovich	.90	.55
104	Jon Sundvold	.90	.55
105	Reggie Theus	1.25	.70
106	Isiah Thomas	10.00	6.50
107	LaSalle Thompson	.90	.55
108	Mychal Thompson	.90	.55
109	Otis Thorpe (R)	8.50	5.00
110	Sedale Threatt	1.25	.70
111	Wayman Tisdale	1.50	.90
112	Kelly Tripucka	1.00	.60
113	Trent Tucker (R)	1.25	.70
114	Terry Tyler	.90	.55
115	Darnell Valentine	.90	.55
116	Kiki Vandeweghe	1.00	.60
117	Darrell Walker	1.25	.70
118	Dominique Wilkins	20.00	12.50
119	Gerald Wilkins	1.50	.90
120	Buck Williams	2.50	1.50
121	Herb Williams	.90	.55
122	John Williams (R)	1.25	.70
123	Hot Rod Williams (R)	4.50	2.75
124	Kevin Willis	3.00	1.75
125	David Wingate (R)	1.25	.70
126	Randy Wittman	.90	.55
127	Leon Wood	.90	.55
128	Mike Woodson	.90	.55
129	Orlando Woolridge	1.25	.70
130	James Worthy	6.50	3.75
131	Danny Young	1.00	.60
132	Checklist (1-132)	1.25	.40

1988-89 Fleer

The cards in this set feature full color photos on the front framed by a thin inner border that mirrors the player's team colors and a wider, outer border in white and gray. The player's name appears in the top left corner of the card while his team name and position are printed in opposite corners at the bottom. The card backs consist of personal data and statistics. A 12-card subset of All-Stars (AS) was included in the set. All cards measure 2-1/2" by 3-1/2".

	MINT	NR/MT
Complete Set (132)	160.00	90.00
Commons	.25	.15

#	Name	MINT	NR/MT
1	Antoine Carr (R)	1.25	.70
2	Cliff Levingston	.25	.15
3	Doc Rivers	.60	.35
4	Spud Webb	1.00	.60
5	Dominique Wilkins	7.00	4.00
6	Kevin Willis	1.50	.90
7	Randy Wittman	.25	.15
8	Danny Ainge	1.50	.90
9	Larry Bird	10.00	6.50
10	Dennis Johnson	.60	.35
11	Kevin McHale	1.50	.90
12	Robert Parish	1.50	.90
13	Tyrone Bogues (R)	4.50	2.75
14	Dell Curry (R)	2.50	1.50
15	Dave Corzine	.25	.15

24 • 1988-89 FLEER

#	Player		
16	Horace Grant (R)	12.50	7.50
17	Michael Jordan	55.00	32.50
18	Charles Oakley	.40	.25
19	John Paxson	1.00	.60
20	Scottie Pippen (R)	60.00	35.00
21	Brad Sellers (R)	.25	.15
22	Brad Daugherty (R)	4.00	2.50
23	Ron Harper	1.50	.90
24	Larry Nance	1.00	.60
25	Mark Price (R)	16.00	10.00
26	Hot Rod Williams	1.00	.60
27	Mark Aguirre	.40	.25
28	Rolando Blackman	.70	.40
29	James Donaldson	.25	.15
30	Derek Harper	.70	.40
31	Sam Perkins	1.25	.70
32	Roy Tarpley (R)	.80	.50
33	Michael Adams (R)	3.50	2.00
34	Alex English	.60	.35
35	Lafayette Lever	.25	.15
36	Blair Rasmussen (R)	.30	.18
37	Danny Schayes	.25	.15
38	Jay Vincent	.30	.18
39	Adrian Dantley	.50	.30
40	Joe Dumars	2.75	1.60
41	Vinnie Johnson	.25	.15
42	Bill Laimbeer	.40	.25
43	Dennis Rodman (R)	10.00	6.50
44	John Salley (R)	1.50	.90
45	Isiah Thomas	3.00	1.75
46	Winston Garland (R)	.40	.25
47	Rod Higgins	.25	.15
48	Chris Mullin	4.00	2.50
49	Ralph Sampson	.40	.25
50	Joe Barry Carroll	.25	.15
51	Sleepy Floyd	.25	.15
52	Rodney McCray	.30	.18
53	Hakeem Olajuwon	10.00	6.50
54	Purvis Short	.25	.15
55	Vern Fleming	.25	.15
56	John Long	.25	.15
57	Reggie Miller (R)	14.00	9.00
58	Chuck Person	.80	.50
59	Steve Stipanovich	.25	.15
60	Waymon Tisdale	.50	.30
61	Benoit Benjamin	.30	.18
62	Michael Cage	.25	.15
63	Mike Woodson	.25	.15
64	Kareem Abdul-Jabbar	4.50	2.75
65	Michael Cooper	.40	.25
66	A.C. Green	2.00	1.25
67	Magic Johnson	12.00	7.50
68	Byron Scott	.50	.30
69	Mychal Thompson	.25	.15
70	James Worthy	2.00	1.25
71	Duane Washington	.25	.15
72	Kevin Williams	.25	.15
73	Randy Breuer (R)	.25	.15
74	Terry Cummings	.75	.45
75	Paul Pressey	.25	.15
76	Jack Sikma	.50	.30
77	John Bagley	.25	.15
78	Roy Hinson	.25	.15
79	Buck Williams	.80	.50
80	Patrick Ewing	8.50	5.00
81	Sidney Green	.25	.15
82	Mark Jackson (R)	3.00	1.75
83	Kenny Walker (R)	.35	.20
84	Gerald Wilkins	.50	.30
85	Charles Barkley	14.00	9.00
86	Maurice Cheeks	.50	.30
87	Mike Gminski	.25	.15
88	Cliff Robinson	.25	.15
89	Armon Gilliam (R)	1.00	.60
90	Eddie Johnson	.50	.30
91	Mark West (R)	.40	.25
92	Clyde Drexler	5.00	3.00
93	Kevin Duckworth (R)	1.00	.60
94	Steve Johnson	.25	.15
95	Jerome Kersey	1.00	.60
96	Terry Porter	2.00	1.25
97	Joe Kleine (R)	.40	.25
98	Reggie Theus	.30	.18
99	Otis Thorpe	2.00	1.25
100	Kenny Smith (R)	3.50	2.00
101	Greg Anderson (R)	.60	.35
102	Walter Berry (R)	.35	.20
103	Frank Brickowski (R)	1.00	.60
104	Johnny Dawkins	.30	.18
105	Alvin Robertson	.40	.25
106	Tom Chambers	1.00	.60
107	Dale Ellis	.60	.35
108	Xavier McDaniel	.75	.45
109	Derrick McKey (R)	2.00	1.25
110	Nate McMillan	.25	.15
111	Thurl Bailey	.25	.15
112	Mark Eaton	.30	.18
113	Bobby Hansen (R)	.30	.18
114	Karl Malone	7.00	4.00
115	John Stockton (R)	25.00	15.00
116	Bernard King	.70	.40
117	Jeff Malone	.80	.50
118	Moses Malone	1.00	.60
119	John Williams	.30	.18
120	Michael Jordan (AS)	18.00	11.00
121	Mark Jackson (AS)	.60	.35
122	Byron Scott (AS)	.30	.18
123	Magic Johnson (AS)	5.00	3.00
124	Larry Bird (AS)	5.00	3.00
125	Dominique Wilkins (AS)	2.50	1.50
126	Hakeem Olajuwon (AS)	4.00	2.50
127	John Stockton (AS)	4.00	2.50
128	Alvin Robertson (AS)	.30	.18
129	Charles Barkley (AS)	6.00	3.50

1989-90 FLEER • 25

130	Patrick Ewing (AS)	3.00	1.75
131	Mark Eaton (AS)	.30	.18
132	Checklist (1-132)	.60	.20

1989-90 Fleer

Fleer increased the size of their set to 168-cards. The card fronts consist of full color action photos framed by multi-colored borders that mirror a player's team colors. The player's name, team and position appear across the top border. The card backs are horizontal and contain personal data, statistics and a basketball fact. The only subset of note are All-Star Game cards (AS). All cards measure 2-1/2" by 3-1/2".

		MINT	NR/MT
	Complete Set (168)	48.00	30.00
	Commons	.12	.07
1	John Battle (R)	.35	.20
2	Jon Koncak (R)	.40	.25
3	Cliff Levingston	.12	.07
4	Moses Malone	.50	.30
5	Glenn Rivers	.12	.07
6	Spud Webb	.30	.18
7	Dominique Wilkins	1.75	1.00
8	Larry Bird	4.00	2.50
9	Dennis Johnson	.20	.12
10	Reggie Lewis (R)	5.00	3.00
11	Kevin McHale	.50	.30
12	Robert Parish	.50	.30
13	Ed Pinckney	.12	.07
14	Brian Shaw (R)	.80	.50
15	Rex Chapman (R)	.80	.50
16	Kurt Rambis	.12	.07
17	Robert Reid	.12	.07
18	Kelly Tripucka	.12	.07
19	Bill Cartwright	.15	.10
20	Horace Grant	1.50	.90
21	Michael Jordan	16.00	10.00
22	John Paxson	.35	.20
23	Scottie Pippen	8.50	5.00
24	Brad Sellers	.12	.07
25	Brad Daugherty	1.00	.60
26	Craig Ehlo (R)	1.25	.70
27	Ron Harper	.40	.25
28	Larry Nance	.30	.18
29	Mark Price	2.00	1.25
30	Mike Sanders	.12	.07
31A	John Williams (Er)	.90	.50
31B	John Williams (Cor)	.30	.18
32	Rolando Blackman	.25	.15
33	Adrian Dantley	.20	.12
34	James Donaldson	.12	.07
35	Derek Harper	.20	.12
36	Sam Perkins	.35	.20
37	Herb Williams	.12	.07
38	Michael Adams	.35	.20
39	Walter Davis	.12	.07
40	Alex English	.25	.15
41	Lafayette Lever	.12	.07
42	Blair Rasmussen	.12	.07
43	Dan Schayes	.12	.07
44	Mark Aguirre	.15	.10
45	Joe Dumars	.70	.40
46	James Edwards	.12	.07
47	Vinnie Johnson	.12	.07
48	Bill Laimbeer	.20	.12
49	Dennis Rodman	1.50	.90
50	Isiah Thomas	1.00	.60
51	John Salley	.15	.10
52	Manute Bol	.12	.07
53	Winston Garland	.12	.07
54	Rod Higgins	.12	.07
55	Chris Mullin	1.00	.60
56	Mitch Richmond (R)	5.00	3.00
57	Terry Teagle	.12	.07
58	Derrick Chievous (R)	.15	.10
59	Sleepy Floyd	.12	.07
60	Tim McCormick	.12	.07
61	Hakeem Olajuwon	4.00	2.50
62	Otis Thorpe	.50	.30
63	Mike Woodson	.12	.07
64	Vern Fleming	.12	.07
65	Reggie Miller	2.00	1.25

26 • 1989-90 FLEER

#	Player	Price 1	Price 2
66	Chuck Person	.35	.20
67	Detlef Schrempf	2.00	1.25
68	Rik Smits (R)	1.75	1.00
69	Benoit Benjamin	.15	.10
70	Gary Grant (R)	.50	.30
71	Dannny Manning (R)	7.50	4.50
72	Ken Norman (R)	1.00	.60
73	Charles Smith (R)	1.50	.90
74	Reggie williams (R)	.80	.50
75	Michael Cooper	.12	.07
76	A.C. Green	.60	.35
77	Magic Johnson	5.00	3.00
78	Byron Scott	.15	.10
79	Mychal Thompson	.12	.07
80	James Worthy	.70	.40
81	Kevin Edwards (R)	.75	.45
82	Grant Long (R)	.75	.45
83	Rony Seikaly (R)	3.00	1.75
84	Rory Sparrow	.12	.07
85	Greg Anderson	.15	.10
86	Jay Humphries	.15	.10
87	Larry Krystkowiak (R)	.35	.20
88	Ricky Pierce	.25	.15
89	Paul Pressey	.12	.07
90	Alvin Robertson	.15	.10
91	Jack Sikma	.20	.12
92	Steve Johnson	.12	.07
93	RicK Mahorn	.15	.10
94	David Rivers (R)	.15	.10
95	Joe Barry Carroll	.12	.07
96	Lester Conner	.12	.07
97	Roy Hinson	.12	.07
98	Mike McGee	.12	.07
99	Chris Morris (R)	.80	.50
100	Patrick Ewing	3.00	1.75
101	Mark Jackson	.40	.25
102	Johnny Newman (R)	.75	.45
103	Charles Oakley	.25	.15
104	Rod Strickland (R)	2.50	1.50
105	Trent Tucker	.12	.07
106	Kiki Vandeweghe	.15	.10
107	Gerald Wilkins	.15	.10
108	Terry Cattledge	.12	.07
109	Dave Corzine	.12	.07
110	Scott Skiles (R)	1.25	.70
111	Reggie Theus	.15	.10
112	Ron Anderson (R)	.15	.10
113	Charles Barkley	4.50	2.75
114	Scott Brooks (R)	.40	.25
115	Maurice Cheeks	.20	.12
116	Mike Gminski	.12	.07
117	Hersey Hawkins (R)	2.75	1.60
118	Chris Welp (R)	.12	.07
119	Tom Chambers	.30	.18
120	Armon Gilliam	.20	.12
121	Jeff Hornacek (R)	2.50	1.50
122	Eddie Johnson	.12	.07
123	Kevin Johnson (R)	7.50	4.50
124	Dan Majerle (R)	6.00	3.75
125	Mark West	.12	.07
126	Richard Anderson	.15	.10
127	Mark Bryant (R)	.25	.15
128	Clyde Drexler	2.00	1.25
129	Kevin Duckworth	.20	.12
130	Jerome Kersey	.30	.18
131	Terry Porter	.75	.45
132	Buck Williams	.25	.15
133	Danny Ainge	.40	.25
134	Ricky Berry	.12	.07
135	Rodney McCray	.15	.10
136	Jim Petersen	.12	.07
137	Harold Pressley	.12	.07
138	Kenny Smith	.40	.25
139	Wayman Tisdale	.25	.15
140	Willie Anderson (R)	.80	.50
141	Frank Brickowski	.12	.07
142	Terry Cummings	.20	.12
143	Johnny Dawkins	.12	.07
144	Vern Maxwell (R)	3.00	1.75
145	Michael Cage	.12	.07
146	Dale Ellis	.20	.12
147	Alton Lister	.12	.07
148	Xavier McDaniel	.25	.15
149	Derrick McKey	.35	.20
150	Nate McMillan	.12	.07
151	Thurl Bailey	.12	.07
152	Mark Eaton	.15	.10
153	Darrell Griffith	.12	.07
154	Eric Leckner (R)	.12	.07
155	Karl Malone	1.75	1.00
156	John Stockton	2.50	1.50
157	Mark Alarie (R)	.15	.10
158	Ledell Eackles (R)	.25	.15
159	Bernard King	.20	.12
160	Jeff Malone	.25	.15
161	Darrell Walker	.12	.07
162A	John Williams (Er)	.35	.20
162B	John Williams (Cor)	.15	.10
163	Karl Malone/John Stockton (AS)	.50	.30
164	Hakeem Olajuwon/Clyde Drexler (AS)	1.50	.90
165	Dominique Wilkins/Moses Malone (AS)	.50	.30
166	Brad Daugherty/Mark Price/Larry Nance (AS)	.40	.25
167	Patrick Ewing/Mark Jackson (AS)	.50	.30
168	Checklist (1-168)	.20	.06

1990-91 Fleer

CHRIS MULLIN
GUARD
FLEER 90

Fleer increased the size of their set to 198-cards in 1990-91. The card fronts feature full color action shots framed by red borders at the top and bottom and blue borders on the sides. The player's name and position appear under the photograph while a team logo is printed in the top left corner. The card backs consist of personal data, statistics and a brief biography. All cards measure 2-1/2" by 3-1/2".

		MINT	NR/MT
	Complete Set (198)	7.50	4.50
	Commond	.05	.02
1	John Battle	.05	.02
2	Cliff Levingston	.05	.02
3	Moses Malone	.15	.10
4	Kenny Smith	.07	.04
5	Spud Webb	.08	.05
6	Dominique Wilkins	.25	.15
7	Kevin Willis	.07	.04
8	Larry Bird	.80	.50
9	Dennis Johnson	.08	.05
10	Joe Kleine	.05	.02
11	Reggie Lewis	.20	.12
12	Kevin McHale	.15	.10
13	Robert Parish	.15	.10
14	Jim Paxson	.05	.02
15	Ed Pinckney	.05	.02
16	Tyrone Bogues	.05	.02
17	Rex Chapman	.08	.05
18	Dell Curry	.05	.02
19	Armon Gilliam	.07	.04
20	J.R. Reid (R)	.15	.10
21	Kelly Tripucka	.05	.02
22	B.J. Armstrong (R)	1.00	.60
23	Bill Cartwright	.07	.04
24	Horace Grant	.20	.12
25	Craig Hodges	.05	.02
26	Michael Jordan	3.00	1.75
27	Stacey King (R)	.15	.10
28	John Paxson	.05	.02
29	Will Perdue (R)	.12	.07
30	Scottie Pippen	.60	.35
31	Brad Daugherty	.20	.12
32	Craig Ehlo	.05	.02
33	Danny Ferry (R)	.10	.06
34	Steve Kerr (R)	.05	.02
35	Larry Nance	.08	.05
36	Mark Price	.20	.12
37	Hot Rod Williams	.08	.05
38	Rolando Blackman	.07	.04
39	Adrian Dantley	.07	.04
40	Brad Davis	.05	.02
41	James Donaldson	.05	.02
42	Derek Harper	.05	.02
43	Sam Perkins	.10	.06
44	Bill Wennington	.05	.02
45	Herb Williams	.05	.02
46	Michael Adams	.08	.05
47	Walter Davis	.07	.04
48	Alex English	.08	.05
49	Bill Hanzlik	.05	.02
50	Lafayette Lever (ER)	.05	.02
51	Todd Lichti (R)	.10	.06
52	Blair Rasmussen	.05	.02
53	Dan Schayes	.05	.02
54	Mark Aguirre	.08	.05
55	Joe Dumars	.15	.10
56	James Edwards	.05	.02
57	Vinnie Johnson	.05	.02
58	Bill Laimbeer	.08	.05
59	Dennis Rodman	.20	.12
60	John Salley	.07	.04
61	Isiah Thomas	.20	.12
62	Manute Bol	.05	.02
63	Tim Hardaway (R)	1.00	.60
64	Rod Higgins	.05	.02
65	Sarunas Marciulionis(R)	.15	.10
66	Chris Mullin	.20	.12
67	Mitch Richmond	.15	.10
68	Terry Teagle	.05	.02
69	Anthony Bowie (R)	.12	.07
70	Eric Floyd	.05	.02
71	Buck Johnson	.07	.04
72	Vernon Maxwell	.07	.04
73	Hakeem Olajuwon	.75	.45
74	Otis Thorpe	.12	.07

28 • 1990-91 FLEER

#	Player		
75	Mitchell Wiggins	.05	.02
76	Vern Fleming	.05	.02
77	George McCloud (R)	.10	.06
78	Reggie Miller	.20	.12
79	Chuck Person	.10	.06
80	Mike Sanders	.05	.02
81	Detlef Schrempf	.10	.06
82	Rik Smits	.07	.04
83	LaSalle Thompson	.05	.02
84	Benoit Benjamin	.07	.04
85	Winston Garland	.05	.02
86	Ron Harper	.08	.05
87	Danny Manning	.25	.15
88	Ken Norman	.08	.05
89	Charles Smith	.12	.07
90	Michael Cooper	.05	.02
91	Vlade Divac (R)	.30	.18
92	A.C. Green	.07	.04
93	Magic Johnson	.70	.40
94	Byron Scott	.07	.04
95	Mychal Thompson	.05	.02
96	Orlando Wooldridge	.05	.02
97	James Worthy	.15	.10
98	Sherman Douglas (R)	.20	.12
99	Kevin Edwards	.05	.02
100	Grant Long	.05	.02
101	Glen Rice (R)	.75	.45
102	Rony Seikaly	.12	.07
103	Billy Thompson (R)	.05	.02
104	Jeff Grayer (R)	.08	.05
105	Jay Humphries	.05	.02
106	Ricky Pierce	.07	.04
107	Paul Pressey	.05	.02
108	Fred Roberts	.05	.02
109	Alvin Robertson	.07	.04
110	Jack Sikma	.07	.04
111	Randy Breuer	.05	.02
112	Tony Campbell (R)	.10	.06
113	Tyrone Corbin	.05	.02
114	Sam Mitchell (R)	.10	.06
115	Tod Murphy (R)	.05	.02
116	Pooh Richardson (R)	.15	.10
117	Mookie Blaylock (R)	.40	.25
118	Sam Bowie	.07	.04
119	Lester Conner	.05	.02
120	Dennis Hopson	.05	.02
121	Chris Morris	.07	.04
122	Charles Shackleford (R)	.05	.02
123	Purvis Short	.05	.02
124	Maurice Cheeks	.07	.04
125	Patrick Ewing	.30	.18
126	Mark Jackson	.07	.04
127	Johnny Newman	.05	.02
128	Charles Oakley	.07	.04
129	Trent Tucker	.05	.02
130	Kenny Walker	.05	.02
131	Gerald Wilkins	.05	.02
132	Nick Anderson (R)	.35	.20
133	Terry Catledge	.05	.02
134	Sidney Green	.05	.02
135	Otis Smith	.05	.02
136	Reggie Theus	.05	.02
137	Sam Vincent	.05	.02
138	Ron Anderson	.05	.02
139	Charles Barkley	.60	.35
140	Scott Brooks	.05	.02
141	Johnny Dawkins	.05	.02
142	Mike Gminski	.05	.02
143	Hersey Hawkins	.10	.06
144	Rick Mahorn	.05	.02
145	Derek Smith	.05	.02
146	Tom Chambers	.10	.06
147	Jeff Hornacek	.12	.07
148	Eddie Johnson	.05	.02
149	Kevin Johnson	.30	.18
150	Dan Majerle	.20	.12
152	Kurt Rambis	.05	.02
153	Mark West	.05	.02
154	Clyde Drexler	.25	.15
155	Kevin Duckworth	.05	.02
156	Byron Irvin (R)	.08	.05
157	Jerome Kersey	.08	.05
158	Terry Porter	.12	.07
159	Cliff Robinson (R)	.75	.45
160	Buck Williams	.07	.04
161	Danny Young	.05	.02
162	Danny Ainge	.08	.05
163	Antoine Carr	.05	.02
164	Pervis Ellison (R)	.20	.12
165	Rodney McCray	.07	.04
166	Harold Pressley	.05	.02
167	Wayman Tisdale	.08	.05
168	Willie Anderson	.07	.04
169	Frank Brickowski	.05	.02
170	Terry Cummings	.08	.05
171	Sean Elliott (R)	.25	.15
172	David Robinson (R)	1.50	.90
173	Rod Strickland	.05	.02
174	David Wingate	.05	.02
175	Dana Barros (R)	.15	.10
176	Michael Cage	.05	.02
177	Dale Ellis	.07	.04
178	Shawn Kemp (R)	3.00	1.75
179	Xavier McDaniel	.08	.05
180	Derrick McKey	.08	.05
181	Nate McMillan	.05	.02
182	Thurl Bailey	.05	.02
183	Mike Brown	.05	.02
184	Mark Eaton	.07	.04
185	Blue Edwards (R)	.15	.10
186	Bob Hansen	.05	.02
187	Eric Leckner	.05	.02
188	Karl Malone	.25	.15
189	John Stockton	.25	.15

1990-91 FLEER ROOKIE SENSATIONS • 29

190	Mark Alarie	.05	.02
191	Ledell Eackles	.07	.04
192	Harvey Grant (R)	.12	.07
193	Tom Hammonds (R)	.08	.05
194	Bernard King	.08	.05
195	Jeff Malone	.08	.05
196	Darrell Walker	.05	.02
197	Checklist	.05	.02
198	Checklist	.05	.02

3	Hakeem Olajuwon	1.50	.90
4	Magic Johnson	1.75	1.00
5	Michael Jordan	4.00	2.50
6	Isiah Thomas	.30	.18
7	Karl Malone	.50	.30
8	Tom Chambers	.25	.15
9	John Stockton	.50	.30
10	David Robinson	2.00	1.25
11	Clyde Drexler	.50	.30
12	Patrick Ewing	1.00	.60

1990-91 Fleer All-Stars

The cards in this limited insert set were distributed randomly in Fleer wax packs. The fronts feature full color photos pictured inside a basketball hoop design. The headline "Fleer '90 All-Stars" appears across the top while the player's name and position are located between two stars below the photograph. The backs contain a paragraph pertaining to career highlights. All cards measure 2-1/2" by 3-1/2".

	MINT	NR/MT
Complete Set (12)	8.00	5.00
Commons	.25	.15

1	Charles Barkley	1.50	.90
2	Larry Bird	1.50	.90

1990-91 Fleer Rookie Sensations

The cards in this limited insert set were distributed randomly in Fleer cello packs. The fronts feature full color action shots with the player's name and position located in a horizontal red box under the photograph. The words "Rookie Sensation" is printed over a small basketball in the lower left corner. The backs contain highlights from the player's college career and rookie season. All cards measure 2-1/2" by 3-1/2".

	MINT	NR/MT
Complete Set (10)	55.00	32.00
Commons	1.00	.60

30 • 1990-91 FLEER ROOKIE SENSATIONS

1	David Robinson	28.00	18.00
2	Sean Elliott	3.00	1.75
3	Glen Rice	8.50	5.00
4	J.R. Reid	1.25	.70
5	Stacey King	1.00	.60
6	Pooh Richardson	1.25	.70
7	Nick Anderson	4.00	2.50
8	Tim Hardaway	12.00	7.00
9	Vlade Divac	2.50	1.50
10	Sherman Douglas	2.50	1.50

1990-91 Fleer Update

This set is comprised of rookies and player's traded during the regular season. The design is identical to the regular Fleer edition except the card backs carry the prefix "U" next to the card number. All cards measure 2-1/2" by 3-1/2".

	MINT	NR/MT
Complete Set (100)	10.00	6.50
Commons	.05	.02

U1	Jon Koncak	.07	.04
U2	Tim McCormick	.05	.02
U3	Glenn Rivers	.05	.02
U4	Rumeal Robinson (R)	.12	.07
U5	Trevor Wilson	.05	.02
U6	Dee Brown (R)	1.00	.60
U7	Dave Popson (R)	.08	.05
U8	Kevin Gamble (R)	.12	.07
U9	Brian Shaw	.07	.04
U10	Michael Smith (R)	.07	.04
U11	Kendall Gill (R)	1.75	1.00
U12	Johnny Newman	.05	.02
U13	Steve Scheffler	.05	.02
U14	Dennis Hopson	.05	.02
U15	Cliff Levingston	.05	.02
U16	Chucky Brown (R)	.10	.06
U17	John Morton (R)	.07	.04
U18	Gerald Paddio (R)	.07	.04
U19	Alex English	.08	.05
U20	Fat Lever	.05	.02
U21	Rodney McCray	.07	.04
U22	Roy Tarpley	.08	.05
U23	Randy White (R)	.12	.07
U24	Anthony Cook (R)	.10	.06
U25	Chris Jackson (R)	1.75	1.00
U26	Marcus Liberty (R)	.08	.05
U27	Orlando Woolridge	.05	.02
U28	William Bedford (R)	.08	.05
U29	Lance Blanks (R)	.08	.05
U30	Scott Hastings	.05	.02
U31	Tyrone Hill (R)	.40	.25
U32	Les Jepsen (R)	.08	.05
U33	Steve Johnson	.05	.02
U34	Kevin Pritchard	.05	.02
U35	Dave Jamerson (R)	.10	.06
U36	Kenny Smith	.05	.02
U37	Greg Dreiling (R)	.08	.05
U38	Kenny Williams (R)	.20	.12
U39	Michael Williams (R)	.12	.07
U40	Gary Grant	.05	.02
U41	Bo Kimble (R)	.08	.05
U42	Loy Vaught (R)	.40	.25
U43	Elden Campbell (R)	.40	.25
U44	Sam Perkins	.08	.05
U45	Tony Smith (R)	.15	.10
U46	Terry Teagle	.05	.02
U47	Willie Burton (R)	.20	.12
U48	Bimbo Coles (R)	.20	.12
U49	Terry Davis (R)	.10	.06
U50	Alec Kessler (R)	.08	.05
U51	Greg Anderson	.07	.04
U52	Frank Brickowski	.05	.02
U53	Steve Henson (R)	.07	.04
U54	Brad Lohaus	.05	.02
U55	Dan Schayes	.05	.02
U56	Gerald Glass (R)	.20	.12
U57	Felton Spencer (R)	.25	.15
U58	Doug West (R)	.75	.45
U59	Jud Buechler (R)	.12	.07
U60	Derrick Coleman (R)	4.00	2.50
U61	Tate George (R)	.07	.04
U62	Reggie Theus	.05	.02
U63	Greg Grant (R)	.07	.04
U64	Jerrod Mustaf (R)	.12	.07

1991-92 Fleer

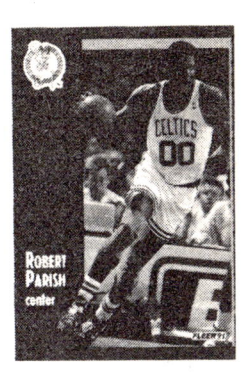

U65 Eddie Lee Wilkins (R)	.08	.05
U66 Michael Ansley (R)	.05	.02
U67 Jerry Reynolds (R)	.05	.02
U68 Dennis Scott (R)	.80	.50
U69 Manute Bol	.05	.02
U70 Armon Gilliam	.05	.02
U71 Brian Oliver (R)	.08	.05
U72 Kenny Payne (R)	.08	.05
U73 Jayson Williams (R)	.10	.06
U74 Kenny Battle (R)	.12	.07
U75 Cedric Ceballos (R)	1.75	1.00
U76 Negele Knight (R)	.15	.10
U77 Xavier McDaniel	.07	.04
U78 Alaa Abdelnaby (R)	.15	.10
U79 Danny Ainge	.08	.05
U80 Mark Bryant	.05	.02
U81 Drazen Petrovic (R)	.80	.50
U82 Anthony Bonner (R)	.20	.12
U83 Duane Causwell (R)	.15	.10
U84 Bobby Hansen	.05	.02
U85 Eric Leckner	.05	.02
U86 Travis Mays (R)	.08	.05
U87 Lionel Simmons (R)	.80	.50
U88 Sidney Green	.05	.02
U89 Tony Massenbug (R)	.05	.02
U90 Paul Pressey	.05	.02
U91 Dwayne Schintzius (R)	.08	.05
U92 Gary Payton (R)	1.75	1.00
U93 Olden Polynice	.05	.02
U94 Jeff Malone	.07	.04
U95 Walter Palmer (R)	.05	.02
U96 Delaney Rudd (R)	.05	.02
U97 Pervis Ellison	.25	.15
U98 A.J. English (R)	.12	.07
U99 Greg Foster (R)	.08	.05
U100 Checklist	.05	.02

The cards in this set were issued in two series and consist of full color action photos on the fronts framed by a blue border with NBA logos superimposed along the border. Horizontal red stripes appear above and below the photograph. A team logo is printed in the top left corner while the player's name and position appear in the lower third of the left border. The flip side includes two additional player photos, a small head shot and a small action shot. Personal data, statistics and a brief biography make up the rest of the card backs. Key subsets include All-Stars (AS), League Leaders (LL), Slam Dunk (SD)(227-232), All-Star Highlights (233-238) and Team Leaders (TL). The set also includes a 12-card insert series featuring Dikembe Mutombo which were randomly distributed in Fleer Series I packs and a 12-card insert set of Dominique Wilkins randomly placed in Fleer Series II packs. Those cards are listed at the end of this checklist but are not included in the complete set price below. All cards measure 2-1/2" by 3-1/2".

	MINT	NR/MT
Complete Set (400)	10.00	6.50
Commons	.05	.02
1 John Battle	.05	.02

32 • 1991-92 FLEER

#	Player			#	Player		
2	Jon Koncak	.05	.02	59	Joe Dumars	.12	.07
3	Rumeal Robinson	.06	.03	60	James Edwards	.05	.02
4	Spud Webb	.06	.03	61	Vinnie Johnson	.05	.02
5	Bob Weiss	.05	.02	62	Bill Laimbeer	.07	.04
6	Dominque Wilkins	.20	.12	63	Dennis Rodman	.12	.07
7	Kevin Willis	.05	.02	64	Isiah Thomas	.15	.10
8	Larry Bird	.50	.30	65	Tim Hardaway	.20	.12
9	Dee Brown	.15	.10	66	Rod Higgins	.05	.02
10	Chris Ford	.05	.02	67	Tyrone Hill	.07	.04
11	Kevin Gamble	.05	.02	68	Sarunas Marciulionis	.08	.05
12	Reggie Lewis	.15	.10	69	Chris Mullin	.15	.10
13	Kevin McHale	.12	.07	70	Don Nelson	.05	.02
14	Robert Parish	.12	.07	71	Mitch Richmond	.10	.06
15	Ed Pinckney	.05	.02	72	Tom Tolbert	.05	.02
16	Brian Shaw	.05	.02	73	Don Chaney	.05	.02
17	Tyrone Bogues	.05	.02	74	Sleepy Floyd	.05	.02
18	Rex Chapman	.07	.04	75	Buck Johnson	.06	.03
19	Dell Curry	.05	.02	76	Vernon Maxwell	.06	.03
20	Kendall Gill	.15	.10	77	Hakeem Olajuwon	.50	.30
21	Eric Leckner	.05	.02	78	Kenny Smith	.05	.02
22	Gene Littles	.05	.02	79	Larry Smith	.05	.02
23	Johnny Newman	.05	.02	80	Otis Thorpe	.08	.05
24	J.R. Reid	.06	.03	81	Vern Fleming	.05	.02
25	B.J. Armstrong	.15	.10	82	Bob Hill	.05	.02
26	Bill Cartwright	.05	.02	83	Reggie Miller	.20	.12
27	Horace Grant	.08	.05	84	Chuck Person	.08	.05
28	Phil Jackson	.05	.02	85	Detlef Schrempf	.10	.06
29	Michael Jordan	1.75	1.00	86	Rik Smits	.05	.02
30	Cliff Levingston	.05	.02	87	LaSalle Thompson	.05	.02
31	John Paxson	.05	.02	88	Michael Williams	.05	.02
32	Will Perdue	.05	.02	89	Gary Grant	.05	.02
33	Scottie Pippen	.35	.20	90	Ron Harper	.06	.03
34	Brad Daugherty	.12	.07	91	Bo Kimble	.05	.02
35	Craig Ehlo	.05	.02	92	Danny Manning	.15	.10
36	Danny Ferry	.06	.03	93	Ken Norman	.06	.03
37	Larry Nance	.06	.03	94	Olden Polynice	.05	.02
38	Mark Price	.10	.06	95	Mike Schuler	.05	.02
39	Darnell Valentine	.05	.02	96	Charles Smith	.10	.06
40	Hot Rod Williams	.07	.04	97	Vlade Divac	.08	.05
41	Lenny Wilkens	.05	.02	98	Mike Dunleavy	.05	.02
42	Richie Adubato	.05	.02	99	A.C. Green	.06	.03
43	Rolando Blackman	.06	.03	100	Magic Johnson	.60	.35
44	James Donaldson	.05	.02	101	Sam Perkins	.06	.03
45	Derek Harper	.06	.03	102	Byron Scott	.06	.03
46	Rodney McCray	.06	.03	103	Terry Teagle	.05	.02
47	Randy White	.05	.02	104	James Worthy	.12	.07
48	Herb Williams	.05	.02	105	Willie Burton	.08	.05
49	Chris Jackson	.12	.07	106	Bimbo Coles	.05	.02
50	Marcus Liberty	.08	.05	107	Sherman Douglas	.08	.05
51	Todd Lichti	.05	.02	108	Kevin Edwards	.05	.02
52	Blair Rasmussen	.05	.02	109	Grant Long	.05	.02
53	Paul Westhead	.05	.02	110	Kevin Loughery	.05	.02
54	Reggie Williams	.06	.03	111	Glen Rice	.15	.10
55	Joe Wolf	.05	.02	112	Rony Seikaly	.08	.05
56	Orlando Woolridge	.05	.02	113	Frank Brickowski	.05	.02
57	Mark Aguirre	.07	.04	114	Dale Ellis	.06	.03
58	Chuck Daly	.05	.02	115	Del Harris	.05	.02

1991-92 FLEER • 33

#	Player		
116	Jay Humphries	.05	.02
117	Fred Roberts	.05	.02
118	Alvin Robertson	.06	.03
119	Dan Schayes	.05	.02
120	Jack Sikma	.05	.02
121	Tony Campbell	.06	.03
122	Tyrone Corbin	.05	.02
123	Sam Mitchell	.05	.02
124	Tod Murphy	.05	.02
125	Pooh Richardson	.07	.04
126	Jim Rodgers	.05	.02
127	Felton Spencer	.08	.05
128	Mookie Blaylock	.07	.04
129	Sam Bowie	.05	.02
130	Derrick Coleman	.40	.25
131	Chris Dudley	.05	.02
132	Bill Fitch	.05	.02
133	Chris Morris	.05	.02
134	Drazen Petrovic	.15	.10
135	Maurice Cheeks	.05	.02
136	Patrick Ewing	.25	.15
137	Mark Jackson	.08	.05
138	Charles Oakley	.05	.02
139	Pat Riley	.05	.02
140	Trent Tucker	.05	.02
141	Kiki Vandeweghe	.06	.03
142	Gerald Wilkins	.05	.02
143	Nick Anderson	.12	.07
144	Terry Catledge	.05	.02
145	Matt Guokas	.05	.02
146	Jerry Reynolds	.05	.02
147	Dennis Scott	.10	.06
148	Scott Skiles	.05	.02
149	Otis Smith	.05	.02
150	Ron Anderson	.05	.02
151	Charles Barkley	.40	.25
152	Johnny Dawkins	.05	.02
153	Armon Gilliam	.05	.02
154	Hersey Hawkins	.07	.04
155	Jim Lynam	.05	.02
156	Rick Mahorn	.05	.02
157	Brian Oliver	.05	.02
158	Tom Chambers	.07	.04
159	Cotton Fitzsimmons	.05	.02
160	Jeff Hornacek	.07	.04
161	Kevin Johnson	.15	.10
162	Negele Knight	.05	.02
163	Dan Majerle	.10	.06
164	Xavier McDaniel	.07	.04
165	Mark West	.05	.02
166	Rick Adelman	.05	.02
167	Danny Ainge	.08	.05
168	Clyde Drexler	.20	.12
169	Kevin Duckworth	.05	.02
170	Jerome Kersey	.07	.04
171	Terry Porter	.08	.05
172	Cliff Robinson	.12	.07
173	Buck Williams	.06	.03
174	Antoine Carr	.05	.02
175	Duane Causwell	.05	.02
176	Jim Les (R)	.08	.05
177	Travis Mays	.08	.05
178	Dick Motta	.05	.02
179	Lionel Simmons	.15	.10
180	Rory Sparrow	.05	.02
181	Wayman Tisdale	.07	.04
182	Willie Anderson	.05	.02
183	Larry Brown	.05	.02
184	Terry Cummings	.07	.04
185	Sean Elliott	.10	.06
186	Paul Pressey	.05	.02
187	David Robinson	.60	.35
188	Rod Strickland	.05	.02
189	Benoit Benjamin	.05	.02
190	Eddie Johnson	.05	.02
191	K.C. Jones	.05	.02
192	Shawn Kemp	.75	.45
193	Derrick McKey	.07	.04
194	Gary Payton	.15	.10
195	Ricky Pierce	.05	.02
196	Sedale Threatt	.05	.02
197	Thurl Bailey	.05	.02
198	Mark Eaton	.05	.02
199	Blue Edwards	.05	.02
200	Jeff Malone	.07	.04
201	Karl Malone	.20	.12
202	Jerry Sloan	.05	.02
203	John Stockton	.20	.12
204	Ledell Eackles	.05	.02
205	Pervis Ellison	.10	.06
206	A.J. English	.08	.05
207	Harvey Grant	.05	.02
208	Bernard King	.07	.04
209	Wes Unseld	.05	.02
210	Kevin Johnson (AS)	.10	.06
211	Michael Jordan (AS)	.80	.50
212	Dominique Wilkins (AS)	.12	.07
213	Charles Barkley (AS)	.25	.15
214	Hakeem Olajuwon (AS)	.25	.15
215	Patrick Ewing (AS)	.15	.10
216	Tim Hardaway (AS)	.15	.10
217	John Stockton (AS)	.12	.07
218	Chris Mullin (AS)	.12	.07
219	Karl Malone (AS)	.15	.10
220	Michael Jordan (LL)	.80	.50
221	John Stockton (LL)	.12	.07
222	Alvin Robertson (LL)	.05	.02
223	Hakeem Olajuwon (LL)	.25	.15
224	Buck Williams (LL)	.05	.02
225	David Robinson (LL)	.25	.15
226	Reggie Miller (LL)	.12	.07
227	Blue Edwards (SD)	.05	.02
228	Dee Brown (SD)	.10	.06
229	Rex Chapman (SD)	.05	.02

34 • 1991-92 FLEER

#	Player		
230	Kenny Smith (SD)	.05	.02
231	Shawn Kemp (SD)	.35	.20
232	Kendall Gill (SD)	.10	.06
233	'91 All Star Game	.05	.02
234	'91 All Star Game	.07	.04
235	'91 All Star Game	.05	.02
236	'91 All Star Game	.08	.05
237	'91 All Star Game	.05	.02
238	'91 All Star Game	.10	.06
239	Checklist	.05	.02
240	Checklist	.05	.02
241	Stacey Augmon (R)	.35	.20
242	Maurice Cheeks	.07	.04
243	Paul Graham (R)	.10	.06
244	Rodney Monroe (R)	.08	.05
245	Blair Rasmussen	.05	.02
246	Alexander Volkov	.05	.02
247	John Bagley	.05	.02
248	Rick Fox (R)	.15	.10
249	Rickey Green	.05	.02
250	Joe Kleine	.05	.02
251	Stojko Vrankovic (R)	.05	.02
252	Allan Bristow	.05	.02
253	Kenny Gattison (R)	.07	.04
254	Mike Gminski	.05	.02
255	Larry Johnson (R)	3.00	1.75
256	Bobby Hansen	.05	.02
257	Craig Hodges	.05	.02
258	Stacey King	.05	.02
259	Scott Williams (R)	.10	.06
260	John Battle	.05	.02
261	Winston Bennett	.05	.02
262	Terrell Brandon (R)	.15	.10
263	Henry James (R)	.05	.02
264	Steve Kerr	.05	.02
265	Jimmy Oliver (R)	.08	.05
266	Brad Davis	.05	.02
267	Terry Davis	.05	.02
268	Donald Hodge (R)	.10	.06
269	Mike Iuzzolino (R)	.07	.04
270	Fat Lever	.05	.02
271	Doug Smith (R)	.15	.10
272	Greg Anderson	.05	.02
273	Kevin Brooks (R)	.08	.05
274	Walter Davis	.05	.02
275	Winston Garland	.05	.02
276	Mark Macon (R)	.15	.10
277	Dikembe Mutombo (R)	1.00	.60
278	William Bedford	.05	.02
279	Lance Blanks	.06	.03
280	John Salley	.05	.02
281	Charles Thomas (R)	.05	.02
282	Darrell Walker	.05	.02
283	Orlando Woolridge	.05	.02
284	Victor Alexander (R)	.15	.10
285	Vincent Askew (R)	.10	.06
286	Mario Elie (R)	.15	.10
287	Alton Lister	.05	.02
288	Billy Owens (R)	.40	.25
289	Matt Bullard (R)	.10	.06
290	Carl Herrera (R)	.25	.15
291	Tree Rollins	.05	.02
292	John Turner	.05	.02
293	Dale Davis (R)	.25	.15
294	Sean Green (R)	.08	.05
295	Kenny Williams	.05	.02
296	James Edwards	.05	.02
297	LeRon Ellis (R)	.12	.07
298	Doc Rivers	.06	.03
299	Loy Vaught	.06	.03
300	Elden Campbell	.10	.06
301	Jack Haley	.05	.02
302	Keith Owens	.05	.02
303	Tony Smith	.05	.02
304	Sedale Threatt	.05	.02
305	Keith Askins	.05	.02
306	Alec Kessler	.05	.02
307	John Morton	.05	.02
308	Alan Ogg (R)	.05	.02
309	Steve Smith (R)	.75	.45
310	Lester Conner	.05	.02
311	Jeff Grayer	.05	.02
312	Frank Hamblen	.05	.02
313	Steve Henson	.05	.02
314	Larry Krystkowiak	.05	.02
315	Moses Malone	.10	.06
316	Thurl Bailey	.05	.02
317	Randy Breuer	.05	.02
318	Scott Brooks	.05	.02
319	Gerald Glass	.08	.05
320	Luc Longley (R)	.10	.06
321	Doug West	.07	.04
322	Kenny Anderson (R)	.80	.50
323	Tate George	.05	.02
324	Terry Mills (R)	.25	.15
325	Greg Anthony (R)	.20	.12
326	Anthony Mason (R)	.30	.18
327	Tim McCormick	.05	.02
328	Xavier McDaniel	.07	.04
329	Brian Quinnett (R)	.05	.02
330	John Starks (R)	.60	.35
331	Stanley Roberts (R)	.12	.07
332	Jeff Turner	.05	.02
333	Sam Vincent	.05	.02
334	Brian Williams (R)	.20	.12
335	Manute Bol	.05	.02
336	Kenny Payne	.05	.02
337	Charles Shackleford	.05	.02
338	Jayson Williams	.05	.02
339	Cedric Ceballos	.12	.07
340	Andrew Lang	.05	.02
341	Jerrod Mustaf	.05	.02
342	Tim Perry	.05	.02
343	Kurt Rambis	.05	.02

1991-92 FLEER PRO VISIONS • 35

344	Alaa Abdelnaby	.08	.05
345	Robert Pack (R)	.15	.10
346	Danny Young	.05	.02
347	Anthony Bonner	.05	.02
348	Pete Chilcutt	.10	.06
349	Rex Hughes	.05	.02
350	Mitch Richmond	.10	.06
351	Dwayne Schintzius	.05	.02
352	Spud Webb	.06	.03
353	Antoine Carr	.05	.02
354	Sidney Green	.05	.02
355	Vinnie Johnson	.05	.02
356	Greg Sutton	.05	.02
357	Dana Barros	.06	.03
358	Michael Cage	.05	.02
359	Marty Conlon (R)	.07	.04
360	Rich King (R)	.07	.04
361	Nate McMillan	.05	.02
362	David Benoit (R)	.10	.06
363	Mike Brown	.05	.02
364	Tyrone Corbin	.05	.02
365	Eric Murdock (R)	.25	.15
366	Delaney Rudd	.05	.02
367	Michael Adams	.05	.02
368	Tom Hammonds	.05	.02
369	Larry Stewart (R)	.12	.07
370	Andre Turner	.05	.02
371	David Wingate	.05	.02
372	Dominique Wilkins (TL)	.15	.10
373	Larry Bird (TL)	.25	.15
374	Rex Chapman (TL)	.05	.02
375	Michael Jordan (TL)	.80	.50
376	Brad Daugherty (TL)	.10	.06
377	Derek Harper (TL)	.07	.04
378	Dikembe Mutombo (TL)	.25	.15
379	Joe Dumars (TL)	.08	.05
380	Chris Mullin (TL)	.10	.06
381	Hakeem Olajuwon (TL)	.25	.15
382	Chuck Person (TL)	.07	.04
383	Charles Smith (TL)	.07	.04
384	James Worthy (TL)	.07	.04
385	Glen Rice (TL)	.08	.05
386	Alvin Robertson (TL)	.05	.02
387	Tony Campbell (TL)	.05	.02
388	Derrick Coleman (TL)	.20	.12
389	Patrick Ewing (TL)	.20	.12
390	Scott Skiles (TL)	.05	.02
391	Charles Barkley (TL)	.25	.15
392	Kevin Johnson (TL)	.10	.06
393	Clyde Drexler (TL)	.12	.07
394	Lionel Simmons (TL)	.10	.06
395	David Robinson (TL)	.25	.15
396	Ricky Pierce (TL)	.05	.02
397	John Stockton (TL)	.12	.07
398	Michael Adams (TL)	.05	.02
399	Checklist	.05	.02
400	Checklist	.05	.02

___	Dikembe Mutombo	.75	.45
	Inserts (1-12) ea.		
___	Dikembe Mutombo	75.00	35.00
	Inserts (Autographed)		
___	Dominique Wilkins	.75	.45
	Inserts (1-12) ea.		
___	Dominique Wilkins	100.00	65.00
	Inserts (Autographed)		

1991-92 Fleer Pro Visions

These limited insert cards feature portraits by noted sports artist Terry Smith and were randomly distributed in Fleer wax packs. The portraits are framed by white borders and the player's name is printed in red ink at the bottom of the card front. The back contains personal data and a biographical sketch of the player. All cards measure 2-1/2" by 3-1/2".

		MINT	NR/MT
Complete Set (6)		3.00	1.75
Commons		.40	.25
1	David Robinson	.80	.50
2	Michael Jordan	2.50	1.50
3	Charles Barkley	.75	.45
4	Patrick Ewing	.50	.32

5	Karl Malone	.40	.25
6	Magic Johnson	.80	.50

1991-82 Fleer Rookie Sensations

The cards in this insert set were randomly distributed in Fleer cello packs. The card fronts include a full color photo superimposed over a basketball hoop. The photos are framed in maroon while the headline "Rookie Sensations" appears in a small oval at the top of the card. The backs include a paragraph of copy devoted to the player's rookie season. All cards measure 2-1/2" by 3-1/2".

		MINT	NR/MT
Complete Set (10)		18.00	12.00
Commons		.50	.32
1	Lionel Simmons	1.75	1.00
2	Dennis Scott	.60	.35
3	Derrick Coleman	8.00	4.75
4	Kendall Gill	2.00	1.25
5	Travis Mays	.50	.30
6	Felton Spencer	.75	.45
7	Willie Burton	.50	.30
8	Chris Jackson	2.50	1.50
9	Gary Payton	2.50	1.50
10	Dee Brown	1.75	1.00

1991-92 Fleer Schoolyard Stars

The cards in this set were distributed one-per-pack in Fleer's rack packs. The fronts feature full color photos that are tilted slightly at an angle and framed in black, pink and yellow border colors. The player's name appears in the upper left corner. The flip side includes a brief description of the player's strengths and a basketball tip. All cards measure 2-1/2" by 3-1/2".

		MINT	NR/MT
Complete Set (6)		3.50	2.00
Commons		.25	.15
1	Chris Mullin	.75	.45
2	Isiah Thomas	.60	.35
3	Kevin McHale	.40	.25
4	Kevin Johnson	.75	.45
5	Karl Malone	1.25	.70
6	Alvin Robinson	.25	.15

1992-93 Fleer

This 444-card set was issued in two series and features full color action photos on the card fronts framed in gold borders. The player's name and position appear vertically in two color bars to the right of the photo. A team logo is printed in the lower right corner. The horizontal card backs contain another full color photo along with personal data and statistics. The main subsets include League Leaders (LL), Award Winners (AW), Pro Visions (PV), Schoolyard Stars (SS) and Slam Dunk (SD). A Larry Johnson 15-card limited insert set, including three mail-in cards, were distributed randomly in Fleer wax packs. Those values are included at the end of this checklist. All cards measure 2-1/2" by 3-1/2".

		MINT	NR/MT
	Complete Set (444)	28.00	18.00
	Commons	.05	.02
1	Stacey Augmon	.15	.10
2	Duane Ferrell	.05	.02
3	Paul Graham	.05	.02
4	Jon Koncak	.05	.02
5	Blair Rasmussen	.05	.02
6	Rumeal Robinson	.07	.04
7	Bob Weiss	.05	.02
8	Dominique Wilkins	.25	.15
9	Kevin Willis	.07	.04
10	John Bagley	.05	.02
11	Larry Bird	.50	.30
12	Dee Brown	.12	.07
13	Chris Ford	.05	.02
14	Rick Fox	.08	.05
15	Kevin Gamble	.05	.02
16	Reggie Lewis	.10	.06
17	Kevin McHale	.12	.07
18	Robert Parish	.12	.07
19	Ed Pinckney	.05	.02
20	Muggsy Bogues	.05	.02
21	Allan Bristow	.05	.02
22	Dell Curry	.05	.02
23	Kenny Gattison	.05	.02
24	Kendall Gill	.12	.07
25	Larry Johnson	.75	.45
26	Johnny Newman	.05	.02
27	J.R. Reid	.07	.04
28	B.J. Armstrong	.12	.07
29	Bill Cartwright	.05	.02
30	Horace Grant	.10	.06
31	Phil Jackson	.05	.02
32	Michael Jordan	1.75	1.00
33	Stacey King	.05	.02
34	Cliff Levingston	.05	.02
35	John Paxson	.08	.05
36	Scottie Pippen	.25	.15
37	Scott Williams	.05	.02
38	John Battle	.05	.02
39	Terrell Brandon	.10	.06
40	Brad Daugherty	.12	.07
41	Craig Ehlo	.05	.02
42	Larry Nance	.07	.04
43	Mark Price	.12	.07
44	Mike Sanders	.07	.04
45	Lenny Wilkens	.05	.02
46	Hot Rod Williams	.07	.04
47	Richie Adubato	.05	.02
48	Terry Davis	.05	.02
49	Derek Harper	.05	.02
50	Donald Hodge	.07	.04
51	Mike Luzzolino	.05	.02
52	Rodney McCray	.07	.04
53	Doug Smith	.07	.04
54	Greg Anderson	.07	.04
55	Winston Garland	.05	.02
56	Dan Issel	.05	.02
57	Chris Jackson	.15	.10
58	Marcus Liberty	.07	.04
59	Mark Macon	.08	.05
60	Dikembe Mutombo	.30	.18
61	Reggie Williams	.05	.02
62	Mark Aguirre	.07	.04
63	Joe Dumars	.10	.06
64	Bill Laimbeer	.07	.04
65	Olden Polynice	.05	.02
66	Dennis Rodman	.10	.06

1992-93 FLEER

#	Player		
67	Ron Rothstein	.05	.02
68	John Salley	.05	.02
69	Isiah Thomas	.12	.07
70	Darrell Walker	.05	.02
71	Orlando Woolridge	.05	.02
72	Victor Alexander	.05	.02
73	Mario Elie	.05	.02
74	Tim Hardaway	.15	.10
75	Tyrone Hill	.05	.02
76	Sarunas Marciulionis	.07	.04
77	Chris Mullin	.15	.10
78	Don Nelson	.05	.02
79	Billy Owens	.15	.10
80	Sleepy Floyd	.05	.02
81	Avery Johnson	.05	.02
82	Buck Johnson	.07	.04
83	Vernon Maxwell	.12	.07
84	Hakeem Olajuwon	.60	.35
85	Kenny Smith	.05	.02
86	Otis Thorpe	.08	.05
87	Rudy Tomjanovich	.05	.02
88	Dale Davis	.10	.06
89	Vern Fleming	.05	.02
90	Bob Hill	.05	.02
91	Reggie Miller	.15	.10
92	Chuck Person	.08	.05
93	Detlef Schrempf	.10	.06
94	Rik Smits	.05	.02
95	LaSalle Thompson	.05	.02
96	Michael Williams	.05	.02
97	Larry Brown	.05	.02
98	James Edwards	.05	.02
99	Gary Grant	.05	.02
100	Ron Harper	.07	.04
101	Danny Manning	.15	.10
102	Ken Norman	.07	.04
103	Doc Rivers	.05	.02
104	Charles Smith	.08	.05
105	Loy Vaught	.05	.02
106	Elden Campbell	.08	.05
107	Vlade Divac	.08	.05
108	A.C. Green	.07	.04
109	Sam Perkins	.07	.04
110	Randy Pfund	.08	.05
111	Byron Scott	.07	.04
112	Sedale Threatt	.05	.02
114	James Worthy	.10	.06
115	Willie Burton	.08	.05
116	Bimbo Coles	.05	.02
117	Kevin Edwards	.05	.02
118	Grant Long	.05	.02
119	Kevin Loughery	.05	.02
120	Glen Rice	.12	.07
121	Rony Seikaly	.08	.05
122	Brian Shaw	.05	.02
123	Steve Smith	.20	.12
124	Frank Brickowski	.05	.02
125	Mike Dunleavy	.05	.02
126	Blue Edwards	.05	.02
127	Moses Malone	.10	.06
128	Eric Murdock	.08	.05
129	Fred Roberts	.05	.02
130	Alvin Robertson	.05	.02
131	Thurl Bailey	.05	.02
132	Tony Campbell	.05	.02
133	Gerald Glass	.05	.02
134	Luc Longley	.05	.02
135	Sam Mitchell	.05	.02
136	Pooh Richardson	.07	.04
137	Jimmy Rodgers	.05	.02
138	Felton Spencer	.07	.04
139	Doug West	.07	.04
140	Kenny Anderson	.20	.12
141	Mookie Blaylock	.07	.04
142	Sam Bowie	.05	.02
143	Derrick Coleman	.20	.12
144	Chuck Daly	.05	.02
145	Terry Mills	.05	.02
146	Chris Morris	.05	.02
147	Drazen Petrovic	.10	.06
148	Greg Anthony	.10	.06
149	Rolando Blackman	.05	.02
150	Patrick Ewing	.35	.20
151	Mark Jackson	.07	.04
152	Anthony Mason	.05	.02
153	Xavier McDaniel	.07	.04
154	Charles Oakley	.05	.02
155	Pat Riley	.05	.02
156	John Starks	.15	.10
157	Gerald Wilkins	.05	.02
158	Nick Anderson	.10	.06
159	Anthony Bowie	.05	.02
160	Terry Catledge	.05	.02
161	Matt Guokas	.05	.02
162	Stanley Roberts	.08	.05
163	Dennis Scott	.08	.05
164	Scott Skiles	.05	.02
165	Brian Williams	.10	.06
166	Ron Anderson	.05	.02
167	Manute Bol	.05	.02
168	Johnny Dawkins	.05	.02
169	Armon Gilliam	.07	.04
170	Hersey Hawkins	.08	.05
171	Jeff Hornacek	.08	.05
172	Andrew Lang	.05	.02
173	Doug Moe	.05	.02
174	Tim Perry	.05	.02
175	Jeff Ruland	.05	.02
176	Charles Shackleford	.05	.02
177	Danny Ainge	.07	.04
178	Charles Barkley	.40	.25
179	Cedric Ceballos	.08	.05
180	Tom Chambers	.07	.04
181	Kevin Johnson	.15	.10

#	Player		
182	Dan Majerle	.08	.05
183	Mark West	.05	.02
184	Paul Westphal	.05	.02
185	Rick Adelman	.05	.02
186	Clyde Drexler	.20	.12
187	Kevin Duckworth	.05	.02
188	Jerome Kersey	.07	.04
189	Robert Pack	.05	.02
190	Terry Porter	.08	.05
191	Cliff Robinson	.10	.06
192	Rod Strickland	.05	.02
193	Buck Williams	.07	.04
194	Anthony Bonner	.05	.02
195	Duane Causwell	.05	.02
196	Mitch Richmond	.10	.06
197	Garry St. Jean	.06	.03
198	Lionel Simmons	.15	.10
199	Wayman Tisdale	.07	.04
200	Spud Webb	.07	.04
201	Willie Anderson	.05	.02
202	Antoine Carr	.05	.02
203	Terry Cummings	.07	.04
204	Sean Elliott	.10	.06
205	Dale Ellis	.05	.02
206	Vinnie Johnson	.05	.02
207	David Robinson	.40	.25
208	Jerry Tarkanian (R)	.15	.10
209	Benoit Benjamin	.05	.02
210	Michael Cage	.05	.02
211	Eddie Johnson	.05	.02
212	George Karl	.05	.02
213	Shawn Kemp	.35	.20
214	Derrick McKey	.05	.02
215	Nate McMillan	.05	.02
216	Gary Payton	.10	.06
217	Ricky Pierce	.05	.02
218	David Benoit	.08	.05
219	Mike Brown	.05	.02
220	Tyrone Corbin	.05	.02
221	Mark Eaton	.05	.02
222	Jay Humphries	.05	.02
223	Larry Krystkowiak	.05	.02
224	Jeff Malone	.08	.05
225	Karl Malone	.25	.15
226	Jerry Sloan	.05	.02
227	John Stockton	.25	.15
228	Michael Adams	.07	.04
229	Rex Chapman	.07	.04
230	Ledell Eackles	.05	.02
231	Pervis Ellison	.08	.05
232	A.J. English	.05	.02
233	Harvey Grant	.05	.02
234	LaBradford Smith	.05	.02
235	Larry Stewart	.05	.02
236	Wes Unseld	.05	.02
237	David Wingate	.05	.02
238	Michael Jordan (LL)	.75	.45
239	Dennis Rodman (LL)	.07	.04
240	John Stockton (LL)	.12	.07
241	Buck Williams (LL)	.05	.02
242	Mark Price (LL)	.07	.04
243	Dana Barros (LL)	.05	.02
244	David Robinson (LL)	.20	.12
245	Chris Mullin (LL)	.08	.05
246	Michael Jordan (MVP)	.75	.45
247	Larry Johnson (ROY)	.25	.15
248	David Robinson (AW)	.20	.12
249	Detlef Schrempf (AW)	.08	.05
250	Clyde Drexler (PV)	.12	.07
251	Tim Hardaway (PV)	.15	.10
252	Kevin Johnson (PV)	.10	.06
253	Larry Johnson (PV)	.25	.15
254	Scottie Pippen (PV)	.20	.12
255	Isiah Thomas (PV)	.10	.06
256	Larry Bird (SS)	.25	.15
257	Brad Daugherty (SS)	.10	.06
258	Kevin Johnson (SS)	.12	.07
259	Larry Johnson (SS)	.25	.15
260	Scottie Pippen (SS)	.15	.10
261	Dennis Rodman (SS)	.08	.05
262	Checklist	.05	.02
263	Checklist	.05	.02
264	Checklist	.05	.02
265	Charles Barkley (SD)	.20	.12
266	Shawn Kemp (SD)	.20	.12
267	Dan Majerle (SD)	.06	.03
268	Karl Malone (SD)	.12	.07
269	Buck Williams (SD)	.06	.03
270	Clyde Drexler (SD)	.12	.07
271	Sean Elliott (SD)	.08	.05
272	Ron Harper (SD)	.05	.02
273	Michael Jordan (SD)	.75	.45
274	James Worthy (SD)	.07	.04
275	Cedric Ceballos (SD)	.07	.04
276	Larry Nance (SD)	.05	.02
277	Kenny Walker (SD)	.05	.02
278	Spud Webb (SD)	.05	.02
279	Dominique Wilkins (SD)	.12	.07
280	Terrell Brandon (SD)	.07	.04
281	Dee Brown (SD)	.08	.05
282	Kevin Johnson (SD)	.10	.06
283	Doc Rivers (SD)	.05	.02
284	Byron Scott (SD)	.05	.02
285	Manute Bol (SD)	.05	.02
286	Dikembe Mutombo (SD)	.15	.10
287	Robert Parish (SD)	.07	.04
288	David Robinson (SD)	.20	.12
289	Dennis Rodman (SD)	.08	.05
290	Blue Edwards (SD)	.05	.02
291	Patrick Ewing (SD)	.20	.12
292	Larry Johnson (SD)	.25	.15
293	Jerome Kersey (SD)	.06	.03
294	Hakeem Olajuwon (SD)	.30	.18
295	Stacey Augmon (SD)	.08	.05

40 • 1992-93 FLEER

#	Player		
296	Derrick Coleman (SD)	.12	.07
297	Kendall Gill (SD)	.10	.06
298	Shaquille O'Neal (SD)	2.50	1.50
299	Scottie Pippen (SD)	.12	.07
300	Darryl Dawkins (SD)	.05	.02
301	Mookie Blaylock	.07	.04
302	Adam Keefe (R)	.12	.07
303	Travis Mays	.05	.02
304	Morton Wiley (R)	.07	.04
305	Sherman Douglas	.07	.04
306	Joe Kleine	.05	.02
307	Xavier McDaniel	.07	.04
308	Tony Bennett (R)	.08	.05
309	Tom Hammonds	.05	.02
310	Kevin Lynch	.05	.02
311	Alonzo Mourning (R)	3.50	2.00
312	David Wingate	.05	.02
313	Rodney McCray	.07	.04
314	Will Perdue	.05	.02
315	Trent Tucker	.05	.02
316	Corey Williams (R)	.10	.06
317	Danny Ferry	.05	.02
318	Jay Guidinger (R)	.08	.05
319	Jerome Lane	.05	.02
320	Gerald Wilkins	.05	.02
321	Stephen Bardo (R)	.05	.02
322	Walter Bond (R)	.07	.04
323	Brian Howard (R)	.07	.04
324	Tracy Moore (R)	.05	.02
325	Sean Rooks (R)	.15	.10
326	Randy White	.07	.04
327	Kevin Brooks	.05	.02
328	LaPhonso Ellis (R)	.80	.50
329	Scott Hastings	.05	.02
330	Todd Lichti	.05	.02
331	Robert Pack	.05	.02
332	Bryant Stith (R)	.30	.18
333	Gerald Glass	.05	.02
334	Terry Mills	.08	.05
335	Isiah Morris (R)	.08	.05
336	Mark Randall	.05	.02
337	Danny Young	.05	.02
338	Chris Gatling	.05	.02
339	Jeff Grayer	.05	.02
340	Byron Houston (R)	.15	.10
341	Keith Jennings (R)	.08	.05
342	Alton Lister	.05	.02
343	Latrell Sprewell (R)	1.75	1.00
344	Scott Brooks	.05	.02
345	Matt Bullard	.05	.02
346	Carl Herrera	.07	.04
347	Robert Horry (R)	1.00	.60
348	Tree Rollins	.05	.02
349	Greg Dreiling	.05	.02
350	George McCloud	.05	.02
351	Sam Mitchell	.05	.02
352	Pooh Richardson	.07	.04
353	Malik Sealy (R)	.12	.07
354	Kenny Williams	.05	.02
355	Jaren Jackson (R)	.08	.05
356	Mark Jackson	.07	.04
357	Stanley Roberts	.08	.05
358	Elmore Spencer (R)	.15	.10
359	Kiki Vandeweghe	.05	.02
360	John Williams	.05	.02
361	Randy Woods (R)	.08	.05
362	Duane Cooper (R)	.10	.06
363	James Edwards	.05	.02
364	Anthony Peeler (R)	.40	.25
365	Tony Smith	.05	.02
366	Keith Askins	.05	.02
367	Matt Geiger (R)	.12	.07
368	Alec Kessler	.05	.02
369	Harold Minor (R)	.50	.30
370	John Salley	.05	.02
371	Anthony Avent (R)	.15	.10
372	Todd Day (R)	.30	.18
373	Blue Edwards	.05	.02
374	Brad Lohaus	.05	.02
375	Lee Mayberry (R)	.20	.12
376	Eric Murdock	.10	.06
377	Dan Schayes	.05	.02
378	Lance Blanks	.05	.02
379	Christian Laettner (R)	.80	.50
380	Bob McCann (R)	.08	.05
381	Chuck Person	.07	.04
382	Brad Sellers	.05	.02
383	Chris Smith (R)	.12	.07
384	Micheal Williams	.05	.02
385	Rafael Addison (R)	.07	.04
386	Chucky Brown	.05	.02
387	Chris Dudley	.05	.02
388	Tate George	.05	.02
389	Rick Mahorn	.05	.02
390	Rumeal Robinson	.07	.04
391	Jayson Williams	.07	.04
392	Eric Anderson (R)	.10	.06
393	Rolando Blackman	.05	.02
394	Tony Campbell	.05	.02
395	Hubert Davis (R)	.30	.18
396	Doc Rivers	.05	.02
397	Charles Smith	.08	.05
398	Herb Williams	.05	.02
399	Litterial Green (R)	.10	.06
400	Greg Kite	.05	.02
401	Shaquille O'Neal (R)	7.00	4.00
402	Jerry Reynolds	.05	.02
403	Jeff Turner	.05	.02
404	Greg Grant	.05	.02
405	Jeff Hornacek	.08	.05
406	Andrew Lang	.05	.02
407	Kenny Payne	.05	.02
408	Tim Perry	.05	.02
409	Clarence Weatherspoon	.75	.45

		MINT	NR/MT
410	Danny Ainge	.07	.04
411	Charles Barkley	.35	.20
412	Negele Knight	.05	.02
413	Oliver Miller (R)	.50	.30
414	Jerrod Mustaf	.05	.02
415	Mark Bryant	.05	.02
416	Mario Elie	.05	.02
417	Dave Johnson (R)	.08	.05
418	Tracy Murray (R)	.15	.10
419	Reggie Smith (R)	.08	.05
420	Rod Strickland	.05	.02
421	Randy Brown	.05	.02
422	Pete Chilcutt	.05	.02
423	Jim Les	.05	.02
424	Walt Williams (R)	.60	.35
425	Lloyd Daniels (R)	.12	.07
426	Vinny Del Negro	.05	.02
427	Dale Ellis	.07	.04
428	Sidney Green	.05	.02
429	Avery Johnson	.05	.02
430	Dana Barros	.07	.04
431	Rich King	.05	.02
432	Isaac Austin (R)	.08	.05
433	John Crotty (R)	.08	.05
434	Stephen Howard (R)	.08	.05
435	Jay Humphries	.05	.02
436	Larry Krystkowiak	.05	.02
437	Tom Gugliotta (R)	.80	.50
438	Buck Johnson	.05	.02
439	Charles Jones	.05	.02
440	Don MacLean (R)	.30	.18
441	Doug Overton	.05	.02
442	Brent Price (R)	.12	.07
443	Checklist	.05	.02
444	Checklist	.05	.02
___	Larry Johnson Inserts (1-15) ea.	1.00	.60
___	Larry Johnson (Autographed)	150.00	90.00

1992-93 Fleer All-Stars

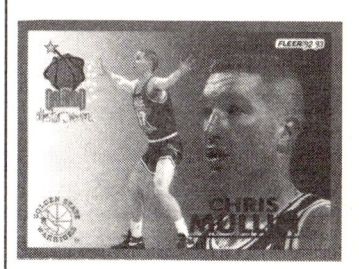

The cards in this limited insert set were distributed randomly in Fleer Series I wax packs. Two full color isolated photographs adorn the horizontal card fronts along with gold-foil stamping. The player's name is printed at the bottom of the card. The backs include personal data and highlights. All cards measure 2-1/2" by 3-1/2".

	MINT	NR/MT
Complete Set (24)	28.50	18.50
Commons	.80	.50

		MINT	NR/MT
1	Michael Adams	.80	.50
2	Charles Barkley	4.00	2.50
3	Brad Daugherty	1.00	.60
4	Joe Dumars	1.00	.60
5	Patrick Ewing	3.50	2.00
6	Michael Jordan	10.00	6.50
7	Reggie Lewis	1.00	.60
8	Scottie Pippen	2.50	1.50
9	Mark Price	1.25	.70
10	Dennis Rodman	1.00	.60
11	Isiah Thomas	1.50	.90
12	Kevin Willis	.80	.50
13	Clyde Drexler	1.75	1.00
14	Tim Hardaway	1.50	.90
15	Jeff Hornacek	.80	.50
16	Dan Majerle	1.00	.60
17	Karl Malone	2.50	1.50

42 • 1992-93 FLEER ALL-STARS

18	Chris Mullin	1.50	.90
19	Dikembe Mutombo	2.00	1.25
20	Hakeem Olajuwon	6.00	3.50
21	David Robinson	4.00	2.50
22	John Stockton	2.00	1.25
23	Otis Thorpe	.80	.50
24	James Worthy	1.00	.60

3	Terrell Brandon	2.50	1.50
4	Rick Fox	2.50	1.50
5	Larry Johnson	30.00	18.50
6	Mark Macon	2.00	1.25
7	Dikembe Mutombo	12.00	7.00
8	Billy Owens	4.50	2.75
9	Stanley Roberts	2.00	1.25
10	Doug Smith	2.00	1.25
11	Steve Smith	10.00	6.50
12	Larry Stewart	2.00	1.25

1992-93 Fleer Rookie Sensations

Rookie Sensations
STACEY AUGMON

The cards in this insert set were distributed randomly in Fleer's Series I cello packs. The card fronts feature gold-foil stamping and full color player photos on a colored background, superimposed over block letters of the team name. The headline "Rookie Sensations" appears under the photo and just above the player's name. Card backs contain personal data and highlights from the player's rookie season. All cards measure 2-1/2" by 3-1/2".

	MINT	NR/MT
Complete Set (12)	55.00	32.00
Commons	2.00	1.25

1	Greg Anthony	2.50	1.50
2	Stacey Augmon	5.00	3.00

1992-93 Fleer Sharpshooters

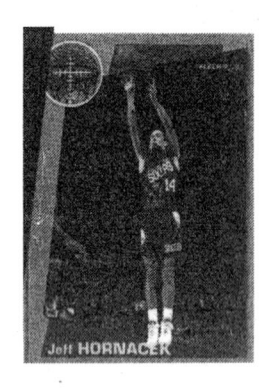

Jeff HORNACEK

These cards were random inserts in Fleer's Series II wax packs. The card fronts include full color action photos with a "Sharpshooters" logo in the top left corner. The player's name appears across the bottom of the card. All cards measure 2-1/2" by 3-1/2".

	MINT	NR/MT
Complete Set (18)	10.00	6.00
Commons	.50	.30

1	Reggie Miller	1.00	.60
2	Dana Barros	.50	.30
3	Jeff Hornacek	.50	.30
4	Drazen Petrovic	.75	.45

1992-93 FLEER TEAM LEADERS • 43

5	Glenn Rice	.60	.35
6	Terry Porter	.75	.45
7	Mark Price	.75	.45
8	Michael Adams	.50	.30
9	Hersey Hawkins	.50	.30
10	Chuck Person	.80	.50
11	John Stockton	1.00	.60
12	Dale Ellis	.50	.30
13	Clyde Drexler	1.25	.70
14	Mitch Richmond	.75	.45
15	Craig Ehlo	.50	.30
16	Dell Curry	.50	.30
17	Chris Mullen	.80	.50
18	Rolando Blackman	.50	.30

1992-93 Fleer Team Leaders

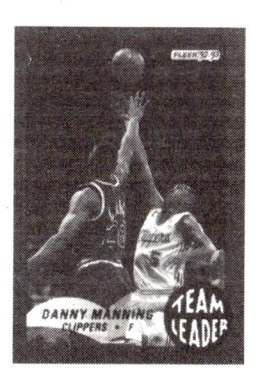

The cards in this limited insert set were found in Fleer's Series I rack packs. The card fronts consist of full color action photos with the player's name stamped in foil at the bottom. A Team Leader logo is located in the lower right corner of the card front. The backs contain another full color head shot and career highlights. All cards measure 2-1/2" by 3-1/2".

		MINT	NR/MT
Complete Set (27)		400.00	275.00
Commons		5.00	3.00

1	Dominique Wilkins	25.00	15.00
2	Reggie Lewis	5.00	3.00
3	Larry Johnson	40.00	25.00
4	Michael Jordan	175.00	100.00
5	Mark Price	8.00	5.00
6	Terry Davis	5.00	3.00
7	Dikembe Mutombo	20.00	12.50
8	Isiah Thomas	12.00	7.00
9	Chris Mullen	12.00	7.00
10	Hakeem Olajuwon	75.00	45.00
11	Reggie Miller	12.00	7.00
12	Danny Manning	12.00	7.00
13	James Worthy	6.50	3.75
14	Glen Rice	7.00	4.00
15	Alvin Robertson	5.00	3.00
16	Tony Campbell	5.00	3.00
17	Derrick Coleman	15.00	10.00
18	Patrick Ewing	35.00	20.00
19	Scott Skiles	5.00	3.00
20	Hersey Hawkins	5.00	3.00
21	Kevin Johnson	10.00	6.00
22	Clyde Drexler	15.00	10.00
23	Mitch Richmond	8.00	5.00
24	David Robinson	45.00	28.00
25	Ricky Pierce	5.00	3.00
26	Karl Malone	25.00	15.00
27	Pervis Ellison	6.00	3.50

1992-93 Fleer Total "D"

The cards in this limited insert set were randomly distributed in Fleer's Series II cello packs. The card fronts feature full color action photos superimposed inside the letter "D". The player's name appears in the lower right corner while a "Total D" logo floats just below the left side of the photograph. All cards measure 2-1/2" by 3-1/2".

		MINT	NR/MT
Complete Set (15)		85.00	50.00
Commons		1.50	.90
1	David Robinson	15.00	10.00
2	Dennis Rodman	2.50	1.50
3	Scottie Pippen	12.00	7.00
4	Joe Dumars	3.00	1.75
5	Michael Jordan	50.00	30.00
6	John Stockton	4.50	2.75
7	Patrick Ewing	12.00	7.00
8	Micheal Williams	1.50	.90
9	Larry Nance	1.50	.90
10	Buck Williams	1.75	1.00
11	Alvin Robinson	1.50	.90
12	Dikembe Mutombo	8.00	5.00
13	Mookie Blaylock	2.50	1.50
14	Hakeem Olajuwon	25.00	15.00
15	Rony Seikaly	2.50	1.50

1992-93 Fleer Ultra

This 375-card set is the first Fleer basketball edition for their premium Ultra brand. The set was released in two series. The card fronts contain full color action photos with the player's name, team and position located in small horizontal color bars below the photograph. The card backs feature two additional full color photos along with personal data and statistics. The key subsets include Draft Picks (193-198) and Jam Session (201-220). A Scottie Pippen Signature Series 10-card insert set was issued in conjunction with this set and randomly distributed in Series I wax packs. Two additional Pippen insert cards were offered through a special mail-in promotion. Those inserts are listed at the end of this checklist but are not included in the complete set price below. All cards measure 2-1/2" by 3-1/2".

		MINT	NR/MT
Complete Set (375)		45.00	28.00
Commons		.10	.06
1	Stacey Augmon	.35	.20
2	Duane Ferrell	.10	.06
3	Paul Graham	.10	.06
4	Blair Rasmussen	.10	.06
5	Rumeal Robinson	.10	.06
6	Dominique Wilkins	.70	.40
7	Kevin Willis	.12	.07

1992-93 FLEER ULTRA • 45

#	Player		
8	John Bagley	.10	.06
9	Dee Brown	.20	.12
10	Rick Fox	.20	.12
11	Kevin Gamble	.10	.06
12	Joe Kleine	.10	.06
13	Reggie Lewis	.20	.12
14	Kevin McHale	.20	.12
15	Robert Parish	.20	.12
16	Ed Pinckney	.10	.06
17	Muggsy Bogues	.10	.06
18	Dell Curry	.10	.06
19	Kenny Gattison	.10	.06
20	Kendall Gill	.30	.18
21	Larry Johnson	2.00	1.25
22	Johnny Newman	.10	.06
23	J.R. Reid	.10	.06
24	B.J. Armstrong	.20	.12
25	Bill Cartwright	.10	.06
26	Horace Grant	.15	.10
27	Michael Jordan	3.50	2.00
28	Stacey King	.12	.07
29	John Paxson	.12	.07
30	Will Perdue	.10	.06
31	Scottie Pippen	.80	.50
32	Scott Williams	.12	.07
33	John Battle	.10	.06
34	Terrell Brandon	.15	.10
35	Brad Daugherty	.25	.15
36	Craig Ehlo	.10	.06
37	Larry Nance	.12	.07
38	Mark Price	.30	.18
39	Mike Sanders	.10	.06
40	John Williams	.10	.06
41	Terry Davis	.10	.06
42	Derek Harper	.12	.07
43	Donald Hodge	.12	.07
44	Mike Iuzzolino	.10	.06
45	Fat Lever	.10	.06
46	Doug Smith	.12	.07
47	Randy White	.10	.06
48	Winston Garland	.10	.06
49	Chris Jackson	.30	.18
50	Marcus Liberty	.10	.06
51	Todd Lichti	.10	.06
52	Mark Macon	.12	.07
53	Dikembe Mutombo	.60	.35
54	Reggie Williams	.10	.06
55	Mark Aguirre	.12	.07
56	Joe Dumars	.25	.15
57	Bill Laimbeer	.12	.07
58	Dennis Rodman	.15	.10
59	Isiah Thomas	.30	.18
60	Darrell Walker	.10	.06
61	Orlando Woolridge	.10	.06
62	Victor Alexander	.10	.06
63	Chris Gatling	.12	.07
64	Tim Hardaway	.40	.25
65	Tyrone Hill	.10	.06
66	Sarunas Marciulionis	.12	.07
67	Chris Mullin	.35	.20
68	Billy Owens	.35	.20
69	Sleepy Floyd	.10	.06
70	Avery Johnson	.10	.06
71	Vernon Maxwell	.20	.12
72	Hakeem Olajuwon	1.50	.90
73	Kenny Smith	.12	.07
74	Otis Thorpe	.12	.07
75	Dale Davis	.15	.10
76	Vern Fleming	.10	.06
77	George McCloud	.10	.06
78	Reggie Miller	.30	.18
79	Detlef Schrempf	.12	.07
80	Rik Smits	.10	.06
81	LaSalle Thompson	.10	.06
82	Gary Grant	.10	.06
83	Ron Harper	.12	.07
84	Mark Jackson	.12	.07
85	Danny Manning	.30	.18
86	Ken Norman	.12	.07
87	Stanley Roberts	.12	.07
88	Loy Vaught	.10	.06
89	Elden Campbell	.12	.07
90	Vlade Divac	.12	.07
91	A.C. Green	.12	.07
92	Sam Perkins	.12	.07
93	Byron Scott	.10	.06
94	Tony Smith	.10	.06
95	Sedale Threatt	.10	.06
96	James Worthy	.20	.12
97	Willie Burton	.12	.07
98	Vernell Coles	.10	.06
99	Kevin Edwards	.10	.06
100	Grant Long	.10	.06
101	Glen Rice	.20	.12
102	Rony Seikaly	.12	.07
103	Brian Shaw	.10	.06
104	Steve Smith	.35	.20
105	Frank Brickowski	.10	.06
106	Moses Malone	.20	.12
107	Fred Roberts	.10	.06
108	Alvin Robertson	.10	.06
109	Thurl Bailey	.10	.06
110	Gerald Glass	.10	.06
111	Luc Longley	.12	.07
112	Felton Spencer	.12	.07
113	Doug West	.15	.10
114	Kenny Anderson	.40	.25
115	Mookie Blaylock	.12	.07
116	Sam Bowie	.10	.06
117	Derrick Coleman	.35	.20
118	Chris Dudley	.10	.06
119	Chris Morris	.10	.06
120	Drazen Petrovic	.20	.12
121	Greg Anthony	.15	.10

46 • 1992-93 FLEER ULTRA

122 Patrick Ewing	.80	.50
123 Anthony Mason	.10	.06
124 Charles Oakley	.10	.06
125 Doc Rivers	.10	.06
126 Charles Smith	.12	.07
127 John Starks	.30	.18
128 Nick Anderson	.30	.18
129 Anthony Bowie	.10	.06
130 Terry Catledge	.10	.06
131 Jerry Reynolds	.10	.06
132 Dennis Scott	.15	.10
133 Scott Skiles	.10	.06
134 Brian Williams	.12	.07
135 Ron Anderson	.10	.06
136 Manute Bol	.10	.06
137 Johnny Dawkins	.10	.06
138 Armon Gilliam	.10	.06
139 Hersey Hawkins	.15	.10
140 Jeff Ruland	.10	.06
141 Charles Shackleford	.10	.06
142 Cedric Ceballos	.12	.07
143 Tom Chambers	.12	.07
144 Kevin Johnson	.30	.18
145 Negele Knight	.10	.06
146 Dan Majerle	.20	.12
147 Mark West	.10	.06
148 Mark Bryant	.10	.06
149 Clyde Drexler	.40	.25
150 Kevin Duckworth	.10	.06
151 Jerome Kersey	.12	.07
152 Robert Pack	.12	.07
153 Terry Porter	.12	.07
154 Cliff Robinson	.30	.18
155 Buck Williams	.12	.07
156 Anthony Bonner	.10	.06
157 Duane Causwell	.10	.06
158 Mitch Richmond	.15	.10
159 Lionel Simmons	.25	.15
160 Wayman Tisdale	.12	.07
161 Spud Webb	.10	.06
162 Willie Anderson	.10	.06
163 Antoine Carr	.10	.06
164 Terry Cummings	.12	.07
165 Sean Elliott	.20	.12
166 Sidney Green	.10	.06
167 David Robinson	1.00	.60
168 Dana Barros	.12	.07
169 Benoit Benjamin	.10	.06
170 Michael Cage	.10	.06
171 Eddie Johnson	.12	.07
172 Shawn Kemp	1.00	.60
173 Derrick McKey	.12	.07
174 Nate McMillian	.10	.06
175 Gary Payton	.20	.12
176 Rickey Pierce	.10	.06
177 David Benoit	.12	.07
178 Mike Brown	.10	.06
179 Tyrone Corbin	.10	.06
180 Mark Eaton	.10	.06
181 Jeff Malone	.15	.10
182 Karl Malone	.75	.45
183 John Stockton	.75	.45
184 Michael Adams	.12	.07
185 Ledell Eackles	.10	.06
186 Pervis Ellison	.12	.07
187 A.J. English	.10	.06
188 Harvey Grant	.10	.06
189 Buck Johnson	.10	.06
190 LaBradford Smith	.10	.06
191 Larry Stewart	.10	.06
192 David Wingate	.10	.06
193 Alonzo Mourning (R)	8.00	5.00
194 Adam Keefe (R)	.20	.12
195 Robert Horry (R)	1.75	1.00
196 Anthony Peeler (R)	.50	.30
197 Tracy Murray (R)	.25	.15
198 Dave Johnson (R)	.15	.10
199 Checklist	.10	.03
200 Checklist	.10	.03
201 David Robinson (Jam)	.35	.20
202 Dikembe Mutombo (Jam)	.20	.12
203 Otis Thorpe (Jam)	.10	.06
204 Hakeem Olajuwon (Jam)	.50	.30
205 Shawn Kemp (Jam)	.30	.18
206 Charles Barkley (Jam)	.35	.20
207 Pervis Ellison (Jam)	.10	.06
208 Chris Morris (Jam)	.10	.06
209 Brad Daugherty (Jam)	.12	.07
210 Derrick Coleman (Jam)	.20	.12
211 Tim Perry (Jam)	.10	.06
212 Duane Causwell (Jam)	.10	.06
213 Scottie Pippen (Jam)	.25	.15
214 Robert Parish (Jam)	.10	.06
215 Stacey Augmon (Jam)	.15	.10
216 Michael Jordan (Jam)	1.00	.60
217 Karl Malone (Jam)	.25	.15
218 John Williams (Jam)	.10	.06
219 Horace Grant (Jam)	.10	.06
220 Orlando Woolridge (Jam)	.10	.06
221 Mookie Blaylock	.10	.06
222 Greg Foster	.10	.06
223 Steve Henson	.10	.06
224 Adam Keefe	.12	.07
225 Jon Koncak	.10	.06
226 Travis Mays	.10	.06
227 Alaa Abdelnaby	.10	.06
228 Sherman Douglas	.12	.07
229 Xavier McDaniel	.12	.07
230 Marcus Webb (R)	.12	.07
231 Tony Bennett (R)	.12	.07
232 Mike Gminski	.10	.06
233 Kevin Lynch	.10	.06
234 Alonzo Mourning	1.50	.90
235 David Wingate	.10	.06

1992-93 FLEER ULTRA • 47

#	Player		
236	Rodney McCray	.12	.07
237	Trent Tucker	.10	.06
238	Corey Williams (R)	.15	.10
239	Danny Ferry	.10	.06
240	Jay Guidinger (R)	.10	.06
241	Jerome Lane	.10	.06
242	Bobby Phills (R)	.15	.10
243	Gerald Wilkins	.10	.06
244	Walter Bond (R)	.12	.07
245	Dexter Cambridge (R)	.12	.07
246	Radisav Curcic (R)	.12	.07
247	Brian Howard (R)	.12	.07
248	Tracy Moore (R)	.12	.07
249	Sean Rooks (R)	.25	.15
250	Kevin Brooks	.10	.06
251	LaPhonso Ellis (R)	1.25	.70
252	Scott Hasting	.10	.06
253	Robert Pack	.12	.07
254	Gary Plummer (R)	.10	.06
255	Bryant Stith (R)	.40	.25
256	Robert Werdann (R)	.12	.07
257	Gerald Glass	.10	.06
258	Terry Mills	.15	.10
259	Olden Polynice	.10	.06
260	Danny Young	.10	.06
261	Jud Buechler	.10	.06
262	Jeff Grayer	.10	.06
263	Bryon Houston (R)	.15	.10
264	Keith Jennings (R)	.12	.07
265	Ed Nealy	.10	.06
266	Latrell Sprewell (R)	2.00	1.25
267	Scott Brooks	.10	.06
268	Matt Bullard	.10	.06
269	Winston Garland	.10	.06
270	Carl Herrera	.12	.07
271	Robert Horry	.40	.25
272	Tree Rollins	.10	.06
273	Greg Dreiling	.10	.06
274	Sean Green	.10	.06
275	Sam Mitchell	.10	.06
276	Pooh Richardson	.12	.07
277	Malik Sealy (R)	.15	.10
278	Kenny Williams	.10	.06
279	Mark Jackson	.12	.07
280	Stanley Roberts	.10	.06
281	Elmore Spencer (R)	.20	.12
282	Kiki Vandeweghe	.10	.06
283	John Williams	.10	.06
284	Randy Woods (R)	.12	.07
285	Alex Blackwell (R)	.10	.06
286	Duane Cooper (R)	.15	.10
287	James Edwards	.10	.06
288	Jack Haley	.10	.06
289	Anthony Peeler	.20	.12
290	Keith Askins	.10	.06
291	Matt Geiger (R)	.12	.07
292	Alec Kessler	.10	.06
293	Harold Miner (R)	.60	.35
294	John Salley	.10	.06
295	Anthony Avent (R)	.12	.07
296	Jon Berry (R)	.12	.07
297	Todd Day (R)	.35	.20
298	Blue Edwards	.10	.06
299	Brad Lohaus	.10	.06
300	Lee Mayberry (R)	.25	.15
301	Eric Murdock	.12	.07
302	Dan Schayes	.10	.06
303	Lance Blanks	.10	.06
304	Christian Laettner (R)	1.00	.60
305	Marlon Maxey (R)	.15	.10
306	Bob McCann (R)	.12	.07
307	Chuck Person	.12	.07
308	Brad Sellers	.10	.06
309	Chris Smith (R)	.15	.10
310	Gundars Vetra (R)	.10	.06
311	Micheal Williams	.10	.06
312	Rafael Addison	.10	.06
313	Chucky Brown	.10	.06
314	Maurice Cheeks	.12	.07
315	Tate George	.10	.06
316	Rick Mahorn	.10	.06
317	Rumeal Robinson	.12	.07
318	Eric Anderson (R)	.12	.07
319	Rolando Blackman	.12	.07
320	Tony Campbell	.10	.06
321	Hubert Davis (R)	.40	.25
322	Doc Rivers	.10	.06
323	Charles Smith	.12	.07
324	Herb Williams	.10	.06
325	Litterial Green (R)	.20	.12
326	Steve Kerr	.10	.06
327	Greg Kite	.10	.06
328	Shaquille O'Neal (R)	8.00	5.00
329	Tom Tolbert	.10	.06
330	Jeff Turner	.10	.06
331	Greg Grant	.10	.06
332	Jeff Hornacek	.12	.07
333	Andrew Lang	.10	.06
334	Tim Perry	.10	.06
335	Clarence Weatherspoon (R)	.80	.50
336	Danny Ainge	.12	.07
337	Charles Barkley	.60	.35
338	Richard Dumas (R)	.25	.15
339	Frank Johnson	.10	.06
340	Tim Kempton (R)	.12	.07
341	Oliver Miller (R)	.60	.35
342	Jerrod Mustaf	.10	.06
343	Mario Elie	.10	.06
344	Dave Johnson	.10	.06
345	Tracy Murray	.15	.10
346	Rod Strickland	.10	.06
347	Randy Brown	.10	.06
348	Pete Chilcutt	.10	.06
349	Marty Conlon	.10	.06

48 • 1992-93 FLEER ULTRA

350	Jim Les	.10	.06
351	Kurt Rambis	.10	.06
352	Walt Williams (R)	.60	.35
353	Lloyd Daniels (R)	.20	.12
354	Vinny Del Negro	.10	.06
355	Dale Ellis	.12	.07
356	Avery Johnson	.10	.06
357	Sam Mack (R)	.12	.07
358	J.R. Reid	.10	.06
359	David Wood	.10	.06
360	Vincent Askew	.10	.06
361	Isaac Austin (R)	.12	.07
362	John Crotty (R)	.12	.07
363	Stephen Howard (R)	.10	.06
364	Jay Humphries	.10	.06
365	Larry Krystkowiak	.10	.06
366	Rex Chapman	.12	.07
367	Tom Gugliotta (R)	.80	.50
368	Buck Johnson	.10	.06
369	Charles Jones	.10	.06
370	Don MacLean (R)	.60	.35
371	Doug Overton	.10	.06
372	Brent Price (R)	.20	.12
373	Checklist	.10	.03
374	Checklist	.10	.03
375	Checklist	.10	.03
___	Scottie Pippen Inserts (1-12) ea.	1.00	.60
___	Scottie Pippen (Autographed)	125.00	70.00

1992-93 Fleer Ultra All-NBA Team

These limited insert cards were issued randomly in Ultra Series I packs. The card fronts feature full color action photos with a shield commemorating the All-NBA Team member in the lower right corner. The player's name appears in the lower left corner. The flip side contains personal data and stats. All cards measure 2-1/2" by 3-1/2"

		MINT	NR/MT
	Complete Set (15)	32.00	20.00
	Commons	1.00	.60
1	Karl Malone	3.00	1.75
2	Chris Mullin	1.75	1.00
3	David Robinson	4.50	2.75
4	Michael Jordan	15.00	9.00
5	Clyde Drexler	2.50	1.50
6	Scottie Pippen	3.50	2.00
7	Charles Barkley	5.00	3.00
8	Patrick Ewing	3.50	2.00
9	Tim Hardaway	1.50	.90
10	John Stockton	2.50	1.50
11	Dennis Rodman	1.50	.90
12	Kevin Willis	1.00	.60
13	Brad Daugherty	1.50	.90
14	Mark Price	1.50	.90
15	Kevin Johnson	1.75	1.00

1992-93 Fleer Ultra Award Winners

These insert cards feature full color action photos on the fronts with an "Award Winner" logo stamped in the lower right corner of the card front. The player's name appears across the bottom. The backs contain personal data and the player's accomplishments. The cards were randomly inserted into Ultra Series I packs. All cards measure 2-1/2" by 3-1/2".

		MINT	NR/MT
	Complete Set (5)	28.00	18.00
	Commons	1.25	.70
1	Michael Jordan	18.00	12.00
2	David Robinson	8.00	5.00
3	Larry Johnson	8.00	5.00
4	Detlef Schrempf	1.50	.90
5	Pervis Ellison	1.25	.70

1992-93 Fleer Ultra Playmakers

The cards in this insert set were randomly distributed in Ultra Series II packs. The card fronts consist of full color action shots with a smaller inset photo in the lower left corner next to a Playmaker logo. The player's name is printed across the bottom of the card. All cards measure 2-1/2" by 3-1/2".

		MINT	NR/MT
	Complete Set (10)	7.00	4.00
	Commons	.40	.25
1	Kenny Anderson	1.25	.70
2	Muggsy Bogues	.40	.25
3	Tim Hardaway	1.00	.60
4	Mark Jackson	.75	.45
5	Kevin Johnson	.75	.45
6	Mark Price	.75	.45
7	Terry Porter	.50	.30
8	Scott Skiles	.40	.25
9	John Stockton	1.50	.90
10	Isiah Thomas	1.25	.70

1992-93 Fleer Ultra Rejectors

The cards in this limited insert set feature full color action photographs on the fronts with a "Rejectors" logo, a small basketball in a diamond, in the lower right corner. The player's name is located in the lower left corner. These cards were randomly inserted into Fleer Series II packs. All cards measure 2-1/2" by 3-1/2".

	MINT	NR/MT
Complete Set (5)	35.00	20.00
Commons	1.50	.90
1 Alonzo Mourning	10.00	6.00
2 Dikembe Mutombo	1.50	.90
3 Hakeem Olajuwon	5.00	3.00
4 Shaquille O'Neal	16.00	10.00
5 David Robinson	4.00	2.75

1992-93 Fleer Ultra Rookie Impact

The cards in this set were random inserts in Ultra Series II packs. The card fronts contain a full length color photo of the player over a background that includes a multi-photo proof sheet of the player. The player's name appears in the lower left corner of the card front while an All-Rookie Team logo is stamped in the lower right side of the card front. All cards measure 2-1/2" by 3-1/2".

	MINT	NR/MT
Complete Set (10)	50.00	32.00
Commons	2.00	1.25
1 LaPhonso Ellis	4.00	2.50
2 Tom Gugliotta	3.00	1.75
3 Robert Horry	4.00	2.50
4 Christian Laettner	3.50	2.00
5 Harold Miner	2.50	1.50
6 Alonzo Mourning	12.00	7.00
7 Shaquille O'Neal	25.00	15.00
8 Latrell Sprewell	10.00	6.00
9 Clarence Weatherspoon	4.00	2.50
10 Walt Williams	2.00	1.25

1993-94 Fleer

The cards in this set feature full-color game action photos on the fronts framed by a white border. The player's name, team and position appear in a day-glow color swatch in the lower corner of the card front. The Fleer logo is printed in the opposite corner at the top. The flip side contains another color photo superimposed over the player's last name which is printed vertically in block letter along the left side of the card back. Personal data and a box containing stats are also printed on the back. Subsets include League Leaders (LL)(221-228), Award Winners (AW)(229-232) and Pro Visions (PV)(233-237). The set also includes a limited 12-cards insert set of Clyde Drexler distributed randomly in Fleer packs. Those cards are listed at the end of this checklist but are not included in the complete set price below. All cards measure 2-1/2" by 3-1/2".

		MINT	NR/MT
	Complete Set (400)	20.00	12.50
	Commons	.05	.02
1	Stacey Augmon	.12	.07
2	Mookie Blaylock	.07	.04
3	Duane Ferrell	.05	.02
4	Paul Graham	.05	.02
5	Adam Keefe	.07	.04
6	Jon Koncak	.05	.02
7	Dominique Wilkins	.25	.15
8	Kevin Willis	.05	.02
9	Alaa Abdelnaby	.05	.02
10	Dee Brown	.10	.06
11	Sherman Douglas	.05	.02
12	Rick Fox	.08	.05
13	Kevin Gamble	.05	.02
14	Reggie Lewis	.08	.05
15	Xavier McDaniel	.05	.02
16	Robert Parrish	.15	.10
17	Muggsy Bogues	.05	.02
18	Dell Curry	.05	.02
19	Kenny Gattison	.05	.02
20	Kendall Gill	.15	.10
21	Larry Johnson	.35	.20
22	Alonzo Mourning	.75	.45
23	Johnny Newman	.05	.02
24	David Wingate	.05	.02
25	B.J. Armstrong	.12	.07
26	Bill Cartwright	.05	.02
27	Horace Grant	.12	.07
28	Michael Jordan	1.75	1.00
29	Stacey King	.05	.02
30	John Paxson	.08	.05
31	Will Perdue	.05	.02
32	Scottie Pippen	.30	.18
33	Scott Williams	.05	.02
34	Terrell Brandon	.08	.05
35	Brad Daugherty	.12	.07
35	Craig Ehlo	.05	.02
37	Danny Ferry	.05	.02
38	Larry Nance	.05	.02
39	Mark Price	.15	.10
40	Mike Sanders	.05	.02
41	Gerald Wilkins	.05	.02
42	John Williams (Cle)	.10	.06
43	Terry Davis	.05	.02
44	Derek Harper	.07	.04
45	Mike Iuzzolino	.05	.02
46	Jim Jackson	.25	.15
47	Sean Rooks	.10	.06
48	Doug Smith	.05	.02
49	Randy White	.05	.02
50	Mahmoud Abdul-Rauf	.15	.10
51	LaPhonso Ellis	.15	.10
52	Marcus Liberty	.05	.02
53	Mark Macon	.08	.05
54	Dikembe Mutombo	.15	.10
55	Robert Pack	.05	.02
56	Bryant Stith	.15	.10
57	Reggie Williams	.05	.02
58	Mark Aquirre	.05	.02
59	Joe Dumars	.15	.10
60	Bill Laimbeer	.05	.02
61	Terry Mills	.05	.02
62	Olden Polynice	.05	.02
63	Alvin Robertson	.05	.02

1993-94 FLEER

#	Player		
64	Dennis Rodman	.10	.06
65	Isiah Thomas	.15	.10
66	Victor Alexander	.05	.02
67	Tim Hardaway	.15	.10
68	Tyrone Hill	.05	.02
69	Byron Houston	.07	.04
70	Sarunas Marciulionis	.05	.02
71	Chris Mullin	.15	.10
72	Billy Owens	.15	.10
73	Latrell Sprewell	.60	.35
74	Scott Brooks	.05	.02
75	Matt Bullard	.05	.02
76	Carl Herrera	.12	.07
77	Robert Hory	.30	.18
78	Vernon Maxwell	.12	.07
79	Hakeem Olajuwon	.75	.45
80	Kenny Smith	.05	.02
81	Otis Thorpe	.05	.02
82	Dale Davis	.10	.06
83	Vern Fleming	.05	.02
84	George McCloud	.05	.02
85	Reggie Miller	.20	.12
86	Sam Mitchell	.05	.02
87	Pooh Richardson	.05	.02
88	Detlef Schrempf	.12	.07
89	Rik Smits	.05	.02
90	Gary Grant	.05	.02
91	Ron Harper	.07	.04
92	Mark Jackson	.10	.06
93	Danny Manning	.15	.10
94	Ken Norman	.05	.02
95	Stanley Roberts	.05	.02
96	Loy Vaught	.05	.02
97	John Williams	.05	.02
98	Elden Campbell	.10	.06
99	Doug Christie	.12	.07
100	Duane Cooper	.05	.02
101	Vlade Divac	.08	.05
102	A.C. Green	.08	.05
103	Anthony Peeler	.15	.10
104	Sedale Threatt	.05	.02
105	James Worthy	.12	.07
106	Bimbo Coles	.05	.02
107	Grant Long	.05	.02
108	Harold Miner	.20	.12
109	Glen Rice	.08	.05
110	John Salley	.05	.02
111	Rony Seikaly	.08	.05
112	Brian Shaw	.05	.02
113	Steve Smith	.20	.12
114	Anthony Avent	.05	.02
115	Jon Barry	.05	.02
116	Frank Brickowski	.05	.02
117	Todd Day	.10	.06
118	Blue Edwards	.05	.02
119	Brad Lohaus	.05	.02
120	Lee Mayberry	.08	.05
121	Eric Murdock	.08	.05
122	Thurl Bailey	.05	.02
123	Christian Laettner	.25	.15
124	Luc Longley	.05	.02
125	Chuck Person	.08	.05
126	Felton Spencer	.08	.05
127	Doug West	.05	.02
128	Michael Williams	.05	.02
129	Rafael Addison	.05	.02
130	Kenny Anderson	.15	.10
131	Sam Bowie	.05	.02
132	Chucky Brown	.07	.04
133	Derrick Coleman	.15	.10
134	Chris Dudley	.05	.02
135	Chris Morris	.05	.02
136	Rumeal Robinson	.05	.02
137	Greg Anthony	.08	.05
138	Rolando Blackman	.05	.02
139	Tony Campbell	.05	.02
140	Hubert Davis	.10	.06
141	Patrick Ewing	.35	.20
142	Anthony Mason	.05	.02
143	Charles Oakley	.10	.06
144	Doc Rivers	.07	.04
145	Charles Smith	.08	.05
146	John Starks	.12	.07
147	Nick Anderson	.10	.06
148	Anthony Bowie	.05	.02
149	Shaquille O'Neal	1.75	1.00
150	Donald Royal	.05	.02
151	Dennis Scott	.08	.05
152	Scott Skiles	.05	.02
153	Tom Tolbert	.05	.02
154	Jeff Turner	.05	.02
155	Ron Anderson	.05	.02
156	Johnny Dawkins	.05	.02
157	Hersey Hawkins	.08	.05
158	Jeff Hornacek	.08	.05
159	Andrew Lang	.05	.02
160	Tim Perry	.05	.02
161	Clarence Weatherspoon	.15	.10
162	Danny Ainge	.10	.06
163	Charles Barkley	.40	.25
164	Cedric Ceballos	.08	.05
165	Tom Chambers	.07	.04
166	Richard Dumas	.10	.06
167	Kevin Johnson	.15	.10
168	Negele Knight	.05	.02
169	Dan Majerle	.12	.07
170	Oliver Miller	.12	.07
171	Mark West	.05	.02
172	Mark Bryant	.05	.02
173	Clyde Drexler	.20	.12
174	Kevin Duckworth	.05	.02
175	Mario Elie	.05	.02
176	Jerome Kersey	.05	.02
177	Terry Porter	.08	.05

1993-94 FLEER • 53

#	Player		
178	Cliff Robinson	.10	.06
179	Rod Stickland	.05	.02
180	Buck Williams	.07	.04
181	Anthony Bonner	.05	.02
182	Duane Causwell	.05	.02
183	Mitch Richmond	.12	.07
184	Lionel Simmons	.20	.12
185	Wayman Tisdale	.07	.04
186	Spud Webb	.05	.02
187	Walt Williams	.15	.10
188	Antoine Carr	.05	.02
189	Terry Cummings	.07	.04
190	Lloyd Daniels	.07	.04
191	Vinny Del Negro	.05	.02
192	Sean Elliott	.10	.06
193	Dale Ellis	.05	.02
194	Avery Johnson	.05	.02
195	J.R. Reid	.05	.02
196	David Robinson	.40	.25
197	Michael Cage	.05	.02
198	Eddie Johnson	.05	.02
199	Shawn Kemp	.35	.20
200	Derrick McKey	.07	.04
201	Nate McMillan	.05	.02
202	Gary Payton	.12	.07
203	Sam Perkins	.07	.04
204	Ricky Pierce	.05	.02
205	David Benoit	.05	.02
206	Tyrone Corbin	.05	.02
207	Mark Eaton	.05	.02
208	Jay Humphries	.05	.02
209	Larry Krystkowiak	.05	.02
210	Jeff Malone	.08	.05
211	Karl Malone	.25	.15
212	John Stockton	.25	.15
213	Michael Adams	.07	.04
214	Rex Chapman	.05	.02
215	Pervis Ellison	.08	.05
216	Harvey Grant	.05	.02
217	Tom Gugliotta	.20	.12
218	Buck Johnson	.05	.02
219	LaBradford Smith	.05	.02
220	Larry Stewart	.05	.02
221	B.J. Armstrong (LL)	.08	.05
222	Cedric Ceballos (LL)	.08	.05
223	Larry Johnson (LL)	.20	.12
224	Michael Jordan (LL)	.75	.45
225	Hakeem Olajuwon (LL)	.40	.25
226	Mark Price (LL)	.08	.05
227	Dennis Rodman (LL)	.08	.05
228	John Stockton (LL)	.12	.07
229	Charles Barkley (AW)	.25	.15
230	Hakeem Olajuwon (AW)	.30	.18
231	Shaquille O'Neal (AW)	.75	.45
232	Cliff Robinson (AW)	.08	.05
233	Shawn Kemp (PV)	.20	.12
234	Alonzo Mourning (PV)	.30	.18
235	Hakeem Olajuwon (PV)	.40	.25
236	John Stockton (PV)	.12	.07
237	Dominique Wilkins (PV)	.12	.07
238	Checklist	.05	.02
239	Checklist	.05	.02
240	Checklist	.05	.02
241	Doug Edwards (R)	.10	.06
242	Craig Ehlo	.05	.02
243	Andrew Lang	.05	.02
244	Ennis Whatley	.05	.02
245	Chris Corchiani	.05	.02
246	Acie Earl (R)	.15	.10
247	Jimmy Oliver	.05	.02
248	Ed Pinckney	.05	.02
249	Dino Radja (R)	.25	.15
250	Matt Wenstrom (R)	.08	.05
251	Tony Bennett	.05	.02
252	Scott Burrell (R)	.15	.10
253	LeRon Ellis	.10	.06
254	Hersey Hawkins	.07	.04
255	Eddie Johnson	.05	.02
256	Corie Blount (R)	.10	.06
257	JoJo English (R)	.12	.07
258	Dave Johnson	.05	.02
259	Steve Kerr	.05	.02
260	Toni Kukoc (R)	.40	.25
261	Pete Myers	.05	.02
262	Bill Wennington	.05	.02
263	John Battle	.05	.02
264	Tyrone Hill	.05	.02
265	Gerald Madkins (R)	.10	.06
266	Chris Mills (R)	.20	.12
267	Bobby Phills	.08	.05
268	Greg Dreiling	.05	.02
269	Lucious Harris (R)	.10	.06
270	Donald Hodge	.05	.02
271	Popeye Jones (R)	.12	.07
272	Tim Legler (R)	.08	.05
273	Fat Lever	.05	.02
274	Jamal Mashburn (R)	.80	.50
275	Darren Morningstar (R)	.08	.05
276	Tom Hammonds	.05	.02
277	Darnell Mee (R)	.10	.06
278	Rodney Rogers (R)	.25	.15
279	Brian Williams	.08	.05
280	Greg Anderson	.05	.02
281	Sean Elliott	.07	.04
282	Allan Houston (R)	.12	.07
283	Lindsey Hunter (R)	.20	.12
284	Marcus Liberty	.05	.02
285	Mark Macon	.07	.04
286	David Wood	.05	.02
287	Jud Buechler	.05	.02
288	Chris Gatling	.07	.04
289	Josh Grant (R)	.12	.07
290	Jeff Grayer	.05	.02
291	Avery Johnson	.05	.02

1993-94 FLEER

#	Player	Price	Price
292	Chris Webber (R)	3.00	1.75
293	Sam Cassell (R)	.50	.30
294	Mario Elie	.05	.02
295	Richard Petruska (R)	.10	.06
296	Eric Riley (R)	.10	.06
297	Antonio Davis (R)	.20	.12
298	Scott Haskin (R)	.10	.06
299	Derrick McKey	.05	.02
300	Byron Scott	.05	.02
301	Malik Sealy	.07	.04
302	LaSalle Thompson	.05	.02
303	Kenny Williams	.05	.02
304	Haywoode Workman	.08	.05
305	Mark Aquirre	.05	.02
306	Terry Dehere (R)	.15	.10
307	Bob Martin (R)	.08	.05
308	Elmore Spencer	.08	.05
309	Tom Tolbert	.05	.02
310	Randy Woods	.05	.02
311	Sam Bowie	.05	.02
312	James Edwards	.05	.02
313	Antonio Harvey (R)	.08	.05
314	George Lynch (R)	.30	.18
315	Tony Smith	.05	.02
316	Nick Van Exel (R)	.40	.25
317	Manute Bol	.05	.02
318	Willie Burton	.07	.04
319	Matt Geiger	.05	.02
320	Alec Kessler	.05	.02
321	Vin Baker (R)	.75	.45
322	Ken Norman	.05	.02
323	Dan Schayes	.05	.02
324	Derek Strong (R)	.10	.06
325	Mike Brown	.05	.02
326	Brian Davis (R)	.10	.06
327	Tellis Frank	.05	.02
328	Marlon Maxey	.05	.02
329	Isaiah Rider (R)	.80	.50
330	Chris Smith	.08	.05
331	Benoit Benjamin	.05	.02
332	P.J. Brown (R)	.12	.07
333	Kevin Edwards	.05	.02
334	Armon Gilliam	.05	.02
335	Rick Mahorn	.05	.02
336	Dwayne Schintzius	.05	.02
337	Rex Walters (R)	.12	.07
338	David Wesley (R)	.08	.05
339	Jayson Williams	.05	.02
340	Anthony Bonner	.05	.02
341	Herb Williams	.05	.02
342	Litterial Green	.05	.02
343	Anfernee Hardaway (R)	2.00	1.25
344	Greg Kite	.05	.02
345	Larry Krystkowiak	.05	.02
346	Todd Lichti	.05	.02
347	Keith Tower (R)	.08	.05
348	Dana Barros	.05	.02
349	Shawn Bradley (R)	.30	.18
350	Michael Curry (R)	.08	.05
351	Greg Graham (R)	.10	.06
352	Warren Kidd (R)	.10	.06
353	Moses Malone	.10	.06
354	Orlando Woolridge	.05	.02
355	Duane Cooper	.05	.02
356	Joe Courtney (R)	.08	.05
357	A.C. Green	.07	.04
358	Frank Johnson	.05	.02
359	Joe Kleine	.05	.02
360	Malcolm Mackey (R)	.12	.07
361	Jerrod Mustaf	.07	.04
362	Chris Dudley	.05	.02
363	Harvey Grant	.05	.02
364	Tracy Murray	.10	.06
365	James Robinson (R)	.12	.07
366	Reggie Smith	.05	.02
367	Kevin Thompson (R)	.08	.05
368	Randy Breuer	.05	.02
369	Randy Brown	.05	.02
370	Evers Burns (R)	.12	.07
371	Pete Chilcutt	.05	.02
372	Bobby Hurley (R)	.30	.18
373	Jim Les	.05	.02
374	Mike Peplowski (R)	.12	.07
375	Willie Anderson	.05	.02
376	Sleepy Floyd	.05	.02
377	Negele Knight	.05	.02
378	Dennis Rodman	.07	.04
379	Chris Whitney (R)	.10	.06
380	Vincent Askew	.05	.02
381	Kendall Gill	.08	.05
382	Ervin Johnson (R)	.12	.07
383	Chris King (R)	.10	.06
384	Rich King	.05	.02
385	Steve Scheffler	.05	.02
386	Detlef Schrempf	.10	.06
387	Tom Chambers	.07	.04
388	John Crotty	.07	.04
389	Byron Russell (R)	.12	.07
390	Felton Spencer	.08	.05
391	Luther Wright (R)	.12	.07
392	Mitchell Butler (R)	.08	.05
393	Calbert Cheaney (R)	.40	.25
394	Kevin Duckworth	.05	.02
395	Don MacLean	.10	.06
396	Gheorghe Muresan (R)	.12	.07
397	Doug Overton	.05	.02
398	Brent Price	.07	.04
399	Checklist	.05	.02
400	Checklist	.05	.02
___	Clyde Drexler (ea.)	.50	.30
___	Clyde Drexler (Auto)	100.00	60.00

1993-94 FLEER NBA INTERNATIONALS • 55

1993-94 Fleer All-Stars

These limited insert cards were randomly issued in Fleer Series I packs. The card fronts consist of full-color action photos framed by a light purple border. Gold foil stamping including a circular All-Star Weekend logo is printed in the bottom corner of the card. All cards measure 2-1/2" by 3-1/2".

		MINT	NR/MT
	Complete Set (24)	32.00	20.00
	Commons	.35	.20
1	Brad Daugherty	.60	.35
2	Joe Dumars	1.50	.90
3	Patrick Ewing	2.00	1.25
4	Larry Johnson	2.00	1.25
5	Michael Jordan	10.00	6.00
6	Larry Nance	.35	.20
7	Shaquille O'Neal	10.00	6.00
8	Scottie Pippen	1.75	1.00
9	Mark Price	.75	.45
10	Detlef Schrempf	.60	.35
11	Isiah Thomas	1.00	.60
12	Dominique Wilkins	1.50	.90
13	Charles Barkley	2.50	1.50
14	Clyde Drexler	1.25	.70
15	Sean Elliott	.50	.30
16	Tim Hardaway	.75	.45
17	Shawn Kemp	2.00	1.25
18	Dan Majerle	.50	.30
19	Karl Malone	1.50	.90
20	Danny Manning	.75	.45
21	Hakeem Olajuwon	5.00	3.00
22	Terry Porter	.35	.20
23	David Robinson	3.50	2.00
24	John Stockton	1.50	.90

1993-94 Fleer NBA Internationals

The cards in this limited insert set feature NBA players who were born outside the USA. The card fronts contain gold foil stamping with full-color action photos superimposed over a background of a map. A small globe appears in the top corner of the card with the words NBA Internationals. The player's name is centered across the bottom of the card in gold type. The cards were issued randomly in Fleer Series I packs and measure 2-1/2" by 3-1/2".

		MINT	NR/MT
	Complete Set (12)	5.00	3.00
	Commons	.30	.18
1	Alaa Abdelnaby	.30	.18
2	Vlade Divac	.50	.30
3	Patrick Ewing	2.00	1.25

56 • 1993-94 FLEER NBA INTERNATIONALS

4	Carl Herrera	.50	.30
5	Luc Longley	.30	.18
6	Sarunas Marciulionis	.30	.18
7	Dikembe Mutombo	1.50	.90
8	Rumeal Robinson	.30	.18
9	Detlef Schrempf	.75	.45
10	Rony Seikaly	.40	.25
11	Rik Smits	.30	.18
12	Dominique Wilkins	1.50	.90

3	Lindsey Hunter	.75	.45
4	Bobby Hurley	.75	.45
5	Toni Kukoc	1.00	.60
6	Jamal Mashburn	2.00	1.25
7	Dino Radja	.75	.45
8	Isaiah Rider	2.50	1.50
9	Nick Van Exel	1.00	.60
10	Chris Webber	5.00	3.00

1993-94 Fleer First Year Phenoms

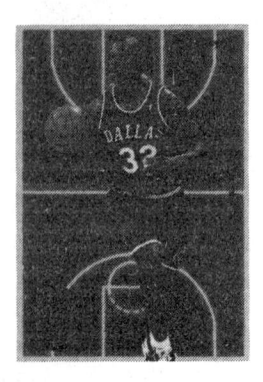

These limited insert cards were randomly issued in Fleer Series II packs. The card fronts consist of a full-color action shot superimposed over the outline of a basketball court. A gold foil stamped First Year Phenoms logo is located in the lower corner of the card while the player's name is printed vertically along with side. All cards measure 2-1/2" by 3-1/2".

	MINT	NR/MT
Complete Set (10)	15.00	10.00
Commons	.75	.45

1	Shawn Bradley	.75	.45
2	Anfernee Hardaway	4.00	2.50

1993-94 Fleer Living Legends

These random inserts were distributed randomly in Fleer Series II packs. The horizontal card fronts feature full-color action photos with a Living Legends logo printed in the lower corner of the card and to the left of the player's name. All cards measure 2-1/2" by 3-1/2".

	MINT	NR/MT
Complete Set (6)	60.00	35.00
Commons	5.00	3.00

1	Charles Barkley	8.50	5.00
2	Larry Bird	15.00	10.00
3	Patrick Ewing	7.00	4.00
4	Michael Jordan	25.00	15.00
5	Hakeem Olajuwon	12.00	7.50
6	Dominique Wilkins	5.00	3.00

1993-94 FLEER ROOKIE SENSATIONS • 57

1993-94 Fleer NBA Superstars

		MINT	NR/MT
17	Mark Price	.40	.25
18	Mitch Richmond	.25	.15
19	David Robinson	1.50	.90
20	Dominique Wilkins	1.25	.70

The cards in this insert set have four photographs on the card fronts including an isolated full-color shot in the foreground and three smaller photos on the right half of the card. The other half of the card front contains the player's last name printed vertically in block letters and the words NBA Superstar. The cards were random inserts in Fleer Series II packs and measure 2-1/2" by 3-1/2".

	MINT	NR/MT
Complete Set (20)	14.00	9.00
Commons	.20	.12

		MINT	NR/MT
1	Mahmoud Abdul-Rauf	.20	.12
2	Charles Barkley	1.25	.70
3	Derrick Coleman	.75	.45
4	Clyde Drexler	.75	.45
5	Joe Dumars	.40	.25
6	Patrick Ewing	1.25	.70
7	Michael Jordan	5.00	3.00
8	Shawn Kemp	1.50	.90
9	Christian Laettner	.75	.45
10	Karl Malone	1.25	.70
11	Danny Manning	.50	.30
12	Reggie Miller	.60	.35
13	Alonzo Mourning	1.75	1.00
14	Chris Mullin	.75	.45
15	Hakeem Olajuwon	2.50	1.50
16	Shaquille O'Neal	5.00	3.00

1993-94 Fleer Rookie Sensations

The cards in this limited insert set were issued in Fleer Series I cello packs. The cards depict the top rookies from the previous season. The card fronts feature gold foil stamping and include an isolated full-color player photo over a purple and blue background with multi-colored spotlights rising from behind a large basketball that the player appears to be standing on. The player's name is printed in the lower corner of the card under a Rookie Sensations logo. All cards measure 2-1/2" by 3-1/2".

	MINT	NR/MT
Complete Set (24)	65.00	38.00
Commons	.75	.45

		MINT	NR/MT
1	Anthony Avent	.75	.45
2	Doug Christie	1.00	.60
3	Lloyd Daniels	.75	.45
4	Hubert Davis	1.25	.70
5	Todd Day	1.25	.70

58 • 1993-94 FLEER ROOKIE SENSATIONS

6	Richard Dumas	.75	.45
7	LaPhonso Ellis	2.50	1.50
8	Tom Gugliotta	2.00	1.25
9	Robert Hory	2.50	1.50
10	Byron Houston	.75	.45
11	Jim Jackson	4.50	2.75
12	Adam Keefe	.75	.45
13	Christian Laettner	2.00	1.25
14	Lee Mayberry	.75	.45
15	Oliver Miller	1.00	.60
16	Harold Miner	1.50	.90
17	Alonzo Mourning	10.00	6.00
18	Shaquille O'Neal	24.00	14.00
19	Anthony Peeler	1.25	.70
20	Sean Rooks	.75	.45
21	Latrell Sprewell	7.00	4.00
22	Bryant Stith	1.00	.60
23	Clarence Weatherspoon	2.00	1.25
24	Walt Williams	1.25	.70

1993-94 Fleer Sharpshooters

These limited insert cards feature two images on the card front including a close-up shot in the foreground and an action shot in the background. A circular Sharpshooters logo appears in the lower corner over an image of a basketball hoop. The cards were distributed randomly in Fleer Series II packs and measure 2-1/2" by 3-1/2".

	MINT	NR/MT
Complete Set (10)	20.00	12.50
Commons	.50	.30

1	Tom Gugliotta	1.50	.90
2	Jim Jackson	3.00	1.75
3	Michael Jordan	12.00	7.00
4	Dan Majerle	.60	.35
5	Mark Price	.75	.45
6	Glen Rice	.50	.30
7	Mitch Richmond	.60	.35
8	Latrell Sprewell	5.00	3.00
9	John Starks	.75	.45
10	Dominique Wilkins	2.00	1.25

1993-94 Fleer Tower of Power

These random insert cards were distributed in Fleer Series II cello packs and consist of a full-color isolated player photo on the card front superimposed in front of tall buildings. A Tower of Power headline is printed in the top corner while the player's name is centered at the bottom. All cards measure 2-1/2" by 3-1/2".

	MINT	NR/MT
Complete Set (30)	38.00	24.00
Commons	.40	.25

1	Charles Barkley	3.00	1.75
2	Shawn Bradley	1.00	.60
3	Derrick Coleman	1.25	.70
4	Brad Daugherty	.60	.35
5	Dale Davis	.50	.30
6	Vlade Divac	.40	.25
7	Patrick Ewing	2.00	1.25
8	Horace Grant	.50	.30
9	Tom Gugliotta	1.00	.60
10	Larry Johnson	2.50	1.50
11	Shawn Kemp	2.00	1.25
12	Christian Laettner	1.00	.60
13	Karl Malone	1.50	.90
14	Danny Manning	.75	.45
15	Jamal Mashburn	2.50	1.50
16	Oliver Miller	.75	.45
17	Alonzo Mourning	4.00	2.50
18	Dikembe Mutombo	1.50	.90
19	Ken Norman	.40	.25
20	Hakeem Olajuwon	5.00	3.00
21	Shaquille O'Neal	8.00	5.00
22	Robert Parish	.50	.30
23	Olden Polynice	.40	.25
24	Cliff Robinson	.60	.35
25	David Robinson	3.00	1.75
26	Dennis Rodman	.60	.35
27	Rony Seikaly	.40	.25
28	Wayman Tisdale	.40	.25
29	Chris Webber	7.00	4.00
30	Dominique Wilkins	1.50	.90

1993-94 Fleer Jam Session

JOHN STOCKTON

The cards in this set measure 2-1/2" by 4-11/16" and feature full-bleed, full-color action hotos on the card fronts. The player's name, team and position appear in a pair of horizontal stripes in the bottom corner of the card opposite an NBA Jam Session logo. Card backs contain another full-color action photo, personal data, a brief highlight and stats.

		MINT	NR/MT
Complete Set (240)		28.00	18.00
Commons		.08	.05
1	Stacey Augmon	.15	.10
2	Mookie Blaylock	.12	.07
3	Doug Edwards (R)	.15	.10
4	Duane Ferrell	.08	.05
5	Paul Graham	.08	.05
6	Adam Keefe	.10	.06
7	Jon Koncak	.08	.05
8	Dominique Wilkins	.35	.20
9	Kevin Willis	.08	.05
10	Alaa Abdelnaby	.08	.05
11	Dee Brown	.15	.10
12	Sherman Douglas	.08	.05

60 • 1993-94 FLEER JAM SESSION

#	Player		
13	Rick Fox	.12	.07
14	Kevin Gamble	.08	.05
15	Xavier McDaniel	.10	.06
16	Robert Parish	.20	.12
17	Muggsy Bogues	.08	.05
18	Scott Burrell (R)	.20	.12
19	Dell Curry	.08	.05
20	Kenny Gattison	.08	.05
21	Hersey Hawkins	.12	.07
22	Eddie Johnson	.10	.06
23	Larry Johnson	.75	.45
24	Alonzo Mourning	1.50	.90
25	Johnny Newman	.08	.05
26	David Wingate	.08	.05
27	B.J. Armstrong	.15	.10
28	Corie Blount (R)	.12	.07
29	Bill Cartwright	.08	.05
30	Horace Grant	.15	.10
31	Stacey King	.08	.05
32	John Paxson	.10	.06
33	Michael Jordan	3.00	1.75
34	Scottie Pippen	.60	.35
35	Scott Williams	.08	.05
36	Terrell Brandon	.08	.05
37	Brad Daugherty	.15	.10
38	Danny Ferry	.08	.05
39	Tyrone Hill	.08	.05
40	Chris Mills (R)	.30	.18
41	Larry Nance	.08	.05
42	Mark Price	.15	.10
43	Gerald Wilkins	.08	.05
44	John Williams (Cle)	.12	.07
45	Terry Davis	.08	.05
46	Derrick Harper	.10	.06
47	Donald Hodge	.08	.05
48	Jim Jackson	.50	.30
49	Jamal Mashburn (R)	1.50	.90
50	Sean Rooks	.15	.10
51	Doug Smith	.08	.05
52	Mahmoud Abdul-Rauf	.15	.10
53	Kevin Brooks	.08	.05
54	LaPhonso Ellis	.25	.15
55	Mark Macon	.12	.07
56	Dikembe Mutombo	.50	.30
57	Rodney Rogers (R)	.35	.20
58	Bryant Stith	.20	.12
59	Reggie Williams	.08	.05
60	Joe Dumars	.20	.12
61	Sean Elliott	.15	.10
62	Bill Laimbeer	.08	.05
63	Terry Mills	.08	.05
64	Olden Polynice	.08	.05
65	Alvin Robertson	.08	.05
66	Isiah Thomas	.25	.15
67	Victor Alexander	.08	.05
68	Chris Gatling	.08	.05
69	Tim Hardaway	.20	.12
70	Byron Houston	.12	.07
71	Sarunas Marciulionis	.10	.06
72	Chris Mullin	.25	.15
73	Billy Owens	.25	.15
74	Latrell Sprewell	.80	.50
75	Chris Webber (R)	3.50	2.00
76	Scott Brooks	.08	.05
77	Matt Bullard	.08	.05
78	Sam Cassell (R)	.60	.35
79	Mario Elie	.08	.05
80	Carl Herrera	.15	.10
81	Robert Hory	.35	.20
82	Vernon Maxwell	.15	.10
83	Hakeem Olajuwon	1.25	.70
84	Kenny Smith	.10	.06
85	Otis Thorpe	.10	.06
86	Dale Davis	.20	.12
87	Vern Fleming	.08	.05
88	Scott Haskin (R)	.15	.10
89	Reggie Miller	.30	.18
90	Sam Mitchell	.08	.05
91	Pooh Richardson	.08	.05
92	Detlef Schrempf	.20	.12
93	Malik Sealy	.12	.07
94	Rik Smits	.08	.05
95	Terry Dehere (R)	.20	.12
96	Ron Harper	.10	.06
97	Mark Jackson	.12	.07
98	Danny Manning	.20	.12
99	Stanley Roberts	.08	.05
100	Loy Vaught	.08	.05
101	John Williams	.08	.05
102	Sam Bowie	.08	.05
103	Elden Campbell	.15	.10
104	Doug Christie	.25	.15
105	Vlade Divac	.12	.07
106	James Edwards	.08	.05
107	George Lynch (R)	.35	.20
108	Anthony Peeler	.25	.15
109	Sedale Threatt	.08	.05
110	James Worthy	.20	.12
111	Bimbo Coles	.08	.05
112	Grant Long	.08	.05
113	Harold Miner	.25	.15
114	Glen Rice	.12	.07
115	John Salley	.08	.05
116	Rony Seikaly	.12	.07
117	Brian Shaw	.08	.05
118	Steve Smith	.25	.15
119	Anthony Avent	.10	.06
120	Vin Baker	.80	.50
121	Jon Barry	.10	.06
122	Frank Brickowski	.08	.05
123	Todd Day	.20	.12
124	Blue Edwards	.08	.05
125	Brad Lohaus	.08	.05
126	Lee Mayberry	.12	.07

1993-94 FLEER JAM SESSION • 61

#	Player		
127	Eric Murdock	.10	.06
128	Ken Norman	.10	.06
129	Thurl Bailey	.08	.05
130	Mike Brown	.08	.05
131	Christian Laettner	.30	.18
132	Luc Longley	.08	.05
133	Chuck Person	.12	.07
134	Chris Smith	.10	.06
135	Doug West	.10	.06
136	Michael Williams	.08	.05
137	Kenny Anderson	.25	.15
138	Benoit Benjamin	.08	.05
139	Derrick Coleman	.25	.15
140	Armon Gilliam	.10	.06
141	Rick Mahorn	.08	.05
142	Chris Morris	.08	.05
143	Rumeal Robinson	.08	.05
144	Rex Walters (R)	.15	.10
145	Greg Anthony	.12	.07
146	Rolando Blackman	.10	.06
147	Tony Campbell	.08	.05
148	Hubert Davis	.15	.10
149	Patrick Ewing	.50	.30
150	Anthony Mason	.08	.05
151	Charles Oakley	.12	.07
152	Doc Rivers	.10	.06
153	Charles Smith	.12	.07
154	John Starks	.20	.12
155	Herb Williams	.08	.05
156	Nick Anderson	.20	.12
157	Anthony Bowie	.08	.05
158	Litterial Green	.08	.05
159	Anfernee Hardaway (R)	3.00	1.75
160	Shaquille O'Neal	3.00	1.75
161	Donald Royal	.08	.05
162	Dennis Scott	.10	.06
163	Scott Skiles	.08	.05
164	Jeff Turner	.08	.05
165	Dana Barros	.10	.06
166	Shawn Bradley (R)	.70	.40
167	Johnny Dawkins	.08	.05
168	Greg Graham (R)	.15	.10
169	Jeff Hornacek	.12	.07
170	Moses Malone	.20	.12
171	Tim Perry	.08	.05
172	Clarence Weatherspoon	.20	.12
173	Danny Ainge	.12	.07
174	Charles Barkley	1.00	.60
175	Cedric Ceballos	.12	.07
176	A.C. Green	.12	.07
177	Frank Johnson	.08	.05
178	Kevin Johnson	.15	.10
179	Negele Knight	.08	.05
180	Malcolm Mackey (R)	.15	.10
181	Dan Majerle	.15	.10
182	Oliver Miller	.15	.10
183	Mark West	.08	.05
184	Clyde Drexler	.35	.20
185	Chris Dudley	.08	.05
186	Harvey Grant	.08	.05
187	Jerome Kersey	.08	.05
188	Terry Porter	.12	.07
189	Cliff Robinson	.15	.10
190	James Robinson (R)	.20	.12
191	Rod Strickland	.08	.05
192	Buck Williams	.10	.06
193	Randy Brown	.08	.05
194	Duane Causwell	.08	.05
195	Bobby Hurley (R)	.70	.40
196	Mitch Richmond	.15	.10
197	Lionel Simmons	.15	.10
198	Wayman Tisdale	.10	.06
199	Spud Webb	.08	.05
200	Walt Williams	.20	.12
201	Willie Anderson	.08	.05
202	Antoine Carr	.08	.05
203	Terry Cummings	.10	.06
204	Lloyd Daniels	.12	.07
205	Vinny Del Negro	.08	.05
206	Sleepy Floyd	.08	.05
207	Avery Johnson	.08	.05
208	J.R. Reid	.08	.05
209	David Robinson	1.00	.60
210	Dennis Rodman	.15	.10
211	Michael Cage	.08	.05
212	Kendall Gill	.15	.10
213	Ervin Johnson (R)	.15	.10
214	Shawn Kemp	.75	.45
215	Derrick McKey	.12	.07
216	Nate McMillan	.08	.05
217	Gary Payton	.15	.10
218	Sam Perkins	.12	.07
219	Ricky Pierce	.08	.05
220	Isaac Austin	.08	.05
221	David Benoit	.08	.05
222	Tom Chambers	.12	.07
223	Tyrone Corbin	.08	.05
224	Mark Eaton	.08	.05
225	Jay Humphries	.08	.05
226	Jeff Malone	.10	.06
227	Karl Malone	.50	.30
228	John Stockton	.50	.30
229	Luther Wright (R)	.20	.12
230	Michael Adams	.12	.07
231	Calbert Cheaney (R)	.75	.45
232	Kevin Duckworth	.08	.05
233	Pervis Ellison	.10	.06
234	Tom Gugliotta	.25	.15
235	Buck Johnson	.08	.05
236	Doug Overton	.08	.05
237	LaBradford Smith	.08	.05
238	Larry Stewart	.08	.05
239	Checklist	.08	.05
240	Checklist	.08	.05

1993-94 Fleer Jam Session Second Year Stars

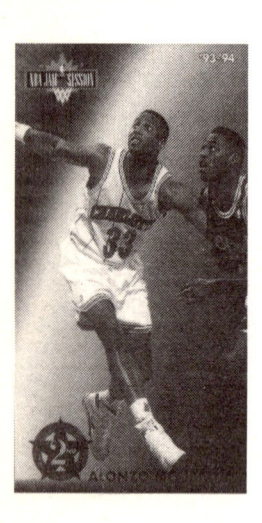

The cards in this set were issued as random inserts in Jam Session foil packs. The cards feauture an isolated full-color action shot on the front with gold foil stamping including a 2nd Year Stars logo in the lower corner. The player's name appears along the bottom of the card opposite the logo. All cards measure 2-1/2" by 4-11/16".

		MINT	NR/MT
Complete Set (8)		8.00	5.00
Commons		.25	.15
1	Tom Gugliotta	.40	.25
2	Jim Jackson	1.00	.60
3	Christian Laettner	.50	.30
4	Oliver Miller	.25	.15
5	Harold Miner	.40	.25
6	Alonzo Mourning	2.00	1.25
7	Shaquille O'Neal	5.00	3.00
8	Walt Williams	.75	.45

1993-94 Fleer Jam Session Slam Dunk Heroes

The cards in this limited edition set were randomly distributed in Fleer Jam Session foil packs. The card fronts consist of a full-bleed, full-color player action shot superimposed over a faded image of the crowd sitting in the stands. A Slam Dunk Heroes logo in stamped in the lower corner while the player's name is printed vertically along the lower quarter of the side of the card. All cards measure 2-1/2" by 4-11/16".

		MINT	NR/MT
Complete Set (8)		10.00	6.50
Commons		.50	.30
1	Patrick Ewing	.75	.45
2	Larry Johnson	1.00	.60
3	Shawn Kemp	.75	.45
4	Karl Malone	.50	.30
5	Alonzo Mourning	2.50	1.50
6	Hakeem Olajuwon	1.50	.90
7	Shaquille O'Neal	4.00	2.50
8	David Robinson	1.50	.90

1993-94 Fleer Jam Session Rookie Standouts

The cards in this set feature full-bleed, full-color action shots superimposed over a multi-colored background with gold foil stamping including a Rookie Standouts logo in the lower corner of the card front. The player's name is printed vertically opposite the logo in the lower third of the card. A Jam Session logo appears in the upper corner. The cards were random inserts in Jam Session foil packs and measure 2-1/2" by 4-11/16".

		MINT	NR/MT
Complete Set (8)		18.00	12.00
Commons		.75	.45
1	Vin Baker	.75	.45
2	Shawn Bradley	1.00	.60
3	Calbert Cheaney	1.25	.70
4	Anfernee Hardaway	6.00	3.75
5	Bobby Hurley	1.25	.70
6	Jamal Mashburn	2.50	1.50
7	Rodney Rogers	.75	.45
8	Chris Webber	7.00	4.00

1993-94 Fleer Jam Session Gamebreakers

These cards feature full-bleed, full-color action shots on the card fronts superimposed over a colorful grid pattern. A Gamebreakers logo is stamped across the bottom of the card just above the player's name. The cards were inserted randomly in Fleer Jam Session foil packs and measure 2-1/2" by 4-11/16".

		MINT	NR/MT
Complete Set (8)		4.00	2.50
Commons		.25	.15
1	Charles Barkley	1.25	.70
2	Tim Hardaway	.40	.25
3	Kevin Johnson	.40	.25
4	Dan Majerle	.25	.15
5	Scottie Pippen	.75	.45
6	Mark Price	.25	.15
7	John Starks	.35	.20
8	Dominique Wilkins	.75	.45

64 • 1993-94 FLEER ULTRA

1993-94 Fleer Ultra

The cards in this set were issued in two series, 200-cards in Series I and175-cards in Series II. The card fronts feature full-bleed, full-color action shots with foil stamping. The player's name, team and position appear in two horizontal color bars under his photo. Cards 361-372 include members of Team USA. A special 10-card insert series featuring Utah Jazz star Karl Malone were randomly distributed in Ultra Series I packs. Two additional Malone cards were available through a special mail-in offer. Those cards are listed at the end of this checklist but are not included in the complete set price below. All cards measure 2-1/2" by 3-1/2".

		MINT	NR/MT
Complete Set (375)		38.00	24.00
Commons		.08	.05
1	Stacey Augman	.12	.07
2	Mookie Blaylock	.12	.07
3	Doug Edwards (R)	.15	.10
4	Duane Ferrell	.08	.05
5	Paul Graham	.08	.05
6	Adam Keefe	.10	.06
7	Dominique Wilkins	.35	.20
8	Kevin Willis	.08	.05
9	Alaa Abdelnaby	.08	.05
10	Dee Brown	.12	.07
11	Sherman Douglas	.08	.05
12	Rick Fox	.12	.07
13	Kevin Gamble	.08	.05
14	Xavier McDaniel	.08	.05
15	Robert Parish	.15	.10
16	Muggsy Bogues	.08	.05
17	Scott Burrell (R)	.20	.12
18	Dell Curry	.08	.05
19	Kenny Gattison	.08	.05
20	Hersey Hawkins	.10	.06
21	Eddie Johnson	.10	.06
22	Larry Johnson	.50	.30
23	Alonzo Mourning	1.00	.60
24	Johnny Newman	.08	.05
25	David Wingate	.08	.05
26	B.J. Armstrong	.15	.10
27	Corie Blount (R)	.12	.07
28	Bill Cartwright	.08	.05
29	Horace Grant	.15	.10
30	Michael Jordan	3.00	1.75
31	Stacey King	.08	.05
32	John Paxson	.10	.06
33	Will Perdue	.08	.05
34	Scottie Pippen	.60	.35
35	Terrell Brandon	.10	.06
36	Brad Daugherty	.15	.10
37	Danny Ferry	.08	.05
38	Chris Mills (R)	.35	.20
39	Larry Nance	.08	.05
40	Mark Price	.15	.10
41	Gerald Wilkins	.08	.05
42	John Williams (Cle)	.12	.07
43	Terry Davis	.08	.05
44	Derek Harper	.10	.06
45	Donald Hodge	.08	.05
46	Jim Jackson	.40	.25
47	Sean Rooks	.12	.07
48	Doug Smith	.08	.05
49	Mahmoud Abdul-Rauf	.15	.10
50	LaPhonso Ellis	.25	.15
51	Mark Macon	.12	.07
52	Dikembe Mutombo	.60	.35
53	Bryant Stith	.20	.12
54	Reggie Williams	.08	.05
55	Mark Aquirre	.10	.06
56	Joe Dumars	.20	.12
57	Bill Laimbeer	.08	.05
58	Terry Mills	.08	.05
59	Olden Polynice	.08	.05
60	Alvin Robertson	.08	.05
61	Dennis Rodman	.15	.10
62	Isiah Thomas	.25	.15
63	Victor Alexander	.08	.05
64	Chris Gatling	.08	.05
65	Tim Hardaway	.20	.12
66	Byron Houston	.12	.07
67	Sarunas Marciulionis	.10	.06
68	Chris Mullin	.25	.15

1993-94 FLEER ULTRA • 65

#	Player	Value 1	Value 2
69	Billy Owens	.20	.12
70	Latrell Sprewell	.75	.45
71	Matt Bullard	.08	.05
72	Sam Cassell (R)	.60	.35
73	Carl Herrera	.15	.10
74	Robert Hory	.30	.18
75	Vernon Maxwell	.15	.10
76	Hakeem Olajuwon	1.25	.70
77	Kenny Smith	.10	.06
78	Otis Thorpe	.10	.06
79	Dale Davis	.15	.10
80	Vern Fleming	.08	.05
81	Reggie Miller	.25	.15
82	Sam Mitchell	.08	.05
83	Pooh Richardson	.08	.05
84	Detlef Schrempf	.15	.10
85	Rik Smits	.08	.05
86	Ron Harper	.10	.06
87	Mark Jackson	.12	.07
88	Danny Manning	.20	.12
89	Stanley Roberts	.08	.05
90	Loy Vaught	.08	.05
91	John Williams	.08	.05
92	Sam Bowie	.08	.05
93	Doug Christie	.20	.12
94	Vlade Divac	.10	.06
95	George Lynch (R)	.30	.18
96	Anthony Peeler	.20	.12
97	James Worthy	.15	.10
98	Bimbo Coles	.08	.05
99	Grant Long	.08	.05
100	Harold Miner	.20	.12
101	Glen Rice	.12	.07
102	Rony Seikaly	.12	.07
103	Brian Shaw	.08	.05
104	Steve Smith	.25	.15
105	Anthony Avent	.12	.07
106	Vin Baker (R)	.80	.50
107	Frank Brickowski	.08	.05
108	Todd Day	.20	.12
109	Blue Edwards	.08	.05
110	Lee Mayberry	.12	.07
111	Eric Murdock	.10	.06
112	Orlando Woolridge	.08	.05
113	Thurl Bailey	.08	.05
114	Christian Laettner	.30	.18
115	Chuck Person	.12	.07
116	Doug West	.12	.07
117	Michael Williams	.08	.05
118	Kenny Anderson	.20	.12
119	Derrick Coleman	.20	.12
120	Rick Mahorn	.08	.05
121	Chris Morris	.08	.05
122	Rumeal Robinson	.08	.05
123	Rex Walters (R)	.15	.10
124	Greg Anthony	.12	.07
125	Rolando Blackman	.10	.06
126	Hubert Davis	.15	.10
127	Patrick Ewing	.50	.30
128	Anthony Mason	.08	.05
129	Charles Oakley	.12	.07
130	Doc Rivers	.10	.06
131	Charles Smith	.12	.07
132	John Starks	.25	.15
133	Nick Anderson	.15	.10
134	Anthony Bowie	.08	.05
135	Shaquille O'Neal	3.00	1.75
136	Dennis Scott	.10	.06
137	Scott Skiles	.08	.05
138	Jeff Turner	.08	.05
139	Shawn Bradley (R)	.60	.35
140	Johnny Dawkins	.08	.05
141	Jeff Hornacek	.12	.07
142	Tim Perry	.08	.05
143	Clarence Weatherspoon	.20	.12
144	Danny Ainge	.12	.07
145	Charles Barkley	1.00	.60
146	Cedric Ceballos	.12	.07
147	Kevin Johnson	.15	.10
148	Negele Knight	.08	.05
149	Malcolm Mackey (R)	.12	.07
150	Dan Majerle	.12	.07
151	Oliver Miller	.15	.10
152	Mark West	.08	.05
153	Mark Bryant	.08	.05
154	Clyde Drexler	.35	.20
155	Jerome Kersey	.08	.05
156	Terry Porter	.12	.07
157	Cliff Robinson	.15	.10
158	Rod Strickland	.08	.05
159	Buck Williams	.10	.06
160	Duane Causwell	.08	.05
161	Bobby Hurley (R)	.60	.35
162	Mitch Richmond	.15	.10
163	Lionel Simmons	.15	.10
164	Wayman Tisdale	.10	.06
165	Spud Webb	.08	.05
166	Walt Williams	.25	.15
167	Willie Anderson	.08	.05
168	Antoine Carr	.08	.05
169	Lloyd Daniels	.12	.07
170	Sean Elliott	.15	.10
171	Dale Ellis	.08	.05
172	Avery Johnson	.08	.05
173	J.R. Reid	.08	.05
174	David Robinson	1.00	.60
175	Michael Cage	.08	.05
176	Kendall Gill	.15	.10
177	Ervin Johnson (R)	.15	.10
178	Shawn Kemp	.75	.45
179	Derrick McKey	.10	.06
180	Nate McMillan	.08	.05
181	Gary Payton	.15	.10
182	Sam Perkins	.10	.06

1993-94 FLEER ULTRA

#	Player		
183	Ricky Pierce	.08	.05
184	David Benoit	.08	.05
185	Tyrone Corbin	.08	.05
186	Mark Eaton	.08	.05
187	Jay Humphries	.08	.05
188	Jeff Malone	.10	.06
189	Karl Malone	.50	.30
190	John Stockton	.50	.30
191	Luther Wright (R)	.15	.10
192	Michael Adams	.10	.06
193	Clabert Cheaney (R)	.60	.35
194	Pervis Ellison	.12	.07
195	Tom Gugliotta	.30	.18
196	Buck Johnson	.08	.05
197	LaBradford Smith	.08	.05
198	Larry Stewart	.08	.05
199	Checklist	.08	.05
200	Checklist	.08	.05
201	Doug Edwards	.10	.06
202	Craig Ehlo	.08	.05
203	Jon Koncak	.08	.05
204	Andrew Lang	.08	.05
205	Ennis Whatley	.08	.05
206	Chris Corchiani	.08	.05
207	Acie Earl (R)	.15	.10
208	Jimmy Oliver	.08	.05
209	Ed Pinckney	.08	.05
210	Dino Radja (R)	.50	.30
211	Matt Wenstrom (R)	.12	.07
212	Tony Bennett	.08	.05
213	Scott Burrell	.12	.07
214	LeRon Ellis	.10	.06
215	Hersey Hawkins	.10	.06
216	Eddie Johnson	.08	.05
217	Rumeal Robinson	.08	.05
218	Corie Blount	.10	.06
219	Dave Johnson	.08	.05
220	Steve Kerr	.08	.05
221	Toni Kukoc (R)	.80	.50
222	Pete Myers	.08	.05
223	Bill Wennington	.08	.05
224	Scott Williams	.08	.05
225	John Battle	.08	.05
226	Tyrone Hill	.08	.05
227	Gerald Madkins (R)	.12	.07
228	Chris Mills	.20	.12
229	Bobby Phills	.12	.07
230	Greg Dreiling	.08	.05
231	Lucious Harris (R)	.12	.07
232	Popeye Jones (R)	.20	.12
233	Tim Legler (R)	.12	.07
234	Fat Lever	.08	.05
235	Jamal Mashburn (R)	1.50	.90
236	Tom Hammonds	.08	.05
237	Darnell Mee (R)	.15	.10
238	Robert Pack	.08	.05
239	Rodney Rogers (R)	.35	.20
240	Brian Williams	.12	.07
241	Greg Anderson	.08	.05
242	Sean Elliott	.10	.06
243	Allan Houston (R)	.20	.12
244	Lindsey Hunter (R)	.30	.18
245	Mark Macon	.12	.07
246	David Wood	.08	.05
247	Jud Buechler	.08	.05
248	Josh Grant (R)	.15	.10
249	Jeff Grayer	.08	.05
250	Keith Jennings	.08	.05
251	Avery Johnson	.08	.05
252	Chris Webber (R)	3.50	2.00
253	Scott Brooks	.08	.05
254	Sam Cassell	.35	.20
255	Mario Elie	.08	.05
256	Richard Petruska (R)	.15	.10
257	Eric Riley (R)	.15	.10
258	Antonio Davis (R)	.25	.15
259	Scott Haskin (R)	.15	.10
260	Derrick McKey	.10	.06
261	Byron Scott	.08	.05
262	Malik Sealy	.10	.06
263	Kenny Williams	.08	.05
264	Haywoode Workman	.10	.06
265	Mark Aquirre	.10	.06
266	Terry Dehere (R)	.20	.12
267	Harold Ellis	.08	.05
268	Gary Grant	.08	.05
269	Bob Martin (R)	.12	.07
270	Elmore Spencer	.15	.10
271	Tom Tolbert	.08	.05
272	Sam Bowie	.08	.05
273	Elden Campbell	.15	.10
274	Antonio Harvey (R)	.15	.10
275	George Lynch	.20	.12
276	Tony Smith	.08	.05
277	Sedale Threatt	.08	.05
278	Nick Van Exel (R)	.80	.50
279	Willie Burton	.10	.06
280	Matt Geiger	.08	.05
281	John Salley	.08	.05
282	Vin Baker	.40	.25
283	Jon Barry	.10	.06
284	Brad Lohaus	.08	.05
285	Ken Norman	.10	.06
286	Derek Strong (R)	.15	.10
287	Mike Brown	.08	.05
288	Brian Davis (R)	.15	.10
289	Tellis Frank	.08	.05
290	Luc Longley	.08	.05
291	Marlon Maxey	.08	.05
292	Isaiah Rider (R)	1.50	.90
293	Chris Smith	.10	.06
294	P.J. Brown (R)	.20	.12
295	Kevin Edwards	.08	.05
296	Armon Gilliam	.10	.06

1993-94 FLEER ULTRA • 67

#	Player		
297	Johnny Newman	.08	.05
298	Rex Walters	.10	.06
299	David Wesley (R)	.12	.07
300	Jayson Williams	.08	.05
301	Anthony Bonner	.08	.05
302	Derek Harper	.10	.06
303	Herb Williams	.08	.05
304	Litterial Green	.08	.05
305	Anfernee Hardaway (R)	3.00	1.75
306	Greg Kite	.08	.05
307	Larry Krystkowiak	.08	.05
308	Keith Tower (R)	.12	.07
309	Dana Barros	.08	.05
310	Shawn Bradley	.30	.18
311	Greg Graham (R)	.15	.10
312	Sean Green	.08	.05
313	Warren Kidd (R)	.12	.07
314	Eric Leckner	.08	.05
315	Moses Malone	.15	.10
316	Orlando Woolridge	.08	.05
317	Duane Cooper	.08	.05
318	Joe Courtney (R)	.12	.07
319	A.C. Green	.12	.07
320	Frank Johnson	.08	.05
321	Joe Kleine	.08	.05
322	Chris Dudley	.08	.05
323	Harvey Grant	.08	.05
324	Jaren Jackson	.08	.05
325	Tracy Murray	.20	.12
326	James Robinson (R)	.20	.12
327	Reggie Smith	.08	.05
328	Kevin Thompson (R)	.12	.07
329	Randy Brown	.08	.05
330	Evers Burns (R)	.15	.10
331	Pete Chilcutt	.08	.05
332	Bobby Hurley	.30	.18
333	Mike Peplowski (R)	.15	.10
334	LaBradford Smith	.08	.05
335	Trevor Wilson	.10	.06
336	Terry Cummings	.10	.06
337	Vinny Del Negro	.08	.05
338	Sleepy Floyd	.08	.05
339	Negele Knight	.08	.05
340	Dennis Rodman	.15	.10
341	Chris Whitney (R)	.15	.10
342	Vincent Askew	.08	.05
343	Kendall Gill	.15	.10
344	Ervin Johnson	.10	.06
345	Chris King (R)	.12	.07
346	Detlef Schrempf	.15	.10
347	Walter Bond	.08	.05
348	Tom Chambers	.12	.07
349	John Crotty	.08	.05
350	Byron Russell (R)	.15	.10
351	Felton Spencer	.12	.07
352	Mitchell Butler (R)	.12	.07
353	Rex Chapman	.12	.07
354	Calbert Cheaney	.30	.18
355	Kevin Duckworth	.08	.05
356	Don MacLean	.15	.10
357	Gheorghe Muresan (R)	.15	.10
358	Doug Overton	.08	.05
359	Brent Price	.10	.06
360	Kenny Walker	.08	.05
361	Derrick Coleman (USA)	.25	.15
362	Joe Dumars (USA)	.20	.12
363	Tim Hardaway (USA)	.20	.12
364	Larry Johnson (USA)	.50	.30
365	Shawn Kemp (USA)	.50	.30
366	Dan Majerle (USA)	.15	.10
367	Alonzo Mourning (USA)	1.00	.60
368	Mark Price (USA)	.15	.10
369	Steve Smith (USA)	.20	.12
370	Isiah Thomas (USA)	.20	.12
371	Dominique Wilkins (USA)	.30	.18
372	D. Nelson/D. Chaney (USA)	.10	.06
373	Checklist	.08	.05
374	Checklist	.08	.05
375	Checklist	.08	.05
___	Karl Malone (ea)	1.00	.60
___	Karl Malone (Auto)	125.00	70.00

1993-94 Fleer Ultra All-NBA Team

The cards in this limited insert set feature a borderless design with foil stamping and four photos on the card front including a large game action shot on one side and three smaller close-up photos stacked along the side of the card. The player's name appears in the lower right corner of the card and an All-NBA Team logo is printed in the top corner. The cards were randomly distributed in Ultra Series I packs and measure 2-1/2" by 3-1/2".

		MINT	NR/MT
	Complete Set (14)	38.00	24.00
	Commons	.75	.45
1	Charles Barkley	4.00	2.50
2	Michael Jordan	12.00	7.00
3	Karl Malone	2.50	1.50
4	Hakeem Olajuwon	5.00	3.00
5	Mark Price	.75	.45
6	Joe Dumars	.75	.45
7	Patrick Ewing	3.50	2.00
8	Larry Johnson	3.50	2.00
9	John Stockton	2.50	1.50
10	Dominique Wilkins	3.00	1.75
11	Derrick Coleman	1.25	.70
12	Tim Hardaway	1.00	.60
13	Scottie Pippen	3.00	1.75
14	David Robinson	4.00	2.50

1993-94 Fleer Ultra All-Rookie Team

These limited insert cards were issued randomly in Ultra Series I foil packs. The card fronts feature an isolated, full-color action shot of the player in the foreground. The player appears to have broken through a wall in the background. The player's name is printed in the lower portion of the card front opposite a V-shaped color bar containing an All-Rookie Team logo. All cards measure 2-1/2" by 3-1/2".

		MINT	NR/MT
	Complete Set (5)	18.00	12.50
	Commons	1.25	.70
1	LaPhonso Ellis	1.50	.90
2	Tom Gugliotta	2.00	1.25
3	Christian Laettner	1.25	.70
4	Alonzo Mourning	5.00	3.00
5	Shaquille O'Neal	10.00	6.50

1993-94 FLEER ULTRA AWARD WINNERS • 69

1993-94 Fleer Ultra All-Defensive Team

The cards in this limited insert set consist of a borderless design with foil stamping and two player images on the card front include a full-color shot along side a ghosted image of the player. A small circular logo with the words All-Defensive Team is stamped in the lower right corner. The player's name is printed across the bottom of the card. The cards were random inserts in Ultra Series I jumbo packs and measure 2-1/2" by 3-1/2".

		MINT	NR/MT
	Complete Set (10)	185.00	100.00
	Commons	7.00	4.00
1	Joe Dumars	8.00	5.00
2	Michael Jordan	100.00	65.00
3	Hakeem Olajuwon	40.00	28.00
4	Scottie Pippen	15.00	10.00
5	Dennis Rodman	8.00	5.00
6	Horace Grant	7.00	4.00
7	Dan Majerle	8.00	5.00
8	Larry Nance	7.00	4.00
9	David Robinson	25.00	15.00
10	John Starks	8.00	5.00

1993-94 Fleer Ultra Award Winners

The cards in this set were randomly distributed in Ultra Series I jumbo packs. The full-bleed, full-color card fronts feature gold foil stamping and an isolated player photo. The words Award Winner are printed vertically along the side of the card. The player's name is centered at the bottom of the card. All cards measure 2-1/2" by 3-1/2".

		MINT	NR/MT
	Complete Set (5)	90.00	55.00
	Commons	7.00	4.00
1	Mahmoud Abdul-Rauf	7.00	4.00
2	Charles Barkley	25.00	15.00
3	Hakeem Olajuwon	30.00	18.00
4	Shaquille O'Neal	50.00	35.00
5	Cliff Robinson	7.00	4.00

1993-94 Fleer Ultra Scoring Kings

The cards in this set consist of full-bleed, full color action shots on the fronts with foil stamping. The player's photo is superimposed over a background of lighning streaks. A Scoring Kings logo is printed in the upper right corner and the player's name is centered under his photograph. The cards were limited inserts packaged randomly in Ultra Series I hobby packs. All cards measure 2-1/2" by 3-1/2".

		MINT	NR/MT
	Complete Set (10)	185.00	110.00
	Commons	4.00	2.50
1	Charles Barkley	12.00	7.00
2	Joe Dumars	4.00	2.50
3	Patrick Ewing	10.00	6.00
4	Larry Johnson	10.00	6.00
5	Michael Jordan	60.00	35.00
6	Karl Malone	10.00	6.00
7	Alonzo Mourning	20.00	12.50
8	Shaquille O'Neal	50.00	35.00
9	David Robinson	15.00	10.00
10	Dominique Wilkins	8.00	5.00

1993-94 Fleer Ultra All-Rookie Series

This limited insert set features the top rookies from the 1993-94 season. The cards were randomly distributed in Ultra Series II foil packs. The full-bleed, full-color card fronts include foil stamping and an action shot of the player with an All-Rookie Series logo in the upper corner. The player's name is printed in the lower corner. All cards measure 2-1/2" by 3-1/2".

		MINT	NR/MT
	Complete Set (15)	40.00	26.00
	Commons	.50	.30
1	Vin Baker	2.50	1.50
2	Shawn Bradley	1.50	.90
3	Calbert Cheaney	1.50	.90
4	Anfernee Hardaway	10.00	6.50
5	Lindsey Hunter	.50	.30
6	Bobby Hurley	1.25	.70
7	Popeye Jones	.50	.30
8	Toni Kukoc	2.00	1.25
9	Jamal Mashburn	5.00	3.00
10	Chris Mills	1.00	.60
11	Dino Radja	1.25	.70
12	Isaiah Rider	5.00	3.00
13	Rodney Rogers	1.00	.60
14	Nick Van Exel	1.50	.90
15	Chris Webber	12.00	7.50

1993-94 FLEER ULTRA INSIDE/OUTSIDE • 71

1993-94 Fleer Ultra Famous Nicknames

These limited insert cards were randomly distributed in Ultra Series II foil packs. The full-bleed, full-color card fronts feature an isolated player photo superimposed over a background that is in the pattern of a basketball net. The player's nickname is printed in bold vertically along the side of the card. A Famous Nicknames logo is located in the lower corner of the card front. All cards measure 2-1/2" by 3-1/2".

		MINT	NR/MT
	Complete Set (15)	20.00	12.50
	Commons	.30	.18
1	Charles Barkley	2.00	1.25
2	Tyrone Bogues	.30	.18
3	Derrick Coleman	.75	.45
4	Clyde Drexler	.75	.45
5	Anfernee Hardaway	5.00	3.00
6	Larry Johnson	1.50	.90
7	Michael Jordan	7.00	4.00
8	Toni Kukoc	1.00	.60
9	Karl Malone	1.25	.70
10	Harold Miner	.50	.30
11	Alonzo Mourning	3.00	1.75
12	Hakeem Olajuwon	5.00	3.00
13	Shaquille O'Neal	7.00	4.00
14	David Robinson	2.50	1.50
15	Dominique Wilkins	1.25	.70

1993-94 Fleer Ultra Inside/Outside

These limited insert cards feature full-bleed, full-color card fronts with foil stamping. A small player shot appears in the foreground set against a larger shot of a basketball hoop. An Inside/Outside logo is printed in the lower corner while the player's name is center across the bottom of the card. The cards were random inserts in Ultra Series II packs and measure 2-1/2" by 3-1/2".

		MINT	NR/MT
	Complete Set (10)	10.00	6.00
	Commons	.50	.30
1	Patrick Ewing	1.25	.70
2	Jim Jackson	1.00	.60
3	Larry Johnson	1.25	.80
4	Michael Jordan	4.00	2.50
5	Dan Majerle	.50	.30
6	Hakeem Olajuwon	2.50	1.50
7	Scottie Pippen	1.25	.70
8	Latrell Sprewell	1.50	.90
9	John Starks	.75	.45
10	Walt Williams	.75	.45

1993-94 Fleer Ultra Jam City

These limited insert cards feature a full-color player shot on the front superimposed over a pattern of tall buildings. The cards were distributed randomly in Fleer Ultra Series II jumbo packs. All cards measure 2-1/2" by 3-1/2".

		MINT	NR/MT
Complete Set (9)		80.00	55.00
Commons		3.00	1.75
1	Charles Barkley	10.00	6.00
2	Derrick Coleman	4.00	2.50
3	Clyde Drexler	4.00	2.50
4	Patrick Ewing	7.00	4.00
5	Shawn Kemp	8.00	5.00
6	Harold Miner	3.00	1.75
7	Shaquille O'Neal	32.00	20.00
8	David Robinson	10.00	6.00
9	Dominique Wilkins	7.00	4.00

1993-94 Fleer Ultra Rebound Kings

These random inserts were distributed in Ultra Series II packs. The full-bleed, full-color card fronts feature three player images, a large action shot, a small action shot and a close-up head shot. A Rebound Kings logo is stamped in the lower corner of the card while the player's name is printed vertically along the opposite side. All cards measure 2-1/2" by 3-1/2".

		MINT	NR/MT
Complete Set (10)		10.00	6.00
Commons		.40	.25
1	Charles Barkley	1.50	.90
2	Derrick Coleman	.75	.45
3	Shawn Kemp	1.50	.90
4	Karl Malone	1.25	.70
5	Alonzo Mourning	2.00	1.25
6	Dikembe Mutombo	1.00	.60
7	Charles Oakley	.40	.25
8	Hakeem Olajuwon	2.50	1.50
9	Shaquille O'Neal	4.00	2.50
10	Dennis Rodman	.50	.30

1993-94 Fleer Ultra Power In The Key

These cards consist of full-bleed, full-color card fronts with foil stamping. The action photograph shows an overhead view of the player superimposed above the crowd and the court. A Power In The Key logo is printed in the top right corner. The player's name is located in the lower corner. The cards were random inserts in Fleer Ultra Series II hobby packs and measure 2-1/2" by 3-1/2".

		MINT	NR/MT
Complete Set (9)		90.00	55.00
Commons		2.00	1.25
1	Larry Johnson	7.00	4.00
2	Michael Jordan	40.00	28.00
3	Karl Malone	4.00	2.50
4	Oliver Miller	2.00	1.25
5	Alonzo Mourning	10.00	6.00
6	Hakeem Olajuwon	12.00	7.00
7	Shaquille O'Neal	25.00	15.00
8	Otis Thorpe	2.00	1.25
9	Chris Webber	10.00	6.00

FRONT ROW

1991 Front Row

This 50-card set contains cards of players selected in the 1991 NBA draft. The card fronts feature full color action photos of player's in their college uniforms. Their names appear in a color bar under the photograph and a Draft Pick '91 logo is located in the lower left corner of the card front. The backs include another color photo and college highlights. The only subset of note is Highlight cards (HL). Limited gold and silver versions of this set were produced with the gold version valued at five times the regular set and the silver version at two times the regular set price. All cards measure 2-1/2" by 3-1/2".

		MINT	NR/MT
Complete Set (50)		6.00	3.50
Commons		.05	.02
1	Larry Johnson	2.00	1.25
2	Kenny Anderson	1.00	.60
3	Rick Fox	.25	.15
4	Pete Chilcutt	.08	.05
5	George Ackles	.05	.02
6	Mark Macon	.12	.07
7	Greg Anthony	.20	.12

74 • 1991 FRONT ROW

8	Mike Iuzzolino	.05	.02
9	Anthony Avent	.12	.07
10	Terrell Brandon	.20	.12
11	Kevin Brooks	.08	.05
12	Myron Brown	.05	.02
13	Chris Corchiani	.08	.05
14	Chris Gatling	.15	.10
15	Marcus Kennedy	.05	.02
16	Eric Murdock	.25	.15
17	Tony Farmer	.05	.02
18	Keith Hughes	.05	.02
19	Kevin Lynch	.05	.02
20	Chad Gallagher	.05	.02
21	Darrin Chancellor	.05	.02
22	Jimmy Oliver	.08	.05
23	Von McDade	.05	.02
24	Donald Hodge	.12	.07
25	Randy Brown	.10	.06
26	Doug Overton	.10	.06
27	LeRon Ellis	.15	.10
28	Sean Green	.05	.02
29	Elliot Perry	.05	.02
30	Richard Dumas	.15	.10
31	Dale Davis	.30	.18
32	Lamont Strothers	.05	.02
33	Steve Hood	.05	.02
34	Joey Wright	.05	.02
35	Patrick Eddie	.05	.02
36	Joe Wylie	.07	.04
37	Bobby Phills	.12	.07
38	Alvaro Teheran	.05	.02
39	Dale Davis (HL)	.12	.07
40	Rick Fox (HL)	.07	.04
41	Terrell Brandon (HL)	.08	.05
42	Greg Anthony (HL)	.10	.06
43	Mark Macon (HL)	.07	.04
44	Larry Johnson (HL)	.40	.25
45	Larry Johnson (HL)	.40	.25
46	Larry Johnson (HL)	.40	.25
47	Larry Johnson (HL)	.40	.25
48	Larry Johnson (HL)	.40	.25
49	Larry Johnson (HL)	.40	.25
50A	Bonus Card	.40	.25
50B	Marty Conlon	.10	.06

1991-92 Front Row Update

This set is an extension of the previous Front Row edition. The design is identical to the first series except the draft pick logo in the lower left corner now reads "Update '92." The card backs contain another small photo, personal data and stats. All cards measure 2-1/2" by 3-1/2".

	MINT	NR/MT
Complete Set (50)	4.50	2.50
Commons	.05	.02

51	Billy Owens	.40	.25
52	Dikembe Mutombo	.80	.50
53	Steve Smith	.75	.45
54	Luc Longley	.10	.06
55	Doug Smith	.12	.07
56	Stacey Augmon	.40	.25
57	Brian Williams	.20	.12
58	Stanley Roberts	.10	.06
59	Rodney Monroe	.07	.04
60	Isaac Austin	.07	.04
61	Rich King	.10	.06
62	Victor Alexander	.15	.10
63	LeBradford Smith	.10	.06
64	Greg Sutton	.05	.02
65	John Turner	.05	.02
66	Joao Viana	.05	.02
67	Charles Thomas	.05	.02
68	Carl Thomas	.05	.02
69	Tharon Mayes	.05	.02

1991-92 Front Row Premier

#	Player	MINT	NR/MT
70	David Benoit	.15	.10
71	Corey Crowder	.05	.02
72	Larry Stewart	.10	.06
73	Steve Bardo	.05	.02
74	Paris McCurdy	.05	.02
75	Robert Pack	.20	.12
76	Doug Lee	.05	.02
77	Tom Copa	.05	.02
78	Keith Owens	.05	.02
79	Mike Goodson	.05	.02
80	John Crotty	.10	.06
81	Sean Muto	.05	.02
82	Chancellor Nichols	.05	.02
83	Stevie Thompson	.05	.02
84	Demetrius Calip	.05	.02
85	Clifford Martin	.05	.02
86	Andy Kennedy	.05	.02
87	Oliver Taylor	.05	.02
88	Gary Waites	.05	.02
89	Matt Roe	.05	.02
90	Cedric Lewis	.05	.02
91	Emanuel Davis	.05	.02
92	Jackie Jones	.05	.02
93	Clifford Scales	.05	.02
94	Cameron Burns	.05	.02
95	Clinton Venable	.05	.02
96	Ken Redfield	.05	.02
97	Melvin Newbern	.05	.02
98	Chris Harris	.05	.02
99	Bonus Card	.40	.25
100	Checklist	.06	.03

This set is another version of Front Row's '91 draft picks set. This set sports a different design from the previous sets. The fronts feature full color action photos framed by a blue and white border. The player's name appears in a silver color bar directly under the picture. The card backs contain personal data, stats and highlights. The only subset is Highlights (HL). Gold and silver limited inserts were randomly distributed in the company's wax packs. The godl versions are valued at 4 X the prices listed below. The Silver versions are valued at 2 X the prices listed below. All cards measure 2-1/2" by 3-1/2"

		MINT	NR/MT
Complete Set (120)		9.00	5.00
Commons		.05	.02
1	Rich King	.10	.06
2	Kenny Anderson	.60	.35
3	Billy Owens	.25	.15
4	Ken Redfield	.05	.02
5	Robert Pack	.20	.12
6	Clinton Venable	.05	.02
7	Tom Copa	.05	.02
8	Rick Fox (HL)	.08	.05
9	Cameron Burns	.05	.02
10	Doug Lee	.05	.02
11	LaBradford Smith	.10	.06

76 • 1991-92 FRONT ROW PREMIER

#	Player		
12	Clifford Scales	.05	.02
13	Mark Peterson	.05	.02
14	Jackie Jones	.05	.02
15	Paris McCurdy	.05	.02
16	Dikembe Mutombo	.30	.18
17	Emanual Davis	.05	.02
18	Michael Cutright	.05	.02
19	Marc Brown	.05	.02
20	Steve Bardo	.05	.02
21	John Turner	.05	.02
22	Anthony Houston	.05	.02
23	Cedric Lewis	.05	.02
24	Matt Roe	.05	.02
25	Larry Stewart	.10	.06
26	Derek Strong	.07	.04
27	Sydney Grider	.05	.02
28	Corey Crowder	.05	.02
29	Gary Waites	.05	.02
30	David Benoit	.15	.10
31	Larry Johnson	.80	.50
32	Oliver Taylor	.05	.02
33	Andy Kennedy	.05	.02
34	Tharon Mayes	.05	.02
35	Carlos Funchess	.05	.02
36	Dale Turnquist	.05	.02
37	Luc Longley	.12	.07
38	Demetrius Calip	.05	.02
39	Anthony Blakley	.05	.02
40	Carl Thomas	.05	.02
41	Charles Thomas	.05	.02
42	Chancellor Nichols	.05	.02
43	Joao Viana	.05	.02
44	Keith Owens	.05	.02
45	Sean Muto	.05	.02
46	Drexel Deveaux	.05	.02
47	Stacey Augmon	.20	.12
48	Mike Goodson	.05	.02
49	Marty Conlon	.05	.02
50	Mark Macon	.12	.07
51	Greg Anthony	.20	.12
52	Dale Davis	.30	.18
53	Isaac Austin	.08	.05
54	Alvaro Teheran	.05	.02
55	Bobby Phills	.12	.07
56	Joe Wylie	.07	.04
57	Patrick Eddie	.05	.02
58	Joey Wright	.05	.02
59	Steve Hood	.05	.02
60	Lamont Strothers	.05	.02
61	Victor Alexander	.15	.10
62	Richard Dumas	.15	.10
63	Elliot Perry	.05	.02
64	Sean Green	.05	.02
65	Rick Fox	.20	.12
66	LeRon Ellis	.20	.12
67	Doug Overton	.10	.06
68	Randy Brown	.10	.06
69	Donald Hodge	.12	.07
70	Von McDade	.05	.02
71	Greg Sutton	.05	.02
72	Jimmy Oliver	.08	.05
73	Terrell Brandon (HL)	.10	.06
74	Darrin Chancellor	.05	.02
75	Chad Gallagher	.05	.02
76	Kevin Lynch	.05	.02
77	Keith Hughes	.05	.02
78	Tony Farmer	.05	.02
79	Eric Murdock	.25	.15
80	Marcus Kennedy	.05	.02
81	Larry Johnson	2.00	1.25
82	Stacey Augmon	.40	.25
83	Dikembe Mutombo	.75	.45
84	Steve Smith	.60	.35
85	Billy Owens	.35	.20
86	Stanley Roberts (Bonus Card #1)	.10	.06
87	Brian Shaw	.10	.06
88	Rodney Monroe (Bonus Card #2)	.10	.06
89	LaBradford Smith (HL)	.07	.04
90	Mark Randall (Bonus Card #3)	.10	.06
91	Brian Williams (Bonus Card #4)	.15	.10
92	Danny Ferry (FB)	.12	.07
93	Shawn Vandiver (Bonus Card #5)	.10	.06
94	Doug Smith (HL)	.08	.05
95	Luc Longley (HL)	.08	.05
96	Billy Owens (HL)	.20	.12
97	Steve Smith (HL)	.20	.12
98	Dikembe Mutombo (HL)	.25	.15
99	Stacey Augmon (HL)	.15	.10
100	Larry Johnson (HL)	.60	.35
101	Chris Gatling	.12	.07
102	Chris Corchiani	.10	.06
103	Myron Brown	.05	.02
104	Kevin Brooks	.08	.05
105	Anthony Avent	.12	.07
106	Steve Smith	.40	.25
107	Mike Iuzzolina	.05	.02
108	George Ackles	.05	.02
109	Melvin Newbern	.05	.02
110	Robert Pack (HL)	.10	.06
111	Darren Henrie	.05	.02
112	Chris Harris	.05	.02
113	John Crotty	.08	.05
114	Terrell Brandon	.15	.10
115	Paul Graham	.08	.05
116	Stevie Thompson	.05	.02
117	Clifford Martin	.05	.02
118	Doug Smith	.12	.07
119	Pete Chilcutt	.08	.05
120	Checklist	.05	.02

1992 Front Row Draft Picks

HAROLD MINER

This 100-card set contains players who were selected in the 1992 NBA Draft. The card fronts feature full color action photos framed by dark blue borders at the top and light blue borders at the bottom. Card backs include personal data, college stats and highlights. All cards measure 2-1/2" by 3-1/2".

		MINT	NR/MT
	Complete Set (100)	10.00	6.50
	Commons	.05	.02
1	Eric Anderson	.08	.05
2	Darin Archbold	.05	.02
3	Woody Austin	.05	.02
4	Mark Baker	.05	.02
5	Jon Barry	.15	.10
6	Elmer Bennett	.05	.02
7	Tony Bennett	.10	.06
8	Alex Blackwell	.05	.02
9	Curtis Blair	.05	.02
10	Ed Book	.05	.02
11	Marques Bragg	.05	.02
12	P.J. Brown	.10	.06
13	Anthony Buford	.05	.02
14	Dexter Cambridge	.07	.04
15	Brian Davis	.10	.06
16	Lucius Davis	.05	.02
17	Todd Day	.50	.30
18	Greg Dennis	.05	.02
19	Randenko Dobras	.05	.02
20	Harold Ellis	.12	.07
21	Chris King	.05	.02
22	Jo Jo English	.12	.07
23	Deron Feldhaus	.05	.02
24	Matt Geiger	.15	.10
25	Lewis Geter	.05	.02
26	George Gilmore	.05	.02
27	Litterial Green	.12	.07
28	Tom Gugliotta	.75	.45
29	Jim Havrilla	.05	.02
30	Robert Horry	.75	.45
31	Stephen Howard	.08	.05
32	Alonzo Jamison	.07	.04
33	Dave Johnson	.10	.06
34	Herb Jones	.05	.02
35	Popeye Jones	.15	.10
36	Adam Keefe	.12	.07
37	Dan Cyrulik	.05	.02
38	Ken Leeks	.05	.02
39	Ricardo Leonard	.05	.02
40	Gerald Madkins	.10	.06
41	Eric Manuel	.07	.04
42	Marlon Maxey	.12	.07
43	Jim McCoy	.05	.02
44	Oliver Miller	.40	.25
45	Sean Miller	.05	.02
46	Darren Morningstar	.05	.02
47	Isiah Morris	.05	.02
48	James Moses	.05	.02
49	Doug Christie	.60	.35
50	Damon Patterson	.05	.02
51	John Pelphrey	.05	.02
52	Brent Price	.15	.10
53	Brett Roberts	.07	.04
54	Steve Rogers	.05	.02
55	Sean Rooks	.20	.12
56	Malik Sealy	.15	.10
57	Tom Schurfranz	.05	.02
58	David Scott	.05	.02
59	Rod Sellers	.05	.02
60	Vernel Singleton	.05	.02
61	Reggie Slater	.05	.02
62	Elmore Spencer	.15	.10
63	Chris Smith	.15	.10
64	Latrell Sprewell	2.00	1.25
65	Matt Steigenga	.05	.02
66	Bryant Stith	.50	.30
67	Daimon Sweet	.05	.02
68	Craig Upchurch	.05	.02
69	Van Usher	.05	.02
70	Tony Watts	.05	.02
71	Clarence Weatherspoon	.75	.45
72	Robert Werdann	.05	.02
73	Benford Williams	.05	.02
74	Corey Williams	.07	.04
75	Henry Williams	.05	.02

78 • 1992 FRONT ROW DRAFT PICKS

76	Tim Burroughs	.05	.02
77	Eric Wilson	.05	.02
78	Randy Woods	.10	.06
79	Kendall Youngblood	.05	.02
80	Terry Boyd	.05	.02
81	Tracy Murray	.25	.15
82	Reggie Smith	.08	.05
83	Lee Mayberry	.20	.12
84	Matthew Fish	.05	.02
85	Hubert Davis	.30	.18
86	Duane Cooper	.10	.06
87	Anthony Peeler	.60	.35
88	Harold Miner	.75	.45
89	Harold Miner	.25	.15
90	Harold Miner	.25	.15
91	Christian Laettner	.80	.50
92	Christian Laettner	.25	.15
93	Christian Laettner	.25	.15
94	Walt Williams	.40	.25
95	Walt Williams	.15	.10
96	Walt Williams	.15	.10
97	LaPhonso Ellis	1.00	.60
98	LaPhonso Ellis	.30	.18
99	LaPhonso Ellis	.30	.18
100	Checklist	.05	.02

HOOPS

1989-90 Hoops

This set marks the premier edition of NBA Hoops, a product of the National Basketball Association. The set was issued in two series, 300-cards in Series I and a 53-card update set. The card fronts contain full color action photographs on a glossy white card stock. The photos are printed inside an oval designed to look like a basketball lane. The player's name is printed in black type above the photo. His team name and position appear under the photo. The card backs contain a small head shot, personal data, statistics and highlights. The only subset of note is All-Stars (AS). Several cards in the set were short-printed when they were dropped from the set during the printing of Series II. Those values are reflected by the letters (SP). All cards measure 2-1/2" by 3-1/2".

	MINT	NR/MT
Complete Set (353)	40.00	25.00
Commons	.05	.02

1	Joe Dumars	.20	.12
2	Tree Rollins	.05	.02
3	Kenny Walker	.05	.02

1989-90 HOOPS • 79

#	Player		
4	Mychal Thompson	.05	.02
5	Alvin Robertson (SP)	.15	.10
6	Vinny Del Negro (R)	.15	.10
7	Greg Anderson (SP)	.15	.10
8	Rod Strickland (R)	.40	.25
9	Ed Pinckney	.05	.02
10	Dale Ellis	.07	.04
11	Chuck Daly (R)	.30	.18
12	Eric Leckner	.05	.02
13	Charles Davis	.05	.02
14	Cotton Fitzsimmons	.05	.02
15	Byron Scott	.10	.06
16	Derrick Chievous (R)	.10	.06
17	Reggie Lewis (R)	1.00	.60
18	Jim Paxson	.07	.04
19	Tony Campbell (R)	.20	.12
20	Rolando Blackman	.10	.06
21	Michael Jordan (AS)	1.50	.90
22	Cliff Levingston	.05	.02
23	Roy Tarpley	.08	.05
24	Harold Pressley	.05	.02
25	Larry Nance	.08	.05
26	Chris Morris (R)	.25	.15
27	Bob Hansen	.05	.02
28	Mark Price (AS)	.15	.10
29	Reggie Miller	.50	.30
30	Karl Malone	.40	.25
31	Sidney Lowe (SP)	.08	.05
32	Ron Anderson	.05	.02
33	Mike Gminski	.05	.02
34	Scott Brooks (R)	.15	.10
35	Kevin Johnson (R)	1.75	1.00
36	Mark Bryant (R)	.15	.10
37	Rik Smits (R)	.30	.18
38	Tim Perry (R)	.15	.10
39	Ralph Sampson	.10	.06
40	Danny Manning (R)	2.00	1.25
41	Kevin Edwards (R)	.20	.12
42	Paul Mokeski	.05	.02
43	Dale Ellis (AS)	.06	.03
44	Walter Berry	.05	.02
45	Chuck Person	.12	.07
46	Rick Mahorn (SP)	.10	.06
47	Joe Kleine	.05	.02
48	Brad Daugherty (AS)	.10	.06
49	Mike Woodson	.05	.02
50	Brad Daugherty	.20	.12
51	Shelton Jones (SP)	.10	.06
52	Michael Adams	.15	.10
53	Wes Unseld	.05	.02
54	Rex Chapman (R)	.20	.12
55	Kelly Tripucka	.05	.02
56	Rickey Green	.05	.02
57	Frank Johnson (SP)	.08	.05
58	Johnny Newman (R)	.20	.12
59	Billy Thompson	.05	.02
60	Stu Jackson	.05	.02
61	Walter Davis	.08	.05
62	Brian Shaw (R)	.60	.35
63	Gerald Wilkins	.05	.02
64	Armon Gilliam	.10	.06
65	Maurice Cheeks	.20	.12
66	Jack Sikma	.07	.04
67	Harvey Grant (R)	.20	.12
68	Jim Lynam	.05	.02
69	Clyde Drexler (AS)	.20	.12
70	Xavier McDaniel	.10	.06
71	Danny Young	.05	.02
72	Fennis Dembo	.05	.02
73	Mark Acres (SP)	.08	.05
74	Brad Lohaus (R)	.20	.12
75	Manute Bol	.05	.02
76	Purvis Short	.07	.04
77	Allen Leavel	.05	.02
78	Johnny Dawkins (SP)	.10	.06
79	Paul Pressey	.05	.02
80	Patrick Ewing	.75	.45
81	Bill Wennington (R)	.08	.05
82	Danny Schayes	.05	.02
83	Derek Smith	.05	.02
84	Moses Malone (AS)	.10	.06
85	Jeff Malone	.10	.06
86	Otis Smith	.07	.04
87	Trent Tucker	.05	.02
88	Robert Reid	.05	.02
89	John Paxson	.15	.10
90	Chris Mullin	.25	.15
91	Tom Garrick	.05	.02
92	Willis Reed	.15	.10
93	Dave Corzine (SP)	.08	.05
94	Mark Alarie	.05	.02
95	Mark Aguirre	.08	.05
96	Charles Barkley (AS)	.50	.30
97	Sidney Green (SP)	.08	.05
98	Kevin Willis	.12	.07
99	Dave Hoppen	.05	.02
100	Terry Cummings	.12	.07
101	Dwayne Washington (SP)	.10	.06
102	Larry Brown	.05	.02
103	Kevin Duckworth	.10	.06
104	Uwe Blab (SP)	.08	.05
105	Terry Porter	.20	.12
106	Craig Ehlo (R)	.25	.15
107	Don Casey	.05	.02
108	Pat Riley	.05	.02
109	John Salley	.07	.04
110	Charles Barkley	1.00	.60
111	Sam Bowie (SP)	.12	.07
112	Earl Cureton	.05	.02
113	Craig Hodges	.05	.02
114	Benoit Benjamin	.05	.02
115A	Spud Webb (Er)	.25	.15
115B	Spud Webb (Cor)	.10	.06

80 • 1989-90 HOOPS

#	Name		
116	Karl Malone (AS)	.20	.12
117	Sleepy Floyd	.05	.02
118	Hot Rod Williams	.15	.10
119	Michael Holton	.05	.02
120	Alex English	.10	.06
121	Dennis Johnson	.10	.06
122	Wayne Cooper	.08	.05
123	Don Chaney	.05	.02
124	A.C. Green	.15	.10
125	Adrian Dantley	.10	.06
126	Del Harris	.05	.02
127	Dick Harter	.05	.02
128	Reggis Williams (R)	.20	.12
129	Bill Hanzlik	.05	.02
130	Dominique Wilkins	.50	.30
131	Herb Williams	.05	.02
132	Steve Johnson (SP)	.08	.05
133	Alex English (AS)	.08	.05
134	Darrell Walker	.05	.02
135	Bill Laimbeer	.08	.05
136	Fred Roberts (R)	.10	.06
137	Hersey Hawkins (R)	.50	.30
138	David Robinson (R)	30.00	18.00
139	Brad Sellers (SP)	.10	.06
140	John Stockton	.60	.35
141	Grant Long (R)	.20	.12
142	Marc Iavaroni (SP)	.08	.05
143	Steve Alford (SP)(R)	.15	.10
144	Jeff Lamp (SP)(R)	.15	.10
145	Buck Williams (SP)	.25	.15
146	Mark Jackson (AS)	.08	.05
147	Jim Petersen	.05	.02
148	Steve Stipanovich (SP)	.08	.05
149	Sam Vincent (SP)	.10	.06
150	Larry Bird	1.00	.60
151	Jon Koncak (R)	.12	.07
152	Olden Polynice (R)	.20	.12
153	Randy Breuer	.05	.02
154	John Battle (R)	.12	.07
155	Mark Eaton	.05	.02
156	Kevin McHale (AS)	.10	.06
157	Jerry Sichting (SP)	.08	.05
158	Pat Cummings (SP)	.08	.05
159	Patrick Ewing (AS)	.25	.15
160	Mark Price	.40	.25
161	Jerry Reynolds	.05	.02
162	Ken Norman (R)	.20	.12
163	John Bagley (SP)	.10	.06
164	Christian Welp (SP)	.08	.05
165	Reggie Theus (SP)	.15	.10
166	Magic Johnson (AS)	.60	.35
167	John Long	.05	.02
168	Larry Smith (SP)	.08	.05
169	Charles Shackleford(R)	.08	.05
170	Tom Chambers	.15	.10
171	John MacLeod	.05	.02
172	Ron Rothstein	.05	.02
173	Joe Wolf	.05	.02
174	Mark Eaton (AS)	.05	.02
175	Jon Sundvold	.05	.02
176	Scott Hastings (SP)	.08	.05
177	Isiah Thomas (AS)	.15	.10
178	Hakeem Olajuwon (AS)	.60	.35
179	Mike Fratello	.05	.02
180	Hakeem Olajuwon	1.25	.70
181	Randolph Keys (R)	.05	.02
182	Richard Anderson	.05	.02
183	Dan Majerle (R)	1.25	.70
184	Derek Harper	.07	.04
185	Robert Parish	.15	.10
186	Ricky Berry (SP)	.08	.05
187	Michael Cooper	.05	.02
188	Vinnie Johnson	.05	.02
189	James Donaldson	.05	.02
190	Clyde Drexler	.30	.18
191	Jay Vincent (SP)	.12	.07
192	Nate McMillan	.05	.02
193	Kevin Duckworth (AS)	.08	.05
194	Ledell Eackles (R)	.10	.06
195	Eddie Johnson	.05	.02
196	Terry Teagle	.05	.02
197	Tom Chambers (AS)	.08	.05
198	Joe Barry Carroll	.05	.02
199	Dennis Hopson (R)	.10	.06
200	Michael Jordan	3.00	1.75
201	Jerome Lane (R)	.12	.07
202	Greg Kite (R)	.10	.06
203	David Rivers (SP)	.10	.06
204	Sylvester Gray	.05	.02
205	Ron Harper	.10	.06
206	Frank Brickowski	.05	.02
207	Rory Sparrow	.05	.02
208	Gerald Henderson	.05	.02
209	Rod Higgins	.05	.02
210	James Worthy	.20	.12
211	Dennis Rodman	.25	.15
212	Ricky Pierce	.10	.06
213	Charles Oakley	.08	.05
214	Steve Colter	.05	.02
215	Danny Ainge	.15	.10
216	Lenny Wilkens	.05	.02
217	Larry Nance (AS)	.07	.04
218	Muggsy Bogues	.10	.06
219	James Worthy (AS)	.10	.06
220	Lafayette Lever	.05	.02
221	Quintin Dailey (SP)	.10	.06
222	Lester Conner	.05	.02
223	Jose Ortiz	.05	.02
224	Micheal Williams (R)	.50	.30
225	Wayman Tisdale	.08	.05
226	Mike Sanders (SP)	.08	.05
227	Jim Farmer (SP)	.08	.05
228	Mark West	.05	.02
229	Jeff Hornacek (R)	.50	.30

1989-90 HOOPS • 81

#	Player	Value 1	Value 2
230	Chris Mullin (AS)	.15	.10
231	Vern Fleming	.05	.02
232	Kenny Smith	.08	.05
233	Derrick McKey	.08	.05
234	Dominique Wilkins (AS)	.20	.12
235	Willie Anderson (R)	.20	.12
236	Keith Lee (R)(SP)	.15	.10
237	Buck Johnson (R)	.15	.10
238	Randy Wittman	.05	.02
239	Terry Catledge (SP)	.10	.06
240	Bernard King	.10	.06
241	Darrell Griffith	.05	.02
242	Horace Grant	.25	.15
243	Rony Seikaly (R)	.50	.30
244	Scottie Pippen	2.00	1.25
245	Michael Cage	.05	.02
246	Kurt Rambis	.05	.02
247	Morlon Wiley (SP)(R)	.12	.07
248	Ronnie Grandison	.05	.02
249	Scott Skiles (SP)(R)	.75	.45
250	Isiah Thomas	.25	.15
251	Thurl Baily	.05	.02
252	Doc Rivers	.07	.04
253	Stuart Gray (SP)	.08	.05
254	John Williams	.05	.02
255	Bill Cartwright	.07	.04
256	Terry Cummings (AS)	.08	.05
257	Rodney McCray	.07	.04
258	Larry Krystkowiak (R)	.15	.10
259	Will Perdue (R)	.15	.10
260	Mitch Richmond (R)	1.50	.90
261	Blair Rasmussen	.05	.02
262	Charles Smith (R)	.30	.18
263	Tyrone Corbin (SP)(R)	.40	.25
264	Kelvin Upshaw	.05	.02
265	Otis Thorpe	.10	.06
266	Phil Jackson	.05	.02
267	Jerry Sloan	.05	.02
268	John Shasky	.05	.02
269	Bernie Bickerstaff	.05	.02
270	Magic Johnson	1.00	.60
271	Vernon Maxwell (R)	.75	.45
272	Tim McCormick	.05	.02
273	Don Nelson	.05	.02
274	Gary Grant (R)	.15	.10
275	Sidney Moncrief (SP)	.20	.12
276	Roy Hinson	.05	.02
277	Jimmy Rodgers	.05	.02
278	Antoine Carr	.05	.02
279	Orlando Woolridge (SP)	.12	.07
280	Kevin McHale	.20	.12
281	LaSalle Thompson	.05	.02
282	Detlef Schrempf	.30	.18
283	Doug Moe	.05	.02
284	James Edwards	.05	.02
285	Jerome Kersey	.10	.06
286	Sam Perkins	.10	.06
287	Sedale Threatt	.07	.04
288	Tim Kempton (SP)	.10	.06
289	Mark McNamara	.05	.02
290	Moses Malone	.15	.10
291	Rick Adelman	.05	.02
292	Dick Versace	.05	.02
293	Alton Lister (SP)	.10	.06
294	Winston Garland	.05	.02
295	Kiki Vandeweghe	.07	.04
296	Brad Davis	.05	.02
297	John Stockton (AS)	.25	.15
298	Jay Humphries	.07	.04
299	Dell Curry	.10	.06
300	Mark Jackson	.15	.10
301	Morton Wiley	.07	.04
302	Reggie Theus	.05	.02
303	Otis Smith	.05	.02
304	Tod Murphy (R)	.08	.05
305	Sidney Green	.05	.02
306	Shelton Jones	.05	.02
307	Mark Acres	.05	.02
308	Terry Catledge	.05	.02
309	Larry Smith	.05	.02
310	David Robinson	4.00	2.50
311	Johnny Dawkins	.05	.02
312	Terry Cummings	.10	.06
313	Sidney Lowe	.05	.02
314	Bill Musselman	.05	.02
315	Buck Williams	.10	.06
316	Mel Turpin	.05	.02
317	Scott Hastings	.05	.02
318	Scott Skiles	.15	.10
319	Tyrone Corbin	.12	.07
320	Maurice Cheeks	.08	.05
321	Matt Goukas	.05	.02
322	Jeff Turner	.05	.02
323	David Wingate	.05	.02
324	Steve Johnson	.07	.04
325	Alton Lister	.05	.02
326	Ken Bannister	.05	.02
327	Bill Fitch	.05	.02
328	Sam Vincent	.05	.02
329	Larry Drew	.05	.02
330	Rick Mahorn	.05	.02
331	Christian Welp	.05	.02
332	Brad Lohaus	.05	.02
333	Frank Johnson	.05	.02
334	Jim Farmer	.05	.02
335	Wayne Cooper	.05	.02
336	Mike Brown (R)	.08	.05
337	Sam Bowie	.05	.02
338	Kevin Gamble (R)	.20	.12
339	Jerry Reynolds	.10	.06
340	Mike Sanders	.05	.02
341	Bill Jones	.05	.02
342	Greg Anderson	.10	.06
343	Dave Corzine	.05	.02

82 • 1989-90 HOOPS

		MINT	NR/MT
344	Micheal Williams	.15	.10
345	Jay Vincent	.05	.02
346	David Rivers	.05	.02
347	Caldwell Jones	.05	.02
348	Brad Sellers	.05	.02
349	Scott Roth	.05	.02
350	Alvin Robertson	.05	.02
351	Steve Kerr (R)	.15	.10
352	Stuart Gray	.05	.02
353A	Pistons Champs	6.00	3.75
353B	Pistons Champs	.60	.35

1990-91 Hoops

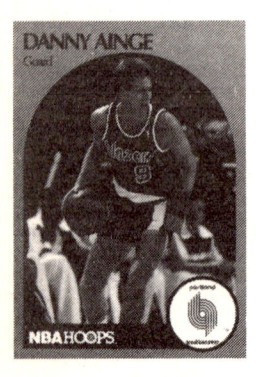

The cards in this set were issued in two series and feature full color action photographs on the front printed inside an oval shaped like a basketball lane. The photographs are bordered in silver except for the All-Star cards which are gold. The player's name and position are printed in the top left corner in his dominent team color while NBA Hoops appears in a color bar that also corresponds to his team colors. A team logo is located in the lower right corner. Card backs consist of a small head shot, personal data, statistics and highlights. Key subsets include All-Stars (AS), Coaches (C), Team Checklists (CL), Inside Stuff (382-385), Message Cards such as Stay In School (386-389) and the Lottery Selections (390-400). The set contains a number of short-prints (SP) including the All-Star selections (1-26). All cards measure 2-1/2" by 3-1/2".

		MINT	NR/MT
	Complete Set (440)	12.50	7.50
	Commons	.05	.02
1	Charles Barkley (AS)	.50	.30
2	Larry Bird (AS)	.75	.45
3	Joe Dumars (AS)	.12	.07
4	Patrick Ewing (AS)	.35	.20
5	Michael Jordan (AS)	2.50	1.50
6	Kevin McHale (AS)	.08	.05
7	Reggie Miller (AS)	.15	.10
8	Robert Parish (AS)	.08	.05
9	Scottie Pippen (AS)	.40	.25
10	Dennis Rodman (AS)	.10	.06
11	Isiah Thomas (AS)	.15	.10
12	Dominique Wilkins (AS)	.25	.15
13A	Checklist (AS w/SP)	.08	.05
13B	Checklist (AS w/no SP)	.35	.10
14	Rolando Blackman (AS)	.07	.04
15	Tom Chambers (AS)	.08	.05
16	Clyde Drexler (AS)	.20	.12
17	A.C. Green (AS)	.07	.04
18	Magic Johnson (AS)	.50	.30
19	Kevin Johnson (AS)	.20	.12
20	Lafayette Lever (AS)	.07	.04
21	Karl Malone (AS)	.20	.12
22	Chris Mullin (AS)	.15	.10
23	Hakeem Olajuwon (AS)	.60	.35
24	David Robinson (AS)	.80	.50
25	John Stockton (AS)	.20	.12
26	James Worthy (AS)	.12	.07
27	John Battle	.05	.02
28	Jon Koncak	.05	.02
29	Cliff Levingston (SP)	.07	.04
30	John Long (SP)	.07	.04
31	Moses Malone	.12	.07
32	Doc Rivers	.05	.02
33	Kenny Smith (SP)	.10	.06
34	Alexander Volkov	.05	.02
35	Spud Webb	.05	.02
36	Dominique Wilkins	.25	.16
37	Kevin Willis	.07	.04
38	John Bagley	.05	.02
39	Larry Bird	.80	.50
40	Kevin Gamble	.10	.06
41	Dennis Johnson (SP)	.12	.07
42	Joe Kleine	.05	.02
43	Reggie Lewis	.20	.12
44	Kevin McHale	.12	.07
45	Robert Parish	.12	.07
46	Jim Paxson (SP)	.07	.04

1990-91 HOOPS • 83

#	Player		
47	Ed Pinckney	.05	.02
48	Brian Shaw	.05	.02
49	Richard Anderson (SP)	.05	.04
50	Muggsy Bogues	.05	.02
51	Rex Chapman	.07	.04
52	Dell Curry	.07	.04
53	Kenny Gattison (R)	.10	.06
54	Armon Gilliam	.07	.04
55	Dave Hoppen	.07	.04
56	Randolph Keys	.05	.02
57	J.R. Reid (R)	.15	.10
58	Robert Reid (SP)	.07	.04
59	Kelly Tripucka	.05	.02
60	B.J. Armstrong (R)	.75	.45
61	Bill Cartwright	.05	.02
62	Charles Davis (SP)	.07	.04
63	Horace Grant	.12	.07
64	Craig Hodges	.05	.02
65	Michael Jordan	2.50	1.50
66	Stacey King (R)	.15	.10
67	John Paxson	.07	.04
68	Will Perdue	.05	.02
69	Scottie Pippen	.50	.30
70	Winston Bennett	.05	.02
71	Chucky Brown (R)	.10	.06
72	Derrick Chievous	.05	.02
73	Brad Daugherty	.20	.12
74	Craig Ehlo	.05	.02
75	Steve Kerr	.05	.02
76	Paul Mokeski (SP)	.07	.04
77	John Morton	.05	.02
78	Larry Nance	.07	.04
79	Mark Price	.20	.12
80	Hot Rod Williams	.08	.05
81	Steve Alford	.05	.02
82	Rolando Blackman	.07	.04
83	Adrian Dantley (SP)	.08	.05
84	Brad Davis	.05	.02
85	James Donaldson	.05	.02
86	Derek Harper	.07	.04
87	Sam Perkins (SP)	.10	.06
88	Roy Tarpley	.08	.05
89	Bill Wennington (SP)	.07	.04
90	Herb Williams	.05	.02
91	Michael Adams	.08	.05
92	Joe Barry Carroll (SP)	.07	.04
93	Walter Davis	.07	.04
94	Alex English (SP)	.08	.05
95	Bill Hanzlik	.05	.02
96	Jerome Lane	.05	.02
97	Lafayette Lever (SP)	.07	.04
98	Todd Lichti (R)	.10	.06
99	Blair Rasmussen	.05	.02
100	Dan Schayes (SP)	.07	.04
101	Mark Aguirre	.07	.04
102	William Bedford (R)	.10	.06
103	Joe Dumars	.20	.12
104	James Edwards	.05	.02
105	Scott Hastings	.05	.02
106	Gerald Henderson (SP)	.07	.04
107	Vinnie Johnson	.05	.02
108	Bill Laimbeer	.07	.04
109	Dennis Rodman	.12	.07
110	John Salley	.05	.02
111	Isiah Thomas	.20	.12
112	Manute Bol (SP)	.07	.04
113	Tim Hardaway (R)	1.25	.70
114	Rod Higgins	.05	.02
115	Sarunas Mariciulionis	.15	.10
116	Chris Mullin	.20	.12
117	Jim Petersen	.05	.02
118	Mitch Richmond	.25	.15
119	Mike Smrek	.05	.02
120	Terry Teagle (SP)	.07	.04
121	Tom Tolbert (R)	.10	.06
122	Christian Welp (SP)	.07	.04
123	Byron Dinkins (SP)	.07	.04
124	Sleepy Floyd	.05	.02
125	Buck Johnson	.05	.02
126	Vernon Maxwell	.12	.07
127	Hakeem Olajuwon	.75	.45
128	Larry Smith	.05	.02
129	Otis Thorpe	.08	.05
130	Mitchell Wiggins (SP)	.07	.04
131	Mike Woodson	.05	.02
132	Greg Dreiling (R)	.10	.06
133	Vern Fleming	.05	.02
134	Rickey Green (SP)	.07	.04
135	Reggis Miller	.25	.15
136	Chuck Person	.10	.06
137	Mike Sanders	.05	.02
138	Detlef Schrempf	.12	.07
139	Rik Smits	.07	.04
140	LaSalle Thompson	.05	.02
141	Randy Wittman	.05	.02
142	Benoit Benjamin	.05	.02
143	Winston Garland	.05	.02
144	Tom Garrick	.05	.02
145	Gary Grant	.05	.02
146	Ron Harper	.07	.04
147	Danny Manning	.30	.18
148	Jeff Martin	.05	.02
149	Ken Norman	.08	.05
150	David Rivers (SP)	.07	.04
151	Charles Smith	.10	.06
152	Joe Wolf (SP)	.08	.05
153	Michael Cooper (SP)	.07	.04
154	Vlade Divac (R)	.25	.15
155	Larry Drew	.05	.02
156	A.C. Green	.07	.04
157	Magic Johnson	.60	.35
158	Mark McNamara (SP)	.07	.04
159	Byron Scott	.07	.04
160	Mychal Thompson	.05	.02

84 • 1990-91 HOOPS

#	Player		
161	Jay Vincent (SP)	.08	.05
162	Orlando Woolridge (SP)	.08	.05
163	James Worthy	.15	.10
164	Sherman Douglas (R)	.20	.12
165	Kevin Edwards	.05	.02
166	Tellis Frank (SP)	.07	.04
167	Grant Long	.05	.02
168	Glen Rice (R)	.60	.35
169	Rony Seikaly	.12	.07
170	Rory Sparrow (SP)	.07	.04
171	Jon Sundvold	.05	.02
172	Billy Thompson	.05	.02
173	Greg Anderson	.07	.04
174	Jeff Grayer (R)	.10	.06
175	Jay Humphries	.05	.02
176	Frank Kornet	.05	.02
177	Larry Krystkowiak	.05	.02
178	Brad Lohaus	.05	.02
179	Ricky Pierce	.05	.02
180	Paul Pressey (SP)	.07	.04
181	Fred Roberts	.05	.02
182	Alvin Robertson	.05	.02
183	Jack Sikma	.07	.04
184	Randy Breuer	.05	.02
185	Tony Campbell	.05	.02
186	Tyrone Corbin	.07	.04
187	Sidney Lowe (SP)	.07	.04
188	Sam Mitchell (R)	.10	.06
189	Tod Murphy	.05	.02
190	Pooh Richardson (R)	.20	.12
191	Scott Roth (SP)	.07	.04
192	Brad Sellers (SP)	.07	.04
193	Mookie Blaylock (R)	.40	.25
194	Sam Bowie	.05	.02
195	Lester Conner	.05	.02
196	Derrick Gervin (R)	.07	.04
197	Jack Haley (R)	.08	.05
198	Roy Hinson	.05	.02
199	Dennis Hopson (SP)	.10	.06
200	Chris Morris	.05	.02
201	Purvis Short (SP)	.10	.06
202	Maurice Cheeks	.08	.05
203	Patrick Ewing	.35	.20
204	Stuart Gray	.05	.02
205	Mark Jackson	.10	.06
206	Johnny Newman (SP)	.08	.05
207	Charles Oakley	.07	.04
208	Trent Tucker	.05	.02
209	Kiki Vandeweghe	.05	.02
210	Kenny Walker	.05	.02
211	Eddie Lee Wilkins	.05	.02
212	Gerald Wilkins	.05	.02
213	Mark Acres	.05	.02
214	Nick Anderson (R)	.50	.30
215	Michael Ansley	.05	.02
216	Terry Catledge	.05	.02
217	Dave Corzine (SP)	.07	.04
218	Sidney Green (SP)	.07	.04
219	Jerry Reynolds	.05	.02
220	Scott Skiles	.05	.02
221	Otis Smith	.05	.02
222	Reggie Theus (SP)	.08	.05
223	Sam Vincent	.05	.02
224	Ron Anderson	.05	.02
225	Charles Barkley	.60	.35
226	Scott Brooks (SP)	.07	.04
227	Johnny Dawkins	.05	.02
228	Mike Gminski	.05	.02
229	Hersey Hawkins	.10	.06
230	Rick Mahorn	.05	.02
231	Derek Smith (SP)	.07	.04
232	Bob Thornton	.05	.02
233	Kenny Battle (R)	.10	.06
234	Tom Chambers	.08	.05
235	Greg Grant (SP)	.07	.04
236	Jeff Hornacek	.10	.06
237	Eddie Johnson	.05	.02
238	Kevin Johnson	.25	.15
239	Dan Majerle	.20	.12
240	Tim Perry	.05	.02
241	Kurt Rambis	.05	.02
242	Mark West	.05	.02
243	Mark Bryant	.05	.02
244	Wayne Cooper	.05	.02
245	Clyde Drexler	.25	.15
246	Kevin Duckworth	.08	.05
247	Jerome Kersey	.10	.06
248	Drazen Petrovic (R)	.50	.30
249	Terry Porter	.15	.10
250	Cliff Robinson (R)	.75	.45
251	Buck Williams	.08	.05
252	Danny Young	.05	.02
253	Danny Ainge (SP)	.12	.07
254	Randy Allen (SP)	.07	.04
255	Antoine Carr	.05	.02
256	Vinny Del Negro (SP)	.08	.05
257	Pervis Ellison (SP)(R)	.25	.15
258	Greg Kite (SP)	.08	.05
259	Rodney McCray (SP)	.08	.05
260	Harold Pressley (SP)	.07	.04
261	Ralph Sampson	.08	.05
262	Wayman Tisdale	.08	.05
263	Willie Anderson	.05	.02
264	Uwe Blab (SP)	.07	.04
265	Frank Brickowski (SP)	.07	.04
266	Terry Cummings	.08	.05
267	Sean Elliott (R)	.30	.18
268	Caldwell Jones (SP)	.08	.05
269	Johnny Moore (SP)	.07	.04
270	David Robinson	1.25	.70
271	Rod Strickland	.05	.02
272	Reggie Williams	.07	.04
273	David Wingate (SP)	.08	.05
274	Dana Barros (R)	.15	.10

1990-91 HOOPS • 85

#	Name	Price 1	Price 2
275	Michael Cage	.05	.02
276	Quintin Dailey	.05	.02
277	Dale Ellis	.07	.04
278	Steve Johnson (SP)	.08	.05
279	Shawn Kemp (R)	3.00	1.75
280	Xavier McDaniel	.08	.05
281	Derrick McKey	.07	.04
282	Nate McMillan	.05	.02
283	Olden Polynice	.05	.02
284	Sedale Threatt	.05	.02
285	Thurl Bailey	.05	.02
286	Mike Brown	.05	.02
287	Mark Eaton	.05	.02
288	Blue Edwards (R)	.15	.10
289	Darrell Griffith	.05	.02
290	Robert Hansen (SP)	.07	.04
291	Eric Leckner (SP)	.07	.04
292	Karl Malone	.25	.15
293	Delaney Rudd	.05	.02
294	John Stockton	.25	.15
295	Mark Alarie	.05	.02
296	Ledell Eackles (SP)	.08	.05
297	Harvey Grant	.07	.04
298	Tom Hammonds (R)	.10	.06
299	Charles Jones	.05	.02
300	Bernard King	.08	.05
301	Jeff Malone (SP)	.15	.10
302	Mel Turpin (SP)	.07	.04
303	Darrell Walker	.05	.02
304	John Williams	.05	.02
305	Bob Weiss (C)	.05	.02
306	Chris Ford (C)	.05	.02
307	Gene Littles (C)	.05	.02
308	Phil Jackson (C)	.05	.02
309	Lenny Wilkens (C)	.05	.02
310	Richie Adubato (C)	.05	.02
311	Doug Moe (C)	.05	.02
312	Chuck Daly (C)	.05	.02
313	Don Nelson (C)	.05	.02
314	Don Chaney (C)	.05	.02
315	Dick Versace (C)	.05	.02
316	Mike Schuler (C)	.05	.02
317	Pat Riley (C)	.05	.02
318	Ron Rothstein (C)	.05	.02
319	Del Harris (C)	.05	.02
320	Bill Musselman (C)	.05	.02
321	Bill Fitch (C)	.05	.02
322	Stu Jackson (C)	.05	.02
323	Matt Guokas (C)	.05	.02
324	Jim Lynam (C)	.05	.02
325	Cotton Fitzsimmons (C)	.05	.02
326	Rick Adelman (C)	.05	.02
327	Dick Motta (C)	.05	.02
328	Larry Brown (C)	.05	.02
329	K.C. Jones (C)	.05	.02
330	Jerry Sloan (C)	.05	.02
331	Wes Unseld (C)	.05	.02
332	Checklist 1 (SP)	.05	.02
333	Checklist 2 (SP)	.05	.02
334	Checklist 3 (SP)	.05	.02
335	Checklist 4 (SP)	.05	.02
336	Danny Ferry (SP)(R)	.15	.10
337	NBA Finals Game 1	.05	.02
338	NBA Finals Game 2	.05	.02
339	NBA Finals Game 3	.05	.02
340	NBA Finals Game 4	.05	.02
341	NBA Finals Game 5	.08	.05
342	Championship Pistons	.10	.06
343	K.C. Jones (C)	.05	.02
344	Wes Unseld (C)	.05	.02
345	Don Nelson (C)	.05	.02
346	Bob Weiss (C)	.05	.02
347	Chris Ford (C)	.05	.02
348	Phil Jackson (C)	.05	.02
349	Lenny Wilkens (C)	.05	.02
350	Don Chaney (C)	.05	.02
351	Mike Dunleavy (C)	.05	.02
352	Matt Guokas (C)	.05	.02
353	Rick Adelman (C)	.05	.02
354	Jerry Sloan (C)	.05	.02
355	Dominique Wilkins (CL)	.15	.10
356	Larry Bird (CL)	.50	.30
357	Rex Chapman (CL)	.05	.02
358	Michael Jordan (CL)	1.25	.70
359	Mark Price (CL)	.08	.05
360	Rolando Blackman (CL)	.05	.02
361	Michael Adams (CL)	.07	.04
362	Joe Dumars (CL)	.08	.05
363	Chris Mullin (CL)	.08	.05
364	Hakeem Olajuwon (CL)	.40	.25
365	Reggie Miller (CL)	.12	.07
366	Danny Manning (CL)	.10	.06
367	Magic Johnson (CL)	.40	.25
368	Rony Seikaly (CL)	.08	.05
369	Alvin Robertson (CL)	.05	.02
370	Pooh Richardson (CL)	.05	.02
371	Chris Morris (CL)	.05	.02
372	Patrick Ewing (CL)	.20	.12
373	Nick Anderson (CL)	.15	.10
374	Charles Barkley (CL)	.25	.15
375	Kevin Johnson (CL)	.12	.07
376	Clyde Drexler (CL)	.12	.07
377	Wayman Tisdale (CL)	.07	.04
378	David Robinson (CL)	.50	.30
379	Xavier McDaniel (CL)	.07	.04
380	Karl Malone (CL)	.15	.10
381	Bernard King (CL)	.07	.04
382	Michael Jordan (Play)	1.25	.70
383	Karl Malone (Lights)	.15	.10
384	Divac/Marcuilionis	.10	.06
385	Magic & Jordan	1.50	.90
386	Johnny Newman	.05	.02
387	Dell Curry	.05	.02
388	Patrick Ewing	.20	.12

86 • 1990-91 HOOPS

389	Isiah Thomas	.12	.07
390	Derrick Coleman (R)	1.75	1.00
391	Gary Payton (R)	.60	.35
392	Chris Jackson (R)	.60	.35
393	Dennis Scott (R)	.30	.18
394	Kendall Gill (R)	.50	.30
395	Felton Spencer (R)	.12	.07
396	Lionel Simmons (R)	.40	.25
397	Bo Kimble (R)	.08	.05
398	Willie Burton (R)	.15	.10
399	Rumeal Robinson (R)	.12	.07
400	Tyrone Hill (R)	.20	.12
401	Tim McCormick	.05	.02
402	Sidney Moncrief	.07	.04
403	Johnny Newman	.05	.02
404	Dennis Hopson	.07	.04
405	Cliff Levingston	.05	.02
406	Danny Ferry	.07	.04
407	Alex English	.08	.05
408	Lafayette Lever	.05	.02
409	Rodney McCray	.07	.04
410	Mike Dunleavy	.05	.02
411	Orlando Woolridge	.07	.04
412	Joe Wolf	.05	.02
413	Tree Rollins	.05	.02
414	Kenny Smith	.07	.04
415	Sam Perkins	.07	.04
416	Terry Teagle	.05	.02
417	Frank Brickowski	.05	.02
418	Danny Schayes	.05	.02
419	Scott Brooks	.05	.02
420	Reggie Theus	.05	.02
421	Greg Grant	.05	.02
422	Paul Westhead	.05	.02
423	Greg Kite	.05	.02
424	Manute Bol	.05	.02
425	Rickey Green	.05	.02
426	Ed Nealy	.05	.02
427	Danny Ainge	.08	.05
428	Bobby Hansen	.05	.02
429	Eric Leckner	.05	.02
430	Rory Sparrow	.05	.02
431	Bill Wennington	.05	.02
432	Paul Pressey	.05	.02
433	David Greenwood	.05	.02
434	Mark McNamara	.05	.02
435	Sidney Green	.05	.02
436	Dave Corzine	.05	.02
437	Jeff Malone	.08	.05
438	Pervis Ellison	.12	.07
439	Checklist 5	.05	.02
440	Checklist 6	.05	.02

1991-92 Hoops

MAGIC JOHNSON

Guard

This set was issued in two series and features full color game action photos on the card fronts printed on a white glossy card stock and framed by various border colors. The player's name is printed in the top left corner while a team logo appears in the lower left corner. The card backs are horizontal and contain a small color photo, personal data, stats and highlights. Key subsets include Coaches (C), All-Stars (AS), Team Cards (274-300), Inside Stuff (302-305), League Leaders (LL), Milestones (314-318), Yearbook (319-324), Supreme Court (SC)(449-502), Art Cards (ART)(503-529), NBA Playoffs (538-543), Draft Picks (546-556) and the USA Basketball Team (USA)(557-588). All cards measure 2-1/2" by 3-1/2".

	MINT	NR/MT
Complete Set (590)	18.50	12.00
Commons	.04	.02

1	John Battle	.04	.02
2	Moses Malone	.10	.06
3	Sidney Moncrief	.07	.04
4	Doc Rivers	.04	.02
5	Rumeal Robinson	.04	.02
6	Spud Webb	.04	.02
7	Dominique Wilkins	.25	.15
8	Kevin Willis	.07	.04
9	Larry Bird	.50	.30
10	Dee Brown	.12	.07

1991-92 HOOPS • 87

#	Player				#	Player		
11	Kevin Gamble	.04	.02		68	Rod Higgins	.04	.02
12	Joe Kleine	.04	.02		69	Tyrone Hill	.04	.02
13	Reggie Lewis	.10	.06		70	Alton Lister	.04	.02
14	Kevin McHale	.12	.07		71	Sarunas Marciulionis	.07	.04
15	Robert Parish	.12	.07		72	Chris Mullin	.15	.10
16	Ed Pinckney	.04	.02		73	Mitch Richmond	.15	.10
17	Brian Shaw	.04	.02		74	Tom Tolbert	.04	.02
18	Muggsy Bogues	.04	.02		75	Sleepy Floyd	.04	.02
19	Rex Chapman	.07	.04		76	Buck Johnson	.04	.02
20	Dell Curry	.04	.02		77	Vernon Maxwell	.07	.04
21	Kendall Gill	.15	.10		78	Hakeem Olajuwon	.50	.30
22	Mike Gminski	.04	.02		79	Kenny Smith	.07	.04
23	Johnny Newman	.04	.02		80	Larry Smith	.04	.02
24	J.R. Reid	.04	.02		81	Otis Thorpe	.07	.04
25	Kelly Tripucka	.04	.02		82	David Wood	.08	.05
26	B.J. Armstrong	.15	.10		83	Vern Fleming	.04	.02
27	Bill Cartwright	.04	.02		84	Reggie Miller	.20	.12
28	Horace Grant	.10	.06		85	Chuck Person	.08	.05
29	Craig Hodges	.04	.02		86	Mike Sanders	.04	.02
30	Michael Jordan	1.75	1.00		87	Detlef Schrempf	.10	.06
31	Stacey King	.04	.02		88	Rik Smits	.04	.02
32	Cliff Levingston	.04	.02		89	LaSalle Thompson	.04	.02
33	John Paxson	.07	.04		90	Micheal Williams	.04	.02
34	Scottie Pippen	.30	.18		91	Winston Garland	.04	.02
35	Chucky Brown	.04	.02		92	Gary Grant	.04	.02
36	Brad Daugherty	.12	.07		93	Ron Harper	.07	.04
37	Craig Ehlo	.04	.02		94	Danny Manning	.15	.10
38	Danny Ferry	.04	.02		95	Jeff Martin	.04	.02
39	Larry Nance	.07	.04		96	Ken Norman	.07	.04
40	Mark Price	.12	.07		97	Olden Polynice	.04	.02
41	Darnell Valentine	.04	.02		98	Charles Smith	.08	.05
42	Hot Rod Williams	.08	.05		99	Vlade Divac	.08	.05
43	Rolando Blackman	.07	.04		100	A.C. Green	.07	.04
44	Brad Davis	.04	.02		101	Magic Johnson	.50	.30
45	James Donaldson	.04	.02		102	Sam Perkins	.07	.04
46	Derek Harper	.07	.04		103	Byron Scott	.04	.02
47	Fat Lever	.04	.02		104	Terry Teagle	.04	.02
48	Rodney McCray	.04	.02		105	Mychal Thompson	.04	.02
49	Roy Tarpley	.07	.04		106	James Worthy	.10	.06
50	Herb Williams	.04	.02		107	Willie Burton	.07	.04
51	Michael Adams	.07	.04		108	Bimbo Coles	.08	.05
52	Chris Jackson	.15	.10		109	Terry Davis	.04	.02
53	Jerome Lane	.04	.02		110	Sherman Douglas	.08	.05
54	Todd Lichti	.04	.02		111	Kevin Edwards	.04	.02
55	Blair Rasmussen	.04	.02		112	Alec Kessler	.04	.02
56	Reggie Williams	.04	.02		113	Glen Rice	.15	.10
57	Joe Wolf	.04	.02		114	Rony Seikaly	.08	.05
58	Orlando Woolridge	.04	.02		115	Frank Brickowski	.04	.02
59	Mark Aguirre	.07	.04		116	Dale Ellis	.07	.04
60	Joe Dumars	.12	.07		117	Jay Humphries	.04	.02
61	James Edwards	.04	.02		118	Brad Lohaus	.04	.02
62	Vinnie Johnson	.04	.02		119	Fred Roberts	.04	.02
63	Bill Laimbeer	.07	.04		120	Alvin Robertson	.04	.02
64	Dennis Rodman	.12	.07		121	Danny Schayes	.04	.02
65	John Salley	.04	.02		122	Jack Sikma	.04	.02
66	Isiah Thomas	.15	.10		123	Randy Breuer	.04	.02
67	Tim Hardaway	.25	.15		124	Tony Campbell	.04	.02

88 • 1991-92 HOOPS

#	Player		
125	Tyrone Corbin	.04	.02
126	Gerald Glass	.04	.02
127	Sam Mitchell	.07	.04
128	Tod Murphy	.04	.02
129	Pooh Richardson	.07	.04
130	Felton Spencer	.07	.04
131	Mookie Blaylock	.07	.04
132	Sam Bowie	.04	.02
133	Jud Buechler	.04	.02
134	Derrick Coleman	.40	.25
135	Chris Dudley	.04	.02
136	Chris Morris	.04	.02
137	Drazen Petrovic	.15	.10
138	Reggie Theus	.04	.02
139	Maurice Cheeks	.04	.02
140	Patrick Ewing	.30	.18
141	Mark Jackson	.07	.04
142	Charles Oakley	.07	.04
143	Trent Tucker	.04	.02
144	Kiki Vandeweghe	.04	.02
145	Kenny Walker	.07	.04
146	Gerald Wilkins	.04	.02
147	Nick Anderson	.15	.10
148	Michael Ansley	.04	.02
149	Terry Catledge	.04	.02
150	Jerry Reynolds	.04	.02
151	Dennis Scott	.10	.06
152	Scott Skiles	.04	.02
153	Otis Smith	.04	.02
154	Sam Vincent	.04	.02
155	Ron Anderson	.04	.02
156	Charles Barkley	.40	.25
157	Manute Bol	.04	.02
158	Johnny Dawkins	.04	.02
159	Armon Gilliam	.04	.02
160	Rickey Green	.04	.02
161	Hersey Hawkins	.08	.05
162	Rick Mahorn	.04	.02
163	Tom Chambers	.07	.04
164	Jeff Hornacek	.07	.04
165	Kevin Johnson	.12	.07
166	Andrew Lang	.04	.02
167	Dan Majerle	.10	.06
168	Xavier McDaniel	.07	.04
169	Kurt Rambis	.04	.02
170	Mark West	.04	.02
171	Danny Ainge	.07	.04
172	Mark Bryant	.04	.02
173	Walter Davis	.04	.02
174	Clyde Drexler	.20	.12
175	Kevin Duckworth	.07	.04
176	Jerome Kersey	.08	.05
177	Terry Porter	.10	.06
178	Cliff Robinson	.12	.07
179	Buck Williams	.07	.04
180	Anthony Bonner	.04	.02
181	Antoine Carr	.04	.02
182	Duane Causwell	.04	.02
183	Bobby Hansen	.04	.02
184	Travis Mays	.04	.02
185	Lionel Simmons	.15	.10
186	Rory Sparrow	.04	.02
187	Wayman Tisdale	.07	.04
188	Willie Anderson	.04	.02
189	Terry Cummings	.07	.04
190	Sean Elliott	.15	.10
191	Sidney Green	.04	.02
192	David Greenwood	.04	.02
193	Paul Pressey	.04	.02
194	David Robinson	.50	.30
195	Dwayne Schintzius	.04	.02
196	Rod Strickland	.04	.02
197	Benoit Benjamin	.04	.02
198	Michael Cage	.04	.02
199	Eddie Johnson	.04	.02
200	Shawn Kemp	.75	.45
201	Derrick McKey	.07	.04
202	Gary Payton	.15	.10
203	Ricky Pierce	.04	.02
204	Sedale Threatt	.04	.02
205	Thurl Bailey	.04	.02
206	Mike Brown	.04	.02
207	Mark Eaton	.04	.02
208	Blue Edwards	.07	.04
209	Darrell Griffith	.04	.02
210	Jeff Malone	.07	.04
211	Karl Malone	.20	.12
212	John Stockton	.20	.12
213	Ledell Eackles	.04	.02
214	Pervis Ellison	.10	.06
215	A.J. English	.04	.02
216	Harvey Grant	.04	.02
217	Charles Jones	.04	.02
218	Bernard King	.07	.04
219	Darrell Walker	.04	.02
220	John Williams	.04	.02
221	Bob Weiss (C)	.04	.02
222	Chris Ford (C)	.04	.02
223	Gene Littles (C)	.04	.02
224	Phil Jackson (C)	.04	.02
225	Lenny Wilkens (C)	.04	.02
226	Richie Adubato (C)	.04	.02
227	Paul Westhead (C)	.04	.02
228	Chuck Daly (C)	.04	.02
229	Don Nelson (C)	.04	.02
230	Don Chaney (C)	.04	.02
231	Bob Hill (C)	.04	.02
232	Mike Schuler (C)	.04	.02
233	Mike Dunleavy (C)	.04	.02
234	Kevin Loughery (C)	.04	.02
235	Del Harris (C)	.04	.02
236	Jimmy Rodgers (C)	.04	.02
237	Bill Fitch (C)	.04	.02
238	Pat Riley (C)	.04	.02

1991-92 HOOPS • 89

#	Name		
239	Matt Guokas (C)	.04	.02
240	Jim Lynam (C)	.04	.02
241	Cotton Fitzsimmons (C)	.04	.02
242	Rick Adelman (C)	.04	.02
243	Dick Motta (C)	.04	.02
244	Larry Brown (C)	.04	.02
245	K.C. Jones (C)	.04	.02
246	Jerry Sloan (C)	.04	.02
247	Wes Unseld (C)	.04	.02
248	Charles Barkley (AS)	.25	.15
249	Brad Daugherty (AS)	.08	.05
250	Joe Dumars (AS)	.08	.05
251	Patrick Ewing (AS)	.20	.12
252	Hersey Hawkins (AS)	.07	.04
253	Michael Jordan (AS)	.75	.45
254	Bernard King (AS)	.07	.04
255	Kevin McHale (AS)	.07	.04
256	Robert Parish (AS)	.07	.04
257	Ricky Pierce (AS)	.04	.02
258	Alvin Robertson (AS)	.04	.02
259	Dominique Wilkins (AS)	.12	.07
260	Chris Ford (C)(AS)	.04	.02
261	Tom Chambers (AS)	.07	.04
262	Clyde Drexler (AS)	.12	.07
263	Kevin Duckworth (AS)	.04	.02
264	Tim Hardaway (AS)	.12	.07
265	Kevin Johnson (AS)	.10	.06
266	Magic Johnson (AS)	.30	.18
267	Karl Malone (AS)	.12	.07
268	Chris Mullen (AS)	.10	.06
269	Terry Porter (AS)	.07	.04
270	David Robinson (AS)	.25	.15
271	John Stockton (AS)	.12	.07
272	James Worthy (AS)	.07	.04
273	Rick Adelman (C)(AS)	.04	.02
274	Atlanta Hawks	.04	.02
275	Boston Celtics	.04	.02
276	Charlotte Hornets	.04	.02
277	Chicago Bulls	.04	.02
278	Cleveland Cavaliers	.04	.02
279	Dallas Mavericks	.04	.02
280	Denver Nuggets	.04	.02
281	Detroit Pistons	.04	.02
282	Gold State Warriors	.04	.02
283	Houston Rockets	.04	.02
284	Indiana Pacers	.04	.02
285	Los Angeles Clippers	.04	.02
286	Los Angeles Lakers	.04	.02
287	Miami Heat	.04	.02
288	Milwaukee Bucks	.04	.02
289	Minnesota Timberwolves	.04	.02
290	New Jersey Nets	.04	.02
291	New York Knicks	.04	.02
292	Orlando Magic	.04	.02
293	Philadelphia 76ers	.04	.02
294	Phoenix Suns	.04	.02
295	Portland Trail Blazers	.04	.02
296	Sacramento Kings	.04	.02
297	San Antonio Spurs	.04	.02
298	Seattle Supersonics	.04	.02
299	Utah Jazz	.04	.02
300	Washington Bullets	.04	.02
301	Centennial Card	.10	.06
302	Kevin Johnson (Stuff)	.08	.05
303	Reggie Miller (Stuff)	.12	.07
304	Hakeem Olajuwon (Stuff)	.25	.15
305	Robert Parish (Stuff)	.07	.04
306	Scoring Leaders	.60	.35
307	3-Point Leaders	.07	.04
308	Free Throw Leaders	.10	.06
309	Blocked Shots Leaders	.40	.25
310	Steals Leaders	.07	.04
311	Rebounds Leaders	.15	.10
312	Assists Leaders	.25	.15
313	Field Goal Leaders	.07	.04
314	Larry Bird (M)	.30	.18
315	A. English/M. Malone (M)	.10	.06
316	Magic Johnson (M)	.35	.20
317	Michael Jordan (M)	.75	.45
318	Moses Malone (M)	.08	.05
319	Larry Bird (YB)	.25	.15
320	Maurice Cheeks (YB)	.07	.04
321	Magic Johnson (YB)	.35	.20
322	Bernard King (YB)	.07	.04
323	Moses Malone (YB)	.08	.05
324	Robert Parish (YB)	.07	.04
325	All Star Jam (Message)	.04	.02
326	All Star Jam (Message)	.04	.02
327	David Robinson (Message)	.30	.18
328	Checklist	.04	.02
329	Checklist	.04	.02
330	Checklist	.04	.02
331	Maurice Cheeks	.04	.02
332	Duane Ferrell	.04	.02
333	Jon Koncak	.04	.02
334	Gary Leonard (R)	.07	.04
335	Travis Mays	.04	.02
336	Blair Rasmussen	.04	.02
337	Alexander Volkov	.04	.02
338	John Bagley	.04	.02
339	Rickey Green	.04	.02
340	Derek Smith	.04	.02
341	Stojko Vrankovic	.04	.02
342	Anthony Frederick (R)	.08	.05
343	Kenny Gattison	.07	.04
344	Eric Leckner	.04	.02
345	Will Perdue	.04	.02
346	Scott Williams (R)	.12	.07
347	John Battle	.04	.02
348	Winston Bennett	.04	.02
349	Henry James	.04	.02
350	Steve Kerr	.04	.02
351	John Morton	.04	.02
352	Terry Davis	.04	.02

90 • 1991-92 HOOPS

#	Player		
353	Randy White	.04	.02
354	Greg Anderson	.07	.04
355	Anthony Cook	.04	.02
356	Walter Davis	.04	.02
357	Winston Garland	.04	.02
358	Scott Hastings	.04	.02
359	Marcus Liberty (R)	.08	.05
360	William Bedford	.04	.02
361	Lance Blanks	.04	.02
362	Brad Sellers	.04	.02
363	Darrell Walker	.04	.02
364	Orlando Woolridge	.04	.02
365	Vincent Askew (R)	.10	.06
366	Mario Elie (R)	.12	.07
367	Jim Petersen	.04	.02
368	Matt Bullard (R)	.10	.06
369	Gerald Henderson	.04	.02
370	Dave Jamerson	.04	.02
371	Tree Rollins	.04	.02
372	Greg Dreiling	.04	.02
373	George McCloud	.04	.02
374	Kenny Williams	.04	.02
375	Randy Wittman	.04	.02
376	Tony Brown	.04	.02
377	Lanard Copeland	.04	.02
378	James Edwards	.04	.02
379	Bo Kimble	.04	.02
380	Doc Rivers	.07	.04
381	Loy Vaught (R)	.10	.06
382	Elden Campbell (R)	.15	.10
383	Jack Haley	.04	.02
384	Tony Smith	.04	.02
385	Sedale Threatt	.04	.02
386	Keith Askins (R)	.08	.05
387	Grant Long	.04	.02
388	Alan Ogg	.04	.02
389	Jon Sundvold	.04	.02
390	Lester Conner	.04	.02
391	Jeff Grayer	.04	.02
392	Steve Henson	.04	.02
393	Larry Krystkowiak	.04	.02
394	Moses Malone	.10	.06
395	Scott Brooks	.04	.02
396	Tellis Frank	.04	.02
397	Doug West	.07	.04
398	Rafael Addison (R)	.08	.05
399	Dave Feitl (R)	.08	.05
400	Tate George	.04	.02
401	Terry Mills (R)	.25	.15
402	Tim McCormick	.04	.02
503	Xavier McDaniel	.07	.04
404	Anthony Mason (R)	.40	.25
405	Brian Quinnett	.04	.02
406	John Starks (R)	.50	.30
407	Mark Acres	.04	.02
408	Greg Kite	.04	.02
409	Jeff Turner	.04	.02
410	Morlon Wiley	.04	.02
411	Dave Hoppen	.04	.02
412	Brian Oliver	.04	.02
413	Kenny Payne	.04	.02
414	Charles Shackleford	.04	.02
415	Mitchell Wiggins	.04	.02
416	Jayson Williams	.04	.02
417	Cedric Ceballos (R)	.15	.10
418	Negele Knight (R)	.12	.07
419	Andrew Lang	.04	.02
420	Jerrod Mustaf	.04	.02
421	Ed Nealy	.04	.02
422	Tim Perry	.04	.02
423	Alaa Abdelnaby	.08	.05
424	Wayne Cooper	.04	.02
425	Danny Young	.04	.02
426	Dennis Hopson	.04	.02
427	Les Jepsen	.04	.02
428	Jim Les (R)	.10	.06
429	Mitch Richmond	.12	.07
430	Dwayne Schintzius	.04	.02
431	Spud Webb	.04	.02
432	Jud Buechler	.04	.02
433	Antonie Carr	.04	.02
435	Sean Higgins (R)	.08	.05
436	Avery Johnson	.04	.02
437	Tony Massenburg	.04	.02
438	Dana Barros	.07	.04
439	Quintin Dailey	.04	.02
440	Bart Kofoed (R)	.07	.04
441	Nate McMillan	.04	.02
442	Delaney Rudd	.04	.02
443	Michael Adams	.07	.04
444	Mark Alarie	.04	.02
445	Greg Foster	.04	.02
446	Tom Hammonds	.04	.02
447	Andre Turner	.04	.02
448	David Wingate	.04	.02
449	Dominique Wilkins (SC)	.15	.10
450	Kevin Willis (SC)	.04	.02
451	Larry Bird (SC)	.25	.15
452	Robert Parish (SC)	.07	.04
453	Rex Chapman (SC)	.06	.03
454	Kendall Gill (SC)	.08	.05
455	Michael Jordan (SC)	.75	.45
456	Scottie Pippen (SC)	.15	.10
457	Brad Daugherty (SC)	.08	.05
468	Larry Nance (SC)	.06	.03
459	Rolando Blackman (SC)	.04	.02
460	Derek Harper (SC)	.04	.02
461	Chris Jackson (SC)	.08	.05
462	Todd Lichti (SC)	.04	.02
463	Joe Dumars (SC)	.07	.04
464	Isiah Thomas (SC)	.10	.06
465	Tim Hardaway (SC)	.15	.10
466	Chris Mullin (SC)	.10	.06
467	Hakeem Olajuwon (SC)	.25	.15

1991-92 HOOPS • 91

#	Name		
468	Otis Thorpe (SC)	.06	.03
469	Reggie Miller (SC)	.15	.10
470	Detlef Schrempf (SC)	.10	.06
471	Ron Harper (SC)	.04	.02
472	Charles Smith (SC)	.06	.03
473	Magic Johnson (SC)	.35	.20
474	James Worthy (SC)	.08	.05
475	Sherman Douglas (SC)	.06	.03
476	Rony Seikaly (SC)	.06	.03
477	Jay Humphries (SC)	.04	.02
478	Alvin Robertson (SC)	.04	.02
479	Tyrone Corbin (SC)	.04	.02
480	Pooh Richardson (SC)	.04	.02
481	Sam Bowie (SC)	.04	.02
482	Derrick Coleman (SC)	.20	.12
483	Patrick Ewing (SC)	.20	.12
484	Charles Oakley (SC)	.04	.02
485	Dennis Scott (SC)	.07	.04
486	Scott Skiles (SC)	.04	.02
487	Charles Barkley (SC)	.25	.15
488	Hersey Hawkins (SC)	.06	.03
489	Tom Chambers (SC)	.06	.03
490	Kevin Johnson (SC)	.08	.05
491	Clyde Drexler (SC)	.12	.07
492	Terry Porter (SC)	.06	.03
493	Lionel Simmons (SC)	.08	.05
494	Wayman Tisdale (SC)	.06	.03
495	Terry Cummings (SC)	.06	.03
496	David Robinson (SC)	.25	.15
497	Shawn Kemp (SC)	.30	.18
498	Ricky Pierce (SC)	.04	.02
499	Karl Malone (SC)	.12	.07
500	John Stockton (SC)	.12	.07
501	Harvey Grant (SC)	.04	.02
502	Bernard King (SC)	.06	.03
503	Travis Mays (SC)	.04	.02
504	Kevin McHale (Art)	.08	.05
505	Muggsy Bogues (Art)	.04	.02
506	Scottie Pippen (Art)	.15	.10
507	Brad Daugherty (Art)	.10	.06
508	Derek Harper (Art)	.04	.02
509	Chris Jackson (Art)	.08	.05
510	Isiah Thomas (Art)	.10	.06
511	Tim Hardaway (Art)	.15	.10
512	Otis Thorpe (Art)	.07	.04
513	Chuck Person (Art)	.06	.03
514	Ron Harper (Art)	.04	.02
515	James Worthy (Art)	.08	.05
516	Sherman Douglas (Art)	.06	.03
517	Dale Ellis (Art)	.04	.02
518	Tony Campbell (Art)	.04	.02
519	Derrick Coleman (Art)	.20	.12
520	Gerald Wilkins (Art)	.04	.02
521	Scott Skiles (Art)	.04	.02
522	Manute Bol (Art)	.04	.02
523	Tom Chambers (Art)	.07	.04
524	Terry Porter (Art)	.07	.04
525	Lionel Simmons (Art)	.08	.05
526	Sean Elliott (Art)	.10	.06
527	Shawn Kemp (Art)	.30	.18
528	John Stockton (Art)	.12	.07
529	Harvey Grant (Art)	.06	.03
530	Michael Adams (LL)	.07	.04
531	Charles Barkley (LL)	.25	.15
532	Larry Bird (LL)	.25	.15
533	Maurice Cheeks (LL)	.06	.03
534	Mark Eaton (LL)	.04	.02
535	Magic Johnson (LL)	.35	.20
536	Michael Jordan (LL)	.75	.45
537	Moses Malone (LL)	.08	.05
538	NBA Finals Game 1	.04	.02
539	NBA Finals Game 2	.04	.02
540	NBA Finals Game 3	.04	.02
541	NBA Finals Game 4	.04	.02
542	NBA Finals Game 5	.08	.05
543	Chicago Bulls Champs	.75	.45
544	Otis Smith (Message)	.04	.02
545	Jeff Turner (Message)	.04	.02
546	Larry Johnson (R)	2.50	1.50
547	Kenny Anderson (R)	.75	.45
548	Billy Owens (R)	.35	.20
549	Dikembe Mutombo (R)	1.00	.60
550	Steve Smith (R)	.75	.45
551	Doug Smith (R)	.12	.07
552	Luc Longley (R)	.08	.05
553	Mark Macon (R)	.12	.07
554	Stacey Augmon (R)	.40	.25
555	Brian Williams (R)	.20	.12
556	Terrell Brandon (R)	.15	.10
557	Walter Davis (USA)	.08	.05
558	Vern Fleming (USA)	.07	.04
559	Joe Kleine (USA)	.07	.04
560	Jon Koncak (USA)	.07	.04
561	Sam Perkins (USA)	.10	.06
562	Alvin Robertson (USA)	.08	.05
563	Wayman Tisdale (USA)	.08	.05
564	Jeff Turner (USA)	.07	.04
565	Willie Anderson (USA)	.07	.04
566	Stacey Augmon (USA)	.25	.15
567	Bimbo Coles (USA)	.08	.05
568	Jeff Grayer (USA)	.08	.05
569	Hersey Hawkins (USA)	.08	.05
570	Dan Majerle (USA)	.10	.06
571	Danny Manning (USA)	.12	.07
572	J.R. Reid (USA)	.07	.04
573	Mitch Richmond (USA)	.10	.06
574	Charles Smith (USA)	.08	.05
575	Charles Barkley (USA)	.80	.50
576	Larry Bird (USA)	1.00	.60
577	Patrick Ewing (USA)	.60	.35
578	Magic Johnson (USA)	1.00	.60
579	Michael Jordan (USA)	3.00	1.75
580	Karl Malone (USA)	.50	.30
581	Chris Mullin (USA)	.25	.15

92 • 1991-92 HOOPS

582	Scottie Pippen (USA)	.40	.25
583	David Robinson (USA)	.80	.50
584	John Stockton (USA)	.40	.25
585	Chuck Daley (USA)	.06	.03
586	Lenny Wilkens (USA)	.06	.03
587	P.J. Carlesimo (USA)	.10	.06
588	Mike Krzyzewski (USA)	.40	.25
589	Checklist	.04	.02
590	Checklist	.04	.02
___	Dr. Naismith (SP)	4.50	2.00
___	Centennial Card	.50	.25
___	USA Title Card	3.00	1.75
___	Head of the Class	20.00	12.50

1991-92 Hoops Slam Dunk Champs

The cards in this insert set were distributed in Hoops Series I rack packs. The set features previous winners of the NBA All-Star Weekend Slam Dunk Contest. The card fronts consist of full color action shots with the player's name printed at the top with a Slam Dunk Champs logo in the lower left corner. The backs contain personal data and a report on each player's dunking ability. All cards measure 2-1/2" by 3-1/2".

		MINT	NR/MT
	Complete Set (6)	12.50	7.50
	Commons	.30	.18
1	Larry Nance	.30	.18
2	Dominique Wilkins	2.00	1.25
3	Spud Webb	.50	.30
4	Michael Jordan	10.00	6.50
5	Kenny Walker	.30	.18
6	Dee Brown	.75	.45

1991-92 Hoops All-Stars MVP's

These insert cards were distributed in Hoops Series II rack packs and follow the numbers from the Slam Dunk Inserts. The cards in this set honor past All-Start MVP's. The card fronts show the winner holding his MVP trophy while the card backs contain an action shot of the player. All cards measure 2-1/2" by 3-1/2".

		MINT	NR/MT
	Complete Set (6)	18.00	12.50
	Commons	.25	.15
7	Isiah Thomas	1.25	.70
8	Tom Chambers	.25	.15
9	Michael Jordan	10.00	6.50

1992-93 HOOPS • 93

10	Karl Malone	2.00	1.25
11	Magic Johnson	4.00	2.50
12	Charles Barkley	3.50	2.00

1992-93 Hoops

The cards in this set were issued in two series. The fronts feature full color action photos framed by a white border. A color stripe reflecting one of the team colors is printed across the bottom of the photo while the player's name is printed vertically along the left side of the card. The horizontal card backs contain another small photo along with personal data, stats and hightlights. The main subsets included Coaches (C)(239-265), Team Cards (266-292), All-Stars (AS)(293-319), League Leaders (LL)(320-327), Magic Moments (328-331) Inside Stuff, Message Cards, Tournament of the Americas featuring Team USA Members (USA)(336-347) and Trivia Cards (481-485). The set also includes a number of random inserts which are listed at the end of this checklist. A Draft Redemption Card wich could be exchanged for a 10-card set of NBA Draft Lottery Picks was also randomly inserted into Hoops packs. That insert set is listed separately in this section. All cards measure 2-1/2" by 31/2".

		MINT	NR/MT
Complete Set (490)		48.00	28.00
Commons		.05	.02
1	Stacey Augmon	.15	.10
2	Maurice Cheeks	.07	.04
3	Duane Ferrell	.05	.02
4	Paul Graham	.05	.02
5	Jon Koncak	.05	.02
6	Blair Rasmussen	.05	.02
7	Rumeal Robinson	.05	.02
8	Dominique Wilkins	.20	.12
9	Kevin Willis	.07	.04
10	Larry Bird	.50	.30
11	Dee Brown	.10	.06
12	Sherman Douglas	.07	.04
13	Rick Fox	.10	.06
14	Kevin Gamble	.05	.02
15	Reggis Lewis	.10	.06
16	Kevin McHale	.10	.06
17	Robert Parish	.10	.06
18	Ed Pinckney	.05	.02
19	Muggsy Bogues	.05	.02
20	Dell Curry	.05	.02
21	Kenny Gattison	.05	.02
22	Kendall Gill	.12	.07
23	Mike Gminski	.05	.02
24	Larry Johnson	.75	.45
25	Johnny Newman	.05	.02
26	J.R. Reid	.05	.02
27	B.J. Armstrong	.12	.07
28	Bill Cartwright	.05	.02
29	Horace Grant	.08	.05
30	Michael Jordan	1.75	1.00
31	Stacey King	.07	.04
32	John Paxson	.07	.04
33	Will Perdue	.05	.02
34	Scottie Pippen	.25	.15
35	Scott Williams	.07	.04
36	John Battle	.05	.02
37	Terrell Brandon	.10	.06
38	Brad Daugherty	.10	.06
39	Craig Ehlo	.05	.02
40	Danny Ferry	.05	.02
41	Henry James	.05	.02
42	Larry Nance	.07	.04
43	Mark Price	.10	.06
44	Hot Rod Williams	.08	.05
45	Rolando Blackman	.07	.04
46	Terry Davis	.05	.02
47	Derek Harper	.07	.04
48	Mike Iuzzolino	.05	.02
49	Fat Lever	.05	.02
50	Rodney McCray	.05	.02
51	Doug Smith	.07	.04
52	Randy White	.05	.02

94 • 1992-93 HOOPS

#	Player		
53	Herb Williams	.05	.02
54	Greg Anderson	.07	.04
55	Winston Garland	.05	.02
56	Chris Jackson	.15	.10
57	Marcus Liberty	.07	.04
58	Todd Lichti	.05	.02
59	Mark Macon	.10	.06
60	Dikembe Mutombo	.25	.15
61	Reggie Williams	.05	.02
62	Mark Aguirre	.07	.04
63	William Bedford	.05	.02
64	Joe Dumars	.10	.06
65	Bill Laimbeer	.07	.04
66	Dennis Rodman	.10	.06
67	John Salley	.05	.02
68	Isiah Thomas	.15	.10
69	Darrell Walker	.05	.02
70	Orlando Woolridge	.05	.02
71	Victor Alexander	.05	.02
72	Mario Elie	.05	.02
73	Chris Gatling	.05	.02
74	Tim Hardaway	.20	.12
75	Tyrone Hill	.05	.02
76	Alton Lister	.05	.02
77	Sarunas Marciulionis	.07	.04
78	Chris Mullin	.15	.10
79	Billy Owens	.20	.12
80	Matt Bullard	.05	.02
81	Eric Floyd	.05	.02
82	Avery Johnson	.05	.02
83	Buck Johnson	.05	.02
84	Vernon Maxwell	.10	.06
85	Hakeem Olajuwon	.60	.35
86	Kenny Smith	.07	.04
87	Larry Smith	.05	.02
88	Otis Thorpe	.07	.04
89	Dale Davis	.08	.05
90	Vern Fleming	.05	.02
91	George McCloud	.05	.02
92	Reggie Miller	.15	.10
93	Chuck Person	.08	.05
94	Detlef Schrempf	.08	.05
95	Rik Smits	.05	.02
96	LaSalle Thompson	.05	.02
97	Michael Williams	.05	.02
98	James Edwards	.05	.02
99	Gary Grant	.05	.02
100	Ron Harper	.07	.04
101	Danny Manning	.15	.10
102	Ken Norman	.07	.04
103	Olden Polynice	.05	.02
104	Doc Rivers	.05	.02
105	Charles Smith	.08	.05
106	Loy Vaught	.05	.02
107	Elden Campbell	.08	.05
108	Vlade Divac	.08	.05
109	A.C. Green	.07	.04
110	Sam Perkins	.07	.04
111	Byron Scott	.05	.02
112	Tony Smith	.05	.02
113	Terry Teagle	.05	.02
114	Sedale Threatt	.05	.02
115	James Worthy	.10	.06
116	Willie Burton	.07	.04
117	Bimbo Coles	.05	.02
118	Kevin Edwards	.05	.02
119	Alec Kessler	.05	.02
120	Grant Long	.05	.02
121	Glen Rice	.10	.06
122	Rony Seikaly	.08	.05
123	Brian Shaw	.05	.02
124	Steve Smith	.20	.12
125	Frank Brickowski	.05	.02
126	Dale Ellis	.07	.04
127	Jeff Grayer	.05	.02
128	Jay Humphries	.05	.02
129	Larry Krystkowiak	.05	.02
130	Moses Malone	.10	.06
131	Fred Roberts	.05	.02
132	Alvin Robertson	.05	.02
133	Dan Schayes	.05	.02
134	Thurl Bailey	.05	.02
135	Scott Brooks	.05	.02
136	Tony Campbell	.05	.02
137	Gerald Glass	.05	.02
138	Luc Longley	.05	.02
139	Sam Mitchell	.05	.02
140	Pooh Richardson	.07	.04
141	Felton Spencer	.07	.04
142	Doug West	.07	.04
143	Rafael Addison	.05	.02
144	Kenny Anderson	.20	.12
145	Mookie Blaylock	.07	.04
146	Sam Bowie	.05	.02
147	Derrick Coleman	.20	.12
148	Chris Dudley	.05	.02
149	Terry Mills	.08	.05
150	Chris Morris	.05	.02
151	Drazen Petrovic	.12	.07
152	Greg Anthony	.12	.07
153	Patrick Ewing	.30	.18
154	Mark Jackson	.07	.04
155	Anthony Mason	.07	.04
156	Xavier McDaniel	.07	.04
157	Charles Oakley	.05	.02
158	John Starks	.20	.12
159	Gerald Wilkins	.05	.02
160	Nick Anderson	.15	.10
161	Terry Catledge	.05	.02
162	Jerry Reynolds	.05	.02
163	Stanley Roberts	.07	.04
164	Dennis Scott	.08	.05
165	Scott Skiles	.05	.02
166	Jeff Turner	.05	.02

1992-93 HOOPS • 95

#	Name		
167	Sam Vincent	.05	.02
168	Brian Williams	.07	.04
169	Ron Anderson	.05	.02
170	Charles Barkley	.40	.25
171	Manute Bol	.05	.02
172	Johnny Dawkins	.05	.02
173	Armon Gilliam	.05	.02
174	Hersey Hawkins	.08	.05
175	Brian Oliver	.05	.02
176	Charles Shackleford	.05	.02
177	Jayson Williams	.05	.02
178	Cedric Ceballos	.08	.05
179	Tom Chambers	.07	.04
180	Jeff Hornacek	.07	.04
181	Kevin Johnson	.12	.07
182	Negele Knight	.07	.04
183	Andrew Lang	.05	.02
184	Dan Majerle	.10	.06
185	Tim Perry	.05	.02
186	Mark West	.05	.02
187	Alaa Abdelnaby	.05	.02
188	Danny Ainge	.07	.04
189	Clyde Drexler	.20	.12
190	Kevin Duckworth	.07	.04
191	Jerome Kersey	.08	.05
192	Robert Pack	.07	.04
193	Terry Porter	.10	.06
194	Cliff Robinson	.10	.06
195	Buck Williams	.07	.04
196	Anthony Bonner	.05	.02
197	Duane Causwell	.05	.02
198	Pete Chilcutt	.05	.02
199	Dennis Hopson	.05	.02
200	Mitch Richmond	.08	.05
201	Lionel Simmons	.15	.10
202	Wayman Tisdale	.07	.04
203	Spud Webb	.05	.02
204	Willie Anderson	.05	.02
205	Antoine Carr	.05	.02
206	Terry Cummings	.07	.04
207	Sean Elliott	.12	.07
208	Sidney Green	.05	.02
209	David Robinson	.40	.25
210	Rod Strickland	.05	.02
211	Greg Sutton	.05	.02
212	Dana Barros	.07	.04
213	Benoit Benjamin	.05	.02
214	Michael Cage	.05	.02
214	Eddie Johnson	.05	.02
216	Shawn Kemp	.40	.25
217	Derrick McKey	.07	.04
218	Nate McMillan	.05	.02
219	Gary Payton	.10	.06
220	Ricky Pierce	.05	.02
221	David Benoit	.08	.05
222	Mike Brown	.05	.02
223	Tyrone Corbin	.05	.02
224	Mark Eaton	.05	.02
225	Blue Edwards	.07	.04
226	Jeff Malone	.07	.04
227	Karl Malone	.25	.15
228	Eric Murdock	.07	.04
229	John Stockton	.25	.15
230	Michael Adams	.07	.04
231	Rex Chapman	.07	.04
232	Ledell Eackles	.05	.02
233	Pervis Ellison	.07	.04
234	A.J. English	.05	.02
235	Harvey Grant	.05	.02
236	Charles Jones	.05	.02
237	LaBradford Smith	.05	.02
238	Larry Stewart	.05	.02
239	Bob Weiss (C)	.05	.02
240	Chris Ford (C)	.05	.02
241	Allan Bristow (C)	.05	.02
242	Phil Jackson (C)	.05	.02
243	Lenny Wilkens (C)	.05	.02
244	Richie Adubato (C)	.05	.02
245	Dan Issel (C)	.05	.02
246	Ron Rothstein (C)	.05	.02
247	Don Nelson (C)	.05	.02
248	Rudy Tomjanovich (C)	.05	.02
249	Bob Hill (C)	.05	.02
250	Larry Brown (C)	.05	.02
251	Randy Pfund (C)	.05	.02
252	Kevin Loughery (C)	.05	.02
253	Mike Dunleavy (C)	.05	.02
254	Jimmy Rodgers (C)	.05	.02
255	Chuck Daly (C)	.05	.02
256	Pat Riley (C)	.05	.02
257	Matt Guokas (C)	.05	.02
258	Doug Moe (C)	.05	.02
259	Paul Westphal (C)	.05	.02
260	Rick Adelman (C)	.05	.02
261	Garry St. Jean CO	.05	.02
262	Jerry Tarkanian (C)	.15	.10
263	George Karl (C)	.05	.02
264	Jerry Sloan (C)	.05	.02
265	Wes Unseld (C)	.05	.02
266	Atlanta Hawks	.05	.02
267	Boston Celtics	.05	.02
268	Charlotte Hornets	.05	.02
269	Chicago Bulls	.05	.02
270	Cleveland Cavaliers	.05	.02
271	Dallas Mavericks	.05	.02
272	Denver Nuggets	.05	.02
273	Detroit Pistons	.05	.02
274	Golden State Warriors	.05	.02
275	Houston Rockets	.05	.02
276	Indiana Pacers	.05	.02
277	Los Angeles Clippers	.05	.02
278	Los Angeles Lakers	.05	.02
279	Miami Heat	.05	.02
280	Milwaukee Bucks	.05	.02

#	Name	Price 1	Price 2
281	Minnesota Timberwolves	.05	.02
282	New Jersey Nets	.05	.02
283	New York Knicks	.05	.02
284	Orlando Magic	.05	.02
285	Philadelphia 76ers	.05	.02
286	Phoenix Suns	.05	.02
287	Portland Trail Blazers	.05	.02
288	Sacramento Kins	.05	.02
289	San Antonio Spurs	.05	.02
290	Seattle Supersonics	.05	.02
291	Utah Jazz	.05	.02
292	Washington Bullets	.05	.02
293	Michael Adams (AS)	.05	.02
294	Charles Barkley (AS)	.20	.12
295	Brad Daugherty (AS)	.07	.04
296	Joe Dumars (AS)	.07	.04
297	Patrick Ewing (AS)	.20	.12
298	Michael Jordan (AS)	.75	.45
299	Reggie Lewis (AS)	.07	.04
300	Scottie Pippen (AS)	.12	.07
301	Mark Price (AS)	.08	.05
302	Dennis Rodman (AS)	.07	.04
303	Isiah Thomas (AS)	.10	.06
304	Kevin Willis (AS)	.05	.02
305	Phil Jackson (C)(AS)	.05	.02
306	Clyde Drexler (AS)	.12	.07
307	Tim Hardaway (AS)	.10	.06
308	Jeff Hornacek (AS)	.07	.04
309	Magic Johnson (AS)	.25	.15
310	Dan Majerle (AS)	.07	.04
311	Karl Malone (AS)	.12	.07
312	Chris Mullin (AS)	.10	.06
313	Dikembe Mutombo (AS)	.12	.07
314	Hakeem Olajuwon (AS)	.30	.18
315	David Robinson (AS)	.20	.12
316	John Stockton (AS)	.12	.07
317	Otis Thorpe (AS)	.07	.04
318	James Worthy (AS)	.08	.05
319	Don Nelson (C)(AS)	.05	.02
320	Scoring Leaders	.50	.30
321	Three Point Percent (LL)	.07	.04
322	Free Throw Percent (LL)	.20	.12
323	Blocks Leaders	.25	.15
324	Steals Leaders	.10	.06
325	Rebounds Leaders	.08	.05
326	Assists Leaders	.12	.07
327	Field Goal Percent(LL)	.07	.04
328	Magic Moments 1980	.25	.15
329	Magic Moments 1985	.25	.15
330	Magic Moments '87,'88	.25	.15
331	Magic Numbers	.25	.15
332	Drazen Petrovic (Stuff)	.07	.04
333	Patrick Ewing (Stuff)	.20	.12
334	David Robinson (Message)	.20	.12
335	Kevin Johnson (Message)	.10	.06
336	Charles Barkley (USA)	.25	.15
337	Larry Bird (USA)	.30	.18
338	Clyde Drexler (USA)	.15	.10
339	Patrick Ewing (USA)	.20	.12
340	Magic Johnson (USA)	.30	.18
341	Michael Jordan (USA)	.75	.40
342	Christian Laettner(USA)	1.00	.60
343	Karl Malone (USA)	.15	.10
344	Chris Mullin (USA)	.10	.06
345	Scottie Pippen (USA)	.15	.10
346	David Robinson (USA)	.25	.15
347	John Stockton (USA)	.15	.10
348	Checklist	.05	.02
349	Checklist	.05	.02
350	Checklist	.05	.02
351	Mookie Blaylock	.08	.05
352	Adam Keefe (R)	.15	.10
353	Travis Mays	.05	.02
354	Morton Wiley	.05	.02
355	Joe Kleine	.05	.02
356	Bart Kofoed	.05	.02
357	Xavier McDaniel	.07	.04
358	Tony Bennett (R)	.10	.06
359	Tom Hammonds	.05	.02
360	Kevin Lynch	.05	.02
361	Alonzo Mourning (R)	6.00	3.50
362	Rodney McCray	.05	.02
363	Trent Tucker	.05	.02
364	Corey Williams (R)	.08	.05
365	Steve Kerr	.05	.02
366	Jerome Lane	.05	.02
367	Bobby Phills (R)	.15	.10
368	Mike Sanders	.05	.02
369	Gerald Wilkins	.05	.02
370	Donald Hodge	.07	.04
371	Brian Howard (R)	.10	.06
372	Tracy Moore (R)	.08	.05
373	Sean Rooks (R)	.30	.18
374	Kevin Brooks	.05	.02
375	LaPhonso Ellis	1.75	1.00
376	Scott Hastings	.05	.02
377	Robert Pack	.07	.04
378	Bryant Stith (R)	.60	.35
379	Robert Werdann (R)	.10	.06
380	Lance Blanks	.05	.02
381	Terry Mills	.10	.06
382	Isaiah Morris (R)	.10	.06
383	Olden Polynice	.05	.02
384	Brad Sellers	.05	.02
385	Jud Buechler	.05	.02
386	Jeff Grayer	.05	.02
387	Byron Houston (R)	.15	.10
388	Keith Jennings (R)	.15	.10
389	Latrell Sprewell (R)	3.50	2.00
390	Scott Brooks	.05	.02
391	Carl Herrera	.08	.05
392	Robert Horry (R)	1.50	.90

1992-93 HOOPS • 97

#	Player	Value1	Value2
393	Tree Rollins	.05	.02
394	Ken Winchester	.05	.02
395	Greg Dreiling	.05	.02
396	Sean Green	.05	.02
397	Sam Mitchell	.07	.04
398	Pooh Richardson	.07	.04
399	Malik Sealy (R)	.15	.10
400	Kenny Williams	.05	.02
401	Jaren Jackson (R)	.10	.06
402	Mark Jackson	.07	.04
403	Stanley Roberts	.07	.04
404	Elmore Spencer (R)	.25	.15
405	Kiki Vandeweghe	.05	.02
406	John Williams	.05	.02
407	Randy Woods (R)	.10	.06
408	Alex Blackwell	.05	.02
409	Duane Cooper (R)	.12	.07
410	Anthony Peeler (R)	.75	.45
411	Keith Askins	.05	.02
412	Matt Geiger (R)	.20	.12
413	Harold Miner (R)	1.00	.60
414	John Salley	.05	.02
415	Alaa Abdelnaby	.05	.02
416	Todd Day (R)	.75	.45
417	Blue Edwards	.07	.04
418	Brad Lohaus	.05	.02
419	Lee Mayberry (R)	.20	.12
420	Eric Murdock	.08	.05
421	Christian Laettner (R)	1.00	.60
422	Bob McCann (R)	.08	.05
423	Chuck Person	.07	.04
424	Chris Smith (R)	.15	.10
425	Gundars Vetra (R)	.10	.06
426	Michael Williams	.05	.02
427	Chucky Brown	.05	.02
428	Tate George	.05	.02
429	Rick Mahorn	.05	.02
430	Rumeal Robinson	.05	.02
431	Jayson Williams	.05	.02
432	Eric Anderson (R)	.10	.06
433	Rolando Blackman	.07	.04
434	Tony Campbell	.05	.02
435	Hubert Davis (R)	.60	.35
436	Bo Kimble	.05	.02
437	Doc Rivers	.05	.02
438	Charles Smith	.08	.05
439	Anthony Bowie	.05	.02
440	Litterial Green (R)	.20	.12
441	Greg Kite	.05	.02
442	Shaquille O'Neal (R)	12.00	7.00
443	Donald Royal	.05	.02
444	Greg Grant	.05	.02
445	Jeff Hornacek	.07	.04
446	Andrew Lang	.05	.02
447	Kenny Payne	.05	.02
448	Tim Perry	.05	.02
449	C. Weatherspoon (R)	1.25	.70
450	Danny Ainge	.07	.04
451	Charles Barkley	.80	.50
452	Tim Kempton	.07	.04
453	Oliver Miller (R)	.80	.50
454	Mark Bryant	.05	.02
455	Mario Elie	.05	.02
456	Dave Jamerson (R)	.10	.06
457	Tracy Murray (R)	.20	.12
458	Rod Strickland	.05	.02
459	Vincent Askew	.05	.02
460	Randy Brown	.07	.04
461	Marty Conlon	.07	.04
462	Jim Les	.05	.02
463	Walt Williams (R)	1.00	.60
464	William Bedford	.05	.02
465	Lloyd Daniels (R)	.25	.15
466	Vinny Del Negro	.07	.04
467	Dale Ellis	.07	.04
468	Larry Smith	.05	.02
469	David Wood	.05	.02
470	Rich King	.05	.02
471	Isaac Austin (R)	.10	.06
472	John Crotty (R)	.10	.06
473	Stephen Howard (R)	.08	.05
474	Jay Humphries	.05	.02
475	Larry Krystowiak	.05	.02
476	Tom Gugliotta (R)	1.50	.90
477	Buck Johnson	.05	.02
478	Don MacLean (R)	.60	.35
479	Doug Overton	.07	.04
480	Brent Price (R)	.20	.12
481	David Robinson (Trivia)	.50	.30
482	Magic Johnson (Trivia)	.50	.30
483	John Stockton (Trivia)	.15	.10
484	Patrick Ewing (Trivia)	.20	.12
485	Trivia Answers	.25	.15
486	John Stockton (Message)	.15	.10
487	Inside Stuff	.05	.02
488	Rookie Checklist	.10	.02
489	Checklist	.05	.02
490	Checklist	.05	.02
__	Chicago Bulls Champs	2.00	1.25
__	USA Team Card	2.50	1.50
__	Olympic Archer Card	35.00	20.00
__	Magic Commemorative	2.50	1.50
__	Magic (Autographed)	250.00	125.00
__	Patrick Ewing Art Card	1.50	.90
__	Patrick Ewing Game	1.50	.90
__	Ewing (Autographed)	150.00	75.00
__	John Stockton Game	3.00	1.75
__	John Stockton Game (Autographed)	100.00	50.00

98 • 1992-93 HOOPS DRAFT REDEMPTION

1992-93 Hoops Draft Redemption

The cards in this set were available by mail with the draft redemption card that was inserted randomly into 1992-93 Hoops basketball packs. The card fronts feature full color close-up photos of the top lottery picks from the 1992 NBA draft with the number of their draft position located in the top corner of the card front. The player's name is printed in a horizontal stripe below the photograph. All cards measure 2-1/2" by 3-1/2".

		MINT	NR/MT
	Complete Set (10)	175.00	100.00
	Commons	2.00	1.25
A	Shaquille O'Neal	75.00	45.00
B	Alonzo Mourning	40.00	25.00
C	Christian Laettner	7.00	4.00
D	LaPhonso Ellis	12.00	7.00
E	Tom Gugliotta	7.00	4.00
F	Walt Williams	5.00	3.00
G	Todd Day	4.00	2.50
H	C. Weatherspoon	7.00	4.00
I	Adam Keefe	2.00	1.25
J	Robert Horry	10.00	6.00

1992-93 Hoops Magic's Rookie Team

The cards in this limited insert set were random inserts in 1992-93 Hoops Series II packs. The card fronts feature full color action photos with the player's name printed vertically in a color bar along the left border in gold foil stamping. A Magic's Rookie Team Logo appears in the lower left corner. The flip side contains personal data and Magic's comments about each prospect. All cards measure 2-1/2" by 3-1/2".

		MINT	NR/MT
	Complete Set (10)	365.00	220.00
	Commons	12.00	7.50
1	Shaquille O'Neal	150.00	90.00
2	Alonzo Mourning	80.00	50.00
3	Christian Laettner	18.00	12.00
4	LaPhonso Ellis	25.00	15.00
5	Tom Gugliotta	18.00	12.00
6	Walt Williams	12.00	7.50
7	Todd Day	12.00	7.50
8	C. Weatherspoon	20.00	12.50
9	Robert Horry	20.00	12.50
10	Harold Miner	14.00	9.00
MM1	Magic Moments (Training Camp)	12.00	7.50
MM2	Magic Moments (L.A. vs 76er's)	12.00	7.50
MM3	Magic Moments (Last Game)	12.00	7.50

1992-93 Hoops Supreme Court

These limited inserts were distributed randomly in 1992-93 Hoops Sries II packs. The card fronts feature full color action photos with the player's name stamped in gold vertically along the left border. A Supreme Court logo appears in the lower left corner and the words "The Fans Choice" appears in a color bar under the photo. The flip side contains another player photo and comments about the player. All cards measure 2-1/2" by 3-1/2".

		MINT	NR/MT
Complete Set (10)		24.00	15.00
Commons		1.00	.60
1	Michael Jordan	10.00	6.50
2	Scottie Pippen	2.50	1.50
3	David Robinson	4.00	2.50
4	Patrick Ewing	3.50	2.00
5	Clyde Drexler	1.50	.90
6	Karl Malone	1.75	1.00
7	Charles Barkley	4.00	2.50
8	John Stockton	1.75	1.00
9	Chris Mullin	1.00	.60
10	Magic Johnson	4.00	2.50

1993-94 Hoops

The cards in this set were issued in two series, 300-cards in Series I and 121-cards in Series II. The fronts feature full-bleed, full-color game action photos with the player's name printed in a horizontal stripe across the bottom of the card in a color that corresponds to his dominate team color. A team logo appears in the lower left corner. The card backs contain a small head shot, personal data, stats and a highlight. Key subsets include Coaches (230-256), All-Stars (257-282), League Leaders (283-290) and Tribute cards (292-297). One card in each pack contained a special foil stamped Hoops Fifth Anniversary logo. These cards are valued at 1-1/4 to 3-1/2 times the value of the regular cards listed below. David Robinson was honored with a special 5-card limited series. Those cards were randomly packed in Series I foil packs. Those cards are listed at the end of this checklist but are not included in the complete set price below. Special commemorative cards featuring Robinson and Magic Johnson with Larry Bird were also random inserts, including autographed versions. Those cards are also listed following this checklist. All cards measure 2-1/2" by 3-1/2".

	MINT	NR/MT
Complete Set (421)	20.00	12.50
Commons	.05	.02

1993-94 HOOPS

#	Player		
1	Stacey Augmon	.12	.07
2	Mookie Blaylock	.10	.06
3	Duane Ferrell	.05	.02
4	Paul Graham	.05	.02
5	Adam Keefe	.07	.04
6	Blair Rasmussen	.05	.02
7	Dominique Wilkins	.25	.15
8	Kevin Willis	.05	.02
9	Alaa Abdelnaby	.05	.02
10	Dee Brown	.10	.06
11	Sherman Douglas	.07	.04
12	Rick Fox	.10	.06
13	Kevin Gamble	.05	.02
14	Joe Kleine	.05	.02
15	Xavier McDaniel	.05	.02
16	Robert Parish	.12	.07
17	Tony Bennett	.05	.02
18	Muggsy Bogues	.05	.02
19	Dell Curry	.05	.02
20	Kenny Gattison	.05	.02
21	Kendall Gill	.12	.07
22	Larry Johnson	.35	.20
23	Alonzo Mourning	1.00	.60
24	Johnny Newman	.05	.02
25	B.J. Armstrong	.12	.07
26	Bill Cartwright	.05	.02
27	Horace Grant	.10	.06
28	Michael Jordan	1.50	.90
29	Stacey King	.05	.02
30	John Paxson	.07	.04
31	Will Perdue	.05	.02
32	Scottie Pippen	.25	.15
33	Scott Williams	.05	.02
34	Moses Malone	.10	.06
35	John Battle	.05	.02
36	Terrell Brandon	.07	.04
37	Brad Daugherty	.12	.07
38	Craig Ehlo	.05	.02
39	Danny Ferry	.05	.02
40	Larry Nance	.05	.02
41	Mark Price	.10	.06
42	Gerald Wilkins	.05	.02
43	John Williams (Cle)	.08	.05
44	Terry Davis	.05	.02
45	Derek Harper	.07	.04
46	Donald Hodge	.05	.02
47	Mike Iuzzolino	.05	.02
48	Jim Jackson	.30	.18
49	Sean Rooks	.08	.05
50	Doug Smith	.05	.02
51	Randy White	.05	.02
52	Mahmoud Abdul-Rauf	.12	.07
53	LaPhonso Ellis	.20	.12
54	Marcus Liberty	.05	.02
55	Mark Macon	.08	.05
56	Dikembe Mutombo	.30	.18
57	Robert Pack	.05	.02
58	Bryant Stith	.10	.06
59	Reggie Williams	.05	.02
60	Mark Aquirre	.07	.04
61	Joe Dumars	.12	.07
62	Bill Laimbeer	.05	.02
63	Terry Mills	.05	.02
64	Olden Polynice	.05	.02
65	Alvin Robertson	.05	.02
66	Dennis Rodman	.10	.06
67	Isiah Thomas	.15	.10
68	Victor Alexander	.05	.02
69	Tim Hardaway	.15	.10
70	Tyrone Hill	.05	.02
71	Byron Houston	.10	.06
72	Sarunas Marciulionis	.07	.04
73	Chris Mullin	.15	.10
74	Billy Owens	.15	.10
75	Latrell Sprewell	.75	.45
76	Scott Brooks	.05	.02
77	Matt Bullard	.05	.02
78	Carl Herrera	.12	.07
79	Robert Horry	.30	.18
80	Vernon Maxwell	.12	.07
81	Hakeem Olajuwon	.75	.45
82	Kenny Smith	.07	.04
83	Otis Thorpe	.07	.04
84	Dale Davis	.08	.05
85	Vern Fleming	.05	.02
86	George McCloud	.05	.02
87	Reggie Miller	.20	.12
88	Sam Mitchell	.05	.02
89	Pooh Richardson	.05	.02
90	Detlef Schrempf	.12	.07
91	Malik Sealy	.10	.06
92	Rik Smits	.05	.02
93	Gary Grant	.05	.02
94	Ron Harper	.07	.04
95	Mark Jackson	.10	.06
96	Danny Manning	.15	.10
97	Ken Norman	.05	.02
98	Stanley Roberts	.05	.02
99	Elmore Spencer	.10	.06
100	Loy Vaught	.05	.02
101	John Williams	.05	.02
102	Randy Woods	.05	.02
103	Benoit Benjamin	.05	.02
104	Elden Campbell	.10	.06
105	Doug Christie	.20	.12
106	Vlade Divac	.10	.06
107	Anthony Peeler	.20	.12
108	Tony Smith	.05	.02
109	Sedale Threatt	.05	.02
110	James Worthy	.10	.06
111	Bimbo Coles	.05	.02
112	Grant Long	.05	.02
113	Harold Miner	.15	.10
114	Glen Rice	.10	.06

1993-94 HOOPS • 101

#	Name		
115	John Salley	.05	.02
116	Rony Seikaly	.08	.05
117	Brian Shaw	.05	.02
118	Steve Smith	.15	.10
119	Anthony Avent	.10	.06
120	Jon Barry	.10	.06
121	Frank Brickowski	.05	.02
122	Todd Day	.15	.10
123	Blue Edwards	.05	.02
124	Brad Lohaus	.05	.02
125	Lee Mayberry	.08	.05
126	Eric Murdock	.07	.04
127	Derek Strong (R)	.12	.07
128	Thurl Bailey	.05	.02
129	Christian Laettner	.25	.15
130	Luc Longley	.05	.02
131	Marlon Maxey	.05	.02
132	Chuck Person	.08	.05
133	Chris Smith	.07	.04
134	Doug West	.08	.05
135	Michael Williams	.05	.02
136	Rafael Addison	.05	.02
137	Kenny Anderson	.20	.12
138	Sam Bowie	.05	.02
139	Chucky Brown	.05	.02
140	Derrick Coleman	.20	.12
141	Chris Morris	.05	.02
142	Rumeal Robinson	.05	.02
143	Greg Anthony	.08	.05
144	Rolando Blackman	.05	.02
145	Hubert Davis	.12	.07
146	Patrick Ewing	.35	.20
147	Anthony Mason	.10	.06
148	Charles Oakley	.10	.06
149	Doc Rivers	.07	.04
150	Charles Smith	.07	.04
151	John Starks	.12	.07
152	Nick Anderson	.12	.07
153	Anthony Bowie	.05	.02
154	Latterial Green	.05	.02
155	Shaquille O'Neal	1.50	.90
156	Donald Royal	.05	.02
157	Dennis Scott	.08	.05
158	Scott Skiles	.05	.02
159	Tom Tolbert	.05	.02
160	Jeff Turner	.05	.02
161	Ron Anderson	.05	.02
162	Johnny Dawkins	.05	.02
163	Hersey Hawkins	.08	.05
164	Jeff Hornacek	.08	.05
165	Andrew Lang	.05	.02
166	Tim Perry	.05	.02
167	Clarence Weatherspoon	.15	.10
168	Danny Ainge	.10	.06
169	Charles Barkley	.50	.30
170	Cedric Ceballos	.08	.05
171	Richard Dumas	.10	.06
172	Kevin Johnson	.12	.07
173	Dan Majerle	.10	.06
174	Oliver Miller	.12	.07
175	Mark West	.05	.02
176	Clyde Drexler	.20	.12
177	Kevin Duckworth	.05	.02
178	Mario Elie	.05	.02
179	Dave Johnson	.05	.02
180	Jerome Kersey	.05	.02
181	Tracy Murray	.10	.06
182	Terry Porter	.10	.06
183	Cliff Robinson	.10	.06
184	Rod Strickland	.05	.02
185	Buck Williams	.07	.04
186	Anthony Bonner	.05	.02
187	Randy Brown	.05	.02
188	Duane Causwell	.05	.02
189	Pete Chilcutt	.05	.02
190	Mitch Richmond	.12	.07
191	Lionel Simmons	.15	.10
192	Wayman Tisdale	.07	.04
193	Spud Webb	.05	.02
194	Walt Williams	.15	.10
195	Willie Anderson	.05	.02
196	Antoine Carr	.05	.02
197	Terry Cummings	.07	.04
198	Lloyd Daniels	.07	.04
199	Sean Elliott	.12	.07
200	Dale Ellis	.07	.04
201	Avery Johnson	.05	.02
202	J.R. Reid	.05	.02
203	David Robinson	.40	.25
204	Dana Barros	.05	.02
205	Michael Cage	.05	.02
206	Eddie Johnson	.05	.02
207	Shawn Kemp	.30	.18
208	Derrick McKey	.07	.04
209	Nate McMillan	.05	.02
210	Gary Payton	.12	.07
211	Sam Perkins	.07	.04
212	Ricky Pierce	.05	.02
213	David Benoit	.05	.02
214	Tyrone Corbin	.05	.02
215	Mark Eaton	.05	.02
216	Jay Humphries	.05	.02
217	Jeff Malone	.07	.04
218	Karl Malone	.25	.15
219	John Stockton	.25	.15
220	Michael Adams	.07	.04
221	Rex Chapman	.08	.05
222	Pervis Ellison	.10	.06
223	Harvey Grant	.05	.02
224	Tom Gugliotta	.20	.12
225	Don MacLean	.15	.10
226	Doug Overton	.05	.02
227	Brent Price	.07	.04
228	LaBradford Smith	.05	.02

#	Name		
229	Larry Stewart	.05	.02
230	Lenny Wilkens (C)	.05	.02
231	Chris Ford (C)	.05	.02
232	Allan Bristow (C)	.05	.02
233	Phil Jackson (C)	.07	.04
234	Mike Fratello (C)	.05	.02
235	Quinn Buckner (C)	.05	.02
236	Dan Issel (C)	.08	.05
237	Don Chaney (C)	.05	.02
238	Don Nelson (C)	.05	.02
239	Rudy Tomjanovich (C)	.05	.02
240	Larry Brown (C)	.05	.02
241	Bob Weiss (C)	.05	.02
242	Randy Pfund (C)	.05	.02
243	Kevin Loughery (C)	.05	.02
244	Mike Dunleavy (C)	.05	.02
245	Sidney Lowe (C)	.05	.02
246	Chuck Daly (C)	.05	.02
247	Pat Riley (C)	.08	.05
248	Brian Hill (C)	.05	.02
249	Fred Carter (C)	.05	.02
250	Paul Westphal (C)	.05	.02
251	Rick Adelman (C)	.05	.02
252	Garry St. Jean (C)	.05	.02
253	John Lucas (C)	.05	.02
254	George Karl (C)	.05	.02
255	Jerry Sloan (C)	.05	.02
256	Wes Unseld (C)	.05	.02
257	Michael Jordan (AS)	.75	.45
258	Isiah Thomas (AS)	.10	.06
259	Scottie Pippen (AS)	.12	.07
260	Larry Johnson (AS)	.15	.10
261	Dominique Wilkins (AS)	.12	.07
262	Joe Dumars (AS)	.08	.05
263	Mark Price (AS)	.08	.05
264	Shaquille O'Neal (AS)	.60	.35
265	Patrick Ewing (AS)	.15	.10
266	Larry Nance (AS)	.05	.02
267	Detlef Schrempf (AS)	.07	.04
268	Brad Daugherty (AS)	.08	.05
269	Charles Barkley (AS)	.25	.15
270	Clyde Drexler (AS)	.12	.07
271	Sean Elliott (AS)	.07	.04
272	Tim Hardaway (AS)	.08	.05
273	Shawn Kemp (AS)	.15	.10
274	Dan Majerle (AS)	.07	.04
275	Karl Malone (AS)	.15	.10
276	Danny Manning (AS)	.10	.06
277	Hakeem Olajuwon (AS)	.40	.25
278	Terry Porter (AS)	.07	.04
279	David Robinson (AS)	.20	.12
280	John Stockton (AS)	.15	.10
281	East Team (AS)	.10	.06
282	West Team (AS)	.08	.05
283	Scoring Leaders (Jordan/Malone Wilkins)	.40	.25
284	Rebound Leaders (Mutombo/O'Neal Rodman)	.25	.15
285	Field Goal Percent (Ceballos)	.07	.04
286	Assist Leaders (Stockton)	.10	.06
287	Free Throw Leaders (L. Johnson/M. Price)	.12	.07
288	Three-Point Leaders (B.J. Armstrong)	.07	.04
289	Steals Leaders (Jordan/Blaylock/Stockton)	.30	.18
290	Blocked Shots Leaders (Olajuwon/O'Neal Mutombo)	.40	.25
291	Hoops Tribute (David Robinson)	.20	.12
292	Hoops Tribute	.05	.02
293	Hoops Tribute (Scottie Pippen)	.12	.07
294	Hoops Tribute	.05	.02
295	Hoops Tribute (Charles Barkley)	.20	.12
296	Hoops Tribute	.05	.02
297	Hoops Tribute	.05	.02
298	Checklist	.05	.02
299	Checklist	.05	.02
300	Checklist	.05	.02
301	Craig Ehlo	.05	.02
302	Jon Koncak	.05	.02
303	Andrew Lang	.05	.02
304	Chris Corchiani	.05	.02
305	Acie Earl (R)	.12	.07
306	Dino Radja (R)	.25	.15
307	Scott Burrell (R)	.12	.07
308	Hersey Hawkins	.07	.04
309	Eddie Johnson	.05	.02
310	David Wingate	.05	.02
311	Corie Blount (R)	.10	.06
312	Steve Kerr	.05	.02
313	Toni Kukoc (R)	.35	.20
314	Pete Myers	.05	.02
315	Jay Guidinger	.05	.02
316	Tyrone Hill	.05	.02
317	Gerald Madkins (R)	.10	.06
318	Chris Mills (R)	.20	.12
319	Bobby Phills	.10	.06
320	Lucious Harris (R)	.10	.06
321	Popeye Jones (R)	.12	.07
322	Fat Lever	.05	.02
323	Jamal Mashburn (R)	.80	.50
324	Darren Morningstar (R)	.08	.05
325	Kevin Brooks	.05	.02
326	Tom Hammonds	.05	.02
327	Darnell Mee (R)	.10	.06
328	Rodney Rogers (R)	.25	.15

1993-94 HOOPS • 103

#	Player	Price 1	Price 2
329	Brian Williams	.10	.06
330	Greg Anderson	.05	.02
331	Sean Elliott	.10	.06
332	Allan Houston (R)	.15	.10
333	Lindsey Hunter (R)	.25	.15
334	David Wood	.05	.02
335	Jud Buechler	.05	.02
336	Chris Gatling	.05	.02
337	Josh Grant (R)	.12	.07
338	Jeff Grayer	.05	.02
339	Keith Jennings	.05	.02
340	Avery Johnson	.05	.02
341	Chris Webber (R)	3.00	1.75
342	Sam Cassell (R)	.60	.35
343	Mario Elie	.05	.02
344	Eric Riley (R)	.10	.06
345	Antonio Davis (R)	.15	.10
346	Scott Haskin (R)	.10	.06
347	Gerald Paddio	.05	.02
348	LaSalle Thompson	.05	.02
349	Ken Williams	.05	.02
350	Mark Aquirre	.07	.04
351	Terry Dehere (R)	.12	.07
352	Henry James	.05	.02
353	Sam Bowie	.05	.02
354	George Lynch (R)	.30	.18
355	Kurt Rambis	.05	.02
356	Nick Van Exel (R)	.40	.25
357	Trevor Wilson	.10	.06
358	Keith Askins	.05	.02
359	Manute Bol	.05	.02
360	Willie Burton	.07	.04
361	Matt Geiger	.05	.02
362	Alec Kessler	.05	.02
363	Vin Baker (R)	.60	.35
364	Ken Norman	.05	.02
365	Dan Schayes	.05	.02
366	Mike Brown	.05	.02
367	Isaiah Rider (R)	.80	.50
368	Benoit Benjamin	.05	.02
369	P.J. Brown (R)	.12	.07
370	Kevin Edwards	.05	.02
371	Armon Gilliam	.07	.04
372	Rick Mahorn	.05	.02
373	Dwayne Schintzius	.05	.02
374	Rex Walters (R)	.12	.07
375	Jayson Williams	.05	.02
376	Eric Anderson	.05	.02
377	Anthony Bonner	.05	.02
378	Tony Campbell	.05	.02
379	Herb Williams	.05	.02
380	Anfernee Hardaway (R) 1.50		2.50
381	Greg Kite	.05	.02
382	Larry Krystkowiak	.05	.02
383	Todd Lichti	.05	.02
384	Dana Barros	.05	.02
385	Shawn Bradley (R)	.30	.18
386	Greg Graham (R)	.10	.06
387	Warren Kidd (R)	.08	.05
388	Eric Leckner	.05	.02
389	Moses Malone	.10	.06
390	A.C. Green	.08	.05
391	Frank Johnson	.05	.02
392	Joe Kleine	.05	.02
393	Malcolm Mackey (R)	.10	.06
394	Jerrod Mustaf	.05	.02
395	Mark Bryant	.05	.02
396	Chris Dudley	.05	.02
397	Harvey Grant	.05	.02
398	James Robinson (R)	.12	.07
399	Reggie Smith	.05	.02
400	Randy Brown	.05	.02
401	Bobby Hurley (R)	.25	.15
402	Jim Les	.05	.02
403	Vinny Del Negro	.05	.02
404	Sleepy Floyd	.05	.02
405	Dennis Rodman	.08	.05
406	Chris Whitney (R)	.08	.05
407	Vincent Askew	.05	.02
408	Kendall Gill	.10	.06
409	Ervin Johnson (R)	.10	.06
410	Rich King	.05	.02
411	Detlef Schrempf	.10	.06
412	Tom Chambers	.07	.04
413	John Crotty	.07	.04
414	Felton Spencer	.12	.07
415	Luther Wright (R)	.12	.07
416	Calbert Cheaney (R)	.30	.18
417	Kevin Duckworth	.05	.02
418	Gheorghe Muresan (R)	.10	.06
419	Checklist		
420	Checklist		
421	Checklist		
___	David Robinson Best (1-5) ea.	.60	.35
___	David Robinson Commemorative	.60	.35
___	David Robinson (Autographed)	150.00	90.00
___	Magic/Bird Commemorative	.75	.45
___	Magic/Bird (Autographed)	350.00	200.00

1993-94 Hoops Admiral's Choice

The cards in this limited insert set were available randomly in Hoops Series II packs. The cards feature full-bleed, full-color player photos with an Admiral's Choice logo printed in the lower corner. The player's name is located across the top of the card. The player's in the set were selected by All-Star center David Robinson and his comments about heach player appear on the card backs. All cards measure 2-1/2" by 3-1/2".

		MINT	NR/MT
	Complete Set (5)	6.00	3.75
	Commons	.30	.20
1	Shawn Kemp	1.00	.60
2	Derrick Coleman	.40	.25
3	Kenny Anderson	.30	.18
4	Shaquille O'Neal	3.00	1.75
5	Chris Webber	2.50	1.50

1993-94 Hoops Face To Face

These limited insert cards feature a full-bleed design and full-color action photos of player's on both sides of the card. A Face-To-Face logo appears in the lower corner of each side while the player's name is centered at the bottom of the card. The cards were randomly distributed in Hoops Series I packs and measure 2-1/2" by 3-1/2".

		MINT	NR/MT
	Complete Set (12)	38.00	24.00
	Commons	1.50	.90
1	Shaquille O'Neal/ David Robinson	10.00	6.50
2	Alonzo Mourning/ Patrick Ewing	6.00	3.50
3	Christian Laettner/ Shawn Kemp	3.00	1.75
4	Jim Jackson/ Clyde Drexler	2.00	1.25
5	LaPhonso Ellis/ Larry Johnson	3.00	1.75
6	Tom Gugliotta/ Karl Malone	3.00	1.75
7	Walt Williams/ Magic Johnson	4.00	2.50
8	Todd Day/ Chris Mullin	1.50	.90
9	C. Weatherspoon/	3.50	2.00

1993-94 HOOPS SUPREME COURT • 105

	Charles Barkley		
10	Robert Horry/	2.50	1.50
	Scottie Pippen		
11	Harold Miner/	12.00	7.50
	Michael Jordan		
12	Richard Dumas/	2.00	1.25
	Dominique Wilkins		

3	Anfernee Hardaway	20.00	12.50
4	Jamal Mashburn	12.00	7.00
5	Isaiah Rider	12.00	7.00
6	Clabert Cheaney	5.00	3.00
7	Bobby Hurley	4.00	2.50
8	Vin Baker	7.50	4.50
9	Lindsay Hunter	3.50	2.00
10	Toni Kukoc	5.00	3.00

1993-94 Hoops Magic's All-Rookies

These random insert cards were distributed in Hoops Series II foil packs and feature some of the NBA's top rookies as selected by Magic Johnson. The card fronts consist of full-bleed, full-color player photos with the player's name printed in a horizontal stripe across the bottom of the card. A Magic's All-Rookie logo appears as part of a small basketball graphic in the lower corner of the card front. All cards measure 2-1/2" by 3-1/2".

	MINT	NR/MT
Complete Set (10)	90.00	55.00
Commons	3.50	2.00

| 1 | Chris Webber | 25.00 | 15.00 |
| 2 | Shawn Bradley | 4.00 | 2.50 |

1993-94 Hoops Supreme Court

The limited inserts in this 11-card set were selected by a vote of the hobby media and were randomly distributed in Hoops Series II foil packs. The cards feature an isolated full-color action shot on the card front over a split background. The player's name is printed across the top of the card while a Supreme Court logo is located in the lower corner. Card numbers contain the prefix SC and all cards measure 2-1/2" by 3-1/2".

	MINT	NR/MT
Complete Set (11)	16.00	10.00
Commons	1.00	.60

| 1 | Charles Barkley | 1.50 | .90 |
| 2 | David Robinson | 1.50 | .90 |

106 • 1993-94 HOOPS SUPREME COURT

		MINT	NR/MT
3	Patrick Ewing	1.25	.70
4	Shaquille O'Neal	4.00	2.50
5	Larry Johnson	1.50	.90
6	Karl Malone	1.25	.70
7	Alonzo Mourning	2.50	1.50
8	John Stockton	1.00	.60
9	Hakeem Olajuwon	3.00	1.75
10	Scottie Pippen	1.00	.60
11	Michael Jordan	5.00	3.00

1993-94 Hoops Hoops Scoops

The cards in this 28-card subset were originally meant to be part of the Hoops regular edition (#422-#450). However they were mistakenly numbered 1-28 with an HS prefix next to the number. The error was never corrected. The cards appeared with the same frequency as other regular edition cards in Hoops Series II and should not be considered limited insert cards. The card fronts feature a Hoops Scoops logo in the top corner while the player's name and team are printed in a color bar under the photograph. All cards measure 2-1/2" by 3-1/2".

		MINT	NR/MT
Complete Set (28)		1.00	.60
Commons		.05	.02
1	Dominique Wilkins	.20	.12
2	Robert Parish	.10	.06
3	Alonzo Mourning	.35	.20
4	Scottie Pippen	.15	.10
5	Larry Nance	.05	.02
6	Derek Harper	.05	.02
7	Reggie Williams	.05	.02
8	Bill Laimbeer	.05	.02
9	Tim Hardaway	.10	.06
10	Hakeem Olajuwon	.40	.25
11	LaSalle Thompson	.05	.02
12	Danny Manning	.10	.06
13	James Worthy	.08	.05
14	Grant Long	.05	.02
15	Blue Edwards	.05	.02
16	Christian Laettner	.12	.07
17	Derrick Coleman	.12	.07
18	Patrick Ewing	.20	.12
19	Nick Anderson	.10	.06
20	Clarence Weatherspoon	.12	.07
21	Charles Barkley	.20	.12
22	Cliff Robinson	.08	.05
23	Lionel Simmons	.12	.07
24	David Robinson	.20	.12
25	Shawn Kemp	.20	.12
26	Karl Malone	.20	.12
27	Rex Chapman	.05	.02
28	Answer Card	.05	.02

SKYBOX

1990-91 SkyBox

1990-91 SKYBOX • 107

This set marks the premier edition of Skybox basketball cards. The set was issued in two series, 300-cards in Series I and 123-cards in Series II. The fronts feature full color player photos superimposed over a computer-generated color background. The photos are framed in gold. The player's name appears in a black bar at the bottom of the card and to the right of a team logo. The card backs contain another full color photo and the player's statistics. Numerous cards were considered short prints (SP) when they were removed from the second series print run. Subsets include Coaches (C) and Team Checklist Cards (328-354) and Lottery Picks (355-365). All cards measure 2-1/2" by 3-1/2".

		MINT	NR/MT
	Complete Set (423)	18.50	12.50
	Commons	.05	.02
1	John Battle	.05	.02
2	Duane Ferrell (R)(SP)	.20	.12
3	Jon Koncak	.05	.02
4	Cliff Levingston (SP)	.07	.04
5	John Long (SP)	.07	.04
6	Moses Malone	.12	.07
7	Glenn Rivers	.05	.02
8	Kenny Smith (SP)	.08	.05
9	Alexander Volkov	.05	.02
10	Spud Webb	.05	.02
11	Dominique Wilkins	.35	.20
12	Kevin Willis	.07	.04
13	John Bagley	.05	.02
14	Larry Bird	1.00	.60
15	Kevin Gamble	.08	.05
16	Dennis Johnson (SP)	.10	.06
17	Joe Kleine	.05	.02
18	Reggie Lewis	.25	.15
19	Kevin McHale	.15	.10
20	Robert Parish	.15	.10
21	Jim Paxson (SP)	.07	.04
22	Ed Pinckney	.05	.02
23	Brian Shaw	.05	.02
24	Michael Smith (R)	.07	.04
25	Richard Anderson (SP)	.06	.03
26	Tyrone Bogues	.05	.02
27	Rex Chapman	.08	.05
28	Dell Curry	.07	.04
29	Armon Gilliam	.07	.04
30	Michael Holton (SP)	.06	.03
31	Dave Hoppen	.05	.02
32	J.R. Reid (R)	.20	.12
33	Robert Reid (SP)	.06	.03
34	Brian Rowsom (SP)	.06	.03
35	Kelly Tripucka	.05	.02
36	Michael Williams (SP)	.08	.05
37	B.J. Armstrong (R)	.80	.50
38	Bill Cartwright	.05	.02
39	Horace Grant	.20	.12
40	Craig Hodges	.05	.02
41	Michael Jordan	3.50	2.00
42	Stacey King (R)	.20	.12
43	Ed Nealy (SP)	.06	.03
44	John Paxson	.07	.04
45	Will Perdue	.07	.04
46	Scottie Pippen	.75	.45
47	Jeff Sanders (R)(SP)	.08	.05
48	Winston Bennett	.05	.02
49	Chucky Brown (R)	.12	.07
50	Brad Daugherty	.25	.15
51	Craig Ehlo	.05	.02
52	Steve Kerr	.05	.02
53	Paul Mokeski (SP)	.06	.03
54	John Morton	.05	.02
55	Larry Nance	.07	.04
56	Mark Price	.25	.15
57	Tree Rollins (SP)	.08	.05
58	Hot Rod Williams	.10	.06
59	Steve Alford	.05	.02
60	Rolando Blackman	.07	.04
61	Adrian Dantley (SP)	.10	.06
62	Brad Davis	.05	.02
63	James Donaldson	.05	.02
64	Derek Harper	.07	.04
65	Anthony Jones (SP)	.06	.03
66	Sam Perkins	.07	.04
67	Roy Tarpley	.07	.04
68	Bill Wennington (SP)	.07	.04
69	Randy White (R)	.12	.07
70	Herb Williams	.05	.02
71	Michael Adams	.08	.05
72	Joe Barry Carroll (SP)	.08	.05
73	Walter Davis	.07	.04
74	Alex English (SP)	.12	.07
75	Bill Hanzlik	.05	.02
76	Tim Kempton (SP)	.08	.05
77	Jerome Lane	.05	.02
78	Lafayette Lever (SP)	.07	.04
79	Todd Lichti (R)	.10	.06
80	Blair Rasmussen	.05	.02
81	Dan Schayes (SP)	.07	.04
82	Mark Aguirre	.08	.05
83	William Bedford (R)	.10	.06
84	Joe Dumars	.20	.12
85	James Edwards	.05	.02
86	David Greenwood (SP)	.08	.05
87	Scott Hastings	.05	.02
88	Gerald Henderson (SP)	.06	.03
89	Vinnie Johnson	.07	.04

1990-91 SKYBOX

#	Player	Price 1	Price 2
90	Bill Laimbeer	.08	.05
91	Dennis Rodman	.20	.12
92	John Salley	.05	.02
93	Isiah Thomas	.25	.15
94	Manute Bol (SP)	.08	.05
95	Tim Hardaway (R)	1.25	.70
96	Rod Higgins	.05	.02
97	Sarunas Marciulionis(R)	.20	.12
98	Chris Mullin	.30	.18
99	Jim Petersen	.05	.02
100	Mitch Richmond	.30	.18
101	Mike Smrek	.05	.02
102	Terry Teagle (SP)	.07	.04
103	Tom Tolbert (R)	.10	.06
104	Kelvin Upshaw (SP)	.06	.03
105	Anthony Bowie (R)(SP)	.20	.12
106	Adrian Caldwell	.05	.02
107	Sleepy Floyd	.05	.02
108	Buck Johnson	.05	.02
109	Vern Maxwell	.15	.10
110	Hakeem Olajuwon	1.00	.60
111	Larry Smith	.05	.02
112	Otis Thorpe	.08	.05
113	Mitchell Wiggins (SP)	.06	.03
114	Vern Fleming	.05	.02
115	Rickey Green (SP)	.07	.04
116	George McCloud (R)	.12	.07
117	Reggie Miller	.30	.18
118	Dyron Nix (SP)	.08	.05
119	Chuck Person	.08	.05
120	Mike Sanders	.05	.02
121	Detlef Schrempf	.15	.10
122	Rik Smits	.07	.04
123	LaSalle Thompson	.05	.02
124	Benoit Benjamin	.05	.02
125	Winston Garland	.05	.02
126	Tom Garrick	.05	.02
127	Gary Grant	.05	.02
128	Ron Harper	.07	.04
129	Danny Manning	.30	.18
130	Jeff Martin (R)	.08	.05
131	Ken Norman	.08	.05
132	Charles Smith	.12	.07
133	Joe Wolf (SP)	.07	.04
134	Michael Cooper (SP)	.08	.05
135	Vlade Divac (R)	.30	.18
136	Larry Drew	.05	.02
137	A.C. Green	.07	.04
138	Magic Johnson	1.00	.60
139	Mark McNamara (SP)	.06	.03
140	Byron Scott	.07	.04
141	Mychal Thompson	.05	.02
142	Orlando Woolridge (SP)	.08	.05
143	James Worthy	.15	.10
144	Terry Davis (R)	.10	.06
145	Sherman Douglas (R)	.30	.18
146	Kevin Edwards	.05	.02
147	Tellis Frank (SP)	.06	.03
148	Scott Haffner (SP)	.06	.03
149	Grant Long	.05	.02
150	Glen Rice (R)	1.00	.60
151	Rony Seikaly	.15	.10
152	Rory Sparrow (SP)	.07	.04
153	Jon Sundvold	.05	.02
154	Billy Thompson	.05	.02
155	Greg Anderson	.07	.04
156	Ben Coleman (SP)	.06	.03
157	Jeff Grayer (R)	.12	.07
158	Jay Humphries	.05	.02
159	Frank Kornet	.05	.02
160	Larry Krystkowiak	.05	.02
161	Brad Lohaus	.05	.02
162	Ricky Pierce	.05	.02
163	Paul Pressey (SP)	.07	.04
164	Fred Roberts	.05	.02
165	Alvin Robertson	.07	.04
166	Jack Sikma	.07	.04
167	Randy Breuer	.05	.02
168	Tony Campbell	.05	.02
169	Tyrone Cobin	.05	.02
170	Sidney Lowe (SP)	.07	.04
171	Sam Mitchell (R)	.15	.10
172	Tod Murphy	.05	.02
173	Pooh Richardson (R)	.25	.15
174	Donald Royal (R)(SP)	.20	.12
175	Brad Sellers (SP)	.07	.04
176	Mookie Blaylock (R)	.60	.35
177	Sam Bowie	.07	.04
178	Lester Conner	.05	.02
179	Derrick Gervin (R)	.08	.05
180	Jack Haley (R)	.08	.05
181	Roy Hinson	.05	.02
182	Dennis Hopson (SP)	.08	.05
183	Chris Morris	.05	.02
184	Pete Myers (SP)	.15	.10
185	Purvis Short (SP)	.08	.05
186	Maurice Cheeks	.10	.06
187	Patrick Ewing	.60	.35
188	Stuart Gray	.05	.02
189	Mark Jackson	.07	.04
190	Johnny Newman	.05	.02
191	Charles Oakley	.05	.02
192	Brian Quinnett (R)	.07	.04
193	Trent Tucker	.05	.02
194	Kiki Vandeweghe	.05	.02
195	Kenny Walker	.07	.04
196	Eddie Lee Wilkins	.05	.02
197	Gerald wilkins	.05	.02
198	Mark Acres	.05	.02
199	Nick Anderson (R)	.60	.35
200	Michael Ansley (R)	.07	.04
201	Terry Catledge	.05	.02
202	Dave Corzine (SP)	.06	.03
203	Sidney Green (SP)	.06	.03

1990-91 SKYBOX • 109

#	Player		
204	Jerry Reynolds	.05	.02
205	Scott Skiles	.07	.04
206	Otis Smith	.05	.02
207	Reggie Theus (SP)	.08	.05
208	Jeff Turner	.05	.02
209	Sam Vincent	.05	.02
210	Ron Anderson	.05	.02
211	Charles Barkley	.75	.45
212	Scott Brooks (SP)	.07	.04
213	Lanard Copeland (SP)	.06	.03
214	Johnny Dawkins	.05	.02
215	Mike Gminski	.05	.02
216	Hersey Hawkins	.12	.07
217	Rick Mahorn	.05	.02
218	Derek Smith (SP)	.07	.04
219	Bob Thornton	.05	.02
220	Tom Chambers	.10	.06
221	Greg Grant (R)(SP)	.15	.10
222	Jeff Hornacek	.15	.10
223	Eddie Johnson	.05	.02
224	Kevin Johnson	.30	.18
225	Andrew Lang (R)	.15	.10
226	Dan Majerle	.25	.15
227	Mike McGee (SP)	.06	.03
228	Tim Perry	.05	.02
229	Kurt Rambis	.05	.02
230	Mark West	.05	.02
231	Mark Bryant	.05	.02
232	Wayne Cooper	.05	.02
233	Clyde Drexler	.30	.18
234	Kevin Duckworth	.07	.04
235	Byron Irvin (SP)	.07	.04
236	Jerome Kersey	.08	.05
237	Drazen Petrovic (R)	.75	.45
238	Terry Porter	.20	.12
239	Cliff Robinson (R)	.80	.50
240	Buck Williams	.08	.05
241	Danny Young	.05	.02
242	Danny Ainge (SP)	.10	.06
243	Randy Allen (SP)	.07	.04
244	Antoine Carr (SP)	.08	.05
245	Vinny Del Negro (SP)	.10	.06
246	Pervis Ellison (R)(SP)	.50	.30
247	Greg Kite (SP)	.07	.04
248	Rodney McCray (SP)	.07	.04
249	Harold Pressley (SP)	.07	.04
250	Ralph Sampson	.08	.05
251	Waymen Tisdale	.08	.05
252	Willie Anderson	.05	.02
253	Uwe Blab (SP)	.07	.04
254	Frank Brickowski (SP)	.08	.05
255	Terry Cummings	.10	.06
256	Sean Elliott (R)	.40	.25
257	Caldwell Jones (SP)	.08	.05
258	Johnny Moore (SP)	.06	.03
259	Zarko Paspalj (SP)	.07	.04
260	David Robinson	1.50	.90
261	Rod Strickland	.05	.02
262	David Wingate (SP)	.08	.05
263	Dana Barros (R)	.20	.12
264	Michael Cage	.05	.02
265	Quintin Dailey	.05	.02
266	Dale Ellis	.07	.04
267	Steve Johnson (SP)	.08	.05
268	Shawn Kemp (R)	3.00	1.75
269	Xavier McDaniel	.08	.05
270	Derrick McKey	.07	.04
271	Nate McMillan (SP)	.07	.04
272	Olden Polynice	.05	.02
273	Sedale Threatt	.05	.02
274	Thurl Bailey	.05	.02
275	Mike Brown	.05	.02
276	Mark Eaton	.05	.02
277	Blue Edwards (R)	.25	.15
278	Darrell Griffith	.07	.04
279	Bobby Hansen (SP)	.07	.04
280	Eric Johnson	.05	.02
281	Eric Leckner (SP)	.07	.04
282	Karl Malone	.40	.25
283	Delaney Rudd	.05	.02
284	John Stockton	.35	.20
285	Mark Alarie	.05	.02
286	Steve Colter (SP)	.06	.03
287	Ledell Eackles (SP)	.08	.05
288	Harvey Grant	.12	.07
289	Tom Hammonds (R)	.15	.10
290	Charles Jones	.05	.02
291	Bernard King	.08	.05
292	Jeff Malone (SP)	.12	.07
293	Darrell Walker	.05	.02
294	John Williams	.05	.02
295	Checklist (SP)	.07	.02
296	Checklist (SP)	.07	.02
297	Checklist (SP)	.07	.02
298	CHecklist (SP)	.07	.02
299	Checklist (SP)	.07	.02
300	Danny Ferry (R)(SP)	.20	.12
301	Bob Weiss (C)	.05	.02
302	Chris Ford (C)	.05	.02
303	Gene Littles (C)	.05	.02
304	Phil Jackson (C)	.07	.04
305	Lenny Wilkens (C)	.07	.04
306	Richie Adubato (C)	.05	.02
307	Paul Westhead (C)	.05	.02
308	Chuck Daly (C)	.05	.02
309	Don Nelson (C)	.05	.02
310	Don Chaney (C)	.05	.02
311	Dick Versace (C)	.05	.02
312	MIke Schuler (C)	.05	.02
313	Mike Dunleavy (C)	.05	.02
314	Ron Rothstein (C)	.05	.02
315	Del Harris (C)	.05	.02
316	Bill Musselman (C)	.05	.02
317	Bill Fitch (C)	.05	.02

1990-91 SKYBOX

#	Name		
318	Stu Jackson (C)	.05	.02
319	Matt Guokas (C)	.05	.02
320	Jim Lynam (C)	.05	.02
321	Cotton Fitzsimmons (C)	.05	.02
322	Rick Adelman (C)	.05	.02
323	Dick Motta (C)	.05	.02
324	Larry Brown (C)	.05	.02
325	K.C. Jones (C)	.07	.04
326	Jerry Sloan (C)	.05	.02
327	Wes Unseld (C)	.05	.02
328	Atlanta Hawks	.05	.02
329	Boston Celtics	.05	.02
330	Charlotte Hornets	.05	.02
331	Chicago Bulls	.05	.02
332	Cleveland Cavaliers	.05	.02
333	Dallas Mavericks	.05	.02
334	Denver Nuggest	.05	.02
335	Detroit Pistons	.05	.02
336	Golden State Warriors	.05	.02
337	Houston Rockets	.05	.02
338	Indiana Pacers	.05	.02
339	Los Angeles Clippers	.05	.02
340	Los Angeles Lakers	.05	.02
341	Miami Heat	.05	.02
342	Milwaukee Bucks	.05	.02
343	Minnesota Timberwolves	.05	.02
344	New Jersey Nets	.05	.02
345	New York Knicks	.05	.02
346	Orlando Magic	.05	.02
347	Philadelpha 76ers	.05	.02
348	Phoenix Suns	.05	.02
349	Portland Trail Blazers	.05	.02
350	Sacramento Kings	.05	.02
351	San Antonio Spurs	.05	.02
352	Seattle SuperSonics	.05	.02
353	Utah Jazz	.05	.02
354	Washington Bullets	.05	.02
355	Rumeal Robinson (R)	.20	.12
356	Kendall Gill (R)	1.00	.60
357	Chris Jackson (R)	1.25	.70
358	Tyrone Hill (R)	.25	.15
359	Bo Kimble (R)	.08	.05
360	Willie Burton (R)	.20	.12
361	Felton Spencer (R)	.25	.15
362	Derrick Coleman (R)	2.50	1.50
363	Dennis Scott (R)	.60	.35
364	Lionel Simmons (R)	1.00	.60
365	Gary Payton (R)	1.00	.60
366	Tim McCormick	.05	.02
367	Sidney Moncrief	.08	.05
368	Kenny Gattison (R)	.15	.10
369	Randolph Keys	.05	.02
370	Johnny Newman	.05	.02
371	Dennis Hopson	.05	.02
372	Cliff Levingston	.05	.02
373	Derrick Chievous	.05	.02
374	Danny Ferry	.08	.05
375	Alex English	.10	.06
376	Lafayette Lever	.05	.02
377	Rodney McCray	.07	.04
378	T.R. Dunn	.05	.02
379	Corey Gaines	.07	.04
380	Avery Johnson (R)	.20	.12
381	Joe Wolf	.05	.02
382	Orlando Woolridge	.07	.04
383	Tree Rollins	.05	.02
384	Steve Johnson	.05	.02
385	Kenny Smith	.07	.04
386	Mike Woodson	.05	.02
387	Greg Dreiling	.08	.05
368	Michael Williams	.07	.04
369	Randy Wittman	.05	.02
390	Ken Bannister	.05	.02
391	Sam Perkins	.08	.05
392	Terry Teagle	.05	.02
393	Milt Wagner	.05	.02
394	Frank Brickowski	.05	.02
395	Dan Schayes	.05	.02
396	Scott Brooks	.05	.02
397	Doug West (R)	.50	.35
398	Chris Dudley (R)	.15	.10
399	Reggie Theus	.07	.04
400	Greg Grant	.05	.02
401	Greg Kite	.05	.02
402	Mark McNamara	.05	.02
403	Manute Bol	.05	.02
404	Rickey Green	.05	.02
405	Kenny Battle	.08	.05
406	Ed Nealy	.05	.02
407	Danny Ainge	.10	.06
408	Steve Colter	.05	.02
409	Bobby Hansen	.05	.02
410	Eric Leckner	.05	.02
411	Rory Sparrow	.05	.02
412	Bill Wennington	.05	.02
413	Sidney Green	.05	.02
414	David Greenwood	.05	.02
415	Paul Pressey	.05	.02
416	Reggie Williams	.07	.04
417	Dave Corzine	.05	.02
418	Jeff Malone	.08	.05
419	Pervis Ellison	.15	.10
420	Byron Irvin	.08	.05
421	Checklist	.05	.02
422	Checklist	.05	.02
423	Checklist	.05	.02
___	SkyBox Salutes NBA	5.00	2.00

1991-92 SkyBox

Clyde Drexler

SkyBox issued this set in two series and expanded the size of their set to 659-cards. The fronts feature full color player photos set against a colorful computer-generated geometric background. The borderless cards are printed on a white glossy card stock. The player's name is printed in multi-colored lettering in the lower left corner of the card front while a team logo appears in the lower right corner. The flip side contains another full color picture along with personal data and stats. Key subsets include Stats Leaders (298-307), Best Single Game Performances(SG)(308-312) All-Star Highlights (313-317), All-Rookie Team (318-322), GQ All-Star Style (323-327), Centennial Highlights (328-332, 524-529), NBA FInals (333-337), Message Cards (338-344, 610-614), Team Logos (351-377), Coaches (378-404), Game Frames (GF)(405-431), Sixth men (432-458), Teamwork (TW) (459-485), Rising Stars (RS)(486-512), Lottery Picks (513-523), Team USA (530-563), Magic of SkyBox (564-571), SkyBox Salutes (SS)(572-576), Skymasters(SM)(577-588), Shooting Stars (589-602), and Small School Sensations (603-609). All cards measure 2-1/2" by 3-1/2".

	MINT	NR/MT
Complete Set (659)	28.00	18.00
Commons	.05	.02

1	John Battle	.05	.02
2	Duane Ferrell	.07	.04
3	Jon Koncak	.05	.02
4	Moses Malone	.10	.06
5	Tim McCormick	.05	.02
6	Sidney Moncrief	.08	.05
7	Doc Rivers	.05	.02
8	Rumeal Robinson	.07	.04
9	Spud Webb	.05	.02
10	Dominique Wilkins	.25	.15
11	Kevin Willis	.07	.04
12	Larry Bird	.75	.45
13	Dee Brown	.20	.12
14	Kevin Gamble	.05	.02
15	Joe Kleine	.05	.02
16	Reggie Lewis	.15	.10
17	Kevin McHale	.12	.07
18	Robert Parish	.12	.07
19	Ed Pinckney	.05	.02
20	Brian Shaw	.05	.02
21	Michael Smith	.05	.02
22	Stojko Vrankovic	.05	.02
23	Muggsy Bogues	.05	.02
24	Rex Chapman	.07	.04
25	Dell Curry	.05	.02
26	Kenny Gattison	.05	.02
27	Kendall Gill	.25	.15
28	Mike Gminski	.05	.02
29	Randolph Keys	.05	.02
30	Eric Leckner	.05	.02
31	Johnny Newman	.05	.02
32	J.R. Reid	.08	.05
33	Kelly Tripucka	.05	.02
34	B.J. Armstrong	.15	.10
35	Bill Cartwright	.05	.02
36	Horace Grant	.12	.07
37	Craig Hodges	.05	.02
38	Dennis Hopson	.05	.02
39	Michael Jordan	2.00	1.25
40	Stacey King	.07	.04
41	Cliff Levingston	.05	.02
42	John Paxson	.07	.04
43	Will Perdue	.07	.04
44	Scottie Pippen	.35	.20
45	Winston Bennett	.05	.02
46	Chucky Brown	.07	.04
47	Brad Daugherty	.15	.10
48	Craig Ehlo	.05	.02
49	Danny Ferry	.05	.02
50	Steve Kerr	.05	.02
51	John Morton	.05	.02
52	Larry Nance	.07	.04
53	Mark Price	.15	.10
54	Darnell Valentine	.05	.02
55	John Williams	.05	.02
56	Steve Alford	.05	.02
57	Rolando Blackman	.07	.04

1991-92 SKYBOX

#	Player		
58	Brad Davis	.05	.02
59	James Donaldson	.05	.02
60	Derek Harper	.07	.04
61	Fat Lever	.05	.02
62	Rodney McCray	.07	.04
63	Roy Tarpley	.07	.04
64	Kelvin Upshaw	.05	.02
65	Randy White	.05	.02
66	Herb Williams	.05	.02
67	Michael Adams	.08	.05
68	Greg Anderson	.07	.04
69	Anthony Cook	.05	.02
70	Chris Jackson	.20	.12
71	Jerome Lane	.05	.02
72	Marcus Liberty	.08	.05
73	Todd Lichti	.05	.02
74	Blair Rasmussen	.05	.02
75	Reggie Williams	.07	.04
76	Joe Wolf	.05	.02
77	Orlando Woolridge	.07	.04
78	Mark Aguirre	.07	.04
79	William Bedford	.07	.04
80	Lance Blanks	.05	.02
81	Joe Dumars	.15	.10
82	James Edwards	.05	.02
83	Scott Hastings	.05	.02
84	Vinnie Johnson	.05	.02
85	Bill Laimbeer	.07	.04
86	Dennis Rodman	.15	.10
87	John Salley	.05	.02
88	Isiah Thomas	.20	.12
89	Mario Elie (R)	.15	.10
90	Tim Hardaway	.25	.15
91	Rod Higgins	.05	.02
92	Tyrone Hill	.07	.04
93	Les Jepsen	.05	.02
94	Alton Lister	.05	.02
95	Sarunas Marciulionis	.08	.05
96	Chris Mullin	.20	.12
97	Jim Petersen	.05	.02
98	Mitch Richmond	.12	.07
99	Tom Tolbert	.05	.02
100	Adrian Caldwell	.05	.02
101	Sleepy Floyd	.05	.02
102	Dave Jamerson	.05	.02
103	Buck Johnson	.05	.02
104	Vernon Maxwell	.12	.07
105	Hakeem Olajuwon	.75	.45
106	Kenny Smith	.07	.04
107	Larry Smith	.05	.02
108	Otis Thorpe	.07	.04
109	Ken Winchester (R)	.10	.06
110	David Wood (R)	.08	.05
111	Greg Dreiling	.05	.02
112	Vern Fleming	.05	.02
113	George McCloud	.05	.02
114	Reggie Miller	.20	.12
115	Chuck Person	.07	.04
116	Mark Sanders	.05	.02
117	Detlef Schrempf	.12	.07
118	Rik Smits	.05	.02
119	LaSalle Thompson	.05	.02
120	Kenny Williams	.05	.02
121	Michael Williams	.05	.02
122	Ken Bannister	.05	.02
123	Winston Garland	.05	.02
124	Gary Grant	.05	.02
125	Ron Harper	.07	.04
126	Bo Kimble	.05	.02
127	Danny Manning	.20	.12
128	Jeff Martin	.05	.02
129	Ken Norman	.07	.04
130	Olden Polynice	.05	.02
131	Charles Smith	.10	.06
132	Loy Vaught	.08	.05
133	Elden Campbell	.15	.10
134	Vlade Divac	.10	.06
135	Larry Drew	.05	.02
136	A.C. Green	.07	.04
137	Magic Johnson	.60	.35
138	Sam Perkins	.07	.04
139	Byron Scott	.05	.02
140	Tony Smith	.05	.02
141	Terry Teagle	.05	.02
142	Mychal Thompson	.05	.02
143	James Worthy	.10	.06
144	Willie Burton	.07	.04
145	Bimbo Coles	.08	.05
146	Terry Davis	.05	.02
147	Sherman Douglas	.10	.06
148	Kevin Edwards	.05	.02
149	Alec Kessler	.05	.02
150	Grant Long	.05	.02
151	Glen Rice	.25	.15
152	Rony Seikaly	.08	.05
153	Jon Sundvold	.05	.02
154	Billy Thompson	.05	.02
155	Frank Brickowski	.05	.02
156	Lester Conner	.05	.02
157	Jeff Grayer	.05	.02
158	Jay Humphries	.05	.02
159	Larry Krystkowiak	.05	.02
160	Brad Lohaus	.05	.02
161	Dale Ellis	.07	.04
162	Fred Roberts	.05	.02
163	Alvin Robertson	.05	.02
164	Danny Schayes	.05	.02
165	Jack Sikma	.05	.02
166	Randy Breuer	.05	.02
167	Scott Brooks	.05	.02
168	Tony Campbell	.05	.02
169	Tyrone Corbin	.05	.02
170	Gerald Glass	.05	.02
171	Sam Mitchell	.07	.04

1991-92 SKYBOX • 113

#	Player			#	Player		
172	Tod Murphy	.05	.02	229	Xavier McDaniel	.08	.05
173	Pooh Richadson	.07	.04	230	Kurt Rambis	.05	.02
174	Felton Spencer	.15	.10	231	Mark West	.05	.02
175	Bob Thornton	.05	.02	232	Alaa Abdelnaby	.08	.05
176	Doug West	.20	.12	233	Danny Ainge	.08	.05
177	Mookie Blaylock	.10	.06	234	Mark Bryant	.05	.02
178	Sam Bowie	.07	.04	235	Wayne Cooper	.05	.02
179	Jud Buechler	.05	.02	236	Walter Davis	.07	.04
180	Derrick Coleman	.50	.30	237	Clyde Drexler	.25	.15
181	Chris Dudley	.05	.02	238	Kevin Duckworth	.07	.04
182	Tate George	.05	.02	239	Jerome Kersey	.08	.05
183	Jack Haley	.05	.02	240	Terry Porter	.10	.06
184	Terry Mills (R)	.40	.25	241	Cliff Robinson	.15	.10
185	Chris Morris	.05	.02	242	Buck Williams	.07	.04
186	Drazen Petrovic	.20	.12	243	Anthony Bonner	.05	.02
187	Reggie Theus	.05	.02	244	Antoine Carr	.05	.02
188	Maurice Cheeks	.07	.04	245	Duane Causwell	.05	.02
189	Patrick Ewing	.35	.20	246	Bobby Hansen	.05	.02
190	Mark Jackson	.07	.04	247	Jim Les (R)	.10	.06
191	Jerrod Mustaf	.08	.05	248	Travis Mays	.05	.02
192	Charles Oakley	.08	.05	249	Ralph Sampson	.08	.05
193	Brian Quinnett	.05	.02	250	Lionel Simmons	.20	.12
194	John Starks (R)	.80	.50	251	Rory Sparrow	.05	.02
195	Trent Tucker	.05	.02	252	Wayman Tisdale	.08	.05
196	Kiki Vandeweghe	.05	.02	253	Bill Wennington	.05	.02
197	Kenny Walker	.05	.02	254	Willie Anderson	.05	.02
198	Gerald Wilkins	.05	.02	255	Terry Cummings	.08	.05
199	Mark Acres	.05	.02	256	Sean Elliott	.20	.12
200	Nick Anderson	.20	.12	257	Sidney Green	.05	.02
201	Michael Ansley	.05	.02	258	David Greenwood	.05	.02
202	Terry Catledge	.05	.02	259	Avery Johnson	.07	.04
203	Greg Kite	.05	.02	260	Paul Pressey	.05	.02
204	Jerry Reynolds	.05	.02	261	David Robinson	.60	.35
205	Dennis Scott	.15	.10	262	Dwayne Schintzius	.05	.02
206	Scott Skiles	.05	.02	263	Rod Strickland	.05	.02
207	Otis Smith	.05	.02	264	David Wingate	.05	.02
208	Jeff Turner	.05	.02	265	Dana Barros	.07	.04
209	Sam Vincent	.05	.02	266	Benoit Banjamin	.05	.02
210	Ron Anderson	.05	.02	267	Michael Cage	.05	.02
211	Charles Barkley	.40	.25	268	Quintin Dailey	.05	.02
212	Manute Bol	.05	.02	269	Ricky Pierce	.05	.02
213	Johnny Dawkins	.05	.02	270	Eddie Johnson	.05	.02
214	Armon Gilliam	.07	.04	271	Shawn Kemp	1.00	.60
215	Rickey Green	.05	.02	272	Derrick McKey	.07	.04
216	Hersey Hawkins	.08	.05	273	Nate MacMillan	.05	.02
217	Rick Mahorn	.05	.02	274	Gary Payton	.20	.12
218	Brian Oliver	.05	.02	275	Sedale Threatt	.05	.02
219	Andre Turner	.05	.02	276	Thurl Bailey	.05	.02
220	Jayson Williams	.05	.02	277	Mike Brown	.05	.02
221	Joe Barry Carroll	.05	.02	278	Tony Brown	.05	.02
222	Cedric Ceballos	.15	.10	279	Mark Eaton	.05	.02
223	Tom Chambers	.08	.05	280	Blue Edwards	.08	.05
224	Jeff Hornacek	.08	.05	281	Darrell Griffith	.05	.02
225	Kevin Johnson	.20	.12	282	Jeff Malone	.08	.05
226	Negele Knight	.08	.05	283	Karl Malone	.25	.15
227	Andrew Lang	.05	.02	284	Delaney Rudd	.05	.02
228	Dan Majerle	.15	.10	285	John Stockton	.25	.15

1991-92 SKYBOX

#	Name		
286	Andy Toolson	.05	.02
287	Mark Alarie	.05	.02
288	Ledell Eackles	.05	.02
289	Pervis Ellison	.12	.07
290	A.J. English	.05	.02
291	Harvey Grant	.07	.04
292	Tom Hammonds	.07	.04
293	Charles Jones	.05	.02
294	Bernard King	.07	.04
295	Darrell Walker	.05	.02
296	John Williams	.05	.02
297	Haywoode Workman (R)	.15	.10
298	Muggsy Bogues (LL)	.05	.02
299	Lester Conner (LL)	.05	.02
300	Michael Adams (LL)	.07	.04
301	Chris Mullin (LL)	.10	.06
302	Otis Thorpe (LL)	.07	.04
303	Mitch Richmond (LL) / Chris Mullin (LL) / Tim Hardaway (LL)	.15	.10
304	Darrell Walker (LL)	.05	.02
305	Jerome Lane (LL)	.05	.02
306	John Stockton (LL)	.12	.07
307	Michael Jordan (LL)	1.00	.60
308	Michael Adams (SG)	.07	.04
309	Larry Smith/Jerome Lane (SG)	.05	.02
310	Scott Skiles (SG)	.05	.02
311	Hakeem Olajuwon/ David Robinson (SG)	.50	.30
312	Alvin Robertson (SG)	.05	.02
313	Stay in School Jam	.05	.02
314	Craig Hodges (3 pt Shootout)	.05	.02
315	Dee Brown (Slam Dunk Champ)	.10	.06
316	Charles Bakley (AS MVP)	.25	.15
317	Behind the Scenes	.12	.07
318	Derrick Coleman (AR)	.20	.12
319	Lionel Simmons (AR)	.12	.07
320	Dennis Scott (AR)	.10	.06
321	Kendall Gill (AR)	.15	.10
322	Dee Brown (AR)	.10	.06
323	Magic Johnson (GQ)	.25	.15
324	Hakeem Olajawon (GQ)	.30	.18
325	Reggie Theus (GQ)	.07	.04
326	Dominique Wilkins/ Kevin Willis (GQ)	.15	.10
327	Gerald Wilkins (GQ)	.05	.02
328	Centennial Logo	.10	.06
329	Old fashioend ball	.05	.02
330	Women Players	.05	.02
331	The Peach Basket	.05	.02
332	Dr. James A. Naismith	.10	.06
333	Magic Johnson/Michael Jordan (Finals)	1.00	.60
334	Michael Jordan (Finals)	1.00	.60
335	Vlade Divac (Finals)	.08	.05
336	John Paxson (Finals)	.07	.04
337	Chicago Bulls (Finals)	.20	.12
338	Stay In School	.05	.02
339	Stay In School	.05	.02
340	Stay In School	.05	.02
341	Stay in School	.05	.02
342	Stay in School	.05	.02
343	Stay in School	.05	.02
344	Stay in School	.05	.02
345	Checklist 1	.05	.02
346	Checklist 2	.05	.02
347	Checklist 3	.05	.02
348	Checklist 4	.05	.02
349	Checklist 5	.05	.02
350	Checklist 6	.05	.02
351	Atlanta Hawks	.05	.02
352	Boston Celtics	.05	.02
353	Charlotte Hornets	.05	.02
354	Chicago Bulls	.05	.02
355	Cleveland Cavaliers	.05	.02
356	Dallas Mavericks	.05	.02
357	Denver Nuggets	.05	.02
358	Detroit Pistons	.05	.02
359	Golden State Warriors	.05	.02
360	Houston Rockets	.05	.02
361	Indiana Pacers	.05	.02
362	Los Angeles Clippers	.05	.02
363	Los Angeles Lakers	.05	.02
364	Miami Heat	.05	.02
365	Milwaukee Bucks	.05	.02
366	Minnesota Timberwolves	.05	.02
367	New Jersey Nets	.05	.02
368	New York Knicks	.05	.02
369	Orlando Magic	.05	.02
370	Philadelphia 76ers	.05	.02
371	Phoenix Suns	.05	.02
372	Portland Trail Blazers	.05	.02
373	Sacramento Kings	.05	.02
374	San Antonio Spurs	.05	.02
375	Seattle Supersonics	.05	.02
376	Utah Jazz	.05	.02
377	Washington Bullets	.05	.02
378	Bob Weiss (C)	.05	.02
379	Chris Ford (C)	.05	.02
380	Allan Bristow (C)	.05	.02
381	Phil Jackson (C)	.07	.04
382	Lenny Wilkens (C)	.07	.04
383	Richie Adubato (C)	.05	.02
384	Paul Westhead (C)	.05	.02
385	Chuck Daly (C)	.05	.02
386	Don Nelson (C)	.05	.02
387	Don Chaney (C)	.05	.02
388	Bob Hill (C)	.05	.02
389	Mike Schuler (C)	.05	.02
390	Mike Dunleavy (C)	.05	.02

1991-92 SKYBOX • 115

#	Name		
391	Kevin Loughery (C)	.05	.02
392	Del Harris (C)	.05	.02
393	Jimmy Rodgers (C)	.05	.02
394	Bill Fitch (C)	.05	.02
395	Pat Riley (C)	.07	.04
396	Matt Guokas (C)	.05	.02
397	Jim Lynam (C)	.05	.02
398	Cotton Fitzsimmons (C)	.05	.02
399	Rick Adelman (C)	.05	.02
400	Dick Motta (C)	.05	.02
401	Larry Brown (C)	.05	.02
402	K.C. Jones (C)	.07	.04
403	Jerry Sloan (C)	.05	.02
404	Wes Unseld (C)	.05	.02
405	Atlanta Hawks (GF)	.05	.02
406	Boston Celtics (GF) (Dee Brown)	.10	.06
407	Charlotte Hornets (GF)	.05	.02
408	Chicago Bulls (GF) (Michael Jordan)	1.00	.60
409	Cleveland Cavaliers (GF)	.05	.02
410	Dallas Mavericks (GF)	.05	.02
411	Denver Nuggets (GF) (Dikembe Mutombo)	.30	.18
412	Detroit Pistons (GF) (Isiah Thomas)	.10	.06
413	Golden State (GF) (Tim Hardaway)	.15	.10
414	Houston Rockets (GF) (Hakeem Olajuwon)	.30	.18
415	Indiana Pacers (GF)	.05	.02
416	L.A. Clippers (GF) (Danny Manning)	.12	.07
417	L.A. Lakers (GF) (Magic Johnson)	.30	.18
418	Miami Heat (GF)	.05	.02
419	Milwaukee Bucks (GF)	.05	.02
420	Timberwolves (GF)	.05	.02
421	New Jersey Nets (GF)	.05	.02
422	New York Knicks (GF)	.05	.02
423	Orlando Magic (GF)	.05	.02
424	Philadelphia 76ers (GF) (Charles Barkley)	.20	.12
425	Phoenix Suns (GF) (Dan Majerle)	.08	.05
426	Trail Blazers (GF)	.05	.02
427	Sacramento Kings (GF)	.05	.02
428	San Antonio Spurs (GF) (David Robinson)	.25	.15
429	Supersonics (GF)	.05	.02
430	Utah Jazz (GF) (Karl Malone)	.15	.10
431	Washington Bullets (GF)	.05	.02
432	Duane Ferrell (6th)	.05	.02
433	Kevin McHale (6th)	.08	.05
434	Dell Curry (6th)	.05	.02
435	B.J. Armstrong (6th)	.10	.06
436	Hot Rod Williams (6th)	.05	.02
437	Brad Davis (6th)	.05	.02
438	Marcus Liberty (6th)	.05	.02
439	Mark Aguirre (6th)	.07	.04
440	Rod Higgins (6th)	.05	.02
441	Sleepy Floyd (6th)	.05	.02
442	Detlef Schrempf (6th)	.08	.05
443	Loy Vaught (6th)	.05	.02
444	Terry Teagle (6th)	.05	.02
445	Kevin Edwards (6th)	.05	.02
446	Dale Ellis (6th)	.05	.02
447	Tod Murphy (6th)	.05	.02
448	Chris Dudley (6th)	.05	.02
449	Mark Jackson (6th)	.07	.04
450	Jerry Reynolds (6th)	.05	.02
451	Ron Anderson (6th)	.05	.02
452	Dan Majerle (6th)	.08	.05
453	Danny Ainge (6th)	.08	.05
454	Jim Les (6th)	.05	.02
455	Paul Pressy (6th)	.05	.02
456	Ricky Pierce (6th)	.05	.02
457	Mike Brown (6th)	.05	.02
458	Ledell Eackles (6th)	.05	.02
459	Atlanta Hawks (TW)	.10	.06
460	Boston Celtics (TW)	.25	.15
461	Charlotte Hornets (TW)	.12	.07
462	Chicago Bulls (TW)	.80	.50
463	Cleveland Cavaliers (TW)	.08	.05
464	Dallas Mavericks (TW)	.07	.04
465	Denver Nugget (TW)	.08	.05
466	Detroit Pistons (TW)	.10	.06
467	Golden State (TW)	.20	.12
468	Houston Rockets (TW)	.07	.04
469	Indiana Pacers (TW)	.10	.06
470	L.A. Clippers (TW)	.12	.07
471	L.A. Lakers (TW)	.30	.18
472	Miami Heat (TW)	.10	.06
473	Milwaukee Bucks (TW)	.05	.02
474	Timberwolves (TW)	.05	.02
475	New Jersey Nets (TW)	.15	.10
476	New York Knicks (TW)	.15	.10
477	Orlando Magic (TW)	.07	.04
478	Philadelphia 76ers (TW)	.20	.12
479	Phoenix Suns (TW)	.10	.06
480	Trail Blazers (TW)	.12	.07
481	Sacramento Kings (TW)	.10	.06
482	San Antonio Spurs (TW)	.10	.06
483	Supersonics (TW)	.05	.02
484	Utah Jazz (TW)	.15	.10
485	Washington Bullets (TW)	.07	.04
486	Rumeal Robinson (RS)	.07	.04
487	Dee Brown (RS)	.10	.06
488	Kendall Gill (RS)	.12	.07
489	B.J. Armstrong (RS)	.12	.07
490	Danny Ferry (RS)	.05	.02
491	Randy White (RS)	.05	.02
492	Chris Jackson (RS)	.10	.06

116 • 1991-92 SKY BOX

#	Name		
493	Lance Blanks (RS)	.05	.02
494	Tim Hardaway (RS)	.15	.10
495	Vernon Maxwell (RS)	.08	.05
496	Michael Williams (RS)	.05	.02
497	Charles Smith (RS)	.07	.04
498	Vlade Divac (RS)	.07	.04
499	Willie Burton (RS)	.07	.04
500	Jeff Grayer (RS)	.07	.04
501	Pooh Richardson (RS)	.07	.04
502	Derrick Coleman (RS)	.25	.15
503	John Starks (RS)	.20	.12
504	Dennis Scott (RS)	.07	.04
505	Hersey Hawkins (RS)	.08	.05
506	Negele Knight (RS)	.07	.04
507	Cliff Robinson (RS)	.10	.06
508	Lionel Simmons (RS)	.12	.07
509	David Robinson (RS)	.40	.25
510	Gary Payton (RS)	.10	.06
511	Blue Edwards (RS)	.08	.05
512	Harvey Grant (RS)	.07	.04
513	Larry Johnson (R)	3.00	1.75
514	Kenny Anderson (R)	1.25	.70
515	Billy Owens (R)	.75	.45
516	Dikembe Mutombo (R)	1.25	.70
517	Steve Smith (R)	1.00	.60
518	Doug Smith (R)	.15	.10
519	Luc Longley (R)	.12	.07
520	Mark Macon (R)	.12	.07
521	Stacey Augmon (R)	.75	.45
522	Brian Williams (R)	.25	.15
523	Terrell Brandon (R)	.20	.12
524	The Ball	.05	.02
525	The Basket	.05	.02
526	24-Second Shot Clock	.05	.02
527	The Game Program	.05	.02
528	The Championship Gift	.05	.02
529	Championship Trophy	.05	.02
530	Charles Barkley (USA)	1.00	.60
531	Larry Bird (USA)	1.00	.60
532	Patrick Ewing (USA)	.75	.45
533	Magic Johnson (USA)	1.25	.70
534	Michael Jordan (USA)	3.00	1.75
535	Karl Malone (USA)	.60	.35
536	Chris Mullin (USA)	.40	.25
537	Scottie Pippen (USA)	.60	.35
538	David Robinson (USA)	1.25	.70
539	John Stockton (USA)	.60	.35
540	Chuck Daly (USA)	.10	.06
541	P.J. Carlesimo (USA)	.20	.12
542	Mike Krzyzewski (USA)	.50	.30
543	Lenny Wilkens (USA)	.10	.06
544	Team USA Card 1	1.25	.70
545	Team USA Card 2	1.25	.70
546	Team USA Card 3	1.25	.70
547	Willie Anderson (USA)	.07	.04
548	Stacey Augmon (USA)	.40	.25
549	Bimbo Coles (USA)	.08	.05
550	Jeff Grayer (USA)	.07	.04
551	Hersey Hawkins (USA)	.08	.05
552	Dan Majerle (USA)	.10	.06
553	Danny Manning (USA)	.15	.10
554	J.R. Reid (USA)	.07	.04
555	Mitch Richmond (USA)	.10	.06
556	Charles Smith (USA)	.08	.05
557	Vern Fleming (USA)	.07	.04
558	Joe Kleine (USA)	.07	.04
559	Jon Koncak (USA)	.07	.04
560	Sam Perkins (USA)	.07	.04
561	Alvin Robertson (USA)	.07	.04
562	Wayman Tisdale (USA)	.07	.04
563	Jeff Turner (USA)	.07	.04
564	Tony Campbell (Magic)	.05	.02
565	Joe Dumars (Magic)	.10	.06
566	Horace Grant (Magic)	.07	.04
567	Reggie Lewis (Magic)	.10	.06
568	Hakeem Olajuwon(Magic)	.30	.18
569	Sam Perkins (Magic)	.07	.04
570	Chuck Person (Magic)	.07	.04
571	Buck Williams (Magic)	.07	.04
572	Michael Jordan (Magic)	1.00	.60
573	Bernard King (SS)	.07	.04
574	Moses Malone (SS)	.08	.05
575	Robert Parish (SS)	.08	.05
576	Pat Riley (SS)	.07	.04
577	Dee Brown (SM)	.10	.06
578	Rex Chapman (SM)	.07	.04
579	Clyde Drexler (SM)	.12	.07
580	Blue Edwards (SM)	.07	.04
581	Ron Harper (SM)	.05	.02
582	Kevin Johnson (SM)	.12	.07
583	Michael Jordan (SM)	1.00	.60
584	Shawn Kemp (SM)	.40	.25
585	Xavier McDaniel (SM)	.07	.04
586	Scottie Pippen (SM)	.15	.10
587	Kenny Smith (SM)	.05	.02
588	Dominique Wilkins(SM)	.15	.10
589	Michael Adams (SS)	.07	.04
590	Dany Ainge (SS)	.07	.04
591	Larry Bird (SS)	.35	.20
592	Dale Ellis (SS)	.05	.02
593	Hersey Hawkins (SS)	.08	.05
594	Jeff Hornacek (SS)	.08	.05
595	Jeff Malone (SS)	.07	.04
596	Reggie Miller (SS)	.12	.07
597	Chris Mullin (SS)	.10	.06
598	John Paxson (SS)	.07	.04
599	Drazen Petrovic (SS)	.10	.06
600	Ricky Pierce (SS)	.05	.02
601	Mark Price (SS)	.10	.06
602	Dennis Scott (SS)	.08	.05
603	Manute Bol (Small School)	.05	.02
604	Jerome Kersey (Small School)	.07	.04

1992 SKYBOX TEAM USA • 117

605	Charles Oakley (Small School)	.05	.02
606	Scottie Pippen (Small School)	.15	.10
607	Terry Porter (Small School)	.08	.05
608	Dennis Rodman (Small School)	.08	.05
609	Sedale Threatt (Small School)	.05	.02
610	Stay In School	.05	.02
611	Stay In School	.05	.02
612	Stay In School	.05	.02
613	Stay In School	.05	.02
614	Stay In School	.05	.02
615	Maurice Cheeks	.07	.04
616	Travis Mays	.05	.02
617	Blair Rasmussen	.05	.02
618	Alexander Volkov	.05	.02
619	Rickey Green	.05	.02
620	Bobby Hansen	.05	.02
621	John Battle	.05	.02
622	Terry Davis	.05	.02
623	Walter Davis	.07	.04
624	Winston Garland	.05	.02
625	Scott Hastings	.05	.02
626	Brad Sellers	.05	.02
627	Darrell Walker	.05	.02
628	Orlando Woolridge	.07	.04
629	Tony Brown	.05	.02
630	James Edwards	.05	.02
631	Doc Rivers	.05	.02
632	Jack Haley	.05	.02
633	Sedale Threatt	.05	.02
634	Moses Malone	.10	.06
635	Thurl Bailey	.05	.02
636	Rafael Addison (R)	.08	.05
637	Tim McCormick	.05	.02
638	Xavier McDaniel	.07	.04
639	Charles Shackleford	.05	.02
640	Mitchell Wiggins	.05	.02
641	Jerrod Mustaf	.05	.02
642	Dennis Hopson	.05	.02
643	Les Jepsen	.05	.02
644	Mitch Richmond	.12	.07
645	Dwayne Schintzius	.05	.02
646	Spud Webb	.05	.02
647	Jud Buechler	.05	.02
648	Antoie Carr	.05	.02
649	Tyrone Corbin	.05	.02
650	Michael Adams	.07	.04
651	Ralph Sampson	.07	.04
652	Andre Turner	.05	.02
653	David Wingate	.05	.02
654	Checklist	.05	.02
655	Checklist	.05	.02
656	Checklist	.05	.02
657	Checklist	.05	.02
658	Checklist	.05	.02
659	Checklist	.05	.02
___	Team USA Gold Card	15.00	10.00
___	Clyde Drexler USA	50.00	28.00

1992 SkyBox Team USA

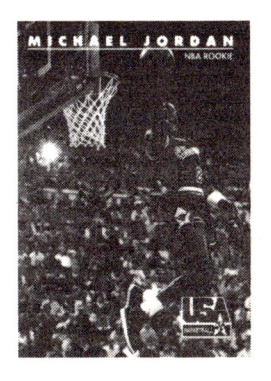

This 110-card set was issued to coincide with the 1992 Summer Olympic Games in Barcelona. It features 9-cards each of the top ten players on Team USA, along with two cards of the coaches and a subset featuring Magic Johnson's review of each player. The card fronts include full color, full bleed action photos with the player's name printed across the top just above the title of the card. The backs consist of another full color action photo and highlights. All cards measure 2-1/2" by 3-1/2".

		MINT	NR/MT
	Complete Set (110)	30.00	18.00
	Commons	.15	.10
1	Charles Barkley (Update)	.50	.30
2	Charles Barkley	.40	.25

1992 SKYBOX TEAM USA

#	Card	Price 1	Price 2
	(Rookie)		
3	Charles Barkley (Strategy)	.40	.25
4	Charles Barkley (Best Game)	.40	.25
5	Charles Barkley (Off the Court)	.40	.25
6	Charles Barkley (Shooting)	.40	.25
7	Charles Barkley (All-Star Record)	.40	.25
8	Charles Barkley Shooting)	.40	.25
9	Charles Barkley (Rebounding)	.40	.25
10	Larry Bird (Update)	.75	.45
11	Larry Bird (Rookie)	.75	.45
12	Larry Bird (Strategy)	.75	.45
13	Larry Bird (Best Game)	.75	.45
14	Larry Bird (Off the Court)	.75	.45
15	Larry Bird (Playoffs)	.75	.45
16	Larry Bird (All-Star Record)	.75	.45
17	Larry Bird (Shooting)	.75	.45
18	Larry Bird (Rebounding)	.75	.45
19	Patrick Ewing (Update)	.35	.20
20	Patrick Ewing (Rookie)	.35	.20
21	Patrick Ewing (Strategy)	.35	.20
22	Patrick Ewing (Best Game)	.35	.20
23	Patrick Ewing (Off the Court)	.35	.20
24	Patrick Ewing (Playoffs)	.35	.20
25	Patrick Ewing (All-Star Record)	.35	.20
26	Patrick Ewing (Shooting)	.35	.20
27	Patrick Ewing (Rebounding)	.35	.20
28	Magic Johnson (Update)	.75	.45
29	Magic Johnson (Rookie)	.75	.45
30	Magic Johnson (Strategy)	.75	.45
31	Magic Johnson (Best Game)	.75	.45
32	Magic Johnson (Off the Court)	.75	.45
33	Magic Johnson (Playoffs)	.75	.45
34	Magic Johnson (All-Star Record)	.75	.45
35	Magic Johnson (Shooting)	.75	.45
36	Magic Johnson (Assists)	.75	.45
37	Michael Jordan (Update)	1.50	.90
39	Michael Jordan (Strategy)	1.50	.90
40	Michael Jordan (Best Game)	1.50	.90
41	Michael Jordan (Off the Court)	1.50	.90
42	Michael Jordan (Playoffs)	1.50	.90
43	Michael Jordan (All-Star Record)	1.50	.90
44	Michael Jordan (Shooting)	1.50	.90
45	Michael Jordan (All-Time Records)	1.50	.90
46	Karl Malone (Update)	.25	.15
47	Karl Malone (Rookie)	.25	.15
48	Karl Malone (Strategy)	.25	.15
49	Karl Malone (Best Game)	.25	.15
50	Karl Malone (Off the Court)	.25	.15
51	Karl Malone (Playoffs)	.25	.15
52	Karl Malone (All-Star Record)	.25	.15
53	Karl Malone (Shooting)	.25	.15
54	Karl Malone (Rebounds)	.25	.15
55	Chris Mullin (Update)	.20	.12
56	Chris Mullin (Rookie)	.20	.12
57	Chris Mullin (Strategy)	.20	.12
58	Chris Mullin (Best Game)	.20	.12
59	Chris Mullin (Off the Court)	.20	.12
60	Chris Mullin	.20	.12

1992 SKYBOX TEAM USA • 119

	(Playoffs)		
61	Chris Mullin (All-Star Record)	.20	.12
62	Chris Mullin (Shooting)	.20	.12
63	Chris Mullin (Minutes)	.20	.12
64	Scottie Pippen (Update)	.20	.12
65	Scottie Pippen (Rookie)	.20	.12
66	Scottie Pippen (Strategy)	.20	.12
67	Scottie Pippen (Best Game)	.20	.12
68	Scottie Pippen (Off the Court)	.20	.12
69	Scottie Pippen (Playoffs)	.20	.12
70	Scottie Pippen (All-Star Record)	.20	.12
71	Scottie Pippen (Shooting)	.20	.12
72	Scottie Pippen (Steals and Blocks)	.20	.12
73	David Robinson (Update)	.75	.45
74	David Robinson (Rookie)	.75	.45
75	David Robinson (Strategy)	.75	.45
76	David Robinson (Best Game)	.75	.45
77	David Robinson (Off the Court)	.75	.45
78	David Robinson (Playoffs)	.75	.45
79	David Robinson (All-Star)	.75	.45
80	David Robinson (Shooting)	.75	.45
81	David Robinson (All-Around)	.75	.45
82	John Stockton (Update)	.20	.12
83	John Stockton (Rookie)	.20	.12
84	John Stockton (Strategy)	.20	.12
85	John Stockton (Best Game)	.20	.12
86	John Stockton (Off the Court)	.20	.12
87	John Stockton (Playoffs)	.20	.12
88	John Stockton (All-Star Record)	.20	.12
89	John Stockton (Shooting)	.20	.12
90	John Stockton (Assists)	.20	.12
91	P.J. Carlesimo (C) (College Coaching)	.15	.10
92	P.J. Carlesimo (C) (NCAA Record)	.15	.10
93	Chuck Daly (C) (NBA Coaching)	.15	.10
94	Chuck Daly (C) (NCAA Record)	.15	.10
95	Mike Krzyzewski (C) (College Coaching)	.15	.10
96	Mike Krzyzewski (C) (NCAA Record)	.15	.10
97	Lenny Wilkens (C) (NBA Coaching)	.15	.10
98	Lenny Wilkens (C) (NBA Record)	.15	.10
99	Checklist	.15	.10
100	Checklist	.15	.10
101	Magic on Barkley	.40	.25
102	Magic on Bird	.75	.45
103	Magic on Ewing	.35	.20
104	Magic on Magic	.75	.45
105	Magic on Jordan	1.00	.60
106	Magic on Malone	.30	.18
107	Magic on Mullin	.20	.12
108	Magic on Pippen	.25	.15
109	Magic on Robinson	.50	.30
110	Magic on Stockton	.25	.15

1992-93 SkyBox

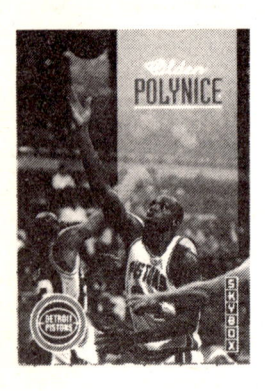

The cards in this set were issued in two series and, for the first time, SkyBox combined full color game action photos over a background of computer-generated designs on the card fronts. The full-bleed fronts feature the player's name in block letters in the upper corner of the photograph. The flip side contains another full color photograph along with stats and a one-line biographical sketch. Key subsets include Coaches (C)(255-281), Team Tix (TT)(282-308), All-Star Highlights (AS)(309-313), NBA Finals (314-318), and Public Service Cards (320-321). Gold foil limited insert cards of Magic Johnson and David Robinson were distributed randomly in SkyBox foil packs. Those cards are listed at the end of the checklist. All cards measure 2-1/2" by 3-1/2".

	MINT	NR/MT
Complete Set (413)	48.00	28.00
Commons	.05	.02

#	Player	MINT	NR/MT
1	Stacey Augmon	.20	.12
2	Maurice Cheeks	.07	.04
3	Duane Ferrell	.05	.02
4	Paul Graham	.05	.02
5	Jon Koncak	.05	.02
6	Blair Rasmussen	.05	.02
7	Rumeal Robinson	.05	.02
8	Dominique Wilkins	.30	.18
9	Kevin Willis	.07	.04
10	Larry Bird	.75	.45
11	Dee Brown	.12	.07
12	Sherman Douglas	.08	.05
13	Rick Fox	.08	.05
14	Kevin Gamble	.05	.02
15	Reggie Lewis	.12	.07
16	Kevin McHale	.12	.07
17	Robert Parish	.12	.07
18	Ed Pinckney	.05	.02
19	Muggsy Bogues	.05	.02
20	Dell Curry	.05	.02
21	Kenny Gattison	.05	.02
22	Kendall Gill	.15	.10
23	Mike Gminski	.05	.02
24	Tom Hammonds	.05	.02
25	Larry Johnson	1.75	1.00
26	Johnny Newman	.05	.02
27	J.R. Reid	.05	.02
28	B.J. Armstrong	.12	.07
29	Bill Cartwright	.05	.02
30	Horace Grant	.07	.04
31	Michael Jordan	2.50	1.50
32	Stacey King	.07	.04
33	John Paxson	.07	.04
34	Will Perdue	.05	.02
35	Scottie Pippen	.35	.20
36	Scott Williams	.05	.02
37	John Battle	.05	.02
38	Terrell Brandon	.10	.06
39	Brad Daugherty	.12	.07
40	Craig Ehlo	.05	.02
41	Danny Ferry	.05	.02
42	Henry James	.05	.02
43	Larry Nance	.07	.04
44	Mark Price	.12	.07
45	Mike Sanders	.05	.02
46	Hot Rod Williams	.07	.04
47	Rolando Blackman	.07	.04
48	Terry Davis	.05	.02
49	Derek Harper	.07	.04
50	Donald Hodge	.05	.02
51	Mike Iuzzolino	.05	.02
52	Fat Lever	.05	.02
53	Rodney McCray	.05	.02
54	Doug Smith	.07	.04
55	Randy White	.05	.02
56	Herb Williams	.05	.02
57	Greg Anderson	.07	.04
58	Walter Davis	.07	.04
59	Winston Garland	.05	.02
60	Chris Jackson	.15	.10
61	Marcus Liberty	.07	.04
62	Todd Lichti	.05	.02
63	Mark Macon	.08	.05
64	Dikembe Mutombo	.40	.25
65	Reggie Williams	.05	.02

1992-93 SKYBOX • 121

#	Player		
66	Mark Aguirre	.07	.04
67	William Bedford	.05	.02
68	Lance Blanks	.05	.02
69	Joe Dumars	.15	.10
70	Bill Laimbeer	.07	.04
71	Dennis Rodman	.10	.06
72	John Salley	.05	.02
73	Isiah Thomas	.20	.12
74	Darrell Walker	.05	.02
75	Orlando Woolridge	.05	.02
76	Victor Alexander	.05	.02
77	Mario Elie	.05	.02
78	Chris Gatling	.05	.02
79	Tim Hardaway	.20	.12
80	Tyrone Hill	.05	.02
81	Alton Lister	.05	.02
82	Sarunas Marciulionis	.07	.04
83	Chris Mullin	.20	.12
84	Billy Owens	.20	.12
85	Matt Bullard	.05	.02
86	Sleepy Floyd	.05	.02
87	Avery Johnson	.05	.02
88	Buck Johnson	.05	.02
89	Vernon Maxwell	.12	.07
90	Hakeem Olajuwon	.75	.45
91	Kenny Smith	.07	.04
92	Larry Smith	.05	.02
93	Otis Thorpe	.07	.04
94	Dale Davis	.08	.05
95	Vern Fleming	.05	.02
96	George McCloud	.05	.02
97	Reggie Miller	.25	.15
98	Chuck Person	.07	.04
99	Detlef Schrempf	.12	.07
100	Rik Smits	.05	.02
101	LaSalle Thompson	.05	.02
102	Michael Williams	.05	.02
103	James Edwards	.05	.02
104	Gary Grant	.05	.02
105	Ron Harper	.07	.04
106	Bo Kimble	.05	.02
107	Danny Manning	.20	.12
108	Ken Norman	.07	.04
109	Olden Polynice	.05	.02
110	Doc Rivers	.05	.02
111	Charles Smith	.08	.05
112	Loy Vaught	.07	.04
113	Elden Campbell	.10	.06
114	Vlade Divac	.08	.05
115	A.C. Green	.07	.04
116	Jack Haley	.05	.02
117	Sam Perkins	.07	.04
118	Byron Scott	.05	.02
119	Tony Smith	.05	.02
120	Sedale Threatt	.05	.02
121	James Worthy	.10	.06
122	Keith Askins	.05	.02
123	Willie Burton	.07	.04
124	Bimbo Coles	.05	.02
125	Kevin Edwards	.05	.02
126	Alec Kessler	.05	.02
127	Grant Long	.05	.02
128	Glen Rice	.15	.10
129	Rony Seikaly	.08	.05
130	Brian Shaw	.05	.02
131	Steve Smith	.25	.15
132	Frank Brickowski	.05	.02
133	Dale Ellis	.05	.02
134	Jeff Grayer	.05	.02
135	Jay Humphries	.05	.02
136	Larry Krystkowiak	.05	.02
137	Moses Malone	.10	.06
138	Fred Roberts	.05	.02
139	Alvin Robertson	.05	.02
140	Dan Schayes	.05	.02
141	Thurl Bailey	.05	.02
142	Scott Brooks	.05	.02
143	Tony Campbell	.05	.02
144	Gerald Glass	.07	.04
145	Luc Longley	.05	.02
146	Sam Mitchell	.07	.04
147	Pooh Richardson	.07	.04
148	Felton Spencer	.10	.06
149	Doug West	.07	.04
150	Rafael Addison	.05	.02
151	Kenny Anderson	.25	.15
152	Mookie Blaylock	.07	.04
153	Sam Bowie	.05	.02
154	Derrick Coleman	.25	.15
155	Chris Dudley	.05	.02
156	Tate George	.05	.02
157	Terry Mills	.08	.05
158	Chris Morris	.05	.02
159	Drazen Petrovic	.15	.10
160	Greg Anthony	.10	.06
161	Patrick Ewing	.40	.25
162	Mark Jackson	.07	.04
163	Anthony Mason	.05	.02
164	Tim McCormick	.05	.02
165	Xavier McDaniel	.07	.04
166	Charles Oakley	.07	.04
167	John Starks	.20	.12
168	Gerald Wilkins	.05	.02
169	Nick Anderson	.20	.12
170	Terry Catledge	.05	.02
171	Jerry Reynolds	.05	.02
172	Stanley Roberts	.08	.05
173	Dennis Scott	.08	.05
174	Scott Skiles	.05	.02
175	Jeff Turner	.05	.02
176	Sam Vincent	.05	.02
177	Brian Williams	.10	.06
178	Ron Anderson	.05	.02
179	Charles Barkley	.40	.25

122 • 1992-93 SKYBOX

#	Player		
180	Manute Bol	.05	.02
181	Johnny Dawkins	.05	.02
182	Armon Gilliam	.05	.02
183	Greg Grant	.05	.02
184	Hersey Hawkins	.08	.05
185	Brian Oliver	.05	.02
186	Charles Shackleford	.05	.02
187	Jayson Williams	.05	.02
188	Cedric Ceballos	.08	.05
189	Tom Chambers	.07	.04
190	Jeff Hornacek	.07	.04
191	Kevin Johnson	.12	.07
192	Negele Knight	.07	.04
193	Andrew Lang	.05	.02
194	Dan Majerle	.10	.06
195	Jerrod Mustaf	.05	.02
196	Tim Perry	.05	.02
197	Mark West	.05	.02
198	Alaa Abdelnaby	.05	.02
199	Danny Ainge	.10	.06
200	Mark Bryant	.05	.02
201	Clyde Drexler	.25	.15
202	Kevin Duckworth	.07	.04
203	Jerome Kersey	.08	.05
204	Robert Pack	.05	.02
205	Terry Porter	.08	.05
206	Cliff Robinson	.10	.06
207	Buck Williams	.07	.04
208	Anthony Bonner	.05	.02
209	Randy Brown	.05	.02
210	Duane Causwell	.05	.02
211	Pete Chilcutt	.05	.02
212	Dennis Hopson	.05	.02
213	Jim Les	.05	.02
214	Mitch Richmond	.15	.10
215	Lionel Simmons	.15	.10
216	Waymen Tisdale	.07	.04
217	Spud Webb	.05	.02
218	Willie Anderson	.05	.02
219	Antoine Carr	.05	.02
220	Terry Cummings	.08	.05
221	Sean Elliott	.12	.07
222	Sidney Green	.05	.02
223	Vinnie Johnson	.05	.02
224	David Robinson	.60	.35
225	Rod Strickland	.05	.02
226	Greg Sutton	.05	.02
227	Dana Barros	.07	.04
228	Benoit Benjamin	.05	.02
229	Michael Cage	.05	.02
230	Eddie Johnson	.05	.02
231	Shawn Kemp	.60	.35
232	Derrick McKey	.07	.04
233	Nate McMillan	.05	.02
234	Gary Payton	.12	.07
235	Ricky Pierce	.05	.02
236	David Benoit	.08	.05
237	Mike Brown	.05	.02
238	Tyrone Corbin	.05	.02
239	Mark Eaton	.05	.02
240	Blue Edwards	.07	.04
241	Jeff Malone	.07	.04
242	Karl Malone	.30	.18
243	Eric Murdock	.07	.04
244	John stockton	.25	.15
245	Michael Adams	.07	.04
246	Rex Chapman	.05	.02
247	Ledell Eackles	.05	.02
248	Pervis Ellison	.08	.05
249	A.J. English	.05	.02
250	Harvey Grant	.05	.02
251	Charles Jones	.05	.02
252	Bernard King	.07	.04
253	LaBradford Smith	.05	.02
254	Larry Stewart	.05	.02
255	Bob Weiss (C)	.05	.02
256	Chris Ford (C)	.05	.02
257	Allan Bristow (C)	.05	.02
258	Phil Jackson (C)	.07	.04
259	Lenny Wilkens (C)	.07	.04
260	Richie Adubato (C)	.05	.02
261	Dan Issel (C)	.07	.04
262	Ron Rothstein (C)	.05	.02
263	Don Nelson (C)	.05	.02
264	Rudy Tomjanovich (C)	.05	.02
265	Bob Hill (C)	.05	.02
266	Larry Brown (C)	.05	.02
267	Randy Pfund (C)	.05	.02
268	Kevin Loughery (C)	.05	.02
269	Mike Dunleavy (C)	.05	.02
270	Jimmy Rodgers (C)	.05	.02
271	Chuck Daly (C)	.05	.02
272	Pat Riley (C)	.07	.04
273	Matt Guokas (C)	.05	.02
274	Doug Moe (C)	.05	.02
275	Paul Westphal (C)	.05	.02
276	Rick Adelman (C)	.05	.02
277	Garry St. Jean (C)	.05	.02
278	Jerry Tarkanian (C)(R)	.15	.10
279	George Karl (C)	.05	.02
280	Jerry Sloan (C)	.05	.02
281	Wes Unseld (C)	.05	.02
282	Dominique Wilkins (TT)	.20	.12
283	Reggie Lewis (TT)	.08	.05
284	Kendall Gill (TT)	.10	.06
285	Horace Grant (TT)	.05	.02
286	Brad Daugherty (TT)	.08	.05
287	Derek Harper (TT)	.05	.02
288	Chris Jackson (TT)	.08	.05
289	Isiah Thomas (TT)	.10	.06
290	Chris Mullin (TT)	.10	.06
291	Kenny Smith (TT)	.05	.02
292	Reggie Miller (TT)	.12	.07
293	Ron Harper (TT)	.05	.02

1992-93 SKYBOX • 123

#	Name		
294	Vlade Divac (TT)	.05	.02
295	Glen Rice (TT)	.10	.06
296	Moses Malone (TT)	.08	.05
297	Doug West (TT)	.05	.02
298	Derrick Coleman (TT)	.15	.10
299	Patrick Ewing (TT)	.25	.15
300	Scott Skiles (TT)	.05	.02
301	Hesey Hawkins (TT)	.06	.03
302	Kevin Johnson (TT)	.10	.06
303	Cliff Robinson (TT)	.07	.04
304	Anthony Webb (TT)	.05	.02
305	David Robinson (TT)	.30	.18
306	Shawn Kemp (TT)	.25	.15
307	John Stockton (TT)	.12	.07
308	Pervis Ellison (TT)	.06	.03
309	Craig Hodges (AS)	.05	.02
310	Magic Johnson(AS-MVP)	.35	.20
311	Cedric Ceballos (AS)	.08	.05
312	West in Action (AS)	.05	.02
313	East in Action (AS)	.05	.02
314	Michael Jordan (MVP)	1.00	.60
315	Clyde Drexler (Finals)	.15	.10
316	Danny Ainge (Finals)	.07	.04
317	Scottie Pippen (Finals)	.15	.10
318	Chicago Bulls Champs	.10	.06
319	Larry Johnson (ROY)	.50	.30
320	Stay In School	.05	.02
321	Boys & Girls Clubs	.05	.02
322	Checklist	.05	.02
323	Checklist	.05	.02
324	Checklist	.05	.02
325	Checklist	.05	.02
326	Checklist	.05	.02
327	Checklist	.05	.02
328	Adam Keefe (R)	.20	.12
329	Sean Rooks (R)	.30	.18
330	Xavier McDaniel	.07	.04
331	Kiki Vandeweghe	.05	.02
332	Alonzo Mourning (R)	6.00	3.50
333	Rodney McCray	.05	.02
334	Gerald Wilkins	.05	.02
335	Tony Bennett (R)	.12	.07
336	LaPhonso Ellis (R)	1.75	1.00
337	Bryant Stith (R)	.50	.30
338	Isaiah Morris (R)	.12	.07
339	Olyden Polynice	.05	.02
340	Jeff Grayer	.05	.02
341	Byron Houston (R)	.25	.15
342	Latrell Sprewell (R)	3.50	2.00
343	Scott Brooks	.05	.02
344	Frank Johnson	.05	.02
345	Robert Horry (R)	1.75	1.00
346	David Wood	.05	.02
347	Sam Mitchell	.07	.04
348	Pooh Richardson	.07	.04
349	Malik Sealy (R)	.12	.07
350	Morton Wiley	.05	.02
351	Mark Jackson	.07	.04
352	Stanley Roberts	.08	.05
353	Elmore Spencer (R)	.25	.15
354	John Williams	.05	.02
355	Randy Woods (R)	.10	.06
356	James Edwards	.05	.02
357	Jeff Sanders	.05	.02
358	Magic Johnson	.40	.25
359	Anthony Peeler (R)	.50	.30
360	Harold Miner (R)	.80	.50
361	John Salley	.05	.02
362	Alaa Abdelnaby	.05	.02
363	Todd Day (R)	.50	.30
364	Blue Edwards	.07	.04
365	Lee Mayberry (R)	.20	.12
366	Eric Murdock	.08	.05
367	Mookie Blaylock	.07	.04
368	Anthony Avent (R)	.15	.10
369	Christian Laettner (R)	1.75	1.00
370	Chuck Person	.07	.04
371	Chris Smith (R)	.20	.12
372	Michael Williams	.05	.02
373	Rolando Blackman	.07	.04
374	Tony Campbell	.05	.02
375	Hubert Davis (R)	.50	.30
376	Travis Mays	.05	.02
377	Doc Rivers	.05	.02
378	Charles Smith	.08	.05
379	Rumeal Robinson	.05	.02
380	Vinny Del Negro	.05	.02
381	Steve Kerr	.05	.02
382	Shaquille O'Neal (R)	12.00	7.50
383	Donald Royal	.05	.02
384	Jeff Hornacek	.08	.05
385	Andrew Lang	.05	.02
386	Tim Perry	.05	.02
387	C. Weatherspoon (R)	1.25	.70
388	Danny Ainge	.07	.04
389	Charles Barkley	.40	.25
390	Tim Kempton	.05	.02
391	Oliver Miller (R)	.75	.45
392	Dave Johnson (R)	.12	.07
393	Tracy Murray (R)	.20	.12
394	Rod Strickland	.05	.02
395	Marty Conlon	.05	.02
396	Walt Williams (R)	.60	.35
397	Lloyd Daniels (R)	.20	.12
398	Dale Ellis	.05	.02
399	Dave Hoppen	.05	.02
400	Larry Smith	.05	.02
401	Doug Overton	.05	.02
402	Isaac Austin (R)	.10	.06
403	Jay Humphries	.05	.02
404	Larry Krystowiak	.05	.02
405	Tom Gugliotta (R)	1.25	.70
406	Buck Johnson	.05	.02
407	Don MacLean (R)	.75	.45

124 • 1992-93 SKYBOX

408	Marlon Maxey (R)	.15	.10
409	Corey Williams (R)	.15	.10
410	Special Olympics	.05	.02
411	Checklist	.05	.02
412	Checklist	.05	.02
413	Checklist	.05	.02
___	Magic Johnson Insert	15.00	8.50
___	David Robinson Insert	15.00	6.50

1992-93 SkyBox David Robinson

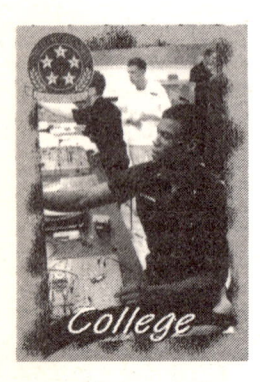

The cards in this limited insert set were distributed randomly in SkyBox packs. The cards feature biographical photographs of David Robinson at various stages in his life. All cards measure 2-1/2" by 3-1/2".

		MINT	NR/MT
	Complete Set (10)	5.00	3.00
	Commons	.50	.30
R1	David Robinson (Childhood)	.50	.30
R2	David Robinson (At Ease)	.50	.30
R3	David Robinson (College)	.50	.30
R4	David Robinson (College)	.50	.30
R5	David Robinson (At Ease)	.50	.30
R6	David Robinson (College)	.50	.30
R7	David Robinson (College)	.50	.30
R8	David Robinson (Awards)	.50	.30
R9	David Robinson (Awards)	.50	.30
R10	David Robinson (At Ease)	.50	.30

1992-93 SkyBox Draft Picks

The cards in this limited insert set feature the top draft picks from the 1992 NBA draft. Two cards, #4 and #17, were never issued. The cards feature full color photos of the players on the front with their names in white letters in the top corner and an NBA Draft logo in the lower corner. The cards were randomly inserted into SkyBox foil packs. All cards measure 2-1/2" by 3-1/2".

		MINT	NR/MT
	Complete Set (25)	100.00	60.00
	Commons	.75	.45
1	Shaquille O'Neal	32.00	20.00

1992-93 SKYBOX THUNDER & LIGHTNING • 125

2	Alonzo Mourning	20.00	12.50
3	Christian Laettner	6.00	3.50
5	LaPhonso Ellis	6.00	3.50
6	Tom Gugliotta	5.00	3.00
7	Walt Williams	3.00	1.75
8	Todd Day	2.00	1.25
9	C. Weatherspoon	3.50	2.00
10	Adam Keefe	.80	.50
11	Robert Horry	5.00	3.00
12	Harold Miner	3.50	2.00
13	Bryant Stith	2.00	1.25
14	Malik Sealy	.80	.50
15	Anthony Peeler	2.00	1.25
16	Randy Woods	.75	.45
18	Tracy Murray	1.00	.60
19	Don MacLean	2.50	1.50
20	Hubert Davis	2.50	1.50
21	Jon Barry	.75	.45
22	Oliver Miller	3.00	1.75
23	Lee Mayberry	.80	.50
24	Latrell Sprewell	12.00	7.00
25	Elmore Spencer	1.00	.60
26	Dave Johnson	.75	.45
27	Byron Houston	1.00	.60

1992-93 SkyBox Olympic Team

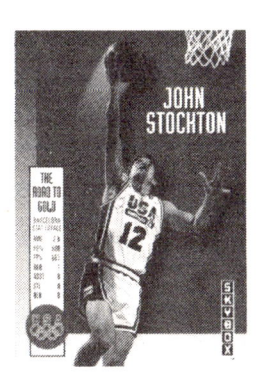

The cards in this limited insert set feature the players on the 1992 USA Olympic Dream Team. The card fronts include full color action photos of the player set against a colorful computer-generated background. A vertical strip containing the player's statistics is located in the lower corner of the card front while his name is printed in white lettering in the top corner. The card numbers contain the prefix USA. These cards were randomly inserted in SkyBox foil packs. All cards measure 2-1/2" by 3-1/2".

		MINT	NR/MT
	Complete Set (12)	28.00	18.00
	Commons	1.25	.70
1	Clyde Drexler	1.50	.90
2	Chris Mullin	1.25	.70
3	John Stockton	1.50	.90
4	Karl Malone	2.00	1.25
5	Scottie Pippen	2.00	1.25
6	Larry Bird	5.00	3.00
7	Charles Barkley	4.00	2.50
8	Patrick Ewing	3.00	1.75
9	Christian Laettner	4.00	2.50
10	David Robinson	4.00	2.50
11	Michael Jordan	10.00	6.50
12	Magic Johnson	4.00	2.50

1992-93 SkyBox Thunder & Lightning

The cards in this limited insert set feature full color action photos of players on each side. The players name is printed in script in the bottom third of the photograph with either

126 • 1992-93 SKYBOX THUNDER & LIGHTNING

the words Thunder or Lightning printed directly under his name. The cards were randomly inserted into SkyBox Series II packs. All cards measure 2-1/2" by 3-1/2".

	MINT	NR/MT
Complete Set (9)	75.00	45.00
Commons	2.50	1.50

1	Mutombo/Macon	7.00	4.00
2	Drexler/Williams	5.00	3.00
3	Barkley/Johnson	20.00	12.50
4	Adams/Ellison	2.50	1.50
5	Bogues/Johnson	20.00	12.50
6	Daugherty/Price	3.00	1.75
7	Kemp/Payton	18.00	12.00
8	Malone/Stockton	12.00	7.00
9	Owens/Hardaway	3.50	2.00

1993-94 SkyBox

The cards in this set feature full-color game action player photos on the card fronts. A white stripe along one side of the card contains the player's name and position at the top and a team logo at the bottom. The printing corresponds with the player's team colors. The card backs contain another full-color head shot on the top half with personal data, a scouting report and stats on the lower half. Subsets include Playoff Performanc (P)(4-21), Changing Faces (CF)(292-318) and Costacos Brothers Poster Cards (PC)(319-338). The set also includes two Draft Pick insert cards of player's who were not included in SkyBox's 1992-93 set, DP 4 Jim Jackson and DP 17 Doug Christie. Those cards are listed at the end of this checklist. All cards measure 2-1/2" by 3-1/2".

	MINT	NR/MT
Complete Set (341)	28.00	18.00
Commons	.05	.02

1	Checklist	.05	.02
2	Checklist	.05	.02
3	Checklist	.05	.02
4	Larry Johnson (P)	.30	.18
5	Alonzo Mourning (P)	.40	.25
6	Hakeem Olajuwon (P)	.50	.30
7	Brad Daugherty (P)	.08	.05
8	Oliver Miller (P)	.08	.05
9	David Robinson (P)	.25	.15
10	Patrick Ewing (P)	.20	.12
11	Ricky Pierce (P)	.05	.02
12	Sam Perkins (P)	.05	.02
13	John Starks (P)	.08	.05
14	Michael Jordan (P)	1.00	.60
15	Dan Majerle (P)	.08	.05
16	Scottie Pippen (P)	.20	.12
17	Shawn Kemp (P)	.25	.15
18	Charles Barkley (P)	.30	.18
19	Horace Grant (P)	.05	.02
20	Kevin Johnson (P)	.07	.04
21	John Paxson (P)	.05	.02
22	Inside Stuff	.05	.02
23	NBA On NBC	.05	.02
24	Stacey Augmon	.15	.10
25	Mookie Blaylock	.10	.06
26	Craig Ehlo	.05	.02
27	Adam Keefe	.05	.02
28	Dominique Wilkins	.25	.15
29	Kevin Willis	.05	.02
30	Dee Brown	.10	.06
31	Sherman Douglas	.07	.04
32	Rick Fox	.08	.05
33	Kevin Gamble	.05	.02
34	Xavier McDaniel	.05	.02
35	Robert Parish	.12	.07
36	Muggsy Bogues	.05	.02
37	Dell Curry	.05	.02
38	Kendall Gill	.12	.07
39	Larry Johnson	.40	.25
40	Alonzo Mourning	.75	.45
41	Johnny Newman	.05	.02

1993-94 SKYBOX • 127

#	Player		
42	B.J. Armstrong	.12	.07
43	Bill Cartwright	.05	.02
44	Horace Grant	.05	.02
45	Michael Jordan	2.00	1.25
46	John Paxson	.07	.04
47	Scottie Pippen	.30	.18
48	Scott Williams	.05	.02
49	Terrell Brandon	.07	.04
50	Brad Daugherty	.10	.06
51	Larry Nance	.05	.02
52	Mark Price	.12	.07
53	Gerald Wilkins	.05	.02
54	John Williams (Cle)	.08	.05
55	Terry Davis	.05	.02
56	Derek Harper	.07	.04
57	Jim Jackson	.40	.25
58	Sean Rooks	.12	.07
59	Doug Smith	.05	.02
60	Mahmoud Abdul-Rauf	.15	.10
61	LaPhonso Ellis	.25	.15
62	Mark Macon	.08	.05
63	Dikembe Mutombo	.30	.18
64	Bryant Stith	.15	.10
65	Reggie Williams	.05	.02
66	Joe Dumars	.15	.10
67	Bill Laimbeer	.05	.02
68	Terry Mills	.05	.02
69	Alvin Robertson	.05	.02
70	Dennis Rodman	.12	.07
71	Isiah Thomas	.20	.12
72	Victor Alexander	.05	.02
73	Tim Hardaway	.15	.10
74	Tyrone Hill	.05	.02
75	Sarunas Marciulionis	.07	.04
76	Chris Mullin	.15	.10
77	Billy Owens	.15	.10
78	Latrell Sprewell	.75	.45
79	Robert Horry	.35	.20
80	Vernon Maxwell	.12	.07
81	Hakeem Olajuwon	.75	.45
82	Kenny Smith	.07	.04
83	Otis Thorpe	.07	.04
84	Dale Davis	.10	.06
85	Reggie Miller	.25	.15
86	Pooh Richardson	.05	.02
87	Detlef Schrempf	.12	.07
88	Malik Sealy	.08	.05
89	Rik Smits	.05	.02
90	Ron Harper	.07	.04
91	Mark Jackson	.08	.05
92	Danny Manning	.15	.10
93	Stanley Roberts	.05	.02
94	Loy Vaught	.05	.02
95	Randy Woods	.05	.02
96	Sam Bowie	.05	.02
97	Doug Christie	.15	.10
98	Vlade Divac	.10	.06
99	Anthony Peeler	.15	.10
100	Sedale Threatt	.05	.02
101	James Worthy	.10	.06
102	Grant Long	.05	.02
103	Harold Miner	.20	.12
104	Glen Rice	.08	.05
105	John Salley	.05	.02
106	Rony Seikaly	.08	.05
107	Steve Smith	.15	.10
108	Anthony Avent	.08	.05
109	Jon Barry	.07	.04
110	Frank Brickowski	.05	.02
111	Blue Edwards	.05	.02
112	Todd Day	.15	.10
113	Lee Mayberry	.08	.05
114	Eric Murdock	.07	.04
115	Thurl Bailey	.05	.02
116	Christian Laettner	.25	.15
117	Chuck Person	.08	.05
118	Doug West	.08	.05
119	Michael Williams	.05	.02
120	Kenny Anderson	.20	.12
121	Benoit Benjamin	.05	.02
122	Derrick Coleman	.20	.12
123	Chris Morris	.05	.02
124	Rumeal Robinson	.05	.02
125	Rolando Blackman	.05	.02
126	Patrick Ewing	.35	.20
127	Anthony Mason	.08	.05
128	Charles Oakley	.08	.05
129	Doc Rivers	.07	.04
130	Charles Smith	.07	.04
131	John Starks	.15	.10
132	Nick Anderson	.12	.07
133	Shaquille O'Neal	2.00	1.25
134	Donald Royal	.05	.02
135	Dennis Scott	.08	.05
136	Scott Skiles	.05	.02
137	Brian Williams	.15	.10
138	Johnny Dawkins	.05	.02
139	Hersey Hawkins	.08	.05
140	Jeff Hornacek	.08	.05
141	Andrew Lang	.05	.02
142	Tim Perry	.05	.02
143	Clarence Weatherspoon	.15	.10
144	Danny Ainge	.08	.05
145	Charles Barkley	.40	.25
146	Cedric Ceballos	.08	.05
147	Kevin Johnson	.12	.07
148	Oliver Miller	.10	.06
149	Dan Majerle	.10	.06
150	Clyde Drexler	.20	.12
151	Harvey Grant	.05	.02
152	Jerome Kersey	.05	.02
153	Terry Porter	.10	.06
154	Cliff Robinson	.12	.07
155	Rod Strickland	.05	.02

128 • 1993-94 SKYBOX

#	Player		
156	Buck Williams	.07	.04
157	Mitch Richmond	.15	.10
158	Lionel Simmons	.15	.10
159	Wayman Tisdale	.07	.04
160	Spud Webb	.05	.02
161	Walt Williams	.15	.10
162	Antoine Carr	.05	.02
163	Lloyd Daniels	.08	.05
164	Sean Elliott	.12	.07
165	Dale Ellis	.07	.04
166	Avery Johnson	.05	.02
167	J.R. Reid	.05	.02
168	David Robinson	.40	.25
169	Shawn Kemp	.40	.25
170	Derrick McKey	.07	.04
171	Nate McMillan	.05	.02
172	Gary Payton	.12	.07
173	Sam Perkins	.07	.04
174	Ricky Pierce	.05	.02
175	Tyrone Corbin	.05	.02
176	Jay Humphries	.05	.02
177	Jeff Malone	.07	.04
178	Karl Malone	.30	.18
179	John Stockton	.25	.15
180	Michael Adams	.07	.04
181	Kevin Duckworth	.05	.02
182	Pervis Ellison	.10	.06
183	Tom Gugliotta	.25	.15
184	Don MacLean	.20	.12
185	Brent Price	.07	.04
186	George Lynch (R)	.35	.20
187	Rex Walters (R)	.15	.10
188	Shawn Bradley (R)	.40	.25
189	Ervin Johnson (R)	.12	.07
190	Luther Wright (R)	.20	.12
191	Calbert Cheaney (R)	.35	.20
192	Craig Ehlo	.05	.02
193	Duane Ferrell	.05	.02
194	Paul Graham	.05	.02
195	Andrew Lang	.05	.02
196	Chris Corchiani	.05	.02
197	Acie Earl (R)	.20	.12
198	Dino Radja (R)	.30	.18
199	Ed Pinckney	.05	.02
200	Tony Bennett	.05	.02
201	Scott Burrell (R)	.20	.12
202	Kenny Gattison	.05	.02
203	Hersey Hawkins	.07	.04
204	Eddie Johnson	.05	.02
205	Corie Blount (R)	.15	.10
206	Steve Kerr	.05	.02
207	Toni Kukoc (R)	.50	.30
208	Pete Myers	.05	.02
209	Danny Ferry	.05	.02
210	Tyrone Hill	.05	.02
211	Gerald Madkins (R)	.10	.06
212	Chris Mills (R)	.25	.15
213	Lucious Harris (R)	.12	.07
214	Ron Jones (R)	.12	.07
215	Jamal Mashburn (R)	1.25	.70
216	Darnell Mee (R)	.12	.07
217	Rodney Rogers (R)	.25	.15
218	Brian Williams	.10	.06
219	Greg Anderson	.05	.02
220	Sean Elliott	.10	.06
221	Allan Houston (R)	.20	.12
222	Lindsey Hunter (R)	.25	.15
223	Chris Gatling	.05	.02
224	Josh Grant (R)	.12	.07
225	Keith Jennings	.05	.02
226	Avery Johnson	.05	.02
227	Chris Webber (R)	3.00	1.75
228	Sam Cassell (R)	.40	.25
229	Mario Elie	.05	.02
230	Richard Petruska (R)	.15	.10
231	Eric Riley (R)	.12	.07
232	Antonio Davis (R)	.20	.12
233	Scott Haskin (R)	.15	.10
234	Derrick McKey	.07	.04
235	Mark Aquirre	.07	.04
236	Terry Dehere (R)	.20	.12
237	Gary Grant	.05	.02
238	Randy Woods	.05	.02
239	Sam Bowie	.05	.02
240	Elden Campbell	.10	.06
241	Nick Van Exel (R)	.40	.25
242	Manute Bol	.05	.02
243	Brian Shaw	.05	.02
244	Vin Baker (R)	.75	.45
245	Brad Lohaus	.05	.02
246	Ken Norman	.07	.04
247	Derek Strong (R)	.12	.07
248	Dan Schayes	.05	.02
249	Mike Brown	.05	.02
250	Luc Longley	.05	.02
251	Isaiah Rider (R)	.80	.50
252	Kevin Edwards	.05	.02
253	Armon Gilliam	.05	.02
254	Greg Anthony	.07	.04
255	Anthony Bonner	.05	.02
256	Tony Campbell	.05	.02
257	Hubert Davis	.15	.10
258	Litterial Green	.05	.02
259	Anfernee Hardaway (R)	2.50	1.50
260	Larry Krystkowiak	.05	.02
261	Todd Lichti	.05	.02
262	Dana Barros	.05	.02
263	Greg Graham (R)	.12	.07
264	Warren Kidd (R)	.10	.06
265	Moses Malone	.10	.06
266	A.C. Green	.08	.05
267	Joe Kleine	.05	.02
268	Malcolm Mackey (R)	.15	.10
269	Mark Bryant	.05	.02

1993-94 SKYBOX • 129

#	Name		
270	Chris Dudley	.05	.02
271	Harvey Grant	.05	.02
272	James Robinson (R)	.15	.10
273	Duane Causwell	.05	.02
274	Bobby Hurley (R)	.30	.18
275	Jim Les	.05	.02
276	Willie Anderson	.05	.02
277	Terry Cummings	.07	.04
278	Vinny Del Negro	.05	.02
279	Eric Floyd	.05	.02
280	Dennis Rodman	.08	.05
281	Vincent Askew	.05	.02
282	Kendall Gill	.08	.05
283	Steve Schfler	.05	.02
284	Detlef Schrempf	.10	.06
285	David Benoit	.05	.02
286	Tom Chambers	.07	.04
287	Felton Spencer	.12	.07
288	Rex Chapman	.05	.02
289	Kevin Duckworth	.05	.02
290	Gheorghe Muresan (R)	.12	.07
291	Kenny Walker	.05	.02
292	Atlanta (CF) (Edwards)	.10	.06
293	Boston (CF) (Earl/Rauja)	.15	.10
294	Charlotte (CF) (Burrell)	.08	.05
295	Chicago (CF) (Blount/Kukoc)	.15	.10
296	Cleveland (CF) (C. Mills)	.08	.05
297	Dallas (CF) (P.Jones/Mashburn)	.25	.15
298	Denver (CF) (R. Rogers)	.08	.05
299	Detroit (CF) (Houston/Hunter)	.10	.06
300	Golden State (CF) (C. Webber)	.75	.45
301	Houston (CF) (Cassell)	.15	.10
302	Indiana (CF) (Haskins)	.07	.04
303	L.A. Clippers (CF) (Dehere)	.07	.04
304	L.A Lakers (CF) (Lynch/Van Exel)	.20	.12
305	Miami (CF) (Graham)	.05	.02
306	Milwaukee (CF) (V. Baker/Norman)	.15	.10
307	Minnesota (CF) (M. Brown/I. Rider)	.25	.15
308	New Jersey (CF) (Walters)	.05	.02
309	New York (CF)	.05	.02
310	Orlando (CF) (A. Hardaway)	.60	.35
311	Philadelphia (CF) (S.Bradley/M.Malone)	.10	.06
312	Phoenix (CF) (Mackey)	.07	.04
313	Portland (CF) (J. Robinson)	.07	.04
314	Sacramento (CF) (Hurley/Richmond)	.10	.06
315	San Antonio (CF) (Whitney)	.05	.02
316	Seattle (CF) (E. Johnson)	.05	.02
317	Utah (CF) (Wright)	.08	.05
318	Washington (CF) (Cheaney)	.10	.06
319	Karl Malone (PC)	.20	.12
320	Alonzo Mourning (PC)	.40	.25
321	Scottie Pippen (PC)	.15	.10
322	Mark Price (PC)	.08	.05
323	LaPhonso Ellis (PC)	.15	.10
324	Joe Dumars (PC)	.08	.05
325	Chris Mullin (PC)	.08	.05
326	Ron Harper (PC)	.05	.02
327	Glen Rice (PC)	.07	.04
328	Christian Laettner (PC)	.10	.06
329	Kenny Anderson (PC)	.10	.06
330	John Starks (PC)	.10	.06
331	Shaquille O'Neal (PC)	1.00	.60
332	Charles Barkley (PC)	.30	.18
333	Cliff Robinson (PC)	.08	.05
334	Clyde Drexler (PC)	.15	.10
335	Mitch Richmond (PC)	.08	.05
336	David Robinson (PC)	.25	.15
337	Shawn Kemp (PC)	.20	.12
338	John Stockton (PC)	.15	.10
339	Checklist	.05	.02
340	Checklist	.05	.02
341	Checklist	.05	.02
DP4	Jim Jackson	2.50	1.50
DP17	Doug Christie	.75	.45

1993-94 SkyBox NBA All-Rookies

The cards in this limited insert set were randomly inserted in SkyBox Series I foil packs. The card fronts feature full-color player photos and gold foil stamping with an All-Rookies Logo in the lower corner. The player's name is printed in a color bar that runs vertically along one side of the card. Card numbers contain the prefix AR. All cards measure 2-1/2" by 3-1/2".

	MINT	NR/MT
Complete Set (5)	30.00	20.00
Commons	1.75	1.00
1 Shaquille O'Neal	20.00	12.50
2 Alonzo Mourning	10.00	6.50
3 Christian Laettner	2.00	1.25
4 Tom Gugliotta	1.75	1.00
5 LaPhonso Ellis	3.00	1.75

1993-94 SkyBox Center Stage

These full-bleed, full-color inserts were distributed randomly in SkyBox Series I foil packs. The card fronts contain an isolated action shot of the player with a gold foil stamped Center Stage logo in the lower corner. The player's name is printed in large type across the top of the card. The letters CS preceeds the card numbers on the backs. All cards measure 2-1/2" by 3-1/2".

	MINT	NR/MT
Complete Set (9)	28.00	18.00
Commons	.60	.35
1 Michael Jordan	10.00	6.50
2 Shaquille O'Neal	10.00	6.50
3 Charles Barkley	4.00	2.50
4 John Starks	.75	.45
5 Larry Johnson	1.75	1.00
6 Hakeem Olajuwon	4.00	2.50
7 Kenny Anderson	.75	.45
8 Mahmoud Abdul-Rauf	.75	.45
9 Cliff Robinson	.60	.35

1993-94 SkyBox NBA Draft Picks

The cards in this limited insert set were randomly distributed in SkyBox Series I and Series II packs. The card fronts consist of photos of the top selections in the 1993 NBA draft. The pictures include a large photo of the player wearing street clothes. A smaller isolated action shot appears in the lower corner of the card. The player's name is printed in block letters across the top of the card just above the name of the team and the draft pick used to select him. Card numbers contain the prefix DP. All cards measure 2-1/2" by 3-1/2".

		MINT	NR/MT
Complete Set (26)		85.00	55.00
Commons		1.00	.60
1	Chris Webber	25.00	15.00
2	Shawn Bradley	3.00	1.75
3	Anfernee Hardaway	20.00	12.50
4	Jamal Mashburn	10.00	6.50
5	Isaiah Rider	8.50	5.00
6	Calbert Cheaney	3.00	1.75
7	Bobby Hurley	2.50	1.50
8	Vin Baker	5.00	3.00
9	Rodney Rogers	2.00	1.25
10	Lindsey Hunter	2.50	1.50
11	Allan Houston	1.50	.90
12	George Lynch	2.50	1.50
13	Terry Dehere	1.00	.60
14	Scott Haskins	1.00	.60
15	Doug Edwards	1.00	.60
16	Rex Walters	1.00	.60
17	Greg Graham	1.00	.60
18	Luther Wright	1.25	.70
19	Acie Earl	1.25	.70
20	Scott Burrell	1.50	.90
21	James Robinson	1.25	.70
22	Chris Mills	2.50	1.50
23	Ervin Johnson	1.00	.60
24	Sam Cassell	4.00	2.50
25	Corie Blunt	1.00	.60
26	Malcolm Mackey	1.00	.60

1993-94 SkyBox Dynamic Dunks

The limited insert cards in this set were randomly distributed in SkyBox Series II packs and feature an isolated action shot of the player dunking the basketball on the horizontal card fronts. The words Dynamic Dunks with a huge letter "D" printed in script appears in the right half of the card. The player's name is printed under the headline. All cards measure 2-1/2" by 3-1/2".

	MINT	NR/MT
Complete Set (9)	80.00	50.00
Commons	1.50	.90

132 • 1993-94 SKYBOX DYNAMIC DUNKS

1	Nick Anderson	1.50	.90
2	Charles Barkley	8.00	5.00
3	Robert Hory	4.00	2.50
4	Michael Jordan	30.00	18.00
5	Shawn Kemp	8.00	5.00
6	Anthony Mason	1.50	.90
7	Alonzo Mourning	15.00	10.00
8	Hakeem Olajuwon	15.00	10.00
9	Dominique Wilkins	5.00	3.00

1993-94 SkyBox Shaq Talk

These insert cards featuring Shaquille O'Neal were distributed randomly in all SkyBox foil packs. The cards include action shots of O'Neal highlighting all facets of his game. All cards measure 2-1/2" by 3-1/2".

	MINT	NR/MT
Complete Set (11)	30.00	18.00
Commons	3.00	1.75

1	The Rebound	3.00	1.75
2	The Block	3.00	1.75
3	The Postup	3.00	1.75
4	The Dunk	3.00	1.75
5	Defense	3.00	1.75
6	Scoring	3.00	1.75
7	Passing	3.00	1.75
8	Rejections	3.00	1.75
9	Confidence	3.00	1.75
10	Legends	3.00	1.75

1993-94 SkyBox Showdown Series

These limited insert cards feature full-bleed, full-color action photos on the fronts with a horizontal stripe across the bottom of the photo with the names of the two players featured on the card. The card numbers contain the prefix SS. The inserts were distributed randomly in SkyBox Series I and Series II packs and all cards measure 2-1/2" by 3-1/2".

	MINT	NR/MT
Complete Set (12)	20.00	12.50
Commons	1.00	.60

1	Mourning vs Ewing	1.50	.90
2	O'Neal vs Ewing	3.00	1.75
3	Mourning vs O'Neal	5.00	3.00
4	Olajuwon vs Mutombo	2.50	1.50
5	Robinson vs Oajuwon	2.50	1.50
6	Robinson vs Mutombo	2.00	1.25
7	Kemp vs K. Malone	1.50	.90
8	L. Johnson vs Barkley	2.00	1.25
9	D. Wilkins vs Pippen	1.00	.60

10	Dumars vs R. Miller 1.00	.60
11	Drexler vs M. Jordan 5.00	3.00
12	M. Johnson vs L. Bird 3.00	1.75

1993-94 SkyBox Thunder & Lightning

These cards feature full-bleed, full-color action shots of players on each side of the card. The player's name is centered near the bottom of the card and directly above the word Thunder or Lightning. A SkyBox logo appears in the top corner. The cards were randomly inserted in SkyBox Series II foil packs. All cards measure 2-1/2" by 3-1/2".

	MINT	NR/MT
Complete Set (9)	45.00	30.00
Commons	1.50	.90
1 Mashburn/Jackson	7.50	4.50
2 Miner/S. Smith	2.50	1.50
3 Rider/M. Williams	5.00	3.00
4 Coleman/Anderson	2.50	1.50
5 Ewing/Starks	2.50	1.50
6 O'Neal/Hardaway	25.00	15.00
7 Bradley/Hornacek	1.50	.90
8 W. Williams/Hurley	1.50	.90
9 Rodman/D. Robinson	3.50	2.00

STAR COMPANY

1983-84 Star Company

The cards in this 275-card set feature color player photos on the fronts framed by border colors that mirror the team colors. The player's name and team appear under the photograph and next to a team logo. The words "Star '84" are located in the top right corner. The horizontal card backs contain personal data and stats. These cards were issued in team sets in polybags and distributed regionally in each team's market area. There is a shortage of Series I cards (1-100) due to severe miscuts which were destroyed. Some team sets are more difficult to find that others and the value of those common cards are higher. This set was the only regular edition NBA set issued during the 1983-1984 season. All cards measure 2-1/2" by 3-1/2".

	MINT	NR/MT
Complete Set (275)	3,350.00	2,000.00
Commons (1-60)	5.00	3.00
Commons (61-275)	2.75	1.75
1 Julius Erving	100.00	65.00

1983-84 STAR COMPANY

#	Player		
2	Maurice Cheeks	20.00	12.50
3	Franklin Edwards	5.00	3.00
4	Marc Iavaroni	5.00	3.00
5	Clemon Johnson	5.00	3.00
6	Bobby Jones	8.50	5.00
7	Moses Malone	40.00	28.00
8	Leo Ratlins	5.00	3.00
9	Clint Richardson	5.00	3.00
10	Sedale Threatt (R)	30.00	18.50
11	Andrew Toney	10.00	6.50
12	Sam Williams	5.00	3.00
13	Magic Johnson	200.00	125.00
14	Kareem Abdul-Jabbar	50.00	32.00
15	Michael Cooper	12.50	7.50
16	Calvin Garrett	5.00	3.00
17	Mitch Kupchak	7.00	4.50
18	Bob McAdoo	15.00	10.00
19	Mike McGee	6.00	3.75
20	Swen Nater	6.00	3.75
21	Kurt Rambis	10.00	6.50
22	Byron Scott (R)	35.00	22.00
23	Larry Spriggs	5.00	3.00
24	Jamaal Wilkes	8.00	5.00
25	James Worthy (R)	80.00	50.00
26	Larry Bird	400.00	275.00
27	Danny Ainge (R)	100.00	60.00
28	Quinn Buckner	10.00	6.50
29	M.L. Carr	9.00	6.00
30	Carlos Clark	8.00	5.00
31	Gerald Henderson	9.00	6.00
32	Dennis Johnson	24.00	14.00
33	Cedric Maxwell	12.00	7.50
34	Kevin McHale	75.00	45.00
35	Robert Parish	75.00	45.00
36	Scott Wedman	8.00	5.00
37	Greg Kite	12.00	7.50
38	Sidney Moncrief	18.00	10.00
39	Nate Archibald	12.00	7.50
40	Randy Breuer (R)	6.00	3.75
41	Junior Bridgeman	6.00	3.75
42	Harvey Catchings	5.00	3.00
43	Kevin Grevey	5.00	3.00
44	Marques Johnson	8.50	5.50
45	Bob Lanier	24.00	14.00
46	Alton Lister (R)	7.00	4.50
47	Paul Mokeski	6.00	3.75
48	Paul Pressey (R)	7.50	4.50
49	Mark Aguirre	90.00	50.00
50	Rolando Blackman (R)	100.00	60.00
51	Pat Cummings	30.00	18.50
52	Brad Davis (R)	38.00	25.00
53	Dale Ellis (R)	100.00	65.00
54	Bill Garnett	30.00	18.50
55	Derek Harper (R)	100.00	65.00
56	Kurt Nimphius	30.00	18.50
57	Jim Spanarkel	30.00	18.50
58	Elston Turner	30.00	18.50
59	Jay Vincent	40.00	28.00
60	Mark West (R)	35.00	22.00
61	Bernard King	10.00	6.50
62	Bill Cartwright	9.00	6.00
63	Len Elmore	2.75	1.75
64	Eric Fernsten	2.75	1.75
65	Ernie Grunfeld	2.75	1.75
66	Louis Orr	2.75	1.75
67	Leonard Robinson	2.75	1.75
68	Rory Sparrow (R)	3.50	2.00
69	Trent Tucker (R)	6.00	3.75
70	Darrell Walker (R)	5.00	3.00
71	Marvin Webster	2.75	1.75
72	Ray Williams	2.75	1.75
73	Ralph Sampson (R)	7.50	4.50
74	James Bailey	2.75	1.75
75	Phil Ford	3.50	2.00
76	Elvin Hayes	15.00	10.00
77	Caldwell Jones	2.75	1.75
78	Major Jones	2.75	1.75
79	Allen Leavell	2.75	1.75
80	Lewis Lloyd	2.75	1.75
81	Rodney McCray (R)	5.00	3.00
82	Robert Reid	2.75	1.75
83	Terry Teagle	6.00	3.75
84	Wally Walker	2.75	1.75
85	Kelly Tripucka	5.00	3.00
86	Kent Benson	2.75	1.75
87	Earl Cureton	2.75	1.75
88	Lionel Hollins	2.75	1.75
89	Vinnie Johnson	4.50	2.75
90	Bill Laimbeer	7.50	4.50
91	Cliff Levingston	5.00	3.00
92	John Long	2.75	1.75
93	David Thirdkill	2.75	1.75
94	Isiah Thomas (R)	170.00	100.00
95	Ray Tolbert	2.75	1.75
96	Terry Tyler	2.75	1.75
97	Jim Paxson	3.50	2.25
98	Kenny Carr	2.75	1.75
99	Wayne Cooper	2.75	1.75
100	Clyde Drexler (R)	375.00	225.00
101	Jeff Lamp (R)	3.50	2.00
102	Lafayette Lever (R)	8.50	5.50
103	Calvin Natt	5.00	3.00
104	Audie Norris	2.75	1.75
105	Tom Piotrowski	2.75	1.75
106	Mychal Thompson	4.50	2.75
107	Darnell Valentine (R)	5.00	3.00
108	Pete Verhoeven	2.75	1.75
109	Walter Davis	5.00	3.00
110	Alvan Adams	3.00	2.00
111	James Edwards	4.00	2.75
112	Rod Foster (R)	3.00	2.00
113	Maurice Lucas	4.00	2.75
114	Kyle Macy	2.75	1.75

1983-84 STAR COMPANY • 135

#	Player		
115	Larry Nance (R)	65.00	38.00
116	Charles Pittman	2.75	1.75
117	Rick Robey	2.75	1.75
118	Mike Sanders (R)	4.00	2.75
119	Alvin Scott	2.75	1.75
120	Paul Westphal	8.00	5.00
121	Bill Walton	24.00	14.00
122	Michael Brooks	2.75	1.75
123	Terry Cummings (R)	24.00	14.00
124	James Donaldson (R)	3.00	2.00
125	Craig Hodges (R)	7.50	4.50
126	Greg Kelser (R)	2.75	1.75
127	Hank McDowell	2.75	1.75
128	Billy McKinney	2.75	1.75
129	Norm Nixon	4.00	2.50
130	Ricky Pierce (R)	40.00	28.00
131	Derek Smith (R)	3.00	2.00
132	Jerome Whitehead	2.75	1.75
133	Adrian Dantley	7.50	4.50
134	Mitch Anderson	2.75	1.75
135	Thurl Bailey (R)	5.00	3.00
136	Tom Boswell	2.75	1.75
137	John Drew	2.75	1.75
138	Mark Eaton (R)	12.00	7.50
139	Jerry Eaves	2.75	1.75
140	Rickey Green (R)	3.50	2.25
141	Darrell Griffith	3.00	2.00
142	Bobby Hansen (R)	3.50	2.25
143	Rich Kelley	2.75	1.75
144	Jeff Wilkins	2.75	1.75
145	Buck Williams (R)	45.00	32.00
146	Otis Birdsong	3.00	2.00
147	Darwin Cook	2.75	1.75
148	Darryl Dawkins	5.00	3.00
149	Mike Gminski	3.50	2.25
150	Reggie Johnson	2.75	1.75
151	Albert King (R)	3.50	2.25
152	Mike O'Koren	2.75	1.75
153	Kelvin Ransey	2.75	1.75
154	M.R. Richardson	2.75	1.75
155	Clarence Walker	2.75	1.75
156	Bill Willoughby	2.75	1.75
157	Steve Stipanovich (R)	3.50	2.25
158	Butch Carter	2.75	1.75
159	Edwin Leroy Combs	2.75	1.75
160	George L. Johnson	2.75	1.75
161	Clark Kellogg	3.50	2.00
162	Sidney Lowe (R)	4.50	2.75
163	Kevin McKenna	2.75	1.75
164	Jerry Sichting (R)	3.50	2.00
165	Brook Steppe	2.75	1.75
166	Jimmy Thomas	2.75	1.75
167	Granville Waiters	2.75	1.75
168	Herb Williams (R)	7.00	4.00
169	Dave Corzine	2.75	1.75
170	Wallace Bryant	2.75	1.75
171	Quintin Dailey (R)	3.50	2.25
172	Sidney Green (R)	4.50	2.75
173	David Greenwood	3.50	2.25
174	Rod Higgins (R)	3.50	2.25
175	Clarence Johnson	2.75	1.75
176	Ronnie Lester	2.75	1.75
177	Jawann Oldham	2.75	1.75
178	Ennis Whatley (R)	3.00	2.00
179	Mitchell Wiggins (R)	3.50	2.25
180	Orlando Woolridge (R)	15.00	10.00
181	Kiki Vandeweghe (R)	12.00	7.50
182	Richard Anderson	2.75	1.75
183	Howard Carter	2.75	1.75
184	T.R. Dunn	2.75	1.75
185	Keith Edmonson	2.75	1.75
186	Alex English	10.00	6.50
187	Mike Evans	2.75	1.75
188	Bill Hanzlik	3.00	2.00
189	Dan Issel	15.00	10.00
190	Anthony Roberts	2.75	1.75
191	Danny Schayes (R)	6.50	4.00
192	Rob Williams	2.75	1.75
193	Jack Sikma	7.00	4.00
194	Fred Brown	3.50	2.25
195	Tom Chambers (R)	48.00	28.00
196	Steve Hawes	2.75	1.75
197	Steve Hayes	2.75	1.75
198	Reggie King	2.75	1.75
199	Scooter McCray	2.75	1.75
200	Jon Sundvold (R)	3.00	2.00
201	Danny Vranes	2.75	1.75
202	Gus Williams	3.00	2.00
203	Al Wood	2.75	1.75
204	Jeff Ruland (R)	3.00	2.00
205	Greg Ballard	2.75	1.75
206	Charles Davis	2.75	1.75
207	Darren Daye	2.75	1.75
208	Michael Gibson	2.75	1.75
209	Frank Johnson (R)	3.50	2.25
210	Joe Kopicki	2.75	1.75
211	Rick Mahorn	3.50	2.25
212	Jeff Malone (R)	35.00	20.00
213	Tom McMillen	3.50	2.25
214	Ticky Sobers	2.75	1.75
215	Bryan Warrick	2.75	1.75
216	Billy Knight	3.00	2.00
217	Don Buse	2.75	1.75
218	Larry Drew (R)	3.50	2.25
219	Eddie Johnson (R)	24.00	14.00
220	Joe Meriweather	2.75	1.75
221	Larry Micheaux	2.75	1.75
222	Ed Nealy (R)	3.00	2.00
223	Mark Olberding	2.75	1.75
224	Dave Robisch	2.75	1.75
225	Reggie Theus	4.00	2.50
226	LaSalle Thompson (R)	4.00	2.50
227	Mike Woodson	2.75	1.75
228	World B. Free	4.00	2.50

136 • 1984-85 STAR COMPANY

		MINT	NR/MT
229	John Bagley (R)	5.00	3.00
230	Jeff Cook	2.75	1.75
231	Geoff Crompton	2.75	1.75
232	John Garris	2.75	1.75
233	Stewart Granger	2.75	1.75
234	Roy Hinson (R)	3.00	2.00
235	Phil Hubbard	2.75	1.75
236	Geoff Huston	2.75	1.75
237	Ben Poquette	2.75	1.75
238	Cliff Robinson	4.00	2.75
239	Lonnie Shelton	2.75	1.75
240	Paul Thompson	2.75	1.75
241	George Gervin	15.00	10.00
242	Gene Banks	2.75	1.75
243	Ron Brewer	2.75	1.75
244	Artis Gilmore	7.50	4.50
245	Edgar Jones	2.75	1.75
246	John Lucas	7.00	4.00
247A	Mike Mitchell (Er)	5.00	3.00
247B	Mike Mitchell (Cor)	2.75	1.75
248A	Mark McNamara (Er)	5.00	3.00
248B	Mark McNamara (Cor)	2.75	1.75
249	Johnny Moore	2.75	1.75
250	John Paxson (R)	25.00	15.00
251	Fred Roberts (R)	5.00	3.00
252	Joe Barry Carroll	3.00	2.00
253	Mike Bratz	2.75	1.75
254	Don Collins	2.75	1.75
255	Lester Conner	3.00	2.00
256	Chris Engler	2.75	1.75
257	Sleepy Floyd (R)	10.00	6.50
258	Wallace Johnson	2.75	1.75
259	Pace Mannion	2.75	1.75
260	Purvis Short	3.50	2.25
261	Larry Smith	3.00	2.00
262	Darren Tillis	2.75	1.75
263	Dominique Wilkins (R)	425.00	300.00
264	Rickey Brown	2.75	1.75
265	Johnny Davis	2.75	1.75
266	Mike Glenn	2.75	1.75
267	Scott Hastings (R)	4.00	2.50
268	Eddie Johnson	2.75	1.75
269	Mark Landsberger	2.75	1.75
270	Billy Paultz	2.75	1.75
271	Doc Rivers (R)	25.00	15.00
272	Tree Rollins	3.50	2.25
273	Dan Roundfield	3.00	2.00
274	Sly Williams	2.75	1.75
275	Randy Wittman (R)	3.00	2.00

1984-85 Star Company

The cards in this set feature full color photos on the fronts framed by different colored borders according to team. The player's name, position and team name appear under the photograph and to the right of a team logo. "Star '85" is printed in the top right corner. The horizontal card backs include personal data and statistics. The cards were distributed in polybags as team sets and shipped regionally to each team's regional market. Two subsets are included in the set, a 6-card 1984 Olympic Team subset (OLY) (195-200) and an NBA Special Highlights series (HL)(281-288). This set contains the first cards of Michael Jordan, Charles Barkley, John Stockton and Hakeem Olajuwon. All cards measure 2-1/2" by 3-1/2".

	MINT	NR/MT
Complete Set (288)	8,500.00	6,250.00
Commons	2.75	1.75

		MINT	NR/MT
1	Larry Bird	190.00	115.00
2	Danny Ainge	30.00	18.00
3	Quinn Buckner	2.75	1.75
4	Rick Carlisle	2.75	1.75
5	M.L. Carr	2.75	1.75
6	Dennis Johnson	6.00	3.50
7	Greg Kite	2.75	1.75

1984-85 STAR COMPANY • 137

#	Player			#	Player		
8	Cedric Maxwell	3.50	2.00	65	Gene Banks	2.75	1.75
9	Kevin McHale	20.00	12.50	66	Ron Brewer	2.75	1.75
10	Robert Parish	20.00	12.50	67	George Gervin	15.00	10.00
11	Scott Wedman	2.75	1.75	68	Edgar Jones	2.75	1.75
12	Larry Bird (MVP)	95.00	60.00	69	Ozell Jones	2.75	1.75
13	Marques Johnson	4.00	2.50	70	Mark McNamara	2.75	1.75
14	Junior Bridgeman	2.75	1.75	71	Mike Mitchell	2.75	1.75
15	Michael Cage (R)	6.50	3.75	72	Johnny Moore	2.75	1.75
16	Harvey Catchings	2.75	1.75	73	John Paxson	9.00	6.00
17	James Donaldson	2.75	1.75	74	Fred Roberts	2.75	1.75
18	Lancaster Gordon	2.75	1.75	75	Alvin Robertson (R)	20.00	12.50
19	Jay Murphy	2.75	1.75	76	Dominique Wilkins	180.00	110.00
20	Norm Nixon	4.00	2.50	77	Rickey Brown	2.75	1.75
21	Derek Smith	2.75	1.75	78	Antoine Carr (R)	10.00	6.50
22	Bill Walton	20.00	12.50	79	Mike Glenn	2.75	1.75
23	Bryan Warrick	2.75	1.75	80	Scott Hastings	2.75	1.75
24	Rory White	2.75	1.75	81	Eddie Johnson	2.75	1.75
25	Bernard King	7.50	4.50	82	Cliff Levingston	3.50	2.25
26	James Bailey	2.75	1.75	83	Leo Raulins	2.75	1.75
27	Ken Bannister	2.75	1.75	84	Doc Rivers	10.00	6.50
28	Butch Carter	2.75	1.75	85	Tree Rollins	3.00	2.00
29	Bill Cartwright	5.00	3.00	86	Randy Wittman	2.75	1.75
30	Pat Cummings	2.75	1.75	87	Sly Williams	2.75	1.75
31	Ernie Grunfeld	2.75	1.75	88	Darryl Dawkins	5.00	3.00
32	Louis Orr	2.75	1.75	89	Otis Birdsong	2.75	1.75
33	Leonard Robinson	2.75	1.75	90	Darwin Cook	2.75	1.75
34	Rory Sparrow	2.75	1.75	91	Mike Gminski	3.00	2.00
35	Trent Tucker	3.00	2.00	92	George L. Johnson	2.75	1.75
36	Darrell Walker	2.75	1.75	93	Albert King	2.75	1.75
37	Eddie Lee Wilkins (R)	3.00	2.00	94	Mike O'Koren	2.75	1.75
38	Alvan Adams	3.00	2.00	95	Kelvin Ransey	2.75	1.75
39	Walter Davis	5.00	3.00	96	Michael Ray Richardson	2.75	1.75
40	James Edwards	3.00	2.00	97	Wayne Sappleton	2.75	1.75
41	Rod Foster	2.75	1.75	98	Jeff Turner (R)	3.50	2.25
42	Michael Holton	2.75	1.75	99	Buck Williams	15.00	10.00
43	Jay Humphries (R)	9.00	6.00	100	Michael Wilson	2.75	1.75
44	Charles Jones	2.75	1.75	101	Michael Jordan(R)	4,800.00	3000.00
45	Maurice Lucas	3.50	2.25	102	Dave Corzine	2.75	1.75
46	Kyle Macy	2.75	1.75	103	Quintin Dailey	2.75	1.75
47	Larry Nance	22.00	13.00	104	Sidney Green	2.75	1.75
48	Charles Pittman	2.75	1.75	105	David Greenwood	2.75	1.75
49	Rick Robey	2.75	1.75	106	Rod Higgins	2.75	1.75
50	Mike Sanders	3.00	2.00	107	Steve Johnson	2.75	1.75
51	Alvin Scott	2.75	1.75	108	Caldwell Jones	2.75	1.75
52	Clark Kellogg	4.50	2.75	109	Wes Matthews	2.75	1.75
53	Tony Brown	4.00	2.50	110	Jawann Oldham	2.75	1.75
54	Devin Durrant	4.00	2.50	111	Ennis Whatley	2.75	1.75
55	Vern Fleming (R)	18.00	11.00	112	Orlando Woolridge	6.00	3.50
56	Bill Garnett	4.00	2.50	113	Tom Chambers	15.00	10.00
57	Stuart Gray	4.00	2.50	114	Cory Blackwell	2.75	1.75
58	Jerry Sichting	4.00	2.50	115	Frank Brickowski (R)	8.50	5.50
59	Terence Stansbury	4.00	2.50	116	Gerald Henderson	2.75	1.75
60	Steve Stipanovich	4.50	2.75	117	Reggie King	2.75	1.75
61	Jimmy Thomas	4.00	2.50	118	Tim McCormick (R)	3.00	2.00
62	Granville Waiters	4.00	2.50	119	John Schweitz	2.75	1.75
63	Herb Williams	7.50	4.50	120	Jack Sikma	4.50	2.75
64	Artis Gilmore	5.00	3.00	121	Ricky Sobers	2.75	1.75

138 • 1984-85 STAR COMPANY

#	Player		
122	Jon Sundvold	2.75	1.75
123	Danny Vranes	2.75	1.75
124	Al Wood	2.75	1.75
125	Terry Cummings	10.00	6.50
126	Randy Breuer	2.75	1.75
127	Charles Davis	2.75	1.75
128	Mike Dunleavy	3.50	2.25
129	Kenny Fields	2.75	1.75
130	Kevin Grevey	2.75	1.75
131	Craig Hodges	3.50	2.25
132	Alton Lister	2.75	1.75
133	Larry Micheaux	2.75	1.75
134	Paul Mokeski	2.75	1.75
135	Sidney Moncrief	8.00	5.00
136	Paul Pressey	3.50	2.25
137	Alex English	8.00	5.00
138	Wayne Cooper	2.75	1.75
139	T.R. Dunn	2.75	1.75
140	Mike Evans	2.75	1.75
141	Bill Hanzlik	2.75	1.75
142	Dan Issel	18.00	11.00
143	Joe Kopicki	2.75	1.75
144	Lafayete Lever	3.00	2.00
145	Calvin Natt	3.00	2.00
146	Danny Schayes	3.00	2.00
147	Elston Turner	2.75	1.75
148	Willie White	2.75	1.75
149	Purvis Short	3.00	2.00
150	Chuck Aleksinas	2.75	1.75
151	Mike Bratz	2.75	1.75
152	Steve Burtt	2.75	1.75
153	Lester Conner	2.75	1.75
154	Sleepy Floyd	5.00	3.00
155	Mickey Johnson	2.75	1.75
156	Gary Plummer	2.75	1.75
157	Larry Smith	3.00	2.00
158	Peter Thibeaux	2.75	1.75
159	Jerome Whitehead	2.75	1.75
160	Othell Wilson	2.75	1.75
161	Kiki Vandeweghe	4.00	2.50
162	Sam Bowie (R)	10.00	6.50
163	Kenny Carr	2.75	1.75
164	Steve Colter	2.75	1.75
165	Clyde Drexler	140.00	85.00
166	Audie Norris	2.75	1.75
167	Jim Paxson	3.00	2.00
168	Tom Scheffler	2.75	1.75
169	Bernard Thompson	2.75	1.75
170	Mychal Thompson	3.00	2.00
171	Darnell Valentine	2.75	1.75
172	Magic Johnson	175.00	110.00
173	Kareem Abdul-Jabbar	35.00	22.00
174	Michael Cooper	4.00	2.50
175	Earl Jones	2.75	1.75
176	Mitch Kupchak	2.75	1.75
177	Ronnie Lester	2.75	1.75
178	Bob McAdoo	5.00	3.00
179	Mike McGee	2.75	1.75
180	Kurt Rambis	3.50	2.25
181	Byron Scott	8.00	5.00
182	Larry Spriggs	2.75	1.75
183	Jamaal Wilkes	4.00	2.50
184	James Worthy	32.00	20.00
185	Gus Williams	3.00	2.00
186	Greg Ballard	2.75	1.75
187	Dudley Bradley	2.75	1.75
188	Darren Daye	2.75	1.75
189	Frank Johnson	3.00	2.00
190	Charles Jones	2.75	1.75
191	Rick Mahorn	3.00	2.00
192	Jeff Malone	12.00	7.50
193	Tom McMillen	3.50	2.25
194	Jeff Ruland	2.75	1.75
195	Michael Jordan(OLY)	675.00	450.00
196	Vern Fleming (OLY)	4.00	2.50
197	Sam Perkins (OLY)	12.00	7.50
198	Alvin Robertson(OLY)	10.00	6.50
199	Jeff Turner (OLY)	3.00	2.00
200	Leon Wood (OLY)	3.00	2.00
201	Moses Malone	18.00	12.00
202	Charles Barkley (R)	600.00	350.00
203	Maurice Cheeks	6.00	3.50
204	Julius Erving	45.00	30.00
205	Clemon Johnson	2.75	1.75
206	George Johnson	2.75	1.75
207	Bobby Jones	3.50	2.25
208	Clint Richardson	2.75	1.75
209	Sedale Threatt	8.00	5.00
210	Andrew Toney	3.00	2.00
211	Sam Williams	2.75	1.75
212	Leon Wood (R)	3.00	2.00
213	Mel Turpin (R)	3.00	2.00
214	Ron Anderson (R)	5.00	3.00
215	John Bagley	3.00	2.00
216	Johnny Davis	2.75	1.75
217	World B. Free	3.50	2.25
218	Roy Hinson	3.00	2.00
219	Phil Hubbard	2.75	1.75
220	Edgar Jones	2.75	1.75
221	Ben Poquette	2.75	1.75
222	Lonnie Shelton	2.75	1.75
223	Mark West	2.75	1.75
224	Kevin Williams	2.75	1.75
225	Mark Eaton	5.00	3.00
226	Mitchell Anderson	2.75	1.75
227	Thurl Bailey	3.50	2.25
228	Adrian Dantley	6.00	3.50
229	Rickey Green	3.00	2.00
230	Darrell Griffith	3.50	2.25
231	Rich Kelley	2.75	1.75
232	Pace Mannion	2.75	1.75
233	Billy Paultz	2.75	1.75
234	Fred Roberts	3.00	2.00
235	John Stockton (R)	300.00	175.00

1985-86 Star Company

KIKI VANDEWEGHE
1986 Court King

This set consists of 172-cards issued in team sets and distributed mainly in each team's home region. The card fronts feature full color player photos wrapped in various border colors, usually mirroring the team colors. The player's name, position and team are printed across the bottom border to the right of the team logo. "Star '86" is printed in the upper right corner. The flip side contains personal data and statistics. This set contains the first card of Patrick Ewing. All cards measure 2-1/2" by 3-1/2".

	MINT	NR/MT
Complete Set (172)	2,950.00	1,875.00
Commons	2.75	1.75

		MINT	NR/MT
236	Jeff Wilkins	2.75	1.75
237	Hakeem Olajuwon (R)	650.00	375.00
238	Craig Ehlo (R)	25.00	15.00
239	Lionel Hollins	2.75	1.75
240	Allen Leavell	2.75	1.75
241	Lewis Lloyd	2.75	1.75
242	John Lucas	5.00	3.00
243	Rodney McCray	3.00	2.00
244	Hank McDowell	2.75	1.75
245	Larry Micheaux	2.75	1.75
246	Jim Peterson (R)	3.00	2.00
247	Robert Reid	2.75	1.75
248	Ralph Sampson	3.50	2.25
249	Mitchell Wiggins	2.75	1.75
250	Mark Aguirre	7.00	4.00
251	Rolando Blackman	8.50	5.25
252	Wallace Bryant	2.75	1.75
253	Brad Davis	2.75	1.75
254	Dale Ellis	8.50	5.25
255	Derek Harper	10.00	6.50
256	Kurt Nimphius	2.75	1.75
257	Sam Perkins (R)	35.00	22.00
258	Charlie Sitton	2.75	1.75
259	Tom Sluby	2.75	1.75
260	Jay Vincent	3.00	2.00
261	Isiah Thomas	50.00	35.00
262	Kent Benson	2.75	1.75
263	Earl Cureton	2.75	1.75
264	Vinnie Johnson	3.50	2.25
265	Bill Laimbeer	6.00	3.75
266	John Long	2.75	1.75
267	Dan Roundfield	2.75	1.75
268	Kelly Tripucka	3.00	2.00
269	Terry Tyler	2.75	1.75
270	Reggie Theus	3.50	2.25
271	Don Buse	2.75	1.75
272	Larry Drew	2.75	1.75
273	Eddie Johnson	7.50	4.50
274	Billy Knight	2.75	1.75
275	Joe Meriweather	2.75	1.75
276	Mark Olberding	2.75	1.75
277	LaSalle Thompson	3.00	2.00
278	Otis Thorpe (R)	32.00	20.00
279	Pete Verhoeven	2.75	1.75
280	Mike Woodson	2.75	1.75
281	Julius Erving (HL)	25.00	15.00
282	Kareem Abdul-Jabbar (HL)	20.00	12.50
283	Dan Issel (HL)	7.50	4.50
284	Bernard King (HL)	4.00	2.50
285	Moses Malone (HL)	7.50	4.50
286	Mark Eaton (HL)	3.50	2.00
287	Isiah Thomas (HL)	24.00	14.00
288	Michael Jordan (HL)	700.00	425.00
1	Maurice Cheeks	5.00	3.00
2	Charles Barkley	250.00	150.00
3	Julius Erving	40.00	28.00
4	Clemon Johnson	2.75	1.75
5	Bobby Jones	4.00	2.50
6	Moses Malone	10.00	6.50
7	Sedale Threatt	7.00	4.00
8	Andrew Toney	2.75	1.75
9	Leon Wood	2.75	1.75
10	Isiah Thomas	45.00	32.00
11	Kent Benson	2.75	1.75
12	Earl Cureton	2.75	1.75
13	Vinnie Johnson	3.00	2.00

140 • 1985-86 STAR COMPANY

#	Player		
14	Bill Laimbeer	4.50	2.75
15	John Long	2.75	1.75
16	Rick Mahorn	3.00	2.00
17	Kelly Tripucka	3.00	2.00
18	Hakeem Olajuwon	250.00	150.00
19	Allen Leavell	2.75	1.75
20	Lewis Lloyd	2.75	1.75
21	John Lucas	4.50	2.75
22	Rodney McCray	3.00	2.00
23	Robert Reid	2.75	1.75
24	Ralph Sampson	3.50	2.25
25	Mitchell Wiggins	2.75	1.75
26	Kareem Abdul-Jabbar	70.00	40.00
27	Michael Cooper	8.50	5.50
28	Magic Johnson	250.00	160.00
29	Mitch Kupchak	4.50	2.75
30	Maurice Lucas	4.50	2.75
31	Kurt Rambis	6.00	3.75
32	Byron Scott	12.00	7.00
33	James Worthy	45.00	28.00
34	Larry Nance	15.00	10.00
35	Alvan Adams	2.75	1.75
36	Walter Davis	4.00	2.75
37	James Edwards	3.00	2.00
38	Jay Humphries	3.50	2.25
39	Charles Pittman	2.75	1.75
40	Rick Robey	2.75	1.75
41	Mike Sanders	3.00	2.00
42	Dominique Wilkins	125.00	75.00
43	Scott Hastings	2.75	1.75
44	Eddie Johnson	2.75	1.75
45	Cliff Levingston	3.00	2.00
46	Tree Rollins	3.00	2.00
47	Doc Rivers	6.50	4.00
48	Kevin Willis (R)	45.00	32.00
49	Randy Wittman	2.75	1.75
50	Alex English	5.00	3.00
51	Wayne Cooper	2.75	1.75
52	T.R. Dunn	2.75	1.75
53	Mike Evans	2.75	1.75
54	Lafayette Lever	3.00	2.00
55	Calvin Natt	3.00	2.00
56	Danny Schayes	3.00	2.00
57	Elston Turner	2.75	1.75
58	Buck Williams	12.00	7.50
59	Otis Birdsong	2.75	1.75
60	Darwin Cook	2.75	1.75
61	Darryl Dawkins	3.00	2.00
62	Mike Gminski	3.00	2.00
63	Mickey Johnson	2.75	1.75
64	Mike O'Koren	2.75	1.75
65	Michael R. Richardson	2.75	1.75
66	Tom Chambers	12.00	7.00
67	Gerald Henderson	2.75	1.75
68	Tim McCormick	2.75	1.75
69	Jack Sikma	3.50	2.25
70	Ricky Sobers	2.75	1.75
71	Danny Vranes	2.75	1.75
72	Al Wood	2.75	1.75
73	Danny Young	2.75	1.75
74	Reggie Theus	3.00	2.00
75	Larry Drew	3.00	2.00
76	Eddie Johnson	6.00	3.50
77	Mark Olberding	2.75	1.75
78	LaSalle Thompson	3.00	2.00
79	Otis Thorpe	15.00	10.00
80	Mike Woodson	2.75	1.75
81	Clark Kellogg	2.75	1.75
82	Quinn Buckner	2.75	1.75
83	Vern Fleming	4.50	2.75
84	Bill Garnett	2.75	1.75
85	Terence Stansbury	2.75	1.75
86	Steve Stipanovich	2.75	1.75
87	Herb Williams	3.00	2.00
88	Marques Johnson	4.50	2.75
89	Michael Cage	3.50	2.25
90	Franklin Edwards	2.75	1.75
91	Cedric Maxwell	3.00	2.00
92	Derek Smith	2.75	1.75
93	Rory White	2.75	1.75
94	Jamaal Wilkes	3.50	2.25
95	Larry Bird	150.00	90.00
96	Danny Ainge	24.00	14.00
97	Dennis Johnson	5.00	3.00
98	Kevin McHale	18.00	12.00
99	Robert Parish	18.00	12.00
100	Jerry Sichting	2.75	1.75
101	Bill Walton	15.00	10.00
102	Scott Wedman	2.75	1.75
103	Kiki Vandeweghe	3.50	2.25
104	Sam Bowie	4.00	2.50
105	Kenny Carr	3.00	2.00
106	Clyde Drexler	100.00	65.00
107	Jerome Kersey (R)	18.00	12.00
108	Jim Paxson	3.00	2.00
109	Mychal Thompson	3.00	2.00
110	Gus Williams	3.00	2.00
111	Darren Daye	2.75	1.75
112	Jeff Malone	10.00	6.50
113	Tom McMillen	3.50	2.25
114	Cliff Robinson	2.75	1.75
115	Dan Roundfield	2.75	1.75
116	Jeff Ruland	2.75	1.75
117	Michael Jordan	1,400.00	1000.00
118	Gene Banks	2.75	1.75
119	Dave Corzine	2.75	1.75
120	Quintin Dailey	2.75	1.75
121	George Gervin	10.00	6.50
122	Jawann Oldham	2.75	1.75
123	Orlando Woolridge	5.00	3.00
124	Terry Cummings	8.00	5.00
125	Craig Hodges	3.00	2.00
126	Alton Lister	2.75	1.75
127	Paul Mokeski	2.75	1.75

1990 STAR PICS

1990 Star Pics

128	Sidney Moncrief	5.00	3.00
129	Ricky Pierce	8.50	5.25
130	Paul Pressey	3.00	2.00
131	Purvis Short	3.00	2.00
132	Joe Barry Carroll	3.00	2.00
133	Lester Conner	2.75	1.75
134	Sleepy Floyd	4.00	2.50
135	Geoff Huston	2.75	1.75
136	Larry Smith	3.00	2.00
137	Jerome Whitehead	2.75	1.75
138	Adrian Dantley	5.00	3.00
139	Mitchell Anderson	2.75	1.75
140	Thurl Bailey	3.00	2.00
141	Mark Eaton	4.00	2.50
142	Rickey Green	2.75	1.75
143	Darrell Griffith	3.00	2.00
144	John Stockton	120.00	70.00
145	Artis Gilmore	5.00	3.00
146	Marc Iavaroni	2.75	1.75
147	Steve Johnson	2.75	1.75
148	Mike Mitchell	2.75	1.75
149	Johnny Moore	2.75	1.75
150	Alvin Robertson	6.00	3.75
151	Jon Sundvold	2.75	1.75
152	World B. Free	3.00	2.00
153	John Bagley	3.50	2.25
154	Johnny Davis	2.75	1.75
155	Roy Hinson	2.75	1.75
156	Phil Hubbard	2.75	1.75
157	Ben Poquette	2.75	1.75
158	Mel Turpin	2.75	1.75
159	Rolando Blackman	8.00	5.00
160	Mark Aguirre	5.00	3.00
161	Brad Davis	2.75	1.75
162	Dale Ellis	6.00	3.75
163	Derek Harper	8.50	5.25
164	Sam Perkins	10.00	6.50
165	Jay Vincent	3.00	2.00
166	Patrick Ewing (R)	500.00	365.00
167	Bill Cartwright	4.00	2.50
168	Pat Cummings	2.75	1.75
169	Ernie Grunfeld	2.75	1.75
170	Rory Sparrow	2.75	1.75
171	Trent Tucker	2.75	1.75
172	Darrell Walker	2.75	1.75

The cards in this set feature players taken in the 1990 NBA draft. The full color photos on the fronts depict player's wearing their college uniforms. The photo is surrounded by a thin white frame line and a wider border containing the image of basketballs. The player's name appears in a block under the photograph. The card backs include a small head shot, personal data, highlights and a scouting report on each prospect. The only subset is Flashbacks (FB). Star Pics also produced a limited Medallion Set, identical to the regular edition except for a glossy paper stock and metallic ink. That set is valued at two times the regular edition listed below. All cards measure 2-1/2" by 3-1/2".

		MINT	NR/MT
	Complete Set (70)	18.00	12.00
	Commons	.05	.02
1	Checklist Card	.05	.02
2	David Robinson	4.00	2.50
3	Antonio Davis	.35	.20
4	Steve Bardo	.08	.05
5	Jayson Williams	.15	.10

142 • 1990 STAR PICS

#	Player		
6	Alaa Abdelnaby	.15	.10
7	Trevor Wilson	.20	.12
8	Dee Brown	.80	.50
9	Dennis Scott	.70	.40
10	Danny Ferry (FB)	.12	.07
11	Stevie Thompson	.07	.04
12	Anthony Bonner	.35	.20
13	Keith Robinson	.08	.05
14	Sean Higgins	.08	.05
15	Bo Kimble	.10	.06
16	David Jamerson	.15	.10
17	Anthony Pullard	.05	.02
18	Phil Henderson	.10	.06
19	Mike Mitchell	.05	.02
20	Vanberbilt Team	.08	.05
21	Gary Payton	2.00	1.25
22	Tony Massenburg	.08	.05
23	Cedric Ceballos	1.50	.90
24	Dwayne Schintzius	.08	.05
25	Bimbo Coles	.40	.25
26	Scott Williams	.50	.30
27	Willie Burton	.50	.30
28	Tate George	.15	.10
29	Mark Stevenson	.05	.02
30	UNLV Team	1.00	.60
31	Earl Wise	.05	.02
32	Alec Kessler	.12	.07
33	Les Jepsen	.10	.06
34	Boo Harvey	.05	.02
35	Elden Campbell	.75	.45
36	Jud Buechler	.10	.06
37	Loy Vaught	.40	.25
38	Tyrone Hill	.40	.25
39	Toni Kukoc	3.50	2.00
40	Jim Calhoun	.05	.02
41	Felton Spencer	.50	.30
42	Dan Godfread	.05	.02
43	Derrick Coleman	5.00	3.00
44	Terry Mills	1.00	.60
45	Kendall Gill	1.50	.90
46	A.J. English	.40	.25
47	Duane Causwell	.25	.15
48	Jerrod Mustaf	.12	.07
49	Alan Ogg	.08	.05
50	Pervis Ellison (FB)	.50	.30
51	Matt Bullard	.20	.12
52	Melvin Newbern	.07	.04
53	Marcus Liberty	.15	.10
54	Walter Palmer	.05	.02
55	Negele Knight	.35	.20
56	Steve Henson	.12	.07
57	Greg Foster	.10	.06
58	Brian Oliver	.15	.10
59	Travis Mays	.20	.12
60	All-Rookie Team	.75	.45
61	Steve Scheffler	.07	.04
62	Chris Jackson	2.50	1.50
63	Derek Strong	.20	.12
64	David Butler	.07	.04
65	Kevin Pritchard	.15	.10
66	Lionel Simmons	2.50	1.50
67	Gerald Glass	.60	.35
68	Tony Harris	.07	.04
69	Lance Blanks	.12	.07
70	Draft Report	.05	.02

1991 Star Pics

The cards in this set feature full color action photos of the NBA's top 1991 draft picks wearing their college uniforms. The photos are framed by black borders on three sides with a large basketball taking up a portion of the top right border. The player's name is centered in the border under the photograph. Card backs contain a small head shot along with personal data, highlights and a scouting report. The only subset is Flashbacks (FB). Star Pics also produced a limited Medallion Set, identical to the regular issue except for the use of metallic inks. That set is valued at two times the regular set price listed below. All cards measure 2-1/2" by 3-1/2".

	MINT	NR/MT
Complete Set (72)	7.50	4.50
Commons	.05	.02

1992 STAR PICS • 143

#	Name		
1	Draft Overview	.05	.02
2	Derrick Coleman	.35	.20
3	Treg Lee	.05	.02
4	Rich King	.15	.10
5	Kenny Anderson	1.25	.70
6	John Crotty	.10	.06
7	Mark Randall	.10	.06
8	Kevin Brooks	.15	.10
9	Lamont Strothers	.05	.02
10	Tim Hardaway (FB)	.20	.12
11	Eric Murdock	.30	.18
12	Melvin Cheatum	.05	.02
13	Pete Chilcutt	.15	.10
14	Zan Tabak	.05	.02
15	Greg Anthony	.25	.15
16	George Ackles	.10	.06
17	Stacey Augmon	.80	.50
18	Larry Johnson	2.00	1.25
19	Alvaro Teheran	.05	.02
20	Reggie Miller (FB)	.20	.12
21	Steve Smith	.75	.45
22	Sean Green	.10	.06
23	Johnny Pittman	.05	.02
24	Anthony Avent	.20	.12
25	Chris Gatling	.20	.12
26	Mark Macon	.12	.07
27	Joey Wright	.05	.02
28	Von McDade	.05	.02
29	Bobby Phills	.12	.07
30	Larry Fleisher	.05	.02
31	Luc Longley	.20	.12
32	Jean Derouillere	.05	.02
33	Doug Smith	.15	.10
34	Chad Gallagher	.08	.05
35	Marty Dow	.05	.02
36	Tony Farmer	.05	.02
37	John Taft	.05	.02
38	Reggie Hanson	.05	.02
39	Terrell Brandon	.20	.12
40	Dee Brown (FB)	.15	.10
41	Doug Overton	.12	.07
42	Joe Wylie	.05	.02
43	Myron Brown	.05	.02
44	Steve Hood	.07	.04
45	Randy Brown	.12	.07
46	Chris Corchiani	.15	.10
47	Kevin Lynch	.08	.05
48	Donald Hodge	.15	.10
49	LaBradford Smith	.20	.12
50	Shawn Kemp (FB)	.50	.30
51	Brian Shorter	.08	.05
52	Gary Waites	.05	.02
53	Mike Iuzzolino	.08	.05
54	LeRon Ellis	.15	.10
55	Perry Carter	.07	.04
56	Keith Hughes	.08	.05
57	John Turner	.08	.05
58	Marcus Kennedy	.08	.05
59	Randy Ayers	.08	.05
60	All Rookie Team	.50	.30
61	Jackie Jones	.05	.02
62	Shaun Vandiver	.05	.02
63	Dale Davis	.60	.35
64	Jimmy Oliver	.15	.10
65	Elliot Perry	.05	.02
66	Jerome Harmon	.05	.02
67	Darrin Chancellor	.05	.02
68	Roy Fisher	.05	.02
69	Rick Fox	.25	.15
70	Kenny Anderson	.35	.20
71	Richard Dumas	.20	.12
72	Checklist Card	.05	.02
__	American Flag	.10	.06

1992 Star Pics

This set features the top college basketball draft picks. The fronts include full color photos of players wearing their college uniforms. The pictures are framed by solid white borders. The player's name and position appear in vertical color bars along the side border. The flip side consists of a small head shot, personal data, highlights and a scouting report. Subsets include Flashbacks (FB) and Kids Cards. All cards measure 2-1/2" by 3-1/2".

144 • 1992 STAR PICS

		MINT	NR/MT
	Complete Set (90)	8.50	5.00
	Commons	.05	.02
1	Draft Report	.05	.02
2	Bryant Stith	.40	.25
3	Reggie Smith	.10	.06
4	Todd Day	.60	.35
5	Bob Knight	.15	.10
6	Darren Morningstar	.05	.02
7	C. Weatherspoon	.75	.45
8	Matt Geiger	.15	.10
9	Marlon Maxey	.12	.07
10	Christian Laettner	.35	.20
11	Tony Bennett	.15	.10
12	Sean Rooks	.25	.15
13	Tom Gugliotta	.80	.50
14	Chris King	.10	.06
15	Mike Krzyzewski	.10	.05
16	Sam Mack	.05	.02
17	Matt Fish	.05	.02
18	Brian Davis	.08	.05
19	Oliver Miller	.75	.45
20	Daimon Sweet	.05	.02
21	Eric Anderson	.10	.06
22	Henry Williams	.05	.02
23	David Johnson	.10	.06
24	Duane Cooper	.15	.10
25	Lucius Davis	.05	.02
26	Matt Steigenga	.05	.02
27	Robert Horry	.75	.45
28	Brent Price	.15	.10
29	Chris Smith	.20	.12
30	Vlade Divac (FB)	.10	.06
31	Adam Keefe	.15	.10
32	Christian Laettner	1.00	.60
33	LaPhonso Ellis (Kid)	.25	.15
34	Alex Blackwell	.05	.02
35	Popeye Jones	.25	.15
36	Walt Williams	.25	.15
37	Radenko Dobras	.05	.02
38	Latrell Sprewell	2.00	1.25
39	Isaiah Morris	.10	.06
40	Horace Grant (FB)	.10	.06
41	Craig Upchurch	.08	.05
42	Alonzo Jamison	.10	.06
43	Bryant Stith	.20	.12
44	Jon Barry	.12	.07
45	Litterial Green	.15	.10
46	Malik Sealy	.15	.10
47	Anthony Peeler	.50	.30
48	Dexter Cambridge	.08	.05
49	Eric Manuel	.07	.04
50	Kendall Gill (FB)	.15	.10
51	Hubert Davis	.30	.18
52	Steve Rogers	.05	.02
53	Byron Houston	.20	.12
54	Randy Woods	.10	.06
55	Elmer Bennett	.05	.02
56	Smokey McCovery	.05	.02
57	George Gilmore	.05	.02
58	Predrag Danilovic	.05	.02
59	John Pelphrey	.05	.02
60	Dan Majerle (FB)	.15	.10
61	Elmore Spencer	.25	.15
62	Calvin Talford	.05	.02
63	David Booth	.05	.02
64	Herb Jones	.05	.02
65	Benford Williams	.05	.02
66	Greg Dennis	.05	.02
67	James McCoy	.05	.02
68	C. Weatherspoon (Kid)	.15	.10
69	LaPhonso Ellis	1.25	.70
70	Sarunas Marciulioni(FB)	.10	.06
71	Walt Williams	.50	.30
72	Lee Mayberry	.25	.15
73	Doug Christie	.50	.30
74	Jon Barry	.10	.06
75	Adam Keefe	.12	.07
76	Robert Werdann	.07	.04
77	P.J. Brown	.10	.06
78	Tom Gugliotta	.25	.15
79	Terrell Lowery	.15	.10
80	Tracy Murray	.25	.15
81	C. Weatherspoon	.25	.15
82	Melvin Robinson	.08	.05
83	Todd Day (Kid)	.15	.10
84	Harold Miner	.60	.35
85	Tim Burroughs	.05	.02
86	Damon Patterson	.05	.02
87	Corey Williams	.15	.10
88	Harold Ellis	.07	.04
89	LaPhonso Ellis	.50	.30
90	Checklist	.05	.02

TOPPS

1957-58 Topps

This set was the first basketball edition produced by Topps. The card fronts consist of color photographs with the player's name and team located in a small box that is centered in the lower third of the photo. The card backs contain personal data, highlights and statistics. More than half the cards in the set were double printed making them twice as plentiful as the rest. Those cards are lised below with (DP) next to the player's name. All cards measure 2-1/2" by 3-1/2".

		NR/MT	EX
	Complete Set (80)	5,800.00	2,800.00
	Commons	32.00	16.00
	Commons (DP)	22.00	10.00
1	Nat Clifton (R)(DP)	200.00	95.00
2	George Yardley (R) (DP)	55.00	27.00
3	Neil Johnston (R) (DP)	55.00	27.00
4	Carl Braun	32.00	16.00
5	Bill Sharman (R) (DP)	160.00	80.00
6	George King (R)(DP)	30.00	15.00
7	Kenny Sears (R)(DP)	28.00	14.00
8	Dick Ricketts(R)(DP)	30.00	15.00
9	Jack Nichols (DP)	22.00	10.00
10	Paul Arizin (R)(DP)	100.00	48.00
11	Chuck Noble (DP)	22.00	10.00
12	Slater Martin (R)	65.00	32.00
13	Dolph Schayes (R) (DP)	125.00	60.00
14	Dick Atha (DP)	22.00	10.00
15	Frank Ramsey (R) (DP)	80.00	38.00
16	Dick McGuire (R) (DP)	50.00	25.00
17	Bob Cousy (R)(DP)	600.00	290.00
18	Larry Foust (R)(DP)	30.00	15.00
19	Tom Heinsohn (R)	300.00	145.00
20	Bill Thieben (DP)	22.00	10.00
21	Don Meineke (R)	32.00	16.00
22	Tom Marshall	32.00	16.00
23	Dick Garmaker	32.00	16.00
24	Bob Pettit (R)(DP)	225.00	110.00
25	Jim Krebs (R)(DP)	30.00	15.00
26	Gene Shue (R)(DP)	65.00	32.00
27	Ed Macauley (R)(DP)	65.00	32.00
28	Vern Mikkelsen (R)	55.00	27.00
29	Willie Naulls (R)	65.00	32.00
30	Walter Dukes(R)(DP)	35.00	17.50
31	Dave Pointek (DP)	22.00	10.00
32	John Kerr (R)	125.00	60.00
33	Larry Costello (R) (DP)	60.00	28.00
34	Woody Sauldsberry (R) (DP)	30.00	15.00
35	Ray Felix (R)	40.00	20.00
36	Ernie Beck	32.00	16.00
37	Cliff Hagan (R)	125.00	60.00
38	Guy Sparrow (DP)	22.00	10.00
39	Jim Loscutoff (R)	48.00	24.00
40	Arnie Risen	35.00	17.50
41	Joe Graboski	32.00	16.00
42	Maurice Stokes (R) (DP)	110.00	55.00
43	Rod Hundley(R)(DP)	130.00	64.00
44	Tom Gola (R)(DP)	80.00	38.00
45	Med Park (R)	35.00	17.00
46	Mel Hutchins (DP)	22.00	10.00
47	Larry Friend (DP)	22.00	10.00
48	Lennie Rosenbluth (R) (DP)	50.00	25.00
49	Walt Davis	32.00	16.00
50	Richie Regan (R)	35.00	17.00
51	Frank Selvy (R)(DP)	38.00	18.50
52	Art Spoelstra (DP)	22.00	10.00
53	Bob Hopkins (R)	35.00	17.50
54	Earl Lloyd (R)	38.00	19.00
55	Phil Jordan (DP)	22.00	10.00

146 • 1957-58 TOPPS

56	Bob Houbregs(R)(DP)	35.00	17.00
57	Lou Tsioropoulas (DP)	22.00	10.00
58	Ed Conlin (R)	35.00	17.00
59	Al Bianchi (R)	75.00	36.00
60	George Dempsey (R)	35.00	17.00
61	Chuck Share	32.00	16.00
62	Harry Gallatin (R) (DP)	50.00	25.00
63	Bob Harrison	32.00	16.00
64	Bob Burrow (DP)	22.00	10.00
65	Win Wilfong (DP)	22.00	10.00
66	Jack McMahon (R) (DP)	50.00	28.00
67	Jack George	32.00	16.00
68	Charlie Tyra (DP)	22.00	10.00
69	Ron Sobie	32.00	16.00
70	Jack Coleman	32.00	16.00
71	Jack Twyman(R)(DP)	100.00	48.00
72	Paul Seymour (R)	38.00	19.00
73	Jim Paxson (R)(DP)	50.00	24.00
74	Bob Leonard (R)	38.00	19.00
75	Andy Phillip	38.00	19.00
76	Joe Holup	32.00	16.00
77	Bill Russell (R)	2,400.00	1250.00
78	Clyde Lovellette (R) (DP)	100.00	48.00
79	Ed Fleming (DP)	22.00	10.00
80	Dick Schnittker (R)	80.00	25.00

1969-70 Topps

After a ten year abscence from the basketball card scene Topps returned with a 99-card set. The over-sized cards measure 2-1/2" by 4-11/16". The fronts feature posed color photographs in an oval-shaped frame. The borders are white and include small cartoon basketball players in the four corners. The player's name is centered across the top of the card while his position is printed in smaller type under his first name in the top left corner. The team name is printed in large block letters across the bottom. The card backs consist of personal data, a brief biographical note, statistics and a player highlight printed in a small circle at the bottom of the card.

		NR/MT	EX
Complete Set (99)		2,150.00	1,100.00
Commons		3.50	1.75
1	Wilt Chamberlain	240.00	120.00
2	Gail Goodrich (R)	28.00	14.00
3	Cazzie Russell (R)	15.00	7.50
4	Darrall Imhoff (R)	5.00	2.50
5	Bailey Howell	5.00	2.50
6	Lucius Allen (R)	8.50	4.25

1969-70 TOPPS • 147

#	Player		
7	Tom Boerwinkle (R)	7.50	3.75
8	Jimmy Walker (R)	7.00	3.50
9	John Block (R)	5.00	2.50
10	Nate Thurmond (R)	35.00	17.50
11	Gary Gregor	3.50	1.75
12	Gus Johnson (R)	15.00	7.50
13	Luther Rackley	3.50	1.75
14	Jon McGlocklin (R)	5.00	2.50
15	Connie Hawkins (R)	40.00	20.00
16	Johnny Egan	3.50	1.75
17	Jim Washington	3.50	1.75
18	Dick Barnett (R)	8.50	4.25
19	Tom Meschery	3.50	1.75
20	John Havlicek (R)	180.00	90.00
21	Eddie Miles	3.50	1.75
22	Walt Wesley	3.50	1.75
23	Rick Adelman (R)	15.00	7.50
24	Al Attles	5.00	2.50
25	Lew Alcindor (R)	650.00	325.00
26	Jack Marin (R)	7.50	3.75
27	Walt Hazzard (R)	14.00	7.00
28	Connie Dierking	3.50	1.75
29	Keith Erickson (R)	9.00	4.50
30	Bob Rule (R)	5.00	2.50
31	Dick Van Arsdale (R)	9.00	4.50
32	Archie Clark (R)	8.00	4.00
33	Terry Dischinger (R)	7.50	4.50
34	Henry Finkel (R)	5.00	2.50
35	Elgin Baylor	65.00	32.50
36	Ron Williams	3.50	1.75
37	Loy Petersen	3.50	1.75
38	Guy Rodgers	4.50	2.25
39	Toby Kimball	3.50	1.75
40	Billy Cunningham(R)	55.00	27.50
41	Joe Caldwell (R)	6.00	3.00
42	Leroy Ellis (R)	5.00	2.50
43	Bill Bradley (R)	180.00	100.00
44	Len Wilkens	30.00	15.00
45	Jerry Lucas (R)	48.00	24.00
46	Neal Walk (R)	5.00	2.50
47	Emmette Bryant (R)	4.00	2.00
48	Bob Kauffman (R)	4.50	2.25
49	Mel Counts (R)	5.00	2.50
50	Oscar Robertson	80.00	48.00
51	Jim Barnett (R)	4.50	2.75
52	Don Smith	3.50	1.75
53	Jim Davis	3.50	1.75
54	Wally Jones (R)	5.00	2.50
55	Dave Bing (R)	45.00	22.50
56	Wes Unseld (R)	50.00	28.50
57	Joe Ellis	3.50	1.75
58	John Tresvant	3.50	1.75
59	Larry Siegfried (R)	7.00	3.50
60	Willis Reed (R)	55.00	30.00
61	Paul Silas (R)	15.00	7.50
62	Bob Weiss (R)	6.00	3.00
63	Willie McCarter	3.50	1.75
64	Don Kojis (R)	4.00	2.00
65	Lou Hudson (R)	16.00	8.00
66	Jim King	3.50	1.75
67	Luke Jackson (R)	4.00	2.00
68	Len Chappell (R)	5.00	2.50
69	Ray Scott	4.00	2.00
70	Jeff Mullins (R)	9.00	4.50
71	Howie Komives	3.50	1.75
72	Tom Sanders (R)	7.00	3.50
73	Dick Snyder	3.50	1.75
74	Dave Stallworth (R)	6.00	3.00
75	Elvin Hayes (R)	80.00	48.00
76	Art Harris	3.50	1.75
77	Don Ohl	3.50	1.75
78	Bob Love (R)	20.00	10.00
79	Tom Van Arsdale (R)	9.00	4.50
80	Earl Monroe (R)	50.00	28.00
81	Greg Smith	3.50	1.75
82	Don Nelson (R)	32.00	16.00
83	Happy Hairston (R)	10.00	5.00
84	Hal Greer	10.00	5.00
85	Dave DeBusschere (R)	48.00	24.00
86	Bill Bridges (R)	5.00	2.50
87	Herm Billiam (R)	4.00	2.00
88	Jim Fox	3.50	1.75
89	Bob Boozer	5.00	2.50
90	Jerry West	110.00	65.00
91	Chet Walker	15.00	7.50
92	Flynn Robinson (R)	5.00	2.50
93	Clyde Lee	3.50	1.75
94	Kevin Loughery (R)	15.00	7.50
95	Walt Bellamy	10.00	5.00
96	Art Wiliams	3.50	1.75
97	Adrian Smith (R)	4.00	2.00
98	Walt Frazier (R)	100.00	60.00
99	Checklist	280.00	75.00

148 • 1970-71 TOPPS

1970-71 Topps

Topps increased the size of their set to 175-cards and stayed with the large format with cards measuring 2-1/2" by 4-11/16". The card fronts consist of full-color player photos framed by white borders. The player's name, position and team are printed over a basketball in the lower right corner of the front. The flip side contains personal data, highlights, statistics and a brief biographical note. The main subsets include League Leaders (LL)(1-6), All-Stars (AS)(106-115) and Playoffs (168-175)

		NR/MT	EX
Complete Set (175)		1,350.00	725.00
Commons (1-110)		2.25	1.10
Commons (111-175)		3.25	1.60
1	Scoring Leaders	35.00	17.00
	Lew Alcindor		
	Jerry West		
	Elvin Hayes		
2	Scoring Average Ldrs	22.00	11.00
	Jerry West		
	Lew Alcindor		
	Elvin Hayes		
3	Field Goal % Ldrs	5.00	2.50
	Johnny Green		
	Darrall Imhoff		
	Lou Hudson		
4	Free Throw % Ldrs	10.00	5.00
	Flynn Robinson		
	Chet Walker		
	Jeff Mullins		
5	Rebound Leaders	16.00	8.00
	Elvin Hayes		
	Wes Unseld		
	Lew Alcindor		
6	Assist Leaders	10.00	5.00
	Len Wilkens		
	Walt Frazier		
	Clem Haskins		
7	Bill Bradley	80.00	40.00
8	Ron Williams	2.25	1.10
9	Otto Moore	2.25	1.10
10	John Havlicek	80.00	45.00
11	George Wilson (R)	3.00	1.50
12	John Trapp	2.25	1.10
13	Pat Riley (R)	55.00	27.50
14	Jim Washington	2.25	1.10
15	Bob Rule	2.25	1.10
16	Bob Weiss	3.00	1.50
17	Neil Johnson	2.25	1.10
18	Walt Bellamy	6.00	3.00
19	McCoy McLemore	2.25	1.10
20	Earl Monroe	16.00	8.00
21	Wally Anderzunas	2.25	1.10
22	Guy Rodgers	3.00	1.50
23	Rick Roberson	2.25	1.10
24	Checklist (1-110)	50.00	7.50
25	Jimmy Walker	2.25	1.10
26	Mike Riordan (R)	5.00	2.50
27	Henry Finkel	2.75	1.40
28	Joe Ellis	2.25	1.10
29	Mike Davis	2.25	1.10
30	Lou Hudson	5.00	2.50
31	Lucius Allen	6.00	3.00
32	Toby Kimball	2.25	1.10
33	Luke Jackson	2.25	1.10
34	Johnny Egan	2.50	1.25
35	Leroy Ellis	2.25	1.10
36	Jack Marin	6.00	3.00
37	Joe Caldwell	5.00	2.50
38	Keith Erickson	5.00	2.50
39	Don Smith	2.25	1.10
40	Flynn Robinson	2.25	1.10
41	Bob Boozer	2.25	1.10
42	Howie Komives	2.25	1.10
43	Dick Barnett	5.00	2.50
44	Stu Lantz (R)	4.50	2.25
45	Dick Van Arsdale	5.00	2.50
46	Jerry Lucas	15.00	7.50
47	Don Chaney (R)	10.00	5.00
48	Ray Scott	2.25	1.10
49	Dick Cunningham	2.25	1.10
50	Wilt Chamberlain	140.00	75.00

1970-71 TOPPS • 149

#	Player	Price	Price
51	Kevin Loughery	5.00	2.50
52	Stan McKenzie	2.25	1.10
53	Fred Foster	2.25	1.10
54	Jim Davis	2.25	1.10
55	Walt Wesley	2.25	1.10
56	Bill Hewitt	2.25	1.10
57	Darrall Imhoff	2.25	1.10
58	John Block	2.25	1.10
59	Al Attles	5.00	2.50
60	Chet Walker	6.00	3.00
61	Luther Rackley	2.25	1.10
62	Jerry Chambers (R)	4.00	2.00
63	Bob Dandridge (R)	8.50	4.25
64	Dick Snyder	2.25	1.10
65	Elgin Baylor	38.00	19.00
66	Connie Dierking	2.25	1.10
67	Steve Kuberski (R)	3.00	1.50
68	Tom Boerwinkle	3.00	1.50
69	Paul Silas	6.50	3.75
70	Elvin Hayes	35.00	18.00
71	Bill Bridges	3.00	1.50
72	Wes Unseld	10.00	5.00
73	Herm Gilliam	2.25	1.10
74	Bobby Smith (R)	5.00	3.00
75	Lew Alcindor	180.00	100.00
76	Jeff Mullins	3.50	1.75
77	Happy Hairston	3.50	1.75
78	Dave Stallworth	2.25	1.10
79	Fred Hetzel	2.25	1.10
80	Len Wilkens	18.00	9.00
81	Johnny Green	3.50	1.75
82	Erwin Mueller	2.25	1.10
83	Wally Jones	2.25	1.10
84	Bob Love	8.50	4.25
85	Dick Garrett (R)	3.00	1.50
86	Don Nelson	15.00	7.50
87	Neal Walk	2.50	1.25
88	Larry Siegfried	3.50	1.75
89	Gary Gregor	2.25	1.10
90	Nate Thurmond	10.00	5.00
91	John Warren	2.25	1.10
92	Gus Johnson	4.50	2.25
93	Gail Goodrich	8.00	4.00
94	Dorrie Murrey	2.25	1.10
95	Cazzie Russell	9.00	4.50
96	Terry Dischinger	3.50	1.75
97	Norm Van Lier (R)	12.00	6.00
98	Jim Fox	2.25	1.10
99	Tom Meschery	2.25	1.10
100	Oscar Robertson	50.00	28.00
101A	Checklist (111-175)	30.00	6.00
102	Rich Johnson	2.25	1.10
103	Mel Counts	2.25	1.10
104	Bill Hosket (R)	4.00	2.00
105	Archie Clark	3.00	1.50
106	Walt Frazier (AS)	15.00	7.50
107	Jerry West (AS)	35.00	18.00
108	Bill Cunningham (AS)	10.00	5.00
109	Connie Hawkins (AS)	7.50	3.75
110	Willis Reed (AS)	10.00	5.00
111	Nate Thurmond (AS)	4.50	2.25
112	John Havlicek (AS)	32.00	16.00
113	Elgin Baylor (AS)	20.00	12.00
114	Oscar Robertson (AS)	25.00	13.00
115	Lou Hudson (AS)	4.00	2.00
116	Emmette Bryant	3.25	1.60
117	Greg Howard	3.25	1.60
118	Rick Adelman	5.00	2.50
119	Barry Clemens	3.25	1.60
120	Walt Frazier	32.00	16.00
121	Jim Barnes (R)	4.00	2.00
122	Bernie Williams	3.25	1.60
123	Pete Maravich (R)	180.00	100.00
124	Matt Guokas (R)	10.00	5.00
125	Dave Bing	12.00	6.00
126	John Tresvant	3.25	1.60
127	Shaler Halimon	3.25	1.60
128	Don Ohl	3.25	1.60
129	Fred Carter (R)	6.00	3.00
130	Connie Hawkins	15.00	7.50
131	Jim King	3.25	1.60
132	Ed Manning (R)	4.50	2.25
133	Adrian Smith	3.25	1.60
134	Walt Hazzard	6.00	3.00
135	Dave DeBusschere	15.00	7.50
136	Don Kojis	3.25	1.60
137	Calvin Murphy (R)	40.00	20.00
138	Nate Bowman	3.25	1.60
139	Jon McGlocklin	4.00	2.00
140	Billy Cunningham	18.00	9.00
141	Willie McCarter	3.25	1.60
142	Jim Barnett	4.00	2.00
143	JoJo White (R)	18.00	9.00
144	Clyde Lee	3.25	1.60
145	Tom Van Arsdale	4.50	2.25
146	Len Chappell	3.50	1.75
147	Lee Winfield	3.25	1.60
148	Jerry Sloan (R)	12.00	6.00
149	Art Harris	3.25	1.60
150	Willis Reed	22.50	11.50
151	Art Williams	3.25	1.60
152	Don May	3.25	1.60
153	Loy Petersen	3.25	1.60
154	Dave Gambee	3.25	1.60
155	Hal Greer	6.00	3.00
156	Dave Newmark	3.25	1.60
157	Jimmy Collins	3.25	1.60
158	Bill Turner	3.25	1.60
159	Eddie Miles	3.25	1.60
160	Jerry West	75.00	37.50
161	Bob Quick	3.25	1.60
162	Fred Crawford	3.25	1.60
163	Tom Sanders	4.50	2.25
164	Dale Schlueter	3.25	1.60

150 • 1970-71 TOPPS

165	Clem Haskins (R)	7.50	3.75
166	Greg Smith	3.25	1.60
167	Rod Thorn (R)	9.00	4.50
168	Playoff Game 1 (Willis Reed)	7.50	3.75
169	Playoff Game 2 (Dick Garrett)	4.50	2.25
170	Playoff Game 3 (Dave DeBusschere)	6.50	3.25
171	Playoff Game 4 (Jerry West)	15.00	7.50
172	Playoff Game 5 (Bill Bradley)	15.00	7.50
173	Playoff Game 6 (Wilt Chamberlain)	18.50	9.25
174	Playoff Game 7 (Walt Frazier)	10.00	5.00
175	Knicks Champs	22.00	11.00

1971-72 Topps

The cards in this set feature players from both the NBA and the ABA (American Basketball Association). The card fronts consist of mostly posed color player photos wrapped by a white border. Team names appear in bold block type above the picture while the player's name is printed across the bottom just above the team nickname and the player's position which appear in smaller type. The horizontal card backs contain personal data, highlights, statistics and a basketball trivia question. Subsets include League Leaders (LL) and Playoffs (133-137). All cards measure 2-1/2" by 3-1/2".

		NR/MT	EX
Complete Set (233)		900.00	475.00
Commons (1-144)		1.25	.70
Commons (145-233)		1.80	1.00
1	Oscar Robertson	55.00	28.00
2	Bill Bradley	48.00	25.00
3	Jim Fox	1.25	.70
4	John Johnson (R)	2.50	1.40
5	Luke Jackson	1.25	.65
6	Don May	1.25	.65
7	Kevin Loughery	3.50	1.80
8	Terry Dischinger	1.75	.90
9	Neal Walk	1.25	.65
10	Elgin Baylor	28.00	15.00
11	Rick Adelman	3.00	1.60
12	Clyde Lee	1.25	.65
13	Jerry Chambers	1.25	.65
14	Fred Carter	1.50	.80
15	Tom Boerwinkle	1.25	.65
16	John Block	1.25	.65
17	Dick Barnett	1.75	.90
18	Henry Finkel	1.50	.80
19	Norm Van Lier	4.00	2.25
20	Spencer Haywood (R)	15.00	8.00
21	George Johnson	1.25	.65
22	Bobby Lewis	1.25	.65
23	Bill Hewitt	1.25	.65
24	Walt Hazzard	3.50	1.80
25	Happy Hairston	2.00	1.10
26	George Wilson	1.25	.65
27	Lucius Allen	2.00	1.10
28	Jim Washington	1.25	.65
29	Nate Archibald (R)	40.00	22.00
30	Willis Reed	10.00	5.50
31	Erwin Mueller	1.25	.65
32	Art Harris	1.25	.65
33	Pete Cross	1.25	.65
34	Geoff Petrie (R)	6.00	3.25
35	John Havlicek	38.00	20.00
36	Larry Siegfried	1.50	.80
37	John Tresvant	1.25	.65
38	Ron Williams	1.25	.65
39	Lamar Green	1.25	.65
40	Bob Rule	1.25	.65
41	Jim McMillan (R)	2.50	1.35
42	Wally Jones	1.25	.65
43	Bob Boozer	1.25	.65
44	Eddie Miles	1.25	.65
45	Bob Love	4.00	2.25
46	Claude English	1.25	.65
47	Dave Cowens (R)	55.00	28.00

1971-72 TOPPS • 151

#	Player	Price 1	Price 2
48	Emmette Bryant	1.25	.65
49	Dave Stallworth	1.25	.65
50	Jerry West	48.00	25.00
51	Joe Ellis	1.25	.65
52	Walt Wesley	1.25	.65
53	Howie Komives	1.25	.65
54	Paul Silas	4.00	2.25
55	Pete Maravich	50.00	28.00
56	Gary Gregor	1.25	.65
57	Sam Lacey	3.00	1.60
58	Calvin Murphy	7.50	4.00
59	Bob Dandridge	2.50	1.35
60	Hal Greer	4.50	2.40
61	Keith Erickson	1.75	.90
62	Joe Cooke	1.25	.65
63	Bob Lanier (R)	45.00	24.00
64	Don Kojis	1.25	.65
65	Walt Frazier	18.00	10.00
66	Chet Walker	3.50	1.80
67	Dick Garrett	1.25	.65
68	John Trapp	1.25	.65
69	JoJo White	6.50	3.50
70	Wilt Chamberlain	80.00	45.00
71	Dave Sorenson	1.25	.65
72	Jim King	1.25	.65
73	Cazzie Russell	4.50	2.40
74	Jon McGlocklin	1.25	.65
75	Tom Van Arsdale	1.50	.80
76	Dale Schlueter	1.25	.65
77	Gus Johnson	2.50	1.35
78	Dave Bing	7.50	4.00
79	Billy Cunningham	10.00	5.50
80	Len Wilkens	10.00	5.50
81	Jerry Lucas	8.00	4.25
82	Don Chaney	3.50	1.80
83	McCoy McLemore	1.25	.65
84	Bob Kauffman	1.25	.65
85	Dick Van Arsdale	1.50	.80
86	Johnny Green	1.25	.65
87	Jerry Sloan	4.00	2.25
88	Luther Rackley	1.25	.65
89	Shaler Halimon	1.25	.65
90	Jimmy Walker	1.25	.65
91	Rudy Tomjanovich (R)	18.00	10.00
92	Levi Fontaine	1.25	.65
93	Bobby Smith	1.50	.80
94	Bob Arnzen	1.25	.65
95	Wes Unseld	8.00	4.25
96	Clem Haskins	2.00	1.10
97	Jim Davis	1.25	.65
98	Steve Kuberski	1.50	.80
99	Mike Davis	1.25	.65
100	Lew Alcindor	80.00	45.00
101	Willie McCarter	1.25	.65
102	Charlie Paulk	1.25	.65
103	Lee Winfield	1.25	.65
104	Jim Barnett	1.50	.80
105	Connie Hawkins	7.00	3.75
106	Archie Clark	1.50	.80
107	Dave DeBusschere	10.00	5.50
108	Stu Lantz	1.25	.65
109	Don Smith	1.25	.65
110	Lou Hudson	2.50	1.60
111	Leroy Ellis	1.25	.65
112	Jack Marin	2.00	1.10
113	Matt Guokas	3.50	1.80
114	Don Nelson	6.50	3.50
115	Jeff Mullins	1.75	.90
116	Walt Bellamy	5.00	2.75
117	Bob Quick	1.25	.65
118	John Warren	1.25	.65
119	Barry Clemens	1.25	.65
120	Elvin Hayes	18.00	9.50
121	Gail Goodrich	6.50	3.50
122	Ed Manning	1.50	.80
123	Herm Gilliam	1.25	.65
124	Dennis Awtrey (R)	1.75	.90
125	John Hummer	1.25	.65
126	Mike Riordan	1.50	.80
127	Mel Counts	1.50	.80
128	Bob Weiss	1.50	.80
129	Greg Smith	1.25	.65
130	Earl Monroe	12.00	6.50
131	Nate Thurmond	5.00	2.75
132	Bill Bridges	1.50	.80
133	NBA Playoffs 1 (Lew Alcindor)	12.00	6.50
134	NBA Playoffs 2	3.50	1.60
135	NBA Playoffs 3	3.50	1.60
136	NBA Playoffs 4 (Oscar Robertson)	8.50	4.50
137	Bucks Champs	4.50	2.40
138	Scoring Leaders Lew Alcindor Elvin Hayes John Havlicek	15.00	8.00
139	Scoring Average Ldrs Lew Alcindor John Havlicek Elvin Hayes	15.00	8.00
140	Field Goal % Ldrs Johnny Green Lew Alcindor Wilt Chamberlain	15.00	8.00
141	Free Throw Leaders Chet Walker Oscar Robertson Ron Williams	5.50	3.00
142	Rebound Leaders Wilt Chamberlain Elvin Hayes Lew Alcindor	24.00	14.00
143	Assist Leaders Norm Van Lier	8.50	5.00

1971-72 TOPPS

#	Player		
	Oscar Robertson		
	Jerry West		
144	NBA Checklist	16.00	6.00
145	ABA Checklist	16.00	6.00
146	Scoring Leaders	6.00	3.25
	Dan Issel		
	John Brisker		
	Charlie Scott		
147	Scoring Average Ldrs	12.00	6.50
	Dan Issel		
	Rick Barry		
	John Brisker		
148	2pt Field Goal Ldrs	4.00	2.25
	Zelmo Beaty		
	Billy Paultz		
	Roger Brown		
149	Free Throw Leaders	8.50	4.25
	Rick Barry		
	Darrell Carrier		
	Billy Keller		
150	Rebound Leaders	4.00	2.25
	Mel Daniels		
	Julius Keye		
	Mike Lewis		
151	Assist Leaders	4.00	2.25
	Bill Melchionni		
	Mack Calvin		
	Charlie Scott		
152	Larry Brown (R)	24.00	13.00
153	Bob Bedell	1.80	1.00
154	Merv Jackson	1.80	1.00
155	Joe Caldwell	2.50	1.40
156	Billy Paultz (R)	4.00	2.25
157	Les Hunter	1.80	1.00
158	Charlie Williams	1.80	1.00
159	Stew Johnson	1.80	1.00
160	Mack Calvin (R)	6.00	3.25
161	Don Sidle	1.80	1.00
162	Mike Barrett	1.80	1.00
163	Tom Workman	1.80	1.00
164	Joe Hamilton	1.80	1.00
165	Zelmo Beaty (R)	6.50	3.50
166	Dan Hester	1.80	1.00
167	Bob Verga	1.80	1.00
168	Wilbert Jones	1.80	1.00
169	Skeeter Swift	1.80	1.00
170	Rick Barry (R)	90.00	48.00
171	Billy Keller (R)	3.50	1.80
172	Ron Franz	1.80	1.00
173	Roland Taylor	2.00	1.10
174	Julian Hammond	1.80	1.00
175	Steve Jones (R)	4.50	2.40
176	Gerald Govan	1.80	1.00
177	Darrell Carrier (R)	2.00	1.10
178	Ron Boone (R)	3.50	1.80
179	George Peeples	1.80	1.00
180	John Brisker	3.50	1.80
181	Doug Moe (R)	15.00	8.00
182	Ollie Taylor	1.80	1.00
183	Bob Netolicky	2.00	1.10
184	Sam Robinson	1.80	1.00
186	James Jones	1.80	1.00
187	Wayne Hightower	1.80	1.00
188	Warren Armstrong (R)	2.00	1.10
189	Mike Lewis	1.80	1.00
190	Charle Scott (R)	7.50	4.00
191	Jim Ard	1.80	1.00
192	George Lehmann	1.80	1.00
193	Ira Harge	1.80	1.00
194	Willie Wise (R)	4.50	2.40
195	Mel Daniels (R)	8.50	4.50
196	Larry Cannon	1.75	.90
197	Jim Eakins	1.80	1.00
198	Rich Jones	1.80	1.00
199	Bill Melchionni (R)	4.00	2.25
200	Dan Issel (R)	55.00	30.00
201	George Stone	1.80	1.00
202	George Thompson	1.80	1.00
203	Craig Raymond	1.80	1.00
204	Freddie Lewis (R)	3.50	1.80
205	George Carter	1.80	1.00
206	Lonnie Wright	1.80	1.00
207	Cincy Powell	1.80	1.00
208	Larry Miller	2.00	1.10
209	Sonny Dove	1.80	1.00
210	Byron Beck (R)	2.00	1.10
211	John Beasley	1.80	1.00
212	Lee Davis	1.80	1.00
213	Rick Mount (R)	8.00	4.25
214	Walt Simon	1.80	1.00
215	Glen Combs	1.80	1.00
216	Neil Johnson	1.80	1.00
217	Manny Leaks	1.80	1.00
218	Chuck Williams	1.80	1.00
219	Warren Davis	1.80	1.00
220	Donnie Freeman (R)	3.50	1.80
221	Randy Mahaffey	1.80	1.00
222	John Barnhill	1.80	1.00
223	Al Cueto	1.80	1.00
224	Louie Dampier (R)	7.50	4.00
225	Roger Brown (R)	4.50	2.50
226	Joe DePre	1.80	1.00
227	Ray Scott	1.80	1.00
228	Arvesta Kelly	1.80	1.00
229	Vann Williford	1.80	1.00
230	Larry Jones	1.80	1.00
231	Gene Moore	1.80	1.00
232	Ralph Simpson (R)	3.50	1.60
233	Red Robbins (R)	3.50	1.60

1972-73 Topps

CONNIE HAWKINS FORWARD

Topps increase the size of their basketball set to 264-cards and included both NBA players and ABA players in the set. The card fronts consist of mosly posed color player photos framed by a white border. The team name appears in large letters in a diagonal color bar in the bottom third of the photo. The player's name and postion appear in opposite corners in the lower border. The flip side contains personal data, a highlight, statistics and a small cartoon. Subsets include All-Stars(AS), League Leaders (LL), NBA Playoffs (154-159) and ABA Playoffs (241-247). All cards measure 2-1/2" by 3-1/2".

		NR/MT	EX
Complete Set (264)		875.00	460.00
Commons		1.25	.70
1	Wilt Chamberlain	65.00	35.00
2	Stan Love	1.25	.70
3	Geoff Petrie	2.00	1.25
4	Curtis Perry (R)	1.75	1.00
5	Pete Maravich	38.00	22.00
6	Gus Johnson	2.00	1.25
7	Dave Cowens	18.00	10.00
8	Randy Smith (R)	2.50	1.50
9	Matt Guokas	2.50	1.50
10	Spencer Haywood	3.50	2.00
11	Jerry Sloan	2.50	1.50
12	Dave Sorenson	1.25	.70
13	Howie Komives	1.25	.70
14	Joe Ellis	1.25	.70
15	Jerry Lucas	7.50	4.00
16	Stu Lantz	1.25	.70
17	Bill Bridges	1.25	.70
18	Leroy Ellis	1.25	.70
19	Art Williams	1.25	.70
20	Sidney Wicks (R)	10.00	6.00
21	Wes Unseld	6.50	3.50
22	Jim Washington	1.25	.70
23	Fred Hilton	1.25	.70
24	Curtis Rowe (R)	3.00	1.75
25	Oscar Robertson	24.00	14.00
26	Larry Steele (R)	1.75	1.00
27	Charlie Davis	1.25	.70
28	Nate Thurmond	5.00	2.75
29	Fred Carter	1.50	.90
30	Connie Hawkins	5.00	2.75
31	Calvin Murphy	5.00	2.75
32	Phil Jackson (R)	25.00	14.00
33	Lee Winfield	1.25	.70
34	Jim Fox	1.25	.70
35	Dave Bing	6.50	3.75
36	Gary Gregor	1.25	.70
37	Mike Riordan	1.50	.90
38	George Trapp	1.25	.70
39	Mike Davis	1.25	.70
40	Bob Rule	1.25	.70
41	John Block	1.25	.70
42	Bob Dandridge	2.00	1.25
43	John Johnson	1.50	.90
44	Rick Barry	30.00	16.00
45	JoJo White	3.50	2.00
46	Cliff Meely	1.25	.70
47	Charlie Scott	2.00	1.25
48	Johnny Green	1.25	.70
49	Pete Cross	1.25	.70
50	Gail Goodrich	4.00	2.50
51	Jim Davis	1.25	.70
52	Dick Barnett	1.50	.90
53	Bob Christian	1.25	.70
54	Jon McGlocklin	1.25	.70
55	Paul Silas	2.00	1.25
56	Hal Greer	3.50	2.00
57	Barry Clements	1.25	.70
58	Nick Jones	1.25	.70
59	Cornell Warner	1.25	.70
60	Walt Frazier	14.00	8.50
61	Dorrie Murray	1.25	.70
62	Dick Cunningham	1.25	.70
63	Sam Lacey	1.50	.90
64	John Warren	1.25	.70
65	Tom Boerwinkle	1.25	.70
66	Fred Foster	1.25	.70
67	Mel Counts	1.25	.70
68	Toby Kimball	1.25	.70
69	Dale Schlueter	1.25	.70
70	Jack Marin	1.50	.90

1972-73 TOPPS

#	Name		
71	Jim Barnett	1.25	.70
72	Clem Haskins	2.00	1.25
73	Earl Monroe	8.50	4.75
74	Tom Sanders	1.50	.90
75	Jerry West	35.00	20.00
76	Elmore Smith (R)	2.00	1.25
77	Don Adams	1.25	.70
78	Wally Jones	1.25	.70
79	Tom Van Arsdale	1.75	1.00
80	Bob Lanier	14.00	8.50
81	Len Wilkens	6.00	3.50
82	Neal Walk	1.25	.70
83	Kevin Loughery	2.00	1.25
84	Stan McKenzie	1.25	.70
85	Jeff Mullins	1.75	1.00
86	Otto Moore	1.25	.70
87	John Tresvant	1.25	.70
88	Dean Meminger (R)	1.75	1.00
89	Jim McMillian	1.75	1.00
90	Austin Carr (R)	7.50	4.00
91	Clifford Ray (R)	2.50	1.50
92	Don Nelson	5.00	2.75
93	Mahdi Abdul-Rahman	2.00	1.25
94	Willie Norwood	1.25	.70
95	Dick Van Arsdale	1.50	.90
96	Don May	1.25	.70
97	Walt Bellamy	4.00	2.50
98	Garfield Heard (R)	3.50	2.00
99	Dave Wohl	1.25	.70
100	Kareem Abdul-Jabbar	65.00	35.00
101	Ron Knight	1.25	.70
102	Phil Chenier (R)	3.00	1.75
103	Rudy Tomjanovich	6.50	3.50
104	Flynn Robinson	1.25	.70
105	Dave De Busschere	7.50	4.00
106	Dennis Layton	1.25	.70
107	Bill Hewitt	1.25	.70
108	Dick Garrett	1.25	.70
109	Walt Wesley	1.25	.70
110	John Havlicek	28.00	16.00
111	Norm Van Lier	2.50	1.50
112	Cazzie Russell	2.50	1.50
113	Herm Gilliam	1.25	.70
114	Greg Smith	1.25	.70
115	Nate Archibald	10.00	6.00
116	Don Kojis	1.25	.70
117	Rick Adelman	2.00	1.25
118	Luke Jackson	1.25	.70
119	Lamar Green	1.25	.70
120	Archie Clark	1.50	.90
121	Happy Hairston	1.75	1.00
122	Bill Bradley	30.00	18.00
123	Ron Williams	1.25	.70
124	Jimmy Walker	1.25	.70
125	Bob Kauffman	1.25	.70
126	Rick Roberson	1.25	.70
127	Howard Porter (R)	2.00	1.25
128	Mike Newlin (R)	1.75	1.00
129	Willis Reed	8.50	4.75
130	Lou Hudson	2.00	1.25
131	Don Chaney	2.50	1.50
132	Dave Stallworth	1.25	.70
133	Charlie Yelverton	1.25	.70
134	Ken Durrett	1.25	.70
135	John Brisker	1.25	.70
136	Dick Snyder	1.25	.70
137	Jim McDaniels	1.25	.70
138	Clyde Lee	1.25	.70
139	Dennis Awtrey	1.25	.70
140	Keith Erickson	1.75	1.00
141	Bob Weiss	1.50	.90
142	Butch Beard (R)	2.50	1.50
143	Terry Dischinger	1.75	1.00
144	Pat Riley	14.00	8.75
145	Lucius Allen	2.00	1.25
146	John Mengelt (R)	1.75	1.00
147	John Hummer	1.25	.70
148	Bob Love	4.50	2.50
149	Bobby Smith	1.25	.70
150	Elvin Hayes	15.00	9.50
151	Nate Williams	1.25	.70
152	Chet Walker	3.50	2.00
153	Steve Kuberski	1.25	.70
154	NBA Playoffs 1	3.00	1.75
155	NBA Playoffs 2	2.00	1.25
156	NBA Playoffs 3	2.00	1.25
157	NBA Playoffs 4	2.00	1.25
158	NBA Playoffs 6	7.50	4.00
159	NBA Champs Lakers	8.50	4.75
160	NBA Checklist	14.00	4.00
161	John Havlicek (AS)	12.00	6.50
162	Spencer Haywood (AS)	2.00	1.25
163	K. Abdul-Jabbar (AS)	28.00	16.00
164	Jerry West (AS)	16.00	10.00
165	Walt Frazier (AS)	6.50	3.50
166	Bob Love (AS)	2.00	1.25
167	Billy Cunningham (AS)	3.50	2.00
168	Wilt Chamberlain (AS)	28.00	16.00
169	Nate Archibald (AS)	4.00	2.25
170	Archie Clark (AS)	1.75	1.00
171	NBA Scoring Leaders	12.00	6.75
	Kareem Abdul-Jabbar		
	John Havlicek, Nate Archibald		
172	NBA Scoring Avg Ldrs	12.00	6.75
	Kareem Abdul-Jabbar		
	Nate Archibald, John Havlicek		
173	NBA Field Goal Lddrs	12.00	6.75
	Wilt Chamberlain		
	Kareem Abdul-Jabbar		
	Walt Bellamy		
174	NBA Free Throw Ldrs	2.50	1.50
	Jack Marin		
	Calvin Murphy		
	Gail Goodrich		

1972-73 TOPPS • 155

#	Name		
175	NBA Rebound Leaders	15.00	8.75
	Wilt Chamberlain		
	Kareem Abdul-Jabbar		
	Wes Unseld		
176	NBA Assist Leaders	8.50	4.75
	Len Wilkens		
	Jerry West		
	Nate Archibald		
177	Roland Taylor	1.25	.70
178	Art Becker	1.25	.70
179	Mack Calvin	2.50	1.50
180	Artis Gilmore (R)	38.00	22.00
181	Collis Jones	1.25	.70
182	John Roche (R)	2.50	1.50
183	George McGinnis (R)	12.00	7.00
184	Johnny Neumann	1.25	.70
185	Willie Wise	1.75	1.00
186	Bernie Williams	1.25	.70
187	Byron Beck	1.25	.70
188	Larry Miller	1.25	.70
189	Cincy Powell	1.25	.70
190	Donnie Freeman	1.25	.70
191	John Baum	1.25	.70
192	Billy Keller	1.50	.90
193	Wilbert Jones	1.25	.70
194	Glen Combs	1.25	.70
195	Julius Erving (R)	360.00	210.00
196	Al Smith	1.25	.70
197	George Carter	1.25	.70
198	Louie Dampier	2.50	1.50
199	Rich Jones	1.25	.70
200	Mel Daniels	3.50	2.00
201	Gene Moore	1.25	.70
202	Randy Denton	1.25	.70
203	Larry Jones	1.25	.70
204	Jim Ligon	1.25	.70
205	Warren Jabali (R)	1.50	.90
206	Joe Caldwell	1.50	.90
207	Darrell Carrier	1.25	.70
208	Gene Kennedy	1.25	.70
209	Ollie Taylor	1.25	.70
210	Roger Brown	1.75	1.00
211	George Lehmann	1.25	.70
212	Red Robbins	1.25	.70
213	Jim Eakins	1.25	.70
214	Willie Long	1.25	.70
215	Billy Cunningham	8.00	4.50
216	Steve Jones	1.75	1.00
217	Les Hunter	1.25	.70
218	Billy Paultz	2.00	1.25
219	Freddie Lewis	1.75	1.00
220	Zelmo Beaty	2.50	1.50
221	George Thompson	1.25	.70
222	Neil Johnson	1.25	.70
223	Dave Robisch (R)	3.00	1.75
224	Walt Simon	1.25	.70
225	Bill Melchionni	1.50	.90
226	Wendell Ladner (R)	2.00	1.25
227	Joe Hamilton	1.25	.70
228	Bob Netolicky	1.25	.70
229	James Jones	1.25	.70
230	Dan Issel	18.00	10.00
231	Charlie Williams	1.25	.70
232	Willie Sojourner	1.25	.70
233	Merv Jackson	1.25	.70
234	Mike Lewis	1.25	.70
235	Ralph Simpson	1.75	1.00
236	Darnell Hillman	1.25	.70
237	Rick Mount	3.50	2.00
238	Gerald Govan	1.25	.70
239	Ron Boone	1.75	1.00
240	Tom Washington	1.25	.70
241	ABA Playoffs 1	2.00	1.25
242	ABA Playoffs 2	5.00	2.75
243	ABA Playoffs 3	4.00	2.25
244	ABA Playoffs 4	4.50	2.50
245	ABA Playoffs 5	2.00	1.25
246	ABA Playoffs 6	2.00	1.25
247	ABA Champs Pacers	2.00	1.25
248	ABA Checklist	14.00	4.00
249	Dan Issel (AS)	8.00	4.75
250	Rick Barry (AS)	14.00	7.50
251	Artis Gilmore (AS)	7.50	4.00
252	Donnie Freeman (AS)	1.50	.90
253	Bill Melchionni (AS)	1.50	.90
254	Willie Wise (AS)	1.50	.90
255	Julius Erving (AS)	90.00	55.00
256	Zelmo Beaty (AS)	1.75	1.00
257	Ralph Simpson (AS)	1.50	.90
258	Charlie Scott (AS)	2.00	1.25
259	ABA Scoring Avg Ldrs	5.00	2.75
	Rick Barry		
	Dan Issel		
	Charlie Scott		
260	ABA 2pt Field Goal Ldrs	4.00	2.25
	Artis Gilmore		
	Tom Washington		
	Larry Jones		
261	ABA 3pt Field Goal Ldrs	1.75	1.00
	Glen Combs		
	Louie Dampier		
	Warren Jabali		
262	ABA Free Throw Ldrs	4.00	2.25
	Rick Barry		
	Mack Calvin		
	Steve Jones		
263	ABA Rebound Ldrs	22.00	12.50
	Artis Gilmore		
	Julius Erving		
	Mel Daniels		
264	ABA Assist Leaders	4.00	2.25
	Bill Melchionni		
	Larry Brown		
	Louie Dampier		

156 • 1973-74 TOPPS

1973-74 Topps

LAKERS
KEITH ERICKSON

The cards in this feature full color player photos on the card fronts framed by a white border. The team name is printed in large block letters below the photograph. The player's name, in smaller type, appears below the team name. A team logo is printed in the lower corner of the card face. The flip side includes personal data, stats, highlights and a small cartoon. The set contains cards of NBA players (1-176) and ABA players (177-264). Key subsets include All-Stars (AS), League Leaders (153-158, 234-239), and Playoffs (62-68, 202-208). All cards measure 2-1/2" by 3-1/2".

		NR/MT	EX
	Complete Set (264)	390.00	225.00
	Commons	.55	.30
1	Nate Archibald (AS)	8.50	4.50
2	Steve Kuberski	.55	.30
3	John Mengelt	.55	.30
4	Jim McMillan	.60	.35
5	Nate Thurmond	3.50	2.00
6	Dave Wohl	.55	.30
7	John Brisker	.55	.30
8	Charlie Davis	.55	.30
9	Lamar Green	.55	.30
10	Walt Frazier (AS)	9.00	5.00
11	Bob Christian	.55	.30
12	Cornell Warner	.55	.30
13	Calvin Murphy	5.00	2.75
14	Dave Sorenson	.55	.30
15	Archie Clark	.80	.50
16	Clifford Ray	1.00	.60
17	Terry Driscoll	.55	.30
18	Matt Guokas	1.50	.90
19	Elmore Smith	.75	.45
20	John Havlicek (AS)	16.00	10.00
21	Pat Riley	10.00	6.00
22	George Trapp	.55	.30
23	Ron Williams	.55	.30
24	Jim Fox	.55	.30
25	Dick Van Arsdale	.60	.35
26	John Tresvant	.55	.30
27	Rick Adelman	1.00	.60
28	Eddie Mast	.55	.30
29	Jim Cleamons	.55	.30
30	Dave DeBusschere (AS)	6.00	3.50
31	Norm Van Lier	1.50	.90
32	Stan McKenzie	.55	.30
33	Bob Dandridge	.70	.40
34	Leroy Ellis	.55	.30
35	Mike Riordan	.60	.35
36	Fred Hilton	.55	.30
37	Toby Kimball	.55	.30
38	Jim Price	.55	.30
39	Willie Norwood	.55	.30
40	Dave Cowens (AS)	7.50	4.00
41	Cazzie Russell	1.75	1.00
42	Lee Winfield	.55	.30
43	Connie Hawkins	5.00	2.75
44	Mike Newlin	.60	.35
45	Chet Walker	1.75	1.00
46	Walt Bellamy	2.25	1.40
47	John Johnson	.70	.40
48	Henry Bibby (R)	3.50	2.00
49	Bobby Smith	.55	.30
50	Kareem Abdul-Jabbar	48.00	28.00
51	Mike Price	.55	.30
52	John Hummer	.55	.30
53	Kevin Porter (R)	5.00	3.00
54	Nate Williams	.55	.30
55	Gail Goodrich	3.50	2.00
56	Fred Foster	.55	.30
57	Don Chaney	1.75	1.00
58	Bud Stallworth	.55	.30
59	Clem Haskins	.80	.50
60	Bob Love (AS)	2.50	1.50
61	Jimmy Walker	.55	.30
62	NBA East Playoff	1.00	.60
63	NBA East Playoff	1.00	.60
64	NBA West Playoff	7.50	4.00
65	NBA West Playoff	1.00	.60
66	NBA East Finals	3.00	1.75
67	NBA West Finals	1.00	.60
68	NBA Champs Knicks	4.50	2.50
69	Larry Steele	.55	.30

1973-74 TOPPS • 157

#	Player		
70	Oscar Robertson	22.00	13.50
71	Phil Jackson	5.00	2.75
72	John Wetzel	.55	.30
73	Steve Patterson (R)	1.75	1.00
74	Manny Leaks	.55	.30
75	Jeff Mullins	1.00	.60
76	Stan Love	.55	.30
77	Dick Garrett	.55	.30
78	Don Nelson	3.50	2.00
79	Chris Ford (R)	6.50	3.50
80	Wilt Chamberlain	48.00	28.00
81	Dennis Layton	.55	.30
82	Bill Bradley	18.50	11.50
83	Jerry Sloan	1.50	.90
84	Cliff Meely	.55	.30
85	Sam Lacey	.55	.30
86	Dick Snyder	.55	.30
87	Jim Washington	.55	.30
88	Lucius Allen	1.25	.70
89	LaRue Martin	.55	.30
90	Rick Barry	14.00	9.00
91	Fred Boyd	.55	.30
92	Barry Clemens	.55	.30
93	Dean Meminger	.70	.40
94	Henry Finkel	.55	.30
95	Elvin Hayes	10.00	6.00
96	Stu Lantz	.55	.30
97	Bill Hewitt	.55	.30
98	Neal Walk	.55	.30
99	Garfield heard	.75	.45
100	Jerry West (AS)	27.00	17.00
101	Otto Moore	.55	.30
102	Don Kojis	.55	.30
103	Fred Brown (R)	5.00	2.75
104	Dwight Davis	.55	.30
105	Willis Reed	6.00	3.50
106	Herm Gilliam	.55	.30
107	Mickey Davis	.55	.30
108	Jim Barnett	.55	.30
109	Ollie Johnson	.55	.30
110	Bob Lanier	7.00	3.75
111	Fred Carter	.55	.30
112	Paul Silas	2.00	1.25
113	Phil Chenier	1.50	.90
114	Dennis Awtrey	.55	.30
115	Austin Carr	1.75	1.00
116	Bob Kauffman	.55	.30
117	Keith Erickson	.60	.35
118	Walt Wesley	.55	.30
119	Steve Bracey	.55	.30
120	Spencer Haywood (AS)	2.50	1.50
121	NBA Checklist	10.00	1.50
122	Jack Marin	.75	.45
123	Jon McGlocklin	.55	.30
124	Johnny Green	.55	.30
125	Jerry Lucas	5.00	2.75
126	Paul Westphal (R)	24.00	14.00
127	Curtis Rowe	1.00	.60
128	Mahdi Abdul-Rahman	1.25	.70
129	Lloyd Neal (R)	1.75	1.00
130	Pete Maravich (AS)	22.00	13.00
131	Don May	.55	.30
132	Bob Weiss	.80	.50
133	Dave Stallworth	.55	.30
134	Dick Cunningham	.55	.30
135	Bob McAdoo (R)	20.00	12.50
136	Butch Beard	.80	.50
137	Happy Hairston	1.00	.60
138	Bob Rule	.55	.30
139	Don Adams	.55	.30
140	Charlie Scott	1.50	.90
141	Ron Riley	.55	.30
142	Earl Monroe	6.50	3.50
143	Clyde Lee	.55	.30
144	Rick Roberson	.55	.30
145	Rudy Tomjanovich	5.00	3.00
146	Tom Van Arsdale	.60	.35
147	Art Williams	.55	.30
148	Curtis Perry	.55	.30
149	Rich Rinaldi	.55	.30
150	Lou Hudson	1.25	.70
151	Mel Counts	.55	.30
152	Jim McDaniels	.55	.30
153	NBA Scoring Leaders	6.00	3.50
	Nate Archibald		
	Kareem Abdul-Jabbar		
	Spencer Haywood		
154	NBA Scoring Avg Ldrs	6.00	3.50
	Nate Archibald		
	Kareem Abdul-Jabbar		
	Spencer Haywood		
155	NBA Field Goal Ldrs	8.50	4.75
	Wilt Chamberlain		
	Matt Guokas		
	Kareem Abdul-Jabbar		
156	NBA Free Throw Ldrs	2.50	1.50
	Rick Barry		
	Calvin Murphy		
	Mike Newlin		
157	NBA Rebound Leaders	6.50	3.75
	Wilt Chamberlain		
	Nate Thurmond		
	Dave Cowens		
158	NBA Assist Leaders	2.50	1.50
	Nate Archibald		
	Len Wilkens		
	Dave Bing		
159	Don Smith	.55	.30
160	Sidney Wicks	2.50	1.50
161	Howie Komives	.55	.30
162	John Gianelli	.55	.30
163	Jeff Halliburton	.55	.30
164	Kennedy McIntosh	.55	.30
165	Len Wilkens	4.00	2.50

158 • 1973-74 TOPPS

#	Player		
166	Corky Calhoun	.55	.30
167	Howard Porter	.75	.45
168	JoJo White	2.00	1.25
169	John Block	.55	.30
170	Dave Bing	4.50	2.75
171	Joe Ellis	.55	.30
172	Chuck Terry	.55	.30
173	Randy Smith	.75	.45
174	Bill Bridges	.60	.35
175	Geoff Petrie	1.25	.70
176	Wes Unseld	5.00	3.00
177	Skeeter Swift	.55	.30
178	Jim Eakins	.55	.30
179	Steve Jones	.55	.30
180	George McGinnis (AS)	3.50	2.00
181	Al Smith	.55	.30
182	Tom Washington	.55	.30
183	Louie Damper	1.50	.90
184	Simmie Hill	.55	.30
185	George Thompson	.55	.30
186	Cincy Powell	.55	.30
187	Larry Jones	.55	.30
188	Neil Johnson	.55	.30
189	Tom Owens	.60	.35
190	Ralph Simpson (AS)	.75	.45
191	George Carter	.55	.30
192	Rick Mount	1.75	1.00
193	Red Robbins	.55	.30
194	George Lehmann	.55	.30
195	Mel Daniels (AS)	1.75	1.00
196	Bob Warren	.55	.30
197	Gene Kennedy	.55	.30
198	Mike Barr	.55	.30
199	Dave Robisch	.55	.30
200	Billy Cunningham (AS)	6.50	3.50
201	John Roche	.60	.35
202	ABA West Playoffs	1.50	.90
203	ABA West Playoffs	1.50	.90
204	ABA East Playoffs	1.75	1.00
205	ABA East Playoffs	1.75	1.00
206	ABA West Finals	1.50	.90
207	ABA East Finals	2.00	1.25
208	ABA Champs Pacers	1.25	.70
209	Glen Combs	.55	.30
210	Dan Issel (AS)	8.00	4.50
211	Randy Denton	.55	.30
212	Freddie Lewis	.55	.30
213	Stew Johnson	.55	.30
214	Roland Taylor	.55	.30
215	Rich Jones	.55	.30
216	Billy Paultz	1.25	.70
217	Ron Boone	.55	.30
218	Walt Simon	.55	.30
219	Mike Lewis	.55	.30
220	Warren Jabali (AS)	.60	.35
221	Wilbert Jones	.55	.30
222	Don Buse (R)	1.75	1.00
223	Gene Moore	.55	.30
224	Joe Hamilton	.55	.30
225	Zelmo Beaty	.70	.40
226	Brian Taylor (R)	1.50	.90
227	Julius Keye	.55	.30
228	Mike Gale (R)	1.00	.60
229	Warren Davis	.55	.30
230	Mack Calvin (AS)	1.50	.90
231	Roger Brown	.75	.45
232	Chuck Williams	.55	.30
233	Gerald Govan	.55	.30
234	ABA Scoring Avg Ldrs	8.50	4.50
	Julius Erving		
	George McGinnis		
	Dan Issel		
235	ABA 2 Pt. % Leaders	1.50	.90
	Artis Gilmore		
	Gene Kennedy		
	Tom Owens		
236	ABA 3 Pt. % Ldrs	1.50	.90
	Glen Combs		
	Roger Brown		
	Louie Dampier		
237	ABA Free Throw Ldrs	1.50	.90
	Billy Keller		
	Ron Boone		
	Bob Warren		
238	ABA Rebound Ldrs	1.75	1.00
	Mel Daniels		
	Artis Gilmore		
	Bill Paultz		
239	ABA Assist Leaders	1.50	.90
	Bill Melchioinni		
	Chuck Williams		
	Warren Jabali		
240	Julius Erving (AS)	85.00	48.00
241	Jimmy O'Brien	.55	.30
242	ABA Checklist	10.00	1.50
243	Johnny Neumann	.60	.35
244	Darnell Hillman	.55	.30
245	Willie Wise	.60	.35
246	Collis Jones	.55	.30
247	Ted McClain	.55	.30
248	George Irvine (R)	1.75	1.00
249	Bill Melchionni	.60	.35
250	Artis Gilmore (AS)	7.50	4.00
251	Willie Long	.55	.30
252	Larry Miller	.55	.30
253	Lee Davis	.55	.30
254	Donnie Freeman	.60	.35
255	Joe Caldwell	.60	.35
256	Bob Netolicky	.55	.30
257	Bernie Williams	.55	.30
258	Byron Beck	.55	.30
259	Jim Chones (R)	2.00	1.25
260	James Jones (AS)	.75	.45
261	Wendell Ladner	.55	.30

#	Player	NR/MT	EX
262	Ollie Taylor	.55	.30
263	Les Hunter	.55	.30
264	Billy Keller	1.50	.90

1974-75 Topps

The cards in this set contain players from the NBA (1-176) and the ABA (177-264). The card fronts feature full color player photos surrounded by a white border. The team nickname is printed in large block type vertically along the right border. The player's name appears in a color box below his photograph and to the left of his team logo. Card backs are horizontal and consist of personal data, statistics, a brief highlight and a cartoon. Subsets include Team Leaders (TL)(81-98, 221-230), League Leaders (144-149, 207-212), and Playoffs (161-164, 246-249). All cards measure 2-1/2" by 3-1/2".

	NR/MT	EX
Complete Set (264)	380.00	215.00
Commons	.50	.28

#	Player	NR/MT	EX
1	Kareem Abdul-Jabbar (AS)	42.00	26.00
2	Don May	.50	.28
3	Bernie Fryer (R)	.80	.50
4	Don Adams	.50	.28
5	Herm Gilliam	.50	.28
6	Jim Chones	.70	.40
7	Rick Adelman	1.00	.60
8	Randy Smith	.50	.28
9	Paul Silas	1.75	1.00
10	Pete Maravich	20.00	12.00
11	Ron Behagen (R)	.50	.28
12	Kevin Porter	1.00	.60
13	Billy Bridges	.60	.35
14	Charles Johnson (R)	1.00	.60
15	Bob Love	1.50	.90
16	Henry Bibby	1.00	.60
17	Neal Walk	.50	.28
18	John Brisker	.50	.28
19	Lucius Allen	1.00	.60
20	Tom Van Arsdale	.60	.35
21	Larry Steele	.50	.28
22	Curtis Rowe	1.00	.60
23	Dean Meminger	.50	.28
24	Steve Patterson	.50	.28
25	Earl Monroe	6.50	3.50
26	Jack Marin	.60	.35
27	JoJo White	1.75	1.00
28	Rudy Tomjanovich	4.50	2.75
29	Otto Moore	.50	.28
30	Elvin Hayes (AS)	8.00	4.50
31	Pat Riley	7.50	4.00
32	Clyde Lee	.50	.28
33	Bob Weiss	.75	.45
34	Jim Fox	.50	.28
35	Charlie Scott	1.00	.60
36	Cliff Meely	.50	.28
37	Jon McGlocklin	.50	.28
38	Jim McMillan	.50	.28
39	Bill Walton (R)	70.00	40.00
40	Dave Bing (AS)	4.00	2.50
41	Jim Washington	.50	.28
42	Jim Cleamons	.50	.28
43	Mel Davis	.50	.28
44	Garfield Heard	.60	.35
45	Jimmy Walker	.50	.28
46	Don Nelson	2.50	1.50
47	Jim Barnett	.50	.28
48	Manny Leaks	.50	.28
49	Elmore Smith	.75	.45
50	Rick Barry (AS)	12.00	6.50
51	Jerry Sloan	1.25	.70
52	John Hummer	.50	.28
53	Keith Erickson	.50	.28
54	George E. Johnson	.50	.28
55	Oscar Robertson	18.00	11.00
56	Steve Mix (R)	1.25	.70
57	Rick Robertson	.50	.28
58	John Mengelt	.50	.28
59	Dwight Jones (R)	.75	.45
60	Austin Carr	1.25	.70
61	Nick Weatherspoon (R)	1.25	.70

160 • 1974-75 TOPPS

62	Clem Haskins	1.00	.60
63	Don Kojis	.50	.28
64	Paul Westphal	8.50	5.00
65	Walt Bellamy	1.75	1.00
66	John Johnson	.50	.28
67	Butch Beard	.50	.28
68	Happy Hairston	.80	.50
69	Tom Boerwinkle	.50	.28
70	Spencer Haywood (AS)	2.00	1.25
71	Gary Melchionni	.50	.28
72	Ed Ratleff (R)	.90	.55
73	Mickey Davis	.50	.28
74	Dennis Awtrey	.50	.28
75	Fred Carter	.50	.28
76	George Trapp	.50	.28
77	John Wetzel	.50	.28
78	Bobby Smith	.50	.28
79	John Gianelli	.50	.28
80	Bob McAdoo (AS)	7.00	4.00
81	Atlanta Hawks (TL) Pete Maravich Lou Hudson Walt Bellamy	5.00	2.75
82	Boston Celtics (TL) Dave Cowans John Havlicek JoJo White	4.50	2.50
83	Buffalo Braves (TL) Ernie DiGregorio Bob McAdoo	1.00	.60
84	Chicago Bulls (TL) Bob Love Chet Walker Clifford Ray Norm Van Lier	2.50	1.50
85	Cleveland Cavs (TL) Austin Carr Dwight Davis Len Wilkens	1.00	.60
86	Detroit Pistons (TL) Dave Bing Bob Lanier Stu Lantz	1.50	.90
87	Golden State (TL) Rick Barry Nate Thurmond	2.50	1.50
88	Houston Rockets (TL) Calvin Murphy Rudy Tomjanovich Don Smith	1.00	.60
89	Kansas City (TL) San Lacey Jimmy Walker	1.00	.60
90	Los Angeles Lakers (TL) Gail Goodrich Happy Hairston	1.50	.90
91	Milwaukee Bucks (TL) Kareem Abdul-Jabbar Oscar Robertson	8.50	4.50
92	New Orleans Jazz Logo	1.00	.60
93	New York Knicks (TL) Bill Bradley Walt Frazier Dave DeBusschere	6.00	3.50
94	Phildelphia 76ers (TL) Fred Carter Tom Van Arsdale Leroy Ellis	1.00	.60
95	Phoenix Suns (TL) Dick Van Arsdale Charlie Scott Neal Walk	1.00	.60
96	Trail Blazers (TL) Geoff Petrie Rick Roberson Sidney Wicks	1.25	.70
97	Supersonics (TL) Fred Brown Spencer Haywood Dick Snyder	1.00	.60
98	Bullets (TL) Phil Chenier Elvin Hayes Kevin Porter	1.25	.70
99	Sam Lacey	.50	.28
100	John Havlicek (AS)	16.00	9.00
101	Stu Lantz	.50	.28
102	Mike Riordan	.50	.28
103	Larry Jones	.50	.28
104	Connie Hawkins	4.00	2.25
105	Nate Thurmond	3.00	1.75
106	Dick Gibbs	.50	.28
107	Corky Calhoun	.50	.28
108	Dave Wohl	.50	.28
109	Cornell Warner	.50	.28
110	Geoff Petrie	.90	.55
111	Leroy Ellis	.50	.28
112	Chris Ford	2.00	1.25
113	Bill Bradley	18.00	11.00
114	Clifford Ray	.60	.35
115	Dick Snyder	.50	.28
116	Nate Williams	.50	.28
117	Matt Guokas	1.00	.60
118	Henry Finkel	.50	.28
119	Curtis Perry	.50	.28
120	Gail Goodrich (AS)	2.25	1.40
121	Wes Unseld	4.00	2.25
122	Howard Porter	.75	.45
123	Jeff Mullins	.75	.45
124	Mike Bantom (R)	.75	.45
125	Fred Brown	1.25	.70
126	Bob Dandridge	.60	.35
127	Mike Newlin	.50	.28
128	Greg Smith	.50	.28

1974-75 TOPPS • 161

#	Name		
129	Doug Collins (R)	12.00	6.50
130	Lou Hudson	1.00	.60
131	Bob Lanier	5.00	2.75
132	Phil Jackson	4.50	2.50
133	Don Chaney	1.25	.70
134	Jim Brewer (R)	.80	.50
135	Ernie DiGregorio (R)	3.50	2.00
136	Steve Kuberski	.50	.28
137	Jim Price	.50	.28
138	Mike D'Antoni	.50	.28
139	John Brown	.50	.28
140	Norm Van Lier (AS)	1.25	.70
141	NBA Checklist	8.50	1.00
142	Slick Watts (R)	2.00	1.25
143	Walt Wesley	.50	.28
144	NBA Scoring Leaders	9.00	5.00
	Bob McAdoo		
	Kareem Abdul-Jabbar		
	Pete Maravich		
145	NBA Scoring Avg. Ldrs	9.00	5.00
	Bob McAdoo		
	Pete Maravich		
	Kareem Abdul-Jabbar		
146	NBA Field Goal % Ldrs	6.00	3.50
	Bob McAdoo		
	Kareem Abdul-Jabbar		
	Rudy Tomjanovich		
147	NBA Free Throw Ldrs	1.25	.70
	Ernie DiGregorio		
	Rick Barry		
	Jeff Mullins		
148	NBA Rebound Leaders	3.50	2.00
	Elvin Hayes		
	Dave Cowens		
	Bob McAdoo		
149	NBA Assist Leaders	1.00	.60
	Ernie DiGregorio		
	Calvin Murphy		
	Len Wilkens		
150	Walt Frazier (AS)	8.00	4.50
151	Cazzie Russell	1.50	.90
152	Calvin Murphy	3.00	1.75
153	Bob Kauffman	.50	.28
154	Fred Boyd	.50	.28
155	Dave Cowens	7.00	4.00
156	Willie Norwood	.50	.28
157	Les Winfield	.50	.28
158	Dwight Davis	.50	.28
159	Georeg T. Johnson	.50	.28
160	Dick van Arsdale	.60	.35
161	NBA East Playoffs	1.00	.60
162	NBA West Playoffs	1.00	.60
163	NBA Division Finals	1.00	.60
164	NBA Champs Celtics	1.25	.70
165	Phil Chenier	1.00	.60
166	Kermit Washington (R)	2.00	1.25
167	Dale Schlueter	.50	.28
168	John Block	.50	.28
169	Don Smith	.50	.28
170	Nate Archibald	4.00	2.25
171	Chet Walker	1.25	.70
172	Archie Clark	.80	.50
173	Kennedy McIntosh	.50	.28
174	George Thompson	.50	.28
175	Sidney Wicks	1.75	1.00
176	Jerry West	24.00	14.00
177	Dwight Lamar	.50	.28
178	George Carter	.50	.28
179	Will Robinson	.50	.28
180	Artis Gilmore (AS)	5.00	3.00
181	Brian Taylor	.50	.28
182	Darnell Hillman	.50	.28
183	Dave Robisch	.50	.28
184	Gene Littles (R)	1.00	.60
185	Willie Wise (AS)	.60	.35
186	James Silas (R)	2.50	1.50
187	Caldwell Jones (R)	5.00	3.00
188	Roland Taylor	.50	.28
189	Randy Denton	.50	.28
190	Dan Issel (AS)	6.00	3.50
191	Mike Gale	.50	.28
192	Mel Daniels	1.50	.90
193	Steve Jones	.50	.28
194	Marv Roberts	.50	.28
195	Ron Boone (AS)	.60	.35
196	George Gervin (R)	40.00	24.00
197	Flynn Robinson	.50	.28
198	Cincy Powell	.50	.28
199	Glen Combs	.50	.28
200	Julius Erving (AS)	60.00	35.00
201	Billy Keller	.50	.28
202	Willie Long	.50	.28
203	ABA Checklist	8.50	1.00
204	Joe Caldwell	.50	.28
205	Swen Nater (R) (AS)	2.50	1.50
206	Rick Mount	1.75	1.00
207	ABA Scoring Avg Ldrs	9.00	5.00
	Julius Erving		
	George McGinnis		
	Dan Issel		
208	ABA 2 pt Field Goal Ldrs	1.00	.60
	James Jones		
	Swen Nater		
	Tom Owens		
209	ABA 3 pt Field Goal Ldrs	1.00	.60
	Roger Brown		
	Louie Dampier		
	Billy Keller		
210	ABA Free Throw Ldrs	1.00	.60
	Ron Boone		
	Mac Calvin		
	James Jones		
211	ABA Rebound Leaders	1.50	.90
	Artis Gilmore		

162 • 1974-75 TOPPS

	George McGinnis		
	Caldwell Jones		
212	ABA Assist Leaders	1.00	.06
	Louie Dampier		
	Al Smith		
	Chuck Williams		
213	Larry Miller	.50	.28
214	Stew Johnson	.50	.28
215	Larry Finch (R)	2.50	1.50
216	Larry Kenon (R)	2.00	1.25
217	Joe Hamilton	.50	.28
218	Gerald Govan	.50	.28
219	Ralph Simpson	.60	.35
220	George McGinnis (AS)	2.50	1.50
221	Carolina Cougars (TL)	1.25	.70
	Billy Cunningham		
	Mack Calvin		
	Joe Caldwell		
	Tom Owens		
222	Denver Nuggest (TL)	1.00	.60
	Byron Beck		
	Dave Robisch		
	Ralph Simpson		
	Al Smith		
223	Indiana Pacers (TL)	1.00	.60
	Billy Keller		
	Freddie Lewis		
	George McGinnis		
224	Kentucky Colonels (TL)	3.00	1.75
	Dan Issel		
	Louie Dampier		
	Artis Gilmore		
225	Memphis Sounds (TL)	1.00	.60
	Larry Finch		
	Randy Denton		
	George Thompson		
226	New York Nets (TL)	10.00	6.50
	Julius Erving		
	John Roche		
	Larry Kenon		
227	San Antonio Spurs (TL)	5.00	3.00
	George Gervin		
	George Gervin		
	Swen Nater		
	James Silas		
228	San Diego (TL)	1.00	.60
	Stew Johnson		
	Caldwell Jones		
	Dwight Lamar		
	Chuck Williams		
229	Utah Stars (TL)	1.00	.60
	James Jones		
	Gerald Govan		
	Willie Wise		
230	Virginia Squires (TL)	1.00	.60
	George Carter		
	Jim Eakins		
	George Irvine		
	Roland Taylor		
231	Bird Averitt (R)	.60	.35
232	John Roche	.70	.40
233	George Irvine	.80	.50
234	John Williamson (R)	1.25	.70
235	Billy Cunningham	5.00	2.75
236	Jimmy O'Brien	.50	.28
237	Wilbert Jones	.50	.28
238	Johnny Neumann	.60	.35
239	Al Smith	.50	.28
240	Roger Brown	.60	.35
241	Chuck Williams	.50	.28
242	Rich Jones	.50	.28
243	Dave Twardzik (R)	1.75	1.00
244	Wendell Ladner	.50	.28
245	Mack Calvin (AS)	1.25	.70
246	ABA East Playoffs	1.00	.60
247	ABA West Playoffs	1.00	.60
248	ABA Division Finals	1.00	.60
249	ABA Champs Nets	10.00	6.50
250	Wilt Chamberlain	40.00	25.00
251	Ron Robinson	.50	.28
252	Zelmo Beaty	.70	.40
253	Donnie Freeman	.50	.28
254	Mike Green	.50	.28
255	Louie Dampier (AS)	.75	.45
256	Tom Owens	.50	.28
257	George Karl (R)	8.00	5.00
258	Jim Eakins	.50	.28
259	Travis Grant	.50	.28
260	James Jones (AS)	.60	.35
261	Mike Jackson	.50	.28
262	Billy Paultz	.80	.50
263	Freddie Lewis	.50	.28
264	Byron Beck	1.00	.60

1975-76 Topps

Topps increased the size of their set to 330-cards making it the largest basketball card set produced up to this point. The set includes players from both the NBA (1-220) and ABA (221-330). The card fronts feature full color player photos framed by a white border. The team name appears in the upper left corner of the photo and the player's name is centered at the bottom of the photo. Card backs contain personal data, statistics and brief player highlights. The main subsets are League Leaders (1-6, 221-226), Team Leaders (116-133, 278-287), Team Checklists (203-220, 321-330) and Playoffs (188-189, 309-310). All cards measure 2-1/2" by 3-1/2".

		NR/MT	EX
	Complete Set (330)	500.00	280.00
	Commons	.50	.28
1	NBA Scoring Avg Ldrs	12.00	6.50
	Kareem Abdul-Jabbar		
	Rick Barry		
	Bob McAdoo		
2	NBA Field Goal % Ldrs	2.00	1.25
	Butch Beard		
	Don Nelson		
	Rudy Tomjanovich		
3	NBA Free Throw Ldrs	4.00	2.25
	Rick Barry		
	Bill Bradley		
	Calvin Murphy		
4	NBA Rebounds Leaders	1.50	.90
	Dave Cowans		
	Wes Unseld		
	Sam Lacey		
5	NBA Assists Leaders	1.75	1.00
	Nate Archibald		
	Dave Bing		
	Kevin Porter		
6	NBA Steals Leaders	3.00	1.75
	Rick Barry		
	Walt Frazier		
	Larry Steele		
7	Tom Van Arsdale	.60	.35
8	Paul Silas	1.25	.70
9	Jerry Sloan	.80	.50
10	Bob McAdoo (AS)	5.00	3.00
11	Dwight Davis	.50	.28
12	John Mengelt	.50	.28
13	George Johnson	.50	.28
14	Ed Ratleff	.60	.35
15	Nate Archibald (AS)	4.00	2.50
16	Elmore Smith	.60	.35
17	Bob Dandridge	.60	.35
18	Louie Nelson (R)	.70	.40
19	Neal Walk	.50	.28
20	Billy Cunningham	4.50	2.50
21	Gary Melchionni	.50	.28
22	Barry Clemens	.50	.28
23	Jimmy Jones	.50	.28
24	Tom Burleson (R)	2.00	1.25
25	Lou Hudson	1.00	.60
26	Henry Finkel	.50	.28
27	Jim McMillan	.50	.28
28	Matt Guokas	1.00	.60
29	Fred Foster	.50	.28
30	Bob Lanier	4.50	2.50
31	Jimmy Walker	.50	.28
32	Cliff Meely	.50	.28
33	Butch Beard	.50	.28
34	Cazzie Russell	1.00	.60
35	Jon McGlocklin	.50	.28
36	Bernie Fryer	.50	.28
37	Bill Bradley	16.00	9.75
38	Fred Carter	.50	.28
39	Dennis Awtrey	.50	.28
40	Sidney Wicks	1.50	.90
41	Fred Brown	1.00	.60
42	Rowland Garrett	.50	.28
43	Herm Gilliam	.50	.28
44	Don Nelson	2.50	1.50
45	Ernie DiGregorio	.75	.45
46	Jim Brewer	.50	.28
47	Chris Ford	1.25	.70
48	Nick Weatherspoon	.50	.28
49	Zaid Abdul-Aziz	.50	.28
50	Keith Wilkes (R)	15.00	9.00

1975-76 TOPPS

#	Player		
51	Ollie Johnson	.50	.28
52	Lucius Allen	.90	.55
53	Mickey Davis	.50	.28
54	Otto Moore	.50	.28
55	Walt Frazier (AS)	8.00	4.50
56	Steve Mix	.50	.28
57	Nate Hawthorne	.50	.28
58	Lloyd Neal	.50	.28
59	Don Watts	.50	.28
60	Elvin Hayes	8.00	5.00
61	Checklist (1-110)	7.50	.75
62	Mike Sojourner	.50	.28
63	Randy Smith	.60	.35
64	John Block	.50	.28
65	Charlie Scott	1.00	.60
66	Jim Chones	.60	.35
67	Rick Adelman	.90	.55
68	Curtis Rowe	.75	.45
69	Derrek Dickey (R)	.70	.40
70	Rudy Tomjanovich	4.00	2.50
71	Pat Riley	7.50	4.00
72	Cornell Warner	.50	.28
73	Earl Monroe	7.50	4.00
74	Allan Bristow (R)	3.00	1.75
75	Pete Maravich	14.00	8.00
76	Curtis Perry	.50	.28
77	Bill Walton	28.00	16.00
78	Leonard Gray	.50	.28
79	Kevin Porter	.80	.50
80	John Havlicek (AS)	16.00	9.50
81	Dwight Jones	.50	.28
82	Jack Marin	.60	.35
83	Dick Snyder	.50	.28
84	George Trapp	.50	.28
85	Nate Thurmond	2.50	1.50
86	Charles Johnson	.50	.28
87	Ron Riley	.50	.28
88	Stu Lantz	.50	.28
89	Scott Wedman (R)	2.00	1.25
90	Kareem Abdul-Jabbar	36.00	21.00
91	Aaron James	.50	.28
92	Jim Barnett	.50	.28
93	Clyde Lee	.50	.28
94	Larry Steele	.50	.28
95	Mike Riordan	.60	.35
96	Archie Clark	.70	.40
97	Mike Bantom	.50	.28
98	Bob Kauffman	.50	.28
99	Kevin Stacom (R)	.80	.50
100	Rick Barry (AS)	12.50	7.00
101	Ken Charles	.50	.28
102	Tom Boerwinkle	.50	.28
103	Mike Newlin	.50	.28
104	Leroy Ellis	.50	.28
105	Austin Carr	1.25	.70
106	Ron Behagen	.50	.28
107	Jim Price	.50	.28
108	Bud Stallworth	.50	.28
109	Earl Williams	.50	.28
110	Gail Goodrich	2.00	1.25
111	Phil Jackson	4.00	2.25
112	Rod Derline	.50	.28
113	Keith Erickson	.60	.35
114	Phil Lumpkin	.50	.28
115	Wes Unseld	4.50	2.75
116	Atlanta Hawks (TL)	1.00	.60
	John Drew		
	Lou Hudson		
	Dean Meminger		
117	Boston Celtics (TL)	2.00	1.25
	Dave Cowens		
	Kevin Stacom		
	Paul Silas		
	JoJo White		
118	Buffao Braves (TL)	1.00	.60
	Bob McAdoo		
	Jack Marin		
	Bob McAdoo		
	Randy Smith		
119	Chicago Bulls (TL)	1.75	1.00
	Bob Love		
	Chet Walker		
	Nate Thurmond		
	Norm Van Lier		
120	Cleveland Cavs (TL)	1.00	.60
	Jim Chones		
	Jim Cleamons		
	Bobby Smith		
	Dick Snyder		
121	Detroit Pistons (TL)	2.00	1.25
	Dave Bing		
	Bob Lanier		
	John Mengelt		
122	Golden State (TL)	2.00	1.25
	Rick Barry		
	Clifford Ray		
123	Houston Rockets (TL)	1.25	.70
	Rudy Tomjanovich		
	Calvin Murphy		
	Kevin Kunnert		
	Mike Newlin		
	Rudy Tomjanovich		
124	Kansas City Kings (TL)	1.25	.70
	Nate Archibald		
	Sam Lacey		
	Ollie Johnson		
125	Los Angeles Lakers (TL)	1.25	.70
	Gail Goodrich		
	Happy Hairston		
	Cazzie Russell		
126	Milwaukee Bucks (TL)	5.00	2.75
	Kareem Abdul-Jabbar		
	Mickey Davis		
127	New Orleans Jazz (TL)	3.00	1.75

1975-76 TOPPS • 165

	Card	Price	Price
	Pete Maravich		
	E.C. Coleman		
	Stu Lanz		
128	New York Knicks (TL)	3.00	1.75
	Bill Bradley		
	Walt Frazier		
	John Gianelli		
129	Philadelphia 76ers (TL)	1.25	.70
	Fred Carter		
	Doug Collins		
	Billy Cunningham		
130	Phoenix Suns (TL)	1.00	.60
	Dennis Awtrey		
	Charlie Scott		
	Keith Erickson		
	Curtis Perry		
131	Portland Blazers (TL)	1.00	.60
	Geoff Petrie		
	Sidney Wicks		
132	Seattle Sonics (TL)	1.00	.60
	Archie Clark		
	Spencer Haywood		
	Don Watts		
133	Washington Bullets (TL)	2.00	1.25
	Elvin Hayes		
	Clem Haskins		
	Wes Unseld		
	Kevin Porter		
134	John Drew (R)	2.00	1.25
135	JoJo White (AS)	1.75	1.00
136	Garfield Heard	.60	.35
137	Jim Cleamons	.50	.28
138	Howard Porter	.50	.28
139	Phil Smith (R)	1.00	.60
140	Bob Love	1.50	.90
141	John Gianelli	.50	.28
142	Larry McNeill	.60	.35
143	Brian Winters	1.75	1.00
144	George Thompson	.50	.28
145	Kevin Kunnert	.50	.28
146	Henry Bibby	.75	.45
147	John Johnson	.50	.28
148	Doug Collins	4.00	2.50
149	John Brisker	.50	.28
150	Dick Van Arsdale	.60	.35
151	Leonard Robinson (R)	2.50	1.50
152	Dean Meminger	.50	.28
153	Phil Hankinson	.50	.28
154	Dale Schlueter	.50	.28
155	Norm Van Lier	1.25	.70
156	Campy Russell (R)	2.50	1.50
157	Jeff Mullins	.75	.45
158	Sam Lacey	.60	.35
159	Happy Hairston	.75	.45
160	Dave Bing	3.00	1.75
161	Kevin Restani (R)	.60	.35
162	Dave Wohl	.50	.28
163	E.C. Coleman	.50	.28
164	Jim Fox	.50	.28
165	Geoff Petrie	1.00	.70
166	Hawthorne Wingo	.50	.28
167	Fred Boyd	.50	.28
168	Willie Norwood	.50	.28
169	Bob Wilson	.50	.28
170	Dave Cowens	8.00	5.00
171	Tom Henderson (R)	.75	.45
172	Jim Washington	.50	.28
173	Clem Haskins	.70	.40
174	Jim Davis	.50	.28
175	Bobby Smith	.50	.28
176	Mike D'Antoni	.50	.28
177	Zelmo Beaty	.60	.35
178	Gary Brokaw (R)	1.00	.60
179	Mel Davis	.50	.28
180	Calvin Murphy	2.50	1.50
181	Checklist (111-220)	7.50	.75
182	Nate Williams	.50	.28
183	LaRue Martin	.50	.28
184	George McGinnis	2.50	1.50
185	Clifford Ray	.50	.28
186	Paul Westphal	5.00	3.00
187	Talvin Skinner	.50	.28
188	NBA Playoffs	1.00	.60
189	NBA Playoffs	1.00	.60
190	Phil Chenier (AS)	.60	.35
191	John Brown	.50	.28
192	Lee Winfield	.50	.28
193	Steve Patterson	.50	.28
194	Charles Dudley	.50	.28
195	Connie Hawkins	2.50	1.50
196	Leon Benbow	.50	.28
197	Don Kojis	.50	.28
198	Ron Williams	.50	.28
199	Mel Counts	.50	.28
200	Spencer Haywood (AS)	2.00	1.26
201	Greg Jackson	.50	.28
202	Tom Kozelko	.50	.28
203	Atlanta Hawks (CL)	1.50	.90
204	Boston Celtics (CL)	2.00	1.25
205	Buffalo Braves (CL)	1.50	.90
206	Chicago Bulls (CL)	2.00	1.25
207	Cleveland Cavs (CL)	1.50	.90
208	Detroit Pistons (CL)	1.50	.90
209	Golden State (CL)	1.50	.90
210	Houston Rockets (CL)	1.50	.90
211	Kansas City Kings (CL)	1.50	.90
212	Los Angeles Lakers (CL)	1.75	1.00
213	Milwaukee Bucks (CL)	1.50	.90
214	New Orleans Jazz (CL)	1.50	.90
215	New York Knicks (CL)	1.75	1.00
216	Philadelphia 76ers (CL)	1.50	.90
217	Phoenix Suns (CL)	1.50	.90
218	Portland Blazers (CL)	1.50	.90

1975-76 TOPPS

#	Card	Price	Price
219	Seattle Sonics (CL)	6.50	3.75
220	Washington Bullets(CL)	1.50	.90
221	ABA Scoring Avg Ldrs	6.50	3.75
	Ray Boone		
	Julius Erving		
	George McGinnis		
222	ABA 2 Pt Field Goals	6.00	3.50
	Bobby Jones		
	Artis Gilmore		
	Moses Malone		
223	ABA 3 Pt Field Goals	1.25	.70
	Louie Dampier		
	Al Smith		
	Billy Shepherd		
224	ABA Free Throw Ldrs	1.50	.90
	Mack Calvin		
	James Silas		
	Dave Robisch		
225	ABA Rebounds Leaders	1.50	.90
	Marvin Barnes		
	Artis Gilmore		
	Swen Nater		
226	ABA Assists Leaders	1.25	.70
	Mack Calvin		
	George McGinnis		
	Chuck Williams		
227	Mack Calvin (AS)	1.50	.90
228	Billy Knight (R)(AS)	3.00	1.75
229	Bird Averitt	.60	.35
230	George Carter	.50	.28
231	Swen Nater (AS)	1.50	.90
232	Steve Jones	.60	.35
233	George Gervin	12.00	7.00
234	Lee Davis	.50	.28
235	Ron Boone (AS)	.75	.45
236	Mike Jackson	.50	.28
237	Kevin Joyce (R)	1.25	.70
238	Marv Roberts	.50	.28
239	Tom Owens	.50	.28
240	Ralph Simpson	.75	.45
241	Gus Gerard	.50	.28
242	Brian Taylor (AS)	.60	.35
243	Rich Jones	.50	.28
244	John Roche	.60	.35
245	Travis Grant	.50	.28
246	Dave Twardzik	.60	.35
247	Mike Green	.50	.28
248	Billy Keller	.50	.28
249	Stew Johnson	.50	.28
250	Artis Gilmore (AS)	5.00	3.00
251	John Williamson	.60	.35
252	Marvin Barnes (R)(AS)	5.00	3.00
253	James Silas (AS)	1.50	.90
254	Moses Malone (R)	80.00	48.00
255	Willie Wise	.60	.35
256	Dwight Lamar	.50	.28
257	Checklist (221-330)	7.50	.75
258	Byron Beck	.50	.28
259	Len Elmore (R)	3.50	2.00
260	Dan Issel	6.00	3.75
261	Rick Mount	.75	.45
262	Billy Paultz	.75	.45
263	Donnie Freeman	.50	.28
264	George Adams	.50	.28
265	Don Chaney	1.75	1.00
266	Randy Denton	.50	.28
267	Don Washington	.50	.28
268	Roland Taylor	.50	.28
269	Charlie Edge	.50	.28
270	Louie Dampier	.75	.45
271	Collis Jones	.50	.28
272	Al Skinner (R)	1.00	.60
273	Coby Dietrick	.50	.28
274	Tim Bassett	.50	.28
275	Freddie Lewis	.60	.35
276	Gerald Govan	.50	.28
277	Ron Thomas	.50	.28
278	Denver Nuggets (TL)	1.50	.90
	Mack Calvin		
	Mike Green		
	Ralph Simpson		
279	Indiana Pacers (TL)	1.50	.90
	Billy Keller		
	George McGinnis		
280	Kentucky Colonels (TL)	1.75	1.00
	Louie Dampier		
	Artis Gilmore		
281	Memphis Sounds (TL)	1.50	.90
	George Carter		
	Larry Finch		
	Tom Owens		
	Chuck Williams		
282	New York Nets (TL)	9.00	5.00
	Julius Erving		
	John Williamson		
283	St. Louis Spirits (TL)	1.50	.90
	Marvin Barnes		
	Freddie Lewis		
284	San Antonio Spurs (TL)	4.00	2.50
	George Gervin		
	James Silas		
	Swen Nater		
285	San Diego Sails (TL)	1.50	.90
	Travis Grant		
	Caldwell Jones		
	Jimmy O'Brien		
286	Utah Stars (TL)	10.00	6.50
	Ron Boone		
	Moses Malone		
	Al Smith		
287	Virginia Squires (TL)	1.50	.90
	Red Robbins		
	Dave Vaughn		
	Dave Twardzik		

1976-77 Topps

	Willie Wise		
288	Claude Terry	.50	.28
289	Wilbert Jones	.50	.28
290	Darnell Hillman	.50	.28
291	Bill Melchionni	.60	.35
292	Mel Daniels	2.50	1.50
293	Fly Williams (R)	3.00	1.75
294	Larry Kenon	.60	.35
295	Red Robbins	.50	.28
296	Warren Jabali	.70	.40
297	Jim Eakins	.50	.28
298	Bobby Jones (R)	10.00	6.50
299	Don Buse	.50	.28
300	Julius Erving (AS)	65.00	38.00
301	Billy Shepherd	.50	.28
302	Maurice Lucas (R)	12.00	7.00
303	George Karl	2.50	1.50
304	Jim Bradley	.50	.28
305	Caldwell Jones	3.00	1.75
306	Al Smith	.50	.28
307	Jan Van Breda Kolff	1.25	.70
308	Darrell Elston	.50	.28
309	ABA Playoffs	1.25	.70
310	ABA Playoff Finals	1.25	.70
311	Ted McClain	.50	.28
312	Willie Sojourner	.50	.28
313	Bob Warren	.50	.28
314	Bob Netolicky	.50	.28
315	Chuck Williams	.50	.28
316	Gene Kennedy	.50	.28
317	Jimmy O'Brien	.50	.28
318	Dave Robisch	.50	.28
319	Wali Jones	.50	.28
320	George Irvine	.70	.40
321	Denver Nuggets (CL)	1.50	.90
322	Indiana Pacers (CL)	1.50	.90
323	Kentucky Colonels (CL)	1.50	.90
324	Memphis Sounds (CL)	1.50	.90
325	New York Nets (CL)	1.50	.90
326	St. Louis Spirits (CL)	1.50	.90
327	San Antonio Spurs (CL)	1.50	.90
328	San Diego Sails (CL)	1.50	.90
329	Utah Stars (CL)	1.50	.90
330	Virginia Squires (CL)	2.50	1.50

With this editon, Topps reduced the number of cards in their set to 144-cards but increased the size of the individual cards to 3-1/8" by 5-1/4". The card fronts feature full color player photos bordered in white. The team nickname appears in block letters vertically along the left border just above a cartoon of basketballs dropping through a hoop. The player's name and position appear in the border under his photograph. The backs include personal data, statistics, highlights and a small cartoon. There were no major subsets in this issue.

		NR/MT	EX
Complete Set (144)		340.00	210.00
Commons		1.50	.90
1	Julius Erving	55.00	32.00
2	Dick Snyder	1.50	.90
3	Paul Silas	2.00	1.25
4	Keith Erickson	1.75	1.00
5	Wes Unseld	4.00	2.50
6	Butch Beard	1.75	1.00

1976-77 TOPPS

#	Player	Price	Price
7	Lloyd Neal	1.50	.90
8	Tom Henderson	1.75	1.00
9	Jim McMillan	1.50	.90
10	Bob Lanier	5.00	3.00
11	Junior Bridgeman (R)	2.50	1.50
12	Corky Calhoun	1.50	.90
13	Billy Keller	1.50	.90
14	Mickey Johnson (R)	1.75	1.00
15	Fred Brown	2.00	1.25
16	Jamaal Wilkes	2.50	1.50
17	Louie Nelson	1.50	.90
18	Ed Ratleff	1.50	.90
19	Billy Paultz	1.50	.90
20	Nate Archibald	4.00	2.50
21	Steve Mix	1.50	.90
22	Ralph Simpson	1.50	.90
23	Campy Russell	1.75	1.00
24	Charlie Scott	2.00	1.25
25	Artis Gilmore	5.00	3.00
26	Dick Van Arsdale	.60	.35
27	Phil Chenier	.60	.35
28	Spencer Haywood	2.50	1.50
29	Chris Ford	2.00	1.25
30	Dave Cowens	8.50	5.00
31	Sidney Wicks	2.00	1.25
32	Jim Price	1.50	.90
33	Dwight Jones	1.50	.90
34	Lucius Allen	1.75	1.00
35	Marvin Barnes	1.75	1.00
36	Henry Bibby	1.75	1.00
37	Joe Meriweather (R)	2.00	1.25
38	Doug Collins	5.00	3.00
39	Garfield Heard	1.75	1.00
40	Randy Smith	1.75	1.00
41	Tom Burleson	2.00	1.25
42	Dave Twardzik	1.75	1.00
43	Bill Bradley	18.00	10.00
44	Calvin Murphy	2.50	1.50
45	Bob Love	2.00	1.25
46	Brian Winters	1.50	.90
47	Glenn McDonald	1.50	.90
48	Checklist Card	16.00	1.50
49	Bird Averitt	1.50	.90
50	Rick Barry	12.00	6.75
51	Ticky Burden (R)	1.75	1.00
52	Rich Jones	1.50	.90
53	Austin Carr	2.00	1.25
54	Steve Kuberski	1.50	.90
55	Paul Westphal	5.00	3.00
56	Mike Riordan	1.50	.90
57	Bill Walton	28.00	16.00
58	Eric Money (R)	1.75	1.00
59	John Drew	2.00	1.25
60	Pete Maravich	25.00	14.00
61	John Shumate (R)	3.00	1.75
62	Mack Calvin	2.50	1.50
63	Bruce Seals	1.50	.90
64	Walt Frazier	8.00	5.00
65	Elmore Smith	1.75	1.00
66	Rudy Tomjanovich	5.00	3.00
67	Sam Lacey	1.50	.90
68	George Gervin	10.00	6.50
69	Gus Williams	6.00	3.25
70	George McGinnis	2.50	1.50
71	Len Elmore	2.00	1.25
72	Jack Marin	1.75	1.00
73	Brian Taylor	1.75	1.00
74	Jim Brewer	1.50	.90
75	Alvan Adams (R)	4.00	2.50
76	Dave Bing	3.00	1.75
77	Phil Jackson	4.00	2.50
78	Geoff Petrie	1.75	1.00
79	Mike Sojourner	1.50	.90
80	James Silas	1.75	1.00
81	Bob Dandridge	1.75	1.00
82	Ernie DiGregorio	1.75	1.00
83	Cazzie Russell	2.50	1.50
84	Kevin Porter	2.00	1.25
85	Tom Boerwinkle	1.50	.90
86	Darnell Hillman	1.50	.90
87	Herm Gilliam	1.50	.90
88	Nate Williams	1.50	.90
89	Phil Smith	1.50	.90
90	John Havlicek	15.00	9.00
91	Kevin Kunnert	1.50	.90
92	Jimmy Walker	1.50	.90
93	Billy Cunningham	4.00	2.25
94	Dan Issel	5.00	2.75
95	Ron Boone	1.75	1.00
96	Lou Hudson	1.75	1.00
97	Jim Chones	1.75	1.00
98	Earl Monroe	6.00	3.50
99	Tom Van Arsdale	1.75	1.00
100	Kareem Abdul-Jabbar	35.00	20.00
101	Moses Malone	30.00	18.00
102	Ricky Sobers (R)	2.00	1.25
103	Swen Nater	1.75	1.00
104	Leonard Robinson	1.75	1.00
105	Don Watts	1.50	.90
106	Otto Moore	1.50	.90
107	Maurice Lucas	2.50	1.50
108	Norm Van Lier	2.00	1.25
109	Clifford Ray	1.50	.90
110	David Thompson (R)	28.00	16.00
111	Fred Carter	1.50	.90
112	Caldwell Jones	2.00	1.25
113	John Williamson	1.50	.90
114	Bobby Smith	1.50	.90
115	JoJo White	2.00	1.25
116	Curtis Perry	1.50	.90
117	John Gianelli	1.50	.90
118	Curtis Rowe	1.75	1.00
119	Lionel Hollins (R)	3.50	2.00
120	Elvin Hayes	7.00	4.00

1977-78 TOPPS • 169

121	Ken Charles	1.50	.90
122	Dave Meyers (R)	2.50	1.50
123	Jerry Sloan	1.75	1.00
124	Billy Knight	2.00	1.25
125	Gail Goodrich	2.50	1.50
126	K. Abdul-Jabbar (AS)	18.00	11.00
127	Julius Erving (AS)	25.00	14.00
128	George McGinnis (AS)	2.50	1.50
129	Nate Archibald (AS)	2.50	1.50
130	Pete Maravich (AS)	10.00	6.50
131	Dave Cowens (AS)	4.50	2.75
132	Rick Barry (AS)	5.00	3.00
133	Elvin Hayes (AS)	4.00	2.50
134	James Silas (AS)	1.75	1.00
135	Randy Smith (AS)	1.75	1.00
136	Leonard Gray	1.50	.90
137	Charles Johnson	1.50	.90
138	Ron Behagen	1.50	.90
139	Mike Newlin	1.50	.90
140	Bob McAdoo	6.00	3.50
141	Mike Gale	1.50	.90
142	Scott Wedman	1.75	1.00
143	Lloyd Free (R)	4.00	2.25
144	Bobby Jones	5.00	3.00

1977-78 Topps

The cards in this set consist of mostly full color action photos on the card fronts framed by a white border. The team name is printed under the photograph with the city located in a small pennant design and the team nickname in larger type. The player's name appears in the lower right corner of the card while his position is found in a small basketball in the lower left corner of the photograph. The flip side includes personal data, statistics, highlights and a small cartoon. All cards measure 2-1/2" by 3-1/2".

		NR/MT	EX
	Complete Set (132)	125.00	70.00
	Commons	.28	.18
1	Kareem Abdul-Jabbar	24.00	14.00
2	Henry Bibby	.40	.25
3	Curtis Rowe	.40	.25
4	Norm Van Lier	.40	.25
5	Darnell Hillman	.28	.18
6	Earl Monroe	3.50	2.00
7	Leonard Gray	.28	.18
8	Bird Averitt	.28	.18
9	Jim Brewer	.28	.18
10	Paul Westphal	2.00	1.25
11	Bob Gross (R)	.60	.35
12	Phil Smith	.28	.18
13	Dan Roundfield (R)	1.25	.70
14	Brian Taylor	.28	.18
15	Rudy Tomjanovich	1.25	.70
16	Kevin Porter	.40	.25
17	Scott Wedman	.35	.20
18	Lloyd Free	.75	.45
19	Tom Boswell (R)	.35	.20
20	Pete Maravich	10.00	6.50
21	Cliff Poindexter	.28	.18
22	Bubbles Hawkins	.28	.18
23	Kevin Grevey (R)	.80	.50
24	Ken Charles	.28	.18
25	Bob Dandridge	.35	.20
26	Lonnie Shelton (R)	.75	.45
27	Don Chaney	.35	.20
28	Larry Kenon	.28	.18
29	Checklist	3.00	.35
30	Fred Brown	.60	.35
31	John Gianelli	.28	.18
32	Austin Carr	.50	.30
33	Jamaal Wilkes	1.00	.60
34	Caldwell Jones	.35	.20
35	JoJo White	1.00	.60
36	Scott May (R)	1.00	.60
37	Mike Newlin	.28	.18
38	Mel Davis	.28	.18
39	Lionel Hollins	.50	.30
40	Elvin Hayes	4.50	2.50
41	Dan Issel	3.50	2.00
42	Ricky Sobers	.28	.18
43	Don Ford	.28	.18

1977-78 TOPPS

#	Player		
44	John Williamson	.28	.18
45	Bob McAdoo	1.50	.90
46	Geoff Petrie	.35	.20
47	M.L. Carr (R)	1.50	.90
48	Brian Winters	.28	.18
49	Sam Lacey	.28	.18
50	George McGinnis	.80	.50
51	Don Watts	.28	.18
52	Sidney Wicks	.75	.45
53	Wilbur Holland	.28	.18
54	Tim Bassett	.28	.18
55	Phil Chenier	.28	.18
56	Adrian Dantley (R)	12.50	7.00
57	Jim Chones	.28	.18
58	John Lucas (R)	12.50	7.00
59	Cazzie Russell	.40	.25
60	David Thompson	2.50	1.50
61	Bob Lanier	2.50	1.50
62	Dave Twardzik	.28	.18
63	Wilbert Jones	.28	.18
64	Clifford Ray	.35	.20
65	Doug Collins	1.25	.70
66	Tom McMillen (R)	3.50	2.00
67	Rich Kelley (R)	.35	.20
68	Mike Bantom	.28	.18
69	Tom Boerwinkle	.28	.18
70	John Havlicek	8.00	5.00
71	Marvin Webster (R)	.60	.35
72	Curtis Perry	.35	.20
73	George Gervin	6.50	3.75
74	Leonard Robinson	.28	.18
75	Wes Unseld	1.75	1.00
76	Dave Meyers	.50	.28
77	Gail Goodrich	1.25	.70
78	Richard Washington(R)	.80	.50
79	Mike Gale	.28	.18
80	Maurice Lucas	1.00	.60
81	Harvey Catchings (R)	.40	.25
82	Randy Smith	.28	.18
83	Campy Russell	.35	.20
84	Kevin Kunnert	.28	.18
85	Lou Hudson	.60	.35
86	Mickey Johnson	.28	.18
87	Lucius Allen	.40	.25
88	Spencer Haywood	1.00	.60
89	Gus Williams	1.00	.60
90	Dave Cowens	3.50	2.00
91	Al Skinner	.28	.18
92	Swen Nater	.35	.20
93	Tom Henderson	.35	.20
94	Don Buse	.28	.18
95	Alvan Adams	1.00	.60
96	Mack Calvin	.50	.30
97	Tom Burleson	.35	.20
98	John Drew	.35	.20
99	Mike Green	.28	.18
100	Julius Erving	28.00	18.00
101	John Mengelt	.28	.18
102	Howard Porter	.28	.18
103	Billy Paultz	.35	.20
104	John Shumate	.70	.40
105	Calvin Murphy	1.25	.70
106	Elmore Smith	.28	.18
107	Jim McMillan	.28	.18
108	Kevin Stacom	.28	.18
109	Jan Van Breda Kolff	.28	.18
110	Billy Knight	.35	.20
111	Robert Parish (R)	60.00	38.00
112	Larry Wright	.28	.18
113	Bruce Seals	.28	.18
114	Junior Bridgeman	.50	.28
115	Artis Gilmore	2.50	1.50
116	Steve Mix	.28	.18
117	Ron Lee	.28	.18
118	Bobby Jones	1.00	.60
119	Ron Boone	.28	.18
120	Bill Walton	12.00	7.00
121	Chris Ford	.75	.45
122	Earl Tatum	.28	.18
123	E.C. Coleman	.28	.18
124	Moses Malone	12.00	7.00
125	Charlie Scott	.40	.25
126	Bobby Smith	.28	.18
127	Nate Archibald	2.00	1.25
128	Mitch Kupchak (R)	2.50	1.50
129	Walt Frazier	5.00	2.75
130	Rick Barry	6.50	3.50
131	Ernie DiGregorio	.35	.20
132	Darryl Dawkins (R)	7.50	4.00

1978-79 Topps

The cards in this set contain two photographs on the card fronts, a larger full color action shot and a smaller head shot located in a circle in the lower right corner. The photos are framed by a white border and the team name is printed in large type vertically along the left border. The player's name appears vertically in smaller type under the team name. The player's position is found in small type under his head shot. The card backs consist of personal data, statistics and a highlight called "Star Stat". All cards measure 2-1/2" by 3-1/2".

		NR/MT	EX
	Complete Set (132)	85.00	50.00
	Commons	.25	.15
1	Bill Walton	14.00	8.00
2	Doug Collins	1.00	.60
3	Jamaal Wilkes	1.00	.60
4	Wilbur Hollard	.25	.15
5	Bob McAdoo	1.25	.60
6	Lucius Allen	.30	.18
7	Wes Unseld	1.50	.90
8	Dave Meyers	.35	.20
9	Austin Carr	.35	.20
10	Walter Davis (R)	8.50	5.00
11	John Williamson	.25	.15
12	E.c. Coleman	.25	.15
13	Calvin Murphy	1.25	.70
14	Bobby Jones	.90	.55
15	Chris Ford	.70	.40
16	Kermit Washington	.25	.15
17	Butch Beard	.25	.15
18	Steve Mix	.25	.15
19	Marvin Webster	.25	.15
20	George Gervin	3.25	1.80
21	Steve Hawes	.25	.15
22	Johnny Davis (R)	.30	.18
23	Swen Nater	.35	.20
24	Lou Hudson	.50	.28
25	Elvin Hayes	3.50	2.00
26	Nate Archibald	1.50	.90
27	James Edwards (R)	3.00	1.75
28	Howard Porter	.25	.15
29	Quinn Buckner (R)	4.00	2.25
30	Leonard Robinson	.25	.15
31	Jim Cleamons	.25	.15
32	Campy Russell	.25	.15
33	Phil Smith	.25	.15
34	Darryl Dawkins	1.25	.70
35	Don Buse	.25	.15
36	Mickey Johnson	.25	.15
37	Mike Gale	.25	.15
38	Moses Malone	8.00	4.50
39	Gus Williams	.75	.45
40	Dave Cowens	3.00	1.75
41	Bobby Wilkerson (R)	.50	.28
42	Wilbert Jones	.25	.15
43	Charlie Scott	.35	.20
44	John Drew	.35	.20
45	Earl Monroe	3.00	1.75
46	John Shumate	.35	.20
47	Earl Tatum	.25	.15
48	Mitch Kupchak	.40	.25
49	Ron Boone	.25	.15
50	Maurice Lucas	.90	.55
51	Louie Dampier	.35	.20
52	Aaron James	.25	.15
53	John Mengelt	.25	.15
54	Garfield Heard	.35	.20
55	George Johnson	.25	.15
56	Junior Bridgeman	.35	.20
57	Elmore Smith	.25	.15
58	Rudy Tomjanovich	.90	.55
59	Fred Brown	.60	.35
60	Rick Barry	5.00	2.75
61	Dave Bing	1.75	1.00
62	Anthony Roberts	.25	.15
63	Norm Nixon (R)	3.50	2.00
64	Leon Douglas (R)	.35	.20
65	Henry Bibby	.35	.20
66	Lonnie Shelton	.25	.15
67	Checklist	2.00	.25
68	Tom Henderson	.25	.15
69	Dan Roundfield	.40	.25
70	Armond Hill (R)	.35	.20
71	Larry Kenon	.25	.15

172 • 1978-79 TOPPS

72	Billy Knight	.35	.20
73	Artis Gilmore	1.50	.90
74	Lionel Hollins	.35	.20
75	Bernard King (R)	12.00	7.00
76	Brian Winters	.25	.15
77	Alvan Adams	.60	.35
78	Dennis Johnson (R)	15.00	9.00
79	Scott Wedman	.30	.18
80	Pete Maravich	6.50	3.50
81	Dan Issel	2.00	1.25
82	M.L. Carr	.30	.18
83	Walt Frazier	3.50	2.00
84	Dwight Jones	.25	.15
85	JoJo White	.75	.45
86	Robert Parish	12.00	6.50
87	Charlie Criss (R)	.35	.20
88	Jim McMillan	.25	.15
89	Chuck Williams	.25	.15
90	George McGinnis	.60	.35
91	Billy Paultz	.25	.15
92	Bob Dandridge	.30	.18
93	Ricky Sobers	.25	.15
94	Paul Silas	.50	.28
95	Gail Goodrich	1.00	.60
96	Tim Bassett	.25	.15
97	Ron Lee	.25	.15
98	Bob Gross	.25	.15
99	Sam Lacey	.25	.15
100	David Thompson	2.50	1.50
101	John Gianelli	.25	.15
102	Norm Van Lier	.35	.20
103	Caldwell Jones	.30	.18
104	Eric Money	.25	.15
105	Jim Chones	.25	.15
106	John Lucas	2.00	1.25
107	Spencer Haywood	.75	.45
108	Eddie Johnson (R)	.50	.28
109	Sidney Wicks	.50	.28
110	Kareem Abdul-Jabbar	16.00	9.00
111	Sonny Parker (R)	.40	.25
112	Randy Smith	.25	.15
113	Kevin Grevey	.25	.15
114	Rich Kelley	.25	.15
115	Scott May	.35	.20
116	Lloyd Free	.35	.20
117	Jack Sikma (R)	7.50	4.00
118	Kevin Porter	.35	.20
119	Darnell Hillman	.25	.15
120	Paul Westphal	2.00	1.25
121	Richard Washington	.30	.18
122	Dave Twardzik	.25	.15
123	Mike Bantom	.25	.15
124	Mike Newlin	.25	.15
125	Bob Lanier	1.75	1.00
126	Marques Johnson (R)	4.00	2.25
127	Foots Walker	.40	.25
128	Cedric Maxwell (R)	1.75	1.00
129	Ray Williams (R)	.75	.45
130	Julius Erving	20.00	12.50
131	Clifford Ray	.25	.15
132	Adrian Dantley	3.00	1.75

1979-80 Topps

The cards in this set feature full color player photos on the card fronts wrapped in a white border. The player's name appears in a diagonal color stripe below the photograph. His team name appears printed over a basketball in the lower right corner. His position is in small type under his name. The card backs consist of personal data, statistics, highlights and a small cartoon. All cards measure 2-1/2" by 3-1/2".

		MINT	NR/MT
Complete Set (132)		85.00	50.00
Commons		.25	.15
1	George Gervin	3.50	2.00
2	Mitch Kupchak	.30	.18
3	Henry Bibby	.35	.20
4	Bob Gross	.25	.15
5	Dave Cowens	2.50	1.50
6	Dennis Johnson	2.00	1.25
7	Scott Wedman	.30	.18
8	Earl Monroe	2.50	1.50

1979-80 TOPPS • 173

#	Player	Price 1	Price 2
9	Mike Bantom	.25	.15
10	Kareem Abdul-Jabbar	14.00	8.00
11	JoJo White	.70	.40
12	Spencer Haywood	.60	.35
13	Kevin Porter	.30	.18
14	Bernard King	3.00	1.75
15	Mike Newlin	.25	.15
16	Sidney Wicks	.50	.28
17	Dan Issel	1.75	1.00
18	Tom Henderson	.25	.15
19	Jim Chones	.25	.15
20	Julius Erving	18.00	11.00
21	Brian Winters	.25	.15
22	Billy Paultz	.25	.15
23	Cedric Maxwell	.50	.28
24	Eddie Johnson	.30	.18
25	Artis Gilmore	1.00	.60
26	Maurice Lucas	.50	.30
27	Gus Williams	.50	.28
28	Sam Lacey	.25	.15
29	Toby Knight	.25	.15
30	Paul Westphal (AS)	1.00	.60
31	Alex English (R)	15.00	9.00
32	Gail Goodrich	.70	.40
33	Caldwell Jones	.35	.20
34	Kevin Grevey	.25	.15
35	Jamaal Wilkes	.60	.35
36	Sonny Parker	.25	.15
37	John Gianelli	.25	.15
38	John Long (R)	.75	.45
39	George Johnson	.25	.15
40	Lloyd Free (AS)	.30	.18
41	Rudy Tomjanovich	.60	.35
42	Foots Walker	.25	.15
43	Dan Roundfield	.30	.18
44	Reggie Theus (R)	4.00	2.25
45	Bill Walton	7.00	3.75
46	Fred Brown	.40	.25
47	Darnell Hillman	.25	.15
48	Ray Williams	.30	.18
49	Larry Kenon	.25	.15
50	David Thompson	2.00	1.25
51	Billy Knight	.25	.15
52	Alvan Adams	.35	.20
53	Phil Smith	.25	.15
54	Adrian Dantley	1.50	.90
55	John Williamson	.25	.15
56	Campy Russell	.25	.15
57	Armond Hill	.25	.15
58	Bob Lanier	1.50	.90
59	Mickey Johnson	.25	.15
60	Pete Maravich	6.50	3.50
61	Nick Weatherspoon	.25	.15
62	Robert Reid (R)	.75	.45
63	Mychal Thompson (R)	3.00	1.75
64	Doug Collins	.80	.50
65	Wes Unseld	1.25	.70
66	Jack Sikma	1.50	.90
67	Bobby Wilkerson	.25	.15
68	Bill Robinzine	.25	.15
69	Joe Meriweather	.25	.15
70	Marques Johnson (AS)	1.00	.60
71	Ricky Sobers	.25	.15
72	Clifford Ray	.25	.15
73	Tim Bassett	.25	.15
74	James Silas	.25	.15
75	Bob McAdoo	.80	.50
76	Austin Carr	.30	.18
77	Don Ford	.25	.15
78	Steve Hawes	.25	.15
79	Ron Brewer (R)	.35	.20
80	Walter Davis	1.25	.70
81	Calvin Murphy	1.00	.60
82	Tom Boswell	.25	.15
83	Lonnie Shelton	.25	.15
84	Terry Tyler (R)	.40	.25
85	Randy Smith	.25	.15
86	Rich Kelley	.25	.15
87	Otis Birdsong (R)	.75	.45
88	Marvin Webster	.30	.18
89	Eric Money	.25	.15
90	Elvin Hayes (AS)	3.25	1.80
91	Junior Bridgeman	.35	.20
92	Johnny Davis	.25	.15
93	Robert Parish	7.50	4.00
94	Eddie Jordan	.25	.15
95	Leonard Robinson	.25	.15
96	Rick Robey (R)	.40	.25
97	Norm Nixon	.70	.40
98	Mark Olberding	.25	.15
99	Wilbur Holland	.25	.15
100	Moses Malone (AS)	6.50	3.50
101	Checklist	2.50	.35
102	Tom Owens	.25	.15
103	Phil Chenier	.25	.15
104	John Johnson	.25	.15
105	Darryl Dawkins	.80	.50
106	Charlie Scott	.35	.20
107	M.L. Carr	.25	.15
108	Phil Ford (R)	2.75	1.60
109	Swen Nater	.30	.18
110	Nate Archibald	1.25	.70
111	Aaron James	.25	.15
112	Jim Cleamons	.25	.15
113	James Edwards	.75	.45
114	Don Buse	.25	.15
115	Steve Mix	.25	.15
116	Charles Johnson	.25	.15
117	Elmore Smith	.25	.15
118	John Drew	.30	.18
119	Lou Hudson	.40	.25
120	Rick Barry	3.50	2.00
121	Kent Benson (R)	.60	.35
122	Mike Gate	.25	.15

174 • 1979-80 TOPPS

123	Jan Van Breda Kolff	.25	.15
124	Chris Ford	.40	.25
125	George McGinnis	.70	.40
126	Leon Douglas	.25	.15
127	John Lucas	1.25	.70
128	Kermit Washington	.25	.15
129	Lionel Hollins	.30	.18
130	Bob Dandridge (AS)	.35	.20
131	James McElroy	.25	.15
132	Bobby Jones	1.00	.60

1980-81 Topps

FORWARD
JOHN JOHNSON

Knicks
BILL CARTWRIGHT

CENTER
Nuggets
DAN ISSEL

This set contains 176 panels measuring 3-1/2" by 2-1/2". Each panel contains three separate basketball cards which measure 1-1/16" by 2-1/2". Each three-player panel is perforated between cards. However, the values listed below are for uncut panels. Cards that have been separated have lost most of their value. In all, there are 264 players pictured on the various panels. The first 88 panels feature all the players in this edition. The last 88 cards have the same players appearing in a different arrangement with other players. The most valuable card in the set is the Larry Bird, Magic Johnson rookie card in which they appear on the same panel along with Julius Erving. All of the individual cards are numbered on the card backs. For the purpose of creating a checklist, the panels are arranged numerically starting with the lowest number on the left back panel on the card backs. Values listed below are for uncut panels and not for individual cards.

		MINT	NR/MT
Complete Set (176)		725.00	425.00
Common Panel		.35	.20
3	Dan Roundfield	7.50	4.00
	181 Julius Erving		
	258 Ron Brewer		
7	Moses Malone (AS)	2.50	1.50
	185 Steve Mix		
	92 Robert Parish		
12	Gus Williams (AS)	.35	.20
	67 Geoff Huston		
	5 John Drew (AS)		
24	Steve Hawes	1.00	.60
	32 Nate Archibald		
	248 Elvin Hayes		
29	Dan Roundfield	.50	.28
	73 Dan Issel		
	152 Brian Winter		
34	Larry Bird (R)	550.00	325.00
	174 Julius Erving		
	139 Magic Johnson (R)		
36	Dave Cowens	1.25	.70
	186 Paul Westphal		
	142 Jamaal Wilkes		
38	Pete Maravich	3.00	1.75
	264 Lloyd Free		
	194 Dennis Johnson		
40	Rick Robey	.40	.25
	234 Adrian Dantley		
	26 Eddie Johnson		
47	Scott May	.35	.20
	196 Kenny Washington		
	177 Henry Bibby		
55	Don Ford	.35	.20
	145 Quinn Buckner		
	138 Brad Holland		
58	Campy Russell	.35	.20
	247 Kevin Grevey		
	52 Dave Robisch		
60	Foots Walker	.35	.20
	113 Mick Johnson		
	130 Bill Robinzine		
61	Austin Carr	4.00	2.25
	8 Kareem Abdul-Jabbar		
	200 Calvin Natt		
63	Jim Cleamons	.35	.20
	256 Robert Reid		
	22 Charlie Criss		

1980-81 TOPPS • 175

69	Tom LaGarde (R) 215 Swen Nater 213 James Silas	.40	.25
71	Jerome Whitehead (R) 259 Artis Gilmore 184 Caldwell Jones	.50	.30
74	John Roche 99 Clifford Ray 235 Ben Poquette (R)	.35	.20
75	Alex English 2 Marques Johnson 68 Jeff Judkins	2.25	1.40
82	Terry Tyler 21 Armond Hill 171 M.R. Richardson (R)	.35	.20
84	Kent Benson 212 John Shumate 229 Paul Westphal	.35	.20
86	Phil Hubbard 93 Robert Parish 126 Tom Burleson	1.50	.90
88	John Long 1 Julius Erving (AS) 49 Ricky Sobers	3.50	2.00
90	Eric Money 57 Dave Robisch 254 Rick Robey	.35	.20
95	Wayne Cooper (R) 226 John Johnson 45 David Greenwood	.35	.20
97	Robert Parish 187 Leon Robinson 46 Dwight Jones	4.00	2.25
98	Sonny Parker 197 Dave Twardzik 39 Cedric Maxwell	.35	.20
105	Rick Barry 122 Otis Birdsong 48 John Mengelt	1.75	1.00
106	Allen Leavell (R) 53 Foots Walker 223 Freeman Williams	.35	.20
108	Calvin Murphy 176 Maurice Cheeks 87 Greg Kelser	1.00	.60
110	Robert Reid 243 Wes Unseld 50 Reggie Theus	.50	.30
111	Rudy Tomjanovich 13 Eddie Johnson (AS) 179 Doug Collns	.40	.25
112	Mickey Johnson 28 Wayne Rollins 15 M.R. Richardson (AS)	.35	.20
115	Mike Bantom 6 Adrian Dantley (AS) 227 James Bailey	.35	.20
116	Dudley Bradley (R) 155 Eddie Jordan 239 Allan Bristow	.35	.20
118	James Edwards 153 Mike Newlin 182 Lionel Hollins	.35	.20
119	Mickey Johnson 154 George Johnson 193 Leonard Robinson	.35	.20
120	Billy Knight 16 Paul Westphal (AS) 59 Randy Smith	.50	.30
121	George McGinnis 83 Eric Money 65 Mike Bratz (R)	.40	.25
124	Phil Ford 101 Phil Smith 224 Gus Williams	.40	.25
127	Phil Ford 19 John Drew 209 Larry Kenon	.40	.25
131	Scott Wedman 164 Bill Cartwright 23 John Drew	.40	.25
132	K. Abdul-Jabbar 56 Mike Mitchell 81 Terry Tyler	3.50	2.00
135	K. Abdul-Jabbar 79 David Thompson 216 Brian Taylor	7.00	3.75
137	Michael Cooper (R) 103 Moses Malone 148 George Johnson	4.00	2.25
140	Mark Landsberger 10 Bob Lanier (AS) 222 Bill Walton	3.00	1.75
141	Norm Nixon 123 Sam Lacey 54 Kenny Carr (R)	.35	.20
143	Marquis Johnson 30 Larry Bird 232 Jack Sikma	35.00	20.00
146	Junior Bridgeman 31 Larry Bird 198 Ron Brewer	35.00	20.00
147	Quinn Buckner 133 K. Abdul-Jabbar 207 Mike Gale	3.50	2.00
149	Marques Johnson 262 Julius Erving 62 Abdul Jeelani (R)	4.00	2.25
151	Sidney Moncrief 260 Lonnie Shelton 220 Paul Silas	5.50	3.00
156	George Johnson 9 Bill Cartwright (AS) 199 Bob Gross	.40	.25

176 • 1980-81 TOPPS

#	Player	Price 1	Price 2
158	Maurice Lucas	.35	.20
	261 James Edwards		
	157 Eddie Jordan		
159	Mike Newlin	.35	.20
	134 Norm Nixon		
	180 Darryl Dawkins		
160	Roger Phegley (R)	.35	.20
	206 James Silas		
	91 Terry Tyler		
161	Cliff Robinson (R)	.50	.30
	51 Mike Mitchell		
	80 Bobby Wilkerson		
162	Jan V. Breda Kolff	.40	.25
	204 George Gervin		
	117 Johnny Davis		
165	M.R. Richardson	.60	.35
	214 Lloyd Free		
	44 Artis Gilmore		
166	Bill Cartwright (R)	3.50	2.00
	244 Kevin Porter		
	25 Armond Hill		
168	Toby Knight	.50	.30
	14 Lloyd Free (AS)		
	240 Adrian Dantley		
169	Joe Meriweather	.35	.20
	218 Lloyd Free		
	42 David Greenwood		
170	Earl Monroe	1.25	.70
	27 James McElroy		
	85 Leon Douglas		
172	Marvin Webster	.35	.20
	175 Caldwell Jones		
	129 Sam Lacey		
173	Ray Williams	.35	.20
	94 John Lucas		
	202 Dave Twardzik		
178	Maurice Cheeks	35.00	20.00
	18 Magic Johnson (AS)		
	237 Ron Boone		
183	Bobby Jones	.40	.25
	37 Chris Ford		
	66 Joe Hassett		
189	Alvan Adams	1.25	.70
	163 B. Cartwright		
	76 Dan Issel		
190	Don Buse	.35	.20
	242 Elvin Hayes		
	35 M.L. Carr		
191	Walter Davis	.50	.30
	11 George Gervin (AS)		
	136 Jim Chones		
192	Rich Kelley	1.75	1.00
	102 Moses Malone		
	64 Winford Boynes		
201	Tom Owens	.50	.30
	225 Jack Sikma		
	100 Purvis Short (R)		
208	George Gervin	1.25	.70
	72 Dan Issel		
	249 Mitch Kupchak		
217	Joe Bryant	2.50	1.50
	263 Bobby Jones		
	107 Moses Malone		
219	Swen Nater	.35	.20
	17 Calvin Murphy (AS)		
	70 Rich Washington		
221	Brian Taylor	.35	.20
	253 John Shumate		
	167 Larry Demic		
228	Fred Brown	.35	.20
	205 Larry Kenon		
	203 Kermit Washington		
230	John Johnson	.75	.45
	4 Walter Davis (AS)		
	33 Nate Archibald		
231	Lonnie Shelton	.35	.20
	104 Allen Leavell		
	96 John Lucas		
233	Gus Williams	.40	.25
	20 Dan Roundfield		
	211 Kevin Restani		
236	Allan Bristow	.35	.20
	210 Mark Olberding		
	255 James Bailey		
238	Tom Boswell	.80	.50
	109 Billy Paultz		
	150 Bob Lanier		
241	Ben Poquette	.35	.20
	188 Paul Westphal		
	77 Charlie Scott		
245	Greg Ballard	.35	.20
	43 Reggie Theus		
	252 John Williamson		
246	Bob Dandridge	.35	.20
	41 Reggie Theus		
	128 Reggie King		
250	Kevin Porter	.35	.20
	114 Johnny Davis		
	125 Otis Birdsong		
251	Wes Unseld	.60	.35
	195 Tom Owens		
	78 John Roche		
257	Elvin Hayes	.90	.55
	144 Marquis Johnson		
	89 Bob McAdoo		
3	Dan Roundfield	.35	.20
	218 Lloyd Free		
	42 David Greenwood		
7	Moses Malone	1.25	.70
	247 Kevin Grevey		
	52 Dave Robosch		
12	Gus Williams	.40	.25
	210 Mark Olberding		
	255 James Bailey		

1980-81 TOPPS • 177

#	Player	Price	Price
24	Steve Hawes	.35	.20
	226 John Johnson		
	45 David Greenwood		
29	Dan Roundfield	.35	.20
	113 Mick Johnson		
	130 Bill Robinzine		
34	Larry Bird	90.00	55.00
	164 B. Cartwright		
	23 John Drew		
36	Dave Cowens	1.25	.70
	16 Paul Westphal (AS)		
	59 Randy Smith		
38	Pete Maravich	2.00	1.25
	187 Leon. Robinson		
	46 Dwight Jones		
40	Rick Robey	.35	.20
	37 Chris Ford		
	66 Joe Hassett		
47	Scott May	35.00	20.00
	30 Larry Bird		
	232 Jack Sikma		
55	Don Ford	.40	.25
	144 Marquis Johnson		
	89 Bob McAdoo		
58	Campy Russell	.35	.20
	21 Armond Hill		
	171 M.R. Richardson		
60	Foots Walker	.35	.20
	122 Otis Birdsong		
	48 John Mengelt		
61	Austin Carr	.40	.25
	56 Mike Mitchell		
	81 Terry Tyler		
63	Jim Cleamons	.35	.20
	261 James Edwards		
	157 Eddie Jordan		
69	Tom LaGarde	.80	.50
	109 Billy Paultz		
	150 Bob Lanier		
71	Jerome Whitehead	.35	.20
	17 Calvin Murphy		
	70 Richard Washington		
74	John Roche	.75	.45
	28 Wayne Rollins		
	15 M.R. Richardson (AS)		
75	Alex English	2.50	1.50
	102 Moses Malone		
	64 Winford Boynes		
82	Terry Tyler	.50	.30
	79 David Thompson		
	216 Brian Taylor		
84	Kent Benson	.50	.30
	259 Artis Gilmore		
	184 Caldwell Jons		
86	Phil Hubbard	.35	.20
	195 Tom Owens		
	78 John Roche		
88	John Long	35.00	20.00
	18 Magic Johnson (AS)		
	237 Ron Boone		
90	Eric Money	.35	.20
	215 Swen Nater		
	213 James Silas		
95	Wayne Cooper	.35	.20
	154 George Johnson		
	193 Leon Robinson		
97	Robert Parish	5.00	2.75
	103 Moses Malone		
	148 George Johnson		
98	Sonny Parker	.35	.20
	94 John Lucas		
	202 Dave Twardzik		
105	Rick Barry	1.25	.70
	123 Sam Lacey		
	54 Kenny Carr		
106	Allen Leavell	.35	.20
	197 Dave Twardzik		
	38 Cedric Maxwell		
108	Calvin Murphy	.50	.30
	51 Mike Mitchell		
	80 Bobby Wilkerson		
110	Robert Reid	.35	.20
	153 Mike Newlin		
	182 Lionel Hollins		
111	Rudy Tomjanovich	.40	.25
	73 Dan Issel		
	152 Brian Winters		
112	Mick Johnson	.80	.50
	264 Lloyd Free		
	194 Dennis Johnson		
115	Mike Bantom	.50	.30
	204 George Gervin		
	117 Johnny Davis		
116	Dudley Bradley	.35	.20
	186 Paul Westphal		
	142 Jamaal Wilkes		
118	James Edwards	1.25	.70
	32 Nate Archibald		
	248 Elvin Hayes		
119	Mickey Johnson	.50	.30
	72 Dan Issel		
	249 Mitch Kupchak		
120	Billy Knight	.35	.20
	104 Allen Leavell		
	96 John Lucas		
121	George McGinnis	1.50	.90
	10 Bob Lanier (AS)		
	222 Bill Walton		
124	Phil Ford	.40	.25
	234 Adrian Dantley		
	26 Eddie Johnson		
127	Phil Ford	.35	.20
	43 Reggie Theus		
	252 John Williamson		

178 • 1980-81 TOPPS

#	Player	Price 1	Price 2
131	Scott Wedman	.35	.20
	244 Kevin Porter		
	25 Armond Hill		
132	K. Abdul-Jabbar	4.50	2.50
	93 Robert Parish		
	126 Tom Burleson		
135	K. Abdul-Jabbar	6.50	3.50
	253 John Shumate		
	167 Larry Demic		
137	Michael Cooper	2.50	1.50
	212 John Shumate		
	229 Paul Westphal		
140	Mark Landsberger	.50	.30
	214 Lloyd Free		
	44 Artis Gilmore		
141	Norm Nixon	.40	.25
	242 Elvin Hayes		
	35 M. L. Carr		
143	Marquis Johnson	.35	.20
	57 Dave Robisch		
	254 Rick Robey		
146	Junior Bridgeman	3.50	2.00
	1 Julius Erving		
	49 Ricky Sobers		
147	Quinn Buckner	.35	.20
	2 Marquis Johnson (AS)		
	68 Jeff Judkins		
149	Marquis Johnson	.35	.20
	83 Eric Money		
	65 Mike Bratz		
151	Sidney Moncrief (R)	6.50	3.50
	133 K. Abdul-Jabbar		
	207 Mike Gale		
156	George Johnson	.35	.20
	175 Caldwell Jones		
	129 Sam Lacey		
158	Maurice Lucas	4.50	2.50
	262 Julius Erving		
	62 Abdul Jeelani		
159	Mike Newlin	.40	.25
	243 Wes Unseld		
	50 Reggie Theus		
160	Roger Phegley	.35	.20
	145 Quinn Buckner		
	138 Brad Holland		
161	Cliff Robinson	.35	.20
	114 Johnny Davis		
	125 Otis Birdsong		
162	J.V. Breda Kolff	100.00	60.00
	174 Julius Erving		
	139 Magic Johnson		
165	M.R. Richardson	1.50	.90
	185 Steve Mix		
	92 Robert Parish		
166	Bill Cartwright	3.50	2.00
	13 Eddie Johnson (AS)		
	179 Doug Collins		
168	Toby Knight	.40	.25
	188 Paul Westphal		
	77 Charlie Scott		
169	Joe Meriweather	.35	.20
	196 Kermit Washington		
	177 Henry Bibby		
170	Earl Monroe	1.25	.70
	206 James Silas		
	91 Terry Tyler		
172	Marvin Webster	.35	.20
	155 Eddie Jordan		
	239 Allan Bristow		
173	Ray Williams	.35	.20
	225 Jack Sikma		
	100 Purvis Short		
178	Maurice Cheeks	5.00	2.75
	11 George Gervin (AS)		
	136 Jim Chones		
183	Bobby Jones	.40	.25
	99 Clifford Ray		
	235 Ben Poquette		
189	Alvan Adams	.50	.30
	14 Lloyd Free (AS)		
	240 Adrian Dantley		
190	Don Buse	.40	.25
	6 Adrian Dantley (AS)		
	227 James Bailey		
191	Walter Davis	.50	.30
	9 Bill Cartwright (AS)		
	199 Bob Gross		
192	Rich Kelley	2.50	1.50
	263 Bobby Jones		
	107 Moses Malone		
201	Tom Owens	.40	.25
	134 Norm Nixon		
	180 Darryl Dawkins		
208	George Gervin	1.00	.60
	53 Foots Walker		
	223 Freeman Williams		
217	Joe Bryant	3.50	2.00
	8 K. Abdul-Jabbar (AS)		
	200 Calvin Natt		
219	Swen Nater	.35	.20
	101 Phil Smith		
	224 Gus Williams		
221	Brian Taylor	.35	.20
	256 Robert Reid		
	22 Charlie Criss		
228	Fred Brown	30.00	18.00
	31 Larry Bird		
	198 Ron Brewer		
230	John Johnson	1.25	.70
	163 Bill Cartwright		
	76 Dan Issel		
231	Lonnie Shelton	.35	.20
	205 Larry Kenon		
	203 Kermit Washington		

1981-82 TOPPS • 179

233	Gus Williams	.35	.20
	41 Reggie Theus		
	128 Reggie King		
236	Allan Bristow	.35	.20
	260 Lonnie Shelton		
	220 Paul Silas		
238	Tom Boswell	.35	.20
	27 James McElroy		
	85 Leon Douglas		
241	Ben Poquette	.80	.50
	176 Maurice Cheeks		
	87 Greg Kelser		
245	Greg Ballard	.80	.50
	4 Walter Davis (AS)		
	33 Nate Archibald		
246	Bob Dandridge	.35	.20
	19 John Drew		
	209 Larry Kenon		
250	Kevin Porter	.35	.20
	20 Dan Roundfield		
	211 Kevin restani		
251	Wes Unseld	.60	.35
	67 Geoff Huston		
	5 John Drew (AS)		
257	Elvin Hayes	7.50	4.00
	181 Julius Erving		
	258 Ron Brewer		

1981-82 Topps

This set contains a total of 198-cards. However only the first 66-cards were distributed nationally. Three subsets of cards numbered from 67-110 were distributed regionally in the East, Midwest and West. These subsets are preceeded by the Prefix E, M and W in the checklist below. All cards feature the same design. The fronts consist of full color player photos framed by a white border. The player's name, position and team are located in a sunburst design in the lower corner of the card front. The flip side features personal data, statistics and highlights. The only subsets of note are Team Leaders (TL)(44-66) and Super Action cards (SA). All cards measure 2-1/2" by 3-1/2".

	MINT	NR/MT
Complete Set (198)	110.00	65.00
Commons	.10	.06

1	John Drew	.20	.12
2	Dan Roundfield	.15	.10
3	Nate Archibald	.80	.50
4	Larry Bird	35.00	20.00
5	Cedric Maxwell	.25	.15
6	Robert Parish	4.50	2.75
7	Artis Gilmore	.70	.40
8	Ricky Sobbers	.10	.06
9	Mike Mitchell	.10	.06
10	Tom LaGarde	.10	.06
11	Dan Issel	.90	.55
12	David Thompson	.75	.45
13	Lloyd Free	.35	.20
14	Moses Malone	2.25	1.40
15	Calvin Murphy	.35	.20
16	Johnny Davis	.10	.06
17	Otis Birdsong	.12	.07
18	Phil Ford	.25	.15
19	Scott Wedman	.10	.06
20	Kareem Abdul-Jabbar	6.00	3.50
21	Magic Johnson	35.00	20.00
22	Norm Nixon	.25	.15
23	Jamaal Wilkes	.25	.15
24	Marques Johnson	.30	.18
25	Bob Lanier	.80	.50
26	Bill Cartwright	.75	.45
27	M.R. Richardson	.12	.07
28	Ray Williams	.10	.06
29	Darryl Dawkins	.35	.20
30	Julius Erving	7.50	4.00
31	Lionel Holins	.15	.10
32	Bobby Jones	.20	.12
33	Walter Davis	.30	.18
34	Dennis Johnson	.60	.35
35	Leonard Robinson	.10	.06
36	Mychal Thompson	.25	.15

1981-82 TOPPS

#	Player		
37	George Gervin	1.00	.60
38	Swen Nater	.15	.10
39	Jack Sikma	.60	.35
40	Adrian Dantley	.60	.35
41	Darrell Griffith (R)	1.75	1.00
42	Elvin Hayes	1.50	.90
43	Fred Brown	.20	.12
44	Atlanta Hawks (TL)	.15	.10
	John Drew		
	Dan Roundfield		
	Eddie Johnson		
45	Boston Celtics (TL)	2.50	1.50
	Nate Archibald		
	Larry Bird		
46	Chicago Bulls (TL)	.25	.15
	Reggie Theus		
	Artis Gilmore		
47	Cleveland Cavs (TL)	.15	.10
	Mike Bratz		
	Kenny Carr		
	Mike Mitchell		
48	Dallas Mavericks (TL)	.15	.10
	Brad Davis		
	Jim Spanarkel		
	Tom LaGarde		
49	Denver Nuggets (TL)	.25	.15
	Dan Issel		
	David Thompson		
	Kenny Higgs		
50	Detroit Pistons (TL)	.15	.10
	John Long		
	Phil Hubbard		
	Ron Lee		
51	Golden State (TL)	.15	.10
	Lloyd Free		
	John Lucas		
	Larry Smith		
52	Houston Rockets (TL)	.40	.25
	Moses Malone		
	Allen Leavell		
53	Indiana Pacers (TL)	.15	.10
	Johnny Davis		
	Billy Knight		
	James Edwards		
54	Kansas City Kings (TL)	.15	.10
	Otis Birdsong		
	Phil Ford		
	Reggie King		
55	Los Angeles Lakers (TL)	1.50	.90
	Kareem Abdul-Jabbar		
	Norm Nixon		
56	Milwaukee Bucks (TL)	.20	.12
	Quinn Buckner		
	Marques Johnson		
	Mickey Johnson		
57	New Jersey Nets (TL)	.15	.10
	Maurice Lucas		
	Mike Newlin		
58	New York Knicks (TL)	.15	.10
	Bill Cartwright		
	M.R. Richardson		
59	Philadelphia 76ers (TL)	1.50	.90
	Maurice Cheeks		
	Julius Erving		
	Caldwell Jones		
60	Phoenix Suns (TL)	.15	.10
	Alvan Adams		
	Truck Robinson		
61	Portland Blazers (TL)	.25	.15
	Jim Paxson		
	Mychal Thompson		
	Kermit Washington		
62	San Antonio Spurs (TL)	.25	.15
	Dave Corzine		
	George Gervin		
	Johnny Moore		
63	San Diego Clippers (TL)	.15	.10
	Swen Nater		
	Brian Taylor		
	Freeman Williams		
64	Seattle Sonics (TL)	.20	.12
	Vinnie Johnson		
	Jack Sikma		
65	Utah Jazz (TL)	.20	.12
	Allan Bristow		
	Adrian Dantley		
	Ben Poquette		
66	Washington Bullets (TL)	.25	.15
	Elvin Hayes		
	Kevin Porter		
E67	Charlie Criss	.10	.06
E68	Eddie Johnson	.10	.06
E69	Wes Matthews	.10	.06
E70	Tom McMillen	.40	.25
E71	Tree Rollins	.30	.18
E72	M.L. Carr	.12	.07
E73	Chris Ford	.40	.25
E74	Gerald Henderson (R)	.50	.30
E75	Kevin McHale (R)	20.00	12.50
E76	Rick Robey	.15	.10
E77	Darwin Cook (R)	.15	.10
E78	Mike Gminski (R)	1.25	.70
E79	Maurice Lucas	.25	.15
E80	Mike Newlin	.10	.06
E81	Mike O'Koren (R)	.30	.18
E82	Steve Hawes	.10	.06
E83	Foots Walker	.10	.06
E84	Campy Russell	.10	.06
E85	DeWayne Scales	.10	.06
E86	Randy Smith	.10	.06
E87	Marvin Webster	.12	.07
E88	Sly Williams	.10	.06
E89	Mike Woodson (R)	.40	.25
E90	Maurice Cheeks	2.00	1.25

1981-82 TOPPS • 181

E91 Caldwell Jones	.15	.10
E92 Steve Mix	.10	.06
E93 Checklist	.80	.15
E94 Greg Ballard	.10	.06
E95 Don Collins	.10	.06
E96 Kevin Grevey	.10	.06
E97 Mitch Kupchak	.15	.10
E98 Rick Mahorn (R)	1.25	.70
E99 Kevin Porter	.15	.10
E100 Nate Archibald (SA)	.40	.25
E101 Larry Bird (SA)	16.00	9.00
E102 Bill Cartwright (SA)	.35	.20
E103 Darryl Dawkins (SA)	.15	.10
E104 Julius Erving (SA)	4.50	2.50
E105 Kevin Porter (SA)	.12	.07
E106 Bobby Jones (SA)	.20	.12
E107 Cedric Maxwell (SA)	.12	.07
E108 Robert Parish (SA)	2.00	1.25
E109 M.R. Richardson (SA)	.12	.07
E110 Dan Roundfield (SA)	.12	.07
M67 David Greenwood	.15	.10
M68 Dwight Jones	.10	.06
M69 Reggie Theus	.20	.12
M70 Bobby Wilkerson	.10	.06
M71 Mike Bratz	.10	.06
M72 Kenny Carr	.10	.06
M73 Geoff Huston	.10	.06
M74 Bill Laimbeer (R)	5.00	2.75
M75 Roger Phegley	.10	.06
M76 Checklist	.80	.15
M77 Abdul Jeelani	.10	.06
M78 Bill Robinzine	.10	.06
M79 Jim Spanarkel	.10	.06
M80 Kent Benson	.20	.12
M81 Keith Herron	.10	.06
M82 Phil Hubbard	.20	.12
M83 John Long	.15	.10
M84 Terry Tyler	.12	.07
M85 Mike Dunleavy (R)	2.00	1.25
M86 Tom Henderson	.10	.06
M87 Billy Paultz	.10	.06
M88 Robert Reid	.15	.10
M89 Mike Bantom	.10	.06
M90 James Edwards	.35	.20
M91 Billy Knight	.15	.10
M92 George McGinnis	.35	.20
M93 Louis Orr	.12	.07
M94 Ernie Grunfeld (R)	.60	.35
M95 Reggie King	.10	.06
M96 Sam Lacey	.10	.06
M97 Junior Bridgeman	.15	.10
M98 Mickey Johnson	.10	.06
M99 Sidney Moncrief	2.00	1.25
M100 Brian Winters	.10	.06
M101 Dave Corzine (R)	.30	.18
M102 Paul Griffin	.10	.06
M103 Johnny Moore (R)	.30	.18

M104 Mark Olberding	.10	.06
M105 James Silas	.10	.06
M106 George Gervin (SA)	.60	.35
M107 Artis Gilmore (SA)	.40	.25
M108 Marquis Johnson (SA)	.20	.12
M109 Bob Lanier (SA)	.60	.35
M110 Moses Malone (SA)	1.50	.90
W67 T.R. Dunn (R)	.30	.18
W68 Alex English	2.00	1.25
W69 Billy McKinney (R)	.30	.18
W70 Dave Robisch	.10	.06
W71 Joe Barry Carroll (R)	.75	.45
W72 Bernard King	1.50	.90
W73 Sonny Parker	.10	.06
W74 Purvis Short	.30	.18
W75 Larry Smith (R)	.80	.50
W76 Jim Chones	.12	.07
W77 Michael Cooper	1.50	.90
W78 Mark Landsberger	.10	.06
W79 Alvan Adams	.15	.10
W80 Jeff Cook	.10	.06
W81 Rich Kelley	.10	.06
W82 Kyle Macy (R)	.40	.25
W83 Billy Ray Bates (R)	.20	.12
W84 Bob Gross	.10	.06
W85 Calvin Natt	.30	.18
W86 Lonnie Shelton	.10	.06
W87 Jim Paxson (R)	1.25	.70
W88 Kelvin Ransey	.10	.06
W89 Kermit Washington	.12	.07
W90 Henry Bibby	.12	.07
W91 Michael Brooks (R)	.25	.15
W92 Joe Bryant	.10	.06
W93 Phil Smith	.10	.06
W94 Brian Taylor	.10	.06
W95 Freeman Williams	.25	.15
W96 James Bailey	.10	.06
W97 Checklist	.80	.15
W98 John Johnson	.10	.06
W99 Vinnie Johnson (R)	2.00	1.25
W100 Wally Walker (R)	.30	.18
W101 Paul Westphal	.20	.12
W102 Allan Bristow	.15	.10
W103 Wayne Cooper	.10	.06
W104 Carl Nicks	.10	.06
W105 Ben Poquette	.10	.06
W106 K. Abdul-Jabbar (SA)	5.00	2.75
W107 Dan Issel (SA)	.50	.30
W108 Dennis Johnson (SA)	.40	.25
W109 Magic Johnson (SA)	16.00	9.00
W110 Jack Sikma (SA)	.30	.18

1992-93 Topps

This set marks Topps return to basketball after a ten year absence. This edition contains 396-cards. The fronts feature full color action photos surrounded by a thin inside frame line and a larger white border. The player's name and team appear in small color bars under the photo. The flip side consists of a small head shot, personal data, and statistics. The main subsets include Record Breakers (RB)(2-4), All-Stars (AS) (100-126), 50 Point Club (199-215) and 20 Assist Club (216-224). Topps also produced a Gold Set of each card in this set. The Gold set is valued at 10 X the regular edition listed below and common gold cards are valued at 25 cents each. All cards measure 2-1/2" by 3-1/2".

	MINT	NR/MT
Complete Set 396)	18.50	10.50
Commons	.05	.02

		MINT	NR/MT
1	Larry Bird	.50	.30
2	Magic Johnson (RB)	.25	.15
3	Michael Jordan (RB)	.40	.25
4	David Robinson (RB)	.20	.12
5	Johnny Newman	.05	.02
6	Mike Iuzzolino	.05	.02
7	Ken Norman	.07	.04
8	Chris Jackson	.12	.07
9	Duane Ferrell	.05	.02
10	Sean Elliott	.15	.10
11	Bernard King	.07	.04
12	Armon Gilliam	.05	.02
13	Reggie Williams	.05	.02
14	Steve Kerr	.05	.02
15	Anthony Bowie	.05	.02
16	Alton Lister	.05	.02
17	Dee Brown	.10	.06
18	Tom Chambers	.08	.05
19	Otis Thorpe	.07	.04
20	Karl Malone	.20	.12
21	Kenny Gattison	.05	.02
22	Lionel Simmons	.12	.07
23	Vern Fleming	.05	.02
24	John Paxson	.07	.04
25	Mitch Richmond	.08	.05
26	Danny Schayes	.05	.02
27	Derrick McKey	.05	.02
28	Mark Randall	.05	.02
29	Bill Laimbeer	.07	.04
30	Chris Morris	.05	.02
31	Alec Kessler	.05	.02
32	Vlade Divac	.08	.05
33	Rich Fox	.08	.05
34	Charles Shackleford	.05	.02
35	Dominique Wilkins	.25	.15
36	Sleepy Floyd	.05	.02
37	Doug West	.07	.04
38	Pete Chilcutt	.05	.02
39	Orlando Woolridge	.05	.02
40	Eric Leckner	.05	.02
41	Joe Kleine	.05	.02
42	Scott Skiles	.05	.02
43	Jerrod Mustaf	.05	.02
44	John Starks	.20	.12
45	Sedale Threatt	.05	.02
46	Doug Smith	.07	.04
47	Byron Scott	.07	.04
48	Willie Anderson	.05	.02
49	David Benoit	.10	.06
50	Scott Hastings	.05	.02
51	Terry Porter	.08	.05
52	Sidney Green	.05	.02
53	Danny Young	.05	.02
54	Magic Is Back	.30	.18
55	Brian Williams	.07	.04
56	Randy Wittman	.05	.02
57	Kevin McHale	.12	.07
58	Dana Barros	.07	.04
59	Thurl Bailey	.05	.02
60	Kevin Duckworth	.07	.04
61	John Williams	.05	.02
62	Willie Burton	.07	.04
63	Spud Webb	.05	.02
64	Detlef Schrempf	.15	.10
65	Sherman Douglas	.08	.05
66	Patrick Ewing	.25	.15
67	Michael Adams	.08	.05
68	Vernon Maxwell	.07	.04

1992-93 TOPPS • 183

#	Player		
69	Terrell Brandon	.10	.06
70	Terry Catledge	.05	.02
71	Mark Eaton	.05	.02
72	Tony Smith	.05	.02
73	B.J. Armstrong	.12	.07
74	Moses Malone	.10	.06
75	Anthony Bonner	.05	.02
76	George McCloud	.05	.02
77	Glen Rice	.12	.07
78	Jon Koncak	.05	.02
79	Michael Cage	.05	.02
80	Ron Harper	.07	.04
81	Tom Tolbert	.05	.02
82	Brad Sellers	.05	.02
83	Winston Garland	.05	.02
84	Negele Knight	.08	.05
85	Ricky Pierce	.07	.04
86	Mark Aguirre	.08	.05
87	Ron Anderson	.05	.02
88	Loy Vaught	.07	.04
89	Luc Longley	.07	.04
90	Jerry Reynolds	.05	.02
91	Terry Cummings	.08	.05
92	Rony Seikaly	.08	.05
93	Derek Harper	.07	.04
94	Cliff Robinson	.10	.06
95	Kenny Anderson	.20	.12
96	Chris Gatling	.05	.02
97	Stacey Augmon	.12	.07
98	Chris Corchiani	.07	.04
99	Pervis Ellison	.08	.05
100	Larry Bird (AS)	.20	.12
101	John Stockton (AS)	.12	.07
102	Clyde Drexler (AS)	.12	.07
103	Scottie Pippen (AS)	.15	.10
104	Reggie Lewis (AS)	.10	.06
105	Hakeem Olajuwon (AS)	.25	.15
106	David Robinson (AS)	.20	.12
107	Charles Barkley (AS)	.20	.12
108	James Worthy (AS)	.07	.04
109	Kevin Willis (AS)	.05	.02
110	Dikembe Mutombo (AS)	.12	.07
111	Joe Dumars (AS)	.07	.04
112	Jeff Hornacek (AS)	.06	.03
113	Mark Price (AS)	.10	.06
114	Michael Adams (AS)	.07	.04
115	Michael Jordan (AS)	.50	.30
116	Brad Daugherty (AS)	.08	.05
117	Dennis Rodman (AS)	.07	.04
118	Isiah Thomas (AS)	.10	.06
119	Tim Hardaway (AS)	.12	.07
120	Chris Mullin (AS)	.10	.06
121	Patrick Ewing (AS)	.15	.10
122	Dan Majerle (AS)	.08	.05
123	Karl Malone (AS)	.12	.07
124	Otis Thorpe (AS)	.06	.03
125	Dominique Wilkins (AS)	.15	.10
126	Magic Johnson (AS)	.20	.12
127	Charles Oakley	.05	.02
128	Robert Pack	.07	.04
129	Billy Owens	.15	.10
130	Jeff Malone	.07	.04
131	Danny Ferry	.05	.02
132	Sam Bowie	.05	.02
133	Avery Johnson	.05	.02
134	Jayson Williams	.05	.02
135	Fred Roberts	.05	.02
136	Greg Sutton	.05	.02
137	Dennis Rodman	.10	.06
138	John Williams	.05	.02
139	Greg Dreiling	.05	.02
140	Rik Smits	.05	.02
141	Michael Jordan	1.00	.60
142	Nick Anderson	.12	.07
143	Jerome Kersey	.08	.05
144	Fat Lever	.05	.02
145	Tyrone Corbin	.05	.02
146	Robert Parish	.10	.06
147	Steve Smith	.20	.12
148	Chris Dudley	.05	.02
149	Antoine Carr	.05	.02
150	Elden Campbell	.07	.04
151	Randy White	.05	.02
152	Felton Spencer	.08	.05
153	Cedric Ceballos	.08	.05
154	Mark Macon	.10	.06
155	Jack Haley	.05	.02
156	Bimbo Coles	.05	.02
157	A.J. English	.07	.04
158	Kendall Gill	.12	.07
159	A.C. Green	.07	.04
160	Mark West	.05	.02
161	Benoit Benjamin	.05	.02
162	Tyrone Hill	.05	.02
163	Larry Nance	.07	.04
164	Gary Grant	.05	.02
165	Bill Cartwright	.05	.02
166	Greg Anthony	.10	.06
167	Jim Les	.05	.02
168	Johnny Dawkins	.05	.02
169	Alvin Robertson	.05	.02
170	Kenny Smith	.07	.04
171	Gerald Glass	.05	.02
172	Harvey Grant	.07	.04
173	Paul Graham	.05	.02
174	Sam Perkins	.07	.04
175	Manute Bol	.05	.02
176	Muggsy Bogues	.05	.02
177	Mike Brown	.05	.02
178	Donald Hodge	.05	.02
179	Dave Jamerson	.05	.02
180	Mookie Blaylock	.08	.05
181	Randy Brown	.05	.02
182	Todd Lichti	.05	.02

1992-93 TOPPS

#	Player		
183	Kevin Gamble	.05	.02
184	Gary Payton	.12	.07
185	Brian Shaw	.05	.02
186	Grant Long	.05	.02
187	Frank Brickowski	.05	.02
188	Tim Hardaway	.20	.12
189	Danny Manning	.15	.10
190	Kevin Johnson	.15	.10
191	Craig Ehlo	.05	.02
192	Dennis Scott	.08	.05
193	Reggie Miller	.10	.06
194	Darrell Walker	.05	.02
195	Anthony Mason	.10	.06
196	Buck Williams	.07	.04
197	Checklist (1-99)	.05	.02
198	Checklist (100-198)	.05	.02
199	Karl Malone (50 pt)	.12	.07
200	Dominique Wilkins(50)	.15	.10
201	Tom Chambers (50 pt)	.07	.04
202	Bernard King (50 pt)	.06	.03
203	Kiki Vandeweghe(50 pt)	.05	.02
204	Dale Ellis (50 pt)	.05	.02
205	Michael Jordan (50 pt)	.50	.30
206	Michael Adams (50 pt)	.06	.03
207	Charles Smith (50 pt)	.06	.03
208	Moses Malone (50 pt)	.08	.05
209	Terry Cummings (50 pt)	.06	.03
210	Vernon Maxwell(50 pt)	.07	.04
211	Patrick Ewing (50 pt)	.15	.10
212	Clyde Drexler (50 pt)	.12	.07
213	Kevin McHale (50 pt)	.08	.05
214	Hakeem Olajuwon (50)	.25	.15
215	Reggie Miller (50 pt)	.10	.06
216	Gary Grant (20 Ast)	.05	.02
217	Doc Rivers (20 Ast)	.05	.02
218	Mark Price (20 Ast)	.07	.04
219	Isiah Thomas (20 Ast)	.08	.05
220	Nate McMillan (20 Ast)	.05	.02
221	Fat Lever (20 Ast)	.05	.02
222	Kevin Johnson (20 Ast)	.08	.05
223	John Stockton (20 Ast)	.12	.07
224	Scott Skiles (20 Ast)	.05	.02
225	Kevin Brooks	.05	.02
226	Bobby Phills (R)	.08	.05
227	Oliver Miller (R)	.30	.18
228	John Williams	.05	.02
229	Brad Lohaus	.05	.02
230	Derrick Coleman	.15	.10
231	Ed Pinckney	.05	.02
232	Trent Tucker	.05	.02
233	Lance Blanks	.05	.02
234	Drazen Petrovic	.10	.06
235	Mark Bryant	.05	.02
236	Lloyd Daniels (R)	.12	.07
237	Dale Davis	.08	.05
238	Jayson Williams	.05	.02
239	Mike Sanders	.05	.02
240	Mike Gminski	.05	.02
241	Williams Bedford	.05	.02
242	Dell Curry	.05	.02
243	Gerald Paddio	.05	.02
244	Chris Smith (R)	.12	.07
245	Jud Buechler	.05	.02
246	Walter Palmer	.05	.02
247	Larry Krystkowiak	.05	.02
248	Marcus Liberty	.07	.04
249	Sam Mitchell	.05	.02
250	Kiki Vandeweghe	.05	.02
251	Vincent Askew	.05	.02
252	Travis Mays	.05	.02
253	Charles Smith	.08	.05
255	James Worthy	.10	.06
256	Paul Pressey	.05	.02
257	Rumeal Robinson	.07	.04
258	Tom Gugliotta (R)	.35	.20
259	Eric Anderson (R)	.10	.06
260	Hersey Hawkins	.08	.05
261	Terry Davis	.05	.02
262	Rex Chapman	.07	.04
263	Chucky Brown	.07	.04
264	Danny Young	.05	.02
265	Olden Polynice	.05	.02
266	Kevin Willis	.05	.02
267	Shawn Kemp	.40	.25
268	Mookie Blaylock	.08	.05
269	Malik Sealy (R)	.12	.07
270	Charles Barkley	.35	.20
271	Corey Williams (R)	.12	.07
272	Stephen Howard (R)	.08	.05
273	Keith Askins	.05	.02
274	Matt Bullard	.05	.02
275	John Battle	.05	.02
276	Andrew Lang	.05	.02
277	David Robinson	.40	.25
278	Harold Miner (R)	.40	.25
279	Tracy Murray (R)	.15	.10
280	Pooh Richardson	.07	.04
281	Dikembe Mutombo	.20	.12
282	Wayman Tisdale	.07	.04
283	Larry Johnson	.50	.30
284	Todd Day (R)	.30	.18
285	Stanley Roberts	.08	.05
286	Randy Woods (R)	.08	.05
287	Avery Johnson	.05	.02
288	Anthony Peeler (R)	.30	.18
289	Mario Elie	.05	.02
290	Doc Rivers	.05	.02
291	Blue Edwards	.07	.04
292	Sean Rooks (R)	.15	.10
293	Xavier McDaniel	.07	.04
294	C. Weatherspoon (R)	.35	.20
295	Morlon Wiley	.05	.02
296	LaBradford Smith	.05	.02
297	Reggie Lewis	.15	.10

1992-93 TOPPS • 185

#	Player		
298	Chris Mullin	.15	.10
299	Litterial Green (R)	.12	.07
300	Elmore Spencer (R)	.12	.07
301	John Stockton	.20	.12
302	Walt Williams (R)	.30	.18
303	Anthony Pullard (R)	.08	.05
304	Gundars Vetra (R)	.08	.05
305	LaSalle Thompson	.05	.02
306	Nate McMillan	.05	.02
307	Steve Bardo (R)	.08	.05
308	Robert Horry (R)	.60	.35
309	Scott Williams	.05	.02
310	Bo Kimble	.05	.02
311	Tree Rollins	.05	.02
312	Tim Perry	.05	.02
313	Isaac Austin (R)	.10	.06
314	Tate George	.05	.02
315	Kevin Lynch	.05	.02
316	Victor Alexander	.05	.02
317	Doug Overton	.05	.02
318	Tom Hammonds	.07	.04
319	LaPhonso Ellis (R)	.70	.40
320	Scott Brooks	.05	.02
321	Anthony Avent (R)	.15	.10
322	Matt Geiger (R)	.10	.06
323	Duane Causwell	.05	.02
324	Horace Grant	.07	.04
325	Mark Jackson	.07	.04
326	Dan Majerle	.10	.06
327	Chuck Person	.07	.04
328	Buck Johnson	.07	.04
329	Duane Cooper (R)	.10	.06
330	Rod Stickland	.05	.02
331	Isiah Thomas	.12	.07
332	Greg Kite	.05	.02
333	Don MacLean (R)	.20	.12
334	Christian Laettner (R)	.50	.30
335	John Crotty (R)	.08	.05
336	Tracy Moore (R)	.10	.06
337	Hakeem Olajuwon	.50	.30
338	Byron Houston (R)	.12	.07
339	Walter Bond (R)	.10	.06
340	Brent Price (R)	.12	.07
341	Bryant Stith (R)	.20	.12
342	Will Perdue	.05	.02
343	Jeff Hornacek	.08	.05
344	Adam Keefe (R)	.12	.07
345	Rafael Addison	.07	.04
346	Marlon Maxey (R)	.10	.06
347	Joe Dumars	.10	.06
348	Jon Barry (R)	.08	.05
349	Marty Conlan	.05	.02
350	Alaa Abdelnaby	.05	.02
351	Micheal Williams	.05	.02
352	Brad Daugherty	.12	.07
353	Tony Bennett (R)	.10	.06
354	Clyde Drexler	.20	.12
355	Rolando Blackman	.07	.04
356	Tom Tolbert	.05	.02
357	Sarunas Marciulionis	.08	.05
358	Jaren Jackson (R)	.10	.06
359	Stacey King	.07	.04
360	Danny Ainge	.07	.04
361	Dale Ellis	.07	.04
362	Shaquille O'Neal (R)	3.50	2.00
363	Bob McCann (R)	.08	.05
364	Reggie Smith (R)	.10	.06
365	Vinny Del Negro	.05	.02
366	Robert Pack	.07	.04
367	David Wood	.05	.02
358	Rodney McCray	.05	.02
369	Terry Mills	.10	.06
370	Eric Murdoch	.08	.05
371	Alex Blackwell (R)	.08	.05
372	Jay Humphries	.05	.02
373	Eddie Lee Wilkins	.05	.02
374	James Edwards	.05	.02
375	Tim Kempton	.05	.02
376	J.R. Reid	.05	.02
377	Sam Mack (R)	.10	.06
378	Donald Royal	.05	.02
379	Mark Price	.12	.07
380	Mark Acres	.05	.02
381	Hubert Davis (R)	.20	.12
382	Dave Johnson (R)	.10	.06
383	John Salley	.05	.02
384	Eddie Johnson	.05	.02
385	Brian Howard (R)	.08	.05
386	Isaiah Morris (R)	.10	.06
387	Frank Johnson	.05	.02
388	Rick Mahorn	.05	.02
389	Scottie Pippen	.20	.12
390	Lee Mayberry (R)	.15	.10
391	Tony Campbell	.05	.02
392	Latrell Sprewell (R)	.75	.45
393	Alonzo Mourning (R)	1.75	1.00
394	Robert Werdann (R)	.10	.06
395	Checklist (199-297)	.05	.02
396	Checklist (298-396)	.05	.02

1992-93 Topps Beam Team

The cards in this set were random inserts in Topps Series II wax packs. The fronts feature full color action photographs of three players in a horizontal format with the headline "Beam Team" in block letters running vertically along the left side of the card. All cards measure 3-1/2" by 2-1/2".

		MINT	NR/MT
Complete Set (7)		10.00	6.00
Commons		.75	.45
1	Reggie Miller Charles Barkley Clyde Drexler	1.50	.90
2	Patrick Ewing Tim Hardaway Jeff Hornacek	.75	.45
3	Kevin Johnson Michael Jordan Dennis Rodman	3.00	1.75
4	Chris Mullin John Stockton Karl Malone	1.00	.60
5	Hakeem Olajuwon Mark Price Shawn Kemp	2.00	1.25
6	Scottie Pippen David Robinson Jeff Malone	1.25	.70
7	Dominique Wilkins Shaquille O'Neal Glen Rice	3.50	2.00

1992-93 Topps Stadium Club

This 400-card set is Topps first premium basketball edition. The set was issued in two 200-card series. The card fronts, printed on a glossy paper stock with UV coating, feature full color, full bleed game action player photos. The player's appears below the Stadium Club logo in the bottom corner of the card front. The card backs contain personal data, statistics and a miniature version of the player's Topps rookie card. The set includes a 20-card Members Choice (MC) subset. All cards measure 2-1/2" by 3-1/2".

		MINT	NR/MT
Complete Set (400)		70.00	40.00
Commons		.10	.06
1	Michael Jordan	4.50	2.75
2	Greg Anthony	.15	.10
3	Otis Thorpe	.12	.07
4	Jim Les	.10	.06
5	Kevin Willis	.12	.07
6	Derek Harper	.12	.07
7	Elden Campbell	.15	.10
8	A.J. English	.12	.07
9	Kenny Gattison	.10	.06
10	Drazen Petrovic	.35	.20
11	Chris Mullin	.35	.20
12	Mark Price	.35	.20
13	Karl Malone	.60	.35

1992-93 TOPPS STADIUM CLUB • 187

14	Gerald Glass	.10	.06		71	Muggsy Bogues	.10	.06
15	Negele Knight	.12	.07		72	Spud Webb	.10	.06
16	Mark Macon	.12	.07		73	Sedale Threatt	.10	.06
17	Michael Cage	.10	.06		74	Chris Gatling	.10	.06
18	Kevin Edwards	.10	.06		75	Derrick McKey	.12	.07
19	Sherman Douglas	.15	.10		76	Sleepy Floyd	.10	.06
20	Ron Harper	.12	.07		77	Chris Jackson	.25	.15
21	Cliff Robinson	.30	.18		78	Thurl Bailey	.10	.06
22	Bryon Scott	.12	.07		79	Steve Smith	.30	.18
23	Antoine Carr	.10	.06		80	Cedric Ceballos	.15	.10
24	Greg Dreiling	.10	.06		81	Anthony Bowie	.10	.06
25	Bill Laimbeer	.15	.10		82	John Williams	.10	.06
26	Hersey Hawkins	.15	.10		83	Paul Graham	.10	.06
27	Will Perdue	.10	.06		84	Willie Burton	.12	.07
28	Todd Lichti	.10	.06		85	Vernon Maxwell	.15	.10
29	Gary Grant	.10	.06		86	Stacey King	.10	.06
30	Sam Perkins	.12	.07		87	B.J. Armstrong	.20	.12
31	Jayson Williams	.10	.06		88	Kevin Gamble	.10	.06
32	Magic Johnson	1.50	.90		89	Terry Catledge	.10	.06
33	Larry Bird	1.75	1.00		90	Jeff Malone	.15	.10
34	Chris Morris	.10	.06		91	Sam Bowie	.10	.06
35	Nick Anderson	.30	.18		92	Orlando Woolridge	.12	.07
36	Scott Hastings	.10	.06		93	Steve Kerr	.10	.06
37	Ledell Eackles	.10	.06		94	Eric Leckner	.10	.06
38	Robert Pack	.12	.07		95	Loy Vaught	.12	.07
39	Dana Barros	.12	.07		96	Jud Buechler	.10	.06
40	Anthony Bonner	.10	.06		97	Doug Smith	.12	.07
41	J.R. Reid	.10	.06		98	Sidney Green	.10	.06
42	Tyrone Hill	.10	.06		99	Jerome Kersey	.12	.07
43	Rik Smits	.10	.06		100	Patrick Ewing	.80	.50
44	Kevin Duckworth	.12	.07		101	Ed Nealy	.10	.06
45	LaSalle Thompson	.10	.06		102	Shawn Kemp	1.00	.60
46	Brian Williams	.12	.07		103	Luc Longley	.12	.07
47	Willie Anderson	.10	.06		104	George McCloud	.10	.06
48	Ken Norman	.12	.07		105	Ron Anderson	.10	.06
49	Mike Iuzzolino	.10	.06		106	Moses Malone	.25	.15
50	Isiah Thomas	.35	.20		107	Tony Smith	.10	.06
51	Alec Kessler	.10	.06		108	Terry Porter	.15	.10
52	Johnny Dawkins	.10	.06		109	Blair Rasmussen	.10	.06
53	Avery Johnson	.10	.06		110	Bimbo Coles	.10	.06
54	Stacey Augmon	.30	.18		111	Grant Long	.10	.06
55	Charles Oakley	.15	.10		112	John Battle	.10	.06
56	Rex Chapman	.12	.07		113	Brian Oliver	.10	.06
57	Charles Shackleford	.10	.06		114	Tyrone Corbin	.10	.06
58	Jeff Ruland	.10	.06		115	Benoit Benjamin	.10	.06
59	Craig Ehlo	.10	.06		116	Rick Fox	.15	.10
60	Jon Koncak	.10	.06		117	Rafael Addison	.10	.06
61	Danny Schayes	.10	.06		118	Danny Young	.10	.06
62	David Benoit	.15	.10		119	Fat Lever	.10	.06
63	Robert Parish	.20	.12		120	Terry Cummings	.15	.10
64	Mookie Blaylock	.15	.10		121	Felton Spencer	.15	.10
65	Sean Elliott	.30	.18		122	Joe Kleine	.10	.06
66	Mark Aguirre	.12	.07		123	Johnny Newman	.10	.06
67	Scott Williams	.10	.06		124	Gary Payton	.30	.18
68	Doug West	.20	.12		125	Kurt Rambis	.10	.06
69	Kenny Anderson	.35	.20		126	Vlade Divac	.15	.10
70	Randy Brown	.10	.06		127	John Paxson	.12	.07

188 • 1992-93 TOPPS STADIUM CLUB

#	Player		
128	Lionel Simmons	.30	.18
129	Randy Wittman	.10	.06
130	Winston Garland	.10	.06
131	Jerry Reynolds	.10	.06
132	Dell Curry	.10	.06
133	Fred Roberts	.10	.06
134	Michael Adams	.12	.07
135	Charles Jones	.10	.06
136	Frank Brickowski	.10	.06
137	Alton Lister	.10	.06
138	Horace Grant	.12	.07
139	Greg Sutton	.10	.06
140	John Starks	.50	.30
141	Detlef Schrempf	.20	.12
142	Rodney Monroe	.10	.06
143	Pete Chilcutt	.10	.06
144	Mike Brown	.10	.06
145	Rony Seikaly	.12	.07
146	Donald Hodge	.10	.06
147	Kevin McHale	.20	.12
148	Ricky Pierce	.12	.07
149	Brian Shaw	.10	.06
150	Reggie Williams	.10	.06
151	Kendall Gill	.25	.15
152	Tom Chambers	.12	.07
153	Jack Haley	.10	.06
154	Terrell Brandon	.15	.10
155	Dennis Scott	.15	.10
156	Mark Randall	.10	.06
157	Kenny Payne	.10	.06
158	Bernard King	.12	.07
159	Tate George	.10	.06
160	Scott Skiles	.10	.06
161	Pervis Ellison	.15	.10
162	Marcus Liberty	.12	.07
163	Rumeal Robinson	.12	.07
164	Anthony Mason	.25	.15
165	Les Jepsen	.10	.06
166	Kenny Smith	.12	.07
167	Randy White	.10	.06
168	Dee Brown	.25	.15
169	Chris Dudley	.10	.06
170	Armon Gilliam	.10	.06
171	Eddie Johnson	.10	.06
172	A.C. Green	.12	.07
173	Darrell Walker	.10	.06
174	Bill Cartwright	.10	.06
175	Mike Gminski	.10	.06
176	Tom Tolbert	.10	.06
177	Buck Williams	.12	.07
178	Mark Eaton	.10	.06
179	Danny Manning	.30	.18
180	Glen Rice	.20	.12
181	Sarunas Marciulionis	.15	.10
182	Danny Ferry	.10	.06
183	Chris Corchiani	.10	.06
184	Dan Majerle	.20	.12
185	Alvin Robertson	.10	.06
186	Vern Fleming	.10	.06
187	Kevin Lynch	.10	.06
188	John Williams	.10	.06
189	Checklist (1-100)	.10	.03
190	Checklist (101-200)	.10	.03
191	David Robinson (MC)	.50	.30
192	Larry Johnson (MC)	.60	.35
193	Derrick Coleman (MC)	.20	.12
194	Larry Bird (MC)	1.00	.60
195	Billy Owens (MC)	.20	.12
196	Dikembe Mutombo (MC)	.30	.18
197	Charles Barkley (MC)	.60	.35
198	Scottie Pippen (MC)	.35	.20
199	Clyde Drexler (MC)	.25	.15
200	John Stockton (MC)	.25	.15
201	Shaquille O'Neal (MC)	3.50	2.00
202	Chris Mullin (MC)	.25	.15
203	Glen Rice (MC)	.20	.12
204	Isiah Thomas (MC)	.25	.15
205	Karl Malone (MC)	.30	.18
206	Christian Laettner (MC)	.50	.30
207	Patrick Ewing (MC)	.50	.30
208	Dominique Wilkins (MC)	.30	.18
209	Alonzo Mourning (MC)	1.75	1.00
210	Michael Jordan (MC)	2.50	1.50
211	Tim Hardaway	.40	.25
212	Rodney McCray	.10	.06
213	Larry Johnson	1.50	.90
214	Charles Smith	.15	.10
215	Kevin Brooks	.10	.06
216	Kevin Johnson	.25	.15
217	Duane Cooper (R)	.25	.15
218	Christian Laettner (R)	1.75	1.00
219	Tim Perry	.10	.06
220	Hakeem Olajuwon	1.25	.70
221	Lee Mayberry (R)	.20	.12
222	Mark Bryant	.10	.06
223	Robert Horry (R)	1.50	.90
224	Tracy Murray (R)	.25	.15
225	Greg Grant	.10	.06
226	Rolando Blackman	.12	.07
227	James Edwards	.10	.06
228	Stan Green	.10	.06
229	Buck Johnson	.12	.07
230	Andrew Lang	.10	.06
231	Tracy Moore (R)	.12	.07
232	Adam Keefe (R)	.20	.12
233	Tony Campbell	.10	.06
234	Rod Strickland	.10	.06
235	Terry Mills	.20	.12
236	Billy Owens	.20	.12
237	Bryant Stith (R)	.40	.25
238	Tony Bennett (R)	.20	.12
239	David Wood	.10	.06
240	Jay Humphries	.10	.06
241	Doc Rivers	.12	.07

1992-93 TOPPS STADIUM CLUB • 189

242 Wayman Tisdale	.12	.07
243 Litterial Green (R)	.25	.15
244 Jon Barry (R)	.20	.12
245 Brad Daugherty	.25	.15
246 Nate McMillan	.12	.07
247 Shaquille O'Neal	12.00	7.00
248 Chris Smith (R)	.25	.15
249 Duane Ferrell	.10	.06
250 Anthony Peeler (R)	.75	.45
251 Gundars Vetra (R)	.12	.07
252 Danny Ainge	.15	.10
253 Mitch Richmond	.20	.12
254 Malik Sealy (R)	.20	.12
255 Brent Price (R)	.20	.12
256 Xavier McDaniel	.12	.07
257 Bobby Phills (R)	.20	.12
258 Donald Royal	.10	.06
259 Olden Polynice	.10	.06
260 Dominique Wilkins	.70	.40
261 Larry Krystkowiak	.10	.06
262 Duane Causwell	.10	.06
263 Todd Day (R)	.75	.45
264 Sam Mack (R)	.15	.10
265 John Stockton	.75	.45
266 Eddie Lee Wilkins	.10	.06
267 Gerald Glass	.10	.06
268 Robert Pack	.15	.10
269 Gerald Wilkins	.10	.06
270 Reggie Lewis	.30	.18
271 Scott Brooks	.10	.06
272 Randy Woods (R)	.15	.10
273 Dikembe Mutombo	.50	.30
274 Kiki Vandeweghe	.10	.06
275 Rich King	.10	.06
276 Jeff Turner	.10	.06
277 Vinny Del Negro	.10	.06
278 Marlon Maxey (R)	.20	.12
279 Elmore Spencer (R)	.25	.15
280 Cedric Ceballos	.15	.10
281 Alex Blackwell (R)	.12	.07
282 Terry Davis	.10	.06
283 Morton Wiley	.10	.06
284 Trent Tucker	.10	.06
285 Carl Herrera	.15	.10
286 Eric Anderson (R)	.20	.12
287 Clyde Drexler	.50	.30
288 Tom Gugliotta (R)	1.25	.70
289 Dale Ellis	.12	.07
290 Lance Blanks	.10	.06
291 Tom Hammonds	.10	.06
292 Eric Murdoch	.20	.12
293 Walt Williams (R)	.80	.50
294 Gerald Paddio	.10	.06
295 Brian Howard (R)	.15	.10
296 Ken Williams	.10	.06
297 Alonzo Mourning (R)	8.00	5.00
298 Larry Nance	.12	.07
299 Jeff Grayer	.10	.06
300 Dave Johnson (R)	.20	.12
301 Bob McCann (R)	.12	.07
302 Bart Kofoed	.10	.06
303 Anthony Cook	.10	.06
304 Radisav Curcic (R)	.12	.07
305 John Crotty (R)	.15	.10
306 Brad Sellers	.10	.06
307 Marcus Webb (R)	.12	.07
308 Winston Garland	.10	.06
309 Walter Palmer	.10	.06
310 Rod Higgins	.10	.06
311 Travis Mays	.10	.06
312 Alex Stivrins (R)	.12	.07
313 Greg Kite	.10	.06
314 Dennis Rodman	.15	.10
315 Mike Sanders	.10	.06
316 Ed Pinckney	.10	.06
317 Harold Miner (R)	1.00	.60
318 Pooh Richardson	.15	.10
319 Oliver Miller (R)	.60	.35
320 Latrell Sprewell (R)	3.50	2.00
321 Anthony Pullard (R)	.12	.07
322 Mark Randall	.10	.06
323 Jeff Hornacek	.15	.10
324 Rick Mahorn	.10	.06
325 Sean Rooks (R)	.30	.18
326 Paul Pressey	.10	.06
327 James Worthy	.25	.15
328 Matt Bullard	.10	.06
329 Reggie Smith (R)	.15	.10
330 Don MacLean (R)	.75	.45
331 John Williams	.10	.06
332 Frank Johnson	.10	.06
333 Hubert Davis (R)	.50	.30
334 Lloyd Daniels (R)	.25	.15
335 Steve Bardo (R)	.12	.07
336 Jeff Sanders	.10	.06
337 Tree Rollins	.10	.06
338 Micheal Williams	.10	.06
339 Lorenzo Williams (R)	.15	.10
340 Harvey Grant	.12	.07
341 Avery Johnson	.12	.07
342 Bo Kimble	.10	.06
343 LaPhonso Ellis (R)	1.75	1.00
344 Mookie Blaylock	.15	.10
345 Isaiah Morris (R)	.15	.10
346 C. Weatherspoon (R)	1.50	.90
347 Manute Bol	.10	.06
348 Victor Alexander	.10	.06
349 Corey Williams (R)	.15	.10
350 Byron Houston (R)	.20	.12
351 Stanley Roberts	.15	.10
352 Anthony Avent (R)	.25	.15
353 Vincent Askew	.10	.06
354 Herb Williams	.10	.06
355 J.R. Reid	.10	.06

190 • 1992-93 TOPPS STADIUM CLUB

356	Brad Lohaus	.10	.06
357	Reggie Miller	.30	.18
358	Blue Edwards	.12	.07
359	Tom Tolbert	.10	.06
360	Charles Barkley	1.00	.60
361	David Robinson	1.00	.60
362	Dale Davis	.15	.10
363	Robert Werdann (R)	.15	.10
364	Chuck Person	.15	.10
365	Alaa Abdelnaby	.10	.06
366	Dave Jamerson	.10	.06
367	Scottie Pippen	.60	.35
368	Mark Jackson	.15	.10
369	Keith Askins	.10	.06
370	Marty Conlon	.10	.06
371	Chucky Brown	.12	.07
372	LaBradford Smith	.12	.07
373	Tim Kempton	.10	.06
374	Sam Mitchell	.12	.07
375	John Salley	.10	.06
376	Mario Elie	.10	.06
377	Mark West	.10	.06
378	David Wingate	.10	.06
379	Jaren Jackson (R)	.15	.10
380	Rumeal Robinson	.12	.07
381	Ken Winchester	.10	.06
382	Walter Bond (R)	.12	.07
383	Isaac Austin (R)	.15	.10
384	Derrick Coleman	.25	.15
385	Larry Smith	.10	.06
386	Joe Dumars	.25	.15
387	Matt Geiger (R)	.25	.15
388	Stephen Howard (R)	.12	.07
389	William Bedford	.10	.06
390	Jayson Williams	.10	.06
391	Kurt Rambis	.10	.06
392	Keith Jennings (R)	.20	.12
393	Steve Kerr	.10	.06
394	Larry Stewart	.12	.07
395	Danny Young	.10	.06
396	Doug Overton	.10	.06
397	Mark Acres	.10	.06
398	John Bagley	.10	.06
399	Checklist (201-300)	.10	.03
400	Checklist (301-400)	.10	.03

1992-93 Topps Stadium Club Beam Team

The cards in this limited insert set were randomly distributed in Stadium Club Series II foil packs. The card fronts contain full color, full bleed game action player photos with laser light streaks surrounding the edges on the cards. The player's name appears in a horizontal bar centered at the bottom of the card front and the words "Beam Team" are printed in the top corner. The flip side consists of another close up photo, the player's name, team and position and a brief biography. All cards measure 2-1/2" by 3-1/2".

		MINT	NR/MT
Complete Set (21)		275.00	160.00
Commons		3.00	1.75
1	Michael Jordan	80.00	50.00
2	Dominique Wilkins	10.00	6.50
3	Shawn Kemp	18.00	12.00
4	Clyde Drexler	8.00	5.00
5	Scottie Pippen	15.00	10.00
6	Chris Mullin	7.00	4.00
7	Reggie Miller	5.00	3.00
8	Glen Rice	3.00	1.75
9	Jeff Hornacek	3.00	1.75
10	Jeff Malone	3.00	1.75
11	John Stockton	8.00	5.00
12	Kevin Johnson	3.50	2.00

13	Mark Price	3.50	2.00
14	Tim Hardaway	5.00	3.00
15	Charles Barkley	20.00	12.50
16	Hakeem Olajuwon	25.00	15.00
17	Karl Malone	10.00	6.50
18	Patrick Ewing	15.00	10.00
19	Dennis Rodman	3.50	2.00
20	David Robinson	20.00	12.50
21	Shaquille O'Neal	125.00	70.00

1993-94 Topps

The cards in this set feature full-color action photos on the fronts framed by a white border. An inner frame line that corresponds to the player's team color runs along the side of his photo and curves under the picture. The player's name appears in script to the side of his photo near the bottom. The team nickname ps printed in a color bar in the lower right corner of the card opposite the player's position. The flip side contains a smaller full-color action shot along with personal data, stats and a brief career highlight. Key subsets include Highlights (HL)(1-5), 50 Point Club (50 pt), All-Stars (AS), All-Rookie Team (ART), Finals MVP Threat (Th)(199-209) and Scoring Leader Threats (Th)(384-394). Gold versions of each card in the set were produced and inserted one per Topps pack. Those cards are valued at 2X to 5X times the prices listed below. All cards measure 2-1/2" by 3-1/2".

		MINT	NR/MT
Complete Set (396)		20.00	12.50
Commons		.05	.02
Complete Set (Gold)		80.00	48.00
Commons (Gold)		.10	.06

1	Charles Barkley (HL)	.25	.15
2	Hakeem Olajuwon (HL)	.40	.25
3	Shaquille O'Neal (HL)	.75	.45
4	Chris Jackson (HL)	.07	.04
5	Cliff Robinson (HL)	.07	.04
6	Donald Hodge	.05	.02
7	Victor Alexander	.05	.02
8	Chris Morris	.05	.02
9	Muggsy Bogues	.05	.02
10	Steve Smith	.12	.07
11	Dave Johnson	.05	.02
12	Tom Gugliotta	.20	.12
13	Doug Edwards (R)	.12	.07
14	Vlade Divac	.08	.05
15	Corie Blount (R)	.10	.06
16	Derek Harper	.05	.02
17	Mark Bullard	.05	.02
18	Terry Catledge	.05	.02
19	Mark Eaton	.05	.02
20	Mark Jackson	.08	.05
21	Terry Mills	.10	.06
22	Johnny Dawkins	.05	.02
23	Michael Jordan	1.50	.90
24	Rick Fox	.08	.05
25	Charles Oakley	.08	.05
26	Derrick McKey	.07	.04
27	Christian Laettner	.20	.12
28	Todd Day	.10	.06
29	Danny Ferry	.05	.02
30	Kevin Johnson	.12	.07
31	Vinny Del Negro	.05	.02
32	Kevin Brooks	.05	.02
33	Pete Chilcutt	.05	.02
34	Larry Stewart	.05	.02
35	Dave Jamerson	.05	.02
36	Sidney Green	.05	.02
37	J.R. Reid	.05	.02
38	Jimmy Jackson	.25	.15
39	Michael Williams	.05	.02
40	Rex Walters (R)	.10	.06
41	Shawn Bradley (R)	.30	.18
42	Jon Koncak	.05	.02
43	Byron Houston	.08	.05
44	Brian Shaw	.05	.02
45	Bill Cartwright	.05	.02

192 • 1993-94 TOPPS

#	Player		
46	Jerome Kersey	.05	.02
47	Danny Schayes	.05	.02
48	Olden Polynice	.05	.02
49	Anthony Peeler	.10	.06
50	Nick Anderson (50 pt)	.08	.05
51	David Benoit	.05	.02
52	David Robinson (50 pt)	.20	.12
53	Greg Kite	.05	.02
54	Gerald Paddio	.05	.02
55	Don MacLean	.15	.10
56	Randy Woods	.05	.02
57	Reggie Miller (50 pt)	.12	.07
58	Kevin Gamble	.05	.02
59	Sean Green	.05	.02
60	Jeff Hornacek	.07	.04
61	John Starks	.15	.10
62	Gerald Wilkins	.05	.02
63	Jim Les	.05	.02
64	Michael Jordan (50 pt)	.75	.45
65	Alvin Robertson	.05	.02
66	Tim Kempton	.05	.02
67	Bryant Stith	.10	.06
68	Jeff Turner	.05	.02
69	Malik Sealy	.07	.04
70	Dell Curry	.05	.02
71	Brent Price	.07	.04
72	Kevin Lynch	.05	.02
73	Bimbo Coles	.05	.02
74	Larry Nance	.05	.02
75	Luther Wright (R)	.12	.07
76	Willie Anderson	.05	.02
77	Dennis Rodman	.10	.06
78	Anthony Mason	.08	.05
79	Chris Gatling	.05	.02
80	Antoine Carr	.05	.02
81	Kevin Willis	.05	.02
82	Thurl Bailey	.05	.02
83	Reggie Williams	.07	.04
84	Rod Strickland	.05	.02
85	Rolando Blackman	.05	.02
86	Bobby Hurley (R)	.25	.15
87	Jeff Malone	.05	.02
88	James Worthy	.10	.06
89	Alaa Abdelnaby	.05	.02
90	Duane Ferrell	.05	.02
91	Anthony Avent	.08	.05
92	Scottie Pippen	.30	.18
93	Ricky Pierce	.05	.02
94	P.J. Brown (R)	.12	.07
95	Jeff Grayer	.05	.02
96	Jerrod Mustaf	.05	.02
97	Elmore Spencer	.08	.05
98	Walt Williams	.15	.10
99	Otis Thorpe	.08	.05
100	Patrick Ewing (AS)	.15	.10
101	Michael Jordan (AS)	.75	.45
102	John Stockton (AS)	.10	.06
103	Dominique Wilkins (AS)	.10	.06
104	Charles Barkley (AS)	.20	.12
105	Lee Mayberry	.07	.04
106	James Edwards	.05	.02
107	Scott Brooks	.05	.02
108	John Battle	.05	.02
109	Kenny Gattison	.05	.02
110	Pooh Richardson	.07	.04
111	Rony Seikaly	.08	.05
112	Mahmoud Abdul-Rauf	.12	.07
113	Nick Anderson	.10	.06
114	Gundars Vetra	.05	.02
115	Joe Dumars (AS)	.10	.06
116	Hakeem Olajuwon (AS)	.40	.25
117	Scottie Pippen (AS)	.12	.07
118	Mark Price (AS)	.08	.05
119	Karl Malone (AS)	.12	.07
120	Michael Cage	.05	.02
121	Ed Pinckney	.05	.02
122	Jay Humphries	.05	.02
123	Dale Davis	.12	.07
124	Sean Rooks	.08	.05
125	Mookie Blaylock	.08	.05
126	Buck Williams	.07	.04
127	John Williams	.07	.04
128	Stacey King	.05	.02
129	Tim Perry	.05	.02
130	Tim Hardaway (AS)	.08	.05
131	Larry Johnson (AS)	.15	.10
132	Detlef Schrempf (AS)	.08	.05
133	Reggie Miller (AS)	.10	.06
134	Shaquille O'Neal (AS)	.75	.45
135	Dale Ellis	.05	.02
136	Duane Causwell	.05	.02
137	Rumeal Robinson	.05	.02
138	Billy Owens	.12	.07
139	Malcolm Mackey (R)	.10	.06
140	Vernon Maxwell	.10	.06
141	LaPhonso Ellis	.15	.10
142	Robert Parish	.10	.06
143	LaBradford Smith	.05	.02
144	Charles Smith	.08	.05
145	Terry Porter	.08	.05
146	Elden Campbell	.08	.05
147	Bill Laimbeer	.07	.04
148	Chris Mills (R)	.30	.18
149	Brad Lohaus	.05	.02
150	Jimmy Jackson (AR)	.15	.10
151	Tom Gugliotta (AR)	.15	.10
152	Shaquille O'Neal (AR)	.75	.45
153	Latrell Sprewell (AR)	.25	.15
154	Walt Williams (AR)	.10	.06
155	Gary Payton	.12	.07
156	Orlando Woolridge	.05	.02
157	Adam Keefe	.07	.04
158	Calbert Cheaney (R)	.25	.15
159	Rick Mahorn	.05	.02

1993-94 TOPPS • 193

#	Player		
160	Robert Horry	.20	.12
161	John Salley	.05	.02
162	Sam Mitchell	.07	.04
163	Stanley Roberts	.07	.04
164	Clarence Weatherspoon	.15	.10
165	Anthony Bowie	.05	.02
166	Derrick Coleman	.15	.10
167	Negele Knight	.05	.02
168	Marlon Maxey	.05	.02
169	Spud Webb	.05	.02
170	Alonzo Mourning	.60	.35
171	Kevin Johnson	.12	.07
172	Sedale Threatt	.05	.02
173	Mark Macon	.07	.04
174	B.J. Armstrong	.12	.07
175	Harold Miner (AR)	.08	.05
176	Anthony Peeler (AR)	.08	.05
177	Alonzo Mourning (AR)	.35	.20
178	Christian Laettner (AR)	.15	.10
179	C. Weatherspoon(AR)	.15	.10
180	Dee Brown	.08	.05
181	Shaquille O'Neal	1.50	.90
182	Loy Vaught	.05	.02
183	Terrell Brandon	.08	.05
184	Lionel Simmons	.15	.10
185	Mark Aquirre	.07	.04
186	Danny Ainge	.08	.05
187	Reggie Miller	.15	.10
188	Terry Davis	.05	.02
189	Mark Bryant	.05	.02
190	Tyrone Corbin	.07	.04
191	Chris Mullin	.15	.10
192	Johnny Newman	.05	.02
193	Doug West	.07	.04
194	Keith Askins	.05	.02
195	Bo Kimble	.05	.02
196	Sean Elliott	.10	.06
197	Checklist (1-99)	.05	.02
198	Checklist (100-198)	.05	.02
199	Michael Jordan (MVP)	.75	.45
200	Patrick Ewing (Th)	.15	.10
201	John Stockton (Th)	.12	.07
202	Shawn Kemp (Th)	.20	.12
203	Mark Price (Th)	.10	.06
204	Charles Barkley (Th)	.25	.15
205	Hakeem Olajuwon (Th)	.40	.25
206	Clyde Drexler (Th)	.12	.07
207	Kevin Johnson (Th)	.08	.05
208	John Starks (Th)	.10	.06
209	Chris Mullin (Th)	.12	.07
210	Doc Rivers	.05	.02
211	Kenny Walker	.05	.02
212	Doug Christie	.15	.10
213	James Robinson (R)	.15	.10
214	Larry Krystkowiak	.05	.02
215	Manute Bol	.05	.02
216	Carl Herrera	.12	.07
217	Paul Graham	.05	.02
218	Jud Buechler	.05	.02
219	Mike Brown	.05	.02
220	Tom Chambers	.07	.04
221	Kendall Gill	.12	.07
222	Kenny Anderson	.15	.10
223	Larry Johnson	.40	.25
224	Chris Webber (R)	2.50	1.50
225	Randy White	.05	.02
226	Rik Smits	.05	.02
227	A.C. Green	.07	.04
228	David Robinson	.40	.25
229	Sean Elliott	.12	.07
230	Gary Grant	.05	.02
231	Dana Barros	.05	.02
232	Bobby Hurley	.20	.12
233	Blue Edwards	.05	.02
234	Tom Hammonds	.05	.02
235	Pete Myers	.05	.02
236	Acie Earl (R)	.12	.07
237	Tony Smith	.05	.02
238	Bill Wennington	.05	.02
239	Andrew Lang	.05	.02
240	Ervin Johnson (R)	.10	.06
241	Byron Scott	.05	.02
242	Eddie Johnson	.05	.02
243	Anthony Bonner	.05	.02
244	Luther Wright	.10	.06
245	LaSalle Thompson	.05	.02
246	Harold Miner	.20	.12
247	Chris Smith	.08	.05
248	John Williams	.05	.02
249	Clyde Drexler	.20	.12
250	Calbert Cheaney	.20	.12
251	Avery Johnson	.05	.02
252	Steve Kerr	.05	.02
253	Warren Kidd (R)	.10	.06
254	Wayman Tisdale	.07	.04
255	Bob Martin (R)	.08	.05
256	Popeye Jones (R)	.15	.10
257	Jimmy Oliver	.05	.02
258	Kevin Edwards	.05	.02
259	Dan Majerle	.12	.07
260	Jon Barry	.07	.04
261	Allan Houston (R0	.15	.10
262	Dikembe Mutombo	.20	.12
263	Sleepy Floyd	.05	.02
264	George Lynch (R)	.25	.15
265	Stacey Augmon	.15	.10
266	Hakeem Olajuwon	.75	.45
267	Scott Skiles	.05	.02
268	Detlef Schrempf	.12	.07
269	Brian Davis (R)	.10	.06
270	Tracy Murray	.10	.06
271	Gheorghe Muresan (R)	.10	.06
272	Terry Dehere (R)	.12	.07
273	Terry Cummings	.07	.04

#	Player		
274	Keith Jennings	.05	.02
275	Tyrone Hill	.05	.02
276	Hersey Hawkins	.07	.04
277	Grant Long	.05	.02
278	Herb Williams	.05	.02
279	Karl Malone	.25	.15
280	Mitch Richmond	.15	.10
281	Derek Strong (R)	.12	.07
282	Dino Radja (R)	.25	.15
283	Jack Haley	.05	.02
284	Derek Harper	.07	.04
285	Dwayne Schintzius	.05	.02
286	Michael Curry	.05	.02
287	Rodney Rogers (R)	.25	.15
288	Horace Grant	.07	.04
289	Oliver Miller	.12	.07
290	Luc Longley	.05	.02
291	Walter Bond	.05	.02
292	Dominique Wilkins	.25	.15
293	Vern Fleming	.05	.02
294	Mark Price	.12	.07
295	Mark Aquirre	.07	.04
296	Shawn Kemp	.30	.18
297	Pervis Ellison	.10	.06
298	Josh Grant (R)	.12	.07
299	Scott Burrell (R)	.15	.10
300	Patrick Ewing	.25	.15
301	Sam Cassell (R)	.40	.25
302	Nick Van Exel (R)	.30	.18
303	Cliff Robinson	.10	.06
304	Frank Johnson	.05	.02
305	Matt Geiger	.05	.02
306	Vin Baker (R)	.60	.35
307	Benoit Benjamin	.05	.02
308	Shawn Bradley	.20	.12
309	Chris Whitney	.05	.02
310	Eric Riley (R)	.10	.06
311	Isiah Thomas	.20	.12
312	Jamal Mashburn (R)	1.00	.60
313	Xavier McDaniel	.05	.02
314	Mike Peplowski (R)	.10	.06
315	Darnell Mee (R)	.10	.06
316	Toni Kukoc (R)	.35	.20
317	Felton Spencer	.10	.06
318	Sam Bowie	.05	.02
319	Mario Elie	.05	.02
320	Tim Hardaway	.12	.07
321	Ken Norman	.07	.04
322	Isaiah Rider (R)	1.00	.60
323	Rex Chapman	.05	.02
324	Dennis Rodman	.10	.06
325	Derrick McKey	.07	.04
326	Corie Blount	.08	.05
327	Fat Lever	.05	.02
328	Ron Harper	.07	.04
329	Eric Anderson	.05	.02
330	Armon Gilliam	.07	.04
331	Lindsey Hunter (R)	.25	.15
332	Eric Leckner	.05	.02
333	Chris Corchiani	.05	.02
334	Anfernee Hardaway (R)	2.00	1.25
335	Randy Brown	.05	.02
336	Sam Perkins	.07	.04
337	Glen Rice	.07	.04
338	Orlando Woolridge	.05	.02
339	Mike Gminski	.05	.02
340	Latrell Sprewell	.60	.35
341	Harvey Grant	.05	.02
342	Doug Smith	.05	.02
343	Kevin Duckworth	.05	.02
344	Cedric Ceballos	.10	.06
345	Chuck Person	.08	.05
346	Scott Haskin (R)	.10	.06
347	Frank Brickowski	.05	.02
348	Scott Williams	.05	.02
349	Brad Daugherty	.12	.07
350	Willie Burton	.07	.04
351	Joe Dumars	.15	.10
352	Craig Ehlo	.05	.02
353	Lucious Harris (R)	.10	.06
354	Danny Manning	.20	.12
355	Latterial Green	.05	.02
356	John Stockton	.25	.15
357	Nate McMillan	.05	.02
358	Greg Graham (R)	.10	.06
359	Rex Walters	.08	.05
360	Lloyd Daniels	.08	.05
361	Antonio Harvey (R)	.12	.07
362	Brian Williams	.15	.10
363	LeRon Ellis	.10	.06
364	Chris Dudley	.05	.02
365	Hubert Davis	.15	.10
366	Evers Burns (R)	.10	.06
367	Sherman Douglas	.05	.02
368	Sarunas Marciulionis	.07	.04
369	Tom Tolbert	.05	.02
370	Robert Pack	.07	.04
371	Michael Adams	.07	.04
372	Negele Knight	.05	.02
373	Charles Barkley	.40	.25
374	Byron Russell (R)	.12	.07
375	Greg Anthony	.08	.05
376	Ken Williams	.05	.02
377	John Paxson	.07	.04
378	Corey Gaines	.05	.02
379	Eric Murdock	.07	.04
380	Kevin Thompson (R)	.08	.05
381	Moses Malone	.12	.07
382	Kenny Smith	.07	.04
383	Dennis Scott	.08	.05
384	Michael Jordan (LL)	.75	.45
385	Hakeem Olajuwon (Th)	.30	.18
386	Shaquille O'Neal (Th)	.75	.45
387	David Robinson (Th)	.20	.12

388	Derrick Coleman (Th)	.12	.07
389	Karl Malone (Th)	.15	.10
390	Patrick Ewing (Th)	.20	.12
391	Scottie Pippen (Th)	.15	.10
392	Dominique Wilkins (Th)	.15	.10
393	Charles Barkley (Th)	.25	.15
394	Larry Johnson (Th)	.20	.12
395	Checklist	.05	.02
396	Checklist	.05	.02

1993-94 Topps Black Gold

The cards in this limited insert set were randomly distributed in 1993-'94 Topps Series I and Series II packs. The card fronts feature an isolate full-color action shot of the player over a dark background and framed by a white border. Gold swirls appear above and below the player's picture while the player's name is printed across a small horizontal box under his photograph. All cards measure 2-1/2" by 3-1/2".

		MINT	NR/MT
	Complete Set (25)	24.00	14.00
	Commons	.30	.18
1	Sean Elliott	.40	.25
2	Glen Rice	.40	.25
3	Kenny Anderson	.80	.50
4	Alonzo Mourning	4.00	2.50
5	Mahmoud Abdul-Rauf	.50	.30
6	Dennis Scott	.40	.25
7	Jim Jackson	1.50	.90
8	Derrick Coleman	.80	.50
9	Larry Johnson	2.00	1.25
10	Billy Owens	.60	.35
11	Christian Laettner	.75	.45
12	Gary Payton	.50	.30
13	Dikembe Mutombo	1.00	.60
14	Isaiah Rider	3.00	1.75
15	Steve Smith	1.00	.60
16	LaPhonso Ellis	.80	.50
17	Danny Ferry	.30	.18
18	Shaquille O'Neal	8.00	5.00
19	Anfernee Hardaway	7.00	4.00
20	J. R. Reid	.30	.18
21	Shawn Bradley	1.00	.60
22	Pervis Ellison	.30	.18
23	Chris Webber	8.00	5.00
24	Jamal Mashburn	3.50	2.00
25	Kendall Gill	.50	.30

1993-94 Topps Finest

This limited upscale set marks the first Basketball edition produced by Topps under the Finest banner. The card fronts feature full-color action shots with foil stamping and colorful borders. The player's name is printed in a horizontal bar above

1993-94 TOPPS FINEST

his photo while a stamped Topps Finest logo is printed under his picture. Subsets include Tribute cards for ichael Jordan and Larry Bird (1-2) plus each division's finest players, Atlantic (AF)(90-99), Central (CF)(100-109), Midwest (MF)(110-119) and Pacific (PF)(120-129). Topps also produced a parallel 220-card limited insert set called Finest Refractors. These limited inserts were randomly distributed in Topps Finest packs. The values for the Refractor inserts range from 8X to 10X the values listed below for major superstars to 3X to 6X for commons to semi-stars. All cards measure 2-1/2" by 3-1/2".

	MINT	NR/MT
Complete Set (220)	175.00	100.00
Commons	.35	.20
Refractors Set (220)	2,200.00	1,250.00
Commons (Refractors)	2.00	1.25

#	Player	MINT	NR/MT
1	Michael Jordan (Trib)	30.00	18.00
2	Larry Bird (Trib)	12.00	7.00
3	Shaquille O'Neal	25.00	15.00
4	Benoit Benjamin	.35	.20
5	Ricky Pierce	.35	.20
6	Ken Norman	.35	.20
7	Victor Alexander	.40	.25
8	Mark Jackson	.40	.25
9	Mark West	.35	.20
10	Don MacLean	.75	.45
11	Reggie Miller	1.75	1.00
12	Sarunas Marciulionis	.35	.20
13	Craig Ehlo	.35	.20
14	Toni Kukoc (R)	3.00	1.75
15	Glen Rice	.60	.35
16	Otis Thorpe	.40	.25
17	Reggie Williams	.35	.20
18	Charles Smith	.40	.25
19	Michael Williams	.35	.20
20	Tom Chambers	.40	.25
21	David Robinson	8.50	5.00
22	Jamal Mashburn (R)	7.50	4.50
23	Cliff Robinson	.60	.35
24	Acie Earl (R)	.80	.50
25	Danny Ferry	.35	.20
26	Bobby Hurley (R)	3.00	1.75
27	Eddie Johnson	.35	.20
28	Detlef Schrempf	.60	.35
29	Mike Brown	.35	.20
30	Latrell Sprewell	7.00	4.00
31	Derek Harper	.40	.25
32	Stacey Augmon	.75	.45
33	Pooh Richardson	.40	.25
34	Larry Krystkowiak	.35	.20
35	Pervis Ellison	.50	.30
36	Jeff Malone	.35	.20
37	Sean Elliott	.60	.35
38	John Paxson	.40	.25
39	Robert Parish	.75	.45
40	Mark Aquirre	.40	.25
41	Danny Ainge	.60	.35
42	Brian Shaw	.35	.20
43	LaPhonso Ellis	2.00	1.25
44	Carl Herrera	.60	.35
45	Terry Cummings	.40	.25
46	Chris Dudley	.35	.20
47	Anthony Mason	.60	.35
48	Chris Morris	.35	.20
49	Todd Day	.80	.50
50	Nick Van Exel (R)	1.75	1.00
51	Larry Nance	.40	.25
52	Derrick McKey	.40	.25
53	Muggsy Bogues	.35	.20
54	Andrew Lang	.35	.20
55	Chuck Person	.50	.30
56	Michael Adams	.40	.25
57	Spud Webb	.35	.20
58	Scott Skiles	.35	.20
59	A.C. Green	.50	.30
60	Terry Mills	.90	.60
61	Xavier McDaniel	.35	.20
62	B. J. Armstrong	.80	.50
63	Donald Hodge	.35	.20
64	Gary Grant	.35	.20
65	Billy Owens	.75	.45
66	Greg Anthony	.40	.25
67	Jay Humphries	.35	.20
68	Lionel Simmons	1.00	.60
69	Dana Barros	.35	.20
70	Steve Smith	1.50	.90
71	Ervin Johnson (R)	.90	.60
72	Sleepy Floyd	.35	.20
73	Blue Edwards	.35	.20
74	Clyde Drexler	3.00	1.75
75	Elden Campbell	.50	.30
76	Hakeem Olajuwon	10.00	6.50
77	C. Weatherspoon	2.00	1.25
78	Kevin Willis	.35	.20
79	Isaiah Rider (R)	8.00	5.00
80	Derrick Coleman	2.50	1.50
81	Nick Anderson	.80	.50
82	Bryant Stith	.75	.45
83	Johnny Newman	.35	.20
84	Calbert Cheaney (R)	2.00	1.25
85	Oliver Miller	1.00	.60
86	Loy Vaught	.35	.20
87	Isiah Thomas	3.00	1.75
88	Dee Brown	.60	.35
89	Horace Grant	.35	.20
90	Patrick Ewing (AF)	3.50	2.00

1993-94 TOPPS FINEST • 197

#	Player		
91	C. Weatherspoon (AF)	1.00	.60
92	Rony Seikaly (AF)	.40	.25
93	Dino Radja (AF)	1.00	.60
94	Kenny Anderson (AF)	1.00	.60
95	John Starks (AF)	.80	.50
96	Tom Gugliotta (AF)	1.00	.60
97	Steve Smith (AF)	1.00	.60
98	Derrick Coleman (AF)	1.25	.70
99	Shaquille O'Neal (AF)	12.00	7.00
100	Brad Daugherty (CF)	.80	.50
101	Horace Grant (CF)	.50	.30
102	Dominique Wilkins (CF)	2.00	1.25
103	Joe Dumars (CF)	.80	.50
104	Alonzo Mourning (CF)	7.00	4.00
105	Scottie Pippen (CF)	3.50	2.00
106	Reggie Miller (CF)	2.50	1.50
107	Mark Price (CF)	.80	.50
108	Ken Norman (CF)	.40	.25
109	Larry Johnson (CF)	3.50	2.00
110	Jamal Mashburn (MF)	3.00	1.75
111	Christian Laettner (MF)	1.25	.70
112	Karl Malone (MF)	2.00	1.25
113	Dennis Rodman (MF)	.75	.45
114	Mahmoud AbdulRaul (MF)	.75	.45
115	Hakeem Olajuwon (MF)	7.00	4.00
116	Jim Jackson (MF)	2.00	1.25
117	John Stockton (MF)	1.75	1.00
118	David Robinson (MF)	4.00	2.50
119	Dikembe Mutombo (MF)	2.00	1.25
120	Vlade Divac (PF)	.40	.25
121	Dan Majerle (PF)	.60	.35
122	Chris Mullin (PF)	1.25	.70
123	Shawn Kemp (PF)	3.50	2.00
124	Danny Manning (PF)	1.25	.70
125	Charles Barkley (PF)	4.00	2.50
126	Mitch Richmond (PF)	.80	.50
127	Tim Hardaway (PF)	.75	.45
128	Detlef Schrempf (PF)	.60	.35
129	Clyde Drexler (PF)	1.75	1.00
130	Christian Laettner	2.50	1.50
131	Rodney Rogers (R)	1.25	.70
132	Rik Smits	.35	.20
133	Chris Mills (R)	2.00	1.25
134	Corie Blount (R)	.80	.50
135	Mookie Blaylock	.50	.30
136	Jim Jackson	3.50	2.00
137	Tom Gugliotta	1.75	1.00
138	Dennis Scott	.60	.35
139	Vin Baker (R)	4.00	2.50
140	Gary Payton	.75	.45
141	Sedale Threatt	.35	.20
142	Orlando Woolridge	.35	.20
143	Avery Johnson	.35	.20
144	Charles Oakley	.50	.30
145	Harvey Grant	.35	.20
146	Bimbo Coles	.35	.20
147	Vernon Maxwell	.50	.30
148	Danny Manning	2.00	1.25
149	Hersey Hawkins	.40	.25
150	Kevin Gamble	.35	.20
151	Johnny Dawkins	.35	.20
152	Olden Polynice	.35	.20
153	Kevin Edwards	.35	.20
154	Willie Anderson	.35	.20
155	Wayman Tisdale	.40	.25
156	Popeye Jones (R)	1.00	.60
157	Dan Majerle	1.25	.70
158	Rex Chapman	.35	.20
159	Shawn Kemp	6.00	3.75
160	Eric Murdock	.40	.25
161	Randy White	.35	.20
162	Larry Johnson	7.00	4.00
163	Dominique Wilkins	3.50	2.00
164	Dikembe Mutombo	2.50	1.50
165	Patrick Ewing	7.00	4.00
166	Jerome Kersey	.35	.20
167	Dale Davis	.80	.50
168	Ron Harper	.40	.25
169	Sam Cassell (R)	3.00	1.75
170	Bill Cartwright	.35	.20
171	John Williams	.35	.20
172	Dino Radja (R)	2.00	1.25
173	Dennis Rodman	.80	.50
174	Kenny Anderson	2.00	1.25
175	Robert Horry	1.50	.90
176	Chris Mullin	3.00	1.75
177	John Salley	.35	.20
178	Scott Burrell (R)	1.00	.60
179	Mitch Richmond	1.00	.60
180	Lee Mayberry	.40	.25
181	James Worthy	.40	.25
182	Rick Fox	.40	.25
183	Kevin Johnson	.80	.50
184	Lindsey Hunter (R)	1.75	1.00
185	Marlon Maxey	.35	.20
186	Sam Perkins	.40	.25
187	Kevin Duckworth	.35	.20
188	Jeff Hornacek	.40	.25
189	Anfernee Hardaway (R)	15.00	10.00
190	Rex Walters (R)	.80	.50
191	Mahmoud Abdul-Rauf	1.50	.90
192	Terry Dehere (R)	.80	.50
193	Brad Daugherty	.75	.45
194	John Starks	2.00	1.25
195	Rod Strickland	.35	.20
196	Luther Wright (R)	1.50	.90
197	Vlade Divac	.50	.30
198	Tim Hardaway	1.25	.70
199	Joe Dumars	1.25	.70
200	Charles Barkley	8.50	5.00
201	Alonzo Mourning	10.00	6.50

1993-94 TOPPS FINEST

202	Doug West	.40	.25
203	Anthony Avent	.40	.25
204	Lloyd Daniels	.40	.25
205	Mark Price	1.25	.70
206	Rumeal Robinson	.35	.20
207	Kendall Gill	.80	.50
208	Scottie Pippen	6.00	3.75
209	Kenny Smith	.40	.25
210	Walt Williams	1.25	.70
211	Hubert Davis	1.00	.60
212	Chris Webber	20.00	12.50
213	Rony Seikaly	.40	.25
214	Sam Bowie	.35	.20
215	Karl Malone	3.50	2.00
216	Malik Sealy	.40	.25
217	Dale Ellis	.35	.20
218	Harold Miner	1.25	.70
219	John Stockton	3.00	1.75
220	Shawn Bradley (R)	2.00	1.25

7	Mahmoud Abdul-Rauf	3.00	1.75
8	Joe Dumars	4.00	2.50
9	Chris Webber	40.00	25.00
10	Hakeem Olajuwon	20.00	12.50
11	Reggie Miller	4.00	2.50
12	Danny Manning	4.00	2.50
13	Doug Christie	3.00	1.75
14	Steve Smith	4.00	2.50
15	Eric Murdock	3.00	1.75
16	Isaiah Rider	15.00	10.00
17	Derrick Coleman	5.00	3.00
18	Patrick Ewing	10.00	6.50
19	Shaquille O'Neal	48.00	28.00
20	Shawn Bradley	4.00	2.50
21	Charles Barkely	12.50	7.50
22	Clyde Drexler	6.00	3.50
23	Mitch Richmond	3.50	2.00
24	David Robinson	12.50	7.50
25	Shawn Kemp	10.00	6.50
26	Karl Malone	7.50	4.50
27	Tom Gugliotta	4.00	2.50

1993-94 Topps Finest Main Attraction

These limited insert cards were distributed one per Topps Finest jumbo pack. Th ecard fronts feature full-color action shots and foil stamping. The player's photo is superimposed over a colorful foil-typ[e background while his name appears in a box under his picture. A Main Attraction logo is printed in block type in the upper corner of the card. All cards measure 2-1/2" by 3-1/2".

	MINT	NR/MT
Complete Set (27)	160.00	95.00
Commons	3.00	1.75

1	Dominique Wilkins	7.00	4.00
2	Dino Radja	4.00	2.50
3	Larry Johnson	10.00	6.50
4	Scottie Pippen	8.00	5.00
5	Mark Price	3.00	1.75
6	Jamal Mashburn	12.50	7.50

1993-94 Topps Stadium Club

The cards in this set feature full-bleed, full -color game action photos on the card fronts with a gold Stadium Club logo in the top corner and the player's name printed in white and gold lettering and stacked in the lower portion of the card.

1993-94 TOPPS STADIUM CLUB • 199

Two white and gold wavy lines lead into the player's name. Th ecard backs contain another full-color player shot on half the card along with vital information including personal data, stats and brief highlights. Key subsets include Triple-Doubles (TD)(1-11,101-111), High Court (HC)(60-69, 170-178), Frequent Flyers (FF)(181-190, 348-358) and New Wave (NW)(265-276). All cards measure 2-1/2" by 3-1/2".

		MINT	NR/MT
	Complete Set (360)	50.00	32.00
	Commons	.10	.06
1	Michael Jordan (TD)	1.50	.90
2	Kenny Anderson (TD)	.15	.10
3	Steve Smith (TD)	.15	.10
4	Kevin Gamble (TD)	.10	.06
5	Detlef Schrempf (TD)	.12	.07
6	Larry Johnson (TD)	.25	.15
7	Brad Daugherty (TD)	.12	.07
8	Rumeal Robinson (TD)	.10	.06
9	Michael Williams (TD)	.10	.06
10	David Robinson (TD)	.40	.25
11	Sam Perkins (TD)	.10	.06
12	Thurl Bailey	.10	.06
13	Sherman Douglas	.10	.06
14	Larry Stewart	.10	.06
15	Kevin Johnson	.20	.12
16	Bill Cartwright	.10	.06
17	Larry Nance	.12	.07
18	P.J. Brown (R)	.20	.12
19	Tony Bennett	.10	.06
20	Robert Parish	.15	.10
21	David Benoit	.10	.06
22	Detlef Schrempf	.15	.10
23	Hubert Davis	.20	.12
24	Donald Hodge	.10	.06
25	Hersey Hawkins	.12	.07
26	Mark Jackson	.12	.07
27	Reggie Williams	.12	.07
28	Lionel Simmons	.20	.12
29	Ron Harper	.12	.07
30	Chris Mills (R)	.35	.20
31	Danny Schayes	.10	.06
32	J.R. Reid	.10	.06
33	Willie Burton	.12	.07
34	Greg Anthony	.12	.07
35	Elden Campbell	.15	.10
36	Ervin Johnson (R)	.15	.10
37	Scott Brooks	.10	.06
38	Johnny Newman	.10	.06
39	Rex Chapman	.10	.06
40	Chuck Person	.12	.07
41	John Williams	.10	.06
42	Anthony Bowie	.10	.06
43	Negele Knight	.10	.06
44	Tyrone Corbin	.12	.07
45	Jud Buechler	.10	.06
46	Adam Keefe	.12	.07
47	Glen Rice	.15	.10
48	Tracy Murray	.12	.07
49	Rick Mahorn	.10	.06
50	Vlade Divac	.15	.10
51	Eric Murdock	.12	.07
52	Isaiah Morris	.10	.06
53	Bobby Hurley (R)	.60	.35
54	Mitch Richmond	.15	.10
55	Danny Ainge	.15	.10
56	Dikembe Mutombo	.25	.15
57	Jeff Hornacek	.12	.07
58	Tony Campbell	.10	.06
59	Vinny Del Negro	.10	.06
60	Xavier McDaniel (HC)	.10	.06
61	Scottie Pippen (HC)	.20	.12
62	Larry Nance (HC)	.10	.06
63	Dikembe Mutombo (HC)	.15	.10
64	Hakeem Olajuwon (HC)	.60	.35
65	Dominique Wilkins (HC)	.20	.12
66	C. Weatherspoon (HC)	.12	.07
67	Chris Morris (HC)	.10	.06
68	Patrick Ewing (HC)	.20	.12
69	Kevin Willis (HC)	.10	.06
70	Jon Barry	.12	.07
71	Jerry Reynolds	.10	.06
72	Sarunas Marciulionis	.12	.07
73	Mark West	.10	.06
74	B.J. Armstrong	.15	.10
75	Greg Kite	.10	.06
76	LaSalle Thompson	.10	.06
77	Randy White	.10	.06
78	Alaa Abdelnaby	.10	.06
79	Kevin Brooks	.10	.06
80	Vern Fleming	.10	.06
81	Doc Rivers	.12	.07
82	Shawn Bradley (R)	.60	.35
83	Wayman Tisdale	.12	.07
84	Olden Polynice	.10	.06
85	Michael Cage	.10	.06
86	Harold Miner	.15	.10
87	Doug Smith	.10	.06
88	Tom Gugliotta	.20	.12
89	Hakeem Olajuwon	1.00	.60
90	Loy Vaught	.10	.06
91	James Worthy	.15	.10
92	John Paxson	.12	.07
93	Jon Koncak	.10	.06
94	Lee Mayberry	.12	.07
95	Clarence Weatherspoon	.20	.12
96	Mark Eaton	.10	.06

200 • 1993-94 TOPPS STADIUM CLUB

#	Player		
97	Rex Walters (R)	.12	.07
98	Alvin Robertson	.10	.06
99	Dan Majerle	.15	.10
100	Shaquille O'Neal	2.50	1.50
101	Derrick Coleman (TD)	.15	.10
102	Hersey Hawkins (TD)	.10	.06
103	Scottie Pippen (TD)	.20	.12
104	Scott Skiles (TD)	.10	.06
105	Rod Stickland (TD)	.10	.06
106	Pooh Richardson (TD)	.10	.06
107	Tom Gugliotta (TD)	.12	.07
108	Mark Jackson (TD)	.10	.06
109	Dikembe Mutombo (TD)	.15	.10
110	Charles Barkley (TD)	.40	.25
111	Otis Thorpe (TD)	.10	.06
112	Malik Sealy	.12	.07
113	Mark Macon	.12	.07
114	Dee Brown	.15	.10
115	Nate McMillan	.10	.06
116	John Starks	.25	.15
117	Clyde Drexler	.30	.18
118	Antoine Carr	.10	.06
119	Doug West	.10	.06
120	Victor Alexander	.10	.06
121	Kenny Gattison	.10	.06
122	Spud Webb	.10	.06
123	Rumeal Robinson	.10	.06
124	Tim Kempton	.10	.06
125	Karl Malone	.35	.20
126	Randy Woods	.10	.06
127	Calbert Cheaney (R)	.60	.35
128	Johnny Dawkins	.10	.06
129	Dominique Wilkins	.40	.25
130	Horace Grant	.12	.07
131	Bill Laimbeer	.12	.07
132	Kenny Smith	.12	.07
133	Sedale Threatt	.10	.06
134	Brian Shaw	.10	.06
135	Dennis Scott	.12	.07
136	Mark Bryant	.10	.06
137	Xavier McDaniel	.10	.06
138	David Wood	.10	.06
139	Luther Wright (R)	.20	.12
140	Lloyd Daniels	.12	.07
141	Marlon Maxey	.10	.06
142	Pooh Richardson	.12	.07
143	Jeff Grayer	.10	.06
144	LaPhonso Ellis	.25	.15
145	Gerald Wilkins	.10	.06
146	Dell Curry	.10	.06
147	Duane Causwell	.10	.06
148	Tim Hardaway	.15	.10
149	Isiah Thomas	.25	.15
150	Doug Edwards (R)	.15	.10
151	Anthony Peeler	.15	.10
152	Tate George	.10	.06
153	Terry Davis	.10	.06
154	Sam Perkins	.12	.07
155	John Salley	.10	.06
156	Vernon Maxwell	.15	.10
157	Anthony Avent	.15	.10
158	Cliff Robinson	.15	.10
159	Corie Blount (R)	.15	.10
160	Gerald Paddio	.10	.06
161	Blair Rasmussen	.10	.06
162	Carl Herrera	.15	.10
163	Chris Smith	.12	.07
164	Pervis Ellison	.12	.07
165	Rod Strickland	.10	.06
166	Jeff Malone	.12	.07
167	Danny Ferry	.10	.06
168	Kevin Lynch	.10	.06
169	Michael Jordan	2.50	1.50
170	Derrick Coleman (HC)	.15	.10
171	Jerome Kersey (HC)	.10	.06
172	David Robinson (HC)	.40	.25
173	Shawn Kemp (HC)	.30	.18
174	Karl Malone (HC)	.20	.12
175	Shaqquille O'Neal (HC)	1.50	.90
176	Alonzo Mourning (HC)	.50	.30
177	Charles Barkley (HC)	.40	.25
178	Larry Johnson (HC)	.25	.15
179	Checklist	.10	.06
180	Checklist	.10	.06
181	Michael Jordan (FF)	1.50	.90
182	Dominique Wilkins (FF)	.20	.12
183	Dennis Rodman (FF)	.12	.07
184	Scottie Pippen (FF)	.20	.12
185	Larry Johnson (FF)	.25	.15
186	Karl Malone (FF)	.20	.12
187	C. Weatherspoon (FF)	.12	.07
188	Charley Barkley (FF)	.40	.25
189	Patrick Ewing (FF)	.25	.15
190	Derrick Coleman (FF)	.15	.10
191	LaBradford Smith	.10	.06
192	Derek Harper	.12	.07
193	Ken Norman	.10	.06
194	Rodney Rogers (R)	.30	.18
195	Chris Dudley	.10	.06
196	Gary Payton	.15	.10
197	Andrew Lang	.10	.06
198	Billy Owens	.15	.10
199	Byron Russell (R)	.15	.10
200	Patrick Ewing	.50	.30
201	Stacey King	.10	.06
202	Grant Long	.10	.06
203	Sean Elliott	.15	.10
204	Muggsy Bogues	.10	.06
205	Kevin Edwards	.10	.06
206	Dale Davis	.15	.10
207	Dale Ellis	.10	.06
208	Terrell Brandon	.12	.07
209	Kevin Gamble	.10	.06
210	Robert Horry	.20	.12

1993-94 TOPPS STADIUM CLUB • 201

#	Player	Price 1	Price 2
211	Moses Malone	.15	.10
212	Gary Grant	.10	.06
213	Bobby Hurley	.30	.18
214	Larry Krystkowiak	.10	.06
215	A.C. Green	.12	.07
216	Christian Laettner	.20	.12
217	Orlando Woolridge	.10	.06
218	Craig Ehlo	.10	.06
219	Terry Porter	.12	.07
220	Jamal Mashburn (R)	1.50	.90
221	Kevin Duckworth	.10	.06
222	Shawn Kemp	.60	.35
223	Frank Brickowski	.10	.06
224	Chris Webber (R)	3.50	2.00
225	Charles Oakley	.12	.07
226	Jay Humphries	.10	.06
227	Steve Kerr	.10	.06
228	Tim Perry	.10	.06
229	Sleepy Floyd	.10	.06
230	Bimbo Coles	.10	.06
231	Eddie Johnson	.10	.06
232	Terry Mills	.12	.07
233	Danny Manning	.20	.12
234	Isaiah Rider (R)	1.25	.70
235	Darnell Mee (R)	.12	.07
236	Haywood Workman	.10	.06
237	Scott Skiles	.10	.06
238	Otis Thorpe	.12	.07
239	Mike Peplowski (R)	.15	.10
240	Eric Leckner	.10	.06
241	Johnny Newman	.10	.06
242	Benoit Benjamin	.10	.06
243	Doug Christie	.15	.10
244	Acie Earl (R)	.15	.10
245	Luc Longley	.10	.06
246	Tyrone Hill	.10	.06
247	Allan Houston (R)	.15	.10
248	Joe Kleine	.10	.06
249	Mookie Blaylock	.12	.07
250	Anthony Bonner	.10	.06
251	Luther Wright	.12	.07
252	Todd Day	.15	.10
253	Kendall Gill	.15	.10
254	Mario Elie	.10	.06
255	Pete Myers	.10	.06
256	Jim Les	.10	.06
257	Stanley Roberts	.12	.07
258	Michael Adams	.12	.07
259	Hersey Hawkins	.12	.07
260	Shawn Bradley	.30	.18
261	Scott Haskin (R)	.15	.10
262	Corie Blount	.12	.07
263	Charles Smith	.12	.07
264	Armon Gilliam	.12	.07
265	Jamal Mashburn (NW)	.50	.30
266	Anfernee Hardaway (NW)	1.25	.70
267	Shawn Bradley (NW)	.20	.12
268	Chris Webber (NW)	1.75	1.00
269	Bobby Hurley (NW)	.15	.10
270	Isaiah Rider (NW)	.40	.25
271	Dino Radja (NW)	.15	.10
272	Chris Mills (NW)	.15	.10
273	Nick Van Exel (NW)	.15	.10
274	Lindsey Hunter (NW)	.15	.10
275	Toni Kukoc (NW)	.20	.12
276	Popeye Jones (NW)	.12	.07
277	Chris Mills	.20	.12
278	Ricky Pierce	.10	.06
279	Negele Knight	.10	.06
280	Kenny Walker	.12	.07
281	Nick Van Exel (R)	.60	.35
282	Derrick Coleman	.20	.12
283	Popeye Jones (R)	.20	.12
284	Derrick McKey	.12	.07
285	Rick Fox	.12	.07
286	Jerome Kersey	.10	.06
287	Steve Smith	.15	.10
288	Brian Williams	.15	.10
289	Chris Mullin	.25	.15
290	Terry Cummings	.12	.07
291	Donald Royal	.10	.06
292	Alonzo Mourning	1.00	.60
293	Mike Brown	.10	.06
294	Latrell Sprewell	.80	.50
295	Oliver Miller	.15	.10
296	Terry Dehere (R)	.15	.10
297	Detlef Schrempf	.15	.10
298	Sam Bowie	.10	.06
299	Chris Morris	.10	.06
300	Scottie Pippen	.40	.25
301	Warren Kidd (R)	.12	.07
302	Don MacLean	.20	.12
303	Sean Rooks	.12	.07
304	Matt Geiger	.10	.06
305	Dennis Rodman	.12	.07
306	Reggie Miller	.25	.15
307	Vin Baker (R)	1.00	.60
308	Anfernee Hardaway (R)	3.00	1.75
309	Lindsey Hunter (R)	.60	.35
310	Stacey Augmon	.15	.10
311	Randy Brown	.10	.06
312	Anthony Mason	.12	.07
313	John Stockton	.30	.18
314	Sam Cassell (R)	.75	.45
315	Buck Williams	.12	.07
316	Bryant Stith	.15	.10
317	Brad Daugherty	.15	.10
318	Dino Radja (R)	.50	.30
319	Rony Seikaly	.12	.07
320	Charles Barkley	.80	.50
321	Avery Johnson	.10	.06
322	Mahmoud Abdul-Rauf	.15	.10

#	Name	Price1	Price2
323	Larry Johnson	.50	.30
324	Michael Williams	.10	.06
325	Mark Aquirre	.12	.07
326	Jim Jackson	.35	.20
327	Antonio Harvey (R)	.15	.10
328	David Robinson	.80	.50
329	Calbert Cheaney	.30	.18
330	Kenny Anderson	.20	.12
331	Walt Williams	.15	.10
332	Kevin Willis	.10	.06
333	Nick Anderson	.12	.07
334	Rik Smits	.10	.06
335	Joe Dumars	.20	.12
336	Toni Kukoc (R)	.75	.45
337	Harvey Grant	.10	.06
338	Tom Chambers	.12	.07
339	Blue Edwards	.10	.06
340	Mark Price	.20	.12
341	Kevin Johnson	.20	.12
342	Rolando Blackman	.12	.07
343	Scott Burrell (R)	.20	.12
344	Gheorghe Muresan (R)	.15	.10
345	Chris Corchiani	.10	.06
346	Richard Petruska (R)	.15	.10
347	Dana Barros	.10	.06
348	Hakeem Olajuwon (FF)	.75	.45
349	Dee Brown (FF)	.12	.07
350	John Starks (FF)	.15	.10
351	Ron Harper (FF)	.10	.06
352	Chris Webber (FF)	1.25	.70
353	Dan Majerle (FF)	.12	.07
354	Clyde Drexler (FF)	.15	.10
355	Shawn Kemp (FF)	.30	.18
356	David Robinson (FF)	.40	.25
357	Chris Morris (FF)	.10	.06
358	Shaquille O'Neal (FF)	1.50	.90
359	Checklist	.10	.06
360	Checklist	.10	.06

1993-94 Topps Stadium Club Beam Team

The cards in this limited insert set were randomly distributed in Stadium Club foil packs and consist of a full-bleed, full-color action photo on three sides of the card front with the player's name printed in a panel at the bottom of the card, next to a Beam Team logo which appears to be shooting out laser light beams across the lower corner of the card. All cards measure 2-1/2" by 3-1/2".

		MINT	NR/MT
	Complete Set (27)	185.00	110.00
	Commons	1.50	.90
1	Shaquille O'Neal	20.00	12.00
2	Mark Price	1.75	1.00
3	Patrick Ewing	8.50	5.00
4	Michael Jordan	32.00	20.00
5	Charles Barkley	10.00	6.50
6	Reggie Miller	3.00	1.75
7	Derrick Coleman	3.50	2.00
8	Dominique Wilkins	6.00	3.75
9	Karl Malone	5.00	3.00
10	Alonzo Mourning	10.00	6.50
11	Tim Hardaway	2.50	1.50
12	Hakeem Olajuwon	12.00	7.50
13	David Robinson	10.00	6.50
14	Dan Majerle	2.00	1.25
15	Larry Johnson	7.50	4.50

1991-92 UPPER DECK • 203

16	LaPhonso Ellis	4.00	2.50
17	Nick Van Exel	3.50	2.00
18	Scottie Pippen	7.00	4.00
19	John Stockton	5.00	3.00
20	Bobby Hurley	3.50	2.00
21	Chris Webber	20.00	12.00
22	Jamal Mashburn	8.00	5.00
23	Anfernee Hardaway	16.00	9.00
24	Isaiah Rider	8.00	5.00
25	Ken Norman	1.50	.90
26	Danny Manning	2.50	1.50
27	Calbert Cheaney	3.50	2.00

1	Shaquille O'Neal	15.00	10.00
2	Harold Miner	1.00	.60
3	Charles Barkley	4.00	2.50
4	Dominique Wilkins	3.00	1.75
5	Shawn Kemp	3.50	2.00
6	Robert Horry	1.50	.90

UPPER DECK

1993-94 Topps Stadium Club Rim Rockers

1991-92 Upper Deck

The cards in this limited insert set were distributed randomly in 1993-94 Stadium Club Series II foil packs. The card fronts feature full-bleed, full color game action photos with the player's name centered and stacked under his photo. A Rim Rockers logo appears in the top corner. All cards measure 2-1/2" by 3-1/2".

	MINT	NR/MT
Complete Set (6)	22.00	13.50
Commons	1.00	.60

This set marks the permier of Upper Deck basketball. The set was issued in two series, a 400-card low series and a 100-card high series. The card fronts feature full color game action player photos printed on a glossy paper stock. The photos are framed on two sides, the bottom and right, by a hardwood design. The player's name and position appear under his picture while the team name is printed vertically along the right border. A team logo is located in the lower corner of the card front. The flip side consists of another large full color action photo along with personal data and statistics. The main subsets include Draft Picks (1-21), Classic Confrontations (CC)(30-34), the All-Rookie Team (AR)(35-39), All-Stars (AS)(49-72,449-475), Team

204 • 1991-92 UPPER DECK

Checklists (CL)(73-99), Tops Prospects (TP)(438-448) and All-Star Skills (476-484). The set also contains random inserts from a 10-card Jerry West Heroes set. Those cards are listed at the end of this checklist. All Cards measure 2-1/2" by 3-1/2".

		MINT	NR/MT
	Complete Set (500)	26.00	15.00
	Commons	.05	.02
1	Draft (CL) (Stacey Augmon Rodney Monroe)	.20	.12
2	Larry Johnson (R)	5.00	3.00
3	Dikembe Mutombo (R)	3.00	1.75
4	Steve Smith (R)	1.50	.90
5	Stacey Augmon (R)	1.25	.70
6	Terrell Brandon (R)	.25	.15
7	Greg Anthony (R)	.20	.12
8	Rich King (R)	.10	.06
9	Chris Gatling (R)	.25	.15
10	Victor Alexander (R)	.25	.15
11	John Turner (R)	.07	.04
12	Eric Murdock (R)	.50	.30
13	Mark Randall (R)	.08	.05
14	Rodney Monroe (R)	.08	.05
15	Myron Brown (R)	.07	.04
16	Mike Iuzzolino (R)	.10	.06
17	Chris Corchiani (R)	.12	.07
18	Elliot Perry (R)	.08	.05
19	Jimmy Oliver (R)	.08	.05
20	Doug Overton (R)	.08	.05
21	Steve Hood (R)	.08	.05
22	Michael Jordan(School)	.75	.45
23	Kevin Johnson (School)	.10	.06
24	Kurk Lee	.05	.02
25	Sean Higgins (R)	.08	.05
26	Morton Wiley (R)	.07	.04
27	Derek Smith	.05	.02
28	Kenny Payne	.05	.02
29	Magic Johnson(Moment)	.40	.25
30	Larry Bird/ Chuck Person (CC)	.30	.18
31	Karl Malone/ Charles Barkley (CC)	.25	.15
32	Kevin Johnson / John Stockton (CC)	.15	.10
33	Hakeem Olajuwon/ Patrick Ewing (CC)	.30	.18
34	Magic Johnson/ Michael Jordan	.75	.45
35	Derrick Coleman (AR)	.25	.15
36	Lionel Simmons (AR)	.15	.10
37	Dee Brown (AR)	.12	.07
38	Dennis Scott (AR)	.10	.06
39	Kendall Gill (AR)	.12	.07
40	Winston Garland	.05	.02
41	Danny Young	.05	.02
42	Rick Mahorn	.05	.02
43	Michael Adams	.07	.04
44	Michael Jordan	2.00	1.25
45	Magic Johnson	.75	.45
46	Doc Rivers	.07	.04
47	Moses Malone	.10	.06
48	Michael Jordan(AS)(CL)	.80	.50
49	James Worthy (AS)	.07	.04
50	Tim Hardaway (AS)	.15	.10
51	Karl Malone (AS)	.20	.12
52	John Stockton (AS)	.20	.12
53	Clyde Drexler (AS)	.15	.10
54	Terry Porter (AS)	.07	.04
55	Kevin Duckworth (AS)	.05	.02
56	Tom Chambers (AS)	.05	.02
57	Magic Johnson (AS)	.40	.25
58	David Robinson (AS)	.40	.25
59	Kevin Johnson (AS)	.10	.06
60	Chris Mullin (AS)	.12	.07
61	Joe Dumars (AS)	.07	.04
62	Kevin McHale (AS)	.07	.04
63	Brad Daugherty (AS)	.08	.05
64	Alvin Robertson (AS)	.05	.02
65	Bernard King (AS)	.06	.03
66	Dominique Wilkins (AS)	.15	.10
67	Ricky Pierce (AS)	.05	.02
68	Patrick Ewing (AS)	.20	.12
69	Michael Jordan (AS)	1.00	.60
70	Charles Barkley (AS)	.25	.15
71	Hersey Hawkins (AS)	.05	.02
72	Robert Parish (AS)	.07	.04
73	Alvin Robertson (CL)	.05	.02
74	Bernard King (CL)	.06	.03
75	Michael Jordan (CL)	.80	.50
76	Brad Daugherty (CL)	.10	.06
77	Larry Bird (CL)	.50	.30
78	Ron Harper (CL)	.05	.02
79	Dominique Wilkins (CL)	.15	.10
80	Rony Seikaly (CL)	.06	.03
81	Rex Chapman (CL)	.06	.03
82	Mark Eaton (CL)	.05	.02
83	Lionel Simmons (CL)	.12	.07
84	Gerald Wilkins (CL)	.05	.02
85	James Worthy (CL)	.08	.05
86	Scott Skiles (CL)	.06	.03
87	Rolando Blackman (CL)	.06	.03
88	Derrick Coleman (CL)	.25	.15
89	Chris Jackson (CL)	.10	.06
90	Reggie Miller (CL)	.10	.06
91	Isiah Thomas (CL)	.12	.07
92	Hakeem Olajuwon (CL)	.40	.25
93	Hersey Hawkins (CL)	.06	.03
94	David Robinson (CL)	.40	.25

1991-92 UPPER DECK • 205

#	Player		
95	Tom Chambers (CL)	.06	.03
96	Shawn Kemp (CL)	.50	.30
97	Pooh Richardson (CL)	.06	.03
98	Clyde Drexler (CL)	.12	.07
99	Chris Mullin (CL)	.10	.06
100	Checklist (1-100)	.05	.02
101	John Shasky	.05	.02
102	Dana Barros	.10	.06
103	Stojko Vrankovic	.05	.02
104	Larry Drew	.05	.02
105	Randy White	.05	.02
106	Dave Corzine	.05	.02
107	Joe Kleine	.05	.02
108	Lance Blanks	.05	.02
109	Rodney McCray	.05	.02
110	Sedale Threatt	.05	.02
111	Ken Norman	.08	.05
112	Rickey Green	.05	.02
113	Andy Toolson	.05	.02
114	Bo Kimble	.07	.04
115	Mark West	.05	.02
116	Mark Eaton	.07	.04
117	John Paxson	.08	.05
118	Mike Brown	.05	.02
119	Brian Oliver	.05	.02
120	Will Perdue	.05	.02
121	Michael Smith	.05	.02
122	Sherman Douglas	.12	.07
123	Reggie Lewis	.15	.10
124	James Donaldson	.05	.02
125	Scottie Pippen	.30	.18
126	Elden Campbell	.12	.07
127	Michael Cage	.05	.02
128	Tony Smith	.05	.02
129	Ed Pinckney	.05	.02
130	Keith Askins (R)	.10	.06
131	Darrell Griffith	.05	.02
132	Vinnie Johnson	.05	.02
133	Ron Harper	.07	.04
134	Andre Turner	.05	.02
135	Jeff Hornacek	.08	.05
136	John Stockton	.25	.15
137	Derek Harper	.07	.04
138	Loy Vaught	.07	.04
139	Thurl Bailey	.05	.02
140	Olden Polynice	.05	.02
141	Kevin Edwards	.05	.02
142	Byron Scott	.07	.04
143	Dee Brown	.15	.10
144	Sam Perkins	.07	.04
145	Rony Seikaly	.08	.05
146	James Worthy	.12	.07
147	Glen Rice	.20	.12
148	Craig Hodges	.05	.02
149	Bimbo Coles	.05	.02
150	Mychal Thompson	.05	.02
151	Xavier McDaniel	.07	.04
152	Roy Tarpley	.05	.02
153	Gary Payton	.20	.12
154	Rolando Blackman	.07	.04
155	Hersey Hawkins	.10	.06
156	Ricky Pierce	.05	.02
157	Fat Lever	.05	.02
158	Andrew Lang	.05	.02
159	Benoit Benjamin	.05	.02
160	Cedric Ceballos	.12	.07
161	Charles Smith	.08	.05
162	Jeff Martin	.05	.02
163	Robert Parish	.10	.06
164	Danny Manning	.20	.12
165	Mark Aguirre	.07	.04
166	Jeff Malone	.07	.04
167	Bill Laimbeer	.08	.05
168	Willie Burton	.07	.04
169	Dennis Hopson	.05	.02
170	Kevin Gamble	.05	.02
171	Terry Teagle	.05	.02
172	Dan Majerle	.12	.07
173	Shawn Kemp	1.00	.60
174	Tom Chambers	.08	.05
175	Vlade Divac	.08	.05
176	Johnny Dawkins	.05	.02
177	A.C. Green	.07	.04
178	Manute Bol	.05	.02
179	Terry Davis	.05	.02
180	Ron Anderson	.05	.02
181	Horace Grant	.10	.06
182	Stacey King	.07	.04
183	William Bedford	.05	.02
184	B.J. Armstrong	.20	.12
185	Dennis Rodman	.12	.07
186	Nate McMillan	.05	.02
187	Cliff Levingston	.05	.02
188	Quintin Dailey	.05	.02
189	Bill Cartwright	.05	.02
190	John Salley	.05	.02
191	Jayson Williams	.05	.02
192	Grant Long	.05	.02
193	Negele Knight	.08	.05
194	Alec Kessler	.05	.02
195	Gary Grant	.05	.02
196	Billy Thompson	.05	.02
197	Delaney Rudd	.05	.02
198	Alan Ogg	.05	.02
199	Blue Edwards	.07	.04
200	Checklist (101-200)	.05	.02
201	Mark Acres	.05	.02
202	Craig Ehlo	.05	.02
203	Anthony Cook	.05	.02
204	Eric Leckner	.05	.02
205	Terry Catledge	.05	.02
206	Reggie Williams	.07	.04
207	Greg Kite	.05	.02
208	Steve Kerr	.05	.02

1991-92 UPPER DECK

#	Player		
209	Kenny Battle	.05	.02
210	John Morton	.05	.02
211	Kenny Williams	.05	.02
212	Mark Jackson	.10	.06
213	Alaa Abdelnaby	.07	.04
214	Rod Strickland	.05	.02
215	Michael Williams	.05	.02
216	Kevin Duckworth	.07	.04
217	David Wingate	.05	.02
218	LaSalle Thompson	.05	.02
219	John Starks (R)	1.75	1.00
220	Cliff Robinson	.15	.10
221	Jeff Grayer	.05	.02
222	Marcus Liberty	.07	.04
223	Larry Nance	.07	.04
224	Michael Ansley	.05	.02
225	Kevin McHale	.12	.07
226	Scott Skiles	.07	.04
227	Darnell Valentine	.05	.02
228	Nick Anderson	.15	.10
229	Brad Davis	.05	.02
230	Gerald Paddio	.05	.02
231	Sam Bowie	.07	.04
232	Sam Vincent	.05	.02
233	George McCloud	.05	.02
234	Gerald Wilkins	.05	.02
235	Mookie Blaylock	.10	.06
236	Jon Koncak	.05	.02
237	Danny Ferry	.05	.02
238	Vern Fleming	.05	.02
239	Mark Price	.20	.12
240	Sidney Moncrief	.08	.05
241	Jay Humphries	.05	.02
242	Muggsy Bogues	.05	.02
243	Tim Hardaway	.25	.15
244	Alvin Robertson	.05	.02
245	Chris Mullin	.20	.12
246	Pooh Richardson	.08	.05
247	Winston Bennett	.05	.02
248	Kevin Upshaw	.05	.02
249	John Williams	.05	.02
250	Steve Alford	.05	.02
251	Spud Webb	.05	.02
252	Sleepy Floyd	.05	.02
253	Chuck Person	.08	.05
254	Hakeem Olajuwon	.75	.45
255	Dominique Wilkins	.30	.18
256	Reggie Miller	.20	.12
257	Dennis Scott	.12	.07
258	Charles Oakley	.08	.05
259	Sidney Green	.05	.02
260	Detlef Schrempf	.15	.10
261	Rod Higgins	.05	.02
262	J.R. Reid	.05	.02
263	Tyrone Hill	.05	.02
264	Reggie Theus	.07	.04
265	Mitch Richmond	.12	.07
266	Dale Ellis	.07	.04
267	Terry Cummings	.08	.05
268	Johnny Newman	.05	.02
269	Doug West	.15	.10
270	Jim Petersen	.05	.02
271	Otis Thorpe	.08	.05
272	John Williams	.05	.02
273	Ken Winchester (R)	.07	.04
274	Duane Ferrell	.05	.02
275	Vernon Maxwell	.12	.07
276	Kenny Smith	.07	.04
277	Jerome Kersey	.08	.05
278	Kevin Willis	.07	.04
279	Danny Ainge	.10	.06
280	Larry Smith	.05	.02
281	Maurice Cheeks	.08	.05
282	Willie Anderson	.05	.02
283	Tom Tolbert	.05	.02
284	Jerrod Mustaf	.05	.02
285	Randolph Keys	.05	.02
286	Jerry Reynolds	.05	.02
287	Sean Elliott	.20	.12
288	Otis Smith	.05	.02
289	Terry Mills (R)	.75	.45
290	Kelly Tripucka	.05	.02
291	Jon Sundvold	.05	.02
292	Rumeal Robinson	.07	.04
293	Fred Roberts	.05	.02
294	Rik Smits	.05	.02
295	Jerome Lane	.05	.02
296	Dave Jamerson	.05	.02
297	Joe Wolf	.05	.02
298	David Wood (R)	.10	.06
299	Todd Lichti	.05	.02
300	Checklist (201-300)	.05	.02
301	Randy Breuer	.05	.02
302	Buck Johnson	.07	.04
303	Scott Brooks	.05	.02
304	Jeff Turner	.05	.02
305	Felton Spencer	.10	.06
306	Greg Dreiling	.05	.02
307	Gerald Glass	.07	.04
308	Tony Brown	.05	.02
309	Sam Mitchell	.07	.04
310	Adrian Caldwell	.05	.02
311	Chris Dudley	.05	.02
312	Blair Rasmussen	.05	.02
313	Antoine Carr	.05	.02
314	Greg Anderson	.07	.04
315	Drazen Petrovic	.20	.12
316	Alton Lister	.05	.02
317	Jack Haley	.05	.02
318	Bobby Hansen	.05	.02
319	Chris Jackson	.20	.12
320	Herb Williams	.05	.02
321	Kendall Gill	.12	.07
322	Tyrone Corbin	.05	.02

1991-92 UPPER DECK • 207

#	Player	Val1	Val2
323	Kiki Vandeweghe	.05	.02
324	David Robinson	.75	.45
325	Rex Chapman	.07	.04
326	Tony Campbell	.05	.02
327	Dell Curry	.05	.02
328	Charles Jones	.05	.02
329	Kenny Gattison	.05	.02
330	Haywoode Workman (R)	.15	.10
331	Travis Mays	.05	.02
332	Derrick Coleman	.60	.35
333	Isiah Thomas	.20	.12
334	Jud Buechler	.05	.02
335	Joe Dumars	.15	.10
336	Tate George	.05	.02
337	Mike Sanders	.05	.02
338	James Edwards	.05	.02
339	Chris Morris	.05	.02
340	Scott Hastings	.05	.02
341	Trent Tucker	.05	.02
342	Harvey Grant	.07	.04
343	Patrick Ewing	.40	.25
344	Larry Bird	.75	.45
345	Charles Barkley	.60	.35
346	Brian Shaw	.05	.02
347	Kenny Walker	.05	.02
348	Danny Schayes	.05	.02
349	Tom Hammonds	.05	.02
350	Frank Brickowski	.05	.02
351	Terry Porter	.10	.06
352	Orlando Woolridge	.07	.04
353	Buck Williams	.07	.04
354	Sarunas Marciulionis	.08	.05
355	Karl Malone	.30	.18
356	Kevin Johnson	.20	.12
357	Clyde Drexler	.25	.15
358	Duane Causwell	.05	.02
359	Paul Pressey	.05	.02
360	Jim Les (R)	.10	.06
361	Derrick McKey	.07	.04
362	Scott Williams (R)	.15	.10
363	Mark Alarie	.05	.02
364	Brad Daugherty	.20	.12
365	Bernard King	.08	.05
366	Steve Henson	.05	.02
367	Darrell Walker	.05	.02
368	Larry Krystkowiak	.05	.02
369	Henry James	.05	.02
370	Jack Sikma	.07	.04
371	Eddie Johnson	.05	.02
372	Wayman Tisdale	.07	.04
373	Joe Barry Carroll	.05	.02
374	David Greenwood	.05	.02
375	Lionel Simmons	.25	.15
376	Dwayne Schintzius	.05	.02
377	Tod Murphy	.05	.02
378	Wayne Cooper	.05	.02
379	Anthony Bonner	.05	.02
380	Walter Davis	.07	.04
381	Lester Conner	.05	.02
382	Ledell Eackles	.05	.02
383	Brad Lohaus	.05	.02
384	Derrick Gervin	.05	.02
385	Pervis Ellison	.12	.07
386	Tim McCormick	.05	.02
387	A.J. English	.07	.04
388	John Battle	.05	.02
389	Roy Hinson	.05	.02
390	Armon Gilliam	.07	.04
391	Kurt Rambis	.05	.02
392	Mark Bryant	.05	.02
393	Chucky Brown	.07	.04
394	Avery Johnson	.08	.05
395	Rory Sparrow	.05	.02
396	Mario Elie (R)	.15	.10
397	Ralph Sampson	.07	.04
398	Mike Gminski	.05	.02
399	Bill Wennington	.05	.02
400	Checklist (301-400)	.05	.02
401	David Wingate	.05	.02
402	Moses Malone	.10	.06
403	Darrell Walker	.05	.02
404	Antoine Carr	.05	.02
405	Charles Shackleford	.05	.02
406	Orlando Woolridge	.07	.04
407	Robert Pack (R)	.30	.18
408	Bobby Hansen	.05	.02
409	Dale Davis (R)	.75	.45
410	Vincent Askew (R)	.12	.07
411	Alexander Volkov	.05	.02
412	Dwayne Schintzius	.05	.02
413	Tim Perry	.05	.02
414	Tyrone Corbin	.05	.02
415	Pete Chilcutt (R)	.10	.06
416	James Edwards	.05	.02
417	Jerrod Mustaf	.05	.02
418	Thurl Bailey	.05	.02
419	Spud Webb	.05	.02
420	Doc Rivers	.07	.04
421	Sean Green (R)	.10	.06
422	Walter Davis	.07	.04
423	Terry Davis	.05	.02
424	John Battle	.05	.02
425	Vinnie Johnson	.05	.02
426	Sherman Douglas	.12	.07
427	Kevin Brooks (R)	.10	.06
428	Greg Sutton	.05	.02
429	Rafael Addison (R)	.10	.06
430	Anthony Mason (R)	.60	.35
431	Paul Graham (R)	.15	.10
432	Anthony Frederick (R)	.07	.04
433	Dennis Hopson	.05	.02
434	Rory Sparrow	.05	.02
435	Michael Adams	.07	.04
436	Kevin Lynch (R)	.10	.06

208 • 1991-92 UPPER DECK

437 Randy Brown (R)	.15	.10
438 Top Prospects (CL)	.60	.35
(Larry Johnson		
Billy Owens)		
439 Stacey Augmon (TP)	.35	.20
440 Larry Stewart (R)(TP)	.15	.10
441 Terrell Brandon (TP)	.12	.07
442 Billy Owens (R)(TP)	1.00	.60
443 Rick Fox (R)(TP)	.25	.15
444 Kenny Anderson (R)	2.00	1.25
(TP)		
445 Larry Johnson (TP)	2.50	1.50
446 Dikembe Mutombo (TP)	1.00	.60
447 Steve Smith (TP)	.75	.45
448 Greg Anthony (TP)	.10	.06
449 East All-Stars (CL)	.10	.06
450 West All-Stars (CL)	.10	.06
451 Isiah Thomas (AS)	.25	.15
452 Michael Jordan (AS)	1.00	.60
453 Scottie Pippen (AS)	.25	.15
454 Charles Barkley (AS)	.40	.25
455 Patrick Ewing (AS)	.30	.18
456 Michael Adams (AS)	.06	.03
457 Dennis Rodman (AS)	.07	.04
458 Reggie Lewis (AS)	.10	.06
459 Joe Dumars (AS)	.10	.06
460 Mark Price (AS)	.08	.05
461 Brad Daugherty (AS)	.08	.05
462 Kevin Willis (AS)	.05	.02
463 Clyde Drexler (AS)	.15	.10
464 Magic Johnson (AS)	.50	.30
465 Chris Mullin (AS)	.12	.07
466 Karl Malone (AS)	.20	.12
467 David Robinson (AS)	.40	.25
468 Tim Hardaway (AS)	.15	.10
469 Jeff Hornacek (AS)	.06	.03
470 John Stockton (AS)	.20	.12
471 Dikembe Mutombo(AS)	.40	.25
472 Hakeem Olajuwon (AS)	.60	.35
473 James Worthy (AS)	.08	.05
474 Otis Thorpe (AS)	.06	.03
475 Dan Majerle (AS)	.08	.05
476 C. Ceballos (Skills)(CL)	.10	.06
477 Nick Anderson (Skills)	.10	.06
478 Stacey Augmon (Skills)	.25	.15
479 Cedric Ceballos (Skills)	.10	.06
480 Larry Johnson (Skills)	1.00	.60
481 Shawn Kemp (Skills)	.75	.45
482 John Starks (Skills)	.40	.25
483 Doug West (Skills)	.07	.04
484 Craig Hodges (Skills)	.05	.02
485 LaBradford Smith (R)	.15	.10
486 Winston Garland	.05	.02
487 David Benoit (R)	.20	.12
488 John Bagley	.05	.02
489 Mark Macon (R)	.15	.10
490 Mitch Richmond	.15	.10
491 Luc Longley (R)	.15	.10
492 Sedale Threatt	.05	.02
493 Doug Smith (R)	.25	.15
494 Travis Mays	.05	.02
495 Xavier McDaniel	.07	.04
496 Brian Shaw	.05	.02
497 Stanley Roberts (R)	.20	.12
498 Blair Rasmussen	.05	.02
499 Brian Williams (R)	.35	.20
500 Checklist	.05	.02
___ Jerry West Heroes ea.	1.25	.70
___ Jerry West Cover	2.00	1.00
___ Jerry West (Signed)	200.00	100.00

1991-92 Upper Deck Award Winner Holograms

These limited insert cards were randomly distributed in Upper Deck foil packs. The fronts feature full color holograms with the player's name and award winning achievement printed in the lower corner. All cards measure 2-1/2" by 3-1/2".

	MINT	NR/MT
Complete Set (9)	12.00	7.50
Commons	.50	.30

1991-92 UPPER DECK ROOKIE STANDOUTS • 209

1	Michael Jordan	3.50	2.00
2	Alvin Robertson	.50	.30
3	John Stockton	1.00	.60
4	Michael Jordan	3.50	2.00
5	Detlef Schrempf	.50	.30
6	David Robinson	2.00	1.25
7	Derrick Coleman	1.00	.60
8	Hakeem Olajuwon	2.50	1.50
9	Dennis Rodman	.50	.30

1991-92 Upper Deck Rookie Standouts

The cards in this limited insert set were distributed in Upper Deck's jumbo packs and in their Locker Series. The desing is identical to the regular issue except for a Rookie Standout Logo in the lower right corner of the card front. The backs include the "R" prefix before the card number. All cards measure 2-1/2" by 3-1/2".

	MINT	NR/MT
Complete Set (40)	28.00	18.00
Commons	.25	.15

1	Gary Payton	1.25	.70
2	Dennis Scott	.75	.45
3	Kendall Gill	1.00	.60
4	Felton Spencer	.30	.18
5	Bo Kimble	.25	.15
6	Willie Burton	.30	.18
7	Tyrone Hill	.25	.15
8	Loy Vaught	.30	.18
9	Travis Mays	.25	.15
10	Derrick Coleman	3.50	2.00
11	Duane Causwell	.25	.15
12	Dee Brown	.75	.45
13	Gerald Glass	.30	.18
14	Jayson Williams	.25	.15
15	Elden Campbell	.30	.18
16	Negele Knight	.30	.18
17	Chris Jackson	1.25	.70
18	Danny Ferry	.25	.15
19	Tony Smith	.25	.15
20	Cedric Ceballos	.80	.50
21	Victor Alexander	.35	.20
22	Terrell Brandon	.50	.30
23	Rick Fox	.40	.25
24	Stacey Augmon	1.25	.70
25	Mark Macon	.30	.18
26	Larry Johnson	5.00	3.00
27	Paul Graham	.25	.15
28	Stanley Roberts	.30	.18
29	Dikembe Mutombo	3.00	1.75
30	Robert Pack	.40	.25
31	Doug Smith	.25	.15
32	Steve Smith	2.50	1.50
33	Billy Owens	1.50	.90
34	David Benoit	.40	.25
35	Brian Williams	.75	.45
36	Kenny Anderson	2.50	1.50
37	Greg Anthony	.40	.25
38	Dale Davis	.75	.45
39	Larry Stewart	.30	.18
40	Mike Iuzzolino	.25	.15

1992-93 Upper Deck

Charles Barkley

The cards in this set were issued in two series including 310-cards in Series I and 204-cards in Series II. The card fronts feature full color game action photos framed by a white border. The player's name and position appear in a striped horizontal color bar under the photograph. The card backs consist of another full color action photo along with personal data and statistics. Card #1A was an NBA Draft Trade Card which could be redeemed for card #1, Shaquille O'Neal. Card # 32A and card # 33A were dropped from the set in Series II and replaced by rookie cards of Doug Christie and Jim Jackson who didn't sign with their respective teams until later in the season. A limited Larry Bird/Magic Johnson Retirement card was inserted randmly into Upper Deck foil packs. Key subsets include Draft Picks (1-21), Team Checklists (CL)(35-61), Scoring Threats (ST)(62-66,498-505), Team Fact Cards (Fact)(350-376), All-Stars (AS)(421-445), In Your Face (Face)(446-454), Top Prospects (TP)(455-482), Game Faces (GF)(483-497) and Fanimation (Fan)(506-510). Larry Bird and Wilt Chamberlain were each the subject of a limited 10-card Heroes insert set. Those cards were randomly distributed in Series I and Series II foil packs respectively and are listed at the end of this checklist though not included in the complete set price below. All cards measure 2-1/2" by 3-1/2".

		MINT	NR/MT
	Complete Set (514)	60.00	38.50
	Commons	.05	.02
1A	Draft Trade Card	.75	.45
1B	Shaquille O'Neal (Trade Card)	7.00	4.00
1	Shaquille O'Neal (R)	12.00	7.50
2	Alonzo Mourning (R)	3.00	1.75
3	Christian Laettner (R)	.75	.45
4	LaPhonso Ellis (R)	1.25	.70
5	C. Weatherspoon (R)	.80	.50
6	Adam Keefe (R)	.12	.07
7	Robert Horry (R)	1.00	.60
8	Harold Miner (R)	.50	.30
9	Bryant Stith (R)	.35	.20
10	Malik Sealy (R)	.12	.07
11	Anthony Peeler (R)	.35	.20
12	Andy Woods (R)	.07	.04
13	Tracy Murray (R)	.15	.10
14	Tom Gugliotta (R)	.80	.50
15	Hubert Davis (R)	.30	.18
16	Don MacLean (R)	.50	.30
17	Lee Mayberry (R)	.15	.10
18	Corey Williams (R)	.08	.05
19	Sean Rooks (R)	.20	.12
20	Todd Day (R)	.40	.25
21	Draft (CL)	.12	.07
22	Jeff Hornacek	.08	.05
23	Michael Jordan	1.50	.90
24	John Salley	.05	.02
25	Andre Turner	.05	.02
26	Charles Barkley	.50	.30
27	Anthony Federick	.05	.02
28	Mario Elie	.05	.02
29	Olden Polynice	.05	.02
30	Rodney Monroe	.05	.02
31	Tim Perry	.05	.02
32	Doug Christie	.75	.45
32A	Magic Johnson	1.25	.70
33	Jim Jackson (R)	5.00	3.00
33A	Larry Bird	1.25	.70
34	Randy White	.05	.02
35	Bucks (CL)	.05	.02
36	Bullets (CL)	.05	.02
37	Bulls (CL)	.12	.07
38	Cavaliers (CL)	.05	.02
39	Celtics (CL)	.05	.02
40	Clippers (CL)	.08	.05
41	Hawks (CL)	.05	.02
42	Heat (CL)	.08	.05
43	Hornets (CL)	.08	.05
44	Jazz (CL)	.12	.07
45	Kings (CL)	.05	.02
46	Knicks (CL)	.20	.12
47	Lakers (CL)	.05	.02
48	Magic (CL)	.05	.02

1992-93 UPPER DECK • 211

#	Name		
49	Mavericks (CL)	.05	.02
50	Nets (CL)	.05	.02
51	Nuggetts (CL)	.05	.02
52	Pacers (CL)	.05	.02
53	Pistons (CL)	.05	.02
54	Rockets (CL)	.05	.02
55	76ers (CL)	.05	.02
56	Spurs (CL)	.05	.02
57	Suns (CL)	.08	.05
58	Supersonics (CL)	.05	.02
59	Timberwolves (CL)	.05	.02
60	Trail Blazers (CL)	.05	.02
61	Warriors (CL)	.12	.07
62	Michael Jordan (ST) Scottie Pippen	.60	.35
63	Kendall Gill (ST) Larry Johnson	.15	.10
64	Tom Chambers (ST) Kevin Johnson	.10	.06
65	Tim Hardaway (ST) Chris Mullin	.15	.10
66	Karl Malone (ST) John Stockton	.15	.10
67	Michael Jordan (MVP)	.75	.45
68	Stacey Augmon ($6 Mil)	.10	.06
69	Bob Lanier (Message)	.05	.02
70	Alaa Abdelnaby	.05	.02
71	Andrew Lang	.05	.02
72	Larry Krystkowiak	.05	.02
73	Gerald Wilkins	.05	.02
74	Rod Stickland	.05	.02
75	Danny Ainge	.08	.05
76	Chris Corchiani	.07	.04
77	Jeff Grayer	.05	.02
78	Eric Murdoch	.10	.06
79	Rex Chapman	.07	.04
80	LaBradford Smith	.07	.04
81	Jay Humphries	.05	.02
82	David Robinson	.50	.30
83	William Bedford	.05	.02
84	James Edwards	.05	.02
85	Dan Schayes	.05	.02
86	Lloyd Daniels (R)	.15	.10
87	Blue Edwards	.07	.04
88	Dale Ellis	.07	.04
89	Rolando Blackman	.07	.04
90	Checklist	.20	.07
91	Rik Smits	.05	.02
92	Terry Davis	.05	.02
93	Bill Cartwright	.05	.02
94	Avery Johnson	.07	.04
95	Micheal Williams	.05	.02
96	Spud Webb	.05	.02
97	Benoit Benjamin	.05	.02
98	Derek Harper	.07	.04
99	Matt Bullard	.05	.02
100	Tyrone Corbin	.05	.02
101	Doc Rivers	.05	.02
102	Tony Smith	.05	.02
103	Doug West	.08	.05
104	Kevin Duckworth	.07	.04
105	Luc Longley	.07	.04
106	Antoine Carr	.05	.02
107	Cliff Robinson	.15	.10
108	Grant Long	.05	.02
109	Terry Porter	.10	.06
110	Steve Smith	.20	.12
111	Brian Williams	.07	.04
112	Karl Malone	.30	.18
113	Reggie Williams	.07	.04
114	Tom Chambers	.07	.04
115	Winston Garland	.05	.02
116	John Stockton	.25	.15
117	Chris Jackson	.20	.12
118	Mike Brown	.05	.02
119	Kevin Johnson	.15	.10
120	Reggie Lewis	.15	.10
121	Bimbo Coles	.05	.02
122	Drazen Petrovic	.15	.10
123	Reggie Miller	.20	.12
124	Derrick Coleman	.20	.12
125	Chuck Person	.08	.05
126	Glen Rice	.12	.07
127	Kenny Anderson	.15	.10
128	Willie Burton	.07	.04
129	Chris Morris	.05	.02
130	Patrick Ewing	.35	.20
131	Sean Elliott	.15	.10
132	Clyde Drexler	.20	.12
133	Scottie Pippen	.30	.18
134	Pooh Richardson	.08	.05
135	Horace Grant	.10	.06
136	Hakeem Olajuwon	.75	.45
137	John Paxson	.07	.04
138	Kendall Gill	.12	.07
139	Michael Adams	.07	.04
140	Otis Thorpe	.07	.04
141	Dennis Scott	.10	.06
142	Stacey Augmon	.15	.10
143	Robert Pack	.08	.05
144	Kevin Willis	.05	.02
145	Jerome Kersey	.07	.04
146	Paul Graham	.05	.02
147	Stanley Roberts	.08	.05
148	Dominique Wilkins	.30	.18
149	Scott Skiles	.07	.04
150	Rumeal Robinson	.07	.04
151	Mookie Blaylock	.10	.06
152	Elden Campbell	.08	.05
153	Chris Dudley	.05	.02
154	Sedale Threatt	.05	.02
155	Tate George	.05	.02
156	James Worthy	.12	.07
157	B.J. Armstrong	.12	.07

212 • 1992-93 UPPER DECK

#	Player		
158	Gary Payton	.12	.07
159	Ledell Eackles	.05	.02
160	Sam Perkins	.07	.04
161	Nick Anderson	.15	.10
162	Mitch Richmond	.15	.10
163	Buck Williams	.07	.04
164	Blair Rasmussen	.05	.02
165	Vern Fleming	.05	.02
166	Duane Ferrell	.05	.02
167	George McCloud	.05	.02
168	Terry Cummings	.08	.05
169	Detlef Schrempf	.12	.07
170	Willie Anderson	.05	.02
171	Scott Williams	.05	.02
172	Vernon Maxwell	.12	.07
173	Todd Lichti	.05	.02
174	David Benoit	.10	.06
175	Marcus Liberty	.07	.04
176	Kenny Smith	.07	.04
177	Dan Marjerle	.12	.07
178	Jeff Malone	.08	.05
179	Robert Parish	.12	.07
180	Mark Eaton	.05	.02
181	Rony Seikaly	.08	.05
182	Tony Campbell	.05	.02
183	Kevin McHale	.12	.07
184	Thurl Bailey	.05	.02
185	Kevin Edwards	.05	.02
186	Gerald Glass	.05	.02
187	Hersey Hawkins	.08	.05
188	Sam Mitchell	.07	.04
189	Brian Shaw	.05	.02
190	Felton Spencer	.10	.06
191	Mark Macon	.08	.05
192	Jerry Reynolds	.05	.02
193	Dale Davis	.10	.06
194	Sleepy Floyd	.05	.02
195	A.C. Green	.07	.04
196	Terry Catledge	.05	.02
197	Byron Scott	.05	.02
198	Sam Bowie	.07	.04
199	Vlade Divac	.08	.05
200	Checklist	.20	.07
201	Brad Lohaus	.05	.02
202	Johnny Newman	.05	.02
203	Gary Grant	.05	.02
204	Sidney Green	.05	.02
205	Frank Brickowski	.05	.02
206	Anthony Bowie	.05	.02
207	Duane Causwell	.05	.02
208	A.J. English	.07	.04
209	Mark Aguirre	.07	.04
210	Jon Koncak	.05	.02
211	Kevin Gamble	.05	.02
212	Craig Ehlo	.05	.02
213	Herb Williams	.05	.02
214	Cedric Ceballos	.12	.07
215	Mark Jackson	.07	.04
216	John Bagley	.05	.02
217	Ron Anderson	.05	.02
218	John Battle	.05	.02
219	Kevin Lynch	.05	.02
220	Donald Hodge	.05	.02
221	Chris Gatling	.05	.02
222	Muggsy Bogues	.05	.02
223	Bill Laimbeer	.08	.05
224	Anthony Bonner	.05	.02
225	Fred Roberts	.05	.02
226	Larry Stewart	.07	.04
227	Darrell Walker	.05	.02
228	Larry Smith	.07	.04
229	Billy Owens	.15	.10
230	Vinny Johnson	.05	.02
231	Johnny Dawkins	.05	.02
232	Rick Fox	.07	.04
233	Travis Mays	.05	.02
234	Mark Price	.15	.10
235	Derrick McKey	.07	.04
236	Greg Anthony	.10	.06
237	Doug Smith	.07	.04
238	Alec Kessler	.05	.02
239	Anthony Mason	.10	.06
240	Shawn Kemp	.40	.25
241	Jim Les	.05	.02
242	Dennis Rodman	.10	.06
243	Lionel Simmons	.20	.12
244	Pervis Ellison	.10	.06
245	Terrell Brandon	.08	.05
246	Mark Bryan	.05	.02
247	Brad Daugherty	.12	.07
248	Scott Brooks	.05	.02
249	Sarunas Marciulionis	.08	.05
250	Danny Ferry	.05	.02
251	Loy Vaught	.07	.04
252	Dee Brown	.12	.07
253	Alvin Robertson	.05	.02
254	Charles Smith	.08	.05
255	Dikembe Mutombo	.30	.18
256	Greg Kite	.05	.02
257	Ed Pinckney	.05	.02
258	Ron Harper	.07	.04
259	Elliott Perry	.05	.02
260	Rafael Addison	.05	.02
261	Tim Hardaway	.20	.12
262	Randy Brown	.05	.02
263	Isiah Thomas	.15	.10
264	Victor Alexander	.05	.02
265	Waymon Tisdale	.07	.04
266	Harvey Grant	.07	.04
267	Mike Iuzzolino	.05	.02
268	Joe Dumars	.15	.10
269	Xavier McDaniel	.07	.04
270	Jeff Sanders	.05	.02
271	Danny Manning	.15	.10

1992-93 UPPER DECK • 213

#	Player		
272	Jayson Williams	.07	.04
273	Ricky Pierce	.07	.04
274	Will Perdue	.05	.02
275	Dana Barros	.07	.04
276	Randy Brewer	.05	.02
277	Manute Bol	.05	.02
278	Negele Knight	.07	.04
279	Rodney McCray	.05	.02
280	Greg Sutton	.05	.02
281	Larry Nance	.07	.04
282	John Starks	.20	.12
283	Pete Chilcutt	.05	.02
284	Kenny Gattison	.05	.02
285	Stacey King	.07	.04
286	Bernard King	.07	.04
287	Larry Johnson	.50	.30
288	John Williams	.05	.02
289	Dell Curry	.05	.02
290	Orlando Woolridge	.05	.02
291	Nate McMillan	.05	.02
292	Terry Mills	.10	.06
293	Sherman Douglas	.08	.05
294	Charles Shackleford	.05	.02
295	Ken Norman	.07	.04
296	LaSalle Thompson	.05	.02
297	Chris Mullin	.15	.10
298	Eddie Johnson	.05	.02
299	Armon Gilliam	.07	.04
300	Michael Cage	.05	.02
301	Moses Malone	.15	.10
302	Charles Oakley	.08	.05
303	David Wingate	.05	.02
304	Steve Kerr	.05	.02
305	Tyrone Hill	.05	.02
306	Mark West	.05	.02
307	Fat Lever	.05	.02
308	J.R. Reid	.05	.02
309	Ed Nealy	.05	.02
310	Checklist	.20	.07
311	Alaa Abdelnaby	.05	.02
312	Stacey Augmon	.15	.10
313	Anthony Avent (R)	.15	.10
314	Walter Bond (R)	.07	.04
315	Byron Houston (R)	.15	.10
316	Rick Mahorn	.05	.02
317	Sam Mitchell	.07	.04
318	Mookie Blaylock	.10	.06
319	Lance Blanks	.05	.02
320	John Williams	.05	.02
321	Rolando Blackman	.07	.04
322	Danny Ainge	.07	.04
323	Gerald Glass	.05	.02
324	Robert Pack	.08	.05
325	Oliver Miller (R)	.40	.25
326	Charles Smith	.08	.05
327	Duane Ferrell	.05	.02
328	Pooh Richardson	.07	.04
329	Scott Brooks	.05	.02
330	Walt Williams (R)	.40	.25
331	Andrew Lang	.05	.02
332	Eric Murdoch	.08	.05
333	Vinny Del Negro	.07	.04
334	Charles Barkley	.60	.35
335	James Edwards	.05	.02
336	Xavier McDaniel	.07	.04
337	Paul Graham	.05	.02
338	David Wingate	.05	.02
339	Richard Dumas (R)	.25	.15
340	Jay Humphries	.05	.02
341	Mark Jackson	.07	.04
342	John Salley	.05	.02
343	Jon Koncak	.05	.02
344	Rodney McCray	.05	.02
345	Chuck Person	.08	.05
346	Mario Elie	.05	.02
347	Frank Johnson	.05	.02
348	Rumeal Robinson	.07	.04
349	Terry Mills	.10	.06
350	Atlanta (Fact)	.05	.02
351	Boston (Fact)	.05	.02
352	Charlotte (Fact)	.05	.02
353	Chicago (Fact)	.05	.02
354	Cleveland (Fact)	.05	.02
355	Dallas (Fact)	.05	.02
356	Denver (Fact)	.05	.02
357	Detroit (Fact)	.08	.05
358	Golden State (Fact)	.05	.02
359	Houston (Fact)	.05	.02
360	Indiana (Fact)	.05	.02
361	L.A. Clippers (Fact)	.05	.02
362	L.A. Lakers (Fact)	.05	.02
363	Miami (Fact)	.05	.02
364	Milwaukee (Fact)	.05	.02
365	Minnesota (Fact)	.05	.02
366	New Jersey (Fact)	.15	.10
367	New York (Fact)	.05	.02
368	Orlando (Fact)	.08	.05
369	Philadelphia (Fact)	.05	.02
370	Phoenix (Fact)	.05	.02
371	Portland (Fact)	.05	.02
372	Sacramento (Fact)	.05	.02
373	San Antonio (Fact)	.05	.02
374	Seattle (Fact)	.05	.02
375	Utah (Fact)	.05	.02
376	Washington (Fact)	.05	.02
377	Buck Johnson	.07	.04
378	Brian Howard (R)	.08	.05
379	Travis Mays	.05	.02
380	Jud Buechler	.05	.02
381	Matt Geiger (R)	.15	.10
382	Bob McCann (R)	.10	.06
383	Cedric Ceballos	.12	.07
384	Rod Stickland	.05	.02
385	Kiki Vandeweghe	.05	.02

1992-93 UPPER DECK

#	Player		
386	Latrell Sprewell (R)	2.00	1.25
387	Larry Krystkowiak	.05	.02
388	Dale Ellis	.07	.04
389	Trent Tucker	.05	.02
390	Negele Knight	.07	.04
391	Stanley Roberts	.08	.05
392	Tony Campbell	.05	.02
393	Tim Perry	.05	.02
394	Doug Overton	.05	.02
395	Dan Majerle	.12	.07
396	Duane Cooper (R)	.15	.10
397	Kevin Willis	.05	.02
398	Micheal Williams	.05	.02
399	Avery Johnson	.07	.04
400	Dominique Wilkins	.30	.18
401	Chris Smith (R)	.25	.15
402	Blair Rasmussen	.05	.02
403	Jeff Hornacek	.08	.05
404	Blue Edwards	.07	.04
405	Olden Polynice	.05	.02
406	Jeff Grayer	.05	.02
407	Tony Bennett (R)	.10	.06
408	Don MacLean	.20	.12
409	Tom Chambers	.07	.04
410	Keith Jennings (R)	.12	.07
411	Gerald Wilkins	.05	.02
412	Ken Winchester	.05	.02
413	Doc Rivers	.05	.02
414	Brent Price (R)	.12	.07
415	Mark West	.05	.02
416	J.R. Reid	.05	.02
417	Jon Berry (R)	.12	.07
418	Kevin Johnson	.20	.12
419	Checklist	.10	.03
420	Checklist	.10	.03
421	All-Star (CL)	.12	.07
422	Scottie Pippen (AS)	.15	.10
423	Larry Johnson (AS)	.25	.15
424	Shaquille O'Neal (AS)	3.50	2.00
425	Michael Jordan (AS)	1.00	.60
426	Isiah Thomas (AS)	.10	.06
427	Brad Daugherty (AS)	.08	.05
428	Joe Dumars (AS)	.08	.05
429	Patrick Ewing (AS)	.20	.12
430	Larry Nance (AS)	.07	.04
431	Mark Price (AS)	.10	.06
432	Detlef Schrempf (AS)	.08	.05
433	Dominique Wilkins (AS)	.15	.10
434	Karl Malone (AS)	.15	.10
435	Charles Barkley (AS)	.30	.18
436	David Robinson (AS)	.30	.18
437	John Stockton (AS)	.15	.10
438	Clyde Drexler (AS)	.15	.10
439	Sean Elliott (AS)	.08	.05
440	Tim Hardaway (AS)	.12	.07
441	Shawn Kemp (AS)	.25	.15
442	Dan Marjele (AS)	.08	.05
443	Danny Manning (AS)	.08	.05
444	Hakeem Olajuwon (AS)	.35	.20
445	Terry Porter (AS)	.07	.04
446	Harold Minor (Face)	.25	.15
447	David Benoit (Face)	.07	.04
448	Cedric Ceballos (Face)	.07	.04
449	Chris Jackson (Face)	.10	.06
450	Tim Perry (Face)	.07	.04
451	Kevin Smith (Face)	.07	.04
452	C. Weatherspon (Face)	.25	.15
453	Michael Jordan (Face)	1.00	.60
454	Dominique Wilkins(Face)	.15	.10
455	Top Prospects (CL)	.12	.07
456	Adam Keefe (TP)	.10	.06
457	Alonzo Mourning (TP)	2.00	1.25
458	Jim Jackson (TP)	1.25	.70
459	Sean Rooks (TP)	.12	.07
460	LaPhonso Ellis (TP)	.50	.30
461	Bryant Stith (TP)	.15	.10
462	Byron Houston (TP)	.10	.06
463	Latrell Sprewell (TP)	.80	.50
464	Robert Horry (TP)	.40	.25
465	Malik Sealy (TP)	.10	.06
466	Doug Christie (TP)	.15	.10
467	Duane Cooper (TP)	.10	.06
468	Anthony Peeler (TP)	.15	.10
469	Harold Miner (TP)	.25	.15
470	Todd Day (TP)	.20	.12
471	Lee Mayberry (TP)	.10	.06
472	Christian Laettner(TP)	.50	.30
473	Hubert Davis (TP)	.15	.10
474	Shaquille O'Neal (TP)	3.50	2.00
475	C. Weatherspoon (TP)	.40	.25
476	Richard Dumas (TP)	.12	.07
477	Oliver Miller (TP)	.15	.10
478	Tracy Murray (TP)	.12	.07
479	Walt Williams (TP)	.20	.12
480	Lloyd Daniels (TP)	.10	.06
481	Tom Gugliotta (TP)	.40	.25
482	Brent Price (TP)	.10	.06
483	Mark Aguirre (GF)	.07	.04
484	Frank Brickowski (GF)	.05	.02
485	Derrick Coleman (GF)	.15	.10
486	Clyde Drexler (GF)	.15	.10
487	Harvey Grant (GF)	.07	.04
488	Michael Jordan (GF)	1.00	.60
489	Karl Malone (GF)	.15	.10
490	Xavier McDaniel (GF)	.07	.04
491	Drazen Petrovic (GF)	.08	.05
492	John Starks (GF)	.10	.06
493	Robert Parish (GF)	.10	.06
494	Christian Laettner (GF)	.50	.30
495	Ron Harper (GF)	.05	..02
496	David Robinson (GF)	.30	.18
497	John Salley (GF)	.05	.02
498	Brad Daugherty (ST) Mark Price	.08	.05

1992-93 UPPER DECK ALL-NBA TEAM • 215

499	Chris Jackson (ST)	.10	.06
	Dikembe Mutombo		
500	Isiah Thomas (ST)	.15	.10
	Joe Dumars		
501	Hakeem Olajuwon (ST)	.30	.18
	Otis Thorpe		
502	Derrick Coleman (ST)	.15	.10
	Drazen Petrovic		
503	Clyde Drexler (ST)	.12	.07
	Terry Porter		
504	Lionel Simmons (ST)	.12	.07
	Mitch Richmond		
505	Sean Elliott (ST)	.20	.12
	David Robinson		
506	Michael Jordan (Fan)	1.00	.60
507	Larry Bird (Fan)	.40	.25
508	Karl Malone (Fan)	.15	.10
509	Dikembe Mutombo (Fan)	.15	.10
510	L. Bird/M. Jordan (Fan)	1.00	.60
___	L. Bird/Magic Retire	7.00	4.00
___	Larry Bird Heroes ea.	1.25	.70
___	Larry Bird Hero Cover	2.50	1.50
___	Wilt Chamberlain ea.	1.00	.60
___	Chamberlain Cover	2.00	1.25

1992-93 Upper Deck Award Winner Holograms

This limited insert set contains 9-hologram cards with full color player photos on the fronts. The first six cards in the series were distributed randomly in Upper Deck Series I foil packs. The last 3 cards were found in Series II packs. The cards depict League Leaders in various statistical categories. All cards measure 2-1/2" by 3-1/2".

		MINT	NR/MT
	Complete Set (9)	12.00	7.50
	Commons	.60	.35
1	Michael Jordan	4.00	2.50
2	Mike Stockton	.80	.50
3	Dennis Rodman	.60	.35
4	Detlef Schrempf	.60	.35
5	Larry Johnson	1.25	.70
6	David Robinson	1.75	1.00
7	David Robinson	1.75	1.00
8	John Stockton	.80	.50
9	Michael Jordan	4.00	2.50

1992-93 Upper Deck All-NBA Team

The cards in this set were distributed only in the Upper Deck Locker Edition. The card fronts feature full bleed, full color action photos. The player's name appears below the photograph. Gold foil

216 • 1992-93 UPPER DECK ALL-NBA TEAM

stamping adorns the cards of NBA first team members while silver foil is used for players on the All-NBA second team. The backs include a biography of each player and the card numbers contain and "AN" prefix. All cards measure 2-1/2" by 3-1/2".

a horizontal stripe under the photo and next to an All-Rookie Team logo. The words "First Team" or "Second Team" are printed under the player's name. Card numbers on the back use the prefix AR. All cards measure 2-1/2" by 3-1/2".

		MINT	NR/MT
	Complete Set (10)	26.00	16.00
	Commons	1.00	.60
1	Michael Jordan	10.00	6.50
2	Clyde Drexler	1.50	.90
3	David Robinson	3.50	2.00
4	Karl Malone	2.50	1.50
5	Chris Mullin	1.25	.70
6	John Stockton	1.75	1.00
7	Tim Hardaway	1.00	.60
8	Patrick Ewing	3.50	2.00
9	Scottie Pippen	2.50	1.50
10	Charles Barkley	5.00	3.00

		MINT	NR/MT
	Complete Set (10)	9.00	5.50
	Commons	.60	.35
1	Larry Johnson	3.50	2.00
2	Dikembe Mutombo	1.50	.90
3	Billy Owens	.80	.50
4	Steve Smith	1.25	.70
5	Stacey Augmon	.80	.50
6	Rick Fox	.60	.35
7	Terrell Brandon	.60	.35
8	Larry Stewart	.60	.35
9	Stanley Roberts	.60	.35
10	Mark Macon	.60	.35

1992-93 Upper Deck All-Rookie Team

The cards in this limited insert set were available randomly in Upper Deck Series I foil packs. The card fronts feature full bleed, full color action photos with the player's name and position appearing in

1992-93 Upper Deck Jerry West Selects

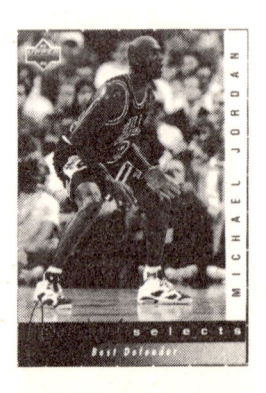

This limited insert set features both current and future NBA greats as selected by former basketball great Jerry West. The card fronts consist of full color action photos with the player's name printed

1992-93 UPPER DECK TEAM MVP's

vertically along the right border. The headline "Jerry West Selects" is printed in a horizontal bar below the photograph and just above the subject of the cards. The flip side includes another photo of the player, a picture of Jerry West and his comments about the player on the card. The card numbers contain the prefix JW. All cards measure 2-1/2" by 3-1/2".

		MINT	NR/MT
	Complete Set (20)	55.00	32.00
	Commons	.50	.30
1	Michael Jordan	10.00	6.50
2	Dennis Rodman	.50	.30
3	David Robinson	3.00	1.75
4	Michael Jordan	10.00	6.50
5	Magic Johnson	5.00	3.00
6	Detlef Schrempf	.50	.30
7	Magic Johnson	5.00	3.00
8	Michael Jordan	10.00	6.50
9	Michael Jordan	10.00	6.50
10	Magic Johnson	5.00	3.00
11	Glen Rice	.50	.30
12	Dikembe Mutombo	1.75	1.00
13	Dikembe Mutombo	1.75	1.00
14	Stacey Augmon	1.00	.60
15	Tim Hardaway	1.00	.60
16	Shawn Kemp	3.00	1.75
17	Danny Manning	1.00	.60
18	Larry Johnson	3.00	1.75
19	Reggie Lewis	.50	.30
20	Tim Hardaway	1.00	.60

1992-93 Upper Deck Team MVP's

This insert set was distributed in Upper Deck's Series I jumbo packs. The cards depict a team MVP from each of the NBA teams. The cards feature game action shots and combine elements of both black and white and full color. The player's name is printed across the white border under his photo and next the the Team MVP designation. Card numbers on the back include the prefix TM. All cards measure 2-1/2" by 3-1/2".

		MINT	NR/MT
	Complete Set (28)	28.00	18.00
	Commons	.40	.25
1	Michael Jordan (CL)	5.00	3.00
2	Dominique Wilkins	2.00	1.25
3	Reggie Lewis	.40	.25
4	Kendall Gill	.60	.35
5	Michael Jordan	10.00	6.50
6	Brad Daugherty	.75	.45
7	Derek Harper	.40	.25
8	Dikembe Mutombo	1.75	1.00
9	Isiah Thomas	1.25	.70
10	Chris Mullin	1.00	.60
11	Hakeem Olajuwon	5.00	3.00
12	Reggie Miller	1.00	.60
13	Ron Harper	.40	.25
14	James Worthy	.50	.30
15	Rony Seikaly	.40	.25

218 • 1992-93 UPPER DECK TEAM MVP's

		MINT	NR/MT
16	Alvin Robertson	.40	.25
17	Pooh Richardson	.40	.25
18	Derrick Coleman	1.00	.60
19	Patrick Ewing	3.50	2.00
20	Scott Skiles	.40	.25
21	Hersey Hawkins	.40	.25
22	Kevin Johnson	1.00	.60
23	Clyde Drexler	1.50	.90
24	Mitch Richmond	.75	.45
25	David Robinson	4.00	2.50
26	Ricky Pierce	.40	.25
27	John Stockton	1.50	.90
28	Pervis Ellison	.50	.30

		MINT	NR/MT
1	Shaquille O'Neal	10.00	6.50
2	Derrick Coleman	.75	.45
3	Glen Rice	.30	.18
4	Reggie Lewis	.30	.18
5	Kenny Anderson	.60	.35
6	Brad Daugherty	.40	.25
7	Dominique Wilkins	1.00	.60
8	Larry Johnson	1.50	.90
9	Michael Jordan	5.00	3.00
10	Mark Price	.50	.30
11	David Robinson	1.50	.90
12	Karl Malone	1.00	.60
13	Sean Elliott	.40	.25
14	John Stockton	.75	.45
15	Derek Harper	.25	.15
16	Kevin Duckworth	.25	.15
17	Chris Mullin	.60	.35
18	Charles Barkley	1.50	.90
19	Tim Hardaway	.50	.30
20	Clyde Drexler	1.00	.60

1992-93 Upper Deck All-Division Inserts

These cards feature full color action photos on the fronts with full-bleed on three sides. The player's name and position are located in a horizontal bar under his photograph. An "All-Division" logo appears in the lower corner of the card front. One card was available in each Upper Deck Hi-Series Jumbo pack. All cards measure 2-1/2" by 3-1/2".

	MINT	NR/MT
Complete Set (20)	20.00	12.50
Commons	.25	.15

1992-93 Upper Deck Foreign Exchange

The cards in this insert set were only distributed in Upper Deck's Hi-Series Locker packs. The card fronts consist of full color action photos with the player's name, position and his native country printed in a color stripe across the bottom of the card. A Foreign Exchange logo in printed in the lower corner of the card

1992-93 UPPER DECK 15,000 POINT CLUB

front and Upper Deck is printed across the top of the card. The letters "FE" preceed the card number on the back. All cards measure 2-1/2" by 3-1/2".

		MINT	NR/MT
	Complete Set (10)	10.00	6.50
	Commons	.40	.25
1	Manute Bol	.40	.25
2	Vlade Divac	.60	.35
3	Patrick Ewing	3.50	2.00
4	Sarunas Marciulionis	.40	.25
5	Dikembe Mutombo	1.75	1.00
6	Hakeem Olajuwon	5.00	3.00
7	Drazen Petrovic	.60	.35
8	Detlef Schrempf	.60	.35
9	Rik Smits	.40	.25
10	Dominique Wilkins	2.00	1.25

1992-93 Upper Deck 15,000 Point Club

The cards in this 20-card set were inserted randomly in Upper Deck's Series II hobby packs. The card fronts feature full color action shots with a 15,000 Point Club headline above the photo. The player's name appears in a small color bar under his photo and next to a small logo in the lower corner of the photo that includes the season the player hit the 15,000 point mark. The card numbers on the back include the prefix PC. All cards measure 2-1/2" by 3-1/2".

		MINT	NR/MT
	Complete Set (20)	28.00	16.00
	Commons	.50	.30
1	Dominique Wilkins	2.00	1.25
2	Kevin McHale	.80	.50
3	Robert Parish	.80	.50
4	Michael Jordan	10.00	6.50
5	Isiah Thomas	1.50	.90
6	Mark Aguirre	.60	.35
7	Kiki Vandeweghe	.50	.30
8	James Worthy	.80	.50
9	Rolando Blackman	.50	.30
10	Moses Malone	1.00	.60
11	Charles Barkley	3.50	2.00
12	Tom Chambers	.50	.30
13	Clyde Drexler	1.50	.90
14	Terry Cummings	.50	.30
15	Eddie Johnson	.50	.30
16	Karl Malone	2.00	1.25
17	Bernard King	.60	.35
18	Larry Nance	.50	.30
19	Jeff Malone	.50	.30
20	Hakeem Olajuwon	5.00	3.00

220 • 1992-93 UPPER DECK ROOKIE STANDOUTS

1992-93 Upper Deck Rookie Standouts

These random inserts feature full color game action photos on the fronts with the player's name printed in a horizontal bar under his picture. A Rookie Standouts logo appears in the lower corner of the card front while Upper Deck is printed vertically along the left side of the photograph. The cards were distributed in Upper Deck HI-Series Jumbo packs. The card numbers on the back are preceeded by the letters RS. All cards measure 2-1/2" by 3-1/2".

		MINT	NR/MT
Complete Set (20)		50.00	30.00
Commons		.50	.30
1	Adam Keefe	.50	.30
2	Alonzo Mourning	10.00	6.50
3	Sean Rooks	.75	.45
4	LaPhonso Ellis	2.50	1.50
5	Latrell Sprewell	6.00	3.75
6	Robert Horry	2.50	1.50
7	Malik Sealy	.50	.30
8	Anthony Peeler	1.00	.60
9	Harold Miner	1.50	.90
10	Anthony Avent	.50	.30
11	Todd Day	1.75	1.00
12	Lee Mayberry	.50	.30
13	Christian Laettner	2.50	1.50
14	Hubert Davis	1.00	.60
15	Shaquille O'Neal	18.00	12.50
16	C. Weatherspoon	2.00	1.25
17	Richard Dumas	.75	.45
18	Walt Williams	1.00	.60
19	Lloyd Daniels	.60	.35
20	Tom Gugliotta	1.50	.90

1993-94 Upper Deck

The cards in this regular edition set were issued in two series and consist of full-color game action player photos on the card fronts. The photos are framed by a white border on the outside of the card with a colored inner border on one side and at the bottom that are printed in the form of a basketball lane. The inner border colors correspond to the player's dominate team color. The player' s name and position are printed in white across the bottom inner border while his team nickname is printed horizontally along the inner side border. An Upper Deck logo is printed in the lower corner of teh card front. The flip side contains a full-color head shot, vital statistics and the player's year-by-year NBA stats. The main subsets include Draft Picks (156-165), Season Leaders (SL)(166-177), Playoffs (178-197), NBA Finals (198-209), Team Schedules (Sch)(210-236), Signature Moves (SM)(237-251). Executive Board (EB)(421-435), Breakaway Threats (BT)(436-455), Game Images (GI)(456-465), Top

1993-94 UPPER DECK • 221

Prospects (TP)(482-497) and highlights from the McDonalds Open (McD)(498-507). A Special card saluting Michael Jordan and Wilt Chamberlain and a card honoring the Chicago Bulls Third World Championship were included in the set and are listed at the end of this checklist. All cards measure 2-1/2" by 3-1/2".

		MINT	NR/MT
Complete Set (510)		38.00	22.00
Commons		.05	.02
1	Muggsy Bogues	.05	.02
2	Kenny Anderson	.15	.10
3	Dell Curry	.05	.02
4	Charles Smith	.08	.05
5	Chuck Person	.08	.05
7	Kevin Johnson	.15	.10
8	Winston Garland	.05	.02
9	John Salley	.05	.02
10	Dale Ellis	.07	.04
11	Otis Thorpe	.08	.05
12	John Stockton	.25	.15
13	Kendall Gill	.12	.07
14	Randy White	.05	.02
15	Mark Jackson	.08	.05
16	Vlade Divac	.08	.05
17	Scott Skiles	.05	.02
18	Xavier McDaniel	.05	.02
19	Jeff Hornacek	.08	.05
20	Stanley Roberts	.07	.04
21	Harold Miner	.15	.10
22	Terrell Brandon	.07	.04
23	Michael Jordan	2.00	1.25
24	Jim Jackson	.30	.18
25	Keith Askins	.05	.02
26	Corey Williams	.07	.04
27	David Benoit	.05	.02
28	Charles Oakley	.10	.06
29	Michael Adams	.07	.04
30	C. Weatherspoon	.20	.12
31	Jon Koncak	.05	.02
32	Gerald Wilkins	.05	.02
33	Anthony Bowie	.05	.02
34	Willie Burton	.07	.04
35	Stacey Augmon	.15	.10
36	Doc Rivers	.07	.04
37	Luc Longley	.05	.02
38	Dee Brown	.12	.07
39	Latterial Green	.05	.02
40	Dan Majerle	.12	.07
41	Doug West	.07	.04
42	Joe Dumars	.15	.10
43	Dennis Scott	.08	.05
44	Mahmud Abdul-Rauf	.15	.10
45	Mark Eaton	.05	.02
46	Danny Ferry	.05	.02
47	Kenny Smith	.07	.04
48	Ron Harper	.08	.05
49	Adam Keefe	.07	.04
50	David Robinson	.50	.30
51	John Starks	.20	.12
52	Jeff Malone	.07	.04
53	Vern Fleming	.05	.02
54	Olden Polynice	.05	.02
55	Dikembe Mutombo	.20	.12
56	Chris Morris	.05	.02
57	Paul Graham	.05	.02
58	Richard Dumas	.12	.07
59	J.R. Reid	.05	.02
60	Brad Daugherty	.15	.10
61	Blue Edwards	.05	.02
62	Mark Macon	.08	.05
63	Latrell Sprewell	.75	.45
64	Mitch Richmond	.15	.10
65	David Wingate	.05	.02
66	LaSalle Thompson	.05	.02
67	Sedale Threatt	.05	.02
68	Larry Krystkowiak	.05	.02
69	John Paxson	.07	.04
70	Frank Brickowski	.05	.02
71	Duane Causwell	.05	.02
72	Fred Roberts	.05	.02
73	Rod Stickland	.05	.02
74	Willie Anderson	.05	.02
75	Thurl Bailey	.05	.02
76	Ricky Pierce	.05	.02
77	Todd Day	.15	.10
78	John Williams	.05	.02
79	Danny Ainge	.10	.06
80	Mark West	.05	.02
81	Marcus Liberty	.07	.04
82	Keith Jennings	.05	.02
83	Derrick Coleman	.20	.12
84	Larry Stewart	.05	.02
85	Tracy Murray	.10	.06
86	Robert Horry	.20	.12
87	Derek Harper	.08	.05
88	Scott Hastings	.05	.02
89	Sam Perkins	.08	.05
90	Clyde Drexler	.25	.15
91	Brent Price	.07	.04
92	Chris Mullin	.20	.12
93	Rafael Addison	.07	.04
94	Tyrone Corbin	.07	.04
95	Sarunas Marciulionis	.07	.04
96	Antoine Carr	.05	.02
97	Tony Bennett	.05	.02
98	Sam Mitchell	.07	.04
99	Lionel Simmons	.20	.12
100	Tim Perry	.05	.02

1993-94 UPPER DECK

#	Player		
101	Horace Grant	.08	.05
102	Tom Hammonds	.05	.02
103	Walter Bonds	.05	.02
104	Detlef Schrempf	.15	.10
105	Terry Porter	.08	.05
106	Dan Schayes	.05	.02
107	Rumeal Robinson	.05	.02
108	Gerald Glass	.07	.04
109	Mike Gminski	.05	.02
110	Terry Mills	.08	.05
111	Loy Vaught	.05	.02
112	Jim Les	.05	.02
113	Byron Houston	.08	.05
114	Randy Brown	.05	.02
115	Anthony Avent	.08	.05
116	Donald Hodge	.05	.02
117	Kevin Willis	.07	.04
118	Robert Pack	.07	.04
119	Dale Davis	.12	.07
120	Grant Long	.05	.02
121	Anthony Bonner	.05	.02
122	Chris Smith	.07	.04
123	Elden Campbell	.10	.06
124	Cliff Robinson	.12	.07
125	Sherman Douglas	.05	.02
126	Alvin Robertson	.05	.02
127	Rolando Blackman	.07	.04
128	Malik Sealy	.08	.05
129	Ed Pinckney	.05	.02
130	Anthony Peeler	.15	.10
131	Scott Brooks	.05	.02
132	Rik Smits	.05	.02
133	Derrick McKey	.07	.04
134	Alaa Abdelnaby	.05	.02
135	Rex Chapman	.05	.02
136	Tony Campbell	.05	.02
137	John Williams	.05	.02
138	Vincent Askew	.05	.02
139	LaBradford Smith	.05	.02
140	Vinny Del Negro	.05	.02
141	Darrell Walker	.05	.02
142	James Worthy	.10	.06
143	Jeff Turner	.05	.02
144	Duane Ferrell	.05	.02
145	Larry Smith	.05	.02
146	Eddie Johnson	.05	.02
147	Chris Gatling	.05	.02
148	Buck Williams	.07	.04
149	Donald Royal	.05	.02
150	Dino Radja (R)	.30	.18
151	Johnny Dawkins	.05	.02
152	Tim Legler (R)	.10	.06
153	Bill Laimbeer	.07	.04
154	Glen Rice	.10	.06
155	Bill Cartwright	.05	.02
156	Luther Wright (R)	.15	.10
157	Rex Walters (R)	.12	.07
158	Doug Edwards (R)	.15	.10
159	George Lynch (R)	.35	.20
160	Chris Mills (R)	.40	.25
161	Sam Cassell (R)	.50	.30
162	Nick Van Exel (R)	.35	.20
163	Shawn Bradley (R)	.40	.25
164	Calbert Cheaney (R)	.40	.25
165	Toni Kukoc (R)	.60	.35
166	Michael Jordan (SL)	1.00	.60
167	Dennis Rodman (SL)	.08	.05
168	John Stockton (SL)	.15	.10
169	B.J. Armstrong (SL)	.08	.05
170	Hakeem Olajuwon (SL)	.50	.30
171	Michael Jordan (SL)	1.00	.60
172	Cedric Ceballos (SL)	.08	.05
173	Mark Price (SL)	.08	.05
174	Charles Barkley (SL)	.25	.15
175	Cliff Robinson (SL)	.08	.05
176	Hakeem Olajuwon (SL)	.50	.30
177	Shaquille O'Neal (SL)	1.00	.60
178	Playoffs (HL)	.05	.02
179	Playoffs (HL)	.05	.02
180	Playoffs (HL) (Michael Jordan)	.75	.45
181	Playoffs (HL)		
182	Playoffs (HL)	.05	.02
183	Playoffs (HL) (David Robinson)	.20	.12
184	Playoffs (HL)	.05	.02
185	Playoffs (HL)	.05	.02
186	Playoffs (HL)	.05	.02
187	Playoffs (HL) (Michael Jordan)	.75	.45
188	Playoffs (HL)	.05	.02
189	Playoffs (HL)	.05	.02
190	Playoffs (HL)	.05	.02
191	Playoffs (HL)	.05	.02
192	Playoffs (HL)	.05	.02
193	Playoffs (HL) (Michael Jordan)	.75	.45
194	Playoffs (HL) (Larry Johnson)	.15	.10
195	Playoffs (HL)	.05	.02
196	Playoffs (HL)	.05	.02
197	Playoffs (HL)	.05	.02
198	NBA Finals (Jordan)	1.00	.60
199	NBA Finals (Pippen)	.15	.10
200	NBA Finals	.07	.04
201	NBA Finals (Jordan)	1.00	.60
202	NBA Finals	.07	.04
203	NBA Finals	.07	.04
204	NBA Finals (Jordan)	1.00	.60
205	NBA Finals	.07	.04
206	NBA Finals	.07	.04
207	NBA Finals	.07	.04
208	1992-93 Chicago Bulls	.07	.04
209	1992-93 Phoenix Suns	.07	.04

1993-94 UPPER DECK • 223

210 Atlanta Hawks (Sch)	.05	.02
211 Boston Celtics (Sch)	.05	.02
212 Charlotte Hornets (Sch)	.05	.02
213 Chicago Bulls (Sch)	.05	.02
214 Cleveland Cavaliers (Sch.)	.05	.02
215 Dallas Mavericks (Sch)	.10	.06
216 Denver Nuggets (Sch)	.05	.02
217 Detroit Pistons (Sch)	.05	.02
218 Golden State (Sch)	.05	.02
219 Houston Rockets (Sch)	.05	.02
220 Indiana Pacers (Sch)	.05	.02
221 L.A. Clippers (Sch)	.05	.02
222 L.A. Lakers (Sch)	.05	.02
223 Miami Heat (Sch)	.05	.02
224 Milwaukee Bucks (Sch)	.05	.02
225 Minnesota T-Wolves (Sch)	.05	.02
226 New Jersey Nets (Sch)	.05	.02
227 New York Knicks (Sch)	.05	.02
228 Orlando Magic (Sch)	.60	.35
229 Philadelphia 76er's(Sch)	.05	.02
230 Phoenix Suns (Sch)	.05	.02
231 Portland T-Blazers (Sch)	.05	.02
232 Sacramento Kings (Sch)	.05	.02
233 San Antonio Spurs (Sch)	.05	.02
234 Seattle SuperSonics (Sch.)	.05	.02
235 Utah Jazz (Sch)	.05	.02
236 Washington Bullets (Sch.)	.05	.02
237 Michael Jordan (SM)	1.00	.60
238 Clyde Drexler (SM)	.15	.10
239 Tim Hardaway (SM)	.08	.05
240 Dominique Wilkins (SM)	.15	.10
241 Brad Daugherty (SM)	.08	.05
242 Chris Mullin (SM)	.10	.06
243 Kenny Anderson (SM)	.08	.05
244 Patrick Ewing (SM)	.20	.12
245 Isiah Thomas (SM)	.10	.06
246 Dikembe Mutombo (SM)	.15	.10
247 Danny Manning (SM)	.08	.05
248 David Robinson (SM)	.25	.15
249 Karl Malone (SM)	.15	.10
250 James Worthy (SM)	.08	.05
251 Shawn Kemp (SM)	.20	.12
252 Checklist	.05	.02
253 Checklist	.05	.02
254 Checklist	.05	.02
255 Checklist	.05	.02
256 Patrick Ewing	.35	.20
257 B.J. Armstrong	.12	.07
258 Oliver Miller	.12	.07
259 Jud Buechler	.05	.02
260 Pooh Richardson	.07	.04
261 Victor Alexander	.05	.02
262 Kevin Gamble	.05	.02
263 Doug Smith	.05	.02
264 Isiah Thomas	.20	.12
265 Doug Christie	.15	.10
266 Mark Bryant	.05	.02
267 Lloyd Daniels	.08	.05
268 Michael Williams	.05	.02
269 Nick Anderson	.10	.06
270 Tom Gugliotta	.20	.12
271 Kenny Gattison	.05	.02
272 Vernon Maxwell	.12	.07
273 Terry Cummings	.07	.04
274 Karl Malone	.30	.18
275 Rick Fox	.08	.05
276 Matt Bullard	.05	.02
277 Johnny Newman	.05	.02
278 Mark Price	.12	.07
279 Mookie Blaylock	.08	.05
280 Charles Barkley	.40	.25
281 Larry Nance	.07	.04
282 Walt Williams	.15	.10
283 Brian Shaw	.05	.02
284 Robert Parish	.12	.07
285 Pervis Ellison	.10	.06
286 Spud Webb	.05	.02
287 Hakeem Olajuwon	.80	.50
288 Jerome Kersey	.05	.02
289 Carl Herrera	.12	.07
290 Dominique Wilkins	.30	.18
291 Billy Owens	.15	.10
292 Greg Anthony	.08	.05
293 Nate McMillan	.05	.02
294 Christian Laettner	.20	.12
295 Gary Payton	.12	.07
296 Steve Smith	.15	.10
297 Anthony Mason	.08	.05
298 Sean Rooks	.08	.05
299 Toni Kukoc	.30	.18
300 Shaquille O'Neal	2.00	1.25
301 Jay Humphries	.05	.02
302 Sleepy Floyd	.05	.02
303 Bimbo Coles	.05	.02
304 John Battle	.05	.02
305 Shawn Kemp	.35	.20
306 Scott Williams	.05	.02
307 Wayman Tisdale	.07	.04
308 Rony Seikaly	.08	.05
309 Reggie Miller	.20	.12
310 Scottie Pippen	.30	.18
311 Chris Webber (R)	3.00	1.75
312 Trevor Wilson	.08	.05
313 Derek Strong (R)	.12	.07
314 Bobby Hurley (R)	.35	.20
315 Herb Williams	.05	.02
316 Rex Walters	.08	.05
317 Doug Edwards	.10	.06
318 Ken Williams	.05	.02
319 Jon Barry	.07	.04

1993-94 UPPER DECK

#	Player		
320	Joe Courtney (R)	.10	.06
321	Ervin Johnson (R)	.12	.07
322	Sam Cassell	.25	.15
323	Tim Hardaway	.12	.07
324	Ed Stokes	.05	.02
325	Steve Kerr	.05	.02
326	Doug Overton	.05	.02
327	Reggie Williams	.08	.05
328	Avery Johnson	.05	.02
329	Stacey King	.05	.02
330	Vin Baker (R)	.60	.35
331	Greg Kite	.05	.02
332	Michael Cage	.05	.02
333	Alonzo Mourning	1.00	.60
334	Acie Earl (R)	.15	.10
335	Terry Dehere (R)	.12	.07
336	Negele Knight	.05	.02
337	Gerald Madkins (R)	.10	.06
338	Lindsey Hunter (R)	.30	.18
339	Luther Wright	.10	.06
340	Mike Peplowski (R)	.10	.06
341	Gerald Paddio	.05	.02
342	Danning Manning	.15	.10
343	Chris Mills	.15	.10
344	Kevin Lynch	.05	.02
345	Shawn Bradley	.20	.12
346	Evers Burns (R)	.10	.06
347	Rodney Rogers (R)	.25	.15
348	Cedric Ceballos	.08	.05
349	Warren Kidd (R)	.10	.06
350	Darnell Mee (R)	.10	.06
351	Matt Geiger	.05	.02
352	Jamal Mashburn (R)	1.50	.90
353	Antonio Davis (R)	.20	.12
354	Calbert Cheaney	.20	.12
355	George Lynch	.15	.10
356	Derrick McKey	.07	.04
357	Jerry Reynolds	.05	.02
358	Don MacLean	.15	.10
359	Scott Haskin (R)	.12	.07
360	Malcolm Mackey (R)	.12	.07
361	Isaiah Rider (R)	1.00	.60
362	Detlef Schrempf	.15	.10
363	Josh Grant (R)	.12	.07
364	Richard Petruska (R)	.12	.07
365	Larry Johnson	.50	.30
366	Felton Spencer	.10	.06
367	Ken Norman	.07	.04
368	Anthony Cook	.05	.02
369	James Robinson (R)	.15	.10
370	Kevin Duckworth	.05	.02
371	Chris Whitney (R)	.10	.06
372	Moses Malone	.10	.06
373	Nick Van Exel	.20	.12
374	Scott Burrell (R)	.15	.10
375	Harvey Grant	.05	.02
376	Benoit Benjamin	.05	.02
377	Henry James	.05	.02
378	Craig Ehlo	.05	.02
379	Ennis Whatley	.05	.02
380	Sean Green	.05	.02
381	Eric Murdock	.07	.04
382	Anfernee Hardaway (R)	2.50	1.50
383	Gheorghe Muresan (R)	.12	.07
384	Kendall Gill	.12	.07
385	David Wood	.05	.02
386	Mario Elie	.05	.02
387	Chris Corchiani	.05	.02
388	Greg Graham (R)	.12	.07
389	Hersey Hawkins	.07	.04
390	Mark Aquirre	.07	.04
391	LaPhonso Ellis	.20	.12
392	Anthony Bonner	.05	.02
393	Lucious Harris (R)	.10	.06
394	Andrew Lang	.05	.02
395	Chris Dudley	.05	.02
396	Dennis Rodman	.08	.05
397	Larry Krystkowiak	.05	.02
398	A.C. Green	.08	.05
399	Eddie Johnson	.05	.02
400	Kevin Edwards	.05	.02
401	Tyrone Hill	.05	.02
402	Greg Anderson	.05	.02
403	P.J. Brown (R)	.12	.07
404	Dana Barros	.07	.04
405	Allan Houston (R)	.15	.10
406	Mike Brown	.05	.02
407	Lee Mayberry	.07	.04
408	Fat Lever	.05	.02
409	Tony Smith	.05	.02
410	Tom Chambers	.07	.04
411	Manute Bol	.05	.02
412	Joe Kleine	.05	.02
413	Bryant Stith	.15	.10
414	Eric Riley	.08	.05
415	Pete Myers	.05	.02
416	Sean Elliott	.10	.06
417	Sam Bowie	.05	.02
418	Armon Gilliam	.07	.04
419	Brian Williams	.12	.07
420	Popeye Jones (R)	.15	.10
421	Dennis Rodman (EB)	.08	.05
422	Karl Malone (EB)	.15	.10
423	Tom Gugliotta (EB)	.12	.07
424	Kevin Willis (EB)	.05	.02
425	Hakeem Olajuwon (EB)	.50	.30
426	Charles Oakley (EB)	.05	.02
427	C. Weatherspoon (EB)	.10	.06
428	Derrick Coleman (EB)	.12	.07
429	Buck Williams (EB)	.05	.02
430	Christian Laettner (EB)	.12	.07
431	Dikembe Mutombo (EB)	.12	.07
432	Rony Seikaly (EB)	.05	.02
433	Brad Daugherty (EB)	.07	.04

1993-94 UPPER DECK ALL-NBA TEAM • 225

434 Horace Grant (EB)	.05	.02
435 Larry Johnson (EB)	.25	.15
436 Dee Brown (BT)	.07	.04
437 Muggsy Bogues (BT)	.05	.02
438 Michael Jordan (BT)	1.00	.60
439 Tim Hardaway (BT)	.08	.05
440 Michael Williams (BT)	.05	.02
441 Gary Payton (BT)	.07	.04
442 Mookie Blaylock (BT)	.07	.04
443 Doc Rivers (BT)	.07	.04
444 Kenny Smith (BT)	.07	.04
445 John Stockton (BT)	.12	.07
446 Alvin Robertson (BT)	.05	.02
447 Mark Jackson (BT)	.07	.04
448 Kenny Anderson (BT)	.10	.06
449 Scottie Pippen (BT)	.15	.10
450 Isiah Thomas (BT)	.10	.06
451 Mark Price (BT)	.08	.05
452 Latrell Sprewell (BT)	.25	.15
453 Sedale Threatt (BT)	.05	.02
454 Nick Anderson (BT)	.08	.05
455 Rod Stickland (BT)	.05	.02
456 Oliver Miller (GI)	.08	.05
457 J. Worthy/V.Divac(GI)	.07	.04
458 Robert Horry (GI)	.10	.06
459 Rockets Players (GI)	.07	.04
460 S. Rooke/J. Jackson (GI)	.12	.07
461 Mitch Richmond (GI)	.08	.05
462 Chris Morris (GI)	.05	.02
463 M. Jackson/G. Grant (GI)	.05	.02
464 David Robinson (GI)	.25	.15
465 Danny Ainge (GI)	.07	.04
466 Michael Jordan (Sky)	1.00	.60
467 Dominique Wilkins (Sky)	.15	.10
468 Alonzo Mourning (Sky)	.40	.25
469 Shaquille O'Neal (Sky)	1.00	.60
470 Tim Hardaway (Sky)	.08	.05
471 Patrick Ewing (Sky)	.20	.12
472 Kevin Johnson (Sky)	.08	.05
473 Clyde Drexler (Sky)	.15	.10
474 David Robinson (Sky)	.25	.15
475 Shawn Kemp (Sky)	.20	.12
476 Dee Brown (Sky)	.07	.04
477 Jim Jackson (Sky)	.15	.10
478 John Stockton (Sky)	.12	.07
479 Robert Horry (Sky)	.15	.10
480 Glen Rice (Sky)	.07	.04
481 M. Williams(School)	.05	.02
482 G.Lynch/T. Dehere (TP)	.10	.02
483 Chris Webber (TP)	1.00	.60
484 Anfemee Hardaway (TP)	.60	.35
485 Shawn Bradley (TP)	.15	.10
486 Jamal Mashburn (TP)	.30	.18
487 Calbert Cheaney (TP)	.15	.10
488 Isaiah Rider (TP)	.30	.18
489 Bobby Hurley (TP)	.12	.07
490 Vin Baker (TP)	.25	.15
491 Rodney Rogers (TP)	.10	.06
492 Lindsey Hunter (TP)	.10	.06
493 Allan Houston (TP)	.08	.05
494 Terry Dehere (TP)	.07	.04
495 George Lynch (TP)	.10	.06
496 Toni Kukoc (TP)	.15	.10
497 Nick Van Exel (TP)	.10	.06
498 Charles Barkley (McD)	.25	.15
499 A.C. Green (McD)	.05	.02
500 Dan Majerle (McD)	.07	.04
501 Jerrod Mustaf (McD)	.05	.02
502 Kevin Johnson (McD)	.08	.05
503 Negele Knight (McD)	.05	.02
504 Danny Ainge (McD)	.07	.04
505 Oliver Miller (McD)	.08	.05
506 Joe Courtney (McD)	.05	.02
507 Checklist (McD)	.05	.02
508 Checklist	.05	.02
509 Checklist	.05	.02
510 Checklist	.05	.02
SP3 Michael Jordan/Wilt Chamberlain	5.00	3.00
SP4 Chicago Bulls Third	5.00	3.00

1993-94 Upper Deck All-NBA Team

These limited insert cards were randomly issued in Upper Deck Series I foil packs. The card fronts feature full-bleed, full-color photos with an All-NBA First or Second Team numerical logo

226 • 1993-94 UPPER DECK ALL-NBA TEAM

printed in the lower corner. Two stripes run vertically from the logo to the top of the card. The inside stripe contains the words First Team or Second Team while the outside stripe contains the player's name. An Upper Deck logo appears in the top corner above the stripe. The prefix AN appears before the card numbers on the flip side. All cards measure 2-1/2" by 3-1/2".

		MINT	NR/MT
	Complete Set (15)	18.00	12.00
	Commons	.40	.25
1	Charles Barkley	2.00	1.25
2	Karl Malone	1.00	.60
3	Hakeem Olajuwon	3.00	1.75
4	Michael Jordan	5.00	3.00
5	Mark Price	.60	.35
6	Dominique Wilkins	1.00	.60
7	Larry Johnson	1.50	.90
8	Patrick Ewing	1.50	.90
9	John Stockton	1.00	.60
10	Joe Dumars	.60	.35
11	Scottie Pippen	1.00	.60
12	Derrick Coleman	1.00	.60
13	David Robinson	1.50	.90
14	Tim Hardaway	.40	.25
15	Michael Jordan (CL)	2.00	1.25

1993-94 Upper Deck All-Rookie Team

This set features some of the top rookies from the previous season and were issued as random inserts in Upper Deck Series I foil packs. The card front sport a full-bleed, full-color design with a game action photo. The player's name appears in a color bar across the bottom portion of the card next to an All-Rookie logo. The words First Team or Second Team are printed in a box in the top corner. The letters AR preceed the card numbers on the backs. All cards measure 2-1/2" by 3-1/2".

		MINT	NR/MT
	Complete Set (10)	40.00	26.00
	Commons	.50	.30
1	Shaquille O'Neal	20.00	12.50
2	Alonzo Mourning	10.00	6.50
3	Christian Laettner	2.00	1.25
4	Tom Gugliotta	1.50	.90
5	LaPhonso Ellis	2.00	1.25
6	Walt Williams	1.25	.70
7	Robert Horry	2.50	1.50
8	Latrell Sprewell	7.00	4.00
9	C. Weatherspoon	2.00	1.25
10	Richard Dumas	.50	.30

1993-94 Upper Deck Michael Jordan's Flight Team

In this limited insert set Michael Jordan picks some of the top player's in the NBA. The card fronts include a full-bleed, full-color game action photo with the player's name, number and team name appearing in a winged-shape logo centered at the bottom of the card. The backs contain another photo of the player along with a photo of Michael Jordan and Jordan's comments about the player. The card numbers sport the prefix FT. The inserts were distributed randomly in Upper Deck Series I hobby packs and measure 2-1/2" by 3-1/2".

		MINT	NR/MT
	Complete Set (20)	125.00	70.00
	Commons	2.00	1.25
1	Stacey Augmon	2.50	1.50
2	Charles Barkley	10.00	6.50
3	David Benoit	2.00	1.25
4	Dee Brown	2.50	1.50
5	Cedric Ceballos	2.50	1.50
6	Derrick Coleman	4.00	2.50
7	Clyde Drexler	5.00	3.00
8	Sean Elliott	2.50	1.50
9	LaPhonso Ellis	6.00	3.50
10	Kendall Gill	2.50	1.50
11	Larry Johnson	10.00	6.50
12	Shawn Kemp	10.00	6.50
13	Karl Malone	6.00	3.50
14	Harold Miner	3.00	1.75
15	Alonzo Mourning	15.00	10.00
16	Shaquille O'Neal	30.00	18.00
17	Scottie Pippen	8.00	5.00
18	C. Weatherspoon	4.00	2.50
19	Spud Webb	2.00	1.25
20	Dominique Wilkins	5.00	3.00

1993-94 Upper Deck Future Heroes

These cards are an extension of the Future Heroes issued in the previous seasons and the card numbers pick up where last year's edition left off. The cards were distributed one per pack in the Upper Deck Locker edition. The card design is similar to the Upper Deck regular edition with a full-color action shot framed on one side and at the bottom by a colorful inner border that resembles a basketball lane and a smaller outside border. The words Future Heroes is printed vertically along the inner border on the side of the card while the player's name appears across the bottom of the card. All cards measure 2-1/2" by 3-1/2".

228 • 1993-94 UPPER DECK FUTURE HEROES

	MINT	NR/MT
Complete Set (10)	20.00	12.50
Commons	.40	.25
28 Derrick Coleman	.80	.50
29 LaPhonso Ellis	1.00	.60
30 Jim Jackson	1.50	.90
31 Larry Johnson	2.00	1.25
32 Shawn Kemp	2.00	1.25
33 Christian Laettner	.80	.50
34 Alonzo Mourning	4.00	2.50
35 Shaquille O'Neal	10.00	6.50
36 Walt Williams	.40	.25
___ L. Ellis/C. Laettner (CL)	.75	.45

	MINT	NR/MT
Complete Set (10)	18.00	12.00
Commons	.30	.18
1 Charles Barkley	3.00	1.75
2 Michael Jordan	10.00	6.50
3 Scottie Pippen	1.75	1.00
4 Detlef Schrempf	.40	.25
5 Mark Jackson	.30	.18
6 Kenny Anderson	.75	.45
7 Larry Johnson	2.00	1.25
8 Dikembe Mutombo	1.25	.70
9 Rumeal Robinson	.30	.18
10 Michael Williams	.30	.18

1993-94 Upper Deck Triple Double Inserts

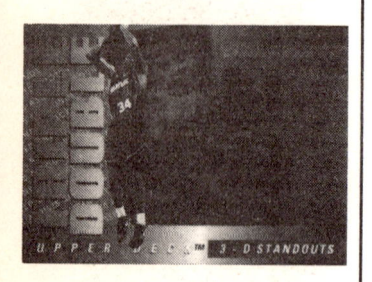

These limited insert cards sport a three-dimensional image on horizontal card fronts. The words Triple-Double are printed vertically along the side of the card while the words Upper Deck 3-D Standouts is printed across the bottom. Th eletters TD preceed the card numbers. The cards were random inserts in Upper Deck Series I packs and measure 3-1/2" by 2-1/2".

1993-94 Upper Deck Locker Talk

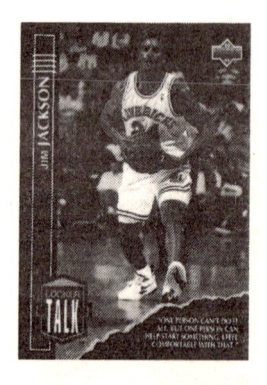

The cards in this set were issued one per Upper Deck Series II Locker pack. The card fronts feature a full-color action shot partially torn in the lower corner where a quote from the player is printed in white type. The player's name appears vertically inside a box along the side of the card. A Locker Talk logo is printed in the lower corner. The card numbers on the flip side contain the letters LT. All cards measure 2-1/2" by 3-1/2".

1993-94 UPPER DECK ROOKIE STANDOUTS • 229

		MINT	NR/MT
	Complete Set (15)	30.00	18.00
	Commons	.40	.25
1	Michael Jordan	10.00	6.50
2	Stacey Augmon	.75	.45
3	Shaquille O'Neal	10.00	6.50
4	Alonzo Mourning	4.00	2.50
5	Harold Miner	.60	.35
6	C. Weatherspoon	.75	.45
7	Derrick Coleman	1.00	.60
8	Charles Barkley	3.50	2.00
9	David Robinson	3.50	2.00
10	Chuck Person	.40	.25
11	Karl Malone	1.50	.90
12	Muggsy Bogues	.40	.25
13	Latrell Sprewell	3.00	1.75
14	John Starks	.75	.45
15	Jim Jackson	1.50	.90

		MINT	NR/MT
	Complete Set (10)	125.00	70.00
	Commons	15.00	10.00
1	Jordan's A Steal	15.00	10.00
2	Jordan's High-Five	15.00	10.00
3	1991 Finals MVP	15.00	10.00
4	35 Point Half	15.00	10.00
5	Three-Point King	15.00	10.00
6	Back-To-Back MVP	15.00	10.00
7	55 Point Game	15.00	10.00
8	Scoring Avg Record	15.00	10.00
9	Jordan's Three-Peat	15.00	10.00
10	Checklist	10.00	2.50

1993-94 Upper Deck Mr. June

The cards in this set spotlight Michael Jordan's playoff exploits and were randomly distributed in Upper Deck Series II hobby packs. The card fronts feature action shots of Jordan taken as the actual events occured along with a Mr. June headline. All cards measure 2-1/2" by 3-1/2".

1993-94 Upper Deck Rookie Standouts

The cards in this limited insert set were randomly distributed in Upper Deck Series II retai packs and Series II jumbo packs. The card fronts consist of full-bleed, full-color action photographs of the player with a Rookie Standouts logo stamped in the lower corner of the card. An RS preceeds the card numbers on the backs. ALl cards measure 2-1/2" by 3-1/2".

	MINT	NR/MT
Complete Set (20)	60.00	38.00
Commons	.60	.35

230 • 1993-94 UPPER DECK ROOKIE STANDOUTS

1	Chris Webber	15.00	10.00
2	Bobby Hurley	2.00	1.25
3	Isaiah Rider	7.00	4.00
4	Terry Dehere	.60	.35
5	Toni Kukoc	3.50	2.00
6	Shawn Bradley	2.00	1.25
7	Allan Houston	.75	.45
8	Chris Mills	1.50	.90
9	Jamal Mashburn	7.00	4.00
10	Greg Graham	.60	.35
11	George Lynch	1.50	.90
12	Scott Burrell	1.00	.60
13	Calbert Cheaney	2.00	1.25
14	Lindsey Hunter	1.50	.90
15	Nick Van Exel	1.50	.90
16	Rex Walters	.60	.35
17	Anfernee Hardaway	10.00	6.50
18	Sam Cassell	3.50	2.00
19	Vin Baker	3.50	2.00
20	Rodney Rogers	1.50	.90

1993-94 Upper Deck Team MVP's

The cards in this limited insert set feature full-color game action photos on the card fronts framed by two borders in all sides. The player's name appears vertically inside a color bar in the top corner of the card/ Team MVP is printed across the inner border at the bottom. The words Upper Deck are located along the inner border across the top of the card. The numbers on the backs are preceeded by the letters TM. The cards were issued randomly in Upper Deck Series II retail and jumbo packs. All cards measure 2-1/2" by 3-1/2".

		MINT	NR/MT
Complete Set (27)		20.00	12.50
Commons		.20	.12

1	Dominique Wilkins	1.00	.60
2	Robert Parish	.35	.20
3	Alonzo Mourning	1.50	.90
4	Michael Jordan	5.00	3.00
5	Mark Price	.40	.25
6	Jim Jackson	1.00	.60
7	Mahmoud Abdul-Rauf	.30	.18
8	Joe Dumars	.50	.30
9	Chris Mullin	.60	.35
10	Hakeem Olajuwon	2.50	1.50
11	Reggie Miller	.75	.45
12	Danning Manning	.60	.35
13	James Worthy	.35	.20
14	Glen Rice	.25	.15
15	Blue Edwards	.20	.12
16	Christian Laettner	.75	.45
17	Derrick Coleman	.75	.45
18	Patrick Ewing	1.25	.70
19	Shaquille O'Neal	5.00	3.00
20	C. Weatherspoon	.75	.45
21	Charles Barkley	1.50	.90
22	Clyde Drexler	1.00	.60
23	Mitch Richmond	.40	.25
24	David Robinson	1.50	.90
25	Shawn Kemp	1.50	.90
26	John Stockton	1.00	.60
27	Tom Gugliotta	.50	.30

1993-94 Upper Deck SE

The cards in this Special Edition premium set feature full-bleed, full-color game action player photos on the card fronts. The player's name, team nickname and the Upper Deck logo are printed with gold foil stamping. The player's name appears vertically in a box in the upper corner of the card front superimposed over his position. The flip side contains another full-color action shot with personal data and a brief biography printed vertically in a small box in the upper corner. Subsets include All-Star Weekend (181-198) and Team Headlines (199-225). Special inserts feature a pair of Michael Jordan cards including one honoring his retirement and another spotlighting his alter ego from his Nike commercial, Johnny Kilroy. Limited inserts also include two 225-card parallel sets, Electric Court (1 card per foil pack) and Electric Gold (shipped randomly in foil packs). Electric Court inserts are valued at 3X to 5X the prices listed below. Electric Gold inserts are valued at 15 X the values listed below for commons up to 50X the values listed below for superstars and hot rookies. All cards measure 2-1/2" by 3-1/2".

		MINT	NR/MT
	Complete Set (225)	32.00	20.00
	Commons	.10	.06
	Electric Court (225)	90.00	55.00
	Commons	.12	.07
	Electric Gold (225)	1,850.00	1,100.00
	Commons	1.50	.90
1	Scottie Pippen	.40	.25
2	Todd Day	.20	.12
3	Detlef Schrempf	.20	.12
4	Chris Webber	3.50	2.00
5	Michael Adams	.12	.07
6	Loy Vaught	.10	.06
7	Doug West	.12	.07
8	A. C. Green	.12	.07
9	Anthony Mason	.15	.10
10	Clyde Drexler	.30	.18
11	Popeye Jones (R)	.25	.15
12	Valde Divac	.12	.07
13	Armon Gilliam	.12	.07
14	Hersey Hawkins	.12	.07
15	Dennis Scott	.15	.10
16	Bimbo Coles	.10	.06
17	Blue Edwards	.10	.06
18	Negele Knight	.10	.06
19	Dale Davis	.15	.10
20	Isiah Thomas	.25	.15
21	Latrell Sprewell	.75	.45
22	Kenny Smith	.10	.06
23	Bryant Stith	.15	.10
24	Terry Porter	.12	.07
25	Spud Webb	.10	.06
26	John Battle	.10	.06
27	Jeff Malone	.12	.07
28	Olden Polynice	.10	.06
29	Kevin Willis	.10	.06
30	Robert Parish	.20	.12
31	Kevin Johnson	.20	.12
32	Shaquille O'Neal	2.50	1.50
33	Willie Anderson	.10	.06
34	Michael Williams	.10	.06
35	Steve Smith	.20	.12
36	Rik Smits	.10	.06
37	Pete Myers	.10	.06
38	Oliver Miller	.15	.10
39	Eddie Johnson	.10	.06
40	Calbert Cheaney (R)	.60	.35
41	Vernon Maxwell	.12	.07
42	James Worthy	.12	.07
43	Dino Radja (R)	.60	.35
44	Derrick Coleman	.20	.12
45	Reggie Williams	.10	.06
46	Dale Ellis	.10	.06
47	Cliff Robinson	.12	.07
48	Doug Christie	.15	.10

1993-94 UPPER DECK SE

#	Player		
49	Ricky Pierce	.10	.06
50	Sean Elliott	.15	.10
51	Anfernee Hardaway (R)	3.00	1.75
52	Dana Barros	.12	.07
53	Reggie Miller	.25	.15
54	Brian Williams	.15	.10
55	Otis Thorpe	.12	.07
56	Jerome Kersey	.10	.06
57	Larry Johnson	.60	.35
58	Rex Chapman	.10	.06
59	Kevin Edwards	.10	.06
60	Nate McMillan	.10	.06
61	Chris Mullin	.20	.12
62	Bill Cartwright	.10	.06
63	Dennis Rodman	.12	.07
64	Pooh Richardson	.12	.07
65	Tyrone Hill	.10	.06
66	Scott Brooks	.10	.06
67	Brad Daugherty	.15	.10
68	Joe Dumars	.20	.12
69	Vin Baker (R)	.80	.50
70	Rod Strickland	.10	.06
71	Tom Chambers	.12	.07
72	Charles Oakley	.12	.07
73	Craig Ehlo	.10	.06
74	LaPhonso Ellis	.25	.15
75	Kevin Gamble	.10	.06
76	Shawn Bradley (R)	.50	.30
77	Kendall Gill	.15	.10
78	Hakeem Olajuwon	1.00	.60
79	Nick Anderson	.15	.10
80	Anthony Peeler	.15	.10
81	Wayman Tisdale	.12	.07
82	Danny Manning	.20	.12
83	John Starks	.15	.10
84	Jeff Hornacek	.12	.07
85	Victor Alexander	.10	.06
86	Mitch Richmond	.15	.10
87	Mookie Blaylock	.12	.07
88	Harvey Grant	.10	.06
89	Doug Smith	.10	.06
90	John Stockton	.30	.18
91	Charles Barkley	.80	.50
92	Gerald Wilkins	.10	.06
93	Mario Elie	.10	.06
94	Ken Norman	.10	.06
95	B.J. Armstrong	.15	.10
96	John Williams	.10	.06
97	Rony Seikaly	.12	.07
98	Sean Rooks	.12	.07
99	Shawn Kemp	.50	.30
100	Danny Ainge	.12	.07
101	Terry Mills	.12	.07
102	Doc Rivers	.12	.07
103	Chuck Person	.12	.07
104	Sam Cassell (R)	.60	.35
105	Kevin Duckworth	.10	.06
106	Dan Majerle	.15	.10
107	Mark Jackson	.12	.07
108	Steve Kerr	.10	.06
109	Sam Perkins	.12	.07
110	C. Weatherspoon	.20	.12
111	Felton Spencer	.12	.07
112	Greg Anthony	.12	.07
113	Pete Chilcutt	.10	.06
114	Malik Sealy	.12	.07
115	Horace Grant	.12	.07
116	Chris Morris	.10	.06
117	Xavier McDaniel	.10	.06
118	Lionel Simmons	.20	.12
119	Dell Curry	.10	.06
120	Moses Malone	.15	.10
121	Lindsey Hunter (R)	.40	.25
122	Buck Williams	.12	.07
123	Mahmoud Abdul-Rauf	.15	.10
124	Rumeal Robinson	.10	.06
125	Chris Mills (R)	.40	.25
126	Scott Skiles	.10	.06
127	Derrick McKey	.12	.07
128	Avery Johnson	.10	.06
129	Harold Miner	.15	.10
130	Frank Brickowski	.10	.06
131	Gary Payton	.15	.10
132	Don MacLean	.20	.12
133	Thurl Bailey	.10	.06
134	Nick Van Exel (R)	.60	.35
135	Matt Geiger	.10	.06
136	Stacey Augmon	.15	.10
137	Sedale Threatt	.10	.06
138	Patrick Ewing	.60	.35
139	Tyrone Corbin	.10	.06
140	Jim Jackson	.35	.20
141	Christian Laettner	.20	.12
142	Robert Horry	.20	.12
143	J.R. Reid	.10	.06
144	Eric Murdock	.12	.07
145	Alonzo Mourning	1.00	.60
146	Sherman Douglas	.10	.06
147	Tom Gugliotta	.20	.12
148	Glen Rice	.15	.10
149	Mark Price	.20	.12
150	Dikembe Mutombo	.30	.18
151	Derek Harper	.12	.07
152	Karl Malone	.40	.25
153	Byron Scott	.10	.06
154	Reggie Jordan (R)	.12	.07
155	Dominique Wilkins	.40	.25
156	Bobby Hurley (R)	.40	.25
157	Ron Harper	.12	.07
158	Byron Russell (R)	.20	.12
159	Frank Johnson	.10	.06
160	Toni Kukoc (R)	.75	.45
161	Lloyd Daniels	.12	.07
162	Jeff Turner	.10	.06

1993-94 UPPER DECK SE ALL-STARS • 233

163	Muggsy Bogues	.10	.06
164	Chris Gatling	.10	.06
165	Kenny Anderson	.20	.12
166	Elmore Spencer	.12	.07
167	Jamal Mashburn (R)	1.25	.70
168	Tim Perry	.10	.06
169	Antonio Davis (R)	.25	.15
170	Isaiah Rider (R)	1.25	.70
171	Dee Brown	.12	.07
172	Walt Williams	.15	.10
173	Elden Campbell	.12	.07
174	Benoit Benjamin	.10	.06
175	Billy Owens	.15	.10
176	Andrew Lang	.10	.06
177	David Robinson	.80	.50
178	Checklist	.10	.06
179	Checklist	.10	.06
180	Checklist	.10	.06
181	Shawn Bradley (ASW)	.15	.10
182	Calbert Cheaney (ASW)	.20	.12
183	Toni Kukoc (ASW)	.25	.15
184	Popeye Jones (ASW)	.12	.07
185	Lindsey Hunter (ASW)	.15	.10
186	Chris Webber (ASW)	1.25	.70
187	Byron Russell (ASW)	.12	.07
188	A. Hardaway(ASW)	1.00	.60
189	Nick Van Exel (ASW)	.20	.12
190	P.J. Brown (ASW)	.12	.07
191	Isaiah Rider (ASW)	.50	.30
192	Chris Mills (ASW)	.15	.10
193	Antonio Davis (ASW)	.12	.07
194	Jamal Mashburn (ASW)	.50	.30
195	Dino Radja (ASW)	.15	.10
196	Sam Cassell (ASW)	.20	.12
197	Isaiah Rider (ASW)(SD)	.50	.30
198	Mark Price (ASW)	.12	.07
199	Atlanta Hawks (TH)	.10	.06
200	Boston Celtics (TH)	.10	.06
201	Charlotte Hornets (TH)	.12	.07
202	Chicago Bulls (TH)	.25	.15
203	Cleveland Cavaliers (TH)	.10	.06
204	Dallas Mavericks (TH)	.20	.12
205	Denver Nuggets (TH)	.10	.06
206	Detroit Pistons (TH)	.10	.06
207	Golden St. Warriors(TH)	.75	.45
208	Houston Rockets (TH)	.10	.06
209	Indiana Pacers (TH)	.10	.06
210	L.A. Clippers (TH)	.10	.06
211	L.A. Lakers (TH)	.10	.06
212	Miami Heat (TH)	.10	.06
213	Milwaukee Bucks (TH)	.12	.07
214	Minnesota T-wolves (TH)	.20	.12
215	New Jersey Nets (TH)	.12	.07
216	New York Knicks (TH)	.20	.12
217	Orlando Magic (TH)	.50	.30
218	Philadelphia 76ers (TH)	.10	.06
219	Phoenix Suns (TH)	.10	.06
220	Portland T'Blazers (TH)	.10	.06
221	Sacramento Kings (TH)	.10	.06
222	San Antonio Spurs (TH)	.20	.12
223	Seattle SuperSonics (TH)	.10	.06
224	Utah Jazz (TH)	.12	.07
225	Washington Bullets (TH)	.10	.06
MJR	Michael Jordan Retire	10.00	6.00
JK	M. Jordan (Kilroy)	10.00	6.00

1993-94 Upper Deck SE All-Stars

The cards in this limited insert set are die-cut at the top to form an arch with a full-color action shot of the player superimposed over a basketball court background. The overall effect makes the cards resemble a basketball lane. The player's name and team nickname are printed vertically along the side of the card. A headline printed in a semi-circle just belowthe top of the die-cut announces the number of times the player was selected to the All-Star team. The cards were distributed randomly and regionally in Upper Deck SE hobby packs with the eastern half of the country getting the East All-Stars with an E prefix next to the card numbers and the western half of the U.S. getting the West All-Stars with a W preceeding the card numbers.

1993-94 UPPER DECK SE ALL-STARS

	MINT	NR/MT
Complete Set (30)	400.00	275.00
Commons	4.00	2.50

		MINT	NR/MT
E1	Dominique Wilkins	10.00	6.50
E2	Alonzo Mourning	20.00	12.50
E3	B.J. Armstrong	4.00	2.50
E4	Scottie Pippen	12.50	7.50
E5	Mark Price	5.00	3.00
E6	Isiah Thomas	6.00	3.50
E7	Harold Miner	4.00	2.50
E8	Vin Baker	10.00	6.50
E9	Kenny Anderson	7.50	4.50
E10	Derrick Coleman	8.00	5.00
E11	Patrick Ewing	15.00	10.00
E12	Anfernee Hardaway	30.00	18.00
E13	Shaquille O'Neal	50.00	35.00
E14	Shawn Bradley	7.50	4.50
E15	Calbert Cheaney	7.50	4.50
W1	Jim Jackson	12.00	7.50
W2	Jamal Mashburn	20.00	12.50
W3	Dikembe Mutombo	7.50	4.50
W4	Latrell Sprewell	20.00	12.50
W5	Chris Webber	40.00	25.00
W6	Hakeem Olajuwon	30.00	18.00
W7	Danny Manning	5.00	3.00
W8	Nick Van Exel	7.50	4.50
W9	Isaiah Rider	18.00	12.00
W10	Charles Barkley	20.00	12.50
W11	Clyde Drexler	10.00	6.50
W12	Mitch Richmond	5.00	3.00
W13	David Robinson	20.00	12.50
W14	Shawn Kemp	18.00	12.00
W15	Karl Malone	12.00	7.50

1993-94 Upper Deck SE Behind-The-Glass

These limited insert cards were distributed randomly in Upper Deck SE retail packs. The cards feature full-bleed, full-color close-up action shots that appear to have been taken fro behind the backboard. The players name appears in a vertical stripe along the side of the card. All cards measure 2-1/2" by 3-1/2".

	MINT	NR/MT
Complete Set (15)	100.00	60.00
Commons	2.00	1.25

		MINT	NR/MT
1	Shawn Kemp	5.00	3.00
2	Patrick Ewing	5.00	3.00
3	Dikembe Mutombo	3.00	1.75
4	Charles Barkley	8.00	5.00
5	Hakeem Olajuwon	10.00	6.50
6	Larry Johnson	7.00	4.00
7	Chris Webber	20.00	12.50
8	John Starks	2.50	1.50
9	Kevin Willis	2.00	1.25
10	Scottie Pippen	5.00	3.00
11	Michael Jordan	25.00	15.00
12	ALonzo Mourning	12.00	7.00
13	Shawn Bradley	3.00	1.75
14	Shaquille O'Neal	25.00	15.00
15	Ron Harper	2.00	1.25

WILD CARD

1991-92 Wild Card College

This set is a Draft Picks set and includes some of the top prospects in basketball pictured in the college uniforms. The card fronts feature full color action photos framed by a dark border with colorful numbers printed within the border. The player's name appears in the lower border under his photograph. A 1st Edition logo is printed in the lower left corner of the card front. Limited edition Wild Cards contain diagonal stripes across the top right corner. These stripes contain denominations that run from 5, 10, 20, 50, 100 to 1,000. A Wild Card with a stripe can be traded for a equal amount of cards corresponding to the amount in the stripe. This checklist only contains values for regular edition cards. To figure the value of the limited Wild Cards multiply the value listed below times the amount on the stripe less 25%. This edition also contains five Suprise Cards which were redeemable for bonus cards. Those cards are listed in the checklist below. All cards measure 2-1/2" by 3-1/2".

		MINT	NR/MT
Complete Set (120)		8.00	5.50
Commons		.04	.02
1	Larry Johnson	.75	.45
2	LeRon Ellis	.10	.06
3	Alvaro Teheran	.04	.02
4	Eric Murdock	.25	.15
5	Suprise Card 1 (Dikembe Mutombo)	.50	.30
6	Anthony Avent	.10	.06
7	Isiah Thomas	.15	.10
8	Abdul Shamsid-Deen	.04	.02
9	Linton Townes	.04	.02
10	Joe Wylie	.04	.02
11	Cozell McQueen	.04	.02
12	David Benoit	.25	.15
13	Chris Mullin	.20	.12
14	Dale Davis	.30	.18
15	Patrick Ewing	.30	.18
16	Greg Anthony	.20	.12
17	Robert Pack	.25	.15
18	Phil Zevenbergen	.04	.02
19	Rick Fox	.25	.15
20	Chris Corchiani	.10	.06
21	Elliott Perry	.04	.02
22	Kevin Brooks	.10	.06
23	Mark Macon	.25	.15
24	Larry Johnson	2.00	1.25
25	George Ackles	.10	.06
26	Suprise Card 5 (Christian Laettner)	1.00	.60
27	Andy Fields	.04	.02
28	Kevin Lynch	.07	.04
29	Graylin Warner	.04	.02
30	James Bullock	.04	.02
31	Steve Bucknall	.04	.02
32	Carl Thomas	.04	.02
33	Doug Overton	.10	.06
34	Brian Shorter	.07	.04
35	Chad Gallagher	.04	.02
36	Antonio Davis	.04	.02
37	Sean Green	.07	.04
38	Randy Brown	.12	.07
39	Richard Dumas	.25	.15
40	Terrell Brandon	.20	.12
41	Marty Embry	.04	.02
42	Ronald Coleman	.04	.02
43	King Rice	.04	.02
44	Perry Carter	.04	.02
45	Andrew Gaze	.04	.02
46	Surprise Card 2 (Billy Owens)	.50	.30
47	Surprise Card 3 (Stacey Augmon)	.50	.30
48	Jimmy Oliver	.08	.05

236 • 1991-92 WILD CARD COLLEGE

49	Treg Lee	.04	.02
50	Ricky Winslow	.04	.02
51	Danny Vranes	.04	.02
52	Jay Murphy	.04	.02
53	Adrian Dantley	.10	.06
54	Joe Arlauckas	.04	.02
55	Moses Scurry	.04	.02
56	Andy Toolson	.04	.02
57	Ramon Rivas	.04	.02
58	Charles Davis	.04	.02
59	Butch Wade	.04	.02
60	John Pinone	.04	.02
61	Bill Wennington	.04	.02
62	Walter Berry	.04	.02
63	Terry Dozier	.04	.02
64	Mitchell Anderson	.04	.02
65	Pace Mannion	.04	.02
66	Pete Myers	.04	.02
67	Eddie Lee Wilkins	.07	.04
68	Mark Hughes	.04	.02
69	Darryl Dawkins	.08	.05
70	Jay Vincent	.10	.06
71	Doug Lee	.04	.02
72	Russ Schoene	.04	.02
73	Tim Kempton	.08	.05
74	Earl Cureton	.07	.04
75	Terence Stansbury	.04	.02
76	Frank Kornet	.04	.02
77	Bob McAdoo	.12	.07
78	Haywoode Workman	.04	.02
79	Vinny Del Negro	.10	.06
80	Harold Pressley	.06	.03
81	Robert Smith	.04	.02
82	Adrian Caldwel	.04	.02
83	Scottie Pippen	.25	.15
84	John Stockton	.25	.15
85	Elwayne Campbell	.04	.02
86	Chris Gatling	.15	.10
87	Cedric Henderson	.04	.02
88	Mike Iuzzolino	.08	.05
89	Fennis Dembo	.07	.04
90	Darnell Valentine	.08	.05
91	Michael Brooks	.04	.02
92	Marty Conlon	.07	.04
93	Lamont Strothers	.07	.04
94	Donald Hodge	.10	.06
95	Pete Chilcutt	.12	.07
96	Kenny Anderson	.75	.45
97	Ian Lockhart	.04	.02
98	Surprise Card 4 (Steve Smith)	.75	.45
99	Larry Lawrence	.04	.02
100	Jerome Mincy	.04	.02
101	Ben Coleman	.07	.04
102	Tom Copa	.04	.02
103	Demetrius Calip	.04	.02
104	Myron Brown	.04	.02
105	Derrick Pope	.04	.02
106	Kelvin Upshaw	.04	.02
107	Andrew Moten	.04	.02
108	Terry Tyler	.07	.04
109	Kevin Magee	.04	.02
110	Tharon Mayes	.04	.02
111	Perry McDonald	.04	.02
112	Jose Ortiz	.04	.02
113	Rick Mahorn	.04	.02
114	David Butler	.04	.02
115	Carl Herrera	.20	.12
116	Darrell Mickens	.04	.02
117	Steve Bardo	.08	.05
118	Checklist 1	.04	.02
119	Checklist 2	.04	.02
120	Checklist 3	.04	.02

1991-92 Wild Card Red Hot Rookies

The cards in this insert set were randomly distributed in Wild Card foil packs. The card fronts are nearly identical to the design of the regular issue except for a Red Hot Rookies logo in the lower corner of the picture. The card backs contain another palyer photo and stats. All cards measure 2-1/2" by 3-1/2".

1991-92 WILD CARD RED HOT ROOKIES • 237

		MINT	NR/MT
Complete Set (10)		20.00	12.50
Commons		.60	.35

1	Dikembe Mutombo	3.00	1.75
2	Larry Johnson	10.00	6.50
3	Steve Smith	2.50	1.50
4	Billy Owens	2.00	1.25
5	Mark Macon	.60	.35
6	Stacey Augmon	2.50	1.50
7	Victor Alexander	1.00	.60
8	Mike Iuzzolino	.60	.35
9	Rick Fox	1.25	.70
10	Terrell Brandon	1.25	.70

Hot Off The Presses (1994-95 Card Sets)

1994 Classic Draft Picks

The cards in this set feature the top picks from the 1994 NBA draft. The card fronts consist of a full-bleed, full-color design and picture players wearing their college uniforms. The player's name appears in a horizontal bar centered under his action photo. Subsets include All-Rookie (AR)(11-15), Centers of Attention (CA)(66-70) and Illustrations (Art)(101-105). Gold versions of each card were produced and are valued at 3X to 7X the value of the regular issue listed below. 500 autographed Shaquille O'Neal cards were issued randomly in Classic packs. Those values are listed at the end of this checklist but are not included in the complete set price. All cards measure 2-1/2" by 3-1/2".

		MINT	NR/MT
	Complete Set (105)	16.00	10.00
	Commons	.05	.02
	Complete Set (Gold)	150.00	90.00
	Commons (Gold)	.15	.10
1	Glenn Robinson	3.00	1.75
2	Jason Kidd	2.50	1.50
3	Charlie Ward	2.00	1.25
4	Grant Hill	2.50	1.50
5	Juwan Howard	.75	.45
6	Eric Montross	.75	.45
7	Carlos Rogers	.60	.35
8	Wesley Person	.60	.35
9	Anthony Miller	.10	.06
10	Dwayne Morton	.25	.15
11	Chris Mills (AR)	.60	.35
12	Jamal Mashburn (AR)	1.00	.60
13	Chris Webber (AR)	1.25	.70
14	Anfernee Hardaway (AR)	1.00	.60
15	Isaiah Rider (AR)	.60	.35
16	Bill McCaffrey	.40	.25
17	Steve Woodberry	.08	.05
18	Damon Bailey	.35	.20
19	Deon Thomas	.25	.15
20	Dontonio Wingfield	.35	.20
21	Albert Burditt	.20	.12
22	Aaron McKie	.35	.20
23	Stevin Smith	.08	.05
24	Tony Dumas	.25	.15
25	Adrian Autry	.15	.10
26	Monty Williams	.60	.35
27	Askia Jones	.12	.07
28	Howard Eisley	.20	.12
29	Brian Grant	.05	.02
30	Eddie Jones	.35	.20
31	Dickey Simpkins	.12	.07
32	Michael Smith	.15	.10
33	Clifford Rozier	.30	.18
34	Travis Ford	.10	.06
35	Jervaughn Scales	.08	.05
36	Tracy Webster	.05	.02
37	Brooks Thompson	.05	.02
38	Jim McIlvaine	.20	.12
39	Eric Piatkowski	.20	.12
40	Arturas Karnishovas	.08	.05
41	Rodney Dent	.12	.07
42	Robert Shannon	.05	.02
43	Derrick Phelps	.10	.06
44	Brian Reese	.08	.05
45	Kevin Salvadon	.05	.02
46	Shon Tarver	.12	.07
47	Anthony Goldwire	.15	.10
48	Jamie Watson	.05	.02
49	Damon Key	.08	.05
50	Kevin Rankin	.05	.02
51	Khalid Reeves	.40	.25
52	Doremus Bennerman	.05	.02
53	Sharone Wright	.25	.15
54	Melvin Simon	.15	.10
55	Andrei Fetisov	.10	.06
56	Barry Brown	.05	.02
57	B.J. Tyler	.25	.15
58	Lawrence Funderburke	.20	.12
59	Darrin Hancock	.05	.02
60	Gaylon Nickerson	.20	.12
61	Jeff Webster	.05	.02

240 • 1994 CLASSIC DRAFT PICKS

62	Derrick Alston	.08	.05
63	Kendrick Warren	.05	.02
64	Yinka Dare	.25	.15
65	Shawnelle Scott	.08	.05
66	Patrick Ewing (CA)	.35	.20
67	Dikembe Mutombo (CA)	.20	.12
68	Alonzo Mourning (CA)	.60	.35
69	Shaquille O'Neal (CA)	1.50	.90
70	Hakeem Olajuwon (CA)	.75	.45
71	Thomas Hamilton	.05	.02
72	Joey Brown	.05	.02
73	Vashon Leonard	.08	.05
74	Donyell Marshall	.60	.35
75	Abdul Fox	.05	.02
76	Checklist	.05	.02
77	Checklist	.05	.02
78	Jalen Rose	.50	.35
79	Trevor Ruffin	.05	.02
80	Sam Mitchell	.08	.05
81	Dick Vitale	.05	.02
82	Charlie Ward (FB)	.75	.45
83	Cornell Parker	.07	.04
84	Clayton Ritter	.05	.02
85	Carl Ray Harris	.05	.02
86	Randy Blocker	.05	.02
87	Chuck Graham	.08	.05
88	Greg Minor	.07	.04
89	Bill Curley	.15	.10
90	Harry Moore	.05	.02
91	Melvin Booker	.05	.02
92	Gary Collier	.05	.02
93	Myron Walker	.05	.02
94	Jamie Brandon	.05	.02
95	Eric Mobley	.10	.06
96	Byron Starks	.05	.02
97	Antonio Lang	.12	.07
98	Jevon Crudup	.12	.07
99	Robert Churchwell	.10	.06
100	Aaron Swinson	.05	.02
101	Glenn Robinson (Art)	1.25	.70
102	Jason Kidd (Art)	1.00	.60
103	Juwan Howard (Art)	.60	.35
104	Charlie Ward (Art)	.75	.45
105	Eric Montross (Art)	.40	.25
___	Shaquille O'Neal (Signed)	200.00	125.00

1994 Classic Dicky V's PTP

The cards in this limited insert set feature broadcaster Dick Vitale's Prime Time Players. The chrome design includes an isolated player shot printed over a swirl of rainbow colors. The player's name appears in a horizontal color bar under his picture and next to a Dicky V logo printed in a star over an oval. All cards measure 2-1/2" by 3-1/2".

		MINT	NR/MT
Complete Set (15)		20.00	12.50
Commons		.40	.25
1	Glenn Robinson	5.00	3.00
2	Jason Kidd	3.50	2.00
3	Grant Hill	3.50	2.00
4	Sharone Wright	.75	.45
5	Juwan Howard	1.25	.70
6	Billy McCraffrey	.75	.45
7	Khalid Reeves	1.00	.60
8	Eddie Jones	1.00	.60
9	Clifford Rozier	.50	.30
10	Charlie Ward	2.50	1.50
11	Eric Montross	1.25	.70
12	Wesley Person	1.00	.60
13	Yinka Dare	.50	.30
14	Dontonio Wingfield	.40	.25
15	Carlos Rogers	.50	.30

1994 Classic Classic Picks

These special foil cards are a continuation of a series and begin with number 6. The card fronts feature a full-color action shot within a brown frame with gold foil stamping. The player'sname appears just under his photo. The cards were inserted randomly in Classic foil packs and measure 2-1/2" by 3-1/2".

	MINT	NR/MT
Complete Set (5)	40.00	28.00
Commons	3.50	2.00

		MINT	NR/MT
6	Glenn Robinson	14.00	8.50
7	Jason Kidd	10.00	6.00
8	Grant Hill	10.00	6.00
9	Eric Montross	3.50	2.00
10	Juwan Howard	3.50	2.00

1994-95 Fleer I

The cards in this set are the first of two series to be issued for the 1994-95 season. The card fronts consist of full-color action shots framed by a white border. The player's name and team appear in the lower corner in foil-stamping over a color swatch that mirrors the player's team colors. A Fleer logo is printed in the top corner. The flips side contains another full-coor action shot on the left side with personal data and statistics on the right side. All cards measure 2-1/2" by 3-1/2".

	MINT	NR/MT
Complete Set (240)	18.00	12.00
Commons	.05	.02

		MINT	NR/MT
1	Stacey Augmon	.07	.04
2	Mookie Blaylock	.07	.04
3	Craig Ehlo	.05	.02
4	Duane Ferrell	.05	.02
5	Adam Keefe	.05	.02
6	Jon Koncak	.05	.02
7	Andrew Lang	.05	.02
8	Danny Manning	.12	.07
9	Kevin Willis	.05	.02
10	Dee Brown	.08	.05
11	Sherman Douglas	.07	.04
12	Acie Earl	.10	.06
13	Rick Fox	.07	.04
14	Kevin Gamble	.05	.02
15	Xavier McDaniel	.05	.02

1994-95 FLEER I

#	Player		
16	Robert Parish	.12	.07
17	Ed Pinckney	.05	.02
18	Dino Radja	.15	.10
19	Muggsy Bogues	.05	.02
20	Frank Brickowski	.05	.02
21	Scott Burrell	.10	.06
22	Dell Curry	.05	.02
23	Kenny Gattison	.05	.02
24	Hersey Hawkins	.07	.04
25	Eddie Johnson	.05	.02
26	Larry Johnson	.25	.15
27	Alonzo Mourning	.40	.25
28	David Wingate	.05	.02
29	B.J. Armstrong	.10	.06
30	Horace Grant	.07	.04
31	Steve Kerr	.05	.02
32	Toni Kukoc	.20	.12
33	Luc Longley	.05	.02
34	Pete Myers	.05	.02
35	Scottie Pippen	.25	.15
36	Bill Wennington	.05	.02
37	Scott Williams	.05	.02
38	Terrell Brandon	.05	.02
39	Brad Daugherty	.10	.06
40	Tyrone Hill	.08	.05
41	Chris Mills	.12	.07
42	Larry Nance	.05	.02
43	Bobby Phills	.07	.04
44	Mark Price	.15	.10
45	Gerald Wilkins	.05	.02
46	John Williams	.05	.02
47	Lucious Harris	.07	.04
48	Donald Hodge	.05	.02
49	Jim Jackson	.25	.15
50	Popeye Jones	.08	.05
51	Tim Legler	.05	.02
52	Fat Lever	.05	.02
53	Jamal Mashburn	.40	.25
54	Sean Rooks	.07	.04
55	Doug Smith	.05	.02
56	Mahmoud Abdul-Rauf	.12	.07
57	LaPhonso Ellis	.15	.10
58	Dikembe Mutombo	.20	.12
59	Robert Pack	.05	.02
60	Rodney Rogers	.12	.07
61	Bryant Stith	.10	.06
62	Brian Williams	.10	.06
63	Reggie Williams	.05	.02
64	Greg Anderson	.05	.02
65	Joe Dumars	.15	.10
66	Sean Elliott	.12	.07
67	Allan Houston	.10	.06
68	Lindsey Hunter	.12	.07
69	Terry Mills	.07	.04
70	Victor Alexander	.05	.02
71	Chris Gatling	.05	.02
72	Tim Hardaway	.12	.07
73	Keith Jennings	.05	.02
74	Avery Johnson	.05	.02
75	Chris Mullin	.15	.10
76	Billy Owens	.12	.07
77	Latrell Sprewell	.35	.20
78	Chris Webber	.80	.50
79	Scott Brooks	.05	.02
80	Sam Cassell	.15	.10
81	Mario Elie	.05	.02
82	Carl Herrera	.08	.05
83	Robert Horry	.15	.10
84	Vernon Maxwell	.08	.05
85	Hakeem Olajuwon	.75	.45
86	Kenny Smith	.07	.04
87	Otis Thorpe	.07	.04
88	Antonio Davis	.05	.02
89	Dale Davis	.10	.06
90	Vern Fleming	.05	.02
91	Derrick McKey	.07	.04
92	Reggie Miller	.25	.15
93	Pooh Richardson	.05	.02
94	Byron Scott	.05	.02
95	Rik Smits	.05	.02
96	Haywoode Workman	.07	.04
97	Terry Dehere	.08	.05
98	Harold Ellis	.08	.05
99	Gary Grant	.05	.02
100	Ron Harper	.08	.05
101	Mark Jackson	.08	.05
102	Stanley Roberts	.05	.02
103	Elmore Spencer	.08	.05
104	Loy Vaught	.05	.02
105	Dominique Wilkins	.25	.15
106	Elden Campbell	.07	.04
107	Doug Christie	.10	.06
108	Vlade Divac	.08	.05
109	George Lynch	.10	.06
110	Anthony Peeler	.10	.06
111	Tony Smith	.05	.02
112	Sedale Threatt	.05	.02
113	Nick Van Exel	.15	.10
114	James Worthy	.10	.06
115	Bimbo Coles	.05	.02
116	Grant Long	.05	.02
117	Harold Miner	.10	.06
118	Glen Rice	.08	.05
119	John Salley	.05	.02
120	Rony Seikaly	.08	.05
121	Brian Shaw	.08	.05
122	Steve Smith	.12	.07
123	Vin Baker	.20	.12
124	Jon Barry	.07	.04
125	Todd Day	.10	.06
126	Blue Edwards	.05	.02
127	Lee Mayberry	.08	.05
128	Eric Murdock	.07	.04
129	Ken Norman	.05	.02

1994-95 FLEER I

#	Player		
130	Derek Strong	.08	.05
131	Thurl Bailey	.05	.02
132	Stacey King	.05	.02
133	Christian Laettner	.12	.07
134	Chuck Person	.07	.04
135	Isaiah Rider	.30	.18
136	Chris Smith	.08	.05
137	Doug West	.05	.02
138	Micheal Williams	.05	.02
139	Kenny Anderson	.15	.10
140	Benoit Benjamin	.05	.02
141	P.J. Brown	.08	.05
142	Derrick Coleman	.20	.12
143	Kevin Edwards	.05	.02
144	Armon Gilliam	.07	.04
145	Chris Morris	.05	.02
146	Johnny Newman	.05	.02
147	Greg Anthony	.07	.04
148	Anthony Bonner	.05	.02
149	Hubert Davis	.12	.07
150	Patrick Ewing	.40	.25
151	Derek Harper	.08	.05
152	Anthony Mason	.08	.05
153	Charles Oakley	.08	.05
154	Doc Rivers	.07	.04
155	Charles Smith	.07	.04
156	John Starks	.12	.07
157	Nick Anderson	.10	.06
158	Anthony Avent	.07	.04
159	Anfernee Hardaway	.75	.45
160	Shaquille O'Neal	1.75	1.00
161	Donald Royal	.05	.02
162	Dennis Scott	.08	.05
163	Scott Skiles	.05	.02
164	Jeff Turner	.05	.02
165	Dana Barros	.07	.04
166	Shawn Bradley	.15	.10
167	Greg Graham	.07	.04
168	Eric Leckner	.05	.02
169	Jeff Malone	.07	.04
170	Moses Malone	.10	.06
171	Tim Perry	.05	.02
172	Clarence Weatherspoon	.10	.06
173	Orlando Woolridge	.05	.02
174	Danny Ainge	.10	.06
175	Charles Barkley	.60	.35
176	Cedric Ceballos	.08	.05
177	A. C. Green	.07	.04
178	Kevin Johnson	.12	.07
179	Joe Kleine	.05	.02
180	Dan Majerle	.10	.06
181	Oliver Miller	.10	.06
182	Mark West	.05	.02
183	Clyde Drexler	.25	.15
184	Harvey Grant	.05	.02
185	Jerome Kersey	.05	.02
186	Tracy Murray	.10	.06
187	Terry Porter	.08	.05
188	Cliff Robinson	.08	.05
189	James Robinson	.12	.07
190	Rod Strickland	.05	.02
191	Buck Williams	.07	.04
192	Duane Causwell	.05	.02
193	Bobby Hurley	.15	.10
194	Olden Polynice	.05	.02
195	Mitch Richmond	.15	.10
196	Lionel Simmons	.15	.10
197	Wayman Tisdale	.07	.04
198	Spud Webb	.05	.02
199	Walt Williams	.12	.07
200	Trevor Wilson	.08	.05
201	Willie Anderson	.05	.02
202	Antoine Carr	.05	.02
203	Terry Cummings	.07	.04
204	Vinny Del Negro	.05	.02
205	Dale Ellis	.07	.04
206	Negele Knight	.05	.02
207	J.R. Reid	.05	.02
208	David Robinson	.60	.35
209	Dennis Rodman	.12	.07
210	Vincent Askew	.05	.02
211	Michael Cage	.05	.02
212	Kendall Gill	.12	.07
213	Shawn Kemp	.35	.20
214	Nate McMillan	.05	.02
215	Gary Payton	.12	.07
216	Sam Perkins	.07	.04
217	Ricky Pierce	.05	.02
218	Detlef Schrempf	.15	.10
219	David Benoit	.05	.02
220	Tom Chambers	.07	.04
221	Tyrone Corbin	.05	.02
222	Jeff Hornacek	.08	.05
223	Jay Humphries	.05	.02
224	Karl Malone	.25	.15
225	Byron Russell	.08	.05
226	Felton Spencer	.08	.05
227	John Stockton	.20	.12
228	Michael Adams	.05	.02
229	Rex Chapman	.05	.02
230	Calbert Cheaney	.15	.10
231	Kevin Duckworth	.05	.02
232	Pervis Ellison	.08	.05
233	Tom Gugliotta	.15	.10
234	Don MacLean	.10	.06
235	Gheorghe Muresan	.08	.05
236	Brent Price	.07	.04
237	Toronto Raptors	.20	.12
238	Checklist	.05	.02
239	Checklist	.05	.02
240	Checklist	.05	.02

1994-95 Fleer NBA All-Stars

The cards in this limited 26-card insert set feature full-bleed full color player photos and foil-stamping on the card fronts. The player's image is isolated over an extreme close-up of a basketball in the background. The player's name and team are printed in the lower corner opposite an All-Star Weekend logo. The cards were distributed randomly in Fleer 15-card packs and measure 2-1/2" by 3-1/2".

		MINT	NR/MT
	Complete Set (26)	28.00	18.00
	Commons	.30	.18
1	Kenny Anderson	.40	.25
2	B. J. Armstrong	.30	.18
3	Mookie Blaylock	.30	.18
4	Derrick Coleman	.60	.35
5	Patrick Ewing	1.50	.90
6	Horace Grant	.30	.18
7	Alonzo Mourning	1.50	.90
8	Charles Oakley	.30	.18
9	Shaquille O'Neal	5.00	3.00
10	Scottie Pippen	1.25	.70
11	Mark Price	.40	.25
12	John Starks	.35	.20
13	Dominique Wilkins	1.00	.60
14	Charles Barkley	1.75	1.00
15	Clyde Drexler	.75	.45
16	Kevin Johnson	.35	.20
17	Shawn Kemp	1.50	.90
18	Karl Malone	1.25	.70
19	Danny Manning	.40	.25
20	Hakeem Olajuwon	2.00	1.25
21	Gary Payton	.30	.18
22	Mitch Richmond	.35	.20
23	Cliff Robinson	.30	.18
24	David Robinson	1.75	1.00
25	Latrell Sprewell	1.00	.60
26	John Stockton	.75	.45

1994-95 Fleer Award Winners

These limited insert cards are horizontal and contain three player images on the card front along with foil stamping. The center photo is a game-action shot while the photos on the sides are isolated close-up shots. The player's name is centered at the bottom of the card between the headline NBA Award Winner and the player's achievement. The cards were issued randomly in Fleer packs and measure 2-1/2" by 3-1/2".

	MINT	NR/MT
Complete Set (4)	8.00	5.00
Commons	.35	.20

1994-95 FLEER CAREER ACHIEVEMENT • 245

		MINT	NR/MT
1	Dell Curry	.35	.20
2	Don MacLean	.35	.20
3	Hakeem Olajuwon	3.00	1.75
4	Chris Webber	5.00	3.00
7	Nate McMillan	.30	.18
8	David Robinson	3.00	1.75
9	Dennis Rodman	.50	.30
10	Latrell Sprewell	1.50	.90

1994-95 Fleer All-Defensive Team

These limited insert cards feature a full-color player shot on the card front superimposed over a black and white game-action background. The words NBA All-Defensive Team are also printed across the card in the background. The player's name is printed under his photo and just above the headline NBA All-Defensive Team. The cards were inserted randomly in Fleer packs and measure 2-1/2" by 3-1/2".

		MINT	NR/MT
Complete Set (10)		10.00	6.50
Commons		.30	.18
1	Mookie Blaylock	.30	.18
2	Charles Oakley	.30	.18
3	Hakeem Olajuwon	3.50	2.00
4	Gary Payton	.40	.25
5	Scottie Pippen	2.00	1.25
6	Horace Grant	.30	.18

1994-95 Fleer Career Achievement

The cards in this limited insert set are all-foil cards and feature two player images on the card front, a large close-up and a smaller action shot. The player's name appears in the lower corner across from a logo in the shape of a plaque that contains the words Career Achievement Award. The cards were distributed randomly in Fleer packs and measure 2-1/2" by 3-1/2".

		MINT	NR/MT
Complete Set (6)		48.00	30.00
Commons		4.00	2.75
1	Patrick Ewing	10.00	6.50
2	Karl Malone	7.00	4.00
3	Hakeem Olajuwon	12.00	7.50
4	Robert Parish	4.00	2.75
5	Scottie Pippen	8.00	5.00
6	Dominique Wilkins	10.00	6.50

1994-95 Fleer League Leaders

The cards in this limited set sport a horizontal design with foil-stamping and feature a full-color action shot of the player over a streaky gold background. The team name is printed in huge type next to the player's photo while the player's name appears in a black stripe the runs the width of the card at the bottom. A League Leader logo is printed in the lower corner of the card. The cards were issued randomly in Fleer Series I packs. All cards measure 3-1/2" by 2-1/2".

		MINT	NR/MT
	Complete Set (8)	14.00	8.50
	Commons	.30	.18
1	Mahmoud Abdul-Rauf	.50	.30
2	Nate McMillan	.30	.18
3	Tracy Murray	.30	.18
4	Dikembe Mutombo	1.25	.70
5	Shaquille O'Neal	10.00	6.50
6	David Robinson	3.00	1.75
7	Dennis Rodman	.50	.30
8	John Stockton	1.00	.60

1994-95 Fleer Pro Visions

These limited insert cards feature a full-bleed, full-color original illustration of the player on the card front. A new interlocking design creates a much larger painting when all nine cards in the set are placed sequentially in a 9-card pocket sleeve. The cards were issued randomly in Fleer packs and measure 2-1/2" by 3-1/2".

		MINT	NR/MT
	Complete Set (9)	7.50	4.50
	Commons	.25	.15
1	Jamal Mashburn	1.00	.60
2	John Starks	.30	.18
3	Toni Kukoc	.75	.45
4	Derrick Coleman	.60	.35
5	Chris Webber	3.50	2.00
6	Dennis Rodman	.25	.15
7	Gary Payton	.25	.15
8	Anfernee Hardaway	2.50	1.50
9	Dan Majerle	.25	.15

1994-95 Fleer Rookie Sensations

These limited insert cards were issued only in Fleer jumbo packs. The full-bleed, full-color card fronts feature foil stamping with an isolated image of the player over a blue background. The player's photo is framed by a jagged border containing a series of high-tech circles including some in the shape of a basketball hoop and net. The player's name is printed in the lower corner opposite a Rookies Sensations logo. All cards measure 2-1/2" by 3-1/2".

		MINT	NR/MT
Complete Set (25)		70.00	48.00
Commons		.75	.45
1	Vin Baker	3.00	1.75
2	Shawn Bradley	3.00	1.75
3	P.J. Brown	.75	.45
4	Sam Cassell	2.00	1.25
5	Calbert Cheaney	3.00	1.75
6	Antonio Davis	.75	.45
7	Acie Earl	.75	.45
8	Harold Ellis	.75	.45
9	Anfernee Hardaway	10.00	6.50
10	Allan Houston	.75	.45
11	Lindsey Hunter	1.00	.60
12	Bobby Hurley	2.50	1.50
13	Popeye Jones	.75	.45
14	Toni Kukoc	5.00	3.00
15	George Lynch	1.00	.60
16	Jamal Mashburn	6.00	3.75
17	Chris Mills	2.00	1.25
18	Gheorghe Muresan	1.00	.60
19	Dino Radja	3.00	1.75
20	Isaiah Rider	6.00	3.75
21	James Robinson	1.50	.90
22	Rodney Rogers	1.50	.90
23	Byron Russell	1.00	.60
24	Nick Van Exel	3.00	1.75
25	Chris Webber	15.00	10.00

1994-95 Fleer Triple Threats

The cards in this limited insert set were randomly distributed in Fleer packs and feature three full-color player photos on the card fronts along with foil stamping and a high-tech background that features multi-colored blueprint-type drawings of a basketball court. The player's photos run from small to large from the background to the foreground. His name is printed in the lower corner and the words Triple Threats are printed vertically along one side of the card. All cards measure 2-1/2" by 3-1/2".

	MINT	NR/MT
Complete Set (10)	12.50	7.50
Commons	.30	.18

248 • 1994-95 FLEER TRIPLE THREATS

1	Mookie Blaylock	.30	.18
2	Patrick Ewing	1.50	.90
3	Shawn Kemp	1.25	.70
4	Karl Malone	1.25	.70
5	Reggie Miller	.80	.50
6	Hakeem Olajuwon	2.50	1.50
7	Shaquille O'Neal	5.00	3.00
8	Scottie Pippen	.80	.50
9	David Robinson	1.75	1.00
10	Latrell Sprewell	1.25	.70

1994 Fleer Flair USA Basketball

The cards in this set were produced under Fleer's upscale Flair banner and honor the 1994 USA Men's Basketball team that won the World Championship in Toronto, Canada. The set consists of eight different cards for each player plus two cards for each coach and a 6-card subset honoring former stars and coaches of some past USA Women's teams. The player cards sport eight seperate designs which explores a different facet of the player's career. All cards measure 2-1/2" by 3-1/2".

	MINT	NR/MT
Complete Set (120)	42.00	26.00
Commons	.15	.10

1	Don Chaney (C)	.15	.10
2	Don Chaney (C)	.15	.10
3	Pete Gillen (C)	.15	.10
4	Pete Gillen (C)	.15	.10
5	Rick Majerus (C)	.15	.10
6	Rick Majerus (C)	.15	.10
7	Don Nelson (C)	.20	.12
8	Don Nelson (C)	.20	.12
9	Derrick Coleman	.40	.25
10	Derrick Coleman	.40	.25
11	Derrick Coleman	.40	.25
12	Derrick Coleman	.40	.25
13	Derrick Colema	.40	.25
14	Derrick Coleman	.40	.25
15	Derrick Coleman	.40	.25
16	Derrick Coleman	.40	.25
17	Joe Dumars	.30	.18
18	Joe Dumars	.30	.18
19	Joe Dumars	.30	.18
20	Joe Dumars	.30	.18
21	Joe Dumars	.30	.18
22	Joe Dumars	.30	.18
23	Joe Dumars	.30	.18
24	Joe Dumars	.30	.18
25	Tim Hardaway	.25	.15
26	Tim Hardaway	.25	.15
27	Tim Hardaway	.25	.15
28	Tim Hardaway	.25	.15
29	Tim Hardaway	.25	.15
30	Tim Hardaway	.25	.15
31	Tim Hardaway	.25	.15
32	Tim Hardaway	.25	.15
33	Larry Johnson	1.00	.60
34	Larry Johnson	1.00	.60
35	Larry Johnson	1.00	.60
36	Larry Johnson	1.00	.60
37	Larry Johnson	1.00	.60
38	Larry Johnson	1.00	.60
39	Larry Johnson	1.00	.60
40	Larry Johnson	1.00	.60
41	Shawn Kemp	1.00	.60
42	Shawn Kemp	1.00	.60
43	Shawn Kemp	1.00	.60
44	Shawn Kemp	1.00	.60
45	Shawn Kemp	1.00	.60
46	Shawn Kemp	1.00	.60
47	Shawn Kemp	1.00	.60
48	Shawn Kemp	1.00	.60
49	Dan Majerle	.25	.15
50	Dan Majerle	.25	.15
51	Dan Majerle	.25	.15
52	Dan Majerle	.25	.15
53	Dan Majerle	.25	.15
54	Dan Majerle	.25	.15
55	Dan Majerle	.25	.15
56	Dan Majerle	.25	.15
57	Reggie Miller	.60	.35

1994-95 HOOPS I • 249

58	Reggie Miller	.60	.35
59	Reggie Miller	.60	.35
60	Reggie Miller	.60	.35
61	Reggie Miller	.60	.35
62	Reggie Miller	.60	.35
63	Reggie Miller	.60	.35
64	Reggie Miller	.60	.35
65	Alonzo Mourning	1.75	1.00
66	Alonzo Mourning	1.75	1.00
67	Alonzo Mourning	1.75	1.00
68	Alonzo Mourning	1.75	1.00
69	Alonzo Mourning	1.75	1.00
70	Alonzo Mourning	1.75	1.00
71	Alonzo Mourning	1.75	1.00
72	Alonzo Mourning	1.75	1.00
73	Shaquille O'Neal	5.00	3.00
74	Shaquille O'Neal	5.00	3.00
75	Shaquille O'Neal	5.00	3.00
76	Shaquille O'Neal	5.00	3.00
77	Shaquille O'Neal	5.00	3.00
78	Shaquille O'Neal	5.00	3.00
79	Shaquille O'Neal	5.00	3.00
80	Shaquille O'Neal	5.00	3.00
81	Mark Price	.30	.18
82	Mark Price	.30	.18
83	Mark Price	.30	.18
84	Mark Price	.30	.18
85	Mark Price	.30	.18
86	Mark Price	.30	.18
87	Mark Price	.30	.18
88	Mark Price	.30	.18
89	Steve Smith	.25	.15
90	Steve Smith	.25	.15
91	Steve Smith	.25	.15
92	Steve Smith	.25	.15
93	Steve Smith	.25	.15
94	Steve Smith	.25	.15
95	Steve Smith	.25	.15
96	Steve Smith	.25	.15
97	Isiah Thomas	.40	.25
98	Isiah Thomas	.40	.25
99	Isiah Thomas	.40	.25
100	Isiah Thomas	.40	.25
101	Isiah Thomas	.40	.25
102	Isiah Thomas	.40	.27
103	Isiah Thomas	.40	.25
104	Isiah Thomas	.40	.25
105	Dominique Wilkins	1.00	.60
106	Dominique Wilkins	1.00	.60
107	Dominique Wilkins	1.00	.60
108	Dominique Wilkins	1.00	.60
109	Dominique Wilkins	1.00	.60
110	Dominique Wilkins	1.00	.60
111	Dominique Wilkins	1.00	.60
112	Dominique Wilkins	1.00	.60
113	Carol Blazejowski	.25	.15
114	Theresa Edwards	.20	.12
115	Nancy Lieberman-Cline	.40	.25
116	Ann Meyers	.40	.25
117	Pat Summitt (C)	.20	.12
118	Lynette Woodard	.40	.25
119	Checklist	.75	.25
120	Checklist	.75	.25

1994-95 Hoops I

The cards in this set feature full-bleed, full-color action photos on the card fronts with the player's name, position and a team logo appearing in a color bar under his photo. The color bar mirrors his dominate team color. The card backs contain a small head shot along with personal data, stats and a summary of the player previous season and career. Key subsets include All-Stars (AS)(224-251), League Leaders (LL)(252-258), Award Winners (AW)259-265), Hoops Tribune (Trib)(2660273) and Coaches (C)(274-295). A commemorative Magic Johnson card was also included in the set (#296) and a Draft Lottery Exchange card was randomly inserted into Hoops packs redeemable for a set of 1994 NBA Draft Lottery picks. The set is the first of two series scheduled for 1994-95 and all cards measure 2-1/2" by 3-1/2".

1994-95 HOOPS I

	MINT	NR/MT
Complete Set (300)	15.00	10.00
Commons	.05	.02

#	Player	MINT	NR/MT
1	Stacey Augmon	.08	.05
2	Mookie Blaylock	.08	.05
3	Doug Edwards	.05	.02
4	Craig Ehlo	.05	.02
5	Jon Koncak	.05	.02
6	Danny Manning	.15	.10
7	Kevin Willis	.05	.02
8	Dee Brown	.08	.05
9	Sherman Douglas	.07	.04
10	Acie Earl	.10	.06
11	Kevin Gamble	.05	.02
12	Xavier McDaniel	.05	.02
13	Robert Parish	.12	.07
14	Dino Radja	.20	.12
15	Tony Bennett	.05	.02
16	Muggsy Bogues	.05	.02
17	Scott Burrell	.12	.07
18	Dell Curry	.05	.02
19	Hersey Hawkins	.07	.04
20	Eddie Johnson	.05	.02
21	Larry Johnson	.25	.15
22	Alonzo Mourning	.40	.25
23	B.J. Armstrong	.12	.07
24	Corie Blount	.10	.06
25	Bill Cartwright	.05	.02
26	Horace Grant	.07	.04
27	Toni Kukoc	.20	.12
28	Luc Longley	.05	.02
29	Pete Myers	.05	.02
30	Scottie Pippen	.25	.15
31	Scott Williams	.05	.02
32	Terrell Brandon	.07	.04
33	Brad Daugherty	.10	.06
34	Tyrone Hill	.08	.05
35	Chris Mills	.15	.10
36	Larry Nance	.07	.04
37	Bobby Phills	.07	.04
38	Mark Price	.15	.10
39	Gerald Williams	.05	.02
40	John Williams	.07	.04
41	Terry Davis	.05	.02
42	Lucious Harris	.08	.05
43	Jim Jackson	.20	.12
44	Popeye Jones	.08	.05
45	Tim Legler	.05	.02
46	Jamal Mashburn	.75	.45
47	Sean Rooks	.10	.06
48	Mahmoud Abdul-Rauf	.15	.10
49	LaPhonso Ellis	.15	.10
50	Dikembe Mutombo	.25	.15
51	Robert Pack	.05	.02
52	Rodney Rogers	.12	.07
53	Bryant Stith	.10	.06
54	Brian Williams	.10	.06
55	Reggie Williams	.05	.02
56	Greg Anderson	.05	.02
57	Joe Dumars	.15	.10
58	Sean Elliott	.12	.07
59	Allan Houston	.10	.06
60	Lindsey Hunter	.15	.10
61	Mark Macon	.08	.05
62	Terry Mills	.07	.04
63	Victor Alexander	.05	.02
64	Chris Gatling	.05	.02
65	Tim Hardaway	.12	.07
66	Avery Johnson	.05	.02
67	Sarunas Marciulionis	.05	.02
68	Chris Mullin	.15	.10
69	Billy Owens	.12	.07
70	Latrell Sprewell	.40	.25
71	Chris Webber	1.50	.90
72	Matt Bullard	.05	.02
73	Sam Cassell	.20	.12
74	Mario Elie	.05	.02
75	Carl Herrera	.08	.05
76	Robert Horry	.15	.10
77	Vernon Maxwell	.08	.05
78	Hakeem Olajuwon	.75	.45
79	Kenny Smith	.07	.04
80	Otis Thorpe	.07	.04
81	Antonio Davis	.10	.06
82	Dale Davis	.10	.06
83	Vern Fleming	.05	.02
84	Scott Haskin	.05	.02
85	Derrick McKey	.07	.04
86	Reggie Miller	.25	.15
87	Byron Scott	.05	.02
88	Rik Smits	.05	.02
89	Haywoode Workman	.07	.04
90	Terry Dehere	.10	.06
91	Harold Ellis	.08	.05
92	Gary Grant	.05	.02
93	Ron Harper	.08	.05
94	Mark Jackson	.08	.05
95	Stanely Roberts	.05	.02
96	Loy Vaught	.05	.02
97	Dominique Wilkins	.25	.15
98	Elden Campbell	.08	.05
99	Doug Christie	.10	.06
100	Vlade Divac	.08	.05
101	Reggie Jordan	.07	.04
102	George Lynch	.12	.07
103	Anthony Peeler	.10	.06
104	Sedale Threatt	.05	.02
105	Nick Van Exel	.20	.12
106	James Worthy	.10	.06
107	Bimbo Coles	.05	.02
108	Matt Geiger	.05	.02
109	Grant Long	.05	.02

1994-95 HOOPS I • 251

#	Player		
110	Harold Miner	.10	.06
111	Glen Rice	.08	.05
112	John Salley	.05	.02
113	Rony Seikaly	.08	.05
114	Brian Shaw	.07	.04
115	Steve Smith	.12	.07
116	Vin Baker	.25	.15
117	Jon Barry	.07	.04
118	Todd Day	.10	.06
119	Lee Mayberry	.08	.05
120	Eric Murdock	.07	.04
121	Ken Norman	.05	.02
122	Mike Brown	.07	.04
123	Stacey King	.05	.02
124	Christian Laettner	.20	.12
125	Chuck Person	.07	.04
126	Isaiah Rider	.60	.35
127	Chris Smith	.10	.06
128	Doug West	.05	.02
129	Michael Williams	.05	.02
130	Kenny Anderson	.15	.10
131	Benoit Benjamin	.05	.02
132	P.J. Brown	.08	.05
133	Derrick Coleman	.20	.12
134	Kevin Edwards	.05	.02
135	Armon Gilliam	.07	.04
136	Chris Morris	.05	.02
137	Rex Walters	.07	.04
138	David Wesley	.05	.02
139	Greg Anthony	.07	.04
140	Anthony Bonner	.05	.02
141	Hubert Davis	.15	.10
142	Patrick Ewing	.35	.20
143	Derek Harper	.08	.05
144	Anthony Mason	.10	.06
145	Charles Oakley	.08	.05
146	Charles Smith	.07	.04
147	John Starks	.10	.06
148	Nick Anderson	.10	.06
149	Anthony Avent	.08	.05
150	Anthony Bowie	.05	.02
151	Anfernee Hardaway	1.25	.70
152	Shaquille O'Neal	1.75	1.00
153	Donald Royal	.05	.02
154	Dennis Scott	.08	.05
155	Scott Skiles	.05	.02
156	Jeff Turner	.05	.02
157	Dana Barros	.07	.04
158	Shawn Bradley	.20	.12
159	Greg Graham	.08	.05
160	Warren Kidd	.07	.04
161	Eric Leckner	.05	.02
162	Jeff Malone	.07	.04
163	Tim Perry	.05	.02
164	Clarence Weatherspoon	.12	.07
165	Danny Ainge	.10	.06
166	Charles Barkley	.40	.25
167	Cedric Ceballos	.08	.05
168	A. C. Green	.07	.04
169	Kevin Johnson	.12	.07
170	Malcolm Mackey	.08	.05
171	Dan Majerle	.10	.06
172	Oliver Miller	.08	.05
173	Mark West	.05	.02
174	Clyde Drexler	.20	.12
175	Chris Dudley	.05	.02
176	Harvey Grant	.05	.02
177	Tracy Murray	.10	.06
178	Terry Porter	.07	.04
179	Cliff Robinson	.10	.06
180	James Robinson	.12	.07
181	Rod Strickland	.05	.02
182	Buck Williams	.07	.04
183	Duane Causwell	.05	.02
184	Bobby Hurley	.20	.12
185	Olden Polynice	.05	.02
186	Mitch Richmond	.15	.10
187	Lionel Simmons	.15	.10
188	Wayman Tisdale	.07	.04
189	Spud Webb	.05	.02
190	Walt Williams	.10	.06
191	Willie Anderson	.05	.02
192	Lloyd Daniels	.08	.05
193	Vinny Del Negro	.05	.02
194	Dale Ellis	.07	.04
195	J.R. Reid	.05	.02
196	David Robinson	.40	.25
197	Dennis Rodman	.10	.06
198	Kendall Gill	.10	.06
199	Ervin Johnson	.08	.05
200	Shawn Kemp	.35	.20
201	Chris King	.07	.04
202	Nate McMillan	.05	.02
203	Gary Payton	.12	.07
204	Sam Perkins	.07	.04
205	Ricky Pierce	.05	.02
206	Detlef Schrempf	.15	.10
207	David Benoit	.05	.02
208	Tom Chambers	.07	.04
209	Tyrone Corbin	.05	.02
210	Jeff Hornacek	.08	.05
211	Karl Malone	.25	.15
212	Byron Russell	.12	.07
213	Felton Spencer	.07	.04
214	John Stockton	.20	.12
215	Luther Wright	.10	.06
216	Michael Adams	.05	.02
217	Mitchell Butler	.05	.02
218	Rex Chapman	.05	.02
219	Calbert Cheaney	.15	.10
220	Pervis Ellison	.07	.04
221	Tom Gugliotta	.15	.10
222	Don MacLean	.12	.07
223	Gheorghe Muresan	.08	.05

252 • 1994-95 HOOPS I

224	Kenny Anderson (AS)	.10	.06
225	B.J. Armstrong (AS)	.08	.05
226	Mookie Blaylock (AS)	.05	.02
227	Derrick Coleman (AS)	.10	.06
228	Patrick Ewing (AS)	.15	.10
229	Horace Grant (AS)	.05	.02
230	Alonzo Mourning (AS)	.25	.15
231	Shaquille O'Neal (AS)	.75	.45
232	Charles Barkley (AS)	.20	.12
233	Scottie Pippen (AS)	.12	.07
234	Mark Price (AS)	.10	.06
235	John Starks (AS)	.07	.04
236	Dominique Wilkins (AS)	.12	.07
237	East Team (AS)	.12	.07
238	Charles Barkley (AS)	.20	.12
239	Clyde Drexler (AS)	.12	.07
240	Kevin Johnson (AS)	.08	.05
241	Shawn Kemp (AS)	.15	.10
242	Karl Malone (AS)	.15	.10
243	Danny Manning (AS)	.10	.06
244	Hakeem Olajuwon (AS)	.35	.20
245	Gary Payton (AS)	.07	.04
246	Mitch Richmond (AS)	.08	.05
247	Cliff Robinson (AS)	.07	.04
248	David Robinson (AS)	.20	.12
249	Latrell Sprewell (AS)	.15	.10
250	John Stockton (AS)	.15	.10
251	West Team	.12	.07
252	Tracy Murray (LL)	.07	.04
253	John Stockton (LL)	.12	.07
254	Shaquille O'Neal (LL)	.75	.45
255	Dikembe Mutombo (LL)	.15	.10
256	Dennis Rodman (LL)	.08	.05
257	David Robinson (LL)	.20	.12
258	Nate McMillan (LL)	.05	.02
259	Chris Webber (AW)	1.00	.60
260	Hakeem Olajuwon (AW)	.35	.20
261	Hakeem Olajuwon (AW)	.35	.20
262	Dell Curry (AW)	.05	.02
263	Scottie Pippen (AW)	.10	.06
264	Anfernee Hardaway (AW)	.50	.30
265	Don MacLean (AW)	.07	.04
266	Game I Finals (Trib)	.05	.02
267	Game 2 Finals (Trib)	.05	.02
268	Game 3 Finals (Trib)	.05	.02
269	Game 4 Finals (Trib)	.05	.02
270	Game 5 Finals (Trib)	.05	.02
271	Game 6 Finals (Trib)	.05	.02
272	Game 7 Finals (Trib)	.05	.02
273	NBA Champions	.05	.02
274	Lenny Wilkins (C)	.10	.06
275	Chris Ford (C)	.05	.02
276	Allan Bristow (C)	.05	.02
277	Phil Jackson (C)	.08	.05
278	Mike Fratello (C)	.05	.02
279	Dick Motta (C)	.05	.02
280	Dan Issel (C)	.08	.05
281	Don Chaney (C)	.05	.02
282	Don Nelson (C)	.08	.05
283	Rudy Tomjanovich (C)	.08	.05
284	Larry Brown (C)	.08	.05
285	Del Harris (C)	.05	.02
286	Kevin Loughery (C)	.05	.02
287	Mike Dunleavy (C)	.05	.02
288	Sidney Lowe (C)	.05	.02
289	Pat Riley (C)	.10	.06
290	Brian Hill (C)	.05	.02
291	John Lucas (C)	.05	.02
292	Paul Westphal (C)	.07	.04
293	Garry St. Jean (C)	.05	.02
294	George Karl (C)	.05	.02
295	Jerry Sloan (C)	.05	.02
296	Magic Johnson (Com)	.40	.25
297	Boys & Girls Club	.05	.02
298	Checklist	.05	.02
299	Checklist	.05	.02
300	Checklist	.05	.02

1994-95 Hoops Big Numbers

The cards in this limited insert set are horizontal and feature a silhouetted photo of the player alongside a number printed in large type that corresponds to his achievement. The flip side contains another action photo and a brief description of the player's highlight. The

1994-95 HOOPS I SUPREME COURT • 253

cards were random inserts in Hoops packs and measure 3-1/2" by 2-1/2".

		MINT	NR/MT
	Complete Set (12)	48.00	28.00
	Commons	2.00	1.25
1	David Robinson	3.50	2.00
2	Jamal Mashburn	2.50	1.50
3	Hakeem Olajuwon	6.00	3.75
4	Patrick Ewing	3.00	1.75
5	Shaquille O'Neal	10.00	6.50
6	Latrell Sprewell	2.50	1.50
7	Chris Webber	8.00	5.00
8	Anfernee Hardaway	4.00	2.75
9	Scottie Pippen	2.00	1.25
10	Isaiah Rider	2.50	1.50
11	Alonzo Mourning	4.00	2.75
12	Charles Barkley	3.50	2.00

1994-95 Hoops I Supreme Court

The cards in this set were inserted randomly in Hoops Series I packs and feature full-color action photos with an embossed gold foil Supreme Court logo on the card fronts. The cards measure 2-1/2" by 3-1/2".

		MINT	NR/MT
	Complete Set (50)	24.00	14.00
	Commons	.25	.15
1	Mookie Blaylock	.25	.15
2	Danny Manning	.35	.20
3	Dino Radja	.50	.30
4	Larry Johnson	1.00	.60
5	Alonzo Mourning	1.25	.70
6	B. J. Armstrong	.30	.18
7	Horace Grant	.25	.15
8	Toni Kukoc	.60	.35
9	Brad Daugherty	.35	.20
10	Mark Price	.40	.25
11	Jim Jackson	.40	.25
12	Jamal Mashburn	.75	.45
13	Dikembe Mutombo	.40	.25
14	Joe Dumars	.30	.18
15	Lindsey Hunter	.30	.18
16	Tim Hardaway	.30	.18
17	Chris Mullin	.35	.20
18	Sam Cassell	.40	.25
19	Hakeem Olajuwon	2.50	1.50
20	Reggie Miller	.75	.45
21	Dominique Wilkins	1.00	.60
22	Nick Van Exel	.40	.25
23	Harold Miner	.30	.18
24	Steve Smith	.30	.18
25	Vin Baker	.40	.25
26	Christian Laettner	.35	.20
27	Isaiah Rider	.75	.45
28	Kenny Anderson	.60	.35
29	Derrick Coleman	.75	.45
30	Patrick Ewing	1.00	.60
31	John Starks	.30	.18
32	Anfernee Hardaway	2.00	1.25
33	Shaquille O'Neal	5.00	3.00
34	Shawn Bradley	.35	.20
35	Clarence Weatherspoon	.30	.18
36	Charles Barkley	.60	.35
37	Kevin Johnson	.35	.20
38	Oliver Miller	.25	.15
39	Clyde Drexler	.40	.25
40	Cliff Robinson	.30	.18
41	Mitch Richmond	.35	.20
42	Bobby Hurley	.40	.25
43	David Robinson	1.50	.90
44	Dennis Rodman	.35	.20
45	Gary Payton	.30	.18
46	Shawn Kemp	1.25	.70
47	John Stockton	1.00	.60
48	Karl Malone	1.25	.70
49	Calbert Cheaney	.40	.25
50	Tom Gugliotta	.30	.18

1994 SkyBox USA

The cards in this set feature the players on the 1994 Team USA Basketball squad. The set consists of six cards of each player pictured in full-bleed, full color shots both in NBA game action and in their USA basketball uniforms. The player's name appears in a banner in the lower third of the card front next to a Team USA logo. Kevin Johnson's cards (90-95) were available through a special mail-in offer. A companion 95-card gold set was issued called Champion Gold with gold cards randomly inserted in SkyBox foil packs. Those cards are valued at 3X to 5X the values listed below. All cards measure 2-1/2" by 3-1/2".

	MINT	NR/MT
Complete Set (95)	18.50	12.50
Commons	.08	.05
Complete Set (Gold)	90.00	60.00
Commons (Gold)	.40	.25

		MINT	NR/MT
1	Alonzo Mourning	.75	.45
2	Alonzo Mourning	.75	.45
3	Alonzo Mourning	.75	.45
4	Alonzo Mourning	.75	.45
5	Alonzo Mourning	.75	.45
6	Alonzo Mourning	.75	.45
7	Larry Johnson	.30	.18
8	Larry Johnson	.30	.18
9	Larry Johnson	.30	.18
10	Larry Johnson	.30	.18
11	Larry Johnson	.30	.18
12	Larry Johnson	.30	.18
13	Shawn Kemp	.40	.25
14	Shawn Kemp	.40	.25
15	Shawn Kemp	.40	.25
16	Shawn Kemp	.40	.25
17	Shawn Kemp	.40	.25
18	Shawn Kemp	.40	.25
19	Mark Price	.15	.10
20	Mark Price	.15	.10
21	Mark Price	.15	.10
22	Mark Price	.15	.10
23	Mark Price	.15	.10
24	Mark Price	.15	.10
25	Steve Smith	.15	.10
26	Steve Smith	.15	.10
27	Steve Smith	.15	.10
28	Steve Smith	.15	.10
29	Steve Smith	.15	.10
30	Steve Smith	.15	.10
31	Dominique Wilkins	.25	.15
32	Dominique Wilkins	.25	.15
33	Dominique Wilkins	.25	.15
34	Dominique Wilkins	.25	.15
35	Dominique Wilkins	.25	.15
36	Dominique Wilkins	.25	.15
37	Derrick Coleman	.20	.12
38	Derrick Coleman	.20	.12
39	Derrick Coleman	.20	.12
40	Derrick Coleman	.20	.12
41	Derrick Coleman	.20	.12
42	Derrick Coleman	.20	.12
43	Isiah Thomas	.15	.10
44	Isiah Thomas	.15	.10
45	Isiah Thomas	.15	.10
46	Isiah Thomas	.15	.10
47	Isiah Thomas	.15	.10
48	Isiah Thomas	.15	.10
49	Joe Dumars	.15	.10
50	Joe Dumars	.15	.10
51	Joe Dumars	.15	.10
52	Joe Dumars	.15	.10
53	Joe Dumars	.15	.10
54	Joe Dumars	.15	.10
55	Dan Majerle	.10	.06
56	Dan Majerle	.10	.06
57	Dan Majerle	.10	.06
58	Dan Majerle	.10	.06
59	Dan Majerle	.10	.06
60	Dan Majerle	.10	.06
61	Tim Hardaway	.12	.07
62	Tim Hardaway	.12	.07
63	Tim Hardaway	.12	.07
64	Tim Hardaway	.12	.07
65	Tim Hardaway	.12	.07
66	Tim Hardaway	.12	.07
67	Shaquille O'Neal	1.50	.90
68	Shaquille O'Neal	1.50	.90

69	Shaquille O'Neal	1.50	.90
70	Shaquille O'Neal	1.50	.90
71	Shaquille O'Neal	1.50	.90
72	Shaquille O'Neal	1.50	.90
73	Reggie Miller	.20	.12
74	Reggie Miller	.20	.12
75	Reggie Miller	.20	.12
76	Reggie Miller	.20	.12
77	Reggie Miller	.20	.12
78	Reggie Miller	.20	.12
79	Don Chaney	.08	.05
80	Pete Gillen	.08	.05
81	Rick Majerus	.08	.05
82	Don Nelson	.08	.05
83	USA Team	.25	.15
84	Rules (Time)	.08	.05
85	Rules (Dimensions)	.08	.05
86	International Rules	.08	.05
87	Magic Johnson (Salutes)	.75	.45
88	David Robinson (Salutes)	.75	.45
89	Checklist	.08	.05
90	Kevin Johnson (Mail)	.15	.10
91	Kevin Johnson (Mail)	.15	.10
92	Kevin Johnson (Mail)	.15	.10
93	Kevin Johnson (Mail)	.15	.10
94	Kevin Johnson (Mail)	.15	.10
95	Kevin Johnson (Mail)	.15	.10

1994 SkyBox USA Dream Play

The cards in this set feature an isolated full-bleed, full-color action shot of the player on the card front in his Team USA uniform. The player's name is printed across the top and a USA logo and Dream Play headline appear in the lower corner. The flip side contains play diagrams and commentary by Hall of Fame coach Jack Ramsay. The prefix DP appears next to the card numbers. Kevin Johnson's card was available by mail. The cards were random inserts in SkyBox USA foil packs and measure 2-1/2" by 3-1/2".

		MINT	NR/MT
Complete Set (14)		120.00	70.00
Commons		3.00	1.75
1	Alonzo Mourning	18.00	12.00
2	Larry Johnson	10.00	6.50
3	Shawn Kemp	15.00	10.00
4	Mark Price	4.00	2.50
5	Steve Smith	4.00	2.50
6	Dominique Wilkins	12.00	7.50
7	Derrick Coleman	6.00	3.75
8	Isiah Thomas	5.00	3.00
9	Joe Dumars	4.00	2.50
10	Dan Majerle	3.00	1.75
11	Tim Hardaway	3.50	2.00
12	Shaquille O'Neal	40.00	28.00
13	Reggie Miller	6.00	3.75
14	Kevin Johnson (Mail)	4.00	2.50

1994 SkyBox USA Portraits

The cards in this limited insert set were randomly distributed in SkyBox USA foil packs and feature a close by portrait shot of each player wearing his USA uniform framed by a wide border. The Kevin Johnson card was available by mail. The backs include the prefix PT next to the card numbers and all cards measure 2-1/2" by 3-1/2".

		MINT	NR/MT
Complete Set (14)		285.00	165.00
Commons		8.00	5.00
1	Alonzo Mourning	35.00	20.00
2	Larry Johnson	20.00	12.50
3	Shawn Kemp	28.00	16.00
4	Mark Price	10.00	6.50
5	Steve Smith	10.00	6.50
6	Dominique Wilkins	20.00	12.50
7	Derrick Coleman	15.00	10.00
8	Isiah Thomas	12.00	7.50
9	Joe Dumars	10.00	6.50
10	Dan Majerle	8.00	5.00
11	Tim Hardaway	9.00	5.75
12	Shaquille O'Neal	100.00	65.00
13	Reggie Miller	18.00	12.00
14	Kevin Johnson (Mail)	10.00	6.50

1994-95 SkyBox Premium I

The cards in this set make up the first of two series of 1994-95 SkyBox Premium cards. The fronts consist of a full-color action photo that appears to be breaking through a black color bar with the player's name printed in large bold type within the bar. A bright fluorescent color creates a shadow for the basketball. The flip side contains a close-up player photo, personal data, statistics and a scouting report by Hall of Fame coach Jack Ramsay. The main subsets include NBA on NBC (NBC)(176-185) and Dynamic Duals (DD)(186-197). All cards measure 2-1/2" by 3-1/2".

		MINT	NR/MT
Complete Set (200)		18.00	12.00
Commons		.05	.02
1	Stacey Augmon	.08	.05
2	Mookie Blaylock	.08	.05
3	Doug Edwards	.08	.05
4	Craig Ehlo	.05	.02
5	Adam Keefe	.05	.02
6	Danny Manning	.12	.07
7	Kevin Willis	.05	.02
8	Dee Brown	.08	.05
9	Sherman Douglas	.07	.04
10	Acie Earl	.08	.05
11	Kevin Gamble	.05	.02

1994 SKYBOX PREMIUM I • 257

#	Player		
12	Xavier McDaniel	.05	.02
13	Dino Radja	.15	.10
14	Muggsy Bogues	.05	.02
15	Scott Burrell	.10	.06
16	Dell Curry	.05	.02
17	LeRon Ellis	.08	.05
18	Hersey Hawkins	.07	.04
19	Larry Johnson	.20	.12
20	Alonzo Mourning	.50	.30
21	B.J. Armstrong	.10	.06
22	Corie Blount	.08	.05
23	Horace Grant	.07	.04
24	Toni Kukoc	.30	.18
25	Luc Longley	.05	.02
26	Scottie Pippen	.20	.12
27	Scott Williams	.05	.02
28	Terrell Brandon	.07	.04
29	Brad Daugherty	.10	.06
30	Tyrone Hill	.07	.04
31	Chris Mills	.15	.10
32	Bobby Phills	.07	.04
33	Mark Price	.15	.10
34	Gerald Wilkins	.05	.02
35	Lucious Harris	.08	.05
36	Jim Jackson	.20	.12
37	Popeye Jones	.08	.05
38	Jamal Mashburn	.60	.35
39	Sean Rooks	.10	.06
40	Mahamoud Abdul-Rauf	.12	.07
41	LaPhonso Ellis	.15	.10
42	Dikembe Mutombo	.20	.12
43	Robert Pack	.05	.02
44	Rodney Rogers	.12	.07
45	Bryant Stith	.10	.06
46	Reggie Williams	.05	.02
47	Joe Dumars	.15	.10
48	Sean Elliott	.12	.07
49	Allan Houston	.10	.06
50	Lindsay Hunter	.12	.07
51	Terry Mills	.05	.02
52	Victor Alexander	.05	.02
53	Tim Hardaway	.12	.07
54	Chris Mullin	.15	.10
55	Billy Owens	.12	.07
56	Latrell Sprewell	.30	.18
57	Chris Webber	1.50	.90
58	Sam Cassell	.30	.18
59	Carl Herrera	.08	.05
60	Robert Horry	.12	.07
61	Vernon Maxwell	.07	.04
62	Hakeem Olajuwon	.75	.45
63	Kenny Smith	.07	.04
64	Otis Thorpe	.07	.04
65	Antonio Davis	.08	.05
66	Dale Davis	.08	.05
67	Derrick McKey	.07	.04
68	Reggie Miller	.25	.15
69	Pooh Richardson	.05	.02
70	Rik Smits	.05	.02
71	Haywoode Workman	.07	.04
72	Terry Dehere	.08	.05
73	Harold Ellis	.07	.04
74	Ron Harper	.08	.05
75	Mark Jackson	.08	.05
76	Loy Vaught	.05	.02
77	Dominique Wilkins	.25	.15
78	Elden Campbell	.08	.05
79	Doug Christie	.10	.06
80	Vlade Divac	.08	.05
81	George Lynch	.15	.10
82	Anthony Peeler	.10	.06
83	Sedale Threatt	.05	.02
84	Nick Van Exel	.25	.15
85	Harold Miner	.10	.06
86	Glen Rice	.08	.05
87	John Salley	.05	.02
88	Rony Seikaly	.08	.05
89	Brian Shaw	.07	.04
90	Steve Smith	.12	.07
91	Vin Baker	.35	.20
92	Jon Barry	.07	.04
93	Todd Day	.10	.06
94	Blue Edwards	.05	.02
95	Lee Mayberry	.07	.04
96	Eric Murdock	.07	.04
97	Mike Brown	.07	.04
98	Stacey King	.05	.02
99	Christian Laettner	.15	.10
100	Isaiah Rider	.60	.35
101	Doug West	.05	.02
102	Micheal Williams	.05	.02
103	Kenny Anderson	.20	.12
104	P. J. Brown	.08	.05
105	Derrick Coleman	.25	.15
106	Kevin Edwards	.05	.02
107	Chris Morris	.05	.02
108	Rex Walters	.08	.05
109	Hubert Davis	.15	.10
110	Patrick Ewing	.35	.20
111	Derek Harper	.08	.05
112	Anthony Mason	.08	.05
113	Charles Oakley	.08	.05
114	Charles Smith	.07	.04
115	John Starks	.10	.06
116	Nick Anderson	.10	.06
117	Anfernee Hardaway	1.25	.70
118	Shaquille O'Neal	1.50	.90
119	Donald Royal	.05	.02
120	Dennis Scott	.08	.05
121	Scott Skiles	.05	.02
122	Dana Barros	.07	.04
123	Shawn Bradley	.20	.12
124	Johnny Dawkins	.05	.02
125	Greg Graham	.08	.05

258 • 1994 SKYBOX PREMIUM I

#	Player		
126	Clarence Weatherspoon	.10	.06
127	Danny Ainge	.10	.06
128	Charles Barkley	.60	.35
129	Cedric Ceballos	.07	.04
130	A. C. Green	.07	.04
131	Kevin Johnson	.12	.07
132	Dan Majerle	.10	.06
133	Oliver Miller	.08	.05
134	Clyde Drexler	.20	.12
135	Harvey Grant	.05	.02
136	Tracy Murray	.10	.06
137	Terry Porter	.08	.05
138	Cliff Robinson	.08	.05
139	James Robinson	.10	.06
140	Rod Strickland	.05	.02
141	Bobby Hurley	.20	.12
142	Olden Polynice	.05	.02
143	Mitch Richmond	.15	.10
144	Lionel Simmons	.15	.10
145	Wayman Tisdale	.07	.04
146	Spud Webb	.05	.02
147	Walt Williams	.10	.06
148	Willie Anderson	.05	.02
149	Vinny Del Negro	.05	.02
150	Dale Ellis	.07	.04
151	J.R. Reid	.05	.02
152	David Robinson	.60	.35
153	Dennis Rodman	.12	.07
154	Kendall Gill	.12	.07
155	Shawn Kemp	.40	.25
156	Nate McMillan	.05	.02
157	Gary Payton	.12	.07
158	Sam Perkins	.07	.04
159	Ricky Pierce	.05	.02
160	Detlef Schrempf	.15	.10
161	David Benoit	.05	.02
162	Tyrone Corbin	.05	.02
163	Jeff Hornacek	.08	.05
164	Jay Humphries	.05	.02
165	Karl Malone	.25	.15
166	Byron Russell	.08	.05
167	Felton Spencer	.08	.05
168	John Stockton	.20	.12
169	Michael Adams	.05	.02
170	Rex Chapman	.05	.02
171	Calbert Cheaney	.25	.15
172	Pervis Ellison	.08	.05
173	Tom Gugliotta	.15	.10
174	Don MacLean	.10	.06
175	Gheorghe Muresan	.12	.07
176	Charles Barkley (NBC)	.25	.15
177	Charles Oakley (NBC)	.07	.04
178	Hakeem Olajuwon (NBC)	.40	.25
179	Dikembe Mutombo (NBC)	.10	.06
180	Scottie Pippen (NBC)	.10	.06
181	Sam Cassell (NBC)	.08	.05
182	Karl Malone (NBC)	.15	.10
183	Reggie Miller (NBC)	.12	.07
184	Patrick Ewing (NBC)	.15	.10
185	Vernon Maxwell (NBC)	.05	.02
186	Hardway vs Smith (DD)	.80	.50
187	Webber vs O'Neal (DD)	1.75	1.00
188	Mashburn vs Rogers (DD)	.30	.18
189	Kukoc vs Radja (DD)	.15	.10
190	Rider vs Anderson (DD)	.25	.15
191	Sprewell vs Jackson (DD)	.25	.15
192	Weatherspoon vs Baker (DD)	.20	.12
193	Cheaney vs Mills (DD)	.20	.12
194	Horry vs Davis (DD)	.10	.06
195	Cassell vs Van Exel (DD)	.15	.10
196	Muresan vs Bradley (DD)	.15	.10
197	Ellis vs Gugliotta (DD)	.10	.06
198	USA Team	.25	.15
199	Checklist	.05	.02
200	Checklist	.05	.02

1994 Upper Deck USA Basketball

The cards in th is set feature full-bleed, full-color photos of the player named to the 1994 Team USA Basketball squad. Each player appears on six different

1994 UPPER DECK USA BASKETBALL • 259

cards with various background designs. The player's name and position appear in a banner type design under his photo and next to a USA logo. The set includes the USA Women's Team (79-84) and All-Time Greats (85-90). All cards measure 2-1/2" by 3-1/2".

		MINT	NR/MT
	Complete Set (90)	15.00	10.00
	Commons	.10	.06
1	Derrick Coleman	.25	.15
2	Derrick Coleman	.25	.15
3	Derrick Coleman	.25	.15
4	Derrick Coleman	.25	.15
5	Derrick Coleman	.25	.15
6	Derrick Coleman	.25	.15
7	Joe Dumars	.15	.10
8	Joe Dumars	.15	.10
9	Joe Dumars	.15	.10
10	Joe Dumars	.15	.10
11	Joe Dumars	.15	.10
12	Joe Dumars	.15	.10
13	Tim Hardaway	.12	.07
14	Tim Hardaway	.12	.07
15	Tim Hardaway	.12	.07
16	Tim Hardaway	.12	.07
17	Tim Hardaway	.12	.07
18	Tim Hardaway	.12	.07
19	Larry Johnson	.30	.18
20	Larry Johnson	.30	.18
21	Larry Johnson	.30	.18
22	Larry Johnson	.30	.18
23	Larry Johnson	.30	.18
24	Larry Johnson	.30	.18
25	Shawn Kemp	.40	.25
26	Shawn Kemp	.40	.25
27	Shawn Kemp	.40	.25
28	Shawn Kemp	.40	.25
29	Shawn Kemp	.40	.25
30	Shawn Kemp	.40	.25
31	Dan Majerle	.10	.06
32	Dan Majerle	.10	.06
33	Dan Majerle	.10	.06
34	Dan Majerle	.10	.06
35	Dan Majerle	.10	.06
36	Dan Majerle	.10	.06
37	Reggie Miller	.25	.15
38	Reggie Miller	.25	.15
39	Reggie Miller	.25	.15
40	Reggie Miller	.25	.15
41	Reggie Miller	.25	.15
42	Reggie MIller	.25	.15
43	Alonzo Mourning	.60	.35
44	Alonzo Mourning	.60	.35
45	Alonzo Mourning	.60	.35
46	Alonzo Mourning	.60	.35
47	Alonzo Mourning	.60	.35
48	Alonzo Mourning	.60	.35
49	Shaquille O'Neal	1.50	.90
50	Shaquille O'Neal	1.50	.90
51	Shaquille O'Neal	1.50	.90
52	Shaquille O'Neal	1.50	.90
53	Shaquille O'Neal	1.50	.90
54	Shaquille O'Neal	1.50	.90
55	Mark Price	.12	.07
56	Mark Price	.12	.07
57	Mark Price	.12	.07
58	Mark Price	.12	.07
59	Mark Price	.12	.07
60	Mark Price	.12	.07
61	Steve Smith	.12	.07
62	Steve Smith	.12	.07
63	Steve Smith	.12	.07
64	Steve Smith	.12	.07
65	Steve Smith	.12	.07
66	Steve Smith	.12	.07
67	Isiah Thomas	.20	.12
68	Isiah Thomas	.20	.12
69	Isiah Thomas	.20	.12
70	Isiah Thomas	.20	.12
71	Isiah Thomas	.20	.12
72	Isiah Thomas	.20	.12
73	Dominique Wilkins	.40	.25
74	Dominique Wilkins	.40	.25
75	Dominique Wilkins	.40	.25
76	Dominique Wilkins	.40	.25
77	Dominique Wilkins	.40	.25
78	Dominique Wilkins	.40	.25
79	Jenifer Azzi	.12	.07
80	Daedra Charles	.12	.07
81	Lisa Leslie	.12	.07
82	Katrina McClain	.12	.07
83	Dawn Staley	.20	.12
84	Steryl Swoopes	.20	.12
85	Michael Jordan	2.00	1.25
86	Larry Bird	1.00	.60
87	Jerry West	.60	.35
88	Adrian Dantley	.12	.07
89	Cheryl Miller	.15	.10
90	Henry Iba	.10	.06
___	Checklist	1.50	.50
___	Checklist	1.50	.50

1994 Upper Deck USA Don Nelson Chalk Talk

The cards in this set were limited inserts packed randomly in Upper Deck USA foil packs. The cards feature a three-dimensional Holoview image on the fronts with a full-color action photo of the player and a small inset photo of head coach Don Nelson in the lower corner. Nelson talks about each player on the card backs. All cards measure 2-1/2" by 3-1/2".

		MINT	NR/MT
Complete Set (14)		110.00	65.00
Commons		4.00	2.50
1	Derrick Coleman	6.00	3.75
2	Joe Dumars	5.00	3.00
3	Tim Hardaway	4.00	2.50
4	Larry Johnson	10.00	6.50
5	Shawn Kemp	12.00	7.50
6	Dan Majerle	4.00	2.50
7	Reggie Miller	8.00	5.00
8	Alonzo Mourning	15.00	10.00
9	Shaquille O'Neal	35.00	20.00
10	Mark Price	5.00	3.00
11	Steve Smith	5.00	3.00
12	Isiah Thomas	5.00	3.00
13	Dominique Wilkins	10.00	6.50
14	Kevin Johnson	4.00	2.50

1994 Upper Deck USA Michael Jordan (HL)

This 5-card limited insert set features highlights from Michael Jordan's international basketball games. The cards were distributed randomly in Upper Deck USA foil packs and consist of action shots of Jordan on the fronts along with his name, the USA logo and the headline Highlights stacked along one side of the card. All cards measure 2-1/2" by 3-1/2".

		MINT	NR/MT
Complete Set (5)		75.00	45.00
Commons		15.00	10.00
1	Michael Jordan ('92 Summer Games)	15.00	10.00
2	Michael Jordan ('92 Americas)	15.00	10.00
3	Michael Jordan ('84 Summer Games)	15.00	10.00
4	Michael Jordan ('84 World Games)	15.00	10.00
5	Michael Jordan (International Games)	15.00	10.00

1994-95 Upper Deck Collectors Choice I

This set marks the debut of Upper Deck's Collectors Choice line of basketball cards. The card fronts feature full-color action photos framed by a white border. The player's name and team nickname are printed in small white type under his photo and next to a box containing a small outline of a basketball figure. The Upper Deck Collectors Choice logo appears in a box in the top corner. The flip side contains another full-color head shot at the top of the card followed by statistics and highlights. Subsets include Tip-Offs (TO)(166-192), All-Star Advice (ASA)(193-198) and Profiles (P)(199-206). Every card in the set also has two parallel insert cards, a silver or gold foil signature series card with the Silver Series valued at 2X to 5X the prices listed below and the Gold Series valued at 30X to 75X the values listed below. All cards measure 2-1/2" by 3-1/2".

	MINT	NR/MT
Complete Set I (210)	15.00	10.00
Commons	.05	.02
Complete Set I(Silver)	70.00	40.00
Commons (Silver)	.10	.06
Complete Set I(Gold)	1,250.00	750.00
Commons (Gold)	2.50	1.50

1	Anfernee Hardaway	.75	.45
2	Moses Malone	.10	.06
3	Steve Smith	.12	.07
4	Chris Webber	1.25	.70
5	Donald Royal	.05	.02
6	Avery Johnson	.05	.02
7	Kevin Johnson	.12	.07
8	Doug Christie	.10	.06
9	Derrick McKey	.05	.02
10	Dennis Rodman	.12	.07
11	Johnny Dawkins	.05	.02
12	Isiah Thomas	.15	.10
13	Kendall Gill	.10	.06
14	Jeff Hornacek	.08	.05
15	Latrell Sprewell	.40	.25
16	Lucious Harris	.08	.05
17	Chris Mullin	.15	.10
18	John Williams	.05	.02
19	Tony Campbell	.05	.02
20	LaPhonso Ellis	.15	.10
21	Gerald Wilkins	.05	.02
22	Clyde Drexler	.20	.12
23	Michael Jordan (Baseball)	2.50	1.50
24	George Lynch	.15	.10
25	Mark Price	.12	.07
26	James Robinson	.12	.07
27	Elmore Spencer	.07	.04
28	Stacey King	.05	.02
29	Corie Blount	.08	.05
30	Dell Curry	.05	.02
31	Reggie Miller	.25	.15
32	Karl Malone	.25	.15
33	Scottie Pippen	.25	.15
34	Hakeem Olajuwon	.75	.45
35	Clarence Weatherspoon	.10	.06
36	Kevin Edwards	.05	.02
37	Pete Myers	.05	.02
38	Jeff Turner	.05	.02
39	Ennis Whatley	.05	.02
40	Calbert Cheaney	.15	.10
41	Glen Rice	.08	.05
42	Vin Baker	.20	.12
43	Grant Long	.05	.02
44	Derrick Coleman	.25	.15
45	Rik Smits	.05	.02
46	Chris Smith	.08	.05
47	Carl Herrera	.08	.05
48	Bob Martin	.07	.04
49	Terrell Brandon	.07	.04
50	David Robinson	.60	.35
51	Danny Ferry	.05	.02
52	Buck Williams	.07	.04
53	Josh Grant	.08	.05
54	Ed Pinckney	.05	.02
55	Dikembe Mutombo	.20	.12
56	Cliff Robinson	.10	.06
57	Luther Wright	.10	.06
58	Scott Burrell	.10	.06

1994-95 UPPER DECK COLLECTORS CHOICE I

#	Player		
59	Stacey Augmon	.08	.05
60	Jeff Malone	.05	.02
61	Byron Houston	.08	.05
62	Anthony Peeler	.10	.06
63	Michael Adams	.05	.02
64	Negele Knight	.05	.02
65	Terry Cummings	.07	.04
66	Christian Laettner	.15	.10
67	Tracy Murray	.10	.06
68	Sedale Threatt	.05	.02
69	Dan Majerle	.10	.06
70	Frank Brickowski	.05	.02
71	Ken Norman	.05	.02
72	Charles Smith	.07	.04
73	Adam Keefe	.05	.02
74	P.J. Brown	.07	.04
75	Kevin Duckworth	.05	.02
76	Shawn Bradley	.20	.12
77	Darnell Mee	.07	.04
78	Nick Anderson	.10	.06
79	Mark West	.05	.02
80	B.J. Armstrong	.10	.06
81	Dennis Scott	.08	.05
82	Lindsay Hunter	.12	.07
83	Derek Strong	.07	.04
84	Mike Brown	.07	.04
85	Antonio Harvey	.07	.04
86	Anthony Bonner	.05	.02
87	Sam Cassell	.15	.10
88	Harold Miner	.10	.06
89	Spud Webb	.05	.02
90	Mookie Blaylock	.07	.04
91	Greg Anthony	.07	.04
92	Richard Petruska	.05	.02
93	Sean Rooks	.10	.06
94	Ervin Johnson	.08	.05
95	Randy Brown	.05	.02
96	Orlando Woolridge	.05	.02
97	Charles Oakley	.07	.04
98	Craig Ehlo	.05	.02
99	Derek Harper	.07	.04
100	Robert Parish	.10	.06
101	Muggsy Bogues	.05	.02
102	Mitch Richmond	.12	.07
103	Mahmoud Abdul-Rauf	.12	.07
104	Joe Dumars	.15	.10
105	Eric Riley	.05	.02
106	Terry Mills	.05	.02
107	Toni Kukoc	.20	.12
108	Jon Koncak	.05	.02
109	Haywoode Workman	.05	.02
110	Todd Day	.10	.06
111	Detlef Schrempf	.12	.07
112	David Wesley	.05	.02
113	Mark Jackson	.07	.04
114	Doug Overton	.05	.02
115	Vinny Del Negro	.05	.02
116	Loy Vaught	.05	.02
117	Mike Peplowski	.05	.02
118	Bimbo Coles	.05	.02
119	Rex Walters	.07	.04
120	Sherman Douglas	.07	.04
121	David Benoit	.05	.02
122	John Salley	.05	.02
123	Cedric Ceballos	.07	.04
124	Chris Mills	.10	.06
125	Robert Horry	.12	.07
126	Johnny Newman	.05	.02
127	Malcolm Mackey	.05	.02
128	Terry Dehere	.08	.05
129	Dino Radja	.12	.07
130	Tree Rollins	.05	.02
131	Xavier McDaniel	.05	.02
132	Bobby Hurley	.15	.10
133	Alonzo Mourning	.60	.35
134	Isaiah Rider	.30	.18
135	Antoine Carr	.05	.02
136	Robert Pack	.05	.02
137	Walt Wiliams	.10	.06
138	Tyrone Corbin	.05	.02
139	Popeye Jones	.07	.04
140	Shawn Kemp	.30	.18
141	Thurl Bailey	.05	.02
142	James Worthy	.10	.06
143	Scott Haskin	.05	.02
144	Hubert Davis	.10	.06
145	A. C. Green	.07	.04
146	Dale Davis	.08	.05
147	Nate McMillan	.05	.02
148	Chris Morris	.05	.02
149	Will Perdue	.05	.02
150	Felton Spencer	.07	.04
151	Rod Strickland	.05	.02
152	Blue Edwards	.05	.02
153	John Williams	.05	.02
154	Rodney Rogers	.10	.06
155	Acie Earl	.08	.05
156	Hersey Hawkins	.07	.04
157	Jamal Mashburn	.35	.20
158	Don MacLean	.10	.06
159	Micheal Williams	.05	.02
160	Kenny Gattison	.05	.02
161	Rich King	.05	.02
162	Allan Houston	.07	.04
163	Hoop-It-Up	.05	.02
164	Hoop-It-Up	.05	.02
165	Hoop-It-Up	.05	.02
166	Danny Manning (TO)	.08	.05
167	Robert Parish (TO)	.07	.04
168	Alonzo Mourning (TO)	.20	.12
169	Scottie Pippen (TO)	.12	.07
170	Mark Price (TO)	.07	.04
171	Jamal Mashburn (TO)	.20	.12
172	Dikembe Mutombo (TO)	.10	.06

1994-95 UPPER DECK COLLECTORS CHOICE I • 263

173	Joe Dumars (TO)	.08	.05
174	Chris Webber (TO)	.40	.25
175	Hakeem Olajuwon (TO)	.40	.25
176	Reggie Miller (TO)	.10	.06
177	Ron Harper (TO)	.05	.02
178	Nick Van Exel (TO)	.08	.05
179	Steve Smith (TO)	.07	.04
180	Vin Baker (TO)	.10	.06
181	Isaiah Rider (TO)	.15	.10
182	Derrick Coleman (TO)	.10	.06
183	Patrick Ewing (TO)	.15	.10
184	Shaquille O'Neal (TO)	.75	.45
185	C. Weatherspoon (TO)	.07	.04
186	Charles Barkley (TO)	.25	.15
187	Clyde Drexler (TO)	.10	.06
188	Mitch Richmond (TO)	.08	.05
189	David Robinson (TO)	.25	.15
190	Shawn Kemp (TO)	.20	.12
191	Karl Malone (TO)	.15	.10
192	Tom Gugliotta (TO)	.08	.05
193	Kenny Anderson (ASA)	.10	.06
194	Alonzo Mourning (ASA)	.20	.12
195	Mark Price (ASA)	.08	.05
196	John Stockton (ASA)	.10	.06
197	Shaquille O'Neal (ASA)	.75	.45
198	Latrell Sprewell (ASA)	.20	.12
199	Charles Barkley (P)	.25	.15
200	Chris Webber (P)	.40	.25
201	Larry Johnson (P)	.10	.06
202	Dennis Rodman (P)	.07	.04
203	Patrick Ewing (P)	.20	.12
204	Michael Jordan (P)	1.25	.70
205	Shaquille O'Neal (P)	.75	.45
206	Shawn Kemp (P)	.20	.12
207	Tim Hardaway (CL)	.07	.04
208	John Stockton (CL)	.10	.06
209	Harold Miner (CL)	.07	.04
210	B.J. Armstrong (CL)	.05	.02